P9-CJX-866

R A D I C A L
HOLLYWOOD

THE UNTOLD STORY BEHIND AMERICA'S FAVORITE MOVIES

PAUL BUHLE
AND DAVE WAGNER

THE NEW PRESS • NEW YORK

To the memory of
Abraham Lincoln Polonsky, 1910–1999

ISBN 1-56584-718-0
CIP data available

The New Press was established in 1990 as a not-for-profit alternative
to the large, commercial publishing houses currently dominating the
book publishing industry. The New Press operates in the public
interest rather than for private gain, and is committed to publishing,
in innovative ways, works of educational, cultural, and community
value that are often deemed insufficiently profitable.

The New Press, 450 West 41st Street, 6th floor, New York, NY 10036
www.thenewpress.com

Book design by Ellen Cipriano
Typesetting by dix!

Printed in the United States of America

2 4 6 8 10 9 7 5 3 1

CONTENTS

INTRODUCTION

I N 1951, THE YEAR OF the fateful (and fatal) second round of House Un-American Activities Committee (HUAC) subpoenas issued against Communists and former Communists in Hollywood, screenwriter Michael Wilson was called to testify. He declined to cooperate, and most of his best work thereafter was done abroad. Newly famous for *A Place in the Sun,* his Oscar-winning adaptation of Theodore Dreiser's classic novel *An American Tragedy,* Wilson was only one of dozens of American filmmakers who lit out for the Continent. In those days, it seemed, Hollywood exiles were everywhere, shifting southward to Mexico or moving eastward across the same longitudes that had seen so many German-speaking artists and intellectuals fleeing Europe for California not so long before. Among the latter was Austrian composer Arnold Schoenberg, in whom fellow California exile Theodor Adorno had located the peculiar genius of twentieth-century music.

Los Angeles, more specifically the upscale suburb of Brentwood, found Schoenberg during that long, difficult spring of 1951. In one of those unforgettable moments that crystallizes a time and place, a former student described the scene that she encountered when she dropped over to the composer's house for dinner. Schoenberg had recently discovered television, she reported, and "no one was more enthralled than he as we sat in front of Hopalong Cassidy with our TV trays in our laps."[1]

The idea that the creator of *Verklärte Nacht* and *Moses und Aron,* and inventor of the twelve-tone musical system that so dominated the serious music of the twentieth century, could in his last year on earth fall into a television reverie over a child's cowboy star overturns certain notions of cultural propriety. It is as though Henry James's character Christopher Newman, so hungry for European culture in *The American* (1878), had crisscrossed Europe to study its history in its cathedrals and then morphed into another "new man," returning to America to gaze upon the vernacular cabins and roadside inns to acquire a sense of the future.

How could this tableau possibly be reconciled with his friend and fellow exile Theodor Adorno's claim that the composer "proclaims the end of infantility within a society which had long been aware that it would be tolerated only as long as it allowed its inmates a quota of juvenile happiness"?[2] To the usual observer on the Left or Right there might be no reconciliation, merely a tragic tableau of artist and student, TV tray and TV set, in the capitulation of a great artist to the banality of popular culture.

But this would be a shallow and ignorant view. If we actually follow Schoenberg's gaze to the television, we might find what really attracted his interest. Perhaps he was watching a 1943 Hoppy movie titled *Colt Comrades.* If so, the old musician may have half-recognized in it some distant flickering of the European critical spirit. Here, Hopalong Cassidy exposes and destroys a banker's monopoly on cattle raising, articulating a code of "no justice, no peace" when banker's law is revealed as lynch-law. The screenwriter was the same Michael Wilson, destined to become one of the medium's most influential, with three titles in the American Film Institute's accredited top one hundred—two of them, *Lawrence of Arabia* and *The Bridge on the River Kwai,* written under other names and their credits restored only after his premature death.

In 1943, the influence of the Hollywood Left had been at its apex, and even B Westerns were often full of this critical spirit, not least in three other Wilson-written Hoppy scripts. Perhaps, at a second guess, Schoenberg was watching Wilson's *Border Patrol* (also notable for the screen debut of Robert Mitchum). In this tale, our aging hero puts an end to a silver-mine owner's reign of terror just north of the Mexican border. One of the most sophisticated Westerns ever made in the historic terms of race and region, its treatment of the legacy of colonization stands second only to left-leaning screenwriter (later semi-friendly witness) Melvin Levy's epic drama of the legendary Mexican-American social bandit Joaquín Murieta in *Robin Hood of El Dorado* (1939).[3] This earlier screen Robin Hood takes to the hills when forty-niner Anglos slaughter his family, and rouses a guerrilla band of resistance before being slaughtered by revenge-takers. Wilson's Hoppy perceives that Mexicans traveling north to work in an Anglo silver mine have suffered the same fate as the Indians of the region under the conquistadores centuries earlier: They are turned into slaves and never heard from again.

Hoppy and his sidekick vow to track down the missing Mexicans. What they find is a corporate mining operation not too far in spirit from the mining company in the celebrated screenplay by Wilson that appeared exactly a decade later under the blacklist (and shortly disappeared, after effectively being banned from commercial viewing), *Salt of the Earth*. The mine owner in the 1943 story has indeed kidnapped the Mexican workers. He takes Hoppy and his pals into custody for trespassing his domain and intends to put them on trial in his own court. Undaunted, Hoppy gives a rousing speech to the workers, helps them free themselves, and informs the mine boss that he will soon face charges for forced labor and peonage made illegal by the New Deal, albeit in a rarely enforced law.

The universal appeal of Hopalong Cassidy and the Western were later to be carefully analyzed by French radical Catholic critic Andre Bazin. In his classic essay "The Western: Or, the American Film Par Excellence," Bazin wrote,

> the durability of the western hero and plots has been demonstrated recently by the fabulous success on television of the old Hopalong Cassidy films. The western does not age. Its world-wide appeal is even more astonishing than its historical survival. What can there possibly be to interest Arabs, Hindus, Latins, Germans or Anglo Saxons, among whom the western has had an uninterrupted success? . . . The western must possess some greater secret than simply the secret of youthfulness. It must be a secret that somehow identifies it with the essence of cinema.[4]

Abraham Polonsky, considered for a half-century until his 1999 death the Marxist savant of Hollywood radicals, added that genres such as the Western (including his own anti-Western *Tell Them Willie Boy Is Here*), far from being created for film, actually reinstated mythic narratives as old as the campfire story. Film, the only truly new art form for centuries, provided the perfect means for this reinstatement because of its evocative power for the mass audience.[5]

Hopalong Cassidy, framed by its savvy creator as the mass culture embodiment of Franklin D. Roosevelt—complete with white hair, chortle, and game leg—thus carried the New Deal message into the center of the American myth. Hoppy's writers and directors were not the only ones reversing the "Winning of the West" narrative in Hollywood's golden era. That the real-life FBI had its agents carefully watching foremost Western director John Ford (guilty of too many friends in the wrong places, and too many endorsements of their activities) as a potential Communist, that screenwriting left-wingers found the historic open plains as the location of European America's original sin (the ravishing of the land and extermination of the Indians) but also, in the hands of Oklahoma home boy Michael Wilson, the possibility of redemption, could not be entirely coincidental.

And it wasn't. A reviewer in *The New York Times Book Review* in September 1944, commenting on a thick volume of published proceedings from a high-profile media "congress" held the previous year in Los Angeles, made a most extraordinary observation: "The screen, radio, publicity, songwriters and cartoonists of the nation," had "made a solemn declaration of their responsibilities and in effect served notice on the entertainment industry that they are about to take over Hollywood."[6]

The participation of leading studio executives at the Los Angeles meetings in June 1943, cosponsored by the Hollywood Writers Mobilization and the University of California at Los Angeles, made it unlikely that any such revolutionary intention had even been suggested. When California State Senator Jack Tenney declared the congress a cause for urgent investigation of the Communist "subversion" of Hollywood, denials were immediately issued from high sources about any scheme or strategy afoot. Film executives understood perfectly well that visionary expectations for a postwar world were, above all, a means to highlight the idealism of the war effort.

And yet *Times* commentator M. McNeil Lowry had captured the wider spirit alive in the movie capital, not only of left-wingers but of many politically indifferent industry participants, including prominent stars, who believed that a struggle for creative control of America's important films would soon be properly on the agenda. Booming with war business and not yet threatened by television, Hollywood had palpably outgrown its plantation-like studio system of rigid and highly arbitrary controls from above, hackneyed plots, and the clichéd star use that abused even the finest, highest-paid talents.

An ongoing technological revolution had in the few previous years greatly enlarged camera techniques, potentially realizing (even without color) many of the possibilities of cinematic expression. Sound films, now more than a decade old, had recently transcended the filmed-play era and begun to experiment widely, from animation to special effects, styles of classic drama to rip-roaring adventure. With *Citizen Kane,* the potential of the writer-director-producer suddenly became burningly evident: The auteur was truly born. Even moderate liberals could see that the cash nexus represented by the studios and their bankers constituted the final obstacle between the collective creators and the eager audience. Escape that smothering effect by whatever method—the independent production company a most obvious expedient—and miracles could surely be realized.

That this dream so shimmered did indeed depend upon the peculiar wartime perspective that, a decade or generation later, seemed in retrospect almost inconceivable. The vision of a reborn world, after the defeat of Nazism, had been constructed out of the experiences of the New Deal and the widespread public sentiment—among powerful sections of elites as well as ordinary folk—of the need for fundamental social and economic reform. By 1948, reform had practically narrowed into another version of a promised chicken in every pot, at its most dramatic the (never-to-be-realized) Fair Deal proposal of universal employment and health care, along with a modest degree of racial equality. A few years earlier, the future had looked very different.

In a society curiously far more divided during wartime unity than it would be under McCarthyism (or perhaps even the Vietnam era), the envisioned postwar return to "normal" had prompted conservatives and the wealthy class to look forward to a wholesale rollback of the New Deal, while large numbers of liberals and union members for their part anticipated a down-structuring of corporate holdings and influence as almost inevitable. Across the seas, the rich and powerful in occupied lands had collaborated widely with the Axis powers, while the Red Army (along with the left-led partisans and aided greatly by U.S. goods) halted and reversed the German advance. The U.S. military did much to finish the war. But capitalism, at least old-style capitalism, still seemed discredited globally, exhausted with fascism and colonialism.

Only American radicals well to the left of the Communists believed that something like socialism (or workers' uprising and "revolution") lay shortly ahead for the world center of private enterprise. But *something* would happen, that was certain, and seemed altogether likely to happen at the epicenter of commercial culture reaching record profits thanks to the cravings of the masses. Hollywood reflected and perceived social realities through a fun-house mirror, distorted but nonetheless recognizable.

During that moment, in the ongoing production of films and the social relations of production within the film community, the entire story of the Hollywood Left could be said to be concentrated. Not because the best films written, directed, or produced by future victims of the 1930s had built up to this moment. And not because the experience for the rest of the 1940s and the fall of America's own cultural iron curtain came with political defeat.

Nor is the story an American one alone. Cultural historians have yet to examine the international context of radical filmmaking from the 1920s to the 1950s, inevitably unique within each national tradition but often strikingly similar at different periods in Rome, Paris, and Berlin, eastward to Moscow, Tokyo, and farther eastward all the way to Hollywood. Pre-Stalin Russia, pre-Hitler Germany, and Popular Front–era France (i.e., 1935–39) were especially rich in experimentation, with the experimenters including Brecht, Eisenstein, and Renoir. These efforts made only a limited impact upon Hollywood of the 1930s, although German exiles both liberal and radical added Expressionist mannerisms as well as social commitments to many of the industry's most interesting films, from horror to light comedy and heroic biopics. The 1940s, climax of Hollywood's classic period, not only realized the promise of international dialogue about film (partly because of the presence there of exiles, including Renoir himself, more through the power of example and the greater freedom of operation) but provided useful models for global filmmakers of the future.

It was no accident that the Italian and Japanese neorealist directors and writers had watched their favorite American films—noirs in particular—very closely. Or that Parisian cinema's detectives looked so curiously American for a long time. Or that British film, slower than others to come of age, would boast Hollywood's forcibly exported artists (above all, Joseph

Losey) as among their best. Or even that Luis Buñuel, an idiosyncratic director of the highest order, assigned a former writer of American family films some of his strangest features and drew examples large and small from his viewing of Hollywood's work.[7]

Further work needs to be done to fill out the suggestion, barely made in the chapters that follow, that film rather than theater was almost certainly the means of communication between social movements and ordinary Americans. A stronger argument is made that within the vicinity of the American Popular Front, some of the most crucial as well as most expansive experiments were realized in this relation; a larger interpretation would be needed to explore pre–Cold War liberalism to understand fully the radicalism of, for instance, non-Communist screenwriter and close ally of the Hollywood Left Dudley Nichols *(The Informer, Stagecoach, How Green Was My Valley)*. Or to grasp fully how much Orson Welles shared with Hollywood's Communists and how much his triumph in *Citizen Kane* meant to them. Feature storytelling, for a historic moment that is still barely understood, constituted more than a remarkably successful populist experiment soon abandoned. It was, in artistic terms, the alternative to an anti-populist modernism, as much as the canvases of John Sloan, Ben Shahn, or the Soyer brothers (and Chagall, across the globe) were to Abstract Expressionism in its Cold War–era triumph.

Film noir, an oddly French title for a supremely American cinematic expression, effectively captured the postwar anticipation of worse to come in American materialism, alienation, and Atomic Age anxiety. Noir might possibly be best seen as the intuitive artistic response to the vanished hopes of 1943. Screenwriters, directors, actors, and also those technicians of camera, score, lighting, and editing poured out their sentiments; audiences intuitively understood the intent and have not ceased to understand it, across ever larger parts of the planet, in the decades to follow. Noir was not the only artistic triumph of the Hollywood intellectuals, by a long shot; but it helped make sense of their other work.

The following pages seek to capture the rich texture of the lives of those people behind the "names": that is to say, Hollywoodites named in congressional hearings during the late 1940s and early 1950s as "subversive."

Few were famous, and only a relative handful ever worked again in films, let alone regained their former positions within the industry. Rather than betray their colleagues, a considerable majority of the accused willingly accepted some form of exile or another from profession and artistic home. Nearly all of the victims were, in our considered view, quietly heroic, their film contributions interesting, however much their higher cinematic aspirations remained unrealized.

To describe them as "subversive" or "Communist" was a convention of the age. Like several million other Americans (including a hugely disproportionate number of Jewish immigrants and their children) during the 1930s and 40s, our subjects passed through a variety of left-wing movements, mostly beginning in the Depression years. They joined unions, belonged to left-tinged fraternal and cultural societies, signed petitions, went on marches, or took part in fund-raising campaigns very much in the way that other American radicals did from the 1840s through the 1860s, 1880s and 1890s, 1900s and 10s, or 1960s and 70s. Undeniably, the Communist Party was the major radical movement from the 1920s through 40s. Therefore, in the iron logic of the Cold War era, the link of Communist associations with multitudinous groups and causes confirmed sins later deemed unforgivable.

It hadn't looked that way to the half million or so for whom left-leaning sentiment was a mark of assorted personal connections and perfectly ordinary experiences—often enough, the experience of Americanization; nor to the millions of union members who voted for Communist-linked officers; nor to Roosevelt voters who resisted the constant conservative association of the New Deal with "Jews" and "Reds." As Jews still facing a large degree of discrimination and resentment (mirroring, in small ways, the terror against their relatives trapped in Europe), they *needed* a different America; the radical culture from Woody Guthrie to Humphrey Bogart, the excitement, the slogans, the movements of the New Deal and wartime afforded the means of transition.

Not everyone named in congressional hearings would be persecuted, and in that fact lies a deeper story of the Hollywood blacklist. Those who agreed to "give names" of their former friends and associates, and to apologize for past behavior of participating in protest movements, could be cleansed and redeemed, although the contraction of the film industry often forecast the end of their careers as well. For most of the others, *not* to give names was a cause considerably greater than the inspiration of either the collapsed political Left or of the Soviet Union (about which disillusionment was rife). Ancient Jewish traditions and even daily prayer proscribed the informer, an ethic that had been held as strongly for other reasons in many contemporary social circles, from blue-collar neighborhoods to British public schools. More to the point, informing constituted, in Hollywood, a personal career move made at the cost of destroying lives. Whether or not to inform, as Walter Bernstein observed later, was not properly a political question at all, but a matter of personal morals and ethics.

The lives described in this book belong mainly if not only to the resisters. Some had developed their predilections with their mothers' milk, so to speak: Their parents and grandparents had been radicals and revolutionaries, and their convictions had been set in childhood. Some had been educated at the point of a policeman's baton during the grim years of the early 1930s. Some were simply fascinated by realist film styles, notably those of 1920s Soviet filmmakers, and followed aesthetic predilections into politics.

A surprising number, however, came straight out of Middle America and made their choice on old-fashioned moral grounds. Their parents and grandparents had been staunch Republicans indifferent to reforms of any kind since at least the Civil War and the ambiguous Union crusade against slavery. In several fascinating cases of what might be called "premature feminism," their mothers had been active in the earlier woman suffrage movement—and still, Republicans. For others of genteel backgrounds, the lowly status of the writer or actor in the "company town" atmosphere of Hollywood during the 1920s and early 1930s was enough to turn them sharply leftward. The emergence of Fascist Italy, Nazi Germany, and ominous anti-Semitism had the same or additive effect on nearly all concerned. The rise of industrial unions as well as their own labor organization, the liberal impulse against racism, and naturally the wartime crusade against fascism all served to drive home the point as much for them (if starting from different premises) as for Jews. Only the career-cautious, the contemptuous rich, or the heartless—and there were plenty of all three types in Hollywood—could easily and completely resist the appeal of the romantic left-connected movements of the late 1930s and the 1940s.

Probably more important than all these particular causes was the change that participation in social circles and social movements brought within "progressive" (a favorite word of their own) film folk themselves. By taking action in social movements, they became new people. The key point of the blacklist, and of the choreographed confession as the only means of escape from it, was to compel the rebels of earlier days into public shame at having rebelled, to compel them to deny their earlier selves. Some certainly did. The resisters, more than 80 percent of those called to testify and many others besides, would likely have already broken the ties with the Communist-linked organizations to which they once belonged—but had kept faith in themselves. They *could* face giving up everything rather than take part in retrospective self-repudiation.

The sensational glare of the newsreels and the private tragedies of blacklistees' lives successfully obscured the large issue of the supposedly subversive films themselves. The prosecutors and their supporters (newspaper columnists like Walter Winchell and Louella Parsons; liberal intellectuals such as Arthur Schlesinger, Jr.; and conservative congressmen like Richard Nixon) had charged that Hollywood films were tainted by Communist ideas and that the "Reds" writing them therefore deserved to be thrown out of the industry. Testimony turned up little evidence of the taint, however, beyond a few lines of script (the most famous spoken by Ginger Rogers in *Tender Comrade:* "Share and share alike, that's democracy") and a small handful of wartime movies romanticizing America's Russian allies. The "issue" was not the "issue"—or was it? Had the Hollywood Left managed to make its own talents, its own aesthetics and politics, an integral part of the American film?

Now that the Cold War is old news, noir filmmaker Abraham Polonsky quipped a few years ago, the Hollywood blacklist has become almost safe for public discussion and an accepted, even regrettable part of American political-cultural history. Neoconservative aestheticians like Hilton Kramer and veteran journalistic combatants like *The New York Times*'s Walter Goodman may be expected to snap and growl at the belated (mostly postmortem) redemption of the blacklistees and their films. But younger generations—which now include practically anyone under fifty—seem to accept the artists and films for what they offer in entertainment, ignoring the political labels. By the time the Soviet Union fell, most of the Cold War antagonists themselves had died off. "Communism" practically ceased to be an issue in an Internet world, if "rebellion" with endless possible implications stubbornly survived.

Since the early 1990s, film festivals have called back survivors of the blacklist to recognition and some acclaim. Award-winning documentaries about the blacklist have added to the interest. For a decade or more, college courses have been showing *Salt of the Earth,* as much a documentary as it is the one unfettered creation of Hollywood's victims. The Hollywood establishment—led by Disney CEO Michael Eisner, himself the son of a black-listee—has meanwhile welcomed back the long-suppressed memories, as some recent Oscar ceremonies remind the careful viewer. If congressional committees and media critics continually demand proof that Hollywood has made deeply moral films, the blacklistees' classic films still offer the decisive evidence.[8]

Perhaps most remarkable of all, many millions of ordinary, escape-seeking television watchers are rehabilitating heretofore forgotten films, simply by tuning them in. American Movie Classics, the various premium film channels, and, above all, Turner Classic Movies run assorted films twenty-four hours every day, reaching by satellite almost every part of the globe, bombarding cable subscribers with massive doses of highly curious but also completely uninterpreted "information."[9] Up to a thousand films with blacklistee writers or directors—not to speak of actors or assorted technicians—make the rounds. The information needed to make sense of the political clues hidden in these films has been lacking. But by endorsing what interests them, perceptive viewers have already begun to decipher, in their own terms, the significance of these half-century-old social themes within the larger popular culture.

Viewers young and old have yet to grasp that so many of the cult classics from the pre-blacklist era, including *The Public Enemy, Little Caesar, Frankenstein, Alice Adams, The Barretts of Wimpole Street, Destry Rides Again, The Thin Man* (and all its sequels), *The House of the Seven Gables,* the first sound version of *A Christmas Carol, Casablanca, Mr. Smith Goes to Washington, A Star Is Born, The Wizard of Oz, The Talk of the Town, The Little Foxes, Murder, My Sweet, The Maltese Falcon, Here Comes Mr. Jordan, Woman of the Year, Watch on the Rhine, Crossfire, Gentleman's Agreement, Laura, Life With Father, Cyrano de Bergerac, Body and Soul, The Naked City, All the King's Men, A Place in the Sun, High Noon,* much of the Blondie and the Henry Aldrich series, along with some of the best Abbott and Costello, Laurel and Hardy, Olsen and Johnson, and even Hopalong Cassidy films, among a score of similarly tainted Westerns starring John Wayne and lesser lights, owe heavily to the Hollywood Left (and are even identified as such by contemporary FBI reports). To go beyond the era of this book, so do *The Robe, The Brave One, The Adventures of Robinson Crusoe, The Defiant Ones, The Servant, Rififi, Odds Against Tomorrow, Lawrence of Arabia, Spartacus, Phaedra, Fail-Safe, The Fixer, Never on Sunday, Norma Rae, The Front, Sounder, The Molly Maguires, The Great White Hope, Tell Them Willie Boy Is Here, Born Free, Planet of the Apes, Two Mules for Sister Sara, M*A*S*H, Zulu, Accident, The Go-Between, Roads to the South, Sands of the Kalahari, Nuts, True Grit, Midnight Cowboy, Serpico,* and *Coming Home*—small tokens of the creative power put on hold or simply destroyed.

Likewise, war and postwar military classics, including *The Story of G.I. Joe, Destination Tokyo, The Negro Soldier, Edge of Darkness, Thirty Seconds Over Tokyo, Action in the North Atlantic, Pride of the Marines, Objective, Burma! Back to Bataan, The Men, A Walk in the Sun, The Guns of Navarone,* and *The Bridge on the River Kwai.* Likewise women's films such as *Kitty Foyle, Holiday, The Philadelphia Story,* Lillian Hellman's *These Three* (later remade under its stage title, *The Children's Hour*), *Possessed,* and *Letter From an Unknown Woman.* Likewise musicals such as *Anchors Aweigh, It Happened in Brooklyn, My Sister Eileen,* and even *The Jolson Story* and *Rhapsody in Blue.* It would be too much, at this point, to begin to delineate the range of slapstick humor, from antic Marx Brothers–style cinematic vaudeville of the early 1930s to the dry wit of Donald Ogden Stewart's drawing room comedies to the best of the Abbott and Costello films in the 1940s. Likewise to delineate the beloved family (or children's) films, many of them animal-related, from early film versions of *The Adventures of Huckleberry Finn* to *Lassie Come Home* and *My Friend Flicka,* not to mention *Cinderella.* Or to describe the bold efforts at crossing the racial barriers in the 1940s when it had become barely possible—*Intruder in the Dust, Home of the Brave, Pinky,* even the musicals *Stormy Weather* and *Cabin in the Sky,* with melodies and "book" by future blacklistees.

It will be crucial to our story, as indicated above, to analyze the rise of film noir as the cinematic triumph of the Left's filmmakers, writers, directors, and the occasional producer over adverse circumstances and ideological resistance from Communist aesthetic reductionism. Here, more than anywhere else, the radicals placed their mark upon contemporary American cinema, but also upon world film for the rest of the century and beyond. The peculiar circumstances at once artistic-mechanical and political

made this development possible, but the inspiration of the artists themselves, facing the probable end of their careers, made the resulting films
unforgettable. *The Strange Love of Martha Ivers, Champion, The Big Clock,
Night and the City, Force of Evil, Gun Crazy, Act of Violence, Thieves' Highway,
He Ran All the Way, The Underworld Story, Kiss the Blood off My Hands, The
Asphalt Jungle*—all of these films appeared shortly before the gatekeepers
slammed the gates shut.

What did it all add up to? The reader will have to judge, based not
only on what is written in the following pages but also on the films that he
or she chooses to watch and consider. Michael Wilson reflected in a late-life
interview that although it proved "extremely difficult to do a truly progressive and honest film in Hollywood," left-wingers "had an obligation to
try our damndest to do so." Notwithstanding everything, it was possible to
accomplish some things "even in the pictures that seemed silly or vapid"—
not the supposed "injection of Communist propaganda" but "honesty and
humanism." [10]

Dalton Trumbo, the best-paid writer in wartime Hollywood, offered
similar observations in his correspondence with friends a decade later, at
the height of the blacklist. "In spite of our mistakes, which were many, and
defeats, which were great," he and his fellow writers had been able to accomplish something, and here was the simple proof: "the content of films
was better in 1943 than it is in 1953." [11] Of course, there were many other
reasons for the lamentable downward plunge of content as well as volume
and prestige of pictures in the latter decade. But the exclusion of idealistic,
radical writers and directors counted heavily in any reasonable calculation.

Hollywood production never did make the turn to creative control by
its workforce, any more than the world advanced from victory over fascism
to world peace or a more cooperative and egalitarian order. The alternatives
have cost us more dearly, as a society and as a source as well as an audience
of popular art, than we dare to guess. Reconstructing the story offers a
glimpse of what might have been, for the American art film and for cinema
at large, and what remains for us of its legacy.

In any case, naming *these* names has the virtue of suggesting what a
rich treasure lies in wait for the viewer of even a fraction of the nearly fifteen
hundred films written, directed, produced, or with an original novel or
story by a certified left-winger. It is Hollywood's biggest secret, surely,
quite despite the notoriety of the blacklist, and is ours to delve for its mys-

teries and joys. We can only hope that the readers of this book will enjoy as much as the authors have the more and less subtle content available in the films themselves, from the highest to the lowest range of production values and formal ratings. When in doubt: See the movie.

There are many people to thank for our intellectual journey back to the films of our childhoods and forward toward clearer views of film culture. The most important is Abraham Polonsky. If he did not live long enough to criticize the manuscript, he inspired many of its insights, directly and indirectly.

Reaching far back to a past that we two authors shared in the 1960s and 70s (taking part in demonstrations and assorted antiwar activities, working on an "underground" newspaper, teaching in an alternative college program, and, most especially, editing two New Left–era journals, *Radical America* and *Cultural Correspondence*), we were further guided by the ideas and personal inspiration of another magnum cultural figure, the Trinidadian-born C. L. R. James (1901–1989), anti-Stalinist Marxist and the last of the great Pan-Africanists. James's fluent writings on sports, music, and literature have been instrumental in our efforts to upturn the cultural critique of the Frankfurt School while keeping the dialectic intact.

So, too, we are grateful to our teachers in Madison, Wisconsin, especially the late George Mosse, for giving us a broad understanding of the European cultural background; to friends and comrades along the way, counting among them fellow film aficionados Robert Hethmon, Michael Tapper, George Lipsitz, David Marc, Danny Czitrom, Franklin Rosemont, Dan Georgakas, Larry Ceplair, and Patrick McGilligan; to the Harburg Foundation, for sponsoring Hollywood interviewing trips and making possible initial purchases of many film videos; to the Southern California Library for Research and Social Change, for assorted assistance, and to the late Marvin Goldsmith in particular for serving as our chauffeur and foot-in-the-door introducer to old-timers; to hardworking research assistants Kirsten Ostherr, Marion Coffey, and Judith Rosenbaum, and to Grace Wagner for special research efforts; to film scholar Judith Smith, for her careful reading of the manuscript; and to interviewees, correspondents, and friends within the shrinking blacklist community, including Norma Barzman, Sylvia Jarrico, William Marshall, Anne Froelick, Maurice Rapf, Jean

Rouverol Butler, Robert Lees, John Randolph, Jules Dassin, Walter Bernstein, Jeff Corey, Marsha Hunt, Adele Ritt, Joan Scott, our late friends Frank Tarloff, Millard Lampell, Paul Jarrico, Carleton Moss, Leonardo Bercovici, and especially the late Ring Lardner, Jr., who supplied names and addresses of potential interviewees early in the game. Darker Image video supplied some especially rare films. John Weber kindly read chapters and generously gave us his criticisms from one who was there, almost literally until his death in May 2001. Thanks also go especially to the gifted Sarah Fan, our editor at The New Press, for seeing this work to a finish.

1. Dika Newlin, *Schoenberg Remembered: Diaries and Recollections, 1938–1976* (New York: Pendragon, 1980), 337.

2. Theodor Adorno, "Arnold Schoenberg 1874–1951," in *Prisms* (London: Nevil Spearman, 1967), translated by Sam and Shierry Weber, 150.

3. Levy, a former playwright whose other credits include a coscript for the hard-hitting *Two Years Before the Mast,* testified cautiously about himself and his former milieu; he left films and later considered himself a victim of the blacklist.

4. Andre Bazin, *What Is Cinema?, Volume II* (Berkeley: University of California, 1971), 141.

5. One of the conceptual gems offered by Abraham Polonsky to us verbally during repeated interviews during 1992–99.

6. W. McNeil Lowry, "A Writers' Congress and Its Credo," *The New York Times Book Review,* September 27, 1944.

7. Buñuel's screenwriter was Hugo Butler, about whom much is written in this volume. Butler scripted for Buñuel, whom he knew well in Mexico in the 1950s, *The Adventures of Robinson Crusoe* (1951) and *The Young One* (1961).

8. The most vivid example was the 1996 ceremony, with Steven Spielberg narrating clips from historic Hollywood "social" films, most of them written by blacklistees; and a similar retrospective of clips from Kirk Douglas's films, from *Champion* to *Spartacus,* with the same suspiciously familiar connections. That same year, the Academy President's Award was given to *Blacklist: Hollywood on Trial,* the documentary made by Howard Koch's son, Christopher Koch, and shown on American Movie Classics. Also that year, radio producer Tony Kahn (the son of blacklistee Gordon Kahn) released a highly praised, six-part reenactment of the high and low points in his father's life from Hol-

lywood, Mexico, New England, and a fatal heart attack at age fifty-two. Pacifica and some National Public Radio stations carried the show.

9. AMC has a backlist of seven hundred film titles to draw from, Turner a list of six thousand. These collections lack for the most part three or four hundred B films, especially low-budget Westerns, and many titles of Republic or the still-smaller Poverty Row studios with blacklist connections. A growing number of these presently "missing" (for the ordinary viewer, and in some cases for the scholar), however, turn up on the eclectic satellite-based stations, or suddenly reappear in film collectors' catalogs.

10. Michael Wilson, "I Am the Sum of My Actions," interview with Joel Gardner, 1975. Oral History Program, UCLA, 121. Among Wilson's own efforts under his real name was coscript credit, with noted liberal Rod Serling, for the original *Planet of the Apes* (1968), an Oscar winner that led to four sequels and two television series. Only the most deadened fans missed the social satire in the original.

11. Helen Manfull, ed., *Additional Dialogue: Letters of Dalton Trumbo, 1942–1962* (New York: M. Evans, 1970), 282–83.

1 ★

THE SCREENWRITER'S FATE

ETERAN WRITER W. R. BURNETT was on hand in 1930 for the Los
Angeles premiere of the pace-setting crime drama *Little Caesar,* but as
the credits were announced, he stirred in his seat, deeply frustrated.
Proud studio officials introduced actors, director, and cinematographer onstage and finally—almost as an afterthought—the ultimate literary source.
The emcee reportedly quipped, "there always has to be a writer," to which
an embittered Burnett claims that he stage-whispered, "Screw you!"
Burnett's description of a primal incident at the birth of sound film,
demonstrating the indignity of the writer's trade, sidesteps one crucial element. Burnett was actually the *novelist* and not even the more important
half of the film's two-man screenwriting team. His characteristic disrespect
for the actual script ("it wasn't very good") typified the ways in which the
ostensibly ignored and abused novelist remained still a head taller than the
screenwriters. Conspicuously unmentioned at the same opening, their absence subtly suggested that perhaps there didn't really need to be that kind
of writer at all.[1]

Francis Faragoh, a Hungarian Jewish immigrant, had taken over the
script from a failed first attempt at adaptation and rewritten it from top
to bottom, slicing away larger and larger parts of the novel to give the
screen version what turned out to be its genre-creating credibility. A
former theatrical avant-gardist hailed by *The New York Times* for his
achievements, Faragoh was to experience ups and downs typical of the
screenwriter's Hollywood, including prestigious assignments in some of
the first color films to enduring family favorites. Unionism and left-wing

politics, scarcely in his mind when he left New York, nevertheless shaped his studio career, his social and personal life. Faragoh offers a picture-perfect example of the truism that radical screenwriters were not born but made. *Little Caesar* also fairly presented for the first time the curious contradiction that the crime story along with women's films offered the right genre for the early exploration of social discontent and the subtle evasion of political censorship by the skilled writer.

In the beginning, with the slow rise of silent film and sudden emergence of producer-merchandisers in giant studios, the writer's job had been truly a mystery. Directors and important actors often composed the film plots as they went along, seeking to avoid repetition of details from some earlier movie while providing essentially the same package of saleable entertainment. Writers first broke in as "captionists," toiling for the studios to develop dialogue through explanatory sentences or "intertitles," and then eventually the plots. As film stories began to become more complex, around 1910, story departments were set up with two main purposes: to analyze material submitted for possible use, and to monitor (or mine) sources like Broadway theater, slick magazine fiction, and best-selling novels for ideas. The increasing difficulty of outright plagiarism, always a quietly happy notion in Hollywood, propelled studio executives to import proven talent. Except for European exiles, the outsiders were mostly New Yorkers.

But hardly radical ones. The sudden spurt of studio growth around 1920 created a demand for more writers—limited to those willing (with the rarest exceptions) to toe the political line. During the "new era" of apparently limitless capitalism (but also of the so-called Soviet Menace), the diversion of the masses' minds from social change to personal escape was openly discussed, and not only in the business or Marxist press but as a ready fact of life. It was as common a topic as scientific management ("Taylorism") or expanded overseas sales of American commodities generally. The steady stream of anti-Bolshevist or antiunion movies seldom drew big audiences, but writers were expected to celebrate the society of abundance even while drawing upon exotic themes, exploiting star appeal with sexual innuendo, and reproaching certain kinds of evildoers.

From a more value-neutral viewpoint, movie production also reorganized along lines already adopted by the makers of automobiles, steel, chemicals, and other commodities rationalized for domestic and international sales. Studio insiders set themselves to the task, complicated by the continuing chaos of the market and by the predilection of rising moguls, to staff their operations with relatives. Contemporary automobile makers if not the machine-tool makers who supplied the parts also had to please the public's current fantasies, even to create them. But there was a difference: Henry Ford and his competitors rarely had to bring in the equivalent of a noted playwright or novelist and then domesticate his or her creative energy. That was the rub, all around. The sound era once more multiplied the demand for writers, this time tenfold, virtually overnight. It also heightened the natural tensions between creative impulses and business practice at the historical moment of capitalist breakdown.

The global movie industry had already faced political and artistic challenges unknown in America. After the First World War, when the French lost their short-lived monopoly on world film production outside the United States (where French films were also heavily distributed), there arose in virtually every film capital from Moscow to Rome to Berlin a new generation of filmmakers whose political allegiances were solidly on the left. They were antiwar as a matter of course, in the wake of the recent horrors, and committed to telling stories of the vast urban populations at a time when censors and conservatives suppressed tales of crime and hunger as insults to national character. And so it was that a new, worldwide popular art with progressive political shading emerged, not only deeply rooted in the century's rapidly developing electromechanical technology but also in the social relations of the emerging industrial-urban population alongside social movements that were most closely identified with that population.[2]

Back in the United States, themes of sympathy for the worthy poor and ridicule for authority had managed to find their way to the silent screen, usually in the guise of the heavily gendered melodrama or the antic Keystone Kops styles, but also in the artistic and overwhelmingly popular "Little Tramp" pictures. With fitting symbolism, the formation of United Artists in 1919 by Charles Chaplin and his star-colleagues Douglas Fairbanks, Sr., and Mary Pickford signaled the first of many efforts to defend creative control as well as distribution and profits from the effects of monopolization (more properly, oligopolization). UA succeeded—but only for its own small production team, spurring limited-scale "artistic" production in later decades. At the "Poverty Row" end of undercapitalized studios, independents grew up almost as fast as they collapsed, and were replaced by fresh contenders without offering serious competition to the mainstream. The giants themselves waxed stronger or weaker, merged and even sometimes collapsed. But they never lost confidence or overall control of the market until the late 1940s, when unexpected weaknesses found them at their most overgrown.

What Abraham Polonsky observed at the end of the century had been true almost from the beginning, that radicals and serious artists had dreamed endlessly of escaping the studio system. Some did. But major filmmaking took place almost exclusively within it, at least through the Second World War. Scatterings of insurgents had to find their way within the maze and monopolies, not even to make peace with the less abusive sections of it but simply to create a workable niche for themselves and their friends. With genius suitable to the rapidly evolving medium, capable of creating a serious as well as brilliantly humorous cinema, the talented writers, along with their acting, directing, producing, and technical counterparts, needed the studios. Their talent for subverting the conservative standards of Hollywood film, usually deployed only within very limited ways until the close of the 1930s and even beyond, found expression in subtleties that managed to evade censors and critics alike.[3]

These needs were likely to come together, in the short run, in sometimes highly curious ways, under the radar of political censorship but verging on the radar screen for censorship of other kinds. Neither crime films nor women's films allowed glimpses of a better world. But rebellious criminals gave audiences license for their outrage at the consequences of the economic collapse, and rebellious women gave female viewers in particular the psychic reinforcement that many craved. Studio assignments found radicalized writers more than prepared to turn in lively scripts on these subjects.

The studios were fortunate in another, closely related sense. By the last few years of silent films, Broadway had entered a lush moment along with the lively neighborhood and college theaters. Plenty of talent was available for the asking, and more on the way with the invention of the stage musical thanks to the concatenation of a sophisticated audience, talented actors, flourishing producers, and a circle of mostly Jewish lyricists and composers. And here we might take a first glance at a curious contradiction from within the consolidating studio system: that the rank and file of the opposition developed deep within the entertainment business at large and frequently from the most unexpected comers. Not a single genre would appear less susceptible to radical intervention than the musical, and no one—neither studio chiefs nor the musical artisans themselves—suspected just how progressive-minded these young men were to become or how heavily they would pay for it.

To commence with a single and improbable example: Ira Gershwin, who would host the anti-blacklist Committee for the First Amendment (CFA) meetings of Hollywood progressives in 1947, emerged as a major popular composer during the 1920s with Broadway hits in collaboration with his more famous brother, George.[4] Ira's film credits stretched from *Shall We Dance* (1937) to *Funny Face* (1957). In 1929, former businessman Yip Harburg—who had been on hand in that famous moment when the first piano was delivered to the Gershwin family flat—began writing lyrics with the encouragement of his lifelong pal Ira, who effectively prepared Yip for future collaborators and film-score writers. By 1932, Yip had a hit show and had written to fellow future blacklistee Jay Gorney's shtetl-inflected melancholy tune the ultimate radicalizing musical statement of the Depression, "Brother, Can You Spare a Dime?"[5] After various ups and (mostly) downs in Hollywood, Harburg recast the structure of a collapsing musical production through his songs, effectively realizing *The Wizard of Oz* (1939). He personally put the age-old radical "rainbow sign" into the movies, a feature absent from *Oz*'s Populist literary original.[6]

To take another fascinating if less spectacular example of the unexpected species of insurgent musical talent, sometime Broadway actor and stage manager Edward Eliscu, who worked with future Hollywood giant (and blacklistee) Sidney Buchman in Adirondacks summer entertainment, also began writing lyrics with some success during the late 1920s. The Depression's crushing effect on Broadway and a fortuitous call from Hollywood offered him a new setting; according to his testimony, he came West without a single self-conscious political impulse. Inside of a year, his songs, along with the gag routines of leftish Henry Myers and a young Joseph Mankiewicz, marked the hilariously anti-Establishment Wheeler and Woolsey vehicle *Diplomaniacs* (1933). Thereafter, Eliscu accommodated his skills to Eddie Cantor (himself soon to be an ardent actor-unionist and outspoken antifascist) in routine studio work.[7]

Like Eliscu's intimate friend Mortimer Offner, a boyhood pal of

Hungarian-Jewish director George Cukor and a frequent early screen-writer for Katharine Hepburn, and like his writing mentor, Francis Faragoh, Eliscu was gaining maturity. Buchman, Gorney, Harburg, Eliscu, Offner, and Faragoh would all go on the blacklist not so much for their deep political attachments—only Faragoh gained any prominence in Communist Party circles or even seems to have belonged for an extended period—as for their personal experiences and their loyalty to one another as Jews and as progressives in an uncertain America.

Hollywood of the early 1930s did not by any means rely wholly upon the training grounds that theater supplied, but it could not have come up with prestigious writers otherwise, or easily filled what Marxists might properly label the "reserve army of mental labor." In the depth of the Depression, studios had on staff something like eight hundred writers, full- or part-time, including lyricists. The story departments also employed within and outside the studios hundreds of "screen readers" of potential film-worthy material, men and a scattering of women from all backgrounds, intellectuals who (with left-wing guidance) eventually formed their own militant union but also often turned their jobs into stepping-stones writing scripts.[8]

Actor-director Irving Pichel, one of the studio insiders who could rightly be called a cinematic theoretician, observed later that the emergence of sound at first seemed to set back film innovation a notch or two. Studio heads, who never lost their low regard for the former caption writers, saw themselves taking full advantage of the availability of theatrical plays by having it both ways. Now that they possessed ready-made scripts for sound production, they immediately sought to simplify movies into "screen plays," minimizing the expenses and trouble of increasingly sophisticated camera work that had been more and more skillfully realized in silent film; meanwhile, they could ignore the intentions of the playwrights as well, ordering rewrites according to formula.[9]

These self-serving assumptions turned out to be doubly false. Audiences demanded and got steadily advancing innovations in technique and narrative, while writers insisted upon the point (without the personal prestige or power to drive it home) that film always began with the story. Studio executives, accepting these realities, nevertheless sought once more to make the best of the situation, subordinating nearly every creative impulse to their own authority.

Formulas came quickly to the sound era, especially as mostly newer film stars were recognized and merchandised through feature after predictable feature, much as earlier stars had been in the silents. In the standard narrative woven by film historians, one cycle of films after another follows in the Golden Age, influenced by the trends of censorship and by the technical integration of the narrative film process, even more by what the studios took to be passing audience fads. At first inspiring dozens of imitations and then exhausting a genre from sheer popular weariness, such cycles simultaneously demanded the birth of new subgenres. Most of the successful writers who were not stuck in the low-budget "series" (like Westerns) followed the trends by virtue of the projects assigned them.[10]

This narrative, repeated so often and so usefully to describe the thinking of studio execs and the films of the most famous Hollywood stars, is less adequate to explain the fuller scope of film production and of screenwriting. The gangster film, for instance, no longer at its apex after the middle-to-late 1930s, never really goes away. Like other styles or models, its elements survive in more complex or sophisticated films; but in reduced form, the gangster film simultaneously sinks into the B genres with endless variations. Likewise, what has been described as the "comedian comedy" predominant in the early 1930s, based upon a vaudeville style of stage action breaking up a thin plot rather than the plot becoming the basis for comedy (as in more sophisticated comedy-drama ascendant in the later 1930s), returns and actually reaches new heights of production during wartime, when low-budget films are turned out at an all-time rapid clip.[11]

The same could also be said of other major genres, from the melodramatic women's film to that all-time B staple, the cowboys. In the usual succession of developments, formula comes to film production, then creative expression, then still more creative expression, and then a lot more formula until television takes over almost all of it, except for the most violent and salacious of the lower genres. Even there, the humblest film spinoff requires a writer.

Much the same story could readily be demonstrated for a handful of other genres less persistent than the Western: the "family comedy," which had its first heyday in the later 1930s; the historical drama and biopic (also in the later 1930s, although with more scattered examples); the war film (its wartime production levels were never approached before or after 1942–45, but the genre was reworked steadily across the eras); the horror film (whose classic 1930s turns into a satiric 1940s, then waves of restored horror and camp ever since); even the screwball and working-class action films, which may indeed have crested respectively in the middle 1930s and middle forties but had ample precursors and more than ample successors. Meanwhile, the productions of near–Poverty Row studios like Republic as well as the B's produced by bigger studios, not to mention the down-deep Poverty Row outfits like Producers Releasing Corporation, figured heavily in the work that average Hollywood writers did and the conditions under which they did it.[12]

Notwithstanding these industry details, the cycles of prestige material unquestionably tell their own story for the public, for the industry, and for the writer. Hollywood had already perfected the star system by the early 1920s; designated the "sin" pictures, exotics, three-hanky melodramas, broad and artistic comedy, sports and college stories, to name only a few themes. Sound required almost a total changeover of stars and the kinds of films written for each, among other adjustments. Most of all, thanks to initial costs of the new technology and the damaging effects of the Depression on receipts, the industry now badly needed to reorient its use of precious resources. Threats of censorship soon sharpened the new focus, and an array of technological developments as well as technical integration of the film narrative moved the picture toward a kind of forced maturity by the opening of the Second New Deal in 1936.

The appearance of the Hollywood Left was tied inextricably to these issues, as was the political and cultural life of millions of other Americans. Technology had repeatedly reinvented screenwriting along with a score of other new film-connected occupations. The Broadway playwright, the famed novelist, and/or the highly paid short-story writer for the slicks took the royal road to the new medium. But the average screenwriter hacking out a bare living found himself (or herself) placed within a contemporary class status analogously described by a historian of social welfare professionalism as simultaneously white-collar proletarian and new middle class, sometimes getting along rather well—occasionally, in the case of the famous screenwriters, spectacularly—but altogether lacking the solid property (land or small business) that the old middle class since the American Revolution had treated as the sacred foundation of citizenship.[13] The screenwriter worked "with his hands" only as much as a bank clerk, social worker, typist, or other white-collar worker; like them, he could be dismissed as readily as a nonunion ditchdigger.

For all the political and social excitement of the disinherited and the industrial worker during the 1930s, the creative response of these white-collar workers to the realities of the Depression etched many of the lasting images of the "Red Decade." The Works Progress Administration (WPA) gatherer of data on local sights, history, and culture; the unfamous muralist or photographer; the neighborhood dentist for ethnic fraternal groups; the public schoolteacher or small businessman who (along with friends or family) patronized and often took part in the higher divisions of radical culture (theater, folk, and choral music), sympathized and empathized with the blue-collar economic movements, and all had their own class-connected dreams and dilemmas. No group (apart from second-generation ethnics, often the same people) responded more enthusiastically and creatively to the appeal of the New Deal. But their attention—especially in the Jewish lower middle class, just one step from their immigrant parents and the memories of sweatshop socialism—had already been aroused by the economic crisis and by the appeal of potential solutions somewhere beyond capitalism.

The screenwriters, uniquely placed but far from alone in their fears and desires, had the distinct advantage of an industry that bounced back fairly quickly from the depths of depressed economics. But their employers, the studios, gave them no cause for gratitude. On the contrary, they had to fight individually and collectively for elementary rights as they faced pay cuts, layoffs, and discrimination. At the same time, they had at least the unique chance to reach millions of movie-mad consumers with images of something interesting and perhaps something important.

Even the highly paid and publicized screenwriter-king could sometimes feel keenly the frustrations and idealist impulses, partly from the influence of less fortunate workmates and colleagues, partly from the world around him (now less often her: The percentages of women screenwriters declined sharply after silent-film production), and very largely from the overwhelming power of the studio corporations in a mini-world where capital seemed to hold all the cards. Philip Dunne, the genial non-Communist (and son of famed columnist Finley Peter Dunne) who at times shared the organizations of the liberal Left and at other times broke with them, was a highly successful screenwriter from the late 1930s onward. Yet for him, too, "Life on the Assembly Line" at Twentieth Century-Fox constantly demonstrated how, even with a highly intelligent executive like Darryl Zanuck, writers faced arbitrary decisions and threats of firing on any given day at work. These creative underbosses, too, hated unions, and for the same reasons as their equivalents outside Hollywood: loss of prerogative and threat to the bottom line.[14]

The film industry's leaders recognized rapidly that studios needed to keep the theaters stocked by further rationalizing production. In the early Depression, only radio prospered among the major media, with falling prices of radios destined to bring down the huge inventory overstock and with continuing profits for the major networks. Most of the big studios, by contrast, lost money hand over fist during the early Depression years. RKO, Paramount, and Fox all went into bankruptcy by 1933, a trend that accelerated consolidation and control of Wall Street that was already under way from investment in equipment for the new sound films.[15] Bankers were good at firing studio workers (and occasionally, if not often, studio executives) but were notably untalented at making films. Movie people soon resumed operations at higher levels, but with a newly burnished corporate-style bureaucracy firmly in place, turning Hollywood from a society of semi-mavericks into a complex and carefully structured system designed to turn out and (just as important) to market a more regularized product. Studio ownership of movie theaters, finally ordered broken up by the Supreme Court in 1948, was only one means to the end.

Some of the strategies meant to achieve this goal had important, if unintended, side effects for our main players. The double feature, already employed to draw crowds in the 1920s, seemed at first to have been wiped out by the cost of producing sound films. By mid-decade, the double feature was back, seized upon first as salvation for the independent exhibitors who could not compete otherwise, and then taken up by the studio-affiliated theaters that needed to meet the competition for a bargain-minded public. Poverty Row and the lesser divisions of large studios determinedly filled the gap with films shot in days and finished for as little as $50,000 (compared with $400,000, and occasionally millions, for the A features). As we shall see, more left-wingers would work at the bottom than anywhere else, especially as film production kicked into its highest gear after 1940 and the low-budget feature inspired independent production.

One more factor would play a crucial role in our story: official censorship. The industry's trade office, the Motion Picture Producers and Distributors of America (MPPDA), hired Will Hays in 1922 to serve as taste czar of product-control. The specter of censorship had haunted the industry since the earliest local ordinance directed at film exhibition had been passed in Chicago in 1907, with many of the same structures maintained for decades afterward. The careful observation of art was more likely, however, to be the supposed control of vice, as progressive reformers contrasted filmgoing to healthful "recreation." The MPPDA, emerging in the late 1910s, safeguarded the reputation of the industry while it set in place the controls of the filmmaking and distributing oligopoly, with Hays supposedly representing the public interest, which is to say, proper morality.

During the dizzy 1920s, when urban sin mocked Main Street, and Broadway was evidently on the side of sin, movie producers were caught at their own game. It is notable that leading Protestant organs of opinion accused Hays of being chosen by certain "shrewd Hebrews" to front for them, a clear foreshadowing of House Un-American Activities Committee charges a decade later that Hollywood operated a Jewish conspiracy against "American" values. An early crisis of credibility for the MPPDA and Hays Office brought a formalization of "the Code" in 1931, with heavy stress upon propriety.[16]

The cash crisis of the industry and the uncertainty of the Code allowed a certain slackness that made Mae West films possible, along with a large genre of titillating "Fallen Women" films. Influential Catholics, working closely with insider Joseph I. Breen, staged a virtual boycott in 1934, with the Catholic Legion of Decency threatening a protest week—an action backed by powerful Catholic bishops and their influential Episcopalian counterparts. Breen thus won his point, cagily counting upon the industry's need to tighten regulation from the inside. Already by 1933, potentially lucrative films were being withheld from release and then drastically reconstructed and in some cases refused certification when studios attempted to rerelease them without significant changes. While the Hays Office sought to establish a widened, respectable, middle-class public for films, Breen's ascendance in 1934 to run the office's Production Code Administration signaled a determination to systematize regulation of limits, based upon the presumed *intended* effect of a film upon the audience.[17]

If no picture could be released that somehow lowered the moral standards of the audience, then movies not only had to have proper conclu-sions—they also had to supply elaborate explanations for apparently unsa-vory events taking place offscreen as well. In the *Dead End* of Sidney Kingsley's stage version, Humphrey Bogart's former moll, clearly a street-walker who had contracted syphilis, became in the film a victim of tu-berculosis, thanks in part to a cough added to the sound track. How thoroughly or exactly this "explained" her fallen quality and made sense of the plot (a final blow to the mobster's ego as he returned to his old neigh-borhood and was rejected by his mother) remained in the gray area along with the question of how the audience actually interpreted the censored material.

Possible political implications of film were not usually so mysterious. Breen himself regarded Communism (or socialism) as an immorality not unlike crime, never to be lauded; outright attacks upon capitalists as a class were also forbidden, however evil this or that individual capitalist might be portrayed. Labor unions, even in the era when President Franklin D. Roosevelt depended heavily upon the Committee for Industrial Organiza-tion for reelection, were systematically denied sympathetic portrayal. As in so many other areas, Hollywood needed years of catching up to supposedly conservative popular values. In public, Breen insisted upon a "balanced" rather than a critical treatment of Hitler and Mussolini, virtually up to wartime, and he openly admired Francisco Franco. In private, he poured out to friends his deep-seated anti-Semitism ("These Jews seem to think of nothing but money making and sexual indulgence," he wrote in 1937. "They are, probably, the scum of the earth." [18])

Conservative Catholic values thus reigned curiously in American life where Catholics had only recently, during the 1920s, been under heavy Protestant attack, and where Jews (often stigmatized by Catholic authori-ties through the centuries) had so large a role to play in entertainment. With far greater success, Breen also prevented the making of films attack-ing Spanish fascism or those supporting the Loyalists, the bête noire of the zealously pro-Franco Church. The banning of divorced characters in films, especially remarried ones who seemed happy, proved more difficult to en-force. By the end of the 1930s, assorted legal questions caused the Code of-fice to back off a bit on many specifics, opening the door to what Breen's adviser, Catholic layman Martin Quigley, described nervously as a rising "Red Propaganda" that the "Hebrew brethren" of Hollywood had allowed to flourish and perhaps even encouraged.[19] In that moment and still under cover of liberal or humanist phraseology, the Hollywood Left would come of age.

The crime story and the women's film might be described as major zones of contention. The original stories and screenwriting tasks of some of the earliest of Hollywood's radical writers, especially John Bright, Sidney Buchman, Donald Ogden Stewart, and John Howard Lawson, show how left-wingers had an early remarkable impact in the face of apparently implacable barriers. They also showed how the promise of a better cinema would inevitably be short-circuited unless and until creative impulse turned into cinematic breakthrough and into the kinds of mobilization that were required to make better films possible. As much as the ordinary writer might wish to rise to the starry heights of fabled (in a handful of cases, real) $1,000 per week salaries and some degree of creative control (still more rare), unionization not so completely different from that of the Depression's restless working stiffs proved a necessary road through the New Deal landscape, with the Popular Front painting on many a horizon the sunset of a happy ending.

Public Enemy or Outsider?

Thanks to *Little Caesar* (1930) and *The Public Enemy* (1931), the first major sound film genre combining enormous popular appeal and critical social significance suddenly came of age.[20] Faragoh's talent in reconstructing the *Little Caesar* script without much regard either for the previous adaptation or the novel surely gives pause. Shifting to Hollywood in 1929, he was barely away from the Neighborhood Playhouse (on Grand Street) production of *Pinwheel* (subtitled "a play of New York"), which mixed jazz, images of Coney Island, automobile horns, and elevated train rattles, all staged on a constructivist set, with two floors of action that included an imagined city street, tenement, cabaret, and movie theater.[21]

Faragoh the newly minted Hollywoodite quickly went on after *Little Caesar* to script: *Frankenstein,* also a genre-setting screen phenomenon; the first color literary adaptation to film (*Becky Sharp,* from William Makepeace Thackeray's *Vanity Fair*); the first color dance-musical (*The Dancing Pirate*); and a handful of gender-heavy romance films. Near the end of a foreshortened career he wrote the children's classic *My Friend Flicka*. Punished by the studios for his pioneering role in the Screen Writers Guild, he received his vindication as chair of the Hollywood Writers Mobilization in 1943. He shared, for that moment, the spotlight with respected academics and top film executives—leaving no doubt that he would be marked for the blacklist a few years later. The talented and highly versatile Faragoh has disappeared from cinema history, popular or scholarly, quite as W. R. Burnett almost escaped the attention of the premiere movie-house audience.

Little Caesar remains a tribute to Faragoh's skill in relating the story of the small-town thief who makes his entry into organized crime by raiding a Manhattan mob nightclub and murdering the crime commissioner who is suspiciously on hand. *Little Caesar* is also a tribute to the persona of unlovable, unforgivable, and unhandsome tough guy Edward G. Robinson (a real-life Hollywood intellectual close to the Left) as the unmistakably Italian-American "Rico." He rises from slum conditions, stepping over former friends to climb upward, brags vulgarly about his successes in the style of Al Capone, until in the final reel, his individualist triumph falls hard on reality: "Mother of God, is this the end of Rico?" is his last line as he drops dead. The opening weekend of its release, *Little Caesar* broke all records for Warner Brothers' showpiece Strand Theater in Manhattan and went on to take the country by storm. Reviewers, failing in these early days even to mention the existence of screenwriters, correctly predicted its inauguration of a movie type.[22]

The distinctly left-wing origins of the second big gangster hit, *The Public Enemy*—its impact so long-lasting that even the noir television hit *The Sopranos* has been added to the list of inspired by the original—have until recent years also been neglected.[23] Both politically and aesthetically, scriptwriter John Bright was, with Faragoh, the first important left-wing innovator in Hollywood. *The Public Enemy* also had the great box office virtue of relating events that the public knew about from the tabloid press, thus blurring boundaries between news and fiction in ways that only the rare literate, socially critical silent films had done earlier.[24]

A native Chicagoan, Bright had been drawn as a youngster toward a fading radical milieu of great significance: hobo-intellectuals, the free-spirited and free-loving bunch around Dr. Ben Reitman (Emma Goldman's longtime lover) and the badly diminished but still evocative Industrial Workers of the World (IWW) headquartered in the Windy City.

Remnant of the war era when President Woodrow Wilson's attorney general had ordered the outright suppression of the Wobs, the survivors fit uncomfortably within a reorganized political Left dominated by would-be American Bolsheviks. On the near north side of the Loop, a "Hobohemia" ruled, with free-speech zones for soapboxing speakers, clubs catering to autodidact proletarians as well as to artists, drug-takers, gays and lesbians, and a general atmosphere of anything-goes.[25]

Intermittently a communist, Bright was always and more profoundly the product of this environment, the roughneck bohemian "sport" who hung out in nightspots and with crowds far below normal Hollywood taste. He didn't, really couldn't, fit into either studio expectations or standard left-wing expectations of dignity and uplift. But for those reasons he proved just right for two transition genres and for one star in particular: James Cagney.[26]

Many of the future blacklistees came from neighborhoods just as rough and interesting as Bright's, with radical ideas in the air. But a special feeling for gangsterism as *the* American epic belonged to Chicagoans, and Bright's perception was nothing if not firsthand. Born in 1908, he left for Manhattan to attend the New School. When the outbreak of the Depression forced a return home, he went to work for Polish-Jewish, small-time bootlegger Kubec Glasmon, who owned a neighborhood drugstore and sold illegal liquor on the side—usually delivered by the young clerk personally. Together, Bright and Glasmon penned a never-to-be-published novel-saga of Chicago gang life, *Beer and Blood,* with lots of action and fairly realistic (if vulgarity-purged) street talk. They so convinced themselves they could sell it to Hollywood that they sailed through the Panama Canal to California. The impulsive Darryl Zanuck, then Harry Warner's right-hand man, knew promising material when he saw it. He compelled the team to cut down on plot complications and to rivet the story to the main character.

Zanuck was dead right: The "Public Enemy" kind of mobster cut a contemporary social figure who needed only the right script and actor to put the concept across. The studio added a self-serving prologue in "documentary" style to establish the legitimacy of the portrayal before the viewer could enjoy the blood and beer. The gangster had appeared in 1920s vernacular as the American individualist closely akin to the ready-at-the-draw cowboy. Prohibition made this new type of individualist at once economically possible and charismatic in public life, as Americans imaginatively paid for their social sins by following the tabloid stories of particular gangsters' spectacular rise and fall. The gangster image reached the mass audience with fresh meaning after the Crash: Repeal remained several years away, and by this time politicians had been discredited along with industrialists as model citizens. The widespread sense of bitterness and the yearning for vicarious revenge found the perfect protagonist here, even if he needed (for purposes of propriety) to be killed off at the end.

Bright and Glasmon's contribution, more creative and more significant by far than Faragoh's in his adaptation, was not confined to the script for *The Public Enemy*—it also included the very creation of movie-star Cagney, whom they successfully pressed upon Zanuck for the film's lead. Like Humphrey Bogart, Paul Muni, John Garfield, Marlon Brando, and so many others, Cagney would serve as protean proletarian, template for the personae of the characters that left-wing screenwriters could spin off into dozens of situations and psychic dilemmas. It was crucial for the movies that Cagney's persona and not his acting (heretofore limited mostly to the stage) had shown the two would-be screenwriters that the young man was perfect for the part. He had the stance and the moves to project what Robert Sklar has described as the "tough/tender" character who can be ruthless but also has a vulnerable, almost feminine side. Unlike Caesar, who is fascinating only in his cruelty and moral corruption, Cagney's character is attractive because his contradictions reveal those of the larger society.[27]

Indeed, in *The Public Enemy,* it is precisely after tender moments with women (in which he notably does not seduce but *is* seduced) that the Cagney character breaks out in raw and sadistic violence. In the crucial scene, after a rendezvous with a gangster's moll that diverts his attention and costs his closest friend's life, Cagney's gangster-protagonist throws himself into an obviously suicidal raid on a rival mob. He escapes immediate death only to be dropped, mortally wounded, upon his mother's doorstep, so swaddled in cloth that he resembles the infant that has never escaped into maturity.

Zanuck, director William Wellman (likewise chosen through fierce lobbying by Bright and Glasmon), and additional-scenario writer Harvey Thew thus gave the Irish former stage actor—memorable for his facility with Yiddish—the space he needed to expand his cinematic self. This was to remain the essence of his screen presence in his best work. Bright along with Glasmon had also been intellectually crucial right from the film's opening scenes in which Cagney and his pal (played by Edward Woods), slum youngsters taking up the bootlegging trade, learn about the social relations of capitalist society by observing the scheming "legitimate" businessman brewery owner be brutal to his employees and eager to get help from the dark side.

Dramatically illustrated in the infamous grapefruit-in-the-moll's-kisser scene that had been taken entire from *Beer and Blood,* their script also advanced a statement on the underlying psychological sources of violence in the relations between men and women. Not only emotionally immature but unable (in his own mind, unwilling) to accept a world of even vaguely equal gender relations, Cagney's character takes out the underlying frustration on everyone around him, from his family to those he sees as thwarting him. That response, with or without the sexual element embedded in it, was, in fact, an important feature of the success and long-lasting influence of *Little Caesar* as well. The two films must be regarded as among the early use of sound film psychologizing its characters within a social context. Like the writers of the *Godfather* epics that four decades later most fully realized the full possibilities of the genre, Faragoh and Bright (along with their collaborators) had struck an authentic American chord.

Socially conscious critics at the time and later, most keenly those in the left-wing press, would complain quite accurately that the implied critique of capitalism always disappeared in gangster films' last reel, with individual madness displacing all else. That was due, in no small part, to the effort to meet censors' demands for a satisfactorily moralistic and individualist conclusion. Hollywood standards forced writers to pull their final punches, then and for decades to come.

Other critics would observe, just as accurately, that the imposition of the ineffective early enforcement of the Production Code by the Hays Office had not been intended to banish screen violence as such but to wall off the psychopathic personality from the idealized family, protected on the other flank from the satires and assorted bohemian messages of the likes of lesbian director Dorothy Arzner and actress-writer Mae West. In *The Public Enemy,* when Cagney's honest brother picks a solid working-class girl for a "normal" family life, Cagney himself turns to Jean Harlow, a free-lover and cynic who represents the disintegration of feminine decency, as well as someone who could never reciprocate his love and help bring him to emotional maturity.

Here as so often, we lack the direct testimony from screenwriters that would suggest what mix of studio pressures, self-censorship, or the effort to concoct a workable story caused these particular narrative contours.[28] The most likely possibility is the last, for the same reasons that limited and shaped the creative contributions of the Hollywood Left at large. Screenwriters quickly gauged what could be done within a genre and resolved to push the edges.

Screenwriter Bright himself pushed onward in the filmic demimonde. His collaborations with Glasmon ended after 1932, about the time (according to Bright's recollections) when he demanded more money for his writing and tried to throw the notoriously imperious and tightfisted Zanuck out a second-story studio window. Within that brief frame, Bright's further explorations into crime and working-class life give us clear indications of how he was working and what a rebellious Hollywood intellectual *could* do.

Blonde Crazy (1931), made a few months after *The Public Enemy,* has not stood up similarly because it etched no genre archetypes; but it is another of Cagney's signature films and contains conceptual dynamite that critics have barely acknowledged. Here, Cagney plays a talented grifter who falls for an apparently ordinary, honest, working-class girl played by Joan Blondell, who had a small part in *The Public Enemy* and was teamed by the studio with Cagney. (*Blonde Crazy* was written expressly for the duo after Bright persuaded Zanuck that she was right for this kind of part.) Blondell slaps him when he makes a pass at her, but she is only intending to put him in his place; he soon draws her into his scams by revealing to her how easy it can be to escape a life of working-class toil. Soon, the two are living in a posh city hotel. There they meet a new accomplice, who turns around to bunko Cagney out of the pair's accumulated stake. Cagney avenges himself on his friend-turned-foe but in the process gets nabbed by the law.

Up to this point, *Blonde Crazy* is unique mainly in the actors' characterizations (which is to say, in what they did with the lines handed them by the screenwriters, and the easygoing direction of Roy Del Ruth). But soon after Blondell's character marries a stockbroker to escape poverty or eventual imprisonment, she learns that much-desired bourgeois life is an intolerably dull series of social events. Sometime in the future, when Cagney comes back from prison, she has one last chance to plead with him to go straight. But he is simply unable to imagine himself as a wage-slave; more important, he cannot see what is morally wrong with stealing from the rich, which is to say, robbing from those who rob everyone else. A master-piece of understatement, *Blonde Crazy*'s slight reputation rests upon the star power of Cagney and Blondell, when it has much more going for it.[29] The built-in limitations were Bright's fate writ large, not very different from nearly all other talented Hollywood writers—and not only those on the Left.

Bright's and Glasmon's next noteworthy assignment was better, even if critics had few kind words for it. *Three On a Match* (1932) had been a modest Broadway success, and the duo did the adaptation with Blondell joined by Ann Dvorak, Bette Davis, and an obscure young Humphrey Bogart in a supporting role. Symbolized in the supposed bad luck of three people lighting cigarettes on a single match, former schoolmates Blondell, Dvorak, and Davis meet accidentally ten years after high school graduation and recount their troubles. Blondell, a working-class girl, earlier let a man get her involved in unspecified criminal activity and did a stretch in jail. Upper-class Dvorak (especially good in this role), terribly restive with life with her stockbroker husband, hangs out in cabarets drinking and dancing with a handsome gigolo. Davis looks on sympathetically as the alcoholic (or perhaps drug addict) Dvorak leaves her husband and young son; Bette moves in and takes over to save the family by marrying the broker (himself brought down by the Crash) and restoring the home. Tragedy strikes as the gigolo tries to recoup his gambling debts by helping two hoods (one of them Bogart) kidnap the son. As cops swarm, a hapless Dvorak melodra-matically plunges to death from a window, with the hidden location scrawled on her blouse.[30]

In retrospect, this is one of those pre-Code gems of sin and tawdry realism (at least by the standards to come). But the experimental use of documentary-looking footage of the stock-market crash—including re-peated predictions of notables that Wall Street is about to recover—drives home a larger point about the era the nation has entered. Laconic marginal comments from a variety of characters reflect the same sentiment: bitter-ness that cannot be salved.

Bright lasted long enough to write several more films for Zanuck and make script contributions to yet another, all of them released in 1932: *Union Depot, If I Had a Million, Taxi!, The Crowd Roars,* and the uncredited *Madison Square Garden.*[31] *Taxi!* was (for at least half the film) the most important by far. Adapted so loosely from Kenyon Nicholson's Broadway play, *Blind Spot,* that almost none of the original remained, it showed Cagney among his Manhattan cabbie pals struggling for a kind of unionization (the strongest statement likely to be tolerated in Hollywood) via association of the independent operators. All the real issues get resolved in the second half of the film through sentimental melodrama, but the glimpse of class resentment resurfaced when a rave appeared in *The Nation.* Zanuck complained about a "review in a magazine I never heard of." Anxiously querying Bright about the social significance attributed to the film, the executive concluded laconically, "I'll be a son of a bitch. I thought it was all cops and robbers."[32]

Bright's high-powered career reached a crashing conclusion with Mae West's *She Done Him Wrong* (1933), considerably adapted from West's own stage play. A film that could not have been made after Breen's rise in 1934, it provided the actress ample opportunity for deathless double entendres and also endless inspirations to future camp. The silliness of the plot—West, the mobster's moll and saloon diva, falls hard for the Christian settlement house worker Cary Grant—scarcely detracted from West's defiance of the double standard ("When a girl goes bad, men go right after her"). Seen in another way, the mixture of radicalism and demimonde mentality in Bright's Chicago background acutely prefigured the gay recuperation of West. Playing with images, these writers/lyricists can be said to have predicted the postmodern attitude. If Bright received nothing more than a salary and a credit out of it, *She Done Him Wrong* achieved an Academy Award nomination for Best Picture, and the National Board of Review amazingly awarded it one of the Top 10 Films of the Year: amazing because Code authorities cited it as precisely the kind of morally corrosive film that had to be eliminated.

She Done Him Wrong was, however, only a temporary diversion from Bright's descent into B pictures, making him the first known radical to pay the price for defying the studio masters through a kind of informal blacklisting. Personally fired by Zanuck, who reputedly told the *Hollywood Reporter* that Bright would never work in pictures again, the writer fell in with rival David Selznick and Samuel Goldwyn at a Hollywood gambling spot, where he was first offered *Stella Dallas* and, turning it down as trash, accepted *She Done Him Wrong* at Paramount.[33] He continued for a few years to sell "originals," the story upon which a script can be based. But he never won rehabilitation as a major screenwriter.

What kind of work could a John Bright do after being driven out of the high-profile mainstream? Not much, but a few of his films over the next few years were at the very least highly intriguing. Bright collaborated with his friend and political comrade Robert Tasker, a former San Quentin inmate destined to die mysteriously in a Mexico City hotel room during the mid-1940s, in *San Quentin* (1937), which followed the wake of real-life prison riots and efforts by California's reformers to overcome the corruption and cruelty of the system.[34] *The Accusing Finger* (1938), also scripted by Bright and Tasker, was a B anti–capital punishment film of considerable strength, with an erstwhile pitiless state's attorney (nicknamed "Hot Seat") himself nearly railroaded into the chair, and Robert Cummings as a repentant teen hillbilly killer who gives him the argument to use, before a State Senate, that no man should act as god over another.[35]

The critically admired if low-budget *Back Door to Heaven* (1939) may be the most important Christian Socialist film in Hollywood for decades before and after. Coscripted with Tasker, it unravels a pathetic saga of class oppression. A poor boy (played by Jimmy Lydon, later the adolescent antihero of the Henry Aldrich series and still later a notably progressive television producer) with a mean drunk for a father is tempted by circumstances to steal a harmonica to play for his grammer school graduation recital. Thrown into reform school, he passes from one abusive institution into another, evidently a lost soul but with a fighting spirit that cannot ever entirely accept degradation. Released, he comes across his former boyhood love and begins the moral climb that climaxes first as he tries to halt a robbery by his acquired pals (resulting only in being charged with a murder) and last as he returns on the run to his hometown, exposing the social cost of class privilege before running toward a certain death from police bullets.

The finest moments in the film, narrated by his kindly former teacher, show each child of the little grade-school class grow into disappointed adulthood, capitalism and the Depression stealing their dreams away. All disappointed, that is, except the haughty banker with a vault for a heart. *Back Door to Heaven,* said to be the fictionalized life-story of producer-director Robert Howard's own childhood chum, ends with a wonderful soliloquy against class hatred, the protagonist pleading with the victims of society to change the world but also to eschew any desire for revenge.[36]

John Bright had a little more to contribute cinematically in the era ahead, from minor noirs to the race and ethnic themes that would mean so much to assorted Hollywood exiles.[37] But basically, Bright was through with any firm attachments to studios. Even by the middle 1930s, his recruitment of Cagney for political defense issues and his pioneering efforts to unionize screenwriters had become more important to him than his film work. Married to Josefina Fierro, the leading Chicana of the Left, he had put his life energies elsewhere.[38] Others faced with his dilemma would more cautiously knuckle under in the short run while seeking collective solutions, including both stronger unionism and the prospects of independent film production. The uncontrollable proletarian pug and pen-pusher Bright thus properly stands for an era in which the studios and censors only gradually reeled in the troublemakers, both in theme and personality. So does that famed inconsolable drinker Dashiell Hammett.

The treatment of the crime theme in 1930s film and in noir films more than a decade later owed more to Hammett's work than to any other novelist, short-story writer, screenwriter, or for that matter producer or director. So much had his characters and literary mise-en-scènes impressed themselves upon the popular reader during the 1920s, and upon producers looking for sure hits, that no fewer than eight films drew upon his work during the 1930s alone (the figure has since risen to at least fifteen). The former Pinkerton agent who might or might not have been present at the murder of Wobbly martyr Frank Little in 1917 was soaking himself in booze and (according to credible accounts of mutual friends) rewriting the southern-born Jewish Lillian Hellman's plays and scripts across the next decade, that is, when he wasn't active in assorted left-wing causes.[39] But by the early years of the Depression, his own serious literary days over, Hammett could hardly bring himself to attempt screenplays.

Hammett blew into Hollywood in 1930 and quickly made friends with some of the most talented and highly paid writers like Ben Hecht and that famed iconoclast of the Algonquin Circle, half-Jewish Dorothy Parker. In an initial burst of enthusiasm, Hammett actually turned out an original script for Paramount director Rouben Mamoulian. *City Streets* (1931) had top stars Gary Cooper and Sylvia Sidney, but a thin plot about a carnie worker who falls into the mob through his relationship with the crime boss's daughter and finds himself reluctantly in charge only to repent and go straight. Still, *City Streets* made money, and the writer meanwhile struck up a relationship with Hellman, married at the time to a rather progressive-minded playwright and screenwriter, Arthur Kober.[40]

A continuing literary success with novels *The Glass Key* and *The Maltese Falcon,* Hammett spent freely, fell into a deep funk, and sold the film rights to *The Thin Man* for $21,000 even before the novel's publication. (Had he retained even a small portion of those rights, the pursuing government investigating committees of McCarthy days might never have been able to bankrupt him with legal fees.) *The Thin Man* model proved to be practically the only good movie rendition of his work that Hammett saw made during the decade; it was a smash in 1934, with the magnetic couple William Powell and Myrna Loy as Nick and Nora Charles, who repeated themselves in *After the Thin Man* (1936) and *Another Thin Man* (1939). *Another Thin Man* was the best if not the last of the series, scripted by the respectful Albert Hackett and Frances Goodrich, a husband and wife team who were also close allies of the Left in the Screen Writers Guild.[41]

Hammett meanwhile worked intermittently but unsuccessfully at several studios, usually no more than weeks at a time, for years. He didn't seem to care that a first film version of *The Maltese Falcon* (1931); a film adaptation (*Woman in the Dark,* 1934) of one of his short stories; a first version of *The Glass Key* (1935); and a second version of *The Maltese Falcon,* retitled *Satan Was a Lady* (1936), were all more or less turkeys, although he may have taken interest in Bette Davis's Bad Girl role in the last one. (Davis herself regarded it as one of the worst movies she ever made.) Had Hammett enjoyed relative hack work with racier angles and a darker tone than post-censorship Hollywood was likely to handle, he might have made his peace with his movies.

No doubt cinematic mediocrity was part of the famed author's general disillusionment, both with Hollywood and with American capitalism. He compensated, like dozens of other left-leaning Hollywood writers, first through politics and later through war duty. He devoted his real energies to causes like the Motion Picture Artists Committee (of which he was chair), raising money for antifascist causes worldwide, and then, as a badly overaged volunteer, editing a GI newspaper in the Aleutians.[42]

Until the famed 1941 *Maltese Falcon,* none of the adaptations of Hammett, notwithstanding the charm of the *Thin Man* series, could stand up to the toughness and crypto-political character of *Little Caesar* and *The Public Enemy.* Other fine crime-related films, many of the best by left-wingers, sentimentalized characters even as they used a steadily improving cinematography and political climate. Those two early entries, however, also continue to remind us of certain limits upon crime-related films until a larger degree of artistic autonomy had been carved out toward the close of the 1940s.

The most notable exceptions in the early talkies can be laid to the dual success of *I Am a Fugitive from a Chain Gang* (1932), one of Paul Muni's best portrayals of victimization, and of *Wild Boys of the Road* (1933), which drew without acknowledgment upon the contemporary Russian film about the homeless, *Road to Life.* The protagonists of these films, not only but especially the children, were guilty at most of being drawn into the social vortex of poverty and low-level crime. In Broadway playwright (and future blacklistee) Edward Chodorov's *The Mayor of Hell* (1933), neighborhood tykes of the later Dead End Kids type—but carefully integrated by both ethnicity and race—are sent to a reformatory run by a swindler-tyrant. Establishing a cooperative survival system among themselves (with a Jewish boy keeping the treasury!), they finally rise up successfully in a rebellion ended only by the arrival of a kindly administrator (himself a spiritual rebel from the corrupt system), played by James Cagney, who is committed to making the penal system work as rehabilitation. Related flatly, without cinematic tricks or sophisticated dialogue, *The Mayor of Hell* was memorably stark in its social message.[43]

Hell's Highway (1932), based on a story by distinguished Jewish novelist Samuel Ornitz and scripted in part by him, was actually released around the same time as the better-produced and bigger-starred *I Was a Prisoner,* denying the other film the lasting attention it might otherwise have earned. But the savagery of conditions in the Kentucky prison camp of *Hell's Highway,* the ways that casual criminals and would-be tough adolescents were drawn into lives and deaths of complete degradation, offered strong social metaphors alongside the inevitable romance. *Road Gang* (1936), the first produced filmscript of Dalton Trumbo, was a more melodramatic Warner Brothers knockoff of *I Am a Fugitive.* An innocent reporter has been placed in a Southern prison by a scheming politician, and from that vantage point he gazes horrified at youngsters marked for brutality and dissenters facing certain doom in a prison mine.[44]

So much for crime, punishment, and social realism in Hollywood until the late 1930s and the evolution of the Warner Brothers social or class drama set piece. For left-wing critics, Hollywood had barely budged from its obsession with the rich, the personalization of social woes, and assorted styles of escapism. Judged in light of studio conservatism and censorship, Hollywood was actually moving forward, albeit in ways scarcely susceptible to old-fashioned Marxist political analysis.

Playing for Women Viewers

The flood of "fallen women" films during the first years of the 1930s jarred moralists of various kinds and gave them something in Hollywood to flail against. Flappers still seemed out of control, the stock-market crash notwithstanding. The movies' young flappers were married women, too: they danced in cabarets and pursued gigolos while their businessmen-husbands toiled at the office. Such themes, popular since the dawn of commercial film, had been accentuated and exaggerated in the last years of the silent era by the superstardom of Clara Bow, Joan Crawford, and Jean Harlow. These developments increasingly offered left-wing writers both a subject and a framework for examining modern mores and the society that made them inevitable.

In the most popular variant, a powerless working-class girl uses her sexuality, through an illicit relationship, to climb upward and then realizes at some late point in the film (often neatly coinciding with motherhood) that she must make things right. Alternatively, the powerless woman is any woman, even an American aristocrat, who seeks love (and lust) in all the wrong places, comes to a tragic end, or manages to pull the emotional irons out of the fire, usually after some calamity. Before the emotion-dripping last reel, our heroine often has a marvelous time in the way that a working-class (or practically any Depression) audience could enjoy vicariously: dancing with a handsome beau, attending nightclubs, talking from a luxurious bedroom on one of the totemic white telephones that connoted excess, generally enjoying the good life by way of compensating for a fall in morality with a rise in class status, hedonistic pleasure, or both.

From one angle, every "women's film," no matter how virtuous the protagonist, rests upon a variation of such melodramatic themes—not so terribly far from the mobster's tragic saga as might seem from first glance. More than one film historian has observed their shared and characteristic American pathos, brought down by the failure hiding within materialistic success.[45]

Her Private Affair (1930), Francis Faragoh's adaptation of a then-current play, gives a fair idea of the contemporary sinner in the early sound film. Actress Ann Harding, the long-suffering and occasionally triumphant heroine of numerous features in the early 1930s, plays a judge's wife who, after a marital spat hardly her fault, vacations alone in Italy, where she falls hard for a slick and handsome society blackmailer. When he follows her home, she slips out from her opera seat, meets the rascal in his apartment, and guns him down. Although much screen time has passed amidst blatant adultery before she is compelled to confess and face the music, Harding's heroine, as the *Variety* reviewer noted, "never manages to lose the sympathy of the audience."[46] In the variant of *Back Pay* (1930), the Faragoh adaptation of a Fannie Hurst novel, a small-town girl revolts against her oppressive environment, abandoning her boyfriend for the city and the luxuries that a war profiteer(!) can afford her. Viewers cannot doubt that when her boyfriend returns from Europe, blinded and almost destroyed by war, the guilt-ridden former immoralist will desert her "merchant of death" lover and come back home. But it is her rebellion, not the final-reel reconciliation, that almost certainly counts for viewers.

Why did so many a heroine choose to become, in the title of another popular film, a *Tarnished Lady* (1931)? In another Faragoh stage adaptation, Carole Lombard's protagonist has a morally improper if logical answer: She can be satisfied by *No One Man* (1932). Dissolute but conflicted, she abandons the Palm Beach polo set for a Viennese physician, then marries a playboy instead and, when he dies in another woman's bedroom, becomes a nurse to the doctor (played by Paul Lukas, a favorite best-when-earnest actor) that she had wrongfully deserted. She has actually been desperate for self-realization, even if that self is realized in a greater purpose with a man. Yet above all she has *The Right to Romance* (1932, written by Sidney Buchman), in this case as a successful woman doctor who has to slip anonymously into the same decadent Palm Beach society and marry a bounder before ending up back in New York with her assistant, a good man who gives her love without taking away her career.

Putting across the message of woman's emancipation from her many bonds, the "modern" girl who has earned the right to make her own life without losing "the right to romance" demanded from the writers a feeling for contemporary actresses and some real talent. Francis Faragoh delivered memorably in the first full-length color film, *Becky Sharp* (1934), his adaptation of Thackeray's *Vanity Fair.* A distinct experiment and not a commercially successful one, it was directed by Rouben Mamoulian for early independent Pioneer Films and budgeted at a cool million dollars. Audience response first seemed promising and then melted away, delaying further full-scale color production for a half-decade (or longer, until the threat of television plunged Hollywood once more into delayed innovation). But like the literary original, *Becky Sharp* was sharply satirical, the story of the powerless orphan in a class-ridden English society who pulls herself up by hook and crook, above all by the manipulation of male aristocrats. Driven to cynicism, she acquires, in a scene that must have startled the Hays Office, the power to humiliate her sanctimoniously religious in-laws. Taking tea at the time of Waterloo, she declares, "Soldiers are dying for their country, and I'm dying for lunch." Despite the predictable ending, it was a remarkable performance for Hollywood (and for Miriam Hopkins, surely her best starring role).[47]

The Chodorov brothers, Edward and the younger Jerome, were both destined for the blacklist, and worked frequently along similar lines. ("Jerry," in many later credits, lacked his sibling's distinguished Broadway background and, like Sidney Buchman's younger brother Harold, had no future outside B films.) The musical *Madame DuBarry* (1934), story and script by Edward Chodorov and directed by left-connected German refugee William Dieterle, has the magnificently spoiled aristocrat of pre-Revolution days (so spoiled that she orders King Louis's entourage to take all the sugar in Paris and sprinkle it about for her sleigh ride on a hot summer day) get her comeuppance in learning that even apparently all-powerful women are only the playthings of class society. *Dancing Feet* (1936), scripted by brother Jerry, brings us up-to-date at the other end of society, where the daughter of a millionaire defects to her proletarian boyfriend with whom she intends to make an honest living by giving tap-dancing lessons over the radio(!).

Edward Chodorov also produced and helped Mary McCall, Jr., write the script for the feminist shocker of the decade—not by accident, also Dorothy Arzner's most important film—*Craig's Wife* (1936). A Pulitzer

Prize–winning play also made in an earlier silent version, this one sparkled mostly due to Rosalind Russell's performance as the strong-minded woman whose obsession with her house (later it could be called agoraphobia) makes her manipulative toward her unsuspecting husband. Behind the potential misogyny of the plot, she is revealed as a victim of her father's abandonment of her mother, decades earlier, and of the consequent belief that no man can be trusted with a woman's fate. Unable to control everything (she even forbids John Boles the right to smoke at home), she finally drives him away and is seen alone in "her" house in the film's final moment. A *New Masses* critic pungently noted that in the stage version, the protagonist was desperately seeking to hold on to a modest middle-class house, her "barrier against poverty." Shifting the location Hollywood-style to a veritable mansion underlined her neurosis; a broken vase can easily be replaced and servants can do the cleaning, while the impoverished understandably struggle over every possession without the benefit of neurosis. A fair criticism, it once again missed the point that Hollywood permitted veracity only in small if sometimes effective doses.[48]

No screenwriter of any political persuasion managed to put the gender or sex-war message across better than Donald Ogden Stewart, genteel opposite of John Bright in everything but political persuasion. Stewart entered Hollywood from the top, already a famed literary figure and playwright. Son of an Ohio judge, Stewart grew up a shy and bespectacled lad who nevertheless managed through geniality and wit to make himself liked at Phillips Exeter Academy and Yale. He soon met all the right people, including F. Scott Fitzgerald, who personally introduced Stewart to the Algonquin Wits of the 1920s. There, Robert Benchley and Dorothy Parker, themselves destined to become serious and important allies of the Hollywood Left, became his fast friends.

Radicalism of any kind, even of the avant-garde variety, nevertheless made no definite impression as the young man settled in at *Vanity Fair*. He devoted himself to writing comic pieces and preparing himself for plays, short stories, and novels with the light touch and wit so famous in the contemporary *New Yorker*. He had adored film since childhood, but was busy giving comic lectures (college audiences were his favorite) and enjoying himself generally. MGM approached him in the middle 1920s, when silents about college life were big, to adapt an action-packed but otherwise vacuous sports drama, *Brown of Harvard,* for the screen. Working in the

Culver Studios in Culver City (then just a year old), Stewart turned in a version worked over heavily by several other writers. Reviewers were not overly impressed by the results, although it was considered no worse and probably a bit better than similar films.[49] Stewart prematurely drew the moral from this and other early disappointments that his writing must not be suited for the screen.

Stewart went on with splendidly successful literary work for several more years. And yet for his circle of intimate friends, more and more of them becoming screenwriters, Hollywood was obviously "in its own orbit" with a reality limited to "whatever was recorded on film at the end of each day's shooting." He speculated later on the guilty pleasure that he, too, could "fit so successfully in this dream world, for I myself was living happily in a personal Paradise in which no essential realities were allowed to disturb my determined play and pleasant dreams . . . "[50] If only he could make a success of it in a second try, Hollywood as a job and as a place seemed to be everything a literary man could want—and more.

Looking back critically at his feckless youth, Stewart the exiled memoirist of the 1950s is obviously setting himself up narratively for conversion to Something More Serious. But there is no reason to doubt his recollection, which runs to continued theatrical triumph (including *Laughter,* one of the ten best plays of the 1929–30 season), European jaunts, boozing, and skirt-chasing until he was lured back to Culver City, this time reporting personally to Irving Thalberg. Actually, two plays had already been optioned, and *Tarnished Lady,* his script for director George Cukor and actress Tallulah Bankhead's joint sound-film debut, was just going into production. Once again, he took the formula the producers gave him—to write for designated stars, produce a triangle, and a happy or morally satisfying ending. But he soon did things with the formula that amused contemporary movie fans enormously and have amazed critics ever since.[51]

Romantic comedy work allowed Stewart to develop cinematic themes that had deep emotional importance for him and went to the heart of his highest success—not forgetting his ability to write snappy dialogue, much of it ridiculing upper-class manners. In his play *Rebound,* considerably rewritten by others before its Hollywood release, his characters come to understand the value of commitment only after the facade of bourgeois complacency cracks and they learn that one must be able to forgive a spouse for "something as trivial as adultery." Much as he envisioned a few years later that socialism would bring to all of humankind the brotherhood he had experienced at Yale, Stewart's work suggested well before his conscious radicalization that through the intimacy of marriage, people found their capacity of sacrifice to something larger than themselves, something approaching a small-scale model for a cooperative society. Disguised in his dialogue as soigné sophistication and world-weariness, the message carried with it possibilities that women viewers in particular could readily understand.

Stewart worked his magic with script contributions to a romantic melodrama like *Red Dust* (1932), an exotic that found rubber-plantation overseer Clark Gable falling in love with engineer's wife Mary Astor before finally realizing that the morally doubtful platinum blonde Jean Harlow (on the lam from the law and evidently a former prostitute) is the spirited woman for him just as he is the rugged right type for her. Likewise, Stewart managed to make *The Barretts of Wimpole Street* (1934)—composed "in almost record time" for Norma Shearer, Fredric March, and Hollywood newcomer Charles Laughton—a great deal more than the sentimental account of the nineteenth-century poets would seem to hold. Laughton was the domineering father who practically kept as prisoner his crippled daughter, the poetess Elizabeth Barrett, played by Shearer; her response to wooing by Robert Browning is an undisguised liberation drama, and the assistance of her sister (played by Maureen O'Sullivan) creates a women's alliance against patriarchy. Even her beloved dog escapes with her—and a good thing, because the perverse Laughton (whose fatherly love seems more and more like emotional incest as the movie goes along) orders the beloved pet executed in revenge.[52] In another vein, adding mordant final lines to the film version of the Broadway smash *Dinner at Eight* (1933), Stewart was said to have provided the quipped response to a high-class courtesan, who has expressed fears that machines would someday abolish jobs, that *her* trade was safe for all time.

Going Hollywood (1933), a Stewart original and pure camp, was an early sound version of the studio-and-star system making fun of itself almost to the extent of an auto-critique. In this chipper musical, shy French teacher Marion Davies falls in love with the imagined figure of radio crooner Bing Crosby (already a Hollywood hit but now debuting at MGM), who surrealistically appears out of the radio—or is it only her fantasy?—to urge her to come to Hollywood. Her fellow academics, wonderfully portrayed as sexually repressed worshipers of dead knowledge, consider Davies a disgrace if not a potential immoralist. Overnight she appears in Tinseltown, snags an understudy part in Crosby's latest film, and fortuitously replaces his current inamorata in film and "real" life. *Going Hollywood,* like *The Public Enemy,* took on the gray zone between reality and films, this time between the fan-magazine craziness with all its gendered content and the film business itself. The back-and-forth between image and image-of-image was brilliant, possible only for a film that refused to take itself seriously. Stewart had supplied Davies and slapstick costar Patsy Kelly in particular everything they needed to be both funny and characterful, something far better than standard sentimental features could provide.

Stewart had to wait for the improvement of Hollywood technology and coordinated production, at the end of the decade, for his greatest triumphs (described in Chapter Four). But *Marie Antoinette* (1938) demonstrated his standing in Hollywood and his capacity for idiosyncratic treatment of the most obvious material. His Marie, played by Norma Shearer in one of MGM's most lavish productions to date, is more victim than predator, with none of Madame DuBarry's taste for excess. King Louis XVI (fabulously portrayed by Robert Morley), a shy and introverted fellow, seems interested only in his hobby of locksmithing. When Marie fails to produce an heir, she is first cast aside and then recovered, bearing son and daughter, only to face the torrent of public hatred toward her as an Austrian and a symbol of royal self-indulgence. Yet somehow, as she goes to the guillotine, it does not seem that the masses have betrayed her so much as the intriguing royalty that somehow survives (especially the Duke d'Orleans scoundrel, brilliantly played by Joseph Schildkraut). Miraculously, in the kind of miracle that only Hollywood can produce, she remains a kind of pre–Princess Di, the "people's queen." [53]

Future blacklistee Sidney Buchman, never as politically minded as Stewart but just as genteel, similarly suited himself to the high end of early sound production and the "women's film" in particular. Like Stewart, if by no means as famous early in his career, Buchman was an experienced and successful playwright gone Hollywood. Born in Duluth, Minnesota, educated first at the state university but leaving for Columbia University and Oxford, Buchman had more academic training than nearly anyone in Hollywood of the day. Still working for Broadway but without impressive success (except in helping to introduce Paul Muni to the English-language audience), he broke into silent films with the society melodrama *Matinee Ladies* (1927) and, after the advent of sound, quickly became one of the industry's fastest and most versatile writers.

Buchman's early, smallish pictures for Columbia were most often quirky romances that, even when originals, worked as if they had been transferred from Broadway. In *I'll Love You Always* (1935), an engineering student woos a local Shakespearean actress, marries her, and later learns to his horror that she is a taxi dancer in a Chicago Chinese restaurant(!). Embittered, he steals money from his employer and prepares to take off for Russia(!!). But they reconcile at the last moment, making it inevitable that she promise to wait for him when he comes out of the Big House.[54] The best of them were women's pictures pitched straight to female audiences with messages close to their collective hearts.

Paramount's lavishly funded *The Sign of the Cross* (1932) offered Buchman his chance at a truly epic film with a women's theme at the center. The earliest budget-busting biblical drama of the sound era, *Variety* grandly if somewhat inaccurately labeled the extravaganza "Religious triumph over paganism [with] . . . the soul . . . stronger than the flesh."[55] Actually, the flesh won quite a few along the way. Cecil B. DeMille directed Fredric March as the prefect of Rome who wants to score with the endangered Christian maiden, played by Elissa Landi, but has no luck. He calls in temptress Joyzelle Joyner, who (in one of the Code-tempting scenes) shows a party-crowd already on the edge of an orgy just how to wiggle for a man. Still no luck: Landi is appalled and horrified. Meanwhile, just as the orgy ensues, Christians can be heard singing and marching outside, en route to their doom in the Arena.

The real action takes place here, with thirty minutes of the goriest scenes imaginable in that era (or in nearly any era) of narrative film with giants, midgets, and muscle-bound women slicing each other up while the Roman crowd yawns and yawps for more blood. Charles Laughton as the mad Nero and Claudette Colbert as his consort (who has her eye on March, and therefore guarantees Landi's doom) are splendid with Buchman's lines. In the film's expansive last moments, March begs Landi to renounce Christianity and, failing, goes into the lion's den to share her bloody fate (offscreen, that is). Corrupted women obviously point the way downward, but the purified woman leads the way to real civilization. Never would future

Jewish biblical drama writers (like Albert Maltz, uncredited author of the original script for *The Robe*) do any better with self-sacrificial Christian themes, although the plot variations and political echoes would continue to fascinate spiritually credulous but obviously thrill-seeking theatergoers.[56]

The women's film with a comic twist became Buchman's forte and the ticket to well-supported work at Columbia, where his work made him a favorite of boss Harry Cohn. The broad, screwballish satire *Theodora Goes Wild* (1936) made his career, pointing the way toward his best and most popular films, including *The Awful Truth* (1937), *Holiday* (1938), *Here Comes Mr. Jordan* (1942), and *The Talk of the Town* (1942). *Theodora,* along with Capra's *It Happened One Night* (1935), arguably set the pace for Columbia's succession of films with beautiful people in fancy dress doing crazy but unquestionably sophisticated things, almost (but not quite) as if the Depression had not ended the witty repartee or stifled the emancipated ladies of the 1920s.

A great vehicle for Irene Dunne and Melvyn Douglas, *Theodora Goes Wild* features a small-town Connecticut unmarried author of a scandalous novel, whose work appears serially in the local paper and horrifies the gentry. Traveling to New York to meet a publisher, she finds herself imitating what she imagines such an author would do, avoids at the last moment actually seducing the artist of her book's cover drawing, and then, in horror at her own behavior, flees the city for home. Artist Douglas (married, but separated) follows her and insists she hire him as a gardener. Eventually she holds a press conference in his Manhattan apartment, revealing her true identity, prompting her aunt to announce that she has "gone wild." After further scandal in which townsfolk believe she has borne an illegitimate child, things work out—very much so for actress Dunne, who had initially tried to avoid playing comedy but got an Oscar nomination for Best Actress. Buchman had other talents, but at his best he was this kind of writer, with dialogue and characterizations daring and improbable enough to overturn the genteel frame of the prevailing comedy-dramas.

Buchman and Stewart's eminently successful transition to films also demonstrated how often sound films through the 1930s were literally "screen plays" in the finest sense, with witty talk at a premium, action strictly secondary, and moody atmosphere often hardly more important than an occasional background for romance. Soon, films would advance beyond this set of conventions, and radicals would play a large role in their further development.

Frustration Politics

There was a large downside to all this. The very success of such screenplays tended to disguise both the bicoastal nature and the creative ambivalence of the best screenwriters, involving the incompatibilities between Broadway and Hollywood. Many of the prestigious writers and directors would emerge from off Broadway and the Federal Theatre in the later 1930s to films during the 1940s and, for a short but happy period, move back and forth between the two. The earlier thirties, by contrast, fostered repeated frustration. Theater remained their true love, literally the "legitimate" part of their lives, while films represented only money, laughs, and occasional opportunities for crypto-political jabs.

John Wexley, to take a less-than-happy example of the playwright-gone-Hollywood, achieved considerable success but never lost the sense of excitement in the Washington Square Playhouse of his youth, or in his dramatic theatrical triumphs of the early 1930s, *The Last Mile* and *They Shall Not Die.* A melodramatic appeal to halt capital punishment, *The Last Mile* ran for 285 performances and established the career of the Broadway lead, Spencer Tracy (Clark Cable, who took over the part in the West Coast production, rode the success to a screen contract). The play received a film treatment so mediocre in 1932 that the killer turned out to be innocent and was saved at the last moment.[57] *They Shall Not Die,* based on the Scottsboro case and mounted to raise funds for the indigent and innocent black defendants of rape charges, got rave reviews and lasted months (it also marked the dramatic debut of Tom Ewell), but proved far too strong for Hollywood. Compared to this, writing in the film colony, if sometimes lucrative, was often creatively less than nothing.[58] An admired dramatist and a nephew of the Yiddish theatrical impresario Maurice Schwartz would seem fated for this kind of comedown. But plenty of other writers felt the same way. Hollywood was bigger than life and just as cruel for those who took their art seriously.

John Howard Lawson lived the contradiction in spades. Hardly the father of class themes, he was arguably the originator of the class-conflict

film in post-silents Hollywood. After deep disappointments and courageous political-labor engagement, he evolved by wartime into a skillful
practitioner of the genuinely cinematic radical film. Destined to be regarded as the Beverly Hills commissar, Lawson was actually an avant-
gardist and, like his colleagues (if more intense), a convert to politics only
at midlife. Scion of a Jewish business family that lost its money (and of a
domineering father who had apparently driven an older, similarly artistically inclined sibling to suicide), he emerged an embittered if abundantly
talented Jewish intellectual at Williams College, a sense of identity that remained with him for life.

Only nineteen when he saw his first play produced by George M.
Cohan, he nevertheless felt himself an abused Jew passed over for the editorship of the college literary magazine, a position obviously reserved for a
Gentile. By 1923, Lawson's semi-Expressionist drama *Roger Bloomer* was
met with real critical respect. His 1925 *Processional* (scholar Bernard F.
Dick calls it a "wedding of drama and pop art, theater and burlesque, sti-
chomythic dialogue and jazz rhythm") offered a dream-like set of often impressive images including silly Communists and whining Jews, taken by
old and new admirers to be proof of the most promising new American
dramatist.[59] Soon after, he helped form the avant-garde New Playwrights,
and the company's production of *The Loud Speaker* in 1927, like Faragoh's
contemporary work (for which Lawson wrote the program notes), was
about as Brechtian as mainstream American theater would become for decades and perhaps forever.

In short, Lawson seemed another natural for a Hollywood seeking
writerly talent. His first assignment, at MGM, in 1926, was to write sound
dialogue for one sequence of Garbo's *Flesh and the Devil*. He quickly fell in
with Albert Lewin—a former Marxist who remained personally affable
while politically distant and, above all, useful as a right-hand man of all-
powerful producer Irving Thalberg, who himself claimed to be a former
adolescent socialist street-corner speaker.[60] Lawson was also on good terms
with actress Bette Davis's husband, future Communist and friendly witness Frank Davis. Before the Depression, Lawson had already been invited
to novelist Samuel Ornitz's Los Angeles home, where he met Lewin, Frank
Davis, and Marian Ainslee, a silent-screen captionist (and intimate to
Theodore Dreiser) who helped Lawson learn film technique.

Thalberg was personally fascinated with Lawson the intellectual even when he could not use the writer's work, and so the playwright was sent to devise titles for an exotic South Seas drama starring Ramon Novarro, *The Pagan* (silent except for "The Pagan Love Song," an international hit). Even here, Lawson found a way to make the native girl socially conscious, unable to betray her people, and the visiting American equally unable to betray his way of living. It was the sort of romantic twist to the familiar themes of the time, but had nothing to do with the realities of middle-class American life.[61] Lawson wanted success as much as anyone, purchasing a large house overlooking Long Island Sound and gaining greater financial security than he and his growing family had ever known. Francis Faragoh moved in close by his artistic comrade. It was obviously a good beginning.[62]

Meanwhile, Cecil B. DeMille had actually seen *Processional* and got the idea that one of its characters, a footloose miner, could be adapted for his own first projected full-sound film, to be titled *Dynamite* (1929). It was a serious assignment, and critics responded with great interest, if more than a little incredulity, at the various improbable turns of the story line. At the star-studded premiere of the film in the Carthay Circle Theatre in Hollywood, DeMille actually called Lawson to the microphone as author.

The coal miner–protagonist played by Charles Bickford is sentenced to death for a crime he did not commit, and agrees, for a cash settlement, to marry a frivolous society girl (played by Kay Johnson) who needs a husband fast in order to receive her family inheritance. Then fate strikes as the real murderer is caught. The miner, finding himself suddenly surrounded by the amoral rich who are Johnson's social circle, returns alone to the coal patch in Pennsylvania, leaving both the dame and the money behind. She heads after him but succeeds only in humiliating him unintentionally with her fancy car, a striking sign of class privilege (underlined through her inability to cook), and makes things worse when her old boyfriend, an upper-class aesthete, shows up to claim her. In the wake of a catastrophic mine explosion, things sort themselves out, and blue-collar boy gets upper-class girl after all. The otherwise motherless child who is Bickford's daughter eases the way for Johnson into the world of miners' women, as improbable as all this seems. If talky, *Dynamite* had at least a fair stretch of rather realistic coal-town scenes and made an effort at portraying working-class social life.[63]

Lawson's next assignment, to script *The Ship from Shanghai* for director Charles Brabin, was more daunting. He had the studio insider's task of introducing Brabin and, by extension, Brabin's wife, Theda Bara (the silents' sex bomb, inactive since 1925), to sound films with a creaking plot about a "hairy ape" captain who leads a rough crew taking a millionaire's wife and friends from Shanghai to San Francisco. All the while plotting to capture the millionairess for himself, the captain leads a mutiny against the passengers, based upon class resentment and murkier Freudian impulses. The ape-looking proletarian is overwhelmed by guilt and self-hatred at the last moment, obligingly committing suicide. *The Ship from Shanghai* was a minor hit, if nothing to brag about from any standpoint. Lawson could enjoy the good life with only some suppressed guilt at having abandoned the avant-garde theater.

Lawson had already shown how to combine class issues with romance, despite all the weaknesses of plotting. His films had powerful moments even when the narratives were weak, a disparity that often marks Hollywood use of class resentments not laughed away. Lawson's original (co-scripted with Bess Meredith), *Our Blushing Brides* (1930), which received hardly better notices, worked the class-gender themes the opposite way far more effectively. Joan Crawford is one of three department store employees (the other two were played by Anita Page and Dorothy Sebastian) and roommates who hate their miserably low salaries, long hours, rat-hole apartment, and cheap meals. Obviously shaped after the semi-silent *Our Dancing Daughters* (1928), which had made Crawford a box office draw, these blushing brides are not "brides" at all, let alone "blushing."

One of them becomes the mistress of a department-store scion who pays her rent (and obviously takes her sexual favors) but will desert her for a woman of his own class; another gets married to a swindler who hides from the police and is finally sent off to jail; according to the film's harshest critics, Crawford alone triumphs because she fends off the capitalist playboy played by Robert Montgomery, preserving that part of the female anatomy that is more sacred than life itself. But at closer glance, Crawford is far more intent on preserving a woman's prerogatives generally, utterly repelled by upper-class men's manipulations on every side, at every pretext. Through asides and confrontations, she asserts the unmistakable young Crawford dignity, not merely to be "free" (as her earlier, adolescent screen self) but to be recognized as a person of value. Her reward, marriage to the reformed playboy, is the expectable and probably inevitable ending. Before that comes, she has taken her stand. As in *Dynamite,* the contrast in production sets, from blue-collar apartment to ruling-class estate complete with luxurious treehouse (plaything for the playboy, where the seduction is attempted), effectively drives the point home.

For Lawson, however, the resistance of his cowriter to this line of feminist-class intent and the almost constant interference of the director, Hunt Stromberg, added up to a terrible frustration. His next assignments, wholly without merit, made him desperate to get away from MGM, even if it meant breaking a contract. Still far from being anything like a Communist, he harkened to the call of spreading Depression, breadlines, and demonstrations of the unemployed. Meanwhile, rising theatrical impresario Harold Clurman contacted him, showing a renewed interest in his past work (now viewing his plays as objects of the 1920s, Lawson had a sudden desire to rewrite them thoroughly) and a broadened consideration of his lyricism. Lawson begged release from MGM, and Thalberg gave it reluctantly, warning that he could not come back so easily. If Lawson had been afraid from the beginning that he would be trapped by Hollywood and almost as afraid that he would not be able to succeed, he had succeeded and quit, with no intention of returning. Little did he know.

Back in New York, Lawson rapidly discovered that the Depression had deflated theater far worse than films. As his hopes nevertheless rose for an early Broadway production, he settled on Long Island—and then realized his plight. Once more, Hollywood called: a romantic comedy for actor-director Lowell Sherman and Mae Mallory. He wrote from Long Island, hopeful for a series of films along the same line; *Bachelor Apartment* was a bomb, Lawson's first. Meanwhile, RKO was falling apart, and as Lawson continued to spend lavishly on his family, he returned to Hollywood and realized that his next script had been essentially rejected. As politics continued to heat up, Lawson spent a weekend with Edmund Wilson, who tried to argue him toward Marxism.[64]

Meanwhile, Lawson's new drama, *Success Story,* produced for the Group Theatre in 1932 and directed by Lee Strasberg, with stage design by Mordecai Gorelik and a stellar cast (among others, Luther Adler, Stella Adler, Franchot Tone, and Morris Carnovsky), gained fulsome praise in the liberal press—and an attack from the Communist-guided *New Masses.* Then in its early sectarian phase of expecting cataclysmic struggle and condemning everything that failed to harden class lines, the magazine complained bitterly of the play's individualistic problems and solutions. Lawson, on the double rebound from Hollywood, felt crestfallen and adrift. Not much later, *Success Story* was purchased by RKO, and Lawson wrote the screen version, *Success at Any Price* (1934), one of the most bitter of the early Depression antibusiness dramas.

Overly stagy and predictable, *Success at Any Price* offers nevertheless a fascinating depiction by Douglas Fairbanks, Jr., of a fanatically determined working-class (if definitely non-Jewish) mug rising from the bottom to become a successful advertising executive and abandoning all his morals in the process. He immediately abandons the childhood sweetheart, Colleen Moore (another Gentile), who got him the entry-level job, and who is the only woman who ever loved him for himself. He as much as propositions the boss's mistress, played by Genevieve Tobin, and although she responds playfully, she lets him know just what he has to do to win her, and he follows her script. By the time he has risen to the top and has begun to fall with the stock-market quotations, the two no longer have anything to talk about, and she spends her nights on the town while he slaves at his desk. Their marriage is a sham. Amid deepening Depression-era business troubles, he experiences a shattering self-realization.

In the stage version, the antiheroic protagonist is a Jewish copywriter from the East Side and an anticapitalist, if somewhat soured on the usual socialist expectations ("I can't help seein' that the revolution ain't gonna happen next week . . . say, I wouldn't be surprised if it didn't happen all summer."). His girlfriend, who grew up with him in the same East Side tenement, is both intelligent and plucky. In short, they are the promise of the proletariat, reaching a dead end in white-collar wage-slavery like so many New York Jews in real life.[65] His old sweetheart shoots him fatally. If an accident, the shooting nevertheless delivers poetic justice upon the creature that he has become. In the film version the characters lose their geopolitical ethnicity long before a typically unrealistic, happy Hollywood ending. Here, a would-be suicidal Fairbanks only wounds himself after Moore rejects his plea for forgiveness. He is now free to recover in her arms, morally redeemed. His stage counterpart had closed the drama (after advising his would-be widow, Sarah, to change her name "from Ginsberg to Grinnell like we talked about") in language more suited to Lawson's protégé, Clifford Odets:

One time there was a Jew named Christ dressed up in a rainbow, he
told the world plenty, maybe there'll be some more like him . . . Me, I
don't care! I'm only thinking of myself. Put me in a solid silver coffin
with gold cupids—don't matter what it costs . . . [Starts to laugh,
stiffens in Sarah's arms.].[66]

In its infernally reworked film version, *Success at Any Price* could almost
be the subconscious autobiography for Lawson, who clung to his Long Island estate for the duration of the 1930s even while making a Communist
political commitment for life. One might easily say that he had committed
spiritual near-suicide by going Hollywood, but determined to redeem
himself in his own eyes. In 1935, after emerging a central non-Communist
figure in the Screen Writers Guild, he suddenly announced in the *New
Masses* his joining the Party. Lawson came as a delayed disciple, all the more
fervent for his initial hesitancy.

No one could call it a career move, quite the opposite. To get rather
ahead of our story chronologically but not aesthetically, independent producer and longtime left-wing ally Walter Wanger had guided director
William Wellman in the controversial warning tale about potential fascism in high places, *The President Vanishes* (1934). Now he decided to make
Lawson his lead writer for the most politically controversial film of the decade, *Blockade,* which finally appeared in 1938. Against the advice of studio
heads who dreaded the certain loss of revenues to German and Italian audiences, and just as much against the American Catholic Church, whose hierarchy (following the Vatican) plumped openly for fascist leader Francisco
Franco, Wanger forged ahead. He threw out previous scripts by Odets and
by Lewis Milestone, redoubtable director of *All Quiet on the Western Front;* it
was the supreme compliment to Lawson.

Despite the censorship that forbade even use of the word "Spain," let
alone "fascism," the film delivered Henry Fonda speaking for an embattled
city of peasants, workers, and citizens desperately in need of supplies that,
in the real world, the U.S. government had embargoed from the Loyalists.
Director William Dieterle (according to Hollywood legend, a Communist
before he left Germany, and according to the FBI, husband of a hard-and-
fast immigrant Red) did his utmost within these obvious constraints. In
Hollywood's nearest approach to the "mass" scenes of Sergei Eisenstein and

Vsevolod Pudovkin until the 1940s war films, *Blockade* almost approached *Battleship Potemkin,* at least in certain spectacular scenes.

Lawson wrote the film around a romance between the daughter of an upper-class smuggler and a shepherd whom she meets when her auto breaks down on a rural road. The next scene finds Fonda, now a lieutenant in the Loyalist army, confronting Madeleine Carroll's father, the very smuggler whom Fonda later kills in self-defense. Slowly, over the course of observing the suffering of the city's inhabitants and especially their milk-starved children, she is converted to the cause (at least the cause of defending the country against the outsiders, a fair estimate of Spanish sentiment versus invading German and Italian fascists). A collaborationist conspiracy by the supposed leading defenders of the city is broken, the lovers united, and even the apparently doomed ship in dock—but disaster has only been temporarily staved off.

The political power of the film was undercut rather than emphasized by the romance, itself not exactly of *Casablanca* quality. But if *Blockade* did poorly at the box office, it was thanks less to plot contrivances or mediocre notices than to a virtual ban in showings abroad and to the Fox theater chain's unwillingness to run it as a first feature. Wanger nevertheless commissioned Lawson to begin another upfront antifascist project, a project that stopped dead when (according to Lawson's later account) Wanger's moneymen told him that he would never be extended another loan if this picture was made. Lawson wrote other films and good films, in fact probably his best and certainly his most favorably received. (See Chapters Four and Five, below.) But the possibilities he envisioned at optimistic moments since the early thirties had passed.[67]

Any hope of an Eisensteinian film was practically over, if it had ever been more than a pipe dream among the handful who had absorbed the Russian cinematic message and kept it close to their hearts. Eisenstein's own failed scheme to make a film in Mexico of Dreiser's *Sister Carrie* confirmed the disappointment. Left-wing scripts had other means, closer to the Hollywood mainstream in form even if meant to tip or subvert them in content. Decades later—after his release from prison and a rumored mental breakdown—Lawson penned his ironclad Stalinist manifesto, *Film in the Battle of Ideas* (1953), which brutally attacked the naïveté of his own earlier work (and, by extension, the praise of its cogency by the left-wing press).

He admitted he had misestimated "class struggle in the field of art." The various limits of *Blockade* and of his career no doubt loomed as large in his mind as the downfall he suffered after his prestige and influence peaked during the Second World War. He had allowed himself to get past bitter disappointment once, only to be struck down again. In that light, the artistic experiment of coalition with liberal filmmakers had proved a failure twice over in politics and art. Lawson retreated to the Communist position of the early 1930s that only organized political pressure on filmmakers could effect real change—a strategy that the Right used far more effectively than the Left.[68]

Nearly two decades younger and more innocent, Lawson had published the first edition of his masterwork as *Theory and Technique of Playwriting* (1936). The first two subjects of the title may have been united successfully in the theater, but otherwise in life and especially in Hollywood were usually at odds, notwithstanding Lawson's later efforts to uphold the Party line on all questions aesthetic, political, and above all international. Lawson's Marxism, in many respects an ill-fitting Russian echo, nevertheless suited studio struggles and race issues. The multiple frustrations of Hollywood also pointed to the self-recognition of the Jewish intellectual, key to a cluster of related matters that could be expressed only, especially in film, in other forms.

Class Conflict Hollywood Style

It would be too easy to attribute to fate or personal psychology, rather than to conscious choice and determined will, Lawson's central role in the screenwriters' effort to raise their collective status. Any mixture of fatalism and psychoanalysis would also disregard the large degree of courage that Lawson and a mere handful of others expressed, decades before he gave in to despair and gave himself over to the worst of Party hacks. Even if Lawson's ideas offered a poor version of screen art and a poorer version of reality, he did the necessary union work that so many well-intended others had sloughed off, and did it through thick and thin. A hard-bitten labor figure like Lawson was badly needed in Hollywood because the odds against writers' or actors' (or technicians') dignity were so heavily outweighed by the studios' power.

Crushing labor opposition and then erasing the evidence had been a way of life in California outside the film industry. The treatment of the organized Left of socialists and Wobblies during wartime and the all-out Red Scare of 1919–21 was among the most severe anywhere, with "criminal syndicalism" indictments and long jail sentences handed out freely.[69] Local police "Red Squads" and FBI agents continued afterward to work overtime with large employers, from shippers to movie moguls, protecting them from unionization as well as from the supposed worse designs of radicals. Not only the tabloid papers but most powerfully the Hearst-owned *Los Angeles Times* and many others right down to neighborhood weeklies casually attributed the "subversive" label to anything that smacked of egalitarian liberalism.

San Franciscans ended the period of employer terror for themselves through the General Strike of 1934. Hereafter, official labor played a prominent role in San Francisco's economic and cultural life, albeit often at the price of keeping the most restless workers in line. Southern California, by vivid contrast, remained a world apart. Since the Gilded Age, it had offered a paradise for manufacturers seeking a union-free environment, a powerful inducement for film studios' move there. It was also more racially divided than the north, with Mexican-Americans, Asians, and Filipinos as a virtual subject class (later a growing number of African-Americans as well). Meanwhile, southern white newcomers joined neofascist movements in large numbers. The region also flaunted a bizarre atmosphere of pseudo-royalty with rampant symbols of aristocracy (like a liveried servant class) elsewhere on the wane in America. Keeping such a system intact was understandably regarded as no easy task. In what can now be viewed as a remnant of an earlier police-state era (and vivid premonition of the "riot prevention" measures in post-1965 Los Angeles), the LAPD handed out pistol permits and gold badges to businessmen and movie executives accorded high honors for the "war on Reds," and into the late 1930s actually provided to the German and Japanese governments detailed information on foreign-born activists.

The union picture in the entertainment industry had been complicated long since by a deeply racist and otherwise exclusionary, generally conservative International Alliance of Theatrical Stage Employees (IATSE). The IATSE had earlier cooperated in breaking strikes by the secretive "White Rats" stage actors' organizations, while maintaining its own ranks through threats of potentially disastrous production shutdowns. Encouraging labor organizations outside their own ranks was far from the intent of IATSE leaders, who customarily limited the union's membership, as far as possible, to relatives of past or current union members. But by virtue of its existence as the only recognized bargaining unit in the film industry, IATSE and its members offered other studio workers reminders of the desperate need for representation.

The very creation of the Academy of Motion Picture Arts and Sciences, in 1927, had been intended to foreclose on organized mental labor as much as raise the dignity of the new profession. Bringing together producers, directors, actors, writers, and technicians, the Academy abstractly offered a commonweal—but with some participants (or would-be participants) working under the absolute control of others. Actually, as open as it claimed to be to all community members who had "contributed in a distinguished way," the Academy was open in fact to anyone whom founder Louis B. Mayer considered worthy, and to no one else. Then came the Depression.

By spring of 1933, most of the studios could not meet their payrolls, and their leaders took up a then-familiar strategy of large and small employers around the nation, i.e., massive wage reductions, in some cases up to 50 percent. Studio employees groaned. But craft unionist IATSE members struck the first blow, against the advice of their leaders, refusing work for a day and in the end taking a cut in some cases of only 20 percent. The impulse for unionization had thus been planted in the minds of many underpaid and overworked employees. In the summer of 1933, IATSE's electricians went out, and several studios briefly closed but then responded with strikebreakers and successfully crushed the strike. Nevertheless, over the next four years, IATSE grew from a few hundred to five thousand, in no small part because Roosevelt's new National Labor Relations Board insisted on the legitimacy of organized labor.[70]

Screenwriters themselves began meeting secretly the same year, combining the famous (Samson Raphaelson, screenwriter of *The Jazz Singer,* the first box office smash in which sound was decisive) and the unfamous, like John Bright, Samuel Ornitz, and fellow future Reds Lester Cole and John Howard Lawson. They had ample reason to organize, with more than half of them then earning less than $4,000 a year, 30 percent earning less than $2,000, and only a princely 10 percent of them earning more than $10,000.

Unlike the IATSE unionists, however, these writers wanted something beyond improvements in wages and conditions: They demanded control over credits. Inasmuch as credits determined salary, the connection was inevitable, but control also implied creative influence, something that was never far from the writers' minds. Affiliating its 175 members with the Authors League of America, the new Screen Writers Guild (SWG) elected Lawson its first president and Joseph Mankiewicz secretary.

Almost by the time the SWG had organized itself (if not the studios), salaries returned to their low normal. The proto-union got nowhere with management. The Screen Actors Guild (SAG) moved first, in part because of the charisma and influence of sympathetic stars, but also because a National Recovery Administration code said to have been written by producers attempted to impose salary ceilings, a limit to free agency (the right of an actor, at the end of a contract, to move on to another studio), and, worst of all, a dictum that actors' (and writers') agents could not negotiate without being licensed by the producers themselves. This added up to nothing less than continued total studio control. Many continued to expect the government to offer a way out by saving the face of the studios while giving Hollywood talent some element of what had been demanded. This was an illusion. Further negotiations were as fruitless for actors as for writers because studio chiefs had no intention of giving in.

But America was changing. A massive drive for industrial unionism followed citywide general strikes and sympathy actions of 1934 in Minneapolis-St. Paul and Toledo as well as San Francisco, and as the critical 1936 elections approached, Roosevelt avidly wooed the unions. The expulsion of the Committee for Industrial Organization (formalized as the Congress of Industrial Organizations) was still to come in 1935, with unprecedented union enrollment of many millions. But even IATSE—its leaders terribly fearful of industrial unionism—was buoyed by the wave of labor energy.

Meanwhile, screenwriters continued to face studio stonewalling. In September 1935, the Academy announced that a new code of practice was being written up; its tenets included the non-revelation that producers would not be legally bound by any decisions on credits made outside their executive domain. The SWG reached nearly a thousand members by the summer of 1936. The SAG moved toward becoming a real union, affiliating directly with the American Federation of Labor (AFL), while the SWG negotiated with the Authors League of America and the Dramatists Guild to form a potentially powerful national writers' organization.

In the controversy to follow, Congress held hearings about the purported crisis in America's favorite entertainment and the rumored "Red danger" that Hearst newspapers dramatized. On behalf of the SWG, Lawson testified to the House Patents' Committee that writers were being treated as mere studio office boys, and demanded union recognition. Producers' warnings against the purported New Yorkers' domination of "their" writers amounted to subtle Red-baiting: Everyone knew that New York was where the Red intellectuals operated. A studio statement calling on screenwriters to abandon "false leaders" was followed by a neat bit of employer strategy. A dissident SWG minority announced its eagerness for a less confrontational relation with the bosses. They evidently meant capitulation, for even as the Guild radicals bent over backward to keep amity among opposing factions, making sure to include conservative screenwriters in the executive committee, the dissatisfied group abandoned ship to form the Screen Playwrights exclusively for the elite.[71]

The studios won another round as an informal blacklist scared off most of the SWG membership. When its rolls fell below a hundred and the faithful abandoned public meetings entirely, the SWG became just about as covert as the small Hollywood Communist Party, whose first branch had just come into existence. Membership in the Party or participation in its study groups was likely no more dangerous than union membership; no wonder some writers active in both organizations could hardly, in later recollections, separate one memory of closed-door meetings from the other.

1. "W. R. Burnett: The Outsider," interviewed by Ken Mate and Patrick McGilligan, in *Backstory 1: Interviews with Screenwriters of Hollywood's Golden Age* (Berkeley: University of California Press, 1986), 58–59. Extracting the anecdote from this interview, Ian Hamilton, in his estimable *Writers in Hollywood* (New York: Carroll & Graf, 1990), 50, seems curiously oblivious to Faragoh's credit, a remarkable and telling lapse for a book about screenwriters.

2. The German case is clearest. See Bruce Murray, *Film and the German Left in the Weimar Republic, from Caligari to Kuhle Wampe* (Austin: University of Texas

Press, 1990), especially Chapter 4, 36–54; Chapters 9–10, 89–138; and Chapters 14–15, 168–222. But for an extended moment it seemed that independent radical and union filmmakers might be able to create genres of commercially successful films with sympathetic themes of labor and class oppression. *The Girl Strike Leader* (1910), *The Long Strike* (1911), and *Toil and Tyranny* (1915) among others demonstrated a greater possibility lost. A second promising genre of union documentary films was abandoned along with the labor-educational movement by AFL leadership in the later 1920s. See Steven J. Ross, *Working-Class Hollywood: Silent Film and the Shaping of Class in America* (Princeton: Princeton University Press, 1998), Chapters 1–3, 11–85.

3. Abraham Polonsky interviewed by Paul Buhle and Dave Wagner, in Patrick McGilligan and Paul Buhle, *Tender Comrades: A Backstory of the Hollywood Blacklist* (New York: St. Martin's Press, 1997), 493.

4. Philip Furia, *Ira Gershwin: The Age of the Lyricist* (Oxford: Oxford University Press, 1996), 44–55.

5. Harold Meyerson and Ernie Harburg, *Who Put the Rainbow in the Wizard of Oz? Yip Harburg, Lyricist* (Ann Arbor: University of Michigan Press, 1993), 30–45.

6. Centuries earlier, communards of the Radical Reformation, seizing cities from royalty and clergy, had adopted the rainbow as their colors; this adoption was rooted in vastly older traditions.

7. Edward Eliscu interviewed by David Eliscu and Patrick McGilligan in McGilligan and Paul Buhle, *Tender Comrades*, 228–34. Eliscu wrote lyrics for the 1930 production of *Whoopee!* for Eddie Cantor, followed by *Roman Scandals* (1933)—directed by future Party member and friendly witness Frank Tuttle—and several more in the next five years. It may be noted that the Communist and near-Communist critics in the *New Masses* thoroughly disapproved of such spectacles. See for instance Nathan Adler, "The Screen," *New Masses* 10 (January 2, 1934), 28–29, on *Roman Scandals* as most improper for the era of mass deprivation and economic crisis.

8. See John Weber interview by Paul Buhle in *Tender Comrades,* 690–91.

9. Irving Pichel, "Creativeness Cannot Be Diffused," *Hollywood Quarterly* 1 (July 1946), 20–22. These issues are further explored in Chapters 2 and 6.

10. Tino Balio, "Production Trends," in Balio, *Grand Design: Hollywood as a Modern Business Enterprise, 1930–1939* (Berkeley: University of California Press, 1993), 179–312, is the most cogent presentation.

11. Henry Jenkins, *What Made Pistachio Nuts? Early Sound Comedy and the Vaude-ville Aesthetic* (New York: Columbia University Press, 1990), especially 6–12, a commentary on the historiography of what Jenkins calls the "anarchistic comedy tradition." Differences with Jenkins's approach will be noted in Chapter 3.

12. See, e.g., Richard Maurice Hurst, *Republic Studios: Between Poverty Row and the Majors* (Metuchen, NJ: Scarecrow Press, 1979).

13. Daniel J. Walkowitz, *Working With Class: Social Workers and the Politics of Mid-dle-Class Identity* (Chapel Hill: University of North Carolina Press, 1999), "Prologue," especially 2–3.

14. See Philip Dunne, "Life on the Assembly Line," Chapter 6 of *Take Two: A Life in Movies and Politics* (New York: McGraw-Hill, 1980), 54–62.

15. Maurice Rapf, *Back Lot: Growing Up with the Movies* (Lanham: Scarecrow Press, 1999), 47–49, is particularly insightful from the standpoint of a mogul's son looking at the practical effects of the Wall Street takeover process.

16. See Richard Maltby, "The Production Code and the Hays Office," in Tino Balio, *Grand Design,* 42–46.

17. Richard Maltby, "The Production Code and the Hays Office," 47–59. Specif-ically forbidden were the undermining of marriage's sanctity, excessive or lustful expression, racial miscegenation and homosexuality, sex hygiene or disease, profanity, ridicule of religion, and so on.

18. Quoted in Clayton R. Koppes, "Regulating the Screen: The Office of War In-formation and the Production Code Administration," in Thomas Schatz, *Boom and Bust: American Cinema in the 1940s* (Berkeley: University of Califor-nia Press, 1997), 265.

19. Richard Maltby, "The Production Code and the Hays Office," in Balio, *Grand Design,* 43–63.

20. Future film scholar Gerald Peary took a close look at the pre-sound origins in "The Rise of the American Gangster Film, 1913–30," unpublished disserta-tion, University of Wisconsin, 1977.

21. J. Brooks Atkinson, "The Play," *The New York Times,* February 4, 1927.

22. "New Gang Film at Strand," *The New York Times,* January 8, 1931. According to the enthusiastic reviewer, Robinson made his protagonist "a figure out of Greek epic tragedy, a cold, ignorant, merciless killer driven on and on by an insatiable lust for power, the play thing of a force that is greater than him-self."

23. Bill Carter, "The Roots of 'Sopranos' Grew from Cagney Film," *The New York Times,* February 26, 2001. An interview with *Sopranos'* writer David Chase notes that *The Public Enemy* started Chase's "love affair with the gangster film," and even inspired his treatment of the much-hailed *Soprano* mobster's mom, Livia.

24. This point owes much to George F. Custen, *Twentieth Century's Fox: Darryl F. Zanuck and the Culture of Hollywood* (New York: Basic Books, 1997), 141; scholar Custen, though, does not even mention the screenwriters, mistakenly attributing the film's innovations to Zanuck alone.

25. This interwar milieu has been identified as a part of "lost Chicago" by a small handful of scholars. See Frank O. Beck, *Hobohemia* (Chicago: Charles H. Kerr Co., 2001).

26. A fact recognized by an early left-wing critic lauding him for "sterling emotional consistency," and calling him "a living definition of the American working class—the most vital creative personification of the energy, courage, cleverness and fatalism of vast numbers of American workers," but suffering under Hollywood's yoke of typecasting. Forrest Clark, "James Cagney," *New Theater* 2 (December 1935), 14–15, 34.

27. Robert Sklar, *City Boys: Cagney, Bogart, Garfield* (Princeton: Princeton University Press, 1992), especially Chapter 2, 57–202.

28. Among the several interviews with Bright bearing upon *The Public Enemy* are John Bright interviewed by Patrick McGilligan, *Tender Comrades,* 128–54; and John Bright interviewed by Lee Server, in Server, *Screenwriter: Words Become Pictures* (Pittstown, NJ: Main Street Press, 1987), 67–92. Faragoh leaves no oral testimony, a considerable gap in what we would wish to know in screenwriters' history.

29. Mordaunt Hall, in "Films," *The New York Times,* December 4, 1931, credited it only with being "lively and cleverly acted."

30. *The New York Times* called it "tedious and distasteful": "M. H." [Mordaunt Hall], "Blackmail and Kidnapping," October 30, 1932.

31. The most embittering one of these for Bright, *The Crowd Roars* was an early location film, this one at the Indianapolis 500 (literally shot there), with the screenwriters on hand, director Howard Hawks quarreling with them every step of the way—and Cagney the boozing race car driver who intrigues against a straight younger brother by making a play for his live-in girlfriend, Dvorak. According to Bright, who was housed by the studio at a real race car drivers' hotel full of gamblers and prostitutes, the idea for the plot came from

a true-to-life story that Bright wrote out as the shooting proceeded and Hawks misappropriated for his own undeserved screenwriting credit.

32. John Bright, interviewed by Patrick McGilligan and Ken Mate, in *Tender Comrades,* 140.

33. *Stella Dallas* was actually scripted by short-term Party member Gertrude Purcell, a collaborator on *Destry Rides Again,* and later a friendly witness. See Chapter 3 on *Destry* and Purcell.

34. Tasker, like Bright, married an important (and reputedly very beautiful) Mexican-American radical, making the foursome a most distinctive Los Angeles set; he also wrote or coscripted several other films most notable for their pre-Code content. *The Great Jasper* (1933) tells the life story of a trolley car operator who has a love affair with the local trolley magnate's wife and, after being fired, ends up (with his illegitimate, sickly son in tow) as a professional mystic.

35. Communist screenwriter Madeleine Ruthven codeveloped the story of *The Accusing Finger,* according to some contemporary accounts. Bright's story for *John Meade's Woman* (1937), scripted by others, even hit the environmental issue as it raked a lumber baron over the social coals. Edward Arnold memorably played the baron who ignores the laws of reforestation as he turns from wood to wheat in search of higher profits. A writer for the *New Masses* called *John Meade's Woman* a "really exciting effort" to smash through the Hollywood conventions, and credited the documentary-style evocation of a dust storm and farmers on the march, adding up to a "vitality achieved by few American films," even if it was reduced in the end by its sappy love story. See Robert White, "Sight and Sounds," *New Masses* 24 (July 27, 1937), 29. An earlier review in the same publication reduced it to the story of a "bad bad capitalist who has a tragic love life." See "The Screen," *New Masses* 22 (March 9, 1937), 30.

36. A *New Masses* writer complained that the story never escaped the frame of the individual victim of capitalism and the maudlin view of small-town life in the past, adding "the dialogue writing does not help," admitting *Back Door to Heaven* was nevertheless a "well-meant picture" but concluding that it "opens upon too little." "J. D.," "Two Tries," *New Masses* 31 (May 16, 1939), 29–30.

37. See Chapter 8, on Bright's late films.

38. Josefina Fierro led the Congress of Spanish Speaking Peoples, a Popular Front organization, centered in Los Angeles, which was briefly influential before being dissolved during World War II.

39. Ring Lardner, Jr., made these observations to Paul Buhle in a conversation; the accuracy cannot be checked.

40. The *Times* greeted it as "quite entertaining" if "incredible" and congratulated the director's "photographic artistry." Mordant Hall, "Beer and Crime," *The New York Times,* April 14, 1931.

41. *New Masses* humor columnist Robert Forsythe merely observed that *The Thin Man* "is a fairly good Hollywood melodrama, with a wire-haired terrier doing the most important acting." Robert Forsythe, "Speaking of the Dance," *New Masses* 12 (July 24, 1934). *New Masses* was kinder to several of the future Hammett story–based films, especially *The Maltese Falcon.* See below, Chapters 3–5.

42. Diane Johnson, *Dashiell Hammett: A Life* (New York: Fawcett Columbine, 1983), 91–167. See more on Hammett and films based on his work in Chapters 2, 5, and 7.

43. It is worth noting that German refugee Michael Curtiz—an ardent antifascist, and later collaborator on some of the best left-written films—stepped into the director's chair for several scenes of *The Mayor of Hell.*

44. See Bernard F. Dick, *Radical Innocence: A Critical Study of the Hollywood Ten* (Lexington: the University Press of Kentucky, 1989), 19–20. Remarkably, for this early period, all three films had sympathetic African-American characters: in the first, the picaresque Billie "Buckwheat" Thomas from the *Our Gang* comedies; in the latter two, several black men as a chorus articulating the sadness of prison fate. *Boy Slaves* (1939), written by future blacklistee Albert Bein and produced by Pandro Berman for RKO, was the last of the genre. Bein, who had lost a leg in his poverty-stricken youth, had his greatest distinction in Broadway dramas of the underprivileged.

45. See Jeanine Basinger, *A Woman's View: How Hollywood Spoke to Women, 1930–1960* (Hanover, NH: New England Universities Press/Weslyan University Press, 1993), a film viewer's interpretation often indifferent to the behind-the-camera logic and the world of the writers in particular.

46. "Her Private Affair," *Variety,* January 15, 1930.

47. The oddest films could do as well with a similar gender message. Faragoh's original for a badly colored *The Dancing Pirate* (1937), an understandably forgotten musical comedy, has a Danny Kaye–type free-spirited but not especially virile dance teacher who is lost at sea off eighteenth-century Latin America make his way to shore, be mistaken for a pirate, and get himself rescued from execution at the hands of the authorities by a collective women's

protest. Spreading the gender-emancipation message from Europe to the colonies, he is once more endangered until the successful invasion of Indians, who have allied themselves with the honest Europeans and share with them an extraordinary ability to dance in Busby Berkeley–like patterns. Our protagonist is victorious because he represents the Other, obviously every Other available, and brings them into an imaginary postcolonial, radically reconstituted society. In this curious way, *The Dancing Pirate* offers a clue to plot strategies of costume dramas, contemporary race and ethnic melodramas, and slapstick comedies alike.

48. Charmion von Wiegand, "The Screen," *New Masses* 21 (October 13, 1936), 27.

49. Mordaunt Hall, "The Screen," *The New York Times,* April 28, 1926.

50. Donald Ogden Stewart, *By a Stroke of Luck: An Autobiography* (London: Paddington Press, 1975), 153. This memoir was prefaced by Katharine Hepburn, who described the screenwriter as "a man who is willing to pay the price of his own passionate beliefs," adding, "He's my friend. I think I'm the lucky one," 9. See also "Donald Ogden Stewart: Politically Conscious," interviewed by Allen Eyles and John Gillett in Pat McGilligan, *Backstory 1: Interviews with Screenwriters of Hollywood's Golden Age* (Berkeley: University of California Press, 1986), 334–56.

51. See the commentary on *Holiday, The Philadelphia Story, Keeper of the Flame,* and *Edward, My Son,* all written by Stewart and directed by Cukor, in Patrick McGilligan, *George Cukor, A Double Life* (New York: St. Martin's Press, 1991), 378–83. All these films are discussed in Chapters 4, 5, and 8.

52. Robert Forsythe unsympathetically called it "the dullest film that has been seen for some time." "Cream Puff and Black Bread," *New Masses* 13 (October 9, 1934), 29.

53. The *New Masses* called it a "bleak, shuddering, cataclysmic bore. It causes audience silences in which you could hear a head drop; in fact, many a head does fall upon many a bosom and blissful, plebian snores respond to the royal salute." James Dugan, "Movies," *New Masses* 28 (August 30, 1938), 30.

54. This film is interesting in another regard: His cowriter was the future blacklistee Vera Caspary, who mainly wrote novels adapted for the screen, including the famed noir *Laura.*

55. "Sign of the Cross," *Variety,* November 30, 1932.

56. Irving Lerner, "More Red Herring Soup," *New Masses* 12 (July 31, 1934), 30. Buchman could also do unrequited fatherly yearning, like the box office

champion of August 1934, *Whom the Gods Destroy*. Here, a successful playwright and ocean liner passenger saves a woman during a shipwreck but
wakes up with women's clothes on (i.e., has apparently preserved his own
coward's life by cross-dressing), and spends the rest of his life apart from his
remarried ex-wife but eventually and secretly in touch with her, watching his
son from a distance and not so curiously like a male Stella Dallas, yearning
but unwilling to bring shame by making his paternity known. We can easily
imagine who bought most of the tickets for this feature; according to contemporary surveys, would-be male viewers regularly yielded in their choice
to wives and daughters.

57. A highly charged, small-budget remake under the same title appeared in
1959, starring Mickey Rooney, which must have offered consolation to the
blacklisted writer; it may also be Rooney's best dramatic film, certainly his
most radical.

58. John Wexley interviewed by Patrick McGilligan and Ken Mate, *Tender Comrades*, 698–713; Edwin Bronner, *The Encyclopedia of the American Theatre,
1900–1975* (San Diego and New York: A. S. Barnes, 1980), 263, 469–70.

59. Dick, *Radical Innocence*, 46.

60. Named for Haymarket riot martyr Albert Parsons by his anarchist parents,
Albert Lewin was a former college professor at Washington University and a
film critic for a St. Louis Jewish weekly; in Hollywood, after Thalberg's
death, Lewin wrote, produced, and directed several of the most surrealistic
films of the age. See Chapter 8. Lewin's friendship with Lawson is recounted
in a memoir by Lawson's son, Jeff Lawson, "An Ordinary Life," in Judy Ka-
plan and Linn Shapiro, editors, *Red Diapers: Growing Up in the Communist Left*
(Urbana: University of Illinois Press, 1998), 54–55.

61. His script for a B sound film, *The Sea Bat* (1931), is a variation: The half-breed
Polynesian girl, her sailor-lover killed at sea, embraces a religious-missionary
figure who turns out to be a criminal on the run but repentant.

62. John Howard Lawson, unpublished memoirs, 201–02, in the Lawson Collection, Southern Illinois University archives.

63. In his treatise on film, dedicated "to the Association of Film Makers of the
USSR," Lawson granted the "crude boldness" of the plot that DeMille had allowed him to compose, but noted that thematically the story was of an aristocratic girl's "frustration and escape," the conclusion of her "return to the man
of her own class." Lawson, *The Creative Process: The Search for an Audio-Visual
Language and Structure* (New York: Hill and Wang, 1964), 105. Lawson's for-

malism would not allow him to touch ambience beyond plot structure and conclusion, except to grant that DeMille's depiction of upper-class decadence served the purpose of a radical screenwriter.

64. Their attempt to write a play together, an imaginary meeting of Lenin and James Joyce in Zurich, came to nothing, but might be said to have planted the seed for Wilson's *To the Finland Station* (1939), marking a memorable artistic-political disillusionment with Communism.

65. John Howard Lawson, *Success Story: A Play* (New York: Farrar & Rinehart, 1928), 40–41.

66. Lawson, *Success Story,* 243. Perhaps it is revealing that in the revised edition of *The Creative Process,* Lawson does not refer to his own films between *Dynamite* and *Blockade,* not even *Success Story.* The advance of the Soviet film and the formation of the Screen Writers Guild fill the screen on his radar, making other developments incidental.

67. Matthew Bernstein, *Walter Wanger: Hollywood Independent* (Berkeley: University of California Press, 1994), 131–33. Inevitably, *Blockade* was a cause célèbre for the Popular Front at large. See James Dugan, "Movies," *New Masses* 28 (August 2, 1938), 30–31, on lobbying to get the movie shown, and in more complete form. The critical judgment of the same writer ("a militant picture; partisan and true") was perhaps the first unequivocal praise of a Hollywood film by an American Marxist publication. See Dugan, "Blockade," *New Masses* 28 (June 28, 1938), 27–28. See also Greg M. Smith, "Blocking Blockade: Partisan Protest, Popular Debate and Encapsulated Texts," *Cinema Journal* 36 (Fall, 1996), 18–38. The never-made film was almost certainly an adaptation of a reporter's discovery of Franco's viciousness and Hitler's anti-Semitism. Breen warned Wanger off the project until 1940, when it was rewritten into Alfred Hitchcock's depoliticized sabotage thriller, *Foreign Correspondent.* See Koppes, "Regulating the Screen," 265.

68. John Howard Lawson, *Film in the Battle of Ideas* (New York: Masses and Mainstream, 1953), 21–22. No doubt the abandonment of the Party by the great majority of his former Hollywood comrades weighed heavily on Lawson's mind as well.

69. This arcane phrase later had to be explained to longtime left sympathizer, invaluable host for fund-raisers, and general Party ally Lucille Ball, on the HUAC witness stand in 1951, when she feigned absolute ignorance. This was not likely a case of disingenuousness on Ball's part; knowledge of pre-Communist radical movements was spotty at best, "syndicalism" a word with

virtually no American past, adopted by prosecutors searching for a criminal phrase to throw at Wobblies. See *Hearings Before the Committee on Un-American Activies, House of Representatives, 83rd Congress, Investigation of Communist Activities in the Los Angeles Area—Part 7, 1953* (Washington, DC: U.S. Government Publications, 1953), 2568–69.

70. See Gerald Horne, *Class Struggle in Hollywood, 1930–1950: Moguls, Mobsters, Stars, Reds, and Trade Unions* (Austin: University of Texas Press, 2001), 43–48. We are grateful to Horne for supplying us with a prepublication copy of the manuscript for this book.

71. Larry Ceplair and Steven Englund, *The Inquisition in Hollywood: Politics in the Film Community, 1930–1960* (Garden City, NY: Anchor Press/Doubleday, 1980), 35–36.

2

THE NEW DEAL, THE RISE OF THE HOLLYWOOD LEFT, AND THE JEWISH QUESTION

HE ONLY WAY TO AVOID HOLLYWOOD," composer Igor Stravinsky famously quipped, "is to live there."[1] Fan magazines, the commercial press, the radio, and every other venue passed gossip to the public about Tinseltown personalities and romances, while *Variety* spread the news far and wide of alliances, dalliances, and deals. Hollywood was everywhere. Yet for the real-life inhabitants of a small town (by New York standards, naturally) and a company town (most especially the areas within the reaches of Beverly Hills), personal contact and communication could be amazingly poor, points of connection beyond employees at various studios practically limited to restaurants and political or social events, often the same thing.

Save for the presence of the sprawling studios, one of British novelist and film correspondent Cedric Belfrage's characters observes about late 1930s Hollywood, "the place was like any other suburb where there was nothing to do and nowhere to go." Life moved ahead with typical American land-boomer self-promotion, radiating along with vast moral hypocrisy a most amazing "insubstantiality," a lostness between past and future.[2] In this world where networking meant everything, the Communist Party's Popular Front was, from the middle thirties until the late forties, *the* network for the cerebral progressive, the inveterate activist, and the determined labor unionist.

But the Popular Front certainly marked an odd gathering point. In other parts of the world and even in New York, political affiliation during the 1930s was central to identity. In Hollywood, where topflight Communist writers often lunched in the studio commissary with their peers instead of their comrades, everyone tended to be judged according to status. The same principle applied to scripts. "All the noble fellows of the left," successful radio writer-producer and blacklistee Leonardo Bercovici observed wryly and without excluding himself from the picture, "what did they write? If they were good, they got the better assignments. And the better assignments were what? Big stars and a certain kind of story."[3] Hollywoodites might shun the glitter and still hardly help thinking in movie terms. Away from the job in Detroit, an autoworker was an anonymous proletarian, but a filmwriter in Hollywood was always a filmwriter in the city where celebrity equaled success and success equaled celebrity.

This was never the whole truth. The majority of screenwriters, proletarian intellectuals by conditions if not by choice, barely made a living and faced constant insecurity. Studio unions at all levels pitted themselves against one of the most profitable industries in the United States. Solidarity with blue-collar Los Angeles just outside studio gates and with the almost inhumanly oppressed agricultural workers beyond was real and important for Hollywoodites who sought reciprocal public sympathy and support. Early dissenters like John Bright had paid the price, in career reverses by the mid-1930s, and many more were to sacrifice opportunities to help create decent working conditions and minimal creative control (at least over credits) en route to the unreachable goal of an artistically independent cinema.

Even the character of the most intense struggles was, however, Hollywoodish and usually Jewish-connected, an extended immigrant-family drama become a sort of middle-class brawl. In the fixed nepotism of the industry, top executives hired brothers, sons-in-law, nephews by the dozens. Meanwhile, progressive writers, actors, and directors enjoyed or at least accepted the prospect that their wives (mostly Jewish wives, even of some Gentile radicals) would take the lead politically, finding within the Popular Front the public role and social-cultural activity otherwise absent for them on the sunshine coast.[4]

Of course, only a minority of American Jews actually heeded the call of the liberal Left, as Jewish Republican studio heads often reminded the press, and only a (albeit large) minority of the Communist Party identified itself as Jewish. But the connection was nevertheless inescapable. Nowhere did Left influence sink so deeply into intellectual culture and with so much lasting effect. Indeed, within the relative vacuum of other progressive forces during the crucial era of antifascist sentiment, unionization, and open anti-Semitism, a kind of Jewishness provided the main lever for radicalism to advance within the Hollywood community, for radicals to raise very considerable sums of money and exert a star power unimaginable otherwise. For banquet goers and fund-pledgers, ghost writers of liberal or labor speeches, the political and economic struggles of the world offered both anodyne and antidote to the inevitable temptations, stresses, and disappointments of career. Popular Front participation thereby became a major avenue of Americanization, redefining an imagined America in which former outsiders could properly belong.[5]

Here, more than anywhere else on earth, a rush of high-profile social events naturally became the major public expression of liberal politics and morals. No Leftists anywhere, not even the postwar celebrity Existentialists of Paris, had such a life of perceived contrasts as Red (or pinkish) couples like Sidney and Beatrice Buchman, Michael and Zelma Wilson, Frank and Tatania Tuttle. Red-baiting gossip columnists who sniped at "swimming-pool Communists" felt no guilt about their own swimming pools and ignored the financially insecure mass of screenwriters. But the incredulity commanded by the damning phrase was nevertheless telling, if the tale could be related sympathetically as the humane commitment of the successful artist rather than caricatured as the vicarious radical adventure of guilty liberal hacks.

The altogether unique circumstances of the 1930s made it possible. Anti-Communism, at the center of bipartisan American politics since the Russian Revolution, reinforced the initial indifference of most Americans to European fascism and to anti-Semitism. Popular disillusionment with the First World War only deepened resistance toward potential reengagement with European events. Fascism, at first sympathetically interpreted among American elites as a last-ditch defense of property and morality against the threat of Communism (often interpreted as the threat of Communistic Jews), had its boosters not only among avowed racists and anti-Semites, but also among Catholic clergy and the presses of newspaper giant William Randolph Hearst. A widespread suspicion of Jews and Jewish influence—the frequency of asides about the "Franklin D. Rosenfeld" administration, about Jewish promoters (and popular as performers) of "jungle music," and about assorted sinners against Christian virtue—made

it difficult even for monied Jewish conservatives to argue against the tolerance of left-wing ideas held by respectable figures. Meanwhile, large sections of Americans across the political spectrum also had the chilling
sensation that capitalism had failed and seemed not especially likely to recover.

The Communists themselves made things immensely easier in 1935
by insisting upon a united opposition to the menace from the Right. The
idea of a global armed alliance against fascism, often seen retrospectively as
a heroic crusade of wise elites and democrats against an irrational Middle
American isolationism, was at first centered considerably outside the Establishment and very largely against its intentions as well as its financial
investments. The same was true of film corporations—even those with
Jewish ownership—that relished foreign bookings and waited until virtually the last moment to give them up in central and southern Europe.

Similarly difficult for later generations to grasp were developments
within popular culture that subtly began to power the popular impulse
toward liberal-left sympathies, and not merely to reflect them. Movies
started off with the lowest possible prestige among American intellectuals.
The educated classes outside Hollywood who went to movies, as virtually
all Americans did, sneered and suffered envy at Hollywoodites' success and
could not really imagine an artistically realized mass culture, let alone any
positive contribution of it to social change. Hollywoodites themselves
hardly knew how such a thing might happen.

Franklin Roosevelt contributed mightily to the change of perception.
A few studio chiefs had embraced the First Family celebrities prematurely—Jack Warner actually staged a "Motion Picture Electrical Parade
and Sports Pageant" at the L.A. Olympic Stadium in early September
1932, promoting the candidate in Busby Berkeley style and foreshadowing
the era in which Warner Brothers would recruit the most New Dealish
(often simultaneously the most left-wing) writers and "social" themes.
Other major players, from Louis B. Mayer on the Right to the Communists
on the Left, took a few years to come around to the New Deal, but eventually jumped in with both feet.

Roosevelt's reelection in 1936 proved decisive to the Hollywood/
White House connection. Along with the popularity of various social pro-
grams of the "Second New Deal" (Social Security, the pro-labor Wagner
Act, and related measures passed in time for the 1936 campaign), Roo-

sevelt's commanding presence in media's fast-growing audience helped him to sweep past the influence of the mainly Republican commercial press that gleefully predicted his defeat. His radio "Fireside Chats" had been vital. But a special relationship with Hollywood steadily gained importance as well.

Eleanor Roosevelt thus wrote in a 1938 issue of *Photoplay* that watching films constituted "the one and only relaxation which my husband has," their family life practically revolving around communal viewing.[6] The First Couple considered movies the ultimate democratic and American form of entertainment, providing a veritable model for lesser families. Roosevelt meanwhile recruited key publicity agents and one of his leading speechwriters (the notably left-liberal, sometime pacifist Robert Sherwood) from Hollywood, while Hollywood glamour (White House visits by stars, including the leftish Fredric March and Marsha Hunt) provided numerous photo-ops. Even a Roosevelt administration filing in 1938 of the antitrust case that would ultimately (but only after a decade of legal wrangling) compel the studios to give up possession of theater chains did not much shake the good feeling.

As FDR the media personality translated the political public into spectators, Hollywood at its most instrumental helped translate the spectators into a growingly self-conscious public if not a body politic. Through the patterns that contemporary films and New Deal wove together, the diverse regions and sections of the American public found or at least imagined many common bonds, for better and for worse. Together, the profit-driven movie corporations and vision- (or power-) driven federal agencies assisted (it would not be too much to say manipulated) the public and consumer into images of self, family member, and citizen.[7]

By 1936, Hollywood Communists cheerfully embraced these equations. Dozens of lifelong Jewish progressives could later have testified to having been loyal Roosevelt supporters (and registered Democrats) *before* becoming Communists, and loyal Democrats long after their Communist experience—"Party members" mainly in the descent of Jefferson rather than Lenin. No substantial Left in the last half of the 1930s could possibly exist far outside the New Deal, just as none could fail to support the war to follow. Roosevelt also badly needed the radicals as publicists, builders of social movements around the Democratic Party and for the electoral machine, even reliable brokers of political compromise with unionists and minorities alienated by Democratic conservatism and presidential inaction.

Amazingly enough, given their expulsion from Hollywood and organized liberalism after Roosevelt's death, the film industry Reds and their supporters had helped forge the necessary compromises here as well. How hard they had to fight back against isolation, and how successfully (at least for a time) they made themselves the respected opponents of philistine careerism, while making careers and (almost always) vigorously supporting the progressive end of mainstream politics may be best revealed initially via that most famous bit of prewar Hollywood Jewish fiction, *What Makes Sammy Run?*

Budd Schulberg's 1941 novel had real psychological penetration because it treated carefully the internal life of the studio intellectuals. Son of a pioneer mogul, the sometime Dartmouth College Marxist organizer and avid young Communist (he provided a model for future Emmy-winning screenwriter Walter Bernstein and recruited the younger man into the CP), young Schulberg spoke with a stammer and viewed Hollywood hijinks from a certain emotional distance.[8] Like his fellow Dartmouthite and future Disney screenwriter Maurice Rapf (whose father, Harry, was another mogul), young Schulberg had been to the Soviet Union, liked what he saw, and didn't have too many illusions about revolutionizing American movies.[9]

Schulberg's film credits before *On the Waterfront* were unimpressive, and his novel achieved its renown only a full decade after publication when the author cited a hostile review in the *Daily Worker* as the reason why he now felt no compunction about testifying against his former comrades. Most ironically at the Cold War moment when anti-Communists pressed the crimes of Stalin against Jews as proof of Communism's perfidy, the Left's cultural commissars were accused (but in distant retrospect) of overreacting to the novel's implied anti-Semitism. The Party's New York leadership, guilty as charged, had not countenanced even the literary ridicule of a dreadful social climber who radiated all the negative qualities that Jewish intellectuals identified among their less principled cohorts. Protagonist Sammy Glick—and this is the important point—was no exploitative sweatshop owner, not a mogul, shyster lawyer, or any other of the probable types identified in previous generations of Jews exploiting Jews in order to join the Gentile rich. He was a screenwriter, and, by dint of undeserved success and calculated connections, a producer as well.[10]

Sammy, a boy from the slums who stepped on and over the people around him, devoted his keenest energies into garnering publicity in the likes of Walter Winchell's columns, making it to Hollywood on the slimmest of actual creative talent. Sammy's political education came in 1934 and was drawn from real life: The studio chiefs decreed that every employee join the drive against Upton Sinclair, best-selling socialist novelist who had captured the Democratic nomination for governor with his End Poverty in California (EPIC) platform. Major studios demanded employees' financial contributions for his Republican opponent and even distributed their own short features during the election season spuriously associating the novelist with riots and rabble. Fictional Sammy insisted that the Communists had taken over the Democratic Party through Sinclair. In actuality, the Communist Party opposed Sinclair as insufficiently left-wing (some critics suggested that the novelist was so left-wing, he offered overpowering competition to the Party's claims on socialism). But many studio employees, including most of the future Communists, saw the broader situation quite differently.

The calculated attack upon Sinclair, a rare decent political figure, offered proof as to why the protections allowed by unionism and an associated political movement of some kind were desperately needed. The 1934 campaign also showed that Hollywood was not only about entertainment or even moneymaking: It was already political in a big way.

Close observers of literary history might have recognized an extended family history in Schulberg's novel from Abraham Cahan's *The Rise of David Levinsky* (1917). Here, an immigrant clothes manufacturer makes himself rich but realizes that in the process he is losing his soul in the land of dollars. He has become an "allrightnik," in the 1910s parlance of the Lower East Side. The novel was, perhaps, the subconscious autobiography of the author, editor of the *Jewish Daily Forward* who drifted gradually from socialism to McCarthyism. Sammy Glick has no conscience and therefore nothing to regret, so naturally Sammy sees in the studio campaign against Sinclair a marvelous opportunity to demonstrate his true loyalty or his moral cynicism, more or less the same thing to the bullying moguls. Sammy was, of course, merely an outstanding sample of the mass of Glicks in Hollywood, known as "Hollywoodniks."

Sammy has the amoral credentials, but he succeeds grandly because he figures out that the great majority of films, including most of the biggest hits, are actually just rewrites of familiar formulas. Not infrequently, stolen ideas add the necessary twist, so Sammy steals ideas as he fortifies his position by betraying the writers who risk their careers for the Screen Writers Guild, all the while pretending to support them. Sammy was also born to be an informer.

Everything Sammy wasn't, the Popular Front came to symbolize for its participants and admirers. They were the Jews (and Gentiles) who didn't sell out, who didn't betray their friends or willingly become studio hacks. And yet even this story could not be the whole Hollywood truth. W. L. River, a reputed political hard-liner with a scant screenwriting career of his own (his most important credit was in 1931, the quaintly proletarian *Way for a Sailor,* starring Wallace Beery), had a point when he quoted a 1940 essay by none other than Schulberg insisting that the "definitive Hollywood novel" would focus not on the glamorous or the corrupt but upon "a cross-section of the thousands of men and women who have become the cogs in a powerful, monopolized industry," that is, the "cutters, make-up men, sound experts, grips, juicers, stenographers, agents, the undiscovered hopefuls, and the broken-down ex-famous."[11]

The studio scion had evidently given up the ghost of this social novel and gone for the juicier if predictable material of the "success story" dark side. The Hollywood of the working stiff and the working stiff intellectuals remained a novel unwritten, a film never made. But its faint prospect drove many Hollywood radicals onward as they earned their bread in the very creation of mainstream Hollywood products that made the uncynical screenwriter grimace.

From New York to Hollywood (and Still Jewish . . .)

The story of the Hollywood Left and the plight of screenwriters needs to be traced from another direction. The vivid ethnic prehistory of theatrical experiments, Old and New World socialist memories, labor-mob involvements, and a continuing intercommunity tension all colored the creation of an improbable vigorous liberal-radical movement.

The diaspora from the East European Pale had begun amid industrialization, urbanization, and anti-Semitism that accentuated the break of Jewish youngsters from the age-old but rapidly fraying rabbinical/merchant hierarchies.[12] The Eastern European immigrant Jews of the 1890s quickly met with indifference or hostility of the earlier-migration German Jews who held positions of financial power and relative respectability in America. (The new immigrants contemptuously called their opposites *Yehudim*, while the Germans responded by christening the newcomers with the hate-word *kikes*.) Henceforth, the Jewish intraclass struggle waxed as fiercely as the common fight against American anti-Semitism. Or rather: As the wealthy counseled respect for property rights and negotiation with the gentility, the radicals urged solidarity among the transethnic and multiracial working class as the proper, only possible winning Jewish strategy.

The swift rise of some of the newer immigrants into sweatshop owners, small manufacturers, Tammany Hall chiselers, and petty (or not so petty) criminals further threw the idealism of the ghetto socialists and syndicalists into stark relief. According to evolving radical doctrine reinforced by the experiences of the First World War, only global socialism could prevent catastrophe for European Jewry in a world where capitalism regularly brought war and depression. A secondary proviso, felt the most strongly by left-wing Yiddishists, dictated that only a vital radical movement guaranteed the continuation of secular Jewish values in a society where the ethnic bourgeoisie, co-opting religion by paying off large portions of the rabbinate, sought both American assimilation and also ruling power in their own nationalistic principality halfway across the world. Even Labor Zionists, a considerable and mainly secular force early in the century, had something very different in mind.

Abraham Polonsky observed generations later that the stock older character in the Jewish drama, whether pronouncing the socialistic moral in theater or a film, was not so much creation as recollection. Every writer had an elderly family member, or knew of someone's elderly family member, who had carried socialistic ideas from the Old World and held fast to them to the end of life, in spite of all apparent disproofs through the advance of American materialism. *Their* proof lay not only in the continued suffering of the racially and ethnically assorted poor in America (and not to speak of the growing danger to Jews abroad), but also in the soullessness of the rich, emphatically including the Jewish rich, and the demoralizing effects of what Marx had called the Philistine "ruling ideas" of the society upon everyone.[13]

It was an old story by 1930, but so was the complex connection of ordinary (many of them socialistic) Jews and film. From early on, Jewish and Gentile mass response to movies seemed to broaden the emancipatory cravings expressed by radical movements but to substitute individual fate—especially, but not merely, via romance. If conservative and radical commentators alike complained that movies were replacing logic with sensation, the ultimate influences that the new art form might exert remained a mystery to all.

The purveyors of the nickelodeons whose constituency hit more than 2 million per day before 1910 and compelled theaters and burlesque and opera houses to install "talking pictures" were not themselves uniformly Jewish, but they were keenly aware of the connection between the new medium and the immigrant Jew. Responding to the growing urban audience (above all, New Yorkers), early moviemakers, notably including Gentile director D. W. Griffith—who personally scripted *Old Isaacs the Pawnbroker* and wrote as well as directed *Romance of a Jewess,* both in 1908— gave the viewers the scenes they demanded via the counterpoising of tradition and modern romance. The latter film happened to be Griffith's biggest box office hit to that time. Subsequent silent hits like *Heart of a Jewess* and *Bleeding Hearts* (both starring a Gentile, Irene Wallace) simultaneously inaugurated the Yiddish age in English language film for "Americans" with Jewish themes, and demonstrated that (Jewish) movie entrepreneurs could expect a continuing heavy turnout from a Yiddish-language crowd.[14]

The favorite plots of such films prefigured favorite talkies on Jewish and non-Jewish subjects alike a generation and more later. On the one hand, daughters broke with their patriarchal fathers' rule in order to marry the men (often idealized WASP American males) of their dreams. Alternatively, sons went through a wrenching process of generational departure in other ways, not usually for love but for the sake of the career (often a teary deathbed reconciliation with the older generation closed the film). Thereby, the youthful protagonist female or male becomes "modern," which is to say Americanized if not wholly assimilated—something left to *their* children, who often flashed suspiciously blond hair and other giveaway Gentile traits. On the other hand, mostly historical and foreign-location epics showed Jews (or others who might be seen as substitutes for Jews) heroically resisting persecution, even going to a martyr's death so that the next generations could live free.

Rising immigrant entrepreneurs, according to legend, eagerly eyed a business where the customers shelled out before being given the product— a most enticing prospect. By 1908, no less than a hundred movie houses had sprouted up in the *Yiddishe gassen* (Jewish streets) of Manhattan and the boroughs. In larger numbers than even the considerable theater audience could boast, Jewish audiences of famed street culture reputedly stood around on the familiar street corners after the films let out, arguing about the respective merits. That year, businessman Thomas Edison (not at all the kindly boy and idealistic young man of the two later biopics scripted in 1940–41 by Communist Hugo Butler) sought a legal monopoly reaffirming the patents that he held on cameras and projectors. Carl Laemmle, the German-Jewish former Midwest clothier who had launched himself from theater owner to film entrepreneur, led a rival syndicate, first by importing European films. Laemmle thus fell into becoming a producer and was followed by William Fox among a succession of other immigrant entrepreneurs, including Louis B. Mayer, the Warner brothers, and Sam Goldfysh aka Goldwyn. A small handful of men raised in mostly poor European communities within five hundred miles of one another resettled in Greater Los Angeles and ruled a kingdom.[15]

According to their boosters, these *makhers* of the film world wanted not only money, power, and social acceptance by their fellow capitalists (also glamorous blond dames: Here reality fulfills a stereotype), but also to establish their names as the royalty of modern entertainment. While the impression of businessmen-outsiders wanting to be accepted by America—in practice, to be admitted to Los Angeles country clubs and to private schools for their children—properly goes comfortably along with their own self-image as paternalistic Jewish godfathers to their employees, neither explains their cravings for undiluted power or their ruthlessness toward the studio workforce.[16] According to the contrary immigrant story passed down through the slums and revived in Hollywood, the perfect willingness to squeeze fellow Jews continued to mark the disreputable route to the top, concluded by rich rascals distancing themselves from their unwashed kinsmen.

In just this atmosphere, among battling narratives, movies became an extraordinarily significant factor in the ways that Jews would affect modern culture at large, as they would rewrite, popularize, and to some degree transform popular music and for that matter become both business force and creative talent behind comic books a generation or so later. Jewish Americans continued to do marvelous things at the highest levels of culture, including poetry, the novel, classical music, and Broadway drama, generation after generation, despite all changes of taste and audience. But it was in film that they could be the entrepreneurs and the writers, scenarists, and even stars for the masses—the more public figures under Gentile names, at least for the first several generations.[17]

The Jazz Singer, first epic of the talkies, rendered stage headliner Al Jolson into the ethnic boy whose character succeeds grandly in the world of commercial entertainment through adopting the minstrel pose, burying his own *Yiddishkayt* in mocking, Mammy-style, an evocation of supposed black characteristics. An unpleasant combination of themes from *Birth of a Nation* or the future *Gone With the Wind* and silent ghetto-dramas, *The Jazz Singer* proved lamentably that Hollywood could play the race card with great effect, and that Jews could actually glory in the celebrity and the profits.

Early sound films offered territory only hitherto imagined. Jewish executives, producers, directors, writers (and, to a lesser extent, actors) operated in an atmosphere in which the only negative rule was the normal restraint against explicit Jewishness. This was quite a rule, as Hitler took power and threatened the majority of world Jewry. But the rewards were ample.

For the most part, Hollywood's Jews simply worked within the studio system that they did so much to erect. As the film descriptions below suggest, there was, for instance, ample room for the gay Jewish-Hungarian George Cukor to shift without strain from the acidic political parlor drama *Dinner at Eight* to pseudo-classic *Camille, Little Women, David Copperfield, Romeo and Juliet,* and on to the gender-heavy *The Women* and *The Philadelphia Story,* rarely (as in *What Price Hollywood?*) even taking up Jewish characters, let alone contemporary Jewish social issues. The same could be said for American-born studio mogul Louis B. Mayer, who turned out one lucrative Andy Hardy episode after another, redefining Americanness through its teenageness.

Hollywood's power brokers did not at first understand the young Jewish radicals, or comprehend what an impact they could potentially exert on the system. These latter Jews were never entirely without Gentile comrades and supporters, and that fact had a signal importance from the beginning. Gentile left-wingers, more often than not "converts" to radicalism after an apolitical or inactive youth, reaffirmed through their sincerity to Jewish writers and directors that "internationalism" (on the home front, real comradeship) was no mere rhetoric. Their cooperative presence as personally successful American radicals reaffirmed Jewish perceptions, in those heady days, that acceptance into the broader America and personal success did not necessarily mean selling out or assimilating into cultural nonidentity, but acceptance as American Jews and Jewish Americans, and as professionals to boot.

The contradictions remained vivid. John Howard Lawson's worst moment before the blacklist days was when he recognized RKO's intention of "Gentile-washing" his script for *Success at Any Price.* He later recalled that he "almost tore up the contract."[18] Instead, amidst Screen Writers Guild negotiations, he swallowed hard. Perhaps the problem (or prospect) never occurred seriously to assorted other Jewish radical screenwriters like the Chodorovs, the Buchmans, or most of the others that they *could* be writing "Jewish" stories. To be sure, implicitly Jewish characters could be found in film, from saucer-eyed singer-comic Eddie Cantor to the Sam Levene archetypes of sentimental mobster who unfailingly revealed a softness of heart. The "Jewish issue" itself hardly surfaced in film, however, until the struggle against Hitler had been adopted by the U.S. government and military. It made box office sense to moguls only in the aftermath of the Holocaust. Even "theatrical" writers like Clifford Odets clearly divided their Hollywood work from what they tried to do on Broadway with at least sub-rosa Jewish messages.

On the reverse side of this promise lay the growing threat of fascism, which could bring a Jewish Republican like Jack Warner together with Jack Lawson, at least until Nazism was crushed and the Reds could safely be outed and ousted. Both kinds of Jews, mogul and writer, right and left, naturally wanted the kind of America where they fit in. Intentionally or unintentionally, in harness or bitterly opposed to each other, they worked to create a cinema that as much as anything else in American culture would actually bring that change about. And yet from the day-to-day viewpoint of ordinary studio workers, including writers, the feelings of solidarity with the boss would remain rare. The studio system of pre-union days was less like a ghetto sweatshop of family memory than a plantation in the Southern California sun.

Here, the class forces—from the viewpoint of Jewish liberals, at any rate—sharply divided. They experienced or knew at one remove what it was like to be despised and exploited; they felt the pain of racial minorities in ways that no future Jewish generation was likely to feel. California offered a particular case in point. New Yorkers of many neighborhoods could go much of a lifetime without direct experience of real race-suffering. The European population of California had, within the previous three generations, all but exterminated Native Americans with a speed and ruthlessness that still shocks scholars, and in the mid-nineteenth-century rush for gold abruptly eliminated most Mexican-American holdings as well. The internment and property theft to come of Japanese-Americans during the Second World War was a natural as well as opportune extension of familiar racial behavior, which also included strict laws against miscegenation and large proscribed zones where African-Americans could not live, eat, or even travel safely. The goal of political repression against the Left since the 1910s was meant to keep California's organized labor, if not entirely prostrate, then divided into two disparate categories: well-paid unionized white craftsmen, and severely downtrodden minorities. Demonizing radicals and driving them from the labor movement proved a most effective means to this end. Wealthy and conservative Jews accepted and evidently enjoyed the many benefits of the race-divided system, while radicals bitterly opposed it.

Organized crime fit the system nicely. A sort of mini-welfare state for certain ethnic clans, it expanded greatly during Prohibition and extended itself soon afterward into many communities of California working people struggling to get back on their feet. Mob infiltration often competed directly with the radicals, especially where race barriers reinforced the ethnic social base of the best available jobs. The highly exclusionary California construction unions had a venerable reputation for casual criminal involvements, as did some other less well paid pockets of labor, from transportation to food services and entertainment.

It was therefore no great surprise—even if subject to much denial and eventual embarrassment—that organized crime was so quick to enter the movies. It did so thanks in no small part to the willingness of studio heads to seek financing wherever they could find it, thanks more to their eagerness to make amicable arrangements with any force capable of curbing militant unionism. If some highly successful Hollywood writers were soon to hold high the "proletarian" banner, and if Jewish actors regularly played Christians, then it should not be surprising in the city of illusions that leading Hollywood craft "unionists" were barely disguised Jewish mobsters.

The most important figure, Willie Bioff, a Jewish immigrant from Russia and former pimp, had boldly taken over a Chicago local of International Alliance of Theatrical Stage Employees (IATSE) during the early 1930s with the assistance of George Browne, a more ordinary hood. Together they set up a soup kitchen for unemployed unionists, skimming off most of the "expenses," meanwhile negotiating a pay cut for local IATSE members and taking "contributions" from movie house management on the side. Al Capone's successor, Frank Nitti, essentially appointed the two as national leaders of IATSE: potential rivals at the 1934 union convention received death threats, and one Chicago IATSE leader mysteriously turned up dead.

Hollywood had been in the sights of the mobsters from the beginning. LA mob leaders quickly set Bioff and Browne up properly, and by the middle 1930s the two met frequently with major studio executives, assuring what was termed "labor peace" at the price of healthy bribes that began a process of mutual (at a minimum, feigned) personal wooing. The most cooperative of the local mob, Johnny Roselli, had in fact already worked as a "labor conciliator" for the film management group, the Motion Picture Producers and Distributors of America (MPPDA), which is to say, almost directly under Will Hays of the Hays Office—a suitable irony because the office had been established mainly to review gangster films. Within a few years, Harry Warner and other moguls were exchanging large personal gifts with Bioff and friends, inviting them to dinners for celebrities, even arranging exquisite vacation dwellings while offering them company stock at bargain rates.[19]

The nationwide union spirit of the middle 1930s brought IATSE new membership and influence, remarkably unresisted by the studios. No doubt executives could be personally intimidated through shakedowns. But as theater chain owners in Chicago who had been Browne and Bioff's quiet partners themselves became major executives in Hollywood, the mob amity with the studios reaped new levels of profits. In return for approximately $100,000 yearly personal salaries plus perks, they delivered the acquiescent labor relations requested. As an investigative reporter later detailed, Music Corporation of America (MCA), chief rival to the William Morris Agency in the Hollywood "talent" field, was soon established by yet another of the mob's former Chicago collaborators; MCA bought top film stars while exerting its main influence through monopolizing the booking of musicians during the flush big band era.

When strict AFL craft union IATSE began to be threatened by the prospect of Hollywood labor reform, IATSE local leaders demanded and received absurdly favorable treatment in *Variety*. Labor conservatives then and later insisted that any and all threats to IATSE supremacy proved Hollywood unionism rife with subversives, ever on the verge of taking over the industry.[20]

The last charge did not lack a certain grain of truth. Without the radical-led unemployed movements and general strikes of the early thirties, the Congress of Industrial Organizations would certainly have lacked the momentum for its big push forward, even if its leaders quickly strategized a careful modulation of militance and New Deal alliances. More important, without the assistance and the personally risk-ridden local initiative of Communists and their allies in the ethnic communities, the necessary groundwork could not have been laid. As of 1940, large and vital units of the CIO, including the biggest union (the United Electrical Workers) and those most actively organizing minorities and women (the Food and Tobacco Workers; the Mine, Mill and Smelter Workers; and the Union of Office and Professional Employees) were indeed led by men and women closely associated with the Communists.

Public school substitute teachers, social case workers, and millions of others in assorted industries or services during the decade after 1935 looked to Communist leaders (or leaders that others insisted were Communist-controlled) for the logical reasons that these leaders were honest and hardworking, especially by the low standards of then mostly craft-based organized labor. In limited but significant measure, the constant stream of Red-baiting, often supplemented by anti-Semitic rhetoric and Negrophobia, actually backfired. Men and women in virtually every movie industry sector who had not a Communist bone in their bodies but who knew their real enemies perfectly well loved to see a radical leader poke his finger into the eye of the studio (and IATSE) establishment.

Yet the real strength of the Hollywood Left (and of the Los Angeles Left at large, excluding certain ethnic pockets of influence) was never among the blue-collar workers whose struggles emerged only tardily from the shadow of company and/or mob unions. Rather, it was within the middle and especially Jewish middle classes for whom antifascism and antiracism became consuming social issues. Nothing in the pre-1935 California Communist rhetoric, with the partial exception of "free speech" issues (and the special appeals to insular ethnic loyalists), foretold winning over this constituency. Like so much else left-wing during the depth of the Depression, Communist attitudes had presumed a near-range capitalist collapse, adding into the miscalculation a dash of Russian aesthetics and a considerably larger dose of down-home materialist reductionism that the vanquished Populists might have recognized. Success as reformers, then, came upon them unwonted, and for a few hard-bitten types, like gravel-voiced actor Lionel Stander who mistrusted the Popular Front, almost undesired.

The Party's inability to see the prospects for Hollywood as a potential political culture has an interesting history of its own. American Communists like those in Europe and elsewhere had already made a swipe at modernism and, for the most part, retreated to safer ground. The *New Masses,* at first claiming the legacy of the 1910s avant-garde *Masses* magazine, had at its 1926 outset announced its intention to guide the liberal and radical intelligentsia toward Marxism *against American commercial culture.* Even the original *Masses,* it may be remembered, had embraced the masses, but not necessarily mass culture.

This condescending view was, in another way, an almost undisputed legacy of European Marxism at large. The German Social Democrats, far and away the most prestigious party before support of the war brought them shame and the wholesale defection of young revolutionaries, evaluated early cinema as mere illusion and entertainment, not the uplift brought by the best of literature and drama.

This view mocked the enthusiasm of the real masses for movies, and not even the shock of war changed the views of left-wing critics whose criticism of popular film's "immorality" differed little from that of conservatives. German Communists, in charge of a considerable apparatus and joined by some of the most creative intellectuals and artists anywhere, at first also considered film a mere distraction from the proletariat's true mission. They came gradually to see in Sergei Eisenstein's Russian film classics, like *Battleship Potemkin,* the possibility of moving the masses' emotions, winning them over with effective modern propaganda. Toward the end of the 1920s and in response to the right-wing control of major German film companies, both socialist and Communist parties supported quasi-documentaries, but without registering real success.[21]

As Weimar's end neared, the Communist-influenced Prometheus Film-Verleih launched a series of fictional films financed thanks to the commercial success of distributing *Potemkin.* But these experiments also proved unsuccessful. By contrast, radical writers and directors working in independent companies with B budgets melded music and drama in the first years of sound (and the very last years of Weimar), above all *Threepenny Opera. Kuhle Wampe,* heavily influenced by Bertolt Brecht's determination to prompt the audience to a new kind of emotional participation, appeared shortly before Hitler took power. *Kuhle Wampe*'s combination of documentary material and the drama around mass unemployment, leading narratively to the impossibility of individual heroism, purposefully disrupted the film spectator's normal passive involvement. Official censorship further damaged the film's coherence, but it may be doubted whether Brechtian film had much of a future outside of art cinema. As assorted left-wing German film collectives planned and dreamed of higher prospects, the end came.

To the last moment, voices within the Left urging the potentially positive emotional appeal of films remained a distinct minority. Didacticism never lost its authority, although another decade of practical experience might have changed the picture dramatically. Marxists had learned too little, even from a combination of Eisenstein and Brecht, to get beyond agit-prop (agitation plus propaganda) to something more definitely rooted in filmmaking experience, including the cravings of the mass audience.[22]

By this time, the Stalinization of the world Communist movement also reflected the isolation of young Soviet Russia and the isolation of Communists almost everywhere from anything resembling a revolutionary transformation of society. At home in the 1920s, with American capitalist consumerism at full tilt and the prestige intelligentsia heading for the Left Bank (or the speakeasies), organized radicalism sunk into a movement composed mostly of poorer immigrants, many of them comfortable only in their native languages. Their press, theater, and choral movements had a distinct cultural character, but it was a folkish, didactic one hardly less hostile toward the corrupting commercial mass culture around them.

The call for "proletarian culture" that went out from Moscow, Berlin, and New York in the early 1930s demanding the creation of new working-class intellectuals to replace the corrupt existing stratum was consequently not nearly so mechanical or Moscow-dictated as future critics (including the later prestigious *Partisan Review* group) would charge. The message could also be interpreted in staggeringly different ways. Left-wing Yiddish theater blossomed in the Arbeter Teater Farband (ARTEF, a workers theater collective), with the formidable Benno Schneider (teacher and role model for future director Jules Dassin) at its head, which operated successfully as an experimental and politically revolutionary institution until its demise in 1939.[23] A heavily Jewish movement of Workers Theater in the early 1930s spawned the Group Theatre, which soon offered some of the best drama of the century.[24] The John Reed Clubs, organized in the same period under Party supervision, recruited and encouraged hundreds of talented real-life proletarians to become novelists, including Richard Wright and Nelson Algren. In all this, Hollywood nevertheless remained the enemy, at least until a bureaucratic turn confirmed in far-off Moscow would give the *New Masses* and radicals entrée into the movies and a renaissance in middle-class life.

In the meantime, the American Communist Party or at least a handful of young and authentically working-class Communists *did* have a real, which is to say alternative, film program. The Workers Film and Photo League, launched in 1930 as an affiliate of Workers International Relief—in turn, an arm of the Communist International (or Comintern)—aspired to follow the German example. German Reds' photography and documentary films of 1920s strikes and demonstrations offered a searing social realism that impressed the likes of Bertolt Brecht and Kurt Weill. Renamed the Film and Photo League in 1933, the New York cadre of artistic-minded, mostly Jewish working-class or lower-middle-class members marched with workers in strikes, produced, and distributed as best they could (which is to say, very meagerly) the few documentaries made by FPL members of such events. The FPL's Advisory Board, as usual in these cases a prestige group useful mainly in fund-raising, featured playwrights (and future screenwriters) Sidney Howard and John Wexley, poet (and sometime screenwriter) Langston Hughes, photographers Margaret Bourke-

White and Berenice Abbott, and Bourke-White's lover, famed southern novelist Erskine Caldwell. Its leaders included future documentarists of note, film scholars, and critics—but, in only a case or two, future Hollywood success stories.

One could almost say that the WFPL had been created to abolish Hollywood. Its leading figure, Harry Alan Potamkin, spoke for the group when he declared in 1930 that

> Capitalist society creates the social mind, the social mind creates the film. Capitalist society also perpetuates itself by deliberate suasions, using the film frequently as purposeful propaganda, underhandedly and sometimes—as in the case of imperialist wars—boldly. The symptomatic propaganda and the deliberate unite to sustain the social mind born of capitalism.[25]

Potamkin was not lashing out against the film narrative as such. His eulogist described him as one of the earliest of "sincere critics of the arts" who struggled to "see as the ground of culture the great masses of productive humanity" and as its enemy "box officialdom."[26] Almost fifty years later, David Platt, Potamkin's cofounder of the short-lived journal *Experimental Cinema,* recalled that they had glimpsed in *Battleship Potemkin* "a new kind of art film" that made them see that another cinema was indeed possible, introducing "hitherto unimaginable fresh concepts of realism to the screen."[27] Like their German comrades, they were converts, but unburdened of much of the heavy theorization of the European Marxist movements.

Practice quickly triumphed over theory as *Experimental Cinema* editors and contributors spent their time on Film and Photo League picket lines, conducting campaigns against Red-baiting films and seeking to make documentary, newsreel-type pictures. The sudden death of Potamkin at age thirty-three considerably dampened the group's prospects. Former editor of an avant-garde literary journal in Philadelphia, Potamkin had moved to New York and made a small name for himself writing for highbrow magazines like *Hound and Horn.* By his leftward turn and personal friendship, his example persuaded Platt also to become a left-wing film reviewer, i.e., a category of intellectual still practically unknown outside Weimar Germany. No doubt Potamkin himself, had he lived, would have become a major film critic as the Communists turned from outright hostility toward accommodation to film's prospects. Platt, for his part, loyally followed the drift. *Experimental Cinema*'s third cofounder, Lewis Jacobs, became the first serious historian of Hollywood, although scarcely a Marxist one.

But the evidence that Potamkin and his circle left behind betrays more political rage than intellectual advance. In Platt's didactic phrase of the time, films "cannot be judged solely as entertainment or mainly for their aesthetic value," but should be judged rather as social statements and almost invariably, when made in Hollywood, reactionary ones.[28] Put a little differently by a future (if never very successful) Hollywood director, Irving Lerner, commercial films *could* be looked upon as art, but should still be seen more accurately as "a reflection of the culture in which they were created," a corrupt bourgeois culture akin to other light industry, bent on producing objects for instant consumption.[29] This was not far from Marx's own observation that the ruling ideas in any epoch are the ideas of the ruling class, but far from Marx's and Engels's appreciation of politically reactionary authors who nevertheless reveal truths about class society—or of religion, which for Marxism's founding fathers expressed the aspirations of the oppressed even while recasting these desires in repressive forms. In an era of mass commercial culture, the Communist view tended toward Manichaeanism, at least until more Communists became screenwriters and more screenwriters became Communists.

The creation of the Harry Alan Potamkin Film School in 1933 (following Potamkin's death) might possibly be described as the first American left-wing workshop in films. But it was far indeed from Hollywood, a group of very young and very Red (also, almost exclusively Jewish) cinephiles expressing Eisensteinian visions that occasionally found print in *Experimental Cinema.* They successfully stirred the pot for the formation of a few local Film and Photo League affiliates, would-be radical filmmakers, including one branch in Los Angeles. If America had been Germany (of the 1920s, that is), a left-wing-film mini-industry might possibly have taken shape. But it was not to be, and not only because the FPL remained small and had no means of distributing its output beyond passing them on to Party affiliates and allies.

From 1934, Platt and Lerner not only wrote frequently for the *New Masses* and the *Daily Worker* on new films, but also produced a newsletter from New York about the working conditions in Hollywood. Almost as if they were the rank-and-file Reds preparing the way for industrial unionism in a factory town through leaflets and local "shop papers" talking about local issues (rather than international politics), they sought to approach the nitty-gritty of studio life. But there were crucial differences. These agitators remained separated by a continent from the sweatshop in question; their main allies were other intellectuals; and in denouncing the reactionary politics of the moguls while appealing to an audience mainly outside the industry, they were in effect culture critics after all. That as young Jews they scarcely mentioned "the Jewish question" was also indicative of their primitive efforts: They all but ignored (despite occasional slaps at studio heads' anti-Semitism) the lower-middle-class reality, often containing the very family memories that would very soon stoke the engine of the Hollywood Left.

In real-life Hollywood, Hitler's capture of power and the declaration of the antifascist Popular Front in 1935 suddenly made Jewishness not only central for the Left but also for the considerable class of Jewish liberals newly empowered from labor to government to the film studios. The rise of pro-Nazi organizations in Southern California drove home the message: Picketing, pamphleteering, and broadcasting by radio against Jews and Jewish influence prompted even the normally conservative moguls and their executive ranks to second thoughts.[30]

The appearance of the Popular Front–era political-artistic films of Jean Renoir and others in France, which were more visually experimental and successful than anything attempted by the Left in Germany before Hitler, proved that radicalism and film were potential allies. The growing sense of fascism's threat to conquer all Europe, and the presence of European exiles in the heart of Hollywood, crystallized new institutions and left-tending celebrities in other ways.

A renowned circle of left-leaning exiles began to meet informally, around this time, at the home of émigré hostess Salka Viertel. One of its key figures was director William Dieterle's wife, Charlotte, who determinedly collected funds for *Europeaischen Hefte,* a Prague-based refugee paper for exiled and underground German antifascists and Communists. Directors Fritz Lang and Ernst Lubitsch, Viertel's screenwriter son Peter Viertel, and "soft left" Peter Lorre were among its better-known members as German intellectuals and artists from Thomas Mann to Theodor Adorno continued to move into Hollywood in search of a living and of allies.

The launching of the Hollywood Anti-Nazi League (HANL) in 1936 marked a sea change. Bringing together liberal Jews from Southern California, relocated New York intellectuals, and recent and fresh exiles from Europe, it presented the most successful self-described "front" (a term, as screenwriter Philip Dunne remarked, with far less sinister undertones than later) of the Left and its allies since the Sacco-Vanzetti defense campaign of the middle 1920s. Exposing horrors in Germany and Italy, attacking American apologists for fascism and their Southern California links, the HANL quickly captured headlines. Leftist Dorothy Parker and liberal Oscar Hammerstein II publicly initiated the organization, with various commissions on culture, women, religion, and so on, dividing up the work.

They could count as sponsors Eddie Cantor, industrialist Rupert Hughes (future mogul Howard Hughes's uncle), Ernst Lubitsch, and Fredric March, and on the organization's executive board such non-Communist notables as Dunne, screenwriter Dudley Nichols, and director Lewis Milestone. Donald Ogden Stewart, in his first important political role, served as hardworking chairman. Religious officeholders, especially high Episcopalians, were successfully pursued for endorsements in a fervor of respectabilization that would have been unthinkable for suspected Communists only two or three years earlier. "I joined the Anti-Nazi League," Dunne would write later, "because I wanted to help fight the most vicious subversion of human dignity in modern history."[31]

Almost overnight, HANL fund-raising played a key role in the Hollywood social whirl. Director Mervyn LeRoy, producer Walter Wanger, studio czar Jack Warner, likewise F. Scott Fitzgerald (who, by this time, insisted that he had become a firm Marxist), and Chico Marx (who certainly hadn't, unless "Marxist" meant something entirely different) listened to Judy Garland sing at a typical event that might have included other standard HANL performers such as Sophie Tucker, Dorothy Lamour, Ray Bolger, Benny Goodman, Fred MacMurray, Ben Blue, the Ritz Brothers, Bert Wheeler, and Martha Raye. Lesser-known (but quietly Communist) screenwriters Paul Trivers and Viola Brothers Shore led auxiliaries or wrote political playlets for small-scale antifascist theater productions.

Altogether, these activities collected the needed sustenance for the League's publicity machine, including its mobilization-minded paper, *Hollywood Now,* later *NOW* (i.e., *News of the World*), each subtitled "A Journal in Defense of Democracy." HANL's key functionaries, especially Stewart, Dorothy Parker, and Parker's husband, Alan Campbell, endured endless committee meetings between equally tireless appearances at fundraisers in a series that merged into the even more furiously active anti-Franco committees for the Spanish Republic.[32]

By 1937, Spain had become the cause of the hour, the Republic as beloved to liberals as it was despised by international Catholic authorities and domestic fascist sympathizers like Father Coughlin. Major Hollywood personalities, including Parker, toured Spain and came home to raise funds for refugees, recruiting her old *New Yorker* magazine colleague Robert Benchley and others to join. The Motion Picture Artists Committee, industry-insider counterpart to the HANL founded in 1936 by Dashiell Hammett and actress Sylvia Sidney to urge a liberal globalist agenda, operated similarly with an overlapping roster of names until the Molotov-Ribbentrop Pact interrupted the liberal adventure in 1939.[33]

A Party in Beverly Hills

In the several years to that point, the Communist Party had transformed itself from its secluded origins into quite the fashionable organization. "Why was I willing to cooperate with Communists, known or suspected?" Philip Dunne asked rhetorically, and provides a persuasive answer that could not possibly have been advanced before 1935:

> Because they seemed so sincere in their devotion to the purely democratic causes these organizations supported, and because never at any formal or informal meeting of any of these organizations did I hear a single word in favor of subversion or revolution.[34]

Decades later, Carl Foreman told a Columbia University interviewer that the Communist branch, a marvelous organization in 1930s Hollywood, had died in 1939 with the Hitler-Stalin Pact but simply not known it.[35] Actually, the Party would enroll more members by far in the years shortly afterward, exercise far more political influence and hugely more artistic importance. But Foreman had a point. The spotless liberal name of the Party, won after an era of ferociously successful Red-baiting, could never quite be regained.

Its life up to 1939 had been brief but vitally connected to the fate of radicalism. The Communist movement of the Euro-American West, as French ex-Marxist historian Francois Furet accurately observed, owed its existence to war, namely the First World War.[36] Minus the war's pointless mass slaughter, minus the betrayal by European social democrats who had earlier as much as promised to resist capitalist war-making, Bolshevism would probably have remained a marginal phenomenon, less important on the revolutionary Left than the ideologies of mass uprising and mobilization of the unskilled workers, not coincidentally at their apex in Europe and the United States (notably with the Industrial Workers of the World) shortly before the outbreak of conflict.

These non-Communist revolutionary movements, strongly associated with the original cultural bohemianism, never recovered. Their energy and some of their allies, by no means all, were absorbed by the new Communist movements. Bolshevism fit large parts of Western experience very badly, and the degeneration of the Russian experiment would disillusion followers again and again. But there was no going back to the era when radical movements based on belief in popular education and in the inevitability of working-class socialism fell short or been crushed by repression. Moreover, only one party held the franchise on Russian sponsorship. The virtual Communist monopoly on anticolonial and antiracist movements modernized the Left, established legitimacy among doubters, and to some degree rationalized abundant sins. The rise of fascism and Nazism, driving the Communists into becoming the heroic defenders of humane liberal values, essentially consolidated their hegemony over the Left and extended their influence far into the mainstream.

Ring Lardner, Jr., liked to say later that he had been exaggerating when he bragged in the 1930s that the Hollywood Reds had the prettiest girls and the deepest thinkers of the movie colony, thanks to Communists being collectively "brighter and more admirable and more likeable than other people" around.[37] There was simply no doubt, however, that the most dedicated and idealistic members of a notoriously cynical film colony belonged to or were often close to these circles, and that the aura (good or bad, depending upon the perception) of bright women with strong character traits had a hard-edged charm compared with the blandly receptive (i.e., easily bedded) blond starlets. As Michael Denning acutely observed, the shock and outrage of anti-Communist critics (during the 1930s and forever after) that leading intellectuals and artists had become Communists *while pursuing their normal careers* registered here as another facet of Hollywood exoticism.[38]

Was it strange to have (as FBI reports suggested) Lucille Ball, Katharine Hepburn, Olivia de Havilland, Rita Hayworth, Humphrey Bogart, Danny Kaye, Fredric March, Bette Davis, Lloyd Bridges, John Garfield, Anne Revere, Larry Parks, some of Hollywood's highest-paid writers, and for that matter the wives of March and Gene Kelly along with Gregory Peck's fiancée all in or close to the Party? Or that a considerably larger number of ostensibly nonpolitical directors, stars, and character actors had their best roles in films written by Reds and deeply if quietly appreciated the effort? No stranger than Hollywood itself, in some light almost a normalizing feature of "real" life amidst the tinsel.

It started small, by common recollection and FBI reports alike. Novelist Samuel Ornitz, not yet a Party member but a serious Marxist thinker by his own estimation, had migrated from New York to Hollywood and begun holding private meetings in his house in 1932 with a very small group of radical-minded intellectuals, including John Bright, Bright's later writing partner Bob Tasker, and a handful of nonwriter studio employees. That same year, two writers fired by Universal, one for refusing to write a reactionary script for a film with a Boulder Dam location and the other for urging his colleagues to publicize the case by speaking at the small Hollywood branch of the John Reed Club, wrote up their grievances in the *New Masses*.[39] But in contrast to New York, where a League of Professional Groups for Foster and Ford (i.e., the 1932 Communist presidential slate) was organized for the fall election with the support of many noted literary intellectuals, Hollywood Reds were few and fearful. They relegated themselves for the moment to other, mostly nonunion and nonelectoral activities.[40]

These activities were not necessarily low-key by choice. Individual Communists Bright and Ornitz soon led small public organizations to defend the Scottsboro boys and to make an investigative trip to the desperate strike of coal miners in Harlan County, Kentucky. Ornitz himself made the journey and gave the public report back in Hollywood. Bright, meanwhile, personally got James Cagney to sign on to a support committee for the strikers of the Joaquin Valley in 1934, a courageous move that backfired when the Hearst papers fingered the two of them. Headliner Cagney had already been nabbed by a photographer with California Communist leader William Schneiderman and Bright on a platform of a meeting in San Francisco appealing for the release of labor prisoner Tom Mooney.[41]

Stung by such experiences and their consequences (in this case, Cagney pulled back from any future public involvement), the Party itself did not actually surface for several years in Hollywood. It also did not *exist*, at least in Hollywood, in anything more than study circles well into 1935.[42] The situation called for a strategy that American Communists had never previously attempted and indeed had been considered unnecessary decades earlier for prestigious socialist and Wobbly sympathizers as various as Helen Keller, Isadora Duncan, or William Dean Howells before the Red Scare had so effectively demonized radicalism. Occasionally, leaders of the California or national Communist Party visited Hollywood to raise money, but no one had ever been sent there to organize a section.

At the very end of 1934 or in the first months of 1935, a young medical resident, red-haired Stanley Lawrence (born Seymour Robbins), arrived in Hollywood with a set of credentials from the Central Committee. He made a living in an area hospital, but his assigned task, he explained to Party members and sympathizers, was to set up a branch directly connected to New York, sans the normal intervening affiliations with city, state, and regional bodies. Soon, the Party would extend this "submarine" benefit to individual leading trade unionists and journalists elsewhere who belonged secretly to the Party but never did so otherwise to an entire secretive *group* as the Hollywoodites.

The timing was right because the Party had only that fall of 1934 opposed the Upton Sinclair campaign that John Bright among (a few) other future Communists boldly or recklessly supported. Before the next election rolled around, the Hollywood Reds had become faithful and influential liberal Democrats, themselves reaping the rewards of a public tired of twenty years' state Republican misrule.

How did it happen? Notwithstanding Lawrence's personal appearance, the flurry of liberal and purely social activities had actually defined the Party milieu. Something as ostensibly nonpolitical (and non-leftist) as the comically titled West Side Writing and Asthma Club, a monthly gathering of Jews who couldn't get into Los Angeles Beach Clubs and didn't want to try to crack the circle of studio big shots at Musso and Frank's Restaurant, quickly if informally became a center of anti-Nazi sentiment. Even Groucho Marx, a rarely public political celebrity but among the early Asthma Club members, could be counted upon for reliable union support and hefty financial contributions to Popular Front causes.

The League of American Writers, a vastly more successful operation than the earlier League of Professional Groups or John Reed Clubs, meanwhile held the first of its national meetings in New York in 1935. Its manifesto was signed by John Howard Lawson and future screenwriter (then still a novelist, en route to Spain) Alvah Bessie, among the artistic types. According to several screenwriters who were later Party members, Franklin Roosevelt himself also signed, but successfully requested anonymity. By 1937, Donald Ogden Stewart had become its wisecracking, affable chair; accorded scholar status, he served as official editor of the meeting's book-length *Proceedings.* Few other screenwriters made the long train trip East until later, and most of the talk about film was by Hollywood's severest critics, i.e., New York literary men. Meanwhile, Bessie wrote the league's pamphlet on anti-Semitism, and by 1939—just as the league was about to lose its influence everywhere but Los Angeles—the LAW could finally claim a handful of prominent screenwriters, including Parker, Hammett, and Langston Hughes, along with Stewart.[43]

The other main source for the Party advance in Hollywood was, naturally, the Screen Writers Guild. The left-wing atmosphere of the earliest days, when practically no one but radicals and a few prestigious writers had been willing to stick their necks out, had been diluted by the upsurge of membership in 1936, then reinforced by the sudden decline of the SWG afterward when those remaining tended to defer to the Party members and to followers willing to take the heat for the profession. It was nevertheless notable that Dudley Nichols, a solid liberal but definitely no Communist, had been the single courageous writer to turn down an Oscar on behalf of his screenwriter colleagues in 1936; and just as notable that SWG members swallowed hard when John Howard Lawson was named by the press as the "leading Hollywood Red" but remained stubbornly unwilling to dump him on that account. In the following few years, some left-wing writer-unionists, including Francis Faragoh and possibly Samuel Ornitz, suffered demotions from which their careers never fully recovered. Other non-Communists or short-time Communists who continued to reject anti-Communism in the face of all pressures carried memories of the early years' moral and personal commitments that even later, bitter disagreements with the Left could not alter; they identified their friends and their enemies by the experiences they regarded as the critical tests of both friendship and professionalism.

By contrast to the dramatic events of the later 1930s and the opportunities that they offered left-wingers in many parts of the country, actual Party organization in Hollywood was not only tardy but downright sluggish. In FBI documents dating from a slightly later period, informers recalling the middle 1930s reaffirm what written recollections of other participants specify. Early unionist-Communists included writer Tess Slesinger and her husband, former film cutter and future scriptwriter Frank Davis, fellow screenwriter Madeleine Ruthven, Lawson, Herbert Biberman, Lester Cole, John Bright, Robert Tasker, actress Jean Muir, and actor Lionel Stander, along with directors Frank Tuttle, Irving Pichel, and Edward Dmytryk.[44]

Within this small if modestly expanding circle, according to an FBI informer, Party dues stamps would be sold, then burned for security's sake, or membership books issued and then retracted. While the Party marched forward nationally through the rise of the industrial union movement and could claim perhaps 40,000 members with a periphery perhaps ten times that size, it had grown in 1937 but to no more than fifty members in Hollywood with perhaps a following of several hundred, counting regular attendees at antifascist events. On the other hand, an FBI source claimed that these members contributed or raised $10,000 every month, a huge sum for such a small group to raise for Party and Party-related activities of various sorts.

By mid-1936, the Party leadership had either yanked Lawrence or he had courageously left on his own to fight in Spain, according to different versions. John Howard Lawson came back from New York because he needed the money and because the Screen Writers Guild needed him. Meanwhile, Party functionary V. J. Jerome (real name Isaac Romain, born in a Russian-Polish village and sent to England for public education, thence moving to the United States) became the head of the Party's Cultural Commission. For a time, Jerome personally assumed responsibility for the Hollywood branches, at once insulating them from the rest of the

Party in Los Angeles and keeping them in direct touch with the national leadership.

A sometime novelist, Jerome was known first for his marriage to Rose Pastor Stokes, the former shop-girl strike leader and charismatic radical heroine of the 1910s–20s—which gained him ready access to the upper realms of Communist cultural critics—but second for his status as a heresy hunter. He had already, by the time of his first visits to Hollywood, attempted to define the proper forms of proletarian literature, seeking to forbid deviating methods to serious revolutionaries. By 1935 he had taken over the Party's theoretical journal, *The Communist,* and remained more or less in that post for twenty years. Destined to play a melancholy role in the Hollywood Left, he made intermittent trips to Hollywood from 1936 onward, cadging funds out of successful writers or directors, assuring listeners of the Soviet leadership's rectitude (especially in the face of discouraging events like the Moscow Trials), and issuing directives that could not actually be followed but that kept official leader Lawson on tenterhooks.[45]

Apart from such public Party activities as passing out leaflets and selling copies of the weekly *Western Worker* (replaced by the *Daily People's World* in 1938), which most Hollywoodites felt they could not do without too much risk to themselves, study groups continued to predominate alongside antifascist and union activities. Frank Tuttle, who had fallen into B directorial assignments after a promising beginning in the silents and would soon make his mark again with *This Gun for Hire,* remembered (in "friendly" testimony) a general Hollywood atmosphere of apathy about Hitler, then the rise of antifascist committees whose fellow members urged him to read some Communist literature. Stanley Lawrence had invited him to sit in on a study class, and he soon after joined the Party, thereafter rising to vice president in the small and largely inactive but symbolically important Screen Directors Guild.[46] In the story-behind-the-story told by other Hollywood veterans, Tuttle took little interest in either politics or unionism, but his Russian-born wife, Tatania, was an enthusiastic Party activist who kept him affiliated (until their divorce) and staged major political benefits in their rambling house near the "Hollywood" sign in the Hills.

Akin to Tuttle's somewhat reluctant interest were reports of those who were said not to qualify as real members but who served (sometimes all the more enthusiastically) as supporters in various venues. One FBI report has Humphrey Bogart attending meetings regularly, and "somewhat of a rebel, adjudged definitely a Party member," although "never considered good party material" apart from his hefty financial contributions. According to various unreliable sources, "Dutch" Reagan was turned down in the later 1930s for being too dumb. Some longtimers would say that lowering the barriers during wartime brought in a host of the barely committed, those most likely to turn up as friendly witnesses in the next period.[47]

Still others with book membership—if uninvolved in study groups during the 1930s—reputedly included actor Franchot Tone, at the time Joan Crawford's husband, also Fredric March and his more politically minded wife, Florence Eldridge, and (even more improbably) director Fritz Lang.[48] The celebrity tone would pick up in wartime with the likes of Lloyd Bridges, Jose Ferrer, Orson Welles, Olivia de Havilland, Rita Hayworth, John Garfield, Ronald Reagan, and Bette Davis herself, albeit strictly as sympathetic but sometimes energetic participants in popular activities rather than as members of the Party.

By 1937–38, the Hollywood Party had become what it remained (despite ups and downs) for a decade: a mobilizing center with so many specific separate causes that Party membership signified a degree of liberal commitment rather than a barrier separating Communist participants from supportive liberals. John Wexley, one of the most successful left-wing Warner Brothers writers, later remembered asking a high Party functionary in New York whether he should join, and being told in confidence that membership would require too many meetings. He was more useful as a full-time screenwriter-unionist.[49]

It was an unusual piece of advice, but not a bad one. A substantial majority of writers tended to drift in and out of Party membership, not so much out of wavering sympathies as because their careers and schedules did not permit them to take a sustained part in activities. So they "lapsed," as many friendly witnesses would shamefacedly remember their membership as ending, rather than in some principled break. The story was not so different outside Hollywood, where local Communist "book membership" west of the Hudson could often turn over 80 percent within a year. Being a conscientious member simply took too much time, and most recruits, working-class or otherwise, found the meetings both dull and lengthy. Whether the credulity demanded for faith in Russian leadership and the practical absence of democracy within the Party nationally were decisive factors depended upon the person. Often enough, not so much the political twists and turns but the wear-and-tear of daily life proved decisive in a country where "politics" never got far from career (or corruption) and "socialism" remained on some distant horizon.

In Hollywood, the higher Party members rose in terms of salary and status—with the important exception of Lawson—the more they tended toward political secrecy. George Beck commented to investigating congressmen that he sometimes felt that he was "the only member of the Communist Party in the United States" because, while he saw plenty of people at assorted meetings, actual membership was never discussed with a lower-down like him.[50] Ring Lardner, Jr., similarly related jocularly to an interviewer that while at the studio he sometimes referred on the phone to Party meetings as "the poker game"—but because he was so embarrassed to be actually involved in high-stakes poker he sometimes referred to the card sessions as "the meeting"![51]

In the same vein, an erstwhile organizer described going to a Hollywood writer's home where he was told of a "great Marxist library" accessed with a button, which, like an Abbott and Costello film, spun the bar around to expose the books—far more rarely absorbed in the course of left-wing Hollywood activities than the contents of the bottles. Paul Jarrico, one of the longtime party leaders in Hollywood, remembered being invited by a former Young Communist League buddy, first to apply for a writer's job at a studio Hollywood, and then to meet some of the more established comrades informally at the Hillcrest Country Club, one of the fanciest places in town.

In a wide assortment of ways like this, the Party had become a social agency as well as a social-political movement, or rather, a social agency that had politics as its premise but operated on a popular basis mainly through parties, banquets, dinner, and drinks. Party members had "assignments" of various kinds, usually where they worked, sometimes where they lived. In either case, they would work with other Party people and sympathizers, meet in caucuses, plan strategies, and proceed upon objectives. But the active participation of members could not be enforced without cutting off a financial lifeline. Abraham Polonsky, who spent some months in Hollywood in 1937 anonymously scripting a light comedy film for radio comedian Gertrude Berg, later observed that becoming a Communist in Hollywood was a great deal like hanging out on Sunset Boulevard: Most of the people came, stayed awhile, left, and were replaced by others who found in it the same, mainly social values until either the potential risks or the tedium overwhelmed commitment. The minority who stayed were not necessarily the brightest or most creative—though some certainly were— but the most active politically, either by personal predilection or by sheer moral commitment.[52]

More than a little guilt, meanwhile, was occasioned on behalf of those authentic proletarian Communists only a short drive from Beverly Hills or Santa Monica. Such men and women dragged themselves out of garment shops back to Yiddish-inflected Boyle Heights, where the main cultural activity apart from Old World–style choruses was the organization of summer camps for the kids. For these deeply ethnic Communists, as for left-wing Hungarians downtown, Croatian longshoremen in San Pedro, and others, Hollywood might as well have been a thousand miles away.[53] But political, union, and general fund-raising activities so much defined Holly-wood life that such guilt had no function except perhaps to increase union support—and to increase financial contributions.[54]

There were important exceptions, loan-outs (to use studio language) of screenwriters' skills to others on the lots. Thus Martin Berkeley, who named more names than any other friendly witness, recalled without animus his assigned task to work with an anti-mob IATSE faction in the middle 1930s editing (really, writing and rewriting) a four-to-eight-page mimeographed, later tabloid weekly bulletin called *The Studio Voice*. Its purpose was to expose and attack the gangster leadership of the IATSE local, which it did (in Berkeley's account) at about the same speed of reve-lations as conservative columnist Westbrook Pegler's muckraking com-mentaries. Perhaps the opposition bulletin's circulation did not really rise to the ten thousand figure claimed by Berkeley, but it did the job and gave the young writer a task that concluded only when IATSE leaders arranged a goon squad to beat him up.[55] Similar loan-outs, of unprestigious writers, mostly, afforded the sort of work as anonymous Los Angeles comrades did, like selling literature. Jokester George Beck claimed that he inadvertently built up his biceps by toting theoretical volumes back and forth from the downtown Party office to public meetings, since no one could be convinced to buy them.[56]

By late 1938, the Hollywood Party had reached several hundred mem-bers and at that point, the quiet (indeed, secret) establishment of a Marxist academy for the film community marked another and distinctly new phase of development. Hitherto, study clubs—now mostly to be put to the side—had been concerned with the fundamentals of Marxism without too much reference to art or culture. The moment had arrived to begin to figure out what to do with movies.

Screenwriters' Blues

That problem, obviously on the minds of writers from the earliest days of sound film in particular, was best illustrated by the disappointments of those who would become Hollywood's Popular Front and openly Communist leaders. Dorothy Parker quipped to a Columbia University interviewer in the 1950s that writers had never been *required* to see their own films, and that in her case the experience would be unbearable.[57]

It was a characteristic Parkeresque remark but she had good reasons to complain. One of the top literary figures of the 1920s, Parker had a biting wit that many thousands of sophisticated Americans admired but few successfully emulated. She could claim, around the table at the Algonquin Hotel, some of the most powerful allies in American letters. She arrived in Hollywood in 1930 and stayed to the end of her life as political activist, blacklistee, and civil libertarian but never, to her own mind, a successful or even worthy screenwriter. She has credits on fifteen films, none of which she cared for. Unlike Dashiell Hammett, with whom she shared more than one event and more than one bottle, she launched no film genre. Much like Hammett, she served memorably as chair of the Joint Anti-Fascist Refugee Committee, organizer of the project Rescue Ship to bring Loyalist veterans from French detention camps to Mexico, as head of Spanish Children's Relief, and as a fixture in virtually every one of the later Left public campaigns in Los Angeles. She was by the later 1930s and remained long thereafter a "name" ever welcome on the dais and in behind-the-scenes fund-raising even when, during later decades, she was severely depressed and virtually destitute. She left her few worldly goods to Martin Luther King, Jr.[58]

A glance at her early credits explains her artistic cynicism. *Suzy* (1936) was merely a Jean Harlow vehicle that Parker was assigned to turn into one of those wartime love-and-separation stiff-upper-lip melodramas that (among other things) only vaguely if at all expressed the writer's personal revulsion at militarism. Cary Grant as a French flier falls in love with the wife of a fellow flier played by Franchot Tone. Spies, fine air footage, and Grant's intoning "Did I Remember?" salvaged some consolation from the melodramatic and stale plot; at rare moments, Parker's witty dialogue shines through. Mostly, the film is pure mush. But by this time she was making $1,500 a week and deeply in love with a younger man, her considerably less talented husband, Alan Campbell, who shared her screen credits. Unlike her happier friends, she could not use screenwriting to make her other writing financially feasible; on the contrary, churning out scripts seemed to kill her real talent.

She and Campbell worked without credit on *Here Is My Heart* (1934), a Bing Crosby vehicle directed by Frank Tuttle that Parker remembered as an assignment for which she was told only to write with either Crosby or the now-forgotten warbler Tullio Carminati in mind, in case one would be substituted at the last minute for the other! *Lady Be Careful* (1936), a navy story based on a 1933 play by Kenyon Nicholson and Charles Robinson, was scarcely thicker, a tale of the brash and shy buddies, highlighted (if that is not too strong a word) by a shivaree dance scene of an enraged dame. In the Broadway original, a bet between two sailors hinges on a seduction; in the film, merely a kiss (Parker jocularly claimed to have offered the studio a more dramatically viable version: The sailors seduce each other). *Three Married Men* (1936), Parker's own boy-meets-then-loses-but-finally-wins-girl script, had little to boast besides the hilarity of the would-be husband listening to an advice record and then donning satin pajamas for his wedding night, provoking his bride's ridicule.

Even *A Star Is Born* (1937), easily Parker's biggest film hit and one of the few color epics of the decade, never got much beyond formula, although a great deal of pathos was wrung out of the saga of a former star (the husband, played by Fredric March) on his way down and a rising star (the wife, played by Janet Gaynor) on her way up. Beyond specifics, it looked enormously like *What Price Hollywood?* (1932), also produced by Zanuck and directed by George Cukor, who would also direct the 1954 *Star Is Born* remake starring Judy Garland and James Mason. Sammy Glick was obviously right about remakes. Nevertheless, exposing the emotional underside of Hollywood in tabloidish style, even drawing upon current events (the funeral of Irving Thalberg) for specific scenes, the 1937 *Star* was the number one moneymaker the year of its production, nominated for Best

Screenplay, and actually got an Oscar for Best Original Story (to William Wellman). Producer David O. Selznick, who had written the original draft, went around claiming that the Parker-Campbell pair had contributed nothing of importance to it (although they had worked long and hard, Dorothy was not sure decades later how much of their effort had been included), but film success did bring Parker useful prestige in social movements as well as the rising price of drinks for the household.[59]

America's keenest wit didn't give herself quite enough credit. Lots of snappy dialogue invented on the set for Wanger allowed Parker and Campbell to work on *Trade Winds* (1938) without the annoyance of collaborating writers or the limitations of a play or novel. But these were most unusual circumstances: During a yachting trip, popular director Tay Garnett had shot considerable ocean footage, and Wanger stepped in to supply money, actors, and writers in short order. The film's plot remained thin, Joan Bennett playing a suspected murderess chased around the world's oceans by detective Fredric March, who in turn is seeking to unload ex-girlfriend Ann Sheridan. The writers put their energy into silly gags and repartee, switching in the second half from conversation against picturesque backgrounds to mystery, unfortunately restoring a rebellious woman (Bennett turned from dumb blonde into the demonstrative type by dyeing her hair dark—and never dyeing it back) into a proper feminine role by the end of the film.[60] Such a collage-like experiment was unlikely to be repeated, still less likely to be improved upon. No wonder Parker, who had few films ahead and never emerged from the blacklist, made Hollywood politics her real interest.

Samuel Ornitz's saga offered still another monument to disappointment, indeed the original disillusionment story of the 1930s Hollywood Left because of his high status, both literary and political, within it. According to the later recollections of Paul Jarrico, it was Ornitz who first argued among his comrades that "you can't do anything in Hollywood" in films, and that to hope otherwise was vain.[61] By a considerably looser standard, Ornitz got quite a bit done in a handful of genres. Virtually all of it came, however, at the bottom-drawer level with his best work never fully realized—although sometimes he came tantalizingly close. If Ornitz shuttled back and forth from Hollywood to Europe from the middle 1930s, building antifascist activities, it was more due to his nature than to the typical screenwriter's prospects.

Destined to be the eldest of the Hollywood Ten, Ornitz was nearly forty by the time he got to the West Coast in 1930. He had been a social worker in New York and a widely respected novelist whose *Haunch, Paunch, and Jowl* (1923) effectively described the assorted corruptions of politics and the law amid the rise of the Jewish-American bourgeoisie. Ornitz was no staid realist, and his experimental *A Yankee Passional* (1927), about a dissenter martyred by American rednecks, was marked by stream-of-consciousness writing. As in the case of Lawson but worse, Hollywood offered him scarce room for further experimentation.

Ornitz sold two original stories to Paramount in 1928, and began to think of himself as a screenwriter when *The Case of Lena Smith* (1929) got made, treating however cautiously the tale of a European peasant woman exploited and abused by the upper classes. *Sins of the Children* (1930) had an interesting first half hour of depression life with a barber struggling to make a living for his motherless family and managing to pull himself up— only to have his daughter go off with a rich sport. Shifting over to RKO, where his scripts could be made into film at lower cost, Ornitz supplied an original story for the first of the chain-gang epics, *Hell's Highway* (1932). *Thirteen Women* (1933), turning popular Yellow Menace stereotypes half-way on their heads, had Myrna Loy as half-Asian conspirator taking her revenge upon racist former sorority sisters who excluded her and thereby drove her mad. *Men of America* (1932), the earliest of left-written Westerns starring William Boyd (not yet Hopalong Cassidy), featured an aging Yankee in the modern West, allied with retiree pals that included a Mexican-American and an Indian, all in need of the future Hoppy's help against mobsters on the run from the law.[62]

Leaving RKO, Ornitz had high artistic hopes, and indeed David Selznick's temporary attention seemed promising. *One Man's Journey* (1933) could be described as the first of the sound-film "good doctor" sagas, with Lionel Barrymore as a broken-down physician who returns to his little hometown to mend hearts and bodies. Ornitz returned to Paramount and a medical drama with *A Doctor's Diary* (1937), in which a physician seeking to discover a cure for polio is accused of negligence and is later fired for willingly testifying for a patient against the hospital, but manages to pull himself back up to research after a series of personal tragedies. (New Zealand, in the midst of a polio epidemic, banned the film, presumably to forestall panic.)

Ornitz's crusading films reached an apex in 1935, with the extraordinary pacifist drama *The Man Who Reclaimed His Head,* drawn from a play by the French left-winger Jean Bart and coauthored with him. In a flashback to events of the First World War era, a radical journalist remembers how he was hired by a seemingly sympathetic publisher-politician, wrote fire-breathing essays of class hatred (signed by the politician, who took credit for them and rose in fame), then watched in horror as his supposed benefactor used the notoriety to commit the paper to rearmament, helping to set off the world slaughter; the unscrupulous figure who set him up then steals his wife while he is off fighting the Germans. "His" head that was stolen is actually the wily politician's own, and by the end we know that the former journalist has sliced it off in revenge and is carrying it about in a box.[63] The power of corruption, the agonies of war (recalled from memories of the front), and above all the evil of the weapons-makers (who plot to lengthen the war, while setting out secret international agreements not to harm one another's resources) could hardly have received a stronger attack. But this was no million-dollar *All Quiet on the Western Front.* Despite starring Claude Rains, it was a small film, quickly forgotten in the antifascist fervor that followed.

Ornitz spent most of the later 1930s at Republic, which allotted stingy budgets for his mostly gentle films about the nobility of the poor and those who try to help the poor. Here, Ornitz had somewhat of an advantage: B films that weren't actioners like the abundant Westerns often concerned themselves more with ordinary people's lives than did A pictures—because the studios lacked the star power and the special effects to do much of anything else.[64] *Three Kids and a Queen* (1935) saw May Robson as a wealthy eccentric on the verge of being declared mentally unfit by her greedy relatives. Three impoverished youngsters accidentally overturn her carriage, then take her home to treat her injured leg. Soon she becomes motherly toward the inhabitants of this slum scene. Eventually she returns to her own world, nevertheless declaring that she never received any love until she found the poor. *Two Wise Maids* (1936) similarly finds a tough old schoolteacher launching a crusade for her poor students, eventually blockading a street so that children can play in safety. *Portia on Trial* (1937), based on a Faith Baldwin novel, features a defense attorney (played vigorously by Frieda Inescort) who specializes in defending downtrodden women; miraculously, in another typical Hollywood miracle, she turns out to be the mother (although never married) of a newspaper magnate's grandson. The Hays Office twice rejected script versions because of the implications of illicit sex.[65]

Ornitz also skillfully adapted a comic strip character, transforming her politics, as he took over *Little Orphan Annie* (1938) in the popular figure's second screen appearance, putting her to the task of defending young Chinese immigrants against racism and reading them the story of Robin Hood along with the Declaration of Independence. In fact, the source of the extremely conservative newspaper strip was "Little Orphant Annie," a poem by James Whitcomb Riley, who had composed Eugene V. Debs's campaign verse for 1900 and remained a drinking buddy of the beloved socialist; Ornitz in effect re-created an unbeaten victim of capitalism that Debs could have recognized.

Ornitz could even turn his hand to musicals, as he showed in the largely plotless *Fatal Lady* (1935) and *Hit Parade* (1937). But only twice, after *The Man Who Reclaimed His Head* and before wartime, did Ornitz get close to the didactic political messages he sought to convey. *It Could Happen to You* (1937), written with his friend Nathanael West, had about fifteen interesting minutes as the film opens in a celebration of democratic ethnic pride (a German-American picnic) and proceeds through a plot by a fascist agent; and in *Three Faces West* (1940), a "B plus" film for director Bernard Vorhaus, John Wayne leads a troop of dust bowl refugees to Oregon in a modern pioneering venture WPA-style, fending off his girl's former fiancé who turns out to be a Nazi agent. Even these projects must have been disappointing to Ornitz, who had by this time worked at every level of films except the top.

No wonder the erstwhile best-selling novelist and occasional playwright (he turned to Broadway in 1934 with *Geraniums in My Window,* an unsuccessful New Deal–inflected play coauthored by fellow left-winger Vera Caspary), as different from Dorothy Parker as might otherwise be imagined within the Left, also put his energy into politics and unionism. He had begun his artistic career as a Jewish critic of Jewish-American society, and if there was great need for the same in Hollywood, there was no room in production for it. Europe, not excluding his own distant relatives, virtually cried for his help; closer to home, the Screen Writers Guild needed every ardent devotee, especially one of theoretical bent (his admirers called it rabbinical) like Ornitz. By contrast to that kind of politics, for Parker or Ornitz in particular, films seemed unpromising and even unimportant, except that they paid the bills and provided a surplus for financing left-wing activities.

New Theater and New Hope

The continuing uncertainty about films was especially evident in the intrigues that customarily surrounded the Party cultural apparatus. Back in the early 1930s, when Mike Gold declared war on Thornton Wilder for writing not only reactionary but downright unmanly novels and plays, theatrical intellectuals around the Left already had broader perspectives than the ideologues. Herbert Kline and Jay Leyda formed *New Theater* magazine in 1934 with Arthur Knight, the distinguished newspaper film reviewer of subsequent decades, as unpaid staffer ("intern" in the language of later generations). *New Theater* got enthusiastic endorsements and cash from the likes of Alfred Lunt, Lee Strasberg, Burgess Meredith, Groucho Marx, and progressive actress Sylvia Sidney's husband, Bennett Cerf (who personally contributed the largest check the publication ever received: $500). Two years later, its name changed to *New Theater and Film,* it attracted first-rate writers on many subjects. Cinematic matters never occupied a majority of the space. But in addition to occasional cinema features, the magazine carried a running (usually wry) paragraph-length roundup of current films and some brief notes about film trends from a left-wing standpoint, naturally.

Most of the commentaries had less to do with Hollywood movies than with signs of studio sympathy for fascism (not entirely a paranoid reflection as the shadowy "Hollywood Hussars" organized, reputedly attracting Gary Cooper as its most public figure), with trends toward censorship, the plight of the film worker, and the vague promise of an entirely different kind of cinema.[66] What the magazine hailed as "Revolutionary Movie Production" was for the most part the work of documentarians, at least in the United States.[67] The accomplishments of European and especially Soviet filmmakers (more precisely, those films made in the 1920s) and occasional translations of essays by the filmmakers themselves seemed to offer the real light ahead. The formation in 1936 of a new left-wing national film society with intentions of publishing its own magazine—even if the project never materialized and the society quickly floundered—showed energetic determination.[68]

Hesitantly, almost furtively, *New Theater* and its short-lived successor went further. The formation of the Screen Directors Guild in early 1936 was dubbed a "brave and important undertaking," heralding hopes of creative control.[69] Frank Capra's *Mr. Deeds Goes to Town* earned accolades as "tremendous and rare," while John Ford came off a technical genius and a courageous figure.[70] The magazine's regular film reviewer observed characteristically that Clifford Odets's *The General Died at Dawn* was not actually a bad film but was oversold by the Left press when "people were given to believe they were going to get *Das Kapital* in eight reels and received instead a better than average melodrama."[71] Like the *Daily Worker* and the *New Masses, New Theater and Film* hammered at day-to-day studio racism and the dreadful roles given minorities in film. But by dropping the usual polemical asides and actually addressing technical as well as political issues, Hollywood contributors also carefully examined the implications of camera work (the decisive technical element setting off film drama from theater), the problems of the "Story Conference," where the plot was hammered out, and the role of the film "original" (original story, that is) in the final product.[72]

In retrospect, *New Theater and Film* appears to have been on its way toward the elucidations that marked the *Hollywood Quarterly* a decade later, and the sort of dialogue between New York and Los Angeles that had been more usually marked by diatribes from East-of-the-Hudson Party cultural leaders. The tragedy of *New Theater and Film,* no less for the broader theatrical and dance milieu around it, was the structural fragility of the operation and its susceptibility to political directives. The latter returned at a most curious time, as the Popular Front held increasing promise, the revival of Yiddish culture and Jewish issues brought new constituencies (in some cases, recuperating ones earlier alienated by what was now derided as assimilationist "abstract internationalism"), and as Communists made special efforts to reach out to liberals.

But every left-wing institution competed for funds and attention with others, in no small part because none of them was ever really financially solvent. By 1935–36, the John Reed Clubs and Workers Lab Theater had dissolved, along with other experiments to build a pure proletarian culture. As theatrical activists moved from collapsing left-wing companies to the WPA's Federal Theater, their own surviving projects faced special dangers. Basking in the Popular Front sunlight, the *New Masses* rapidly improved into an often exciting, well-written, and artfully illustrated weekly for the left-leaning middle class—and quickly threatened to absorb all literary energy and associated cultural fund-raising of the Left magazine audience into itself. *New Theater and Film* thereby became a most curious orphan. Amidst a periodic financial crisis for the magazine during the later months of 1936, John Howard Lawson (then on the New York end of his bicoastal commuting) complained that it had become politically "wishy-washy," according to the recollections of its real editor, Herbert Kline. Perhaps Lawson really meant that *New Theater and Film* had bypassed the political genuflections to Moscow that appeared all too frequently in the *New Masses,* sticking to its own artistic areas of concern; and that absent such a specialized magazine, the *New Masses* would be stronger.

Abandoned to his own devices, Lawson might nevertheless have let matters go along. But from deep within the Party apparatus, V. J. Jerome—rumored to have gained a Hollywood lover and political supporter in veteran screenwriter Viola Brothers Shore—was in turn pushing Lawson hard. Jerome, far more than Lawson, sought instinctively to eradicate competition and possible deviancy in an arena where he could exert authority. Besides, he had his own opinions of the avant-garde. "In a nutshell," recalls an activist in the contemporary labor theater, "Jerome's opinion was that working class theater was irrelevant . . . we were ordered to redirect our enthusiasms."[73]

Kline might have given in to Lawson by degrees, but he had two good reasons to resist. First, he was rightly convinced that a more didactic approach would undercut the progress that the magazine made winning show business allies—and decisively narrow the readership and support. Second, he had already made up his mind to leave for Spain as war correspondent. When he resigned, leaving a committee of four relative unknowns in charge (including a young Eleanor Flexner, destined to become one of the most prominent historians of American women), the magazine continued for a few issues, then folded. Nominally, it was replaced by a slicker *TAC* (for Theater Action Committee) that, however, practically ignored films, failed to gain an audience, and disappeared quickly. Kline records that his friend Bosley Crowther, of *The New York Times,* offered to publicize the real political causes of his resignation at the time, but he (Kline) did not want to damage the already weakened magazine.[74]

This understated precursor of the "Maltz Affair" of 1946 (see Chapter 6) could be seen correctly as the workings of the cold hand of the Party bureaucracy, a smaller version in some ways of the vastly more ominous power of the studios, the Red-baiting gossip columnists, and the censors. Such incidents large or small, publicized or otherwise, could best be judged, as Abraham Polonsky observed, as part of a protracted conflict that pitted political orthodoxy against artistic experimentation. These caused many of the best-trained intellectuals (such as Polonsky himself, during the later 1930s an English instructor at City College) simply to avoid writing for Party-connected publications, while nevertheless retaining the comradeship and shared political activity of fellow members. It was far from an ideal solution—Polonsky's own CCNY literary modernist chums who never went to Hollywood mostly became Trotskyists or anarchists—but the alternatives looked worse in matters of day-to-day mobilizations. Besides, after 1935 (and except for some agonizing months from 1939 to 1941), the Communists were *the* Roosevelt Party of the Left, the Popular Front niche for those left-wing Democrats like Polonsky who were also Communists.

Outbreaks of anti-Semitism could drive home the point even in the worst of times. Isolationist propaganda rarely lacked some anti-Semitic rhetoric after 1937, as left-led antifascism began to crest. Around the time congressman Martin Dies announced in 1939 that he had uncovered a Jewish plot to take over America by guiding a mercenary army up from Mexico, meanwhile manipulating Wall Street into collapse, he claimed to have been stunned by American Legionnaires' files on subversion in Hollywood. Left-wingers opined that the studios had nevertheless invited the Dies Committee (the House Committee on Un-American Activities, founded in 1934 as an investigative body to trace domestic fascism) to Hollywood so as to squelch the Screen Writers Guild. It was a plausible suggestion. The first round of House Committee hearings, held in August 1940, actually came to nothing, but the Senate's own investigation later that year by Gerald Nye of North Dakota offered the muckraking antimonopoly senator the opportunity to pinpoint the media conspiracy dragging Americans into war: "production directors" of "Jewish faith," the very essence of unrepentant "foreigners" in a nation that needed to hang together. The Senate Subcommittee on War Propaganda duly began an investigation of some forty-eight allegedly prowar films, but by the time the subcommittee met, in September 1941, the nearness of war had wiped out the apparent threat of propaganda.[75] These experiences had not seriously damaged the film industry, but they drove home the simple lesson that Hollywood was threatened by outsiders, not by its own community members.

Hollywood Communists had already proven themselves invaluable to get social and union movements going; despite the ideological fog in the Party, they would soon prove themselves almost as valuable in getting serious discussion of film art moving among writers, directors, and critics. They would surely have done so earlier and better without censorious bureaucrats like Jerome (and willing victims-made-functionaries, as Lawson allowed himself to become). But the causes of the day brought the artists into political consciousness and gave them helpful tasks to perform as they worked on their art; the Party framework provided them a common agenda in the unlikely vicinity of Beverly Hills. We might also discern in the promise of *New Theater and Film* an impulse, growing clearer in the war years, for the Popular Front to outgrow the Communist Party, even among those whose political and artistic engagements predated the broad shift toward liberalism. Only the Cold War closed out this particular impulse.

But to appreciate the particularity of the screenwriters' situation, it is also crucial to understand that the intellectuals of the Left, with the rarest exceptions, lacked the kind of cultural education that might have permitted them to think clearly about art forms in general, films in particular. For a party of avowed working-class intellectuals, they had precious few published resources along these lines. The Manhattan-based editors, writers, and functionaries could "appreciate" Russian films and "enjoy" some apparently harmless Hollywood products. William Z. Foster, considered the Party's leading trade union strategist and second only to Earl Browder in global prestige, was a particularly big fan of Westerns and was thoroughly downhearted during a Hollywood visit when the comrades could not introduce him to any of the cowboy stars whom he idolized.[76]

Beyond repeating generalities that some Russians offered about film, Communist leaders simply lacked their own definite aesthetic ideas. Being a long way from Hollywood in every sense, they also had no idea of how films were actually made, and rightly suspected that influencing them

would be problematic at best. To garner the emerging benefits of organization there, they reasoned they would need a reliable man on the job.

Thus the Party dispatched a young organizer, John Weber, to Hollywood in 1938. Previously a mobilizer of hunger marches and assorted
demonstrations, official organizer of left-wing union locals and party districts, Weber had no apparent credentials for Hollywood organizing—
which may have been perceived as safer and more reliable than sending, for
instance, someone from the former *New Theater and Film* milieu.

Environment and personality soon fairly overcame the none-too-
hidden intentions of formal directives. Schooling Hollywood supporters of
the Party in Marxist ideas Moscow-style would have been a didactic misadventure. But the work moved quickly in an entirely different direction.
Weber and Arthur Birnkrandt (a future aide to producer Sidney Buchman,
and late in life a screenwriter for Bill Baird's puppets) split the instruction
of several hundred students through a dozen classes in various private
homes, thus avoiding publicity and career risks to those attending. To
quote Weber, the real purpose of the school, as it actually took shape, was

> to develop the minds of the people who were the creative heart of Hol-
> lywood. Almost all of the people taking courses were writers, direc-
> tors, producers, actors and technicians—three hundred of them. The
> students were mostly not Party members but people who were at-
> tracted by the anti-Fascist movement.[77]

If Hollywoodites thus wanted, for personal even more than for aesthetic or
career reasons, to "understand society and social forces better," the school
influenced them (in Weber's recollection) to "be more confident that they
could present progressive ideas, one way or another, in any phase of their
work as writers, actors, directors, even technicians." It "freed up" the creative powers of dozens and perhaps hundreds of those destined to make a
mark on film in the next decade or so.[78]

Future schools in that period, more formally organized, would continue to play a central role in the Left's relationship with Hollywood. Open
to the public and boasting courses by well-known liberals as well as left-
wingers, the League of American Writers school (1940–41), the Writers'
Clinics (1942–43), and the People's Educational Center (1943–48) drew
thousands more current or would-be studio employees—and, at a mini-

mum, dozens of FBI agents. The first, nameless school guided by Weber and Birnkrandt ended in 1940, when the combination of legal pressure upon the Communist Party, loss of revenues, and a cutback of Party staff abandoned the two educators to their own financial resources, with the usual parting advice to "go into industry," this time not steel or textiles but the movies.

One could easily draw from this early episode the moral that nothing had been decided politically about film. It would be truer to say that Hollywood as producer of films (rather than of funds and politically useful personalities) remained at the outer edges of the American Communist leaders' radar screen, especially from the perspective of New York. Like sports, central to American working-class leisure but never outside the sports page of the *Daily Worker* (according to persistent rumor, the best-read and also the best-written page of the paper), movies remained "there," far below the events in war-torn Europe or Asia, the struggles for unions, the intrigues and conflicts in Washington or Wall Street.[79]

If Communist leaders and intellectuals had instinctively developed a structural model of society in which culture was always the superstructure, novels and theater represented arenas familiar enough to influence or (if possible) control. Films, especially Hollywood films, were so far up the superstructure, and so suspect as escapist products of bourgeois culture, that control of even serious influence upon film content was never seriously contemplated, a conclusion that brought the Hollywood struggle back to fund-raising and publicity.

But Hollywoodites themselves, working within the studios, could not feel this way. For them, the superstructure *was* the structure of the major American industry where they toiled regularly or irregularly, for good wages or bad. The fact that the Hollywood Left was an "underground" *within the Party,* hidden inside the Los Angeles Communist apparatus out of fear of job loss, put another barrier between normal political life and Hollywood. There were still more barriers. Social circles generally remained small, one group of left-wingers (who happened to be friends of Howard Koch, a non-Communist and Gentile) likely to meet for bridge games on Sunday while another group boozed heavily or met for heated discussion in the back room of a well-known Hollywood leftish and rather gay bookshop. The better-known writers, actors, and directors did appear at public events in which Communists were fairly conspicuous, especially fund-raisers for the Hollywood Anti-Nazi League, Spain-related activities, and wartime mobilization. But these were hardly moments for artistic contemplation.

Thus serious discussion about films, whether framed in terms of Marxism (or "historical materialism") or not, began and went right on being informal, public in the sense that classes at various schools were quasi-public but in that circumstance often taught by sympathetic liberals with little knowledge of Marxism. Increasingly interesting reviews (and a few essays) began to appear in the Communist press, and some larger statements of Hollywood writers could be found in the Hollywood Left's own short-lived magazines and the *New Masses* shortly before America entered the war. Little other rumination did.

If hostile reviews in the Party press could hurt left-wing novels and even off-Broadway plays, they were hurtful only to the *writers* of films and then not entirely because the writers were removed so far from the final product as to agree, in the broadest political terms, with many of the criticisms. Often enough they had worked to order and therefore had no more control over the formula than a brassmaker does on a rivet. But they learned from their own experiences, which steadily placed the Hollywood Reds less in line with New York political thinking than with non-Communist Hollywood liberals and experimenters in commercial film form and content. Subtle shifts in orientation brought new recruits and devotees still more like themselves, immeasurably less like the hard-bitten Communists of earlier years and other circumstances.

Appearing as it did at the historical moment when the Popular Front was cresting, the Hollywood Communist movement and its surrounding milieu acted as if American Communism had never existed otherwise or as if its earlier emanations had been no more than a bad memory. From the eternal present of Hollywood, things could easily look that way. This assumption gave the film Left an amazing degree of self-created freedom, if also a naïveté about how swiftly the end could come and how final would be its verdict.

1. Quoted in Otto Frederich, *City of Nets: A Portrait of Hollywood in the 1940s* (Berkeley: University of California Press, 1996), xii.
2. Cedric Belfrage, *Promised Land* (London: Victor Gollancz, 1938), 158–59.

3. Leonardo Bercovici interviewed by Paul Buhle, in Patrick McGilligan and Paul Buhle, *Tender Comrades: A Backstory of the Hollywood Blacklist* (New York: St. Martin's Press, 1997), 42. More in Chapter 8 on Bercovici, a late beginner in Hollywood whose prestige credits included *The Bishop's Wife, Kiss the Blood off My Hands, Portrait of Jennie,* and, in exile, the award-winning *Maddelena.*

4. Indeed, all the subsequent Hollywood "causes," from oppressed farmworkers to endangered whales, have their proper origins here.

5. *The Way We Were* (1973) and *Guilty by Suspicion* (1992), despite the censorious rewriting of scripts and other abundant flaws, captured certain aspects of the 1940s–50s experience. The recent filmic treatment of Dorothy Parker in *Mrs. Parker and the Vicious Circle* (1994) characteristically makes her political life in Hollywood an extension of neurotic and bitchy behavior, rather than a riveting point for her emotionally chaotic life.

6. Quoted in Giuliana Muscio, *Hollywood's New Deal* (Philadelphia: Temple University Press, 1996), 36.

7. Muscio, *Hollywood's New Deal,* 20–35.

8. Bernstein, who went on the blacklist after writing an early version of the script for *Kiss the Blood off My Hands,* became a notable television writer of the 1950s, then returned to films in 1959. As of 2000, he rewrote his 1961 film script for *Fail-Safe* for a new telefilm produced by George Clooney, shown in spring of that year—apparently the very last creation of a blacklist returnee unless Bernstein writes more. Bernstein's other scripts have included *The Front, The Molly Maguires,* and the Emmy-winning script for the 1998 telefilm *Miss Evers' Boys* (1997). Bernstein's autobiography is *Inside Out: A Memoir of the Blacklist* (New York: Knopf, 1996).

9. See Maurice Rapf, *Back Lot: Growing Up With the Movies* (Lantham, MD: Scarecrow Press, 1999), 23–31, 115–22.

10. Rapf insisted that the novel was serialized in Nazi papers, proving that his friend of the time had written a dangerous text and deserved to be criticized for it. No claim was made that the novel should be suppressed, of course, and no action was taken against Schulberg's status in the Party. Rapf, *Back Lot,* 131.

11. W. L. River, "Conniving and Copulating Ghosts," *The Clipper* 1 (June 1941), 20, quoting Schulberg, "The Hollywood Novel," in *Films,* Spring 1940.

12. The best account of this initial alienation is in Hadassa Kosak, *Cultures of Opposition: Jewish Immigrant Workers, New York City, 1881–1903* (Albany: State University of New York Press, 2000), 15–36. The link with Yiddish is sug-

gested in Dan Miron, *A Traveler Disguised: The Rise of Modern Yiddish Fiction in the Nineteenth Century* (New York: Schocken Books, 1973).

13. Even Neil Simon's teleplay *Broadway Bound* (1992) had such an older figure, a grandfather morphed into a Trotskyist, a far safer if improbable figure for idealization than the Communists who outnumbered their factional opponents perhaps a hundred to one in the 1930s–40s American Jewish community.

14. J. Hoberman, *Bridge of Light: Yiddish Film Between Two Worlds* (New York: Schocken Books and the Museum of Modern Art, 1991), 26–28.

15. See Neal Gabler, *An Empire of Their Own: How the Jews Invented Hollywood* (New York: Anchor, 1988), 44–94.

16. Exclusion from the watering spots of the rich was a particular sore point in the 1930s. See Gabler, *An Empire of Their Own,* 272–74.

17. The literature on this subject is prolific, but one fine novel carries the mogul story from East Coast origins to Hollywood: Howard Fast, *Max: A Novel* (Boston: Houghton Mifflin, 1982).

18. Lawson, unpublished memoirs, John Howard Lawson Papers, Southern Illinois University, 173–74; our gratitude to Robert Hethmon, future Lawson biographer, for pointing out Lawson's recollections of particular films.

19. Dan E. Moldea, *Dark Victory: Ronald Reagan, MCA and the Mob* (New York: Viking-Penguin, 1986), 24–27. See also Gerald Horne, *Class Struggle in Hollywood, 1930–1950: Moguls, Mobsters, Stars, Reds and Trade Unionists* (Austin: University of Texas Press, 2001), 39–50, for a close reading of the mob-related materials.

20. Moldea, *Dark Victory,* 27–34.

21. Bruce Murray, *Film and the German Left in the Weimar Republic* (Austin: University of Texas Press, 1990), 19.

22. Murray, *Film and the German Left,* 186–232.

23. Yiddish theater continued, mostly in revivals and musicals, and is still presented today, though largely in bilingual productions.

24. The literature on the Group is abundant. One of the best short treatments is in Foster Hirsch, *A Method to Their Madness: The History of the Actors Studio* (W. W. Norton: New York, 1984), 67–109.

25. Harry Alan Potamkin, "The Film and Revolution," *New Masses* 6 (November 1930), 23.

26. David Wolff, "Harry Alan Potamkin," *New Theater* 2 (February 1936), 28. Wolff further quoted Potamkin rather more didactically describing film as

"at once the response of the mind which the dominant class has effected; and the agent of the dominant class to affect the response."

27. David Platt, "Expansion of Remarks Opening the 1930s–40s Panel at the Alternative Cinema Conference at Bard College, June 12–17, 1979." Manuscript in authors' possession.

28. Platt, "Expansion of Remarks."

29. Quoted in Russell Campbell, *Cinema Strikes Back: Radical Filmmaking in the United States, 1930–1942* (Ann Arbor: UMI Research Press, 1982), 56.

30. Gabler, *An Empire of Their Own,* 341. The executives and their community allies, notably Rabbi Edgar Magnin, launched the Community Relations Committee (CRC) to monitor American Nazi activity; compared with its left-wing counterpart, the CRC was phlegmatic and quiet.

31. Philip Dunne, *Take Two,* 110.

32. *News of the World,* renamed from *Hollywood Now* after its first year of publication, ran tabloid for eighteen months, publicizing HANL's varied activities, including a Women's League, a Youth League, Stewart's comic scripts for radio broadcasts, and numerous public events. The HANL faded into events around the defense of the Spanish Republic even before the Hitler-Stalin Pact and with it, one could argue, the peculiar importance of the German colony in Hollywood. One of the few consecutive runs of *News/Hollywood Now* is in the UCLA Special Collections. Saverio Giovancchini, *Hollywood Modernism: Film and Politics in the Age of the New Deal* (Philadelphia: Temple University Press, 2001), 72–86, provides one of the few accounts of HANL's rise and fall, with heavy emphasis upon the emigrant German role but without much appreciation for the complexities within the Popular Front milieu and the ways in which the Spanish Civil War stole the HANL's thunder even before the Nazi-Soviet Pact killed the organization.

33. Nancy Lynn Schwartz thus lists some celebrities at a typical 1938 MPAC fund-raising banquet held at the home of Ira Gershwin and his wife: Eve Arden, Fanny Brice, Louise Rainer, Gale Sondergaard, Dorothy Parker, Jean Rouverol Butler, Dorshka Raphaelson, Beatrice Buchman, and Karen Morley. See Nancy Lynn Schwartz, *The Hollywood Writers' Wars* (New York: Knopf, 1982), 118.

34. Dunne, *Take Two,* 110.

35. "Reminiscenes of Dorothy Parker," interviewed by Robert and Joan Parker, 1959, Columbia University Oral History Project.

36. See Francois Furet, *The Passing of an Illusion: The Idea of Communism in the Twentieth Century,* translated by Deborah Furet (Chicago: University of Chicago Press, 1999), 19–29.

37. Lardner quoted by Nancy Lynn Schwartz, *The Hollywood Writers' Wars,* 92; but lyricist-scriptwriter Henry Myers jocularly made the claim openly that Hollywood's left-wing events and organizations were hosted and guided by the prettiest, i.e., the most left-wing women: "Beautiful but Undumb," *Black & White* 1 (June 1939), 10.

38. Whittaker Chambers's memoir, *Witness,* later put this sense of rage most eloquently, arguing that the 1930s brought "a small intellectual army" of subversives, obviously including himself, into "all branches of commucation but especially radio, motion pictures, book, magazine and newspaper publishing." Quoted in Denning, *The Cultural Front,* 105. It is notable that the Hollywood Left had more than its fair share of neurotics, but no Whittaker Chambers type involved at first in information passing and then high-profile anti-Communist ideologue of *Time* magazine prestige was ever to emerge here.

39. Patrick Kearney, "They Accuse Universal!" *New Masses* 7 (June 1932), 19–20.

40. It was also noteworthy that the announcements of participants in the League of Professional Groups included no screenwriters. A few later screenwriters were involved in the Los Angeles branches of the John Reed Clubs, the Communist-led literary-political movement that boosted the careers and lives of Richard Wright, Nelson Algren, Tillie Lerner (i.e., Tillie Olsen), and so many others—before being dropped for the Popular Front format of the American Writers Congress in mid-decade. But the several John Reed Clubs of Los Angeles were neighborhood-based, none actually from Hollywood. At the close of the 1930s, the League of American Writers did better, but its Hollywood branch has not found a scholar.

41. Afterward doubly wary, Party leaders reputedly sought to work out a private arrangement with Cagney, who nevertheless shifted rightward after a few years of mentorship in Carmel with Lincoln Steffens and his wife, Ella Winter (who later remarried Donald Ogden Stewart). See "John Bright," interviewed by Patrick McGilligan, *Tender Comrades,* 142–43.

42. *FBI Surveillance Files,* Reel 5, LA 100-15732, 7.

43. See Franklin Folsom, *Days of Anger, Days of Hope* (Boulder: University of Colorado Press, 1994), a memoir of the LAW written by a former New

York LAW staffer, has little concerning the organization's Hollywood activities.

44. The literature on Tess Slesinger (1905–45) is greater than that of almost any other screenwriter, thanks to her reputation as a novelist and because of her connections with the New York intellectuals. Her best-known work, *The Unpossessed* (1934), was a sharp critique of the gender relations within that circle. See, e.g., Alan Wald, *The New York Intellectuals: The Rise and Decline of the Anti-Stalinist Left from the 1930s to the 1980s* (Chapel Hill: University of North Carolina Press, 1987), 64–74. Slesinger's film credits include *The Good Earth* (1937) and *A Tree Grows in Brooklyn* (1945, see Chapters 5 and 8). Madeleine Ruthven, frequently named in FBI documents, had a few credits during the 1930s, entirely in B films, and none afterward.

45. Some of the details of Jerome's life were unavailable until Alan Wald began working on literary personalities in the party's milieu; we gladly extend our thanks to Wald for providing materials and interpretations.

46. "Testimony of Frank Tuttle," *Communist Infiltration of Hollywood Motion-Picture Industry, 82nd Congress, First Session* (Washington: Government Printing Office, 1951), 626–28.

47. *FBI Surveillance Files*, Reel 5, LA 100–15732, 7–12.

48. Ibid., 11.

49. This recollection relayed by John Weber.

50. "Testimony of George Beck," *Communist Infiltration of the Hollywood Motion-Piction Industry*, 1821.

51. Interview with Ring Lardner, Jr., New York City, June 1991.

52. Polonsky's conversations with Paul Buhle and Dave Wagner, Beverly Hills, 1996–98, touched on this and Party issues often, a treasure trove of anecdotes.

53. This impression comes from interviews Paul Buhle did with a variety of left-wingers in Los Angeles in 1980–82; several of these are available in the Oral History of the American Left, Tamiment Library, New York University.

54. Interviews with Hollywoodites, especially left-wing Jews with little knowledge of the progressive Yiddish-speaking community geographically close to them, confirm this view. Thanks to Robert Lees and Abraham Polonsky in particular for this insight.

55. Martin Berkeley HUAC testimony, *Communist Infiltration of the Hollywood Motion-Picture Industry*, 1572. According to later anti-Communist myths, a manipulative and totalitarian organization would have purposely placed him

in danger of a beating, just so as to demonstrate the steely nerves needed for Communist commitment. Berkeley himself, despite his newly ardent anti-Communism, made no such claim and obviously remained proud of his activity.

56. "Testimony of George Beck," 1820–21.

57. "Reminiscences of Dorothy Parker," 1959 interview by Robert and Jean Franklin, Columbia University Oral History Project, transcript at Columbia University Archives.

58. This view has rarely been offered, even in the standard biographies of Parker, e.g., Marion Meade, *Dorothy Parker: What Fresh Hell Is This?* (New York: Villard Books, 1988). For a more politically accurate if brief view, see e.g., Annette Rubinstein, "Dorothy Parker," *Encyclopedia of the American Left* (New York: Oxford University Press, 1998), 580.

59. Meade, *Dorothy Parker,* 262–63.

60. Two years earlier, *The Moon's Our Home* (1936), written for Walter Wanger's unit at Paramount and based on Faith Baldwin's novel of the same name, actually succeeded at moments. More like *Going Hollywood* than *A Star Is Born,* it reflected upon the unreal world of celebrity through a wry gaze hardly distracted by romping sentimentality. The dialogue, as occasionally happens in Parker films, successfully ran away with (or from) the plot. *New Masses* credited the script with having characters "exchanging persiflage as only Parker can write it." James Dugan, "Movies," *New Masses* 30 (December 27, 1938), 28.

61. Paul Jarrico interview by Larry Ceplair, UCLA Oral History Project, 1988.

62. See Dick, *Radical Innocence,* 22–24. *Secrets of the French Police* (1932), another clinker, had in its opening moments a newspaper headline about the French Communist Party, viewed for several seconds, then an exotic conspiracy around a café flower girl kidnapped by a murderously mad White Russian (i.e., anti-Bolshevik).

63. It would appear that the decapitated head of an anti-Semite in the Coen brothers' *Barton Fink* (1991) references *The Man Who Reclaimed His Head,* and that the former film's screenwriter-protagonist could at least in some respects pass for Clifford Odets.

64. Brian Taves, "The B Film: Hollywood's Other Half," in Tino Balio, *Grand Design: Hollywood as a Modern Business Enterprise, 1930–1939* (Berkeley: University of California Press, 1993), 313–50. See also Richard Maurice Hurst,

Republic Studios: Between Poverty Row and the Majors (Metuchen, NJ: Scarecrow Press, 1979).

65. *New Masses* gave one of its rare nods to an Ornitz film with *Two Wise Maids,* suggesting that a small production company (the kinds that "seldom get reviewed in these pages") could do something valuable, like this film, "built around the lack of playgrounds in large cities and around the dramatic idea of mothers putting up an organized fight to get those playgrounds for their children." "Housing and Flood Control in the Films," *New Masses* 26 (January 18, 1937), 29.

66. See Louis Norden, "Boycott Hearst Films," *New Theatre* II (July 1935), 28–29; Joel Faith, "Mayer of MGM," *New Theatre* II (September 1935), 6–8.

67. Ralph Steiner, "Revolutionary Movie Production," *New Theatre* 1 (September, 1934), 4.

68. "The New Film Alliance," *New Theatre* 2 (September 1935), 29. For the time being, according to the announcement, *New Theatre* would continue to be the NFA's outlet, apparently foreshadowing the addition of "and Film" to the magazine's title a year later, in lieu of the new journal. See Campbell, *Cinema Strikes Back,* for a full account of the Left documentary push.

69. George Mansion, "Hollywood's Hundred Grand Union," *New Theatre* 3 (January 1936), 25–26.

70. Robert Stebbins, "Mr. Capra Goes to Town," and Emanuel Eisenberg, "John Ford: Fighting Irish," *New Theatre* 3 (April 1936), 32–33 and 8, 42; Arthur Kober, "Hollywood Story Conference," *New Theatre* 3 (November 1936), 17, 35.

71. Robert Stebbins, "Film Miscellany," *New Theatre and Film* 2 (October 1936), 18.

72. See especially Herbert Biberman, "Theater and Film," *New Theatre* 3 (July 1936), 14–15.

73. Toby Cole to Paul Buhle, September 26, 2000. Cole, author of several books on theater, added that, in retrospect, it was in Jerome's apartment (shared by Cole's friend and Jerome's wife, Alice Evans) where she first heard songs from Brecht and Weill's *Threepenny Opera* "intoned," i.e., sung aloud. It was a saving grace.

74. Herbert Kline, editor, *New Theatre and Film, 1934–37* (New York: Harcourt Brace Jovanovich, 1984), 363–67. Kline says that decades later, in the year of Lawson's death, he pleaded to see Kline again, apologized profusely, and in-

sisted that he (Lawson) would have done better to stick with writing plays and leave politics to others. See the lamentable influence of Jerome on Lawson later, in Chapter 8.

75. Neal Gabler, *An Empire of Their Own,* 345–46.

76. The "New York Critics' Group," on the fringes of the Popular Front, began publishing serious theoretical works at the close of the 1930s, but the work did not survive the Hitler-Stalin Pact. See Chapter 6, on the Critics' Group's most important work, *The Philosophy of Art of Karl Marx* (1938), by the Russian theorist Mikhail Lifshitz. John Weber has confirmed that even a Hollywood instructor in Marxism was unlikely to have heard of these texts.

77. "John Weber," interviewed by Paul Buhle, *Tender Comrades,* 686–87.

78. "John Weber," 687.

79. Lester Rodney, interviewed by Paul Buhle, UCLA Oral History Collection, 1982. Rodney was sports editor of the *Daily Worker* from the middle 1930s to the middle 1950s.

3

GENRE REALIZED:
THE RADICAL WORLD OF THE B FILM

IVING WITHIN THE CULTURAL PUZZLE PALACE, left-wing screenwriters felt less burdened by the usual artistic censorship when their work abandoned all claims to realism. The several genres of make-believe, as they had for centuries in the theater, circus, or carnival, offered different paths of expression. They also offered, through horror and fantasy, opportunities for visual experimentation foreshadowing what might be done later with improved technology and better camera work.

Fantasy had been explored well before sound, most famously in *The Cabinet of Dr. Caligari, Nosferatu,* and *Metropolis,* not to mention *The Golem* (with heavy Jewish symbolism and Yiddish subtitles) and a minor assortment of early Hollywood sci-fi experiments featuring rocket ships and robots. To innovators like Carl Laemmle, Jr., of Universal, eager to make a mark upon films on a relatively skimpy budget and with less-than-shining stars, horror classics offered an irresistible opportunity.

Sophisticated culture critics and those who hammered professionally on the refined gold of political theory generally agreed that nothing so far down the superstructure as fantasy, cops 'n' robbers, slapstick, or cowboys and Indians could possibly contain social criticism. By and large they were right. But just as in the natural sciences, where anomalous phenomena sometimes lead to larger theories and new understanding, the exceptions within popular culture were never entirely absent, and proved important in unexpected ways. For one thing, precisely because the attention of censors and conservative political critics focused elsewhere, artists on the bottom rungs of the genres often had a freer hand than their more exalted counterparts. For another, they were more likely to be in touch with working-class audiences than were the artists whose work was reviewed in the literary press.

The realist-minded Left, including old-school Marxists, usually shared with the gentility the most restricted views. But radicalized youngsters in the 1930s who were experimenting in a variety of popular media saw it differently. From the Jewish socialist sympathizers in mid-1930s Cleveland who created the original comic strip character of Superman as an injustice-fighting super-FDR (or perhaps Socialist Party presidential nominee Norman Thomas) before selling the rights for a pittance; to the leader of the socialistic Workers Alliance (along with the Communist-led Unemployed Leagues the foremost organization of the jobless in the early 1930s), who also worked as an editor of *Science Wonder Stories;* to the teenage Manhattan "Futurions" (including Isaac Asimov and Frederik Pohl), who ranged themselves sympathetically around the Popular Front while learning their writing trade, the new generation made its own experience.[1] None of these particular writers and artists actually happened to find their way into films. But like Hammett's fellow writers in the *Black Mask* detective slicks of the 1920s, they helped establish the styles of fanciful conceptual narrative frameworks within which adept Hollywoodites learned to operate.

They had a near-match in the B (and occasionally A) screenwriters who quickly learned that Westerns could be their own bread and butter on Hollywood's often profitable "Poverty Row." Julian Zimet recalled a half century later that in 1940, snagging a job, he was amazed to find Republic turning out "pictures that never played in New York City," or at least not in the theaters where he'd spent his childhood leisure. Given the chance he, too, could grind out scripts for Gene Autry and Roy Rogers features—but with at least somewhat of a difference. Cowboys often really did act as if they stood on the side of justice, protecting the weak against the unscrupulous, a standard plot feature with enormous possible implications.[2]

The art of making progressive Westerns lay in rendering the villains not as freakish loners nor mere bandit chiefs but more like their counterparts in real-life America: swindling bankers, agents of corporations intent upon monopolizing the land; or, for the especially bold writer, the racists who abused Indians and Mexican-Americans. To perform this alchemy, the writer also had to transform the larger assorted pulp images of pulp writers like Max Brand (and before him, of "yellow back" writers of the nineteenth century) into something more humane and complex, yet simple enough for the studio and audience tastes that often ran to the juvenile. It was no easy task, and not one likely to be much appreciated by the critics.

Perhaps it should not be surprising that several of the giants of the left-wing Western, notably Carl Foreman (*High Noon*), began in another bottom-of-the-barrel genre: slapstick comedy. After all, the Keystone Kops and Charlie Chaplin, ridiculing authority and exalting the little man, had been at the root of film's early popularity, especially among the immigrant working-class audience. Within the artistry of the physical gag might be found subtleties that prestigious writers of theatrical dialogue never understood. The task of renewing and revising the tradition in sound film offered the radical writer the prospect of a modest income if, almost certainly, No Respect.

But progress along these lines did not come easily. Recent scholarship has, albeit with the best intentions, overplayed Depression film's crypto-political advances so as to heighten the purported conservative drift of the war years.[3] Immigrant film writers and directors in the studio mainstream, as historians suggest, did successfully introduce more of the themes of out-siders (like themselves) into American films. But few of the fictive out-siders had a rebellious bone in their bodies. And most of these fresh talents to Hollywood, career-bent and indifferent to politics, were just as capable as American-born writers and film executives of replicating the "white telephone" film glamorizing elites or the action film portraying the poor as degraded and dangerous. Any presence of occasional nonwhite actors, un-derstandably considered a marker for Hollywood progressives, was almost without exception utilized to reinforce racial codes. As credulous darkies offered contrast to rational whites, Polynesian princesses added color (if very little) to the adventuresomeness of American males, and most Indians continued to bite the dust for the crime of challenging wagon trains' intru-sion on what had for a millennia been Indian Territory. Businessmen might be bad in an era when a large proportion of Americans felt "the system" had failed, but they rarely *were* bad unless radical screenwriters made them so.

The most potent Populistic figures of commercial Hollywood up to the mid-1930s were unarguably Charlie Chaplin's "little man" and the down-home, Mark Twain–style comedian realized for a few years by Will Rogers. Charlie was at once the idol of the immigrant neighborhood and one of the first figures of world cinema. Rogers the part-Cherokee who often transgressed racial lines also good-naturedly poked other holes in typical American hypocrisies. He usually played the respectable doctor, judge, farmer, or citizen of the old middle class who redressed the prerogatives of the privileged by aligning himself with the excluded. As Chaplin dominated realms of silent screen comedy, Rogers charmed such huge audiences that by 1934–35 he had become Hollywood's number one money-making star. During the funeral following his fatal airplane accident in 1935, all film production ceased, and some twelve thousand theaters darkened their screens.

Cinematically, Chaplin the writer and director as well as star had invented innumerable gestures of silent screen. He also shocked Red-hunters by embracing labor causes and the new Russian regime. Rogers for his part inspired some of John Ford's best early directing work, with scripts cowritten as originals or coadapted from literary sources by Dudley Nichols, one of the Left's most important collaborating non-Communist allies and, for most of the next ten years, the highest-paid, most artistically respected writer in Hollywood.[4] But neither Chaplin's quirky style nor Rogers's movie martyrdom offered viable models for the left-of-center film drawing upon Hollywood's main lines of production. The problem was to move progressive themes out of isolation into the mainstream. A handful of writers, emphatically including Nichols, along with fewer directors or producers, successfully managed to do so, especially in the first years, revealing just as little as possible of their political intent.[5]

They intuitively worked through existing formulae toward innovation. To discover what possibilities lay within genre required a keen eye to the contradictions at the lowest end of film production, where crude manipulation of the audience was standard and aesthetic considerations apparently nonexistent. There were more slips than successes along the way, outright failures to evade the controlling power of the director and studio or to establish a viable story in its own right. Here and there, more often for one scene or several scenes than otherwise, a clear break nevertheless could be seen. Still more often, it could be seen best in retrospect, because radicals were so painfully aware of the distance between their aspirations and the finished film.

Wonderfully Horrible

During the 1920s, both *Dracula* and *Frankenstein* had been transatlantic stage hits. Screen idol Clara Bow pursued a personal fascination with Bela Lugosi into a yearlong affair of the "vamp" (short for "vampire") with her corresponding male screen persona. Horace Liveright, the Jewish avant-garde publisher and ally of artistic-minded left-wingers, staged some of the U.S. productions of *Dracula* and hoped to make a vampire film with Universal, but lost his fortune in the stock-market crash. Liveright's aesthetic sense was better than his market timing. According to shrewd insiders, this was just the moment for the appearance of screen monsters. The great success of gangsters in the Cagney style suggested the ripeness of the moment for a parallel "psychic lawlessness" in more fantastic versions of monsterdom.[6]

It was no accident that *Dracula* (1931), the first filmed American version of Bram Stoker's novel, would be directed, amid confusion and false starts, by Tod Browning. An extreme oddball and alcoholic best remembered for the widely banned *Freaks* (1932), he was soon to be a collaborator on *Mark of the Vampire* (1935) with future left-wing stalwart Guy Endore, whose 1931 novel *Werewolf of Paris*—in which a creature appears significantly at the moment of the Paris Commune—was one of the best-selling and best-written of the genre. *Dracula* proved, over an extended run, a major hit; *Mark of the Vampire* (with additional script contributions by leftists Hy Kraft and Samuel Ornitz) was at first distinguished by the fear and outrage that it provoked, leading to outright suppression or heavy censorship of horror films across central and eastern Europe.[7] Meanwhile, the early success of *Dracula* had established a Hollywood precedent for the "fantastic" theme, establishing commercial viability for a sound-version *Frankenstein*.

Silent film versions of Mary Shelley's novel had already been produced twice, in 1910 and again in 1915. This time around, Carl Laemmle, Jr., hired British director James Whale to oversee the project. The Universal connection was important in the emerging horror cycle for very materialist reasons: This former giant of a studio had come down with the stock market, and was compelled to cut costs and concentrate distribution in something less than first-run, metropolitan theaters. Although Universal continued to make some very major films, from *All Quiet on the Western Front* to *Destry Rides Again,* its standard low-budget, meal-ticket style operated most efficiently within the horror-fantasy genre. The technicians knew best how to do the necessary work, their creative talents unloosed (within limits) along with those of studio writers and directors. Until Deanna Durbin was discovered in the late 1930s, Boris Karloff remained the studio's top star.[8]

Unanticipated rebelliousness was inscribed in *Frankenstein*'s production. Karloff, previously a little-known silent film actor, later recalled that mistreatment on the set prompted him to become a leader in the formation of the Screen Actors Guild, while letters from children reinforced his own sense that (as in author Shelley's original intention) the "monster" was the real victim of a misunderstanding world. Francis Faragoh, who received "screenplay and dialogue" credit, had made the decisive contribution of softening the monster from theatrical Frankensteins, and he added a large dose of humor as well, mostly ridicule of upper-class manners. His script was also likely responsible, along with the direction and camera work, for the expressionist zest that gives the picture a 1920s, *Metropolis*-inspired *Mittel-Europa* quality vastly superior to the two earlier (silent) screen versions.[9]

This is true not only for many small points of improvement on the literary original, like the child- or animal-like yearning of the creature for the sunlight denied him in the laboratory, but also in the climax with the rage of the villagers, their lust at trapping the monster and burning him alive (still striking out wildly, never grasping either his deeds or his fate). The film shows not justice however brutally realized, but a lynching destined to be restated in leftish films from *They Won't Forget* (1937) to *Superman and the Mole Men* (1951) to the legal and therefore all the more joyous hanging scene Marguerite Roberts penned for *True Grit* (1969), i.e., from lowest to highest grade of film across eras and genres. If conservatives viewed the outsider as the source of chaos to be controlled or eradicated, progressives saw into the souls of the aliens.[10]

Film audiences, in any case, loved *Frankenstein:* It was one of the top money-earners of 1931 and made *The New York Times* list of ten best films of the year. Faragoh was less fortunate. Brushed aside as a rebel after the attempted formation of the Screen Writers Guild (SWG) in 1936 and driven back to stage work in New York (unsuccessful there, and returning a year later to MGM), he received a wide variety of assignments but never got the opportunity to work on the "weird" theme again.

Universal, for its part, was off and running in the horror genre, with MGM in close competition. Moving back and forth between the studios, Guy Endore scripted, co-scripted, or made script contributions to five crucial genre films that appeared in 1935, *The Raven, The Black Room, Mad Love,* and *Mark of the Vampire,* and then (with Erich von Stroheim) *The Devil-Doll,* in 1936. Taken together, they move from psychosexual obsession to revenge against the masters of the stock market. Endore continued to draw heavily upon psychological themes, including his own favorite and most serious novel, *Me Thinks the Lady,* rendered into the mediocre *Whirlpool* in 1949 after Endore's own script was dumped, presumably because of the descending blacklist.[11]

The rarely seen *Devil-Doll* is easily the most political of the series.[12] Directed by Tod Browning, who contributed the story that Endore, Garrett Fort, and Erich von Stroheim adapted for the screen, it has wrongly convicted French businessman Lionel Barrymore sentenced to Devil's Island. He manages an escape to the backwoods Indian country that harbors a scientific husband-and-wife team experimenting with the miniaturization of living creatures, and returns to Paris with the widow. There, the two open up a toy shop as they continue experiments and begin robberies of a wealthy enemy of Barrymore through directing the actions of a miniaturized couple who sneak into an apartment and steal precious jewelry. Barrymore, himself in drag for much of the film, guides the further revenge upon the rich crooks while assisting his daughter, who is affianced to a Paris cabdriver. An odd combination of horror and fantasy, political revenge and social solidarity, with worthy working people, *The Devil-Doll* barely suggests how much further Hollywood horror might have gone.

Though slightly earlier, *Mark of the Vampire* provides the logical climax to the first phase of Hollywood horror films at large. Drawing upon *On the Nightmare,* psychoanalyst Ernest Jones's famed study, *Mark of the Vampire* subtly reimagines vampirism as incest guilt and also provides an implicit commentary upon the whole genre. Unaffiliated left-winger James Wong Howe has been rightly credited with the camera work here that defined for the first time what has been called "Hollywood Gothic," with more creepy *movement* of actors among the shadows than previous American films had managed. In a small German town, an illusionist (played brilliantly by Lugosi) and his daughter lead protagonist Lionel Barrymore and townsfolk on a merry chase over a murder, finally exposing the true murderer and revealing themselves as a touring vaudeville act with something possibly more sexually sinister about them. Demonstrating that horror depends upon the counterfeit, it was also one of Browning's last films, thanks ironically to public protests against the purported effects of extreme horror upon the credulous.[13] In effect, the genre had reached its initial limits, and needed something more to recontinue, whether a distancing humor (or camp), stronger psychological twists, or simply a drive-in audience sufficiently distracted by real-life sex and the setting to pay much attention to the production values.[14]

Isle of the Dead (1945), properly the final left-wing horror classic before the blacklist, was written by talented Austrian exile playwright Josef Mischel, produced by genre veteran Val Lewton, and directed by talented youngster Mark Robson, destined to make an extended series of liberal and left-connected films.[15] Arguably the most psychologically sophisticated of all the horror films (and in line with Lewton's 1942 *Cat People,* which was more horrific but less social-minded), it built upon *Mark of the Vampire*'s conceits while coming as close to a high-flown, general-interest film as any horror low-budget allegory could. This time, Karloff—struggling successfully for almost the last time in film against typecasting—is a tough Greek general in a nineteenth-century war, trapped with English tourists on a remote island where the plague is about to reach and where tale's of vampirism coincidentally abound.[16]

The nonappearance of real vampires does nothing to ease the eeriness of the setting, nor are we to reduce a general's willingness to sacrifice thousands of lives (as he reconstructs battle plans from a distance) to wanton power-lust. Moral monster Karloff sees his own doom approaching, but holds to his sense of duty even in what he recognizes as an ultimately meaningless war. For the ordinary viewer wearying of war propaganda by this time, such a general might have been leading troops on either side, any side, of the real conflict then coming to a close. The officer's evident melancholy cannot absolve him or those who willingly obey his orders from the tragedy unfolding around the planet, perhaps now irreversible despite all the optimistic assurances in real-life 1945 to the contrary.

For film historians, the most important element in this embrace of horror may not have been the public clamor over supposed psychological perversion, but the realization of more German aesthetics in horror than in all the filmed comedies, musicals, and straight drama combined. The aesthetics that otherwise proved a poor match for the studios worked here effectively, probably because American audiences could accept gothic stylization without complaint, unleashing their own imaginations beyond the limits of the usual romance or action film. Indeed, apart from William Dieterle, Fritz Lang, Ernst Lubitsch, the Mankiewicz brothers, and Billy Wilder, the émigrés managed to make, at least given their abundant talents, relatively few films as directors, fewer still as writers—a great loss to film, and not only to American film.

But their work, as the extraordinarily independent-minded (soon also bargain-basement-minded) and left-leaning exiled Jewish auteur Edgar G. Ulmer demonstrated best, had almost limitless possibilities in the assorted realms of fantasy.[17] Ulmer, who worked in virtually all genres among his 150-plus features, and by the early 1940s generally shot a film in under a week with a bare minimum of retakes, had come to the United States with F. W. Murnau during the 1920s as a set designer and worked with Erich von Stroheim, Emil Jannings, Ernst Lubitsch, and other legendary figures. His credits in that capacity included *The Last Laugh, Lady Windermere's Fan,* and DeMille's *King of Kings.* By the early thirties a director of minor Westerns and one of the first solid and financially successful documentaries about the dangers of venereal disease (*Damaged Lives*), he most urgently wanted to do an antiwar film, the kind of project made possible by the success of *All Quiet on the Western Front* (scripted in part by a future blacklistee Gordon Kahn). Ulmer, with his background in expressionism, had a very different notion of how it could be done.

The Black Cat (1936) had next to nothing in common with Edgar Allan Poe's original story. Instead, it was an extraordinary revisiting of a battle scene, years after the shooting had stopped. Rather than analyzing the lives of protagonists as Lewis Milestone and his screenwriters did in *All Quiet,* Ulmer created an elaborate metaphor of stylized horror. Then in his self-described Bauhaus period, Ulmer coscripted and directed the film in and around a replica of a real-life French fortress that had been shelled and attacked by the Germans, with thousands of bodies from both sides still buried beneath the hill. The set alone would have been worth the film, since the mise-en-scène starkness of horror in a sharp-edged, futuristic art deco frame has never been equaled.

Bringing Lugosi and Karloff back together, Ulmer made Lugosi the maddened former German commander who has returned to the site of his military triumph (and human disaster), where the commander of the rival army, played by Karloff, has kept the wife of his nemesis and a growing daughter away from the world. The dead wife, in one of the most bizarre moments of 1930s film, has been preserved in a chaste white dress, hanging lifelike from a ceiling of the castle's catacomb; the daughter is an innocent who knows nothing of the old conflict and ultimately will be murdered by a paternally incestuous Karloff as the entire edifice collapses, bringing final destruction to the saga of war's legacy. We might see it as reminiscent of Poe's collapsing southern mansions, but Ulmer himself described the film as allegory. He had seen the face of the war's horror and rendered it in narrative, symbolic form around the twin commanders driven to lunacy by the consequences of their own deeds. These touches shaded all of Ulmer's subsequent efforts, even his breeziest B comedy-dramas.

Sickened by the studio system and even more by the prospect of his own potential corruption there, Ulmer embarked on a series of nonrealist projects in other directions, including ethnic folk dancers, Harlem habitués, and, above all, the cream of the Yiddish stage (including the 1937 *Green Fields,* the most popular Yiddish-language film ever made)—always at the edge of the Left. By the middle 1940s, as we shall discuss later, he made the classic noir film *Detour* (1945) and several equally dark films, with the participation of his Hollywood Red friends, en route to an obscure fantasy-horror series so strange and low-budget that he might properly be considered the prototype for Ed Wood, Jr., except that even when confined within sharp limits, Ulmer's talent and vision never flagged.[18]

Contrasting with Ulmer's Poverty Row independence, Irving Pichel, occasional actor and prolific director, Christian Socialist, and highly idiosyncratic artist, was one of those Hollywood figures who continued to work the system but also trod his own path. A pioneer in the earlier Little Theatre Movement that Emma Goldman had done so much to popularize, Pichel hailed from Pittsburgh, the son of the composing-room supervisor at a local daily. Struck by footlight fever, he had memorized the first act of *The Merchant of Venice* by age sixteen, and established Boston's Toy Theater before graduating from Harvard. Shifting to California, he experimented in theater for a decade and a half, mostly directing modernist dramas. He came to the attention of Hollywood through the Pasadena Playhouse, where in 1929 he staged the world premiere of Eugene O'Neill's rarely performed *Lazarus Laughed.*

From the studios' standpoint, Pichel was eminently workmanlike, capable of turning out film after film on time and at budget. (On the side, until the end of the thirties, he also casted nearly a dozen major and minor films guided by other directors.) But more like ex-Marxist Albert Lewin than any director except Ulmer, he often chose strange material that would have been unimproved B fare in the hands of others.

His first important directing job came when studio heads realized that the set for *King Kong* could be exploited for another, quickie feature. Pichel was ready to supervise the adaptation of Richard Connell's short story (adapted to film twice later) about a White Russian exile somewhere in Latin America who makes visitors into his prey, stalking them and promising release if they evade his pursuit for a day. *The Most Dangerous Game* (1934), codirected with Ernest B. Schoedsack, was a small gem of an action film resting upon a conceptual premise that many viewers must have missed. In the opening shipboard scene, protagonist Joel McCrea is a two-fisted American who exalts the struggle of the fittest in the human and animal kingdoms alike. He learns his lesson quickly from Count Zaroff—played with fiendish zest by Leslie Banks—and spends most of his screen-time defending fellow captive Fay Wray, a carryover from *King Kong,* including her jungle outfit.

According to later interpreters (or perhaps overinterpreters), the deeply troubled images displayed in early scenes of *The Most Dangerous Game,* from the protagonist's illness onboard and the presence of sharks circling the ship, recur repeatedly through the film, albeit scattered and disguised, at last sharpened in the climax as the two escape successfully and their dying captor falls from a cliff into the jaws of his baying hounds. That the spectator in the real theater "remains suspended between having empathy with and keeping himself detached from the spectacle" may or may not mark the sort of cinematic illustration of British psychoanalyst Melanie Klein's theories as these critics suggest.[19] But the extremely sophisticated Pichel and Schoedsack clearly had the idea of identifying protagonist and audience in some subtle fashion. The horror in Wray's eyes might be seen as a simple continuation of her similar charismatic victim status in *King Kong,* but the recoiling of her would-be savior McCrea at his own past (he suddenly realizes how the animals felt when he was chasing them, as the White Russian hunter prepares to close in for the kill) surely has a larger meaning. The horror belongs to us, to Homo sapiens and organized society, not to some outsized externality.

Thereafter Pichel was off and running: He charted thirty-five more films, including two low-budget biblical classics of the original Christian revolution (or failed revolution against the Empire, in his view) and a 1953 swan song, *Martin Luther,* bearing ample asides to inquisitional American McCarthyism. Most of his movies were standard studio fare, but he atoned with odd features in a half-dozen genres, from children's and sci-fi films to religious, social, and sexual allegories.[20]

Pichel's most elaborate film from any standpoint, including set, direction, and budget, or star power, for at least another decade, was the fantasy *She* (1935). Adapted from the H. Rider Haggard novel, it starred Helen Gahagan. A progressive-minded actress and the wife of Melvyn Douglas, she was later elected to Congress, then defeated through a compulsive Red-baiting campaign (joined to a Jew-baiting campaign against Douglas) decisive to Hollywood politics and to the future career of her opponent, Richard Nixon. Here, Gahagan plays "she who must be obeyed." Shot first in 1921 and again in 1963 as an African epic of the "white goddess," Pichel's fictional *She* has existed for centuries somewhere in the Siberian steppes, protected by slaves who seem curiously Polynesian and by a praetorian guard that bears a strong resemblance to displaced Cossacks. It was spectacularly weird, but unfortunately it lost money.

Although most of the rest of Pichel's work during the 1930s was strictly routine, here and there plots involving psychic phenomena allowed him some more territory approaching the surreal and supernatural. A Party member from 1937, two years later he reached for the heights of Christian Socialist sensibility with one of the strangest (and cheapest) biblical dramas on film, *The Great Commandment.*

An independent feature (from a budgetary standpoint, practically a subfeature) for Episcopalian-based Cathedral Films, *The Great Commandment* portrays with the barest sets and straightforward dialogue the tribal-sect Zealots of Biblical days severely oppressed by the Romans and on the verge of rebellion. The Roman commander (portrayed by Albert Dekker, a longtime progressive later to escape the blacklist by providing friendly testimony) arrives to announce the new tax schedules and to threaten dissidents with prison. Outgunned, so to speak, the villagers send an emissary to Galilee, where a new leader named Jesus may be willing to head up a massive rebellion. (He won't, but the commander martyrs himself for the new cause.) Pichel used only one cinematic trick in all of this: The Savior is the eye of the camera in the only scenes in which He appears, speaking and in effect narrating, but never seen.[21]

By contracting with Cathedral, Pichel achieved control over production, although Fox bought *The Great Commandment* for nearly $200,000 and held on to it for two years, intending apparently to dump it and to make a spectacular film along similar lines. As the war swept Europe, Fox abandoned the project after all, and Cathedral found the film's true niche: private screenings in churches, especially Episcopalian. Ahead for Pichel, beyond a series of sometimes sharp-edged war and home-front films, lay more fantasy (like *Mr. Peabody and the Mermaid*) and the use of religious metaphors (*The Miracle of the Bells*) to make social points. Going his own way within the system, Pichel never had a big hit, but managed many remarkable small moments.[22]

The leading contemporary secular or near-secular version of prewar pacifist-spiritualist yearnings was surely *Lost Horizon* (1937), based upon James Hilton's novel of the same name, with script contributions by Sidney Buchman. But *The Wizard of Oz* (1939) offered utopia from an entirely different and more obviously American angle. Wilder in its way than anything that Walt Disney had to offer, *The Wizard of Oz* has tempted generations of critics toward ever new interpretations of its meaning.

Hollywood had hardly seen a more troubled major production, especially with the advance promise of a story based on the most popular children's novel in U.S. history. From 1933 onward, after the success of *Alice in Wonderland* and Samuel Goldwyn's purchase of the rights to the *Wizard* story written by a turn-of-the-century best-selling Populist author, MGM was looking for a collection of stars to head a production. The smash success of Disney's *Snow White and the Seven Dwarfs* in 1937 made the literary *Wizard* a hot property. When MGM finally moved ahead, resolving to produce a high-prestige film even if no guaranteed money-winner, execs soon had Judy Garland (discovered a few years earlier in Los Angeles by one of Yip Harburg's intermittent collaborators) and the other actors who eventually made the film work. But the studio then ran through eleven screen-writers and three directors, approaching total collapse of the project when Harburg was brought in by associate producer Arthur Freed, himself a sometime lyricist.

Harburg, for all his zesty lyrical radicalism, had no particular sense of Frank Baum's original iconoclastic allegory, with factory worker (i.e., Tin Man) and farmer (i.e., Scarecrow) unable to unite and Democratic-Populist 1896 presidential candidate William Jennings Bryan only a cowardly lion full of windy rhetoric. But even absent this knowledge, Harburg was able to develop a covertly liberating (if also somewhat contradictory) story line that the final crew of director and screenwriters fumbled into execution. The narrative at last collapsed haplessly into the familiar conservative, no-place-like-home message typical for Hollywood films of every kind. But the ambiguous adolescent and perhaps also sexually ambivalent Dorothy would nevertheless experience a lifetime of adventure.

Harburg did it by proposing an integrated score through which the plot developed. The concept had been established on Broadway and in films a bit earlier, then temporarily dropped in both. The Fred Astaire–style musical meanwhile seemed to demand a return to song and dance as a break from the thinly plotted features. To make the more sophisticated formula work, Harburg synthesized previous script drafts and added his own dialogue. Despite the successful transformation of theatrical *Oklahoma!* into film in 1955 and a handful of other such musical spectaculars later, perhaps only fantasy could fully achieve this kind of integration, and for good reason: Almost never, right to the current day, has a lyricist again exercised such an organizing influence on a major production.

Not that his influence was anything like absolute. Harburg's proposed lyrics for the last third of *Wizard,* which would have been drastically less Manichean or sentimental and more whimsical, were rudely cut and the ending that he despised essentially slapped on. "Somewhere Over the Rainbow," bracketing his inventive intentions for the whole film, barely survived postproduction, but the middle forty-five minutes were great. "The Wicked Witch Is Dead" has the feeling of liberation that Harburg and his fellow Popular Front artists dreamed for a Europe free of fascism and for colonial citizens across what become known as the Third World, free of colonialism, both political and economic. Dorothy's companions, like her, actually on a fool's errand, nevertheless realize their own human potential, and so does she—after a silly and film-wasting chase scene. It's a message of hope in a darkening world. Harburg received credits only for "Lyrics by," but along with Harold Arlen he got the consolation of an Oscar for Best Original Song for "Somewhere Over the Rainbow."[23]

Harburg, like so many others, managed to make a dent in Hollywood's facade of clichés—if only a limited one. Abraham Polonsky observed laconically, in later years, that one of the great perennial left-wing discussions in Hollywood was: "Should I be in Hollywood, and should I be writing movies? Or should I try to make films apart from Hollywood that would in some way deal with the theoretical basis of why we are in fact in the Communist Party?" The answer was simpler and more demanding: "Filmmaking in the major studios is the prime way that film art exists . . . [so] there's only one thing to do: you try to make feature films for studios." This was definitely not "the best solution to an artistic problem" and it might "end in the total defeat of every impulse that the writer, the director and actor has." But in truth it was the only real choice, "and that is why so many people who became Communists in Hollywood didn't rush to go anywhere else."[24]

That observation might not be true always, but was certainly true of the historic moment when the Left was moving from the margins toward the center of the Hollywood picture, and from the incidental or "famous" writer on the occasional film to the explicitly left-wing writer whom a producer/director sought out for the kind of film that critics praised and audiences seemed increasingly eager to attend.

Slapstick and Its Relatives

Comic fantasy offered other dimensions, some of the richest that left-wing screenwriters (like other screenwriters) would ever tap, and yet with few exceptions it won the least critical respect. As various critics have observed, the Keystone Kops and vaudeville "blackout" style had origins quite different from the sophisticated dialogue humor of Donald Ogden Stewart: the old "world turned upside down" carnival and modern sideshow rather than the Reformation (later, Victorian) stage, each with their own traditions of subversion but distinctly different class-based sources of appeal.[25]

The slapstick style, so much in evidence during silent films, notoriously peaked in sound films at mid-decade of the 1930s. But this is only one way of looking at the issue. Antic behavior could be found in most musicals, and in the sidekick roles of the second (male) lead in Westerns. Just as important, leading stage comedy acts kept going in films: If Wheeler and Woolsey were finished and the Marx Brothers winding down by 1940, Ole Olsen and Chic Johnson, even the aging Stan Laurel and Oliver Hardy, had more films to do, while Abbott and Costello were at the beginning of an impressive cinematic run, and Martin and Lewis not far over the horizon. Physical comedy series heavily staffed from the Left, including the Bowery Boys, Henry Aldrich, Blondie, and nearly a dozen films about boxer Joe Palooka, had only just been launched at the dawn of the 1940s.

The less sophisticated of these films rarely allowed characters to slip out of their designated roles and deliver monologues to the audience (as Bob Hope did in the more literate and big-budget comedies and as George Burns was to continue on television, previewing the postmodern sitcom). But few viewers over age six could ever have taken the daffy characterization of Blondie and "Daggy" (or Joe Palooka and his blubbery perennial rival, Humphrey) seriously. Broad comedy, with or without the gender references, ruled the game. The star or stars engaged in a dialogue with the imagined crowd, laughing at themselves while laughing at the alternatively picaresque and (especially if upper class) pretentious characters in front of the camera.

Henry Myers, more novelist than screenwriter, had originally studied in Europe to become a composer. Back home in Depression America, he co-scripted *Million Dollar Legs* (1932), a sixty-four-minute feature directed by Edward Cline. His partner was German refugee Joseph L. Mankiewicz, a Screen Writers Guild pioneer who became a director and producer of note in later years.[26] The film offers a truly extraordinary series of laughs, most of them sight gags.

Usually considered just another W. C. Fields picture, *Million Dollar Legs* actually has Fields on camera irregularly, focusing attention instead on the bizarre qualities and trials of a Luxembourg-sized European nation, "Klopstokia." Fuller Brush–style American salesman Jack Oakie just happens to be there and falls for the king's daughter. Fields, as her father, rules literally through strength: He beats back contenders through repeated bouts of arm wrestling. But the country is flat broke in the Depression, and Fields's rule is about to fall to comically sinister plotters when instinctive promoter Oakie suddenly realizes Klopstokians can run faster and jump higher than seemingly possible, making them perfect for the upcoming Olympic Games in Los Angeles. Although not up to the political satire of the Marx Brothers' 1933 *Duck Soup* (whose "Freedonia" may have been inspired by "Klopstokia"), with mock wars and Groucho-style chatter, *Million Dollar Legs* has plenty of contemporary social satire. The plot disappears under the sheer weight of the gags, more varied and crisp than in the W. C. Fields films that follow.

The same script duo's *Diplomaniacs* (1933), from an original story by Mankiewicz, took the famous "back-flipping" vaudeville comedy of Burt Wheeler and Robert Woolsey to its highest political point. Here we have a more savage play on diplomacy, on stuffed shirts and contemporary international intrigue. The film's attack upon world leaders who claim to want peace but really want to continue the arms race and prospective conquest is pungent and unmistakable. Ultimately, the two hapless heroes return home convinced they have brought global amity, only to learn that they have been duped by a phony secret message. World war has broken out, and they have been drafted! As the film closes, they head off to apparent doom with the conspirators now as celestial (also heretical) beings. The working title abandoned was: "In the Red." Most unfortunately, Myers had no real chance to continue his fanciful, frantic style.[27]

A handful of other left-wing writers worked on thirties and early forties antic comedies as well. *Swing It, Professor* (1937), with original story, lyrics, and score by future *Blondie* writer Connie Lee, is a sort of third-rate *Horse Feathers* (1932) with an endangered college firing its music professor because he can't "swing" like the undergraduates. (He takes to the road, and erudite hobos show him the aesthetic meeting points of classical music and jazz: He becomes a hipster bohemian.)[28] The Marx Brothers' *Room Service* (1938), the last of their beloved 1930s cycle, was based upon the hit stage play by Groucho's friend Allen Boretz, another Hollywood Red. Labeled *"meshugina filosof"* by his family, apparently after the beloved literary creation of the same name by Morris Winchevsky (known as the "zeyde," or grandfather, of Yiddish left-wing journalism), Boretz had written several unsuccessfully staged farces until *Room Service* opened in 1937, closed, and reopened (on the initiative of production assistant Garson Kanin) to become a standard theater comedy with endless revivals. RKO paid a then-unprecedented $255,000 for the screen rights.[29] Boretz found his way to

Hollywood at once personally radical, well-to-do from his stage work, and a nonstop ad-libber who put his social intimate Groucho to shame.

The studios immediately turned the talented Boretz into a mere script doctor. Danny Kaye's first film, *Up in Arms* (1944), and Bob Hope's most surrealistically antiauthoritarian film, *The Princess and the Pirate* (1944), both owed considerably to his work.[30] So did *Room Service,* despite large changes from its original: Not only did many of Boretz's own gag lines remain, but so did the basic idea of a cast staying on hotel time and charging expenses like meals, day by day, flattering the manager and meanwhile making with the wisecracks.

Air Raid Wardens (1943), written in part by comedy novice Howard Dimsdale for the aging but still mobile Laurel and Hardy, and *The Daring Young Man* (1942), by the *Blondie* team of Connie Lee and Karen De Wolf, for bigmouthed Joe E. Brown, merged familiar gestures of their established characters into wartime antifascist themes. In both cases our antiheroes find themselves rejected by all branches of the armed forces, and after bumbling projects to defend the home front, somehow expose saboteurs and wind up as heroes. Laurel and Hardy can be charming as bicycle-shop owners, but Brown is best in drag, a hip grandmother who throws loaded dice in the old folks home.

Yet another wisecracking writer, the Marxist bohemian Gordon Kahn, was to script the first pairing of Roy Rogers and Dale Evans (*The Cowboy and the Senorita,* 1944) and wrote the first book-length account of the government attack on Hollywood (*Hollywood on Trial,* 1948). His costory for *World Premiere* (1941) was a farce too complicated to work, but it remains one of the left-written satires of Tinseltown life that criticized celebrity as silliness while ridiculing fascism and fascists.[31] *Buy Me That Town* (1941), a Runyonesque farce scripted entirely by Kahn, offered rather more. Despite its evident low budget and partly because of it, *Variety* called the film "one of the most entertaining B entries of the season," depicting the takeover of a Depression-ridden town by gangsters who save it after all.

Series work offered more steady employment, inevitably also more hack work. If the Three Stooges (known by wartime for their appearances at left-sponsored antifascist events and for urging the labor reform La Follette Seaman's Act) might be considered tenement-district Marx Brothers, the Dead End Kids in all their emanations were a stretched-out version of the Stooges. Never did such bottom-of-the-barrel material owe its origins to such serious drama as *Dead End,* written by Sidney Kingsley for the stage and adapted by Lillian Hellman into one of the dramatic set pieces of Depression Hollywood. The Dead End Kids, with more sympathetic impact upon audiences than Kingsley, Hellman, or director William Wyler expected (or even desired on behalf of these lumpen social by-products), became through a succession of names and cast changes over two decades the most prolific series in Hollywood history. Only the Three Stooges came close in total numbers and duration of short-features productions.

The kids' team had, however, first been relaunched, after *Dead End,* for serious melodrama. Building upon public reception to their mixture of urchin pathos and clowning, the kids (mainly actors Billy Halop, Bobby Jordan, Gabriel Dell, Huntz Hall, Leo Gorcey, and Bernard Punsly) made their mark as symptoms of social distress when *Angels with Dirty Faces* (1938), written by John Wexley, posed them as the descendents of James Cagney's youthful criminality. That same year, the best known of the young actors had already broken off to work at Universal as the Little Tough Guys (nine films between 1938 and 1943), and here they miraculously assumed the mischief-maker, heart-of-gold status for the various later emanations. Typically, these films open with a pan shot of the old Lower East Side, which already looked severely antiquated, streets crowded with pushcarts instead of cars, deeply proletarian (and often Jewish-looking) ethnic crowds jostling, and a musical background of an organ grinder's "Sidewalks of New York." They are evidently coming from an older world into modernity, if they make it at all.

No less a figure than young Carl Foreman broke into films with the second offshoot series, *East Side Kids* (twenty-two films, 1940–45) for the barely existent Banner Films (distributed by Monogram, a Poverty Row survivor), with *Bowery Blitzkrieg* (1941) and *Spooks Run Wild* (1941). The same farcical boys appear in *Live Wires* (1946) and *Hard Boiled Mahoney* (1946), both of these written by future noir specialist (and in exile, major British directorial talent) Cy Endfield.[32] By this time, and for the next decade, the now-renamed acting team didn't have much at all new, but they did have a steady audience.

The Bowery Boys in all their versions would be far too slum-like for the prime-time sitcomic television modes soon to arrive. But their series of films foreshadowed and surrounded several others that would need little to add to the stock of misunderstandings, pet (and horse) humor, and ridicule of petite bourgeois family, teen, home (or suburban) life already familiar to radio writers.

Actually, the Henry Aldrich series for Paramount, an effort to compete with the Andy Hardy series starring Mickey Rooney, was in spots very funny, even if reviewers occasionally complained that the moments of pathos (no doubt written by the left-wingers involved) might be too heavy for bobby-soxer audiences. British-born writer Val Burton, who began his career path as a military school official in England and ended the same way, running a Los Angeles academy while on the blacklist, was serious and sincere in his B efforts, making humor out of points about civil liberties and class privileges that television's Dobie Gillis would occasionally return to a decade later.[33]

Blondie, adapted from the comic strip, was more consistently funny and far more successful than Henry Aldrich, totaling some twenty-eight films, an undoubted precursor to *I Love Lucy* but rather daffier if less well-acted during its extended prime. After the first two entries, shot in the thirties, many of the rest were written by Connie Lee and/or Karen De Wolf, with topical references ranging from wartime women's units (*Blondie for Victory,* 1942) to new housing developments (*It's a Great Life,* 1943), but frequently revolving around Dagwood's dilemmas as employee/flunky of an architectural firm and the hopeless craving of Blondie for him to get ahead. In one of the best moments, *Blondie in Society* (1941), the advance into the local Smart Set is reckoned in terms of dog shows (but the family's borrowed Great Dane can only sing-howl in response to the melodic version of Joyce Kilmer's revered poem "Trees")![34] Released to television in 1966 and widely shown thereafter, the *Blondies* never get close to the burlesque of reality in true farce, but like *Henry Aldrich* nibble more at the edges than sitcomic television before 1970 was likely to go.

Joe Palooka marked several steps further downward in production quality, but with indubitably proletarian and reform themes apparently unnoticed, let alone censored, by Hollywood watchers. The series began near the bottom back in 1934, with Reliance Pictures fronting a cast including Jimmy Durante, Lupe Velez, and Stuart Erwin (as Joe the boxer), and writers Gertrude Purcell, Arthur Kober, and Jack Jevne (a good-natured pal of assorted left-wingers), about the son of a boxing champ who is talked into a series of choreographed mismatches before he comes to his senses and gets the girl. The Palooka series beginning in 1946 substituted veteran comic

Leon Errol for Durante, with assorted Hollywood Reds scripting the comic war against assorted special interests and respectable-looking crooks.[35]

The genius award of left-wing antic comedy must go to quarters and budgets distant from these. Robert Lees, a UCLA dropout, and Fred Rinaldo, a Dartmouth graduate who visited the Soviet Union with Budd Schulberg in 1936, together broke into the Shorts Department at MGM during the middle 1930s and there began writing for Robert Benchley. Their *How to Sleep* (1935) showed a perfect adaptation to Benchley's nervous and self-deprecating humor, the constant self-interruption of the heavy drinking, overweight, and anxious middle-class, middle-aged Manhattanite.[36] Sight gags and confused public conversation (as in their *A Half Hour for Lunch* for Benchley) further ridiculed claims of American-style self-improvement by demonstrating the average citizen's social incompetence. Lees and Rinaldo also wrote sports shorts, a mixture of semiserious instruction, health warnings, sight gags, and humorous asides.

Amid the Hitler-Stalin Pact, incipient Hollywood political-personality Lees followed his partner into the Party and quickly became a sort of local social chairman. By 1940, Lees and Rinaldo had begun furiously writing full-length scripts and looking for a breakthrough. Serious drama (an attempt to show what a millionaire's life was like if he lost his money and identity—*Street of Memories,* 1940) disappointed the pair, but then they fell back successfully into real comedy.[37]

The Invisible Woman (1941), a comedy-romance with Virginia Bruce and John Barrymore, had only about fifteen good minutes. But by playing upon the conventions of *The Invisible Man* (and, more directly, the Topper series of books and films), Lees and Rinaldo created revenge for the shop girl—accidentally rendered invisible—who can return the torment she and coworkers have suffered at her supervisor's hands. Bruce demands improvements of wages and conditions for her fellow workers and wins them, just before embarking on a wild trip that will, predictably, land her happily into the big boss's arms.

Their skill with gags set the writers' path for framing the routines of Abbott and Costello, to that moment perhaps America's most popular prole-style comics. *Buck Privates* (to which they had an uncredited contribution, 1941), *Hold That Ghost* (1941), *Hit the Ice* (1943), *The Wistful Widow of Wagon Gap* (1947), *Buck Privates Come Home* (1947), *Abbott and Costello Meet Frankenstein* (1948), *Abbott and Costello Meet the Invisible Man*

(1951), and *Comin' Round the Mountain* (1951) constituted most of the two comedians' top-grossing films and, with the possible exception of *Little Giant* (1946, from a story by Paul Jarrico and Richard Collins), their funniest as well.

Buck Privates was hardly more than a vaudeville show with Abbott and Costello bits around dance-and-song routines by the likes of the Andrews Sisters. Although Abbott and Costello had a modestly successful film support-role debut in *One Night in the Tropics* (scripted by Gertrude Purcell), they did not impress studio chiefs as big-timers. *Buck Privates* was consequently shot on the back lot at Universal for $180,000 in twenty days; for a studio in such serious financial trouble, the film might have never been made if the Andrews Sisters had not already been under contract and if Abbott and Costello had not been such current radio hits filling in for Fred Allen. Catching the moment perfectly for prospective draftees desperately needing a laugh, *Buck Privates* grossed more than $4 million and made the pair into highly paid screenwriters.[38]

Abbott and Costello were no Marx Brothers, but the perfect timing, the lovingly portrayed sexual ambiguity of Lou, and the constant sight gags were a match for anything else in the medium and the era. Indeed, Mel Brooks had only to add antiracist, sex, and bathroom gags earlier forbidden, along with a new generation of comic actors, including some African-Americans, to re-create the genre-satire form in his string of 1960s–80s hits.

Hold That Ghost stands as one of the best of the four Lees and Rinaldo originals, mainly because female lead Joan Davis is a comedy standout in her own right as a former radio star who specializes in screams. Only Costello's camera-hogging determination to limit Davis's comedic competition prevented the film from reaching its highest potential. More importantly in cinematic terms, Lees and Rinaldo had built into this film a decisive twist in film comedy: the horror burlesque. In retrospect, after decades of postmodern and camp treatments of the theme, it may seem that horror naturally tends toward self-satire. If so, the possibility had not yet been detected by 1940. Lees was to argue later that he had learned from the classics the intimate relation of comedy to tragedy, the opposite direction of the upturned mouth of the mask, embodying virtually identical elements and structure. By distorting the dramatic elements of conflict, character, and background through exaggeration or understatement, dramatic situations become horrific—or comical. In both, the role of the classic hero-protagonist is turned upside down. Even the technique of building the horror detail by detail had its mirror opposite in building the gag in the same fashion, to a crescendo; the shock of surprise served both equally. The power of *Hold That Ghost* rested, as do so many horror films, particularly on *anticipation.* Thus the audience, trained in ghost films, roars with tension-releasing laughter as Costello experiences what they would presumably experience, and then anticipates his astonishment at the accumulating shocks.[39]

Buck Privates Come Home had another quality most remarkable for the politically conservative comedians: the indignation and craving for revenge against their commanding officers that millions of ordinary GIs felt. It was viewed along with *The Wistful Widow of Wagon Gap* as the "return" of the pair who had never been away but lacked a big hit for several years, the more so because a financial shake-up had just created Universal-International Pictures. *Wistful Widow* remains the most artful satire on Westerns ever made, albeit with some rough competition from the various anti-Westerns of the 1960s–70s, when sexual romps became considerably less restrained. But never has there been a more hilarious tough cowlady than Marjorie Main, a real-life Hollywood lesbian who here plays the widow in question. Lou becomes sheriff of the outlaw-ridden Wagon Gap when he accidentally shoots into the air and brings down a notorious figure hovering on a roof. By a law of the West unknown elsewhere he thereby inherits the widow, and thereafter intimidates bad guys by threatening them with a photo of Main, destined to be the bride of anyone who should kill him.

The scene in which Lou compels a whole bar of boozers to follow his example of milk-drinking (a satire on *Destry Rides Again,* itself a satire on cowboy whiskey-swilling manhood) is a film classic. But the conclusion of *Wistful Widow* supplies the topper, for Lou in drag leads the women of the town upon the accursed saloon where the outlaws dwell, and in the name of decency he unleashes a brawl of the best silent-film quality. Leaving town (and the threat of marriage) like two cowpokes of endless films, the pair fade into the proverbial sunset, ready for another jibe at genre.

Abbott and Costello Meet Frankenstein (1948) with Lon Chaney, Jr., and Bela Lugosi (but ironically for the title, without the "real" Frankenstein, i.e., Boris Karloff) playing the Wolfman and Dracula, respectively, may be one of the wildest sound comedies ever made, in part because the creature-actors successfully play it straight; but also because the trusting Lou (in love with the scheming werewoman, Lenore Aubert, who pretends to woo this most unlikely suitor) comes within an inch of losing his brain for a revived Frankenstein's monster. Lowly shipping clerks in a museum, they accept a box containing Dracula (naturally, Lou spots Drac, while Bud refuses to believe such nonsense); meanwhile, the remorseful Wolfman pleads with the boys to lock him in before night when he grows fangs and develops uncontrollable wolfish appetites. The nonstop quality of the film—Lees later claimed that the director and other actors successfully reined in the megalomaniacal Costello, staying close to the script rather than merely providing a framework for the comedians to work their usual routines—is the secret of the film's greatest charms.[40] And the gags are great. Asked a question, Lou answers, "I'll bite," and Lugosi responds politely, "No, I will." Ineffectual and childlike in contrast to these superhumans, Lou somehow emerges unscathed, and remains so through endless Halloween reshowings of the film on television.

No future monster-spoof could go further conceptually, not even with levels of simulated live-action animation that filmmakers of mid-century could not envision. Lees later claimed that monster-film spin-offs suffered for years afterward, but Abbott and Costello went on quickly to make the last clump of their successful pictures as virtual "fright film" clones: *Abbott and Costello Meet the Killer Boris Karloff; Abbott and Costello Meet Dr. Jekyll and Mr. Hyde; Abbott and Costello Meet the Invisible Man;* and *Abbott and Costello Meet the Mummy.* None of them had the coherence of their *Frankenstein.*[41]

Lees and Rinaldo managed one other outstanding comedy. Ole Olsen and Chic Johnson finally got the script they deserved in *Crazy House* (1943), one of those films so full of surrealistic material that it became fodder for the late-night campus cinema of the 1970s, watched alongside certain Betty Boop cartoons such as *Minnie the Moocher* with marijuana-filled enthusiasm. In *Crazy House's* opening, as part of a spectacularly strange Hollywood parade, Olsen and Johnson, who are forbidden to enter the studios because of the ruckus they have caused in past films, have themselves shot from a cannon into the office of a Poverty Row studio ("Miracle Pictures—If It's a Good Picture, It's a Miracle"). The secretary there calmly tells them that the producer is too busy to see them—until she recognizes

the pair and literally jumps into her desk. And so it goes, as full of refer-
ential fun as anything ever to be made on the lots.

Lees and Rinaldo had still other interesting films ahead, like *Holiday
in Havana* (1949), Desi Arnez's debut feature, where a nationwide mambo
contest brings an American-raised girl back into the heart of Cuban culture
(the film set up Lees and Rinaldo to script *I Love Lucy*—until the blacklist
knocked them out of television comedy).[42] But by that time, the era of proletarian humor had already passed. In the Martin and Lewis vehicle *Jumping
Jacks* (1952), from a Lees-Rinaldo wartime script intended for Abbott and
Costello but postponed until another duo took center stage amid another
war, Jerry's persona was merely childish and regressive, neither mentally
bruised grifter nor hopeless hick. Meanwhile, the Stooges—luckily escaping investigation and blacklisting—had Moe and Larry hanging on with
new partners near the end of a low-paid career of shorts that closed in 1957,
with an almost infinite (for the stars, unpaid) return via local television. By
this time, reruns must have looked to suburban kids like they came from
some other century.[43]

Out West

Westerns occupied a different sort of fantasy, however riveted they may
have been to a kind of cinematic pseudo-realism. The "historic" Western
depicting pioneer scenes had usually emphasized the "winning" in "Winning of the West," with Indians, bad men, and other black-hatted types
temporarily blocking the path of honest and productive development. The
Popular Front's leftward tug at New Dealism prompted instead a Populist
interpretation, hinged upon the theft of the "people's land" by the railroads, the bankers, and their criminal and/or political allies.

Robin Hood of El Dorado (1936), coscripted by erstwhile playwright
Melvyn Levy, offered a grand and predictive exception: Chicanos driven off
the land they had settled (with as little discussion as possible of the Indians
previously deprived), their families murdered, creating a heroic outlaw
band whose leader reluctantly chooses force only because he has been deprived of any alternative. In this romantic evocation of the real-life bandito
Joaquín Murieta ("the murderer who murdered the murderers and died for
our honor," in the real-life musical verse of the Mexican-American *corridos*),

Murieta comes to rob a banquet of the Mexican-American elite, finds them impoverished, and adopts the beautiful daughter of a leading figure as his lover and fellow leader. The scenes of his hidden outlaw band in celebration are among the most positive seen in film about Mexican-Americans to this time. The Anglo vigilante slaughter of every single Chicano that follows can only be described as gruesome evidence of the emerging Anglo rule.

Robin Hood of El Dorado was a distinct exception (if not quite the only one) in its admiration for Chicano culture, and even the sympathetic treatment of Indians (so marked in the post-1948 modern Western and written, for decades, most effectively by surviving left-wingers and their friends) remains rare in a B genre of predictable heroes, laughable sidekicks, and unkissed women.[44] But during the late 1930s, Republic Studios of low budgets and straightforward patriotism fostered a reconfiguring of the socially conscious, collective heroes on other grounds. A new Three Mesquiteers series, mainly scripted by later friendly witness Stanley Roberts, finds John Wayne on the job in his first major screen role. As Stony Brooke, he generally pretends to be an outlaw (or is forced to take cover after unjust accusation), revealing his true status in the final reel.

In *Pals of the Saddle* (1938), the first of the series, the United States has just signed the Neutrality Act, making the war-related mineral substance monium illegal to market abroad. A comely secret service agent in disguise draws the Mesquiteers into a series of disguises and intrigues, until they stop the smugglers at the Mexican border, aided by the U.S. Cavalry (!). Likewise, *Red River Range,* made later that year, has Wayne and his pals discovering, after they are deputized by a state attorney general, that the town banker has set up a conspiracy to steal horses.

Those *Heroes of the Hills* (1938), another in the series (but without Wayne this time), help a jailbreaker who has fled because his lungs cannot stand the prison atmosphere. The Mesquiteers, New Dealers all the way, propose that the prison relieve its overcrowding by rendering convicts into trustees who can work usefully on nearby ranches and on rebuilding the prison itself. In the end, prisoners are more honest than the men who intend to make a fortune on the prison system—surely a lesson for the future.[45]

Roberts's scripts had effectively forecast the screenwriting of Morton Grant, Louise Rousseau, and a handful of other B writers for the 1940s Western genre, itself a forecast of the "dark" Western or "anti-Western" of liberals and left-wingers in the era to follow. Indeed, Grant already had written a lively B film, *Timber Stampede* (1939), pitting lumber barons against honest town folk. No wonder the FBI, a few years later, reported warnings of an industry informer that a suspicious tone had entered the seemingly innocent format, locating "a villain in the character of the local banker, crooked rancher with money or other capitalist always behind the plot to rob the ranchers, rustle cattle, prevent farmers coming into the country . . . etc."[46] In *Colorado Sunset* (1941), written by Roberts for Gene Autry, the FBI is still very much on the right side, with the patriotic Gene and Smiley Burnette in tow, exposing a radio station owner and mean-spirited capitalist not at all surprisingly seeking to transmit secret messages to German agents.[47]

Occasionally, such Westerns reached higher levels. Future Hollywood Ten producer Adrian Scott as screenwriter and familiar Hopalong Cassidy producer Harry Sherman managed a remake of *The Parson of Panamint* (1941), a gem among forgotten horse-opera social melodramas. A minister has been invited into the virtual ghost town, formerly a mining center ruined years earlier when an underground river flooded the mine. The town dignitaries predictably turn against the parson when he embraces the dregs of local society, including the saloon singer/prostitute.[48]

All this straining toward social significance followed logically what Julian Zimet was to describe in *The Screen Writer* as the "severe limitations" of the cowboy film. A loner against the collective energy represented in the outlaw gang (or the respectable folk who wrongly mistrust him), the guy in the white hat earns success simply because his heart is pure—a socially bad message for the viewer to follow, because the explanation for personal failure must logically be self-caused. And yet, even in the average Western, "right is more frequently on the side of the poor than on the rich," reflecting a long national history of "little people" against the powerful.[49] Zimet surely exaggerated the virtues of the average Western, especially in regard to Indians, but it's true that, often enough, the sheriff is seen as crooked and the politicians as well, so that decency can't be won without a fight. Or at least this lesson managed to make it via the conventions of what might be called Capraesque or "little guy" Westerns made for ten years or so from the middle thirties onward.

It was a concept easier to use than to explain. Only as recently as 1935 had poet-critic Kenneth Burke, a highly unorthodox left-winger, put forward in an American Writers Congress session the notion that for American life and politics the proper nomenclature was more likely to be "people's culture" than proletarian culture.[50] That this proposed readjustment arose at a Communist-led intellectuals' event cannot be separated from the arrival of the People's, i.e., Popular Front, and the turn toward liberal and middle class "allies" against fascism. But the issues involved ran considerably deeper, down to the structure of the script and the role of the screenwriter as self-conscious producer of a worthy if not necessarily dignified cultural creation.[51]

The trajectory of the socially interesting "A" Western allowed the writer to rise to a higher artistic level. Not only did it offer bigger stars and budgets, a definite issue for the presentation of Big Sky Country and perhaps location shooting, but also the prospect of working out themes with a complexity that the B westerns usually avoided. The Popular Front years thereby opened a window of opportunities that Western fans of earlier and (especially) later years did not often recognize. Thus the later conservative drift of director John Ford's work, particularly in the absence of Dudley Nichols's progressive scripts, appears more obvious in retrospect because Ford steadily turned rightward from the early populistic Will Rogers features and the radical-liberal *The Informer* (1935), *Young Mr. Lincoln* (1939), and *The Grapes of Wrath* (1940), to the Capraesque and cinematically brilliant *Stagecoach* (1939) to the working-class-sentimental *How Green Was My Valley* (1941) to the distinctly conservative-patriotic (and racist) *Fort Apache* (1946) and *She Wore a Yellow Ribbon* (1949), the neocolonialist *Mogambo* (1953, actually an Africa-set remake of the earlier *Red Dust*), and beyond.

Destry Rides Again, appearing the same year as *Stagecoach* and also hailed by contemporary critics, is altogether different if equally "mature." A story of refugees in old California, written in the new California by refugees from New York and Berlin, it is stylistically an invocation of the Western in the spirit of the Viennese social comedy, and the Berlin cabaret film that featured Marlene Dietrich (her casting possible because of a severely reduced salary, thanks to several recent bombs) as the demimonde diva. The very improbability of this consummation and a peculiar genius for satire have set *Destry* apart as a film virtually impervious to criticism as it has been to imitation.

Destry producer and Jewish refugee Joe Pasternak, who turned out many bedroom comedies in both the Viennese- and Doris Day–style over his long careers in Berlin and Hollywood, drew upon a story by a Western pulp writer using the nom de plume Max Brand. The novel had been shot humorlessly in a 1931 version starring Tom Mix that looked almost exactly like all the other Tom Mix films. Something drastic had changed by 1939.

In the novel, Tom Destry is a roustabout in the town of Wham; a hard worker and hard drinker who is framed for a train robbery and returns from six years in prison to track down and kill the twelve jurors who sent him there.[52] Pasternak turned to a couple of left-wingers for the dialogue, Gertrude Purcell and Henry Myers. Purcell was the more predictable of the two, a jack-of-all trades in screenwriting who had moved to Hollywood in 1930. Thereafter, she seems to have been called in when the producers or directors wanted someone skilled at transforming stage matter for the screen or to make certain that the female characters would be rounded out, as with *In Old California,* a 1942 near-remake of the *Destry* plot, where Purcell has a woman take down her washing by shooting the clothespins off the line. Purcell succeeded most famously with *Stella Dallas* (1937), a box office bonanza of virtuoso masochism. A political naif only briefly in the Party, she would name Myers in "friendly" testimony.[53] But she was just right for *Destry.* In the novel, the jurors who are afraid of Destry's return literally head for the hills in fear after shopping for killers who can take care of him while they are gone. To lure them back to Wham (aptly changed to "Bottleneck" for the film), Destry puts on an act of servility and deference that earns him the contempt of everyone around him—until the reassured jurors start to show up to push him around again. They pay for this delusion with their lives, as he reasserts his confidence and his skill with revolvers.

But his meekness also has a larger purpose. In many gestures, particularly in his refusal to wear sidearms and his preference for moralizing to the citizens by anecdote, the new deputy sheriff is shown to be a man of ideas, a modest government official whose understanding of the law contains a view of society that is subtly subversive of the corrupt current power holders. Not even the best of previous left-wing cowboy films has anyone like this. His careful outbursts of civic anger and indignation should be seen as metaphorical but unapologetic defenses of the New Deal, antifascism, and, until the last possible moment, downright pacifism. This is, indeed, the classic displacement of the Marxist intellectual in Hollywood films, one more often made into the figure of the graying doctor (or defrocked professional) with a German accent and played by Paul Lukas.[54]

The possibilities in this remarkable character were seized upon by a gifted and young Jimmy Stewart, fresh from shooting Sidney Buchman's screenplay for *Mr. Smith Goes to Washington,* and still evidently wrapped up in the considerable moral authority of that role. Even though *Destry* is consciously played for satire, notably on familiar Western plot features (as when the women of the town take up their revolutionary rolling pins at the same moment as Destry accepts the necessity of strapping on his guns), Stewart plays his role entirely straight, in homespun Mr. Smith fashion.

Still, the real hero is the collective. With a team of German refugees and sympathetic American leftists, Pasternak was apparently ready to realize a mythic town so crammed with economic refugees that virtually from beginning to end their faces spill into every corner of the screen. In the saloon/cabaret that is the real home of this crowd, even during a Homeric brawl between Dietrich and Stewart, virtually every shot contains at least five other faces and often as many as fifty, filled out to the corners of the frame like lily pads in a Monet. The sound of this crowd's laughter becomes Destry's true orchestral score.

Very few films of the era had offered a righteous gathering not as a dangerous mob but as the true voice of American democracy. *Destry* was indubitably the first high-budget feature in which a kind of collective subjectivity would be presented first in the raucous laughter of the crowd, next in the action taken by the men, and then reasserted uproariously by the women whose action make it a social story, at last leaving the fate of the stars to the side, a virtual footnote. That something else new to American films was also afoot becomes apparent from the start, when the score quotes with sarcasm a few clichéd bars of music familiar from juvenile Westerns, and then pushes enthusiastically into the social life of the scene, spinning through the bar like the Viennese characters in a Siegfried Geyer flirtation comedy.

Complete with Geyeresque wisecracks (now spat with tobacco juice rather than pronounced around elegant cigarette holders), it is as though Viennese society had traveled to Berlin to acquire a cabaret pallor and an apocalyptic sense of humor before moving on to the rustic West. Costar Dietrich epitomized the spirit with her signature tune, "See What the Boys in the Back Room Will Have," so self-stylized (or self-caricatured) that it became one of the all-time favorites of drag queens, marking an odd gay connection with the differently fanciful *Wizard of Oz* (leading to the fifties bar-entry line, "Do you know Dorothy?").[55]

More than a little of the magic of *Destry* was due to good luck of studio talent and literary rights at hand, but it was no political accident. Pasternak soon revealed his penchant for what cynics called "Popular Front kitsch" (in some key respects, above all Jewish ones, a precursor in stylization to what other cynics, a half-century later, would call the "Holocaust kitsch" of liberal descendent Steven Spielberg among others): pro-Russian wartime films that included the stagey musicals *Thousands Cheer,* written by Lester Cole and Paul Jarrico, and *Song of Russia* (by Cole, Jarrico, and Guy Endore). *Destry* was simply the best of the lot.[56]

MGM's *Honky Tonk* (1941) is the other undiscovered political gem of the reimagined horse opera from literalist oater to a finely tuned and ironic work of art. Its main screenwriter was Marguerite Roberts, already a veteran writer who would go on to log a dozen years at MGM as screenwriter for many of the biggest stars. She had her real breakthrough in the backstage musical *Ziegfeld Girl* (1941), the antifascist *Escape* (1941), and, most definitely, *Honky Tonk.*[57] Roberts and her Marxist novel–writing third husband, John Sanford, collaborated for the only time, engaging the themes of what has been called the "outlaw" Western, counter to the "town tamer Western" in the familiar literary-scholarly usage. If the hero Destry overcomes the criminals who impose injustice through empowering the decent folks, in *Honky Tonk* the outlaw takes on the sources of injustice (most especially the railroads) that parade as the agents of progress, dissecting the corruption of the entrepreneurial character and the thrall that it has imposed on local government.[58]

A little outlaw context helps here. The most common of the outlaw Westerns, the Jesse James cycle, saw no less than fourteen features devoted to the famous enemy of the railroads. These include a Republic serial co-scripted by later friendly witness Sol Shor, and the small-budget Samba Productions' *Man from Texas* (1947), whose social-minded bandit wins back an alienated wife and sings tunes written by Earl Robinson.[59] In *Honky Tonk,* slick promoter Clark Gable uses his wit and charm to take over a gambling house of a small Western town, then resolves to take over the entire town as well, running and winning a mayoral election and using the people's taxes to complete his empire. From his point of view, the deal is more than fair. After all, he returns a portion of the tax money to the people in the form of schools and health care. As the head of government, he realizes that people are entitled to some kind of cut (most real-life American officeholders would grant no more). When the citizenry grows restless, even rebellious, he does not hesitate to call his new buddy the governor and have the equivalent of the National Guard ordered in to protect his dirty operation, much as city bosses have used public officials and police to overturn undesired election results and guard against unwanted consequences.

Honky Tonk is about as candid as Hollywood would ever become on issues of class, and as critical an analysis of the true character of politics and government as any Western ever made. Unlike the popular critique of demagoguery made repeatedly during the Cold War–era (the first time by Robert Rossen's award-winning *All the King's Men,* in 1949), Roberts and Sanford went deeper, beyond easy individualist moralisms. The charming gangsters and their corporate partners at the head of government in *Honky Tonk* do not despise democracy, as a fascist or even as a demagogue might (whatever the rhetoric); they merely find it an inconvenience, and sweep it aside without much thought.

To take this energizing idea one or more steps further, from the salability of socially relevant scripts to the understanding of why a good script was good artistically as well as politically—in any genre, the less realist the more difficult to analyze in familiar terms—demanded something that most left-wing Hollywood writers only intuited. Such issues appeared clear in retrospect, if at all. But they could not be avoided for much longer.[60]

Perhaps the famous bundle of critical Modernist observations formulated by the brightest minds of Greenwich Village of the 1910s could not have been refashioned as left-wing cultural theory until a newer social movement took definitive shape among a succeeding generation of American intellectuals. No doubt the aesthetic schematism of the Communist Party (likewise of its political competitors, with few exceptions) failed to advance the radicals' critical effort and as much as invited aestheticism, a demi-European literary high culture to offset vulgar *Homo Americanus,* with Hollywood as the worst example. But by an enormous paradox, it was only Hollywood Communist intellectuals—often acting at first quietly, privately, to think through the issues while presenting a brave public front of complete and unflinching agreement—who were best placed to forge ahead with the notions of what modern intellectuals in touch with the cravings of ordinary Americans for entertainment could do, and how they could do it.

Unbeknownst to American leftists, Walter Benjamin, in his writings of the late 1920s and early 1930s, had most astonishingly warned that the anonymous materials of daily life, not excluding technological developments, were more likely than "culture" (in the old uplifting but also class-bound sense) to bring forward the possibilities of real freedom. As a post-blacklist Abraham Polonsky looking back to childhood would hail the "kitsch, in childhood, in storytelling, in the rubbish of paperbacks and sitting under the streetlights," Benjamin proposed that humanity could outlive "the traditional, solemn, noble image of man, festooned with all the sacrificial offerings of the past."[61] The wild and playful cinematic adventures of the late 1930s and early 1940s, unanticipated and not even particularly desired, nevertheless marked the road toward that end.

1. See Dennis Dooley, "The Man of Tomorrow and the Boys of Yesterday," in Dennis Dooley and Gary Engle, editors, *Superman at Fifty: The Persistence of a Legend* (New York: Collier Books, 1988), 19–34; "The Age of Wonder," an interview with David Lasser, by Eric Leif Davin, in *Fantasy Commentator* 4 (Fall 1987), 4–25; and Frederik Pohl, "The Futurions," *Encyclopedia of the American Left* (New York: Oxford University Press, 1997, Second Edition), 251. Personal thanks go to Pohl for correspondence about his early days in the Young Communist League.

2. "Introduction" to interview with Julian Zimet, by Patrick McGilligan, in Patrick McGilligan and Paul Buhle, *Tender Comrades: A Backstory of the Hollywood Blacklist* (New York: St. Martin's Press, 1997), 724.

3. Lary May's *The Big Tomorrow* (Chicago: University of Chicago Press, 2000) is the most recent claimant of this perspective.

4. Nichols's work is discussed below, in Chapters 4, 5, and 6.

5. One more extended claim might be made: that Nichols's writing influenced John Ford to seize Populist themes in films like *The Grapes of Wrath* and *How Green Was My Valley,* which Nichols himself did not write. See May, *The Big Tomorrow,* Chapter 2, 54–100, for the best statement of the "radical 1930s" view of film that May cannot, however, sustain on the basis of the evidence.

6. See David J. Skal, *The Monster Show: A Cultural History of Horror* (New York: W. W. Norton, 1993), 94–114; and *The New York Times* review, Mordaunt

Hall, "Reviews," December 5, 1931; see also the perceptive comments on *Frankenstein* by noir scholar James Ursini, in "Noir Science," *Film Noir Reader 2* (New York: Limelight Editions, 1999), edited by Alain Silver and James Ursini, 226–27.

7. "Reflections of Guy Endore" (interviewed by Joel Gardner), Oral History Program, UCLA, 1964, 55.

8. David A. Cook, *A History of the Narrative Film* (New York: W. W. Norton, 1996 edition), 295–96.

9. Denis Gifford, *Karloff: The Man, The Monster, The Movies* (New York: Curtis Books, 1973), 44.

10. Skal, *The Monster Show*, 135–45.

11. *King of Paris* was Endore's best-selling novel. He also wrote *Babouk*, a historical novel about the uprising of slaves in eighteenth-century Haiti: See "Reflections of Guy Endore," 57, 67–78. In *The Raven*—nominally based upon Poe's poem, and to which script Endore made an uncredited contribution—the petty criminal played by Karloff is promised a new face by brilliant but mad surgeon Bela Lugosi, who cackles while Karloff, gun in hand, pathetically fires at mirrors all around him as he sees the disfigured creature staring back. This rare, authentically surrealist moment of film is followed by the doctor's obsession with a beautiful singer (whose act includes an almost incredible episode of playful appeal to the dark forces through song-and-dance) played by Irene Ware.

    Mad Love—a remake of *The Hands of Dr. Orlac*—was closely adapted from F. W. Murnau's 1924 silent feature, with Endore as coscripter, and followed the same plot line. This time Peter Lorre is the genius humanitarian surgeon (we know because he saves children from lives of helplessness) who attends every performance of a cheap horror drama in which the apparently tortured protagonist howling out her pain is a stage actress played by Frances Drake. That agony, we immediately see, is his ecstasy. The play's run is about to close, and he learns she will abandon the stage for marriage and children. Lorre even attends a reception for the happy couple, seizing the opportunity to kiss her full on the lips. She turns him away with repugnance and a degree of fear, only to plead with the doctor, soon after, for his help for her pianist-husband, Colin Clive, whose hands have been crushed in an accident. Lorre pretends to give him the hands of an executed murderer, and as in so many subsequent horror films, the victim finds himself drawn by compulsions of apparently out-of-control body parts. However improbable in plot, the movie is brilliantly directed by German refugee cameraman Karl Freund, and Lorre, in his first American film, gives a bravura performance. Himself an antifascist refugee of left leanings as well as a famous depressive and heavy drinker (often with Humphrey Bogart), Lorre would continue to play the same role repeatedly, if in more subdued fashion; his hooded eyes, the center of the visual narrative as he looks out repeatedly from behind curtains at Drake, extend and transform the gaze of Lugosi's Dracula, becoming at once more pathetic and more human.

12. Among others of the same stripe, *The Black Room,* scripted by Henry Myers and forgotten blacklistee Arthur Strawn, is often praised for its under-statement and consequently for Karloff's performance, one of few post-*Frankenstein* outings where the talented actor did not seem commanded to overact. A medieval doubling exercise, the film has a good brother/bad brother division of nobility plotting against itself and the very idea of virtue. Shot with the kind of visual symbolism of romance-and-ruins that Gothic writing had made its forte, *The Black Room* evoked the power of past sins to catch up to evildoers who cannot escape the consequences. The original story was by Strawn, whose later pre-blacklist credits include several sci-fi films.

13. Skal, *The Monster Show,* 190–95. The original story had Lugosi's character committing suicide after revealing the incestuous relationship; the actors balked when director Browning announced the gimmick ending, but of course had no hand in the final decision.

14. *The Devil Commands* (1941)—directed by neophyte Edward Dmytryk, who was destined to go to jail as a member of the Hollywood Ten and then turn on his former comrades—in a few noir-like cinematic innovations an advance over *Mark of the Vampire,* was in its plot and even more in its dialogue a rever-sion to the horror scare show. A scientist played by a very human, apparently rational and kindly Karloff, becomes obsessed with the old spiritualist idea of contacting a dead spouse. He wastes his savings and considerable reputation building a fantastic machine that could theoretically make it happen. Hiding away as a recluse with a former fake spiritualist (played by left-winger Anne Revere), he rushes toward self-destruction. Dmytryk, *It's a Hell of a Life But Not a Bad Living* (New York: Times Books, 1978), 53.

15. *Home of the Brave* was Robson's first major feature, *Avalanche Express* his last. In between, Robson guided several Paul Newman vehicles, including *From the Terrace* and *The Prize,* with strong social themes and possible "graylist" con-tributions.

16. Actually, Karloff was able to escape typecasting now and then on Broadway, and even more in television, where Hannah Weinstein, who produced *The Adventures of Robin Hood,* also produced a season of *Colonel March of Scotland Yard.*

17. John Belton, *The Hollywood Professionals: Howard Hawks, Frank Borzage, Edgar G. Ulmer* (London: The Tantivy Press, 1974), 149–180; astonishingly, this essay remains the only solid biographical work on Ulmer, though George Lipsitz—who staged an Ulmer Film Festival, with widow Shirley Ulmer on hand, in Houston during the 1980s—has an acute overview of the director's work in his *Time Passages: Collective Memory and American Popular Culture* (Minneapolis: University of Minnesota, 1990), 194–207.

18. The all-black *Moon Over Harlem* (1939) was a Popular Front–style melodrama with a reformer pitted against mobsters. See Chapter 7 on some of Ulmer's 1940s films. Among the strangest and most remarkable of Ulmer's later features is *The Naked Dawn* (1955), written by Julian Zimet (as "Julian Halevy") and based on a short story by Maxim Gorky. It is as flawless a film as Ulmer ever made, and among the most daring, an unlikely German-Russian-Yiddish Western, set in Mexico, that measures the promise of love and revolution against their mutual failures. *Beyond the Time Barrier* (1960), an anti-nuke feature with half-human creature-victims of radiation poisoning in a grim future, was followed by *The Cavern* (1965), from a Dalton Trumbo script, allegorically assaulting the four-power occupation of Europe during the Cold War.

19. See, e.g., Francesco Casetti, *Theories of Cinema, 1945–1995* (Austin: University of Texas Press, 1996), translated by Francesca Chiostri and Elizabeth Gard Bartolini-Salimbeni, 168–69. Casetti is here interpreting the writings of the French critic T. Kunzel during the 1970s.

20. See Chapters 5, 6, and 8 on Pichel's later work, as director and critic.

21. See Chapter 6, and *AFI Catalogue, Feature Films, 1931–1940 II* (Berkeley: University of California Press, 1994), 1298–99.

22. In 1940, Pichel made the curiously spiritual *Earthbound,* cowritten by John Howard Lawson (based on a short story by Basil King). As a Parisian couple begin a mountain-climbing vacation, a strange old man beseeches husband Warner Baxter to consider the workings of fate, warning him that his own time on earth is limited. After Baxter's character is murdered by a jealous ex-lover, his ghost protects his widow from conspiracy. As the film ends, he leaves the earth one last time, holding the tiny ghost of a dead bird in his

hand. Made as a silent feature in 1920, it appealed to the morbid instincts of audiences rightly fearing the worst ahead.

23. Harold Meyerson and Ernie Harburg, *Who Put the Rainbow in the Wizard of Oz? Yip Harburg, Lyricist* (Ann Arbor: University of Michigan Press, 1994), 119–160.

24. "Abraham Polonsky," interviewed by Paul Buhle and Dave Wagner, in *Tender Comrades,* 493.

25. See the observations of Mikhail Bakhtin, in *Problems of Dostoevsky's Poetics* (Minneapolis: University of Minnesota Press, 1984), translated by Caryl Emerson, 128–35.

26. Younger brother of Herman J. Mankiewicz and, like his brother, a *Chicago Tribune* correspondent in Berlin before Hitler's rise, Joseph broke into silent films at the end of the era and hit the ground running within the new system. Best remembered as a director (he broke in taking over from an ailing Lubitsch in the leftish *Dragonwyck* in 1946), his films include several credits with left-wing connections: *Escape, 5 Fingers, Cleopatra,* and, with Sidney Lumet, *King: A Filmed Record . . . Montgomery to Memphis.* As producer he worked still more often with lefties: *The Shopworn Angel, The Adventures of Huckleberry Finn, A Christmas Carol, The Philadelphia Story, Woman of the Year,* and *Reunion in France.*

27. Myers also supplied a cowritten story basis for *Merry Go Round of 1938,* scripted by Monte Brice and A. Dorian Otvos, with Bert Lahr among others in a backstage vaudeville comedy-romance. Information and insights about Myers has been most kindly made available to us by his cousin (also a future blacklistee), Norma Barzman.

28. *Swing It, Professor,* made by the independent Conn Features of Maurice Conn, starred Eddie Cantor radio show comedian Pinky Tomlin as the professor. Jerry Chodorov did the script for the exceptionally low quality production of the first Olsen and Johnson (whose stage hit *Hellzapoppin'* had a sort of standing Three Stooges appeal) Hollywood feature. *All Over Town* suffers from a hackneyed plot, but has a sourpussed Ben Blue and many extremely odd moments, some of the best of them with Sally, the Talking Seal.

29. Interestingly, the most notable revival of *Room Service* also marked the liberal Jack Lemmon's Broadway debut, costarring two blacklistees, John Randolph and Stanley Prager, and directed by another blacklistee, former screenwriter Mortimer Offner. Edwin Brommer, *The Encyclopedia of the American Theater 1900–1975* (San Diego: A. S. Barnes, 1980), 402.

30. Boretz was accorded an adaptation credit for *The Princess and the Pirate* and co-script for *Up in Arms*. Abraham Polonsky later suggested that he had proposed the character that Danny Kaye maintained throughout most of the actor's career, that of the characterful little guy or apparent coward.

31. As the film begins, a plot is hatched in Rome and Berlin (already, curiously, under bomb attack: The film was released in August 1941) to destroy a dangerous movie (*The World's on Fire*) being shot in Hollywood. Douglas Fairbanks, Jr., is brilliantly iconoclastic as the megalomaniac artiste producer trying to finish his film and attract attention to its premiere with outrageous publicity schemes, deterred but not quite defeated by narcissistic stars, studio hacks, and Nazi-fascist villains. In a year or two, critics would sound off against German and Italian spies who here seemed almost lovable in their silliness. The pace of *World Premiere*'s gags (escaped lion; hometown crowd ludicrously serenading a star who doesn't show; a stolen film print heaved improbably between two passing trains; and so on), all undercut by the uneven editing and direction, made a film that could easily have been better but, with many limitations, still had hilarious moments.

32. In *Bowery Blitzkrieg*, Leo Gorcey, the most appealing of the boys, has made up his mind to leave behind the life of low-level stickup crimes by becoming a boxing champ. This hope is doomed, but when neighborhood mobsters try to pull him back down to their level, he finds a tough cop (former gang member, played by Warren Hull) and social-reforming dame (Charlotte Henry) reaching out to the neighborhood ragamuffins like him, winning one soul at a time. *Spooks Run Wild*, Foreman's earliest screen credit, shows Bela Lugosi tilting toward self-satire as a magician (and Nazi collaborator) mistaken for a serial killer as the boys spend a night in his supposed haunted house.

Endfield was born in Pennsylvania, but, during his exile years, purposely threw off critics and film scholars by describing his origins as South African. Educated at Yale and the New Theatre League, in New York, he taught drama and produced for the stage, served in the Army Signal Corps, and established himself at the margins with the Bowery Boys and Palooka films before making several cherished noir films discussed in Chapter 8. In a post-1950 British exile, he first wrote under pseudonyms and then emerged as director. He formed a production company with Welsh actor Stanley Baker, and made films in a considerable variety of genres.

33. Typical Burton-scripted features like *Henry Aldrich for President* (1941), *Henry Aldrich, Editor* (1942), and *Henry Aldrich Haunts a House* (1943) had the ado-

lescent star Jimmy Lydon winning contests or class office, staging stunts or otherwise seeking to call attention to himself and win the favors of a potential girlfriend, but actually falling on his face in humiliation. The series ran to nine films, with Burton scripting or coscripting all but two, and all of them starring Lydon. The final Andy Hardy film, *Love Laughs at Andy Hardy,* aka *Uncle Andy Hardy,* had a story basis by another future blacklistee, Howard Dimsdale.

34. Penny Singleton, who played Blondie, is best remembered for her later role as unionist leading the Rockettes of Rockefeller Center out on strike in 1960.

35. Hal A. Chester, who produced the series for Monogram, went on to fame in the UK as film impresario of antic comedies, including *School for Scoundrels* written by but not credited to another American blacklistee, Frank Tarloff. The most frequent writer for the Palooka series was Henry Blankfort, cousin of a more successful left-wing screenwriter and future friendly witness, Michael Blankfort. Henry had a dozen assorted credits in low-budget comedy and drama, taking greatest pride in his theatrical work—but he also wrote one of the unremembered gems of noir, *The Underworld Story* (1950).

36. Lees and Rinaldo also wrote the following for Benchley: *A Night at the Movies, How to Be a Detective, How to Start the Day, How to Train a Dog, An Evening at Home Alone,* and *An Hour for Lunch,* along with more than a dozen shorts, including Pete Smith sports shorts with a modest degree of real instruction, safety tips for amateurs—and plentiful gags in a side monologue. Ironically, even as Lees and Rinaldo faced the blacklist, their patriotic civil libertarian documentary, *The Flag Speaks,* made much earlier for the Shorts Department, was still being shown in high school civics classes.

37. Interview with Robert Lees by Paul Buhle and Dave Wagner in *Tender Comrades,* 420–23.

38. Chris Costello, the star's daughter, with Raymond Strait, *Lou's on First: a Biography* (New York: St. Martin's Press, 1981), 62–75. With some embarrassment, the nominal author (or perhaps her amanuensis) describes her father's ardent sympathy for Joe McCarthy and avid support of the blacklist, but fails even to mention Lees and Rinaldo. Of all their writers, the comedians may have known only veteran gag-writer John Grant on a close personal basis. Grant, never especially political, broke with Costello in the early 1950s rather than sign the anti-Red loyalty oath that the comic himself circulated at the studios where he worked.

39. Robert Lees, unpublished manuscript [1980?], "Comedy," kindly lent to Paul Buhle by Lees, and drawn from lectures given in various Los Angeles venues from the days of the Political Education Center forward.

40. *Little Giant* achieved the same end more directly by separating the two, placing Lou as a hick and would-be salesman who falls for the sales methods on a motivational record, then bumbles continually as shyster-executive Abbott tries to manipulate him.

41. Interview with Lees by Buhle and Wagner, 1998; unpublished Lees manuscript, "Comedy." Howard Dimsdale wrote or coscripted *Abbott and Costello Meet the Invisible Man, Abbott and Costello Meet Dr. Jekyll and Mr. Hyde,* and *Abbott and Costello Meet Captain Kidd,* but his best work, apart from a script contribution to *National Velvet,* was surely *The Traveling Saleswoman* (1949) for Joan Davis, soon to be a minor-league (i.e., Dumont) network television star who singularly gave the fledgling Television Writers of America (TWA) a union contract for the *Joan Davis Show.* Refusing to submit its members to a loyalty oath, the TWA was forced out of business. See "Interview with Dick Powell," in Paul Buhle, *From the Knights of Labor to the New World Order: Essays on Labor and Culture* (New York: Garland Publishers, 1997), 239–48.

42. Lees was through in films, although he continued to display his talent for adaptation irregularly across the decades, in *Alfred Hitchcock Presents, Lassie, Flipper,* and *Daktari.* Rinaldo never worked commercially again, although rumors of his scripting later Three Stooges films circulated.

43. Left-wing writers and their allies, like Dick Powell, were still operating familiar blue-collar, military service, and supernatural themes for the moment, on a variety of these newer shows (including the best of them, *You'll Never Get Rich,* aka *The Phil Silvers Show;* the most inventive, *Topper;* and the most proletarian, *The Life of Riley*). But the frame for comedy had narrowed decisively. Jarrico wrote for Phil Silvers (who was "discovered" by Jarrico for *Tom, Dick and Harry,* and remained sympathetic to his left-wing pals; some said that Silvers's father had been a socialist) and for Nat Hiken, the *You'll Never Get Rich* and *Car 54, Where Are You?* producer who used assorted blacklistees on his shows. Frank Tarloff, the most successful of the television-writing blacklistees (and a close friend of Carl Reiner), delivered dozens of scripts under pseudonyms and his own name for *The Danny Thomas Show* and *The Dick Van Dyke Show.* See "Frank Tarloff," interviewed by Paul Buhle, in *Tender Comrades,* 648–50, for a useful discussion about radio and television writing.

44. Republic's *Rancho Grande* (1940) begins with Mexican-American children singing the regional-standard title song, joined by Gene Autry. The present-day plot, from a story coscripted by Connie Lee, has a tenderfoot brother and sister inheriting the ranch where Gene is foreman, and the predictable attempt by wrongdoers (led by a lawyer) to sabotage irrigation pipes. But the female lead, in the process of abandoning her Manhattan nostalgia for the West and Gene, serves as godmother for a newborn Chicana while a dignified Mexican-American priest gives the homily. The treatment borders on condescension but has no trace of racism: Chicanos are part of the hardworking and honest (almost cooperatively organized) ranch crew. The film ends with all the ranch hands and Gene's sweetheart backing him up as he sings "Rancho Grande," riding and exulting in the modern cowboy's life.

45. In a rather wild extension of historical fantasy, the Mesquiteers are about to be hanged when the female lead nearly reaches President Garfield with the information—a moment after he is assassinated! The sheriff, a quiet ally, has the accused killers "shot" with blanks. See the critical approval in "The Night Riders," *Variety*, April 5, 1939. *New Frontier*, released later that year in Wayne's final series appearance, even posed the rural environment against urban demands upon it. This time, the Mesquiteers, good agents of the federal government, help bring farmers in line with the creation of a reservoir and outwit the politicians who would have deprived the settlers of the benefits from irrigation. *Night Riders* (1939), described by *Variety* as Stanley Roberts's (and coscripter Betty Burbridge's) best effort, has the Mesquiteers defending ranchers thrown off their spreads by a phony land grant, thus endorsing modern Robin Hoods' conduct of fighting a guerrilla war against the land baron to expose false claims and win back their land.

46. *FBI Surveillance Files*, Reel 5, LA–100572, 37.

47. See Chapter 5, for Michael Wilson's Hopalong Cassidy features of the early 1940s.

48. See "The Parson of Panamint," *AFI Catalog: Feature Films, 1941–1950*, II (Berkeley: University of California, 2000), 1819; and "TMP," "At the Roxy," *New York Times*, July 26, 1941. Bernard F. Dick, *Radical Innocence: A Critical Study of the Hollywood Ten* (Lexington: University of Kentucky Press, 1989), 123, has a stirring rendition based upon Scott's role.

49. Julian Zimet, "Regarding the Horse Opera," *The Screen Writer*, 18.

50. This speech and dogmatic Communist criticisms of it have been discussed often in volumes and essays about the 1930s "literary wars," but Michael

Denning throws new light upon its significance in *The Cultural Front: The Laboring of Culture in the Twentieth Century* (New York: Verso, 1996), 102–04.

51. Burke went on to say that the middle-class intellectual "takes an interest in as many imaginative, aesthetic and speculative fields as he can handle—and into this breadth of his concerns interweave a general attitude of sympathy for the oppressed and antipathy toward our oppressive institutions." Quoted in Denning, *The Cultural Front,* 103.

52. The "story," actually an adaptation, was credited to Felix Jackson. The almost supernatural qualities of Destry were already in the literary original, as suggested by Richard W. Eutlain in his introduction to the 1979 edition of *Destry Rides Again* (New York: The Gregg Press, 1979), viii.

53. "Testimony of Gertrude Purcell," *Hearings, Infiltration of Communist Activities in the Los Angeles Area, Part 4, April 7–8, 1953* (Washington: Government Printing Office, 1953), 812.

54. The participating production group was full of antifascist exiles, if not exactly Marxists, including producer Pasternak, who was born in a corner of Transylvania, Hungary, in what was then part of the Austro-Hungarian empire.

55. There were other sexual touches as well. The Hays Office demanded that a near-final line be omitted: "There's gold in them thar hills," which Dietrich murmured as she stuffed gold coins into her bosom. Universal agreed to drop the line, but it reappeared in a print shown in New York, to the delight of audiences and further industry embarrassment. See *American Film Institute Catalog, Feature Films, 1931–1940, I* (Berkeley: University of California Press, 1993), 491.

   Pasternak was keenly aware that Dietrich had had a string of flops before she agreed to work in *Destry,* and her fee of $50,000 was considerably less than the figure that she had received earlier in the decade. See Clive Hirschhorn, *The Universal Story* (New York: Crown, 1983).

56. Universal's sequel *In Old California,* coscripted by Purcell and Frances Hyland, had an interesting plot of humanitarian Boston druggist John Wayne taming a Western town by curing an outbreak of yellow fever in a nearby mining camp, while being torn between a sincere if obviously weathered dance-hall girl and an upper-crust cutie. Another Republic feature that was a truer political sequel to *Destry* was *Three Faces West* (1940), with John Wayne manhandling a New Deal story line (albeit a humorless one) of dust bowl refugees moving determinedly to Oregon for a revitalized community life.

57. For more of Marguerite Roberts's story and her antifascist films, see Chapter 5. *Ziegfeld Girl* was coscripted with Sonia Levien, the most successful female Hollywood writer of the time.

58. See Richard Slotkin, *Gunfighter Nation* (New York: Maxwell-MacMillan, 1992), 379.

59. The serial *Adventures of Frank and Jesse James* (1949) has the brothers out of prison and reformed, but blackmailed by a banker to cooperate in another robbery. After much repetitive action—more than in an average Western—they outwit and outshoot their powerful enemy, prove to the skeptical that reform of outlaws is possible, and recover their good names in the process. Shor shared credit with three other writers, as in his other Republic serials. Although Jesse James is not specifically invoked in *Man from the West,* the tradition is unmistakable in the former highwayman who pledges his reform to a wife who will no longer accept her lot and then finds himself manipulated by unscrupulous bankers until he can take the heroic steps that finally clear his name. Robinson was famed for writing "Ballad for Americans," salvaged from a congressionally canceled Federal Theater show, sung by Paul Robeson on radio and adopted by the Republican Party for its 1940 convention. It proved more popular in wartime than Kate Smith's version of "God Bless America." Later, Robinson was blacklisted.

60. See Chapter 6 for the full discussion of the problems.

61. Walter Benjamin, *Selected Writings, II, 1927–1934* (Cambridge: Harvard University Press, 1999), translated by Rodney Livingstone, et al., edited by Michael W. Jennings, Howard Eiland, and Gary Smith; Polonsky quoted in David Thomson, *A Biographical Dictionary of Film* (New York: Morrow, 1981), 479.

Success, but at Any Price?
The New Deal Film and the
Marketing of the Popular Front

THE *PRESIDENT'S MYSTERY* (1936), written by Lester Cole and Nathanael
West, is occasionally described as an example of the most "political" film
that the Hollywood Left could get past the Hays Office and the studio
chiefs during the Depression.[1] It is better seen as a transition from an era of
hammering on the door of the Roosevelt coalition to one of providing some
of the chief artifacts of the Popular Front. That the transition was made almost unconsciously and often in lower genre features by screenwriters simply working at their jobs was remarkable enough. That many of these same
writers found themselves in high demand shortly afterward had been
hardly imaginable. Still others just arriving in Hollywood were able to
find work easily as the mood of the era shifted from depressed uncertainty
to antifascism and war. Previously disregarded (except where proven commercial successes) when not considered politically dangerous to the industry's profit levels, the screenwriters had become bankable and perhaps even
necessary.

The origins of *The President's Mystery*, save for a presidential detail, are
utterly nondescript. Republic, strategically located between Poverty Row
and the majors, was not created (to put it mildly) with any pretension to serious cinematic art or expectations of Academy Awards. A former executive
of the American Tobacco Company built up a film laboratory during the
1920s; in 1935, it merged with two small-time B studios, Mascot Films
and Monogram, forming Republic Studios. There, working on lean budgets and without big-name stars, the mystery and Western series and more
generally those top or bottom bill run-of-the-mill productions that *Variety*

called "actioners" could be shot within a week for less than $30,000. The very opposite of avant-garde, Republic successfully cultivated the conservative qualities and calculated the censorship potential of its major markets in the mostly small-town Midwest, south, and southwest.

But in 1935, Republic urgently needed more mystery melodrama films to fill its yearly schedules. Studio execs turned to a most unlikely source, an unsuccessful MGM writer named Lester Cole. Republic offered him $200 a week to leave the majors. Burt Kelly, the studio's mildly progressive producer, encouraged Cole to write *Hitch Hike Lady* (1936), an unusual combination of Depression road film and musical comedy about a woman who believes she has inherited a California orange grove and has all sorts of adventures driving from New York to California while entangled with quirky characters, scam artists, and gangsters along the way. For Republic, this was quality, and the film made real money. Cole persuaded the studio to hire his pal Nathanael West, the black-humored novelist who managed to keep working but hadn't had much luck in Hollywood.

During the first months of 1936, the editors of *Liberty* magazine coincidentally proposed to Franklin Roosevelt that if he gave the magazine the idea for a mystery, the publishers would hire a writer and call it "The President's Mystery." Approaching an election campaign that many were convinced he would lose, it seems Roosevelt actually came up with the idea (perhaps from real life, or from the fantasies of a brain truster) of a corporate attorney who becomes disillusioned with the life around him and vanishes from public sight. The resulting *Liberty* serial, penned by a half-dozen writers, was a literary hash. But Cole's producer knew a good thing (and a cheap one, at a $2,000 option) when he saw it. Cole and West, aided by a sympathetic director, Phil Karlson, set out to portray a factory town in desperate trouble, with unemployed workers rallying together, joining farmers, fighting the bankers—and realizing the implications of "the Roosevelt program," that is, putting America back to work.[2]

Only so much of the plot survives the inevitable centrality of the romantic element. Henry Wilcoxon as Wall Street lawyer who lobbies to block a New Deal measure that would have enabled shuttered factories to become cooperatives himself disappears from sight just as his adulterous wife is murdered. He turns up in a little town where he meets a closed canning plant owner's pretty daughter (played by Betty Furness), and at an emergency town meeting shows his change of heart: He outlines the cooperative solution to the local bankruptcy crisis. Together, the two mobilize the citizenry for a cooperative reopening with workers and farmers joining hands in production for use instead of profit. In real-life America, bankers were indeed shutting down such plants, and it was no great stretch to imagine them sending in thugs to stir up a riot to provoke repression and effectively end any such experiment. After a dramatic confrontation, of course, all here is resolved, including the murder mystery, and with it, the problem of how the boy and girl will get each other.

According to Cole's suspiciously apocryphal recollections, Republic's owner Herbert Yates, ordinarily indifferent to anything but the bottom line, took one look at the film and ordered "this Roosevelt commie crap" put on the shelf—if not forever, then at least until after the election. The mini-mogul had bet $200,000 on Republican Alf Landon and had no intention of endangering his own interests, either in particular or as a member of the capitalist class. When Roosevelt won in a landslide, the film duly appeared, made good money, and even won some critical praise. It succeeded in one more way: Within a year, Kelly had moved over to Universal and taken Cole with him.[3] Lester Cole was not destined to be either a hugely paid Dalton Trumbo or a hugely artistic Ring Lardner, Jr. But as the most prolific of all the Hollywood Reds (according to contemporaries, he was also the possessor of the largest ego of the crowd), he proved capable of turning out scripts at a ferocious pace, dramatically if not politically close to what the studios had in mind.

Son of a Polish-Jewish garment cutter, Cole (né Cohen) grew up in a tough slum neighborhood but also in a socialistic home atmosphere. He could remember his father on a soapbox, appealing for unionization and votes for Socialist Party candidates. After his parents divorced, his mother married a modest garments-trade capitalist, and young Lester nearly broke the matron's heart by ditching the dignified path of college education and a profession for pursuit of show business success. Striking a friendship with a left-leaning British film journalist in a Hollywood bookstore, he made his first contacts. After a series of blue-collar jobs and unsuccessful theatrical efforts, he worked as a screen reader and entered the big time, though none too successfully.[4]

His most interesting efforts in the years shortly after *The President's Mystery* came in an odd mixture of stories.[5] *Sinners in Paradise* (1938), directed by James Whale (from an original story by Harold Buckley, who collaborated on the script with Cole and Louis Stevens), has eight American passengers on a small plane successfully survive an emergency landing on a deserted Pacific island. Each has a seemingly good reason to leave home: an heiress who has left behind a strike at her Detroit factories (almost certainly a reference to the famed Flint sit-down strike of the previous year); a mobster and his moll on the run from the law; two munitions salesmen and the pious senator they are lobbying; a nurse fleeing her husband; and a matron on the way to visit her son in Shanghai. They learn quickly that only through cooperative living can they survive—a lesson that the senator is especially loath to grasp. The factory owner herself goes on strike against the assigned labor en route to learning sympathy for the working class, and others gain a variety of lessons about the need for commitment to positive change.

The House of the Seven Gables (1941) could be described as the most social-minded of the film adaptations of Nathaniel Hawthorne's works, and it was Cole's alone. Embroidering upon the radical threads in the original—the corruption of wealth epitomized in the phrase "Drink My Blood, John Marley!"—Cole dramatically changed the protagonist, Holgrave (played by Vincent Price, only rarely able to act out his own real-life progressive instincts), into an ardent abolitionist, his bête noire into a Northern-based slave trader. This Holgrave drove home the fruits of the family's evil, exploitative history and went to prison rather than lose his claim upon the better side of the American political legacy. If more than a few literary fine points were lost, much was gained in the process. According to Cole's account, the executives accused producer Kelly and Cole of sneaking radicalism into the film, a charge not entirely false. But the film was no more radical than Hawthorne's own sentiments, another case of the Hollywood Reds being more true to the original intent than any other screenwriters were likely to be.[6]

Among the Living (1941), subjected to murderous censorship from the Hays Office, should nevertheless be called one of the most radical (also modern gothic) tales of the prewar cinema. As the funeral of the wealthiest man in a southern textile town unfolds at the film's onset, mill hands stand outside the cemetery gates and recall his viciousness. The protagonist, son of the dead man, has returned from the north after twenty-five years, and he quickly discovers that the twin brother (both played by Albert Dekker) he was told had died in their youth is still alive, mentally incompetent, hidden away with the help of an elderly black caretaker. The truth behind the story is more shocking: His brother had been protecting their mother from the evil patriarch-capitalist's beatings. A murder, false accusations, a near-lynching by a rednecked mob (this scene considered particularly unacceptable by the New York Board of Review, fearing export of a film that would bring discredit to supposed American traditions of justice), and some doubling melodrama make up the plot, but class issues and others hinting at the decadence of contemporary southern society survived the cutting.

Cole had begun screenwriting early enough to suffer the extreme disillusionment of an Ornitz or a Wexley. But supremely workmanlike, and with no previous literary or stage success to compare his Hollywood career against, he soldiered on to his real moments of triumph after 1940. As it turned out, the war film worked perfectly for his action-oriented writing.

Meanwhile, *The President's Mystery* had set the stage more generally for what might be described as the dawn of the Social Drama, Hollywood-style. Among the other films that left-wing writers worked on in 1936, one could count *The Raven; Craig's Wife;* the widely praised *The Story of Louis Pasteur* (directed by William Dieterle, with contributions by Sidney Buchman), both *The Moon's Our Home* and *Suzy* (by the team of Dorothy Parker and Alan Campbell); *Road Gang,* by Trumbo, and a score of low-profile B mysteries and comedies. The following year saw, among others, *The Awful Truth,* by Buchman, *Dead End,* by Lillian Hellman, *Marked Woman* and *They Won't Forget* (both coscripted by Robert Rossen), *A Star Is Born,* by Parker and Campbell, *Stella Dallas,* by Gertrude Purcell, and a larger number of B films of all varieties. These offerings constituted the thin beginnings of a rush from 1938 on, fed by a growing network of personal contacts, the increased demonstration of talent by left-wing writers, and above all the emerging sense in the industry that moviegoers wanted to see the kinds of films that these writers scripted.

That the Hollywood of the later 1930s and of the early 1940s— leaving aside for later consideration the key antifascist and war-related films—fulfilled a promise of earlier genres is easy enough to demonstrate in a single case. The characterful but also vulnerable Katharine Hepburn protagonists of *The Little Minister* (1934) and *Alice Adams* (1935), both scripted in part by Mortimer Offner, flowered so magnificently in the hands of other left-wing writers in *Holiday* (1938), *The Philadelphia Story*

(1940), and *Woman of the Year* (1942), that nothing she did afterward could approach these accomplishments.

Women's films with such writers saw cinematically richer and often more sensitively crafted versions than ones by standard writers.[7] Crime films benefited less from theatrical borrowings but improved greatly as they gained character development and social complexity. Historical films often became more than mere costume dramas. Even children's films, especially those with loving animals on the scene, grew from sparse beginnings and sentimental exploitation to serious, memorable renditions of child characters in social themes. From the viewpoint of left-leaning writers, *this* was the beginning of Hollywood's true Golden Age, and it lasted a little more than a decade, marked at the very end by noir.

The years 1936–39 also dated the approaching conclusion of extended negotiations accepting the SWG and SAG as legitimate bargaining units, soon followed by the realization of the SWG's long-pursued goal to determine screen credits according to merit (or at least peer judgment) rather than studio whim. From a left-wing standpoint, if scarcely in Marxist terms, Hollywood was at last coming of age.

Thus did Ella Winter, redoubtable widow of Lincoln Steffens and wife of Donald Ogden Stewart, write in the fearful spring of 1939 that things seemed to be changing within the film colony. In a world of "artists . . . under fire" and "culture . . . being bayoneted," movies held a prospect of becoming at last "real," more truthful. This meant everything for the men and women turning out scripts.

Most screen writers who have any sort of conscience will tell you sad stories of things they have tried to do in pictures, scenes and situations they fashioned, dialog they hammered out, only to have it fail to get by director or producer. Writers have become in many instances office boys, copy readers, glorified stenographers for some producers. This they will be less and less. Those that have something to say will go ahead and say it; and in every producer's mind, as he reads something he would have automatically have laughed out of the studio a few months ago, is bound to come sneaking the shadow of a suspicion. Maybe—maybe—the people I'm supposed to be Giving What They Want—want this?[8]

The changing material conditions of the screenwriting proletarian may not have determined creative consciousness, to borrow from Marx's famous phrase in the *Contribution to the Critique of the Political Economy*. But they certainly played a great role in how writers thought about themselves, about issues of creative control, and about the many analogies between corporate Hollywood and American life at large. By 1940, filmmaking was the nation's twelfth-largest industry, a surge that logically followed the swift rise of first the telegraph, then radio, and predicted the later, equally sudden rise not only of television in the postwar years but of software operations at the end of the century. The development of films as corporate enterprise had been explicit from the beginning but took on new forms as sound, now the harbinger of fresh technology, offered new worlds to conquer.

The continuing corporate shakedown, indeed, constituted a major part of the sound revolution. A handful of smaller studios died, Warners moved from the bottom of the majors toward the top, and new ones like Columbia, RKO, and Twentieth Century-Fox quickly established themselves. But the capital available to make films was always less than the demand, because a large chunk of the studios' paper value was in extensive real estate holdings for shooting purposes; that melancholy fact made the accelerated shift to Wall Street inevitable. Simultaneously, and with the definite encouragement of the bankers, studio execs were determined to run a tighter ship.[9]

As the studios fought the writers' collective tooth and nail for the next five years with various combinations of threats and bribes, the writer-unionists, whatever their politics, correctly counted on the New Deal–established National Labor Relations Board to finalize the victory already won for screenwriters' hearts and minds. Neither the brave and often self-sacrificing pioneer unionists nor the studios had expected that the Junior Writers Departments, where younger writers made a munificent $35 a week and generally earned no screen credits, would prove to be the hidden strength of the Hollywood labor movement. Like the mostly Jewish (and mostly female) substitute teachers in New York State who zealously backed the left-wing Teachers Union, these underlings were the exploited and disregarded. Their commitment offered proof positive that the Screen Writers Guild was a real movement.

The process unquestionably politicized a significant proportion of

Hollywood writers. It was not just the Depression and international issues or proximity to Hollywood's still small if influential Communist Party; it was the sense of becoming part of an ongoing struggle that could presumably be won. Participation in the process posed a kind of writer-intellectual as an almost social force, as a counterpart to the journalists of *J'Accuse*–era Paris or the muckrakers of America's Progressive Era.

Writers' grievances were by now rooted not only in their low status and absence of any control over their creations but in their observation of the success and increasing sophistication of the studios as they gradually climbed out of the Depression slough. They also found comrades and friends on the same side of the camera. Technicians from sound, lighting, and camera departments, and cutters and others from editors to directors, steadily relearned large parts of their crafts as fresh injections of capital and steady technical innovations made a new cinematic realism (likewise non-realism, even surrealism) possible. They, too, yearned for more creative control. Thus, a new day had begun.

Most impressive to cerebral-minded audiences (but not only to them) were the sharp improvements in "continuity." The flow of dialogue in films before 1932 had been problematic, a result of technical problems made worse by actors who still projected stage lines or (like Clara Bow) were flummoxed by the presence and often elusive location of hidden microphones. To follow the visual bouncing ball, writers had to craft question-and-response between actors, while the camera trained upon faces and especially upon eyes (a mode already somewhat established in silent films) to establish an intimate audience identification impossible in theater. Continuity offered a first step toward what recent scholars have called the "dialogical camera," granting audiences a multiplicity of more or less equal faces and even points of view, much as the first-row crowd enjoyed in a theatrical ensemble, but improved by the possibilities of film. Among screenwriters, Left ally Dudley Nichols was arguably the master writer-innovator of all this technological promise.

New roles for music to mobilize the narrative and point up patterns of dialogue meanwhile evolved fairly swiftly, thanks again to technicians and to writers of the score, creating fresh material or adapting it as the situation demanded. Meanwhile, the rapid adoption of moving-camera technologies made possible increased motion while more sustained shooting and vastly improved framing, yielding unprecedented synchronization, allowed ex-

perimentation with all sorts of shooting angles and rapid cuts. All this
came to full fruition by the war years. Optical printers realized the fade-
outs, dissolves, and tricks like superimpositions as the "effects" that audiences quickly came to expect for their money. Even new film stock
contributed considerably to film realism, the increased sensitivity to light
prompting a new clarity and possibilities of depth that the cinematographers of the 1940s (notably those two notoriously close to the Left, Gregg
Toland and James Wong Howe) would deploy more fully.[10]

Much if not all of this improvement also came together in the creation
and construction of sets, one of the literally "artistic" skills that made a
considerable impact in films. Here and there a Left ally, notably Mordecai
Gorelik, transferred formidable stage set-design skills to Hollywood. The
keenly antifascist German refugees created new set models for the film industry at large. Hans Dreier, with a background in German expressionism
and steady employment at Paramount, thus became a major innovator of
the set interior that offered considerably more to the action than mere
background. Indeed, much as the expansive (but not especially expensive)
studio-lot scenery endeared audiences to thinly plotted Westerns, the art
deco look and wildly eclectic designs conveyed the rich fantasy of melodrama and comedy that many directors of the same background, like Ernst
Lubitsch, used to best advantage, but that Middle American directors
could deploy freely without much ruminative effort. Actually, most directors, like producers, had "brains" (of others, that is) to work out the details
for them. The same was notably true in the horror genre that quickly acquired its own specialists and the musicals with lavish sets and chore-
ography.[11]

Here, rather than in studio management decisions, good or bad, was
the true "genius of the system" embodied in the hardworking insiders.
Technicians, creative writers, and directors accepted the realities of star
marketing, for instance, or the craving of large audiences for childish male
action dramas and maudlin three-hanky features. But even in the notoriously cheaply produced B's, more creative efforts were sometimes made
and met with audience approval. At higher levels, studio heads seemed no
more skilled than anyone else at discerning the shifting public interest,
and their autocratic behavior toward actors or others made for a more obviously massive and stupid waste of creative energies.

The studios themselves often pioneered the changes with the goals of cost savings and a cleaner product. But so did professional associations of craftsmen, like the Society of Motion Picture Engineers, the American Society of Cinematographers, or less formal groupings of animationists and others who made themselves felt not by questioning the basic profitability of the industry but by seeking to raise standards of the craft itself. The studios financed the creation and regular improvement of the Moviola, for instance, but the craftsmen, engineers, and skilled workers of the factory improved it in successive models, and only the master craftsman and his assistants could work the machine properly.

All this involved particulars of economic exploitation familiar to those close observers of American factory life who saw inside inventors get $50 or $100 for a patent worth millions. But it had implications for even the most creative of the film production process. The relative handful of high-minded directors complained that most of their colleagues unquestioningly followed the dictates of producers right down to the last detail, efficiently turning out a bland and uniformly predictable product.[12]

Film scholars have rightly pointed to the role of classic Hollywood storytelling in fostering the quality and the pace of technological developments, but this is only part of the truth.[13] If no technological change is politically neutral, the revolutionary changes sweeping Hollywood technology during the 1930s were (at least) double-edged. The possibilities for a different kind of cinema, not necessarily more "political" but more truthful, more imaginative, and more entertaining, struck every writer and technician who was troubled by the philistine character and ruthless application of typical studio methods. The times lent themselves to envisioning challenges as large as the industrial union posed to the great factories, or the New Deal posed (at least *seemed* to pose, for critics and supporters alike) to the old certainties of uncontrolled capitalism.

Realism, Warner Brothers Style

The films written by Robert Rossen up to the early years of World War II define, perhaps better than any others, what the new merged politics of salesmanship, art, and commitment were all about, most especially at Warner Brothers. They offer both continuity (in the analytical sense) and contrast to the small handful of successful 1930s screenwriters—Lester

Cole, Dalton Trumbo, Ring Lardner, Jr., Lillian Hellman, Fred Rinaldo, and Robert Lees—who emerged as political, box office, or artistic powerhouses of the 1940s Hollywood Left.

Unlike the earlier-established Sidney Buchman and Donald Ogden Stewart, this group had no grand early studio success to build on, no inner circle of Hollywood bigwigs to persuade in private social settings. Unlike Dorothy Parker and Sam Ornitz, they were able to roll with the studio punches, and unlike Francis Faragoh, Guy Endore, or John Bright, they had more work ahead of them in 1940 than behind. In short, they were the heart of the ordinary left-wing writers' crowd that was moving upward just before the war, creating the nucleus for the final and in some ways most substantial generation of radical film talent. Through bad projects and promising ones, conceptually thin or thick, they made their way.

A product of the Lower East Side who grew up impoverished and who boxed professionally for a time, Rossen struck coworkers as personally competitive almost to the point of mania. But there was no doubt that he bitterly opposed existing class relations and dreamed of a better society. As he moved through the Off Broadway of the early 1930s, as an actor and as a director, he gravitated naturally to Hollywood. With luck, he landed at Warners, the perfect place for his style of work.[14]

Almost overnight Rossen perfected the distinctive Warners style—a success that arguably confined him to its limits all the way to his final triumph in *The Hustler.* The arch (and heavily stylized) sincerity of the typical Warners feature directed by William Wellman, Anatole Litvak, Mervyn LeRoy, and especially William Dieterle; the stars (who included Muni, Bogart, Cagney, Bette Davis, Barbara Stanwyck, Pat O'Brien, and Edward G. Robinson); and even the low-key lighting adopted to cover the low-financed sets lent a very particular aura. Above all, Warners had the status of a "writer's studio," not because writers were paid more or subjected to fewer rewrites, but because the character of production emphasized the hiring of the director after the script had been approved: The story counted for a good deal, if by no means everything. For that matter, and within the limits of the commercial enterprise, Warners management cared for something rather beyond the bottom line, or more properly committed themselves to a certain kind of quasi-politics, which, even in its later turn to anti-Communist films, expressed a commitment generally lacking at other studios.

Within five years of his Hollywood initiation in 1936, Rossen had co-scripted more than a half dozen successful sharp-edged Warners dramas. In *Marked Woman* (1937), the "fallen woman" cycle of the early 1930s found a worthy successor, now on a bigger budget. Supposedly based on actual criminal trials in New York—indeed, upon the case of Lucky Luciano, a mobster far from unknown to Hollywood's own contemporary mobbed-up craft-union leaders—a group of barroom "hostesses" (cleaned up from prostitutes in the theatrical version) were led by Bette Davis in revolt against a mob takeover of "their" club and the further degradation of their lives.[15] A dashing D.A. (Humphrey Bogart, playing someone who could easily be New York's famed crime fighter Thomas Dewey) props up Davis and her sinning sisters, giving her the protection and moral courage to testify and to clean up one corner of public entertainment. Notably, after the film's courtroom climax the women stride off together arm and arm into the fog, leaving Bogey and the audience wondering about the Hollywood romantic-clasp ending that just didn't happen. With limited room for character development, Davis nonetheless turned in one of her strongest gender-conscious roles.

As in the minor action-drama *Racket Busters* (1938, coscripted with Leonardo Bercovici), also "based on actual events," the plot—in this case, Bogart as a D.A. confronting labor traffickers—was less important than the ways in which ordinary folks talk about their jobs and learn to fight (admittedly against crime lords rather than their employers as such) for their rights. Recruited that year to the Communist Party whose *Daily Worker* praised the implicit union sentiment of *Racket Busters,* Rossen delivered the solid New Dealish message that industrial unionists who had gone all out for Roosevelt's reelection could readily appreciate.

They Won't Forget (1937), coscripted by Aben Kandel from a novel by Ward Greene, was based upon the notorious 1915 trial of a southern Jewish factory supervisor falsely charged with murdering a young woman in the mill where he worked. The courtroom drama that followed underlined American anti-Semitism so clearly that Yiddish newspaper giant Abraham Cahan devoted most of one of the final volumes of his memoirs to the case. Given the temper of Hollywood, the supervisor inevitably lost his Jewish character. But otherwise, the scene of a sleepy southern town that comes alive at the prospect of a rape conviction (and presumed execution of a local teacher, a disliked Yankee), rammed through by a conniving district attorney, offered the most electrifying version of judicial misconduct yet seen in top-star billing. Claude Rains is the D.A., Otto Kruger the northern lawyer who tries to get his client a fair trial, and no less than teenager Lana Turner has her career-making cameo role as the victim. The governor nobly sacrifices his political future for the sake of justice. But the mob has already acted, offering a distinctly unhappy Hollywood ending.

The Roaring Twenties (1939) and *Out of the Fog* (1941), two of Rossen's most interesting gangster-connected films, the Depression-heavy *Dust Be My Destiny* (1939), and *Blues in the Night* (1941) arguably realized older genres as well. The first, to which Rossen made only a modest script contribution with the credited writing by Jerry Wald and Richard Macaulay from a story by Mark Hellinger (who would supply the story and also produce *The Naked City* with Jules Dassin as director almost a decade later), retraces the social moods in the early part of the century from woman suffrage to war and postwar letdown. James Cagney and Humphrey Bogart are pals who size up their prospects and, with good economic logic, go into the rackets. As the two protagonists fall, so does the life of the 1920s, viewed in retrospect with as much nostalgia as repulsion.

Out of the Fog, a sentimental adaptation by the same writing team, based on a Broadway hit by the left-leaning Irwin Shaw, made Garfield the heavy, a Brooklyn wise guy whose money and personal charisma have won over working-class girl Ida Lupino from her honest proletarian boyfriend (played by Eddie Albert). Shaw's title, *The Gentle People,* signifies the blue-collar family, headed by kindly patriarch Thomas Mitchell, whose spirit manages to survive even the shame of a daughter's lost virtue and inspire revitalizing revenge. Critics accurately complained that from stage to film, the father character had traded in his Jewishness for Irishness, just one more of the typical Broadway-to-Hollywood conventions of the times.

Dust Be My Destiny, directed by Edward Seiler, could be described as a mix-and-match combination of other Warners Depression films in its hard-luck theme of a hard-luck boy of the road (Garfield) sent off to a prison farm, where he meets and loves the sympathetic stepdaughter (Priscilla Lane) of a vindictive and perhaps incestuously lustful straw boss. The two escapees hit the road to survive. A single moment, favored by later left-wing observers, shows a broke Garfield asking a milkman for a bottle, and the agreeable fellow proletarian handing it over with the remark that in a better world the basic necessities would be free.

Blues in the Night (1941, directed by Anatole Litvak and adapted by Rossen from a play by Edwin Gilbert, *Hot Nocturne*, said to have been written in part by Elia Kazan) is a rare, almost explicitly Jewish jazz piece marking the escape of the marginally employed working-class New Yorkers from the improbable prospect of upward mobility into the musician's dubious career (which a Jewish "Mama" considers hopeless for her boy, played by a whiny Kazan in his best screen role). The impossibility of a meaningful life of steady social relations for Depression-era losers becomes all the clearer here. An extraordinary independent-minded blues singer, once again Warners contract player Priscilla Lane, struggles to realize her own identity as the group makes its way through boxcars across the south (and through some thick melodrama as well). African-American themes are ubiquitous in this journey, from jailbirds singing to families chopping cotton (in passing efforts to "document" the south, WPA-style), and tragedy is always around the corner, real happiness hard or perhaps impossible to find. Another of the best 1930s films actually made in the forties, *Blues* might be said to finish off the Depression youngsters-on-the-road genre with a flourish—and an Oscar nomination for Johnny Mercer's title song.

The Sea Wolf (1941), a modern rendition of Jack London's novel and uncontestably the best London film adaptation, capped Rossen's prewar production and gave him his finest director in the antifascist Hungarian refugee Michael Curtiz.[16] One of the anarcho-socialist author's most Nietzschean works, it has as would-be Superman the ship's captain, Edward G. Robinson; only this time around, he is more of a fascist than mere twisted intellectual. His informer, ship's doctor Barry Fitzgerald (a delicious irony for Communists and freethinkers who despised the lovable-priest image of Fitzgerald's contemporary film roles), is a detestable Quisling-style collaborator. Among those who resist, the working-class girl with a shady past (Ida Lupino) and a proletarian on the run (John Garfield in his best supporting role after the *Four Daughters* part that made him a film star), struggle to make sense of themselves and to avert or at least escape the common disaster at hand in the ship's inevitable crackup. Robinson himself described the ship as the psychologically perfect portrait of Nazism's social order.[17]

It would be an exaggeration, but not an enormous one, to say that Rossen afterward recombined these themes or even made the same film again and again with different settings. Class oppression, whether simple grinding poverty, the special degradation of women sex workers, seamen under the dictatorial rules of the waves, or the philistinism faced by would-be artists of any kind, invariably wounded deepest through humiliation.[18] Risking all, the courageous individual—only occasionally supported by collective action—struck back, realizing himself (or herself) and establishing a veritable psychology of resistance.

In a way, as Rossen would demonstrate more clearly in *Edge of Darkness* (1943, where the story of Norwegian Resistance against the Nazis begins on a killing field with nearly all of its heroes slain), defeat and personal annihilation are staggeringly irrelevant. A stand has been taken, with the notable help of the swashbuckling British underground agent, played by Errol Flynn, and human dignity trumps approaching death. And with box office success: *Edge* was the top moneymaker of the year. Himself more and more the Jack London–style individualist as he grew more successful (according to Walter Bernstein's memory, a pacing Rossen continually threw punches into the air at an invisible adversary), the writer-director placed himself against every outside authority, be it capitalism, the studios, or the would-be discipline of the Party—far less important to him than the first two, but important for a while longer in maintaining his Hollywood rebel image.[19]

By this time, Rossen had redefined the Warners "realist" film for the whole studio. As Abraham Polonsky observed decades after writing *Body and Soul* (1947) for Rossen's direction, the insecure former proletarian artist desperately wanted to create "real" art, but his art was best suited, after all, to the Warners style. The Steinbeckian naturalism in *Of Mice and Men* (which Columbia bought, chopped badly, and produced), to take another angle on Depression life, was too much of a challenge literally or artistically; it failed despite director Lewis Milestone's game efforts. By contrast, the plays Rossen adapted and some of his original screenplays were just about right for audience expectations, the workmanlike product of a New Deal frame shifted twenty or thirty degrees (but no more) left-ward, with heroes who more often than not curiously resembled Rossen's images of himself. Actually, the more heroic and successfully stylized realism of the 1940 *The Grapes of Wrath* (which Fox, under Zanuck, did very well with, with director John Ford then close enough to the Left to be wrongly identified by the FBI as a Communist) might have suited Rossen even better. But it would have been far beyond Warners' budget expectations and possibly censored in its strongest parts. As Polonsky quipped later, Communists usually had their internal censor working, while the best of liberals could act as though they were unaware of industry censorship.[20]

After Rossen, the most typical New Deal and Warners writer must have been John Wexley. A pioneer of the Hollywood Communist Party and one of the first Left playwrights to feel the bitter regret of abandoning Broadway, Wexley nevertheless had the real Hollywood-style talent to shape James Cagney's character from twisted tough guy into sentimentalist. He'd suffered seeing *The Last Mile* (1932), based on his successful Broadway play, transformed into an anti–capital punishment film with no bite when he accepted John Huston's offer to rework a story by Rowland Brown into *Angels with Dirty Faces* (1938). In one sense, *Angels* was Cagney at his best, the slum kid caught for a petty crime and jailed while his chum (Pat O'Brien, destined to be a priest) escapes. Decades later, while the Father is overseeing the Dead End Kids—the actors fresh from the stage hit of *Dead End*—to try to keep them away from crime, Cagney returns from the state pen to the neighborhood as a local hero. Double-crossed by mob lawyer Humphrey Bogart, he struggles with his conscience as he returns to friendship with O'Brien and begins to romance the honest proletarian neighbor played by Ann Sheridan (who lost an earlier gangster boyfriend in a shoot-out). His fate is sealed by the background of the social environment he cannot escape, and he takes his revenge at the cost of very nearly everything but his pride. In the end, he yields even that.

Against the background of the New Deal, that pride miraculously becomes less important than social ideals of uplift. Foreshadowing those wartime epics in which the heretofore conflicted individual willingly sinks his all for the community, *Angels* offers a social halo to the self-abnegating mobster—albeit through the guidance of one of the most reactionary institutions in contemporary American life, the Church. For all that apparent weakness, *Angels* still had the gritty feel of a Lower East Side neighborhood, with its tenement and street life, and the hope of a redemption more than personal.[21]

Wexley's *City for Conquest* (1940), a solo script (with a polish by Rossen) based on a novel by Aben Kandel, kept to Hollywood's standard of individual solutions but successfully sermonized via the fight game. Two brothers in Manhattan slums face tough choices, and the one who can use his fists (Cagney) resolves to make possible the dream of the one who wants to write a great democratic symphony about the life of the city (Arthur Kennedy, in his screen debut). Cagney's character has also fallen hard for a dame, who betrays him by going over to a partnership with a slick vaudeville dancer. In the tear-jerking climax, a blinded Cagney, his sight ruined by a dirty fighter, is a lowly newsboy listening to his brother's symphony live on the radio from Carnegie Hall when the contrite ex-girlfriend finds him and pleads successfully for his forgiveness. As he soliloquizes a scene or two earlier, "I can see things better now than I could before." So much human capital was expended for the contribution that working stiffs could make; in a different social order they would surely realize their just rewards.

The soulful boxer was already a theatrical standard on the Left for one good reason: Clifford Odets. *Golden Boy* (1939) constituted along with *None But the Lonely Heart* (1944) stage legend Odets's only satisfying film credits before the blacklist, and for the first, Odets merely supplied the theatrical original. The mid-thirties darling of the Left, author of *Waiting for Lefty* and other dramas, he should have been a film icon as well but could not bridge the gap between the Broadway of ethnic accents and Hollywood, where "liberal" stood for "left," a melted-pot "poor" for the working class, and Gentiles for Jews. Actually, *The General Died at Dawn* (1936), his maiden outing, had about fifteen good minutes, as the critics jibed (newspaper zinger: "Odets, Where Is Thy Sting?"). Gary Cooper, playing the soldier of fortune in China, manages to be so sickened by the racist indifference of a fellow American merchant to punch out his headlights for ridiculing the suffering of the peasants. Despite Lewis Milestone's direction, the rest is standard adventure and romance.[22]

But *Golden Boy* was a serious work of film art, performed before the cameras by the Group Theatre with a modest change of cast and with much of the spirit (if virtually none of the obvious Jewishness) of the original. The boxer who was meant to be a violinist (played by William Holden, in his first important role) is an extension of social contradictions in a family of economically hopeless but spiritually rich Depression characters. The un-Hollywoodish feeling of the film, greatly assisted by the astute direction, production, and creative control of Rouben Mamoulian, was perhaps its best quality, notwithstanding the orchestrated escape of the protagonist from the hold of the gangsters and his reuniting with his sweetheart, the improbably Gentile Barbara Stanwyck.

And yet Odets, with all his heartfelt energy, was never quite right for the New Deal film, even this one. Away from the New York scene and shorn of hopes for early revolutionary change, he craved the success and the money Hollywood offered, hated himself for it, despised studio life, but, unlike the film Left, chose no compensating political role. Sidney Buchman, who had the real Hollywood polish, was just right on both scores. As for a few others at the top of their game, Columbia provided the ideal working atmosphere, thanks less to any particular social-reform sentiment than to the shrewd use of resources and gauge for public taste. The sole creation of Harry Cohn, Columbia was the smallest of the major-minor studios (along with Universal, and a large step above Poverty Row), yet nevertheless produced some of the slickest and most sophisticated of the 1930s pictures and a large handful of the best. Cohn's habit of picking up, for a single feature, stars temporarily estranged from their home studios contributed in no small degree to Columbia's successes. But so did his own confidence in the New Dealish, optimistic vision sometimes best realized in Capra films but not infrequently by others also working at Columbia.[23]

Buchman's *She Married Her Boss* (1935) was, by these standards, typically good Columbia. Starring Claudette Colbert and Melvyn Douglas, it has an executive secretary refusing a dream job in Paris because of her apparently unrequited love. At one point, Douglas is so determined to prove he has overcome his obsession with property that he joins her in hurling bricks through his own store's display windows. The film, a good moneymaker, convinced Douglas (a real Hollywood Jewish liberal, later to be baited by HUAC for changing his name) to sign an extended contract with Columbia.

Capra did far more for James Stewart in *Mr. Smith Goes to Washington* (1939). The Sicilian working-class immigrant who started working in films in 1915, directed *Our Gang* and Mack Sennett comedies, and gradually emerged from assorted commercial successes to win an Academy Award for *It Happened One Night* (1934) happened to be a Republican and a pillar of Establishment Hollywood. But he had also, since silent days, been making successful films about the dispossessed, featuring near-broken men and Magdalene-like fallen women. When he responded to Depression suffering with the sensitive *Mr. Deeds Goes to Town* (1936), he found his true métier. Capra was capable of drifting considerably further leftward before turning toward the postwar conservatism that coincided with his collapse as a filmmaker. He had worked intermittently with Sidney Buchman since the stock horse–race drama *Broadway Bill* (neither of them got or wanted credit) and used the screenwriter extensively for rewrites of *Lost Horizon* (1937), a production that ran vastly over budget and kept the director occupied for a precious sixteen months while Columbia was counting on him to bring home the bacon.

In the next two years, Capra continued his drift, at one point arranging for Columbia to buy the rights for *Golden Boy* and then, according to self-created lore, trading it off to Rouben Mamoulian for an unpublished story titled "The Gentleman from Montana." An outsider comes to Washington as a member of Congress, finds a nest of corruption, and throws all his energies against it (in the novel he fails, but that would hardly do for Hollywood). Capra invited Buchman to tour Washington with him by bus in 1938, scouting locations and exchanging ideas. The idea of a civic fighter had been tried out with Gary Cooper in *Mr. Deeds Goes to Town,* but Buchman intensified the lone-man-against-the-system theme, and Stewart was perfectly cast for a mixture of naïveté and idealistic determination. From time to time in later years the director sought to discount the message of urgent resistance against corruption and political misleadership, but he just as often admitted *Mr. Smith* was his masterpiece. As it undoubtedly is: the very best of a thin genre on congressional politics and a supreme statement of populistic sentiment during the New Deal years.

Jefferson Smith, Stewart's character, advances to the Senate by an accident whose implications he is too ignorant to grasp. A political boss has lost through an untimely death his ally for a land swindle, and the governor under his thumb appoints Smith, known only for his leadership of a Boy Rangers (i.e., Boy Scouts) troop and considered malleable. Arriving in Washington, he is met by the senatorial office secretary (Jean Arthur, in one of her best roles), who simply can't believe his patriotism is sincere but then falls in love with the big lug. By that time, he is unknowingly sponsoring a bill for an expanded Rangers camp whose existence will ruin the crooked land deal. The state's senior senator (played by Claude Rains), a once-honest politician who has been corrupted, schemes madly to stop

Smith, even accusing him of corruption and presenting phony evidence that he owns the land in question.

Momentarily depressed as only Jimmy Stewart can be, he visits the Lincoln Memorial and decides to stage a one-man filibuster the next day. This Smith does in one of the most politically dramatic moments of any American film, while his mother back home has rallied the Rangers to spread the word. The crooks, in a jackboot operation, beat up the kids and steal copies of their little newspaper that tells the truth. Exhausting himself from speaking, Smith meanwhile collapses—and Rains, conscience-struck, reveals everything. No wonder the film was met with horror on the real-life Senate floor, where shady deals and trading on privilege were (and are, as much as ever) daily business; and no wonder the conservative press went after Capra and the studio. The wonder is that the trade press and most of the dailies still greeted the film as magnificent. But they were, of course, outside Washington, somewhere in the rest of the country, where *Mr. Smith* was boffo for the cinema palace and the neighborhood theater alike.[24]

Buchman and that other Stewart, Donald Ogden, had together made lasting film history in another way the year before, with *Holiday* (1938), based on the popular Broadway play by Philip Barry and starring Katharine Hepburn. The film adaptation shrewdly repositioned Hepburn's inner strength with ironic turns, fleshing out her surroundings with the useless upper-class twits, genuine reactionaries, and the disappointed ordinary people that Donald Ogden Stewart must have known aplenty in real life.

If there is an unreality to *Holiday* (and what could be more unreal to the audience of ordinary Americans than the domiciles and problems of the very rich?), the craving of Katharine Hepburn's character for freedom was nevertheless compelling almost beyond words. In just one film the actress had more than broken the "box office poison" reputation she had gained since the middle 1930s. By choosing her next parts carefully—virtually all of them vehicles written or adapted for her in the next half dozen years by left-wingers—she made herself into the ideal American woman who didn't happen to be a willing (or unwilling, therefore femme fatale) sex goddess but a strong, lovely, and vulnerable character.

The Philadelphia Story (1940) emphasized her vulnerability and brought out the very best of Jimmy Stewart, who got an Oscar for Best Actor. Written for her by Philip Barry, the theatrical version wowed sophisticated Broadway with more than two hundred performances. Donald Ogden Stewart later modestly wrote that he "got out of the way" for the screen version, but actually he again fleshed out the surroundings and dialogue. Once more the frustrated upper-class woman, she is about to remarry when her ex-husband (played by Grant), the feckless playboy, shows up along with novelist-turned-journalist Jimmy Stewart to provoke (in the journalist's case, also to record) her confusion in finally coming toward consciousness of herself.

No one can quite say what stands in the way of happiness, and any attempt to confine it to the maneuvering of the upper class would be a mistake. But as the usual punches are pulled within American films and social problems seem to be resolved individually, the psychological plight of both the useless rich and the powerless outsiders nevertheless suggests the need for some other possibility. Perhaps the shadow of an approaching Second World War made audiences crave this kind of diffused or sublimated stress. The anguish in *The Philadelphia Story* is so effective dramatically, however, that it defies "escapism."

Irwin Shaw and Buchman's original script for *The Talk of the Town* (1942), produced shortly before the invasion of Pearl Harbor and released in the months afterward, helps fill in the blank. This time, Cary Grant is a homespun American radical, the village atheist type who denounces the high-handness of the local mill owners so successfully that he is framed for setting fire to the mill and for the death of a worker inside. With Grant's character pretending to be a gardener for his potential lover Jean Arthur, and a prominent judge also in the house, Buchman and Shaw set up the scene perfectly for a dialogue about the letter and the spirit of the law, or the heart versus the property-weighted legal rule book. Ultimately, after several of the funniest chase scenes in sound-film history, Grant is vindicated. But the larger point stands out beyond the World War II–era rhetoric: In this America, the outsider understands how the cards are stacked, and the insiders who have a conscience urgently need to listen. It was properly a 1930s message of social restlessness and New Deal appointments to high places, but it carried democratic weight into the following era of enforced unity and martial enthusiasm. So few African-American actors had dignified roles in films up to this point that Rex Ingram, playing the respectful but also respected chauffeur to the judge, offered more evidence that Buchman, by this time promoted to producer, was bringing Hollywood into modern times.

A handful of other Left writers made headway in the same direction as Sidney Buchman, blending their talents with the themes of the New Deal. None of them being screen pioneers like him, they had little of the sense of disappointment that overcame the likes of Sam Ornitz or John Bright. Most of them were, like Lester Cole, fighting their way upward from the B's, so they experienced the first whiffs of major production values as incentives to devote themselves to craft along with the politics of unionism and the Popular Front.

Foremost in prolific writing (and sales of his scripts) was undoubtedly Dalton Trumbo, whose career closely resembled Rossen's in a few key respects. Born and raised in Colorado, the grandson of a two-gun sheriff in a troubled family of Christian Scientists, Trumbo set out for college but abandoned it, thanks to the usual financial problems of the day. He worked eight long years in a Los Angeles bakery as he steadily wrote short stories and searched for something greater. It came first as journalist at a Hollywood trade paper and then, on the basis of a novel and short stories, a hire at Warners in 1935. *Road Gang* was his first picture, strictly B material, but with unusual moments, shortly followed by run-of-the-mill work. A rebel by instinct, Trumbo quickly found his way to the circle of left-wing writers and the SWG, a bold move that ended him at Warners—although he remained formally outside the Communist Party until 1943, with unionism (and family life on his ranch) the only serious distractions from his writing career. He made his breakthrough to RKO, the smallest and least financially stable of the majors but nonetheless notable for its literary adaptations and for its one outstanding star, Katharine Hepburn.

A Man to Remember (1938) was a lower-middle-class and Middle American version of a Rossenesque saga of the man against the system. By taking unpopular action to postpone a county fair and outraging the county medical association by making injections against polio available to the public, a small-town physician brought hope in many ways to a beset town—just before he died, hopelessly in debt. Scarcely more than a remake of *One Man's Journey* (1933), it received welcome attention from *The New York Times* and made up for a good deal of hackwork. Trumbo's panache and RKO's low budgets even made possible the occasional film with a political edge, like *Heaven with a Barbed Wire Fence* (1939), in which an orphaned survivor of the fascist attacks during the Spanish Civil War travels across the United States, is arrested as an illegal alien, and after more troubles resolves to build a ranch out of rough Arizona territory.[25] Further down in B material, Anne Shirley (who married Adrian Scott, then named him as she instituted divorce proceedings) became the innocent of *Sorority House* (1938), a coed who realizes just how snooty and backstabbing the class system of Greek college life can be when a friend commits suicide.[26]

Five Came Back (1939), coscripted with Nathanael West and Jerry Cady, is one of Trumbo's B-budget best, a wrongfully neglected small-budget exotic drama in which the survivors of a plane crash in Central America face the need to work together. An angst-filled version of *Sinners in Paradise,* it gives an anarchist (played with great pathos by Joseph Calleia) the opportunity to play the self-sacrificing hero as he explains the collectivist necessity to the endangered little society.

All this brought Trumbo to *Kitty Foyle* (1940), the film adaptation that got him out of the B circuit and made his career. Based on a popular novel by Christopher Morley, it earned the screenwriter a nomination, and its star, Ginger Rogers, an Oscar. It was also a major box office triumph for RKO. Donald Odgen Stewart, who had worked first on the adaptation, proposed a flashback to capture the first-person character of the narrative. Trumbo usefully complicated an inner dialogue in which Kitty looks back on her choice either to marry a heroically struggling physician or a Main Line plutocrat. Film historians have themselves often reflected upon *Kitty Foyle's* totemic status, the mixture of class, Irish-American ethnicity (probably the film's least important aspect), and gender, as Kitty becomes entangled with the wealthy and handsome publisher (played by Dennis Morgan). Pregnant with an heir but unable to bear the domination of their prospective married lives by his haughty upper-crust family, she walks out. As she considers a reconciliation, she reads about his engagement to a woman of his own class. When her baby dies, she realizes that she belongs with the doctor and his social mission.

Kitty Foyle was bound to become the film standard that feminists and post-feminists in particular tirelessly analyzed. As retold recently by a film scholar, the critical moment comes when the smart Kitty confronts the misguided Kitty in the mirror, the potential wife and mother versus the potential mistress. Her fate has been sealed by that of every white-collar girl who seeks to enter the bachelorhood of a man's world and sinks unhappily until she realizes that it is not meant for women.[27]

But this trendy end-of-the-century interpretation is not fair either to Trumbo or to *Kitty Foyle.* What made Trumbo special was his ability to take perfectly ordinary material and make something different, more emphatic, more humane. Kitty never chose bachelorhood of her own will, but because of her entanglement with the mighty; her alternative lay with the good doctor (in a variety of guises) that Cole, Trumbo, Ring Lardner, Jr., and a handful of other writers all lionized in the same years. Choosing her role as helpmeet to a humanitarian, she takes on the Greer Garson status (filmically solidified as defender of orphans in the 1941 *Blossoms in the Dust,* with script contributions by Hugo Butler), prefeminist but definitely humane and even idealistic. After the critical and box office triumph of *Kitty Foyle,* his biographer notes, Trumbo gained the courage to become more determinedly antifascist, more didactic, also more interesting artistically in some ways, but arguably less a Hollywood-style storyteller.[28]

Ring Lardner, Jr., was just right for a certain kind of humane comedy film for an America seeking momentary escape from the darkness of war themes. The only radical Hollywood screenwriter who could claim to be the son of another famous writer, Lardner also had the driest wit; like his father, he was a hard-drinking, laconic newspaperman by habit and trade. Thanks to his family name he was invited to Hollywood in 1937, where he entered near the top but also proved almost immediately too left-wing for the studio chiefs to adopt comfortably. He later recalled that his initial work with Selznick brought him only two years of disappointment, and two more years at Warners (with Jerry Wald, soon to be a sort of sponsor of left-wing material while stealing writers' credits for himself on a regular basis) were no more satisfying.[29]

Thanks to the connections of his new writing partner, Ian McClellan Hunter, whom he had worked with on the New York *Daily Mirror,* Lardner, Jr., placed himself at a small independent production company, Stephens-Lange. Set up by two agents of radio favorite Jean Hersholt, the company projected several features based on Hersholt's popular current show, *Dr. Christian.* With *Meet Dr. Christian* (1939), Lardner had in effect started over again at the Hollywood B level. His director, Bernard Vorhaus, was another comrade who had already collaborated with Hunter on low-budget Bobby Breen musicals made for an equally tiny independent production company (Principal Productions/Bobby Breen Productions, Inc.).

A script had already been written for *Meet Dr. Christian,* but Vorhaus persuaded producer William Stephens to turn it over to Hunter and Lardner, whose combined talents were perfect for it. The kindly doctor has given up a big career in Chicago to help the country folk of a small town, and when a mayor is replaced, he accepts the job of health department chief. Questioning the priority (or justice) of building roads when a hospital is badly needed, he is angrily dismissed, in front of the townsfolk, by the new mayor. Then the situation suddenly reverses when the mayor's own daughter suffers a cerebral hemorrhage. In the end, even politicians grasp the practicality of humanitarianism. *Meet Dr. Christian* cost barely more than $100,000 to produce and made back almost four times that much.

The Courageous Dr. Christian (1940) was right down the line from Trumbo's *A Man to Remember,* with superior star power and more warm-hearted humor; or, from another angle, a *Meet Dr. Christian* with slightly more political punch. This time, the good doctor faces a typical dilemma posed by massive thirties homelessness. "Squatterstown" badly needs some public housing, but the town council will agree to build only if the doctor can persuade a rich widow to donate the property. Happily for the plot, spinal meningitis—which is to say, a threat to the whole community—is discovered, and the hearts of the lady and the townsfolk are moved. This, as it turned out, marked Lardner's swan song in the B's.

Woman of the Year (1942) was to Lardner what *Kitty Foyle* was to Trumbo, and as vastly more artistic as Hepburn was beyond Ginger Rogers's acting abilities. Notwithstanding the success of the *Dr. Christian* features, Lardner ran promptly into a stone wall: His leading role in the SWG and his reputation as a Red cost him dearly. But a close friend of Katharine Hepburn, Broadway writer Michael Kanin, pitched to his brother Garson Kanin and to Lardner the idea of juxtaposing a sports columnist and a woman columnist. With Hepburn's encouragement, the two came up with a script, easily one of the wittiest ever written about gender conflict and certainly perfect for Hepburn, fresh from her triumph with *The Philadelphia Story.* She gave it to MGM without the writers' names on the script copy, and they bought it for the highest amount ever paid for an original screenplay to that time. Thanks to Hepburn and to producer Joe

Mankiewicz (who helped with a second draft and suggested the title), Hepburn got very nearly the vehicle that she wanted, and the two screenwriters had a probable triumph.[30]

Despite the studio-forced conclusion that put the crusading liberal quasi-diplomat heroine back into the wifely role and the bumbling reporter in the proper place as the husband and family head, *Woman of the Year* scored endless points in women's self-assertion, their capacities to achieve, and, perhaps most of all, their capacities to make men look silly. Along with Sidney Buchman's adaptation for *Holiday* and Donald Ogden Stewart's for *The Philadelphia Story* (both from successful Broadway plays by Philip Barry), it was also the best material Hepburn would have to work with, ever.[31] Lardner himself would have to wait another quarter-century for its equal, despite some remarkable films in between.

Paul Jarrico, one of the younger writers to race toward a conomination for an Oscar, offered another interesting case of rapid mobility to the big time. Son of a prominent Labor Zionist and host to visiting Yiddish literary personalities, Jarrico had been born and ritually bathed in L.A.'s left-leaning Jewish culture. He joined the Young Communist League at UCLA in 1930 and got into film writing by the middle of the decade. His first major credit, after a Columbia B romance picture (*No Time to Marry,* 1938), was for coscripting a Lucille Ball vehicle with three other writers, *Beauty for the Asking* (1939).[32] *Tom, Dick and Harry* (1941), for which Jarrico supplied the story and coscript (with Garson Kanin) for RKO, was intended to be a critique or satirical attack upon the bourgeois version of the Cinderella story. Proletarian Ginger Rogers (Jarrico had urged Jean Arthur for the part, and she would have been miles better) has three suitors: a worker, a capitalist, and a middling fellow. Jarrico later commented wryly about his efforts that every attempt to say something semipolitical falls back into a Hollywood cliché—in this case, a bell that rings when she kisses the proletarian proves not that working-class love or character is superior but merely that Love Conquers All. It was nevertheless a cliché perfect, by implication at least, for the democratizing spirit of the times.[33]

Tom, Dick and Harry was also a career-making credit with an Oscar nomination for the script. Jarrico had already done an original for *Men of the Timberland* (1940), a B Universal film that featured Andy Devine and some slum kids helping the Civilian Conservation Corps (CCC) of the New Deal fight the ruthless timber barons.[34] Like Cole, Jarrico was ready to step into major war films, achieving both career success and political influence impossible before or after.

Director and sometimes writer Bernard Vorhaus was one of those who never quite made it, coming so close that only a bad break or a poor choice held him back. A doctor's son born in New York near the turn of the century, Vorhaus began literally playing with film stock when his older sister, a budding titlist of the silents, took him along to one of the early studios in New Jersey. By his early twenties he was a junior writer at Columbia, then Metro, then director of a two-reel dramatic silent film (*Sunlight,* 1928) that attracted so little attention in Hollywood that he removed himself to the British film industry, in those days turning out reels of "quota" films demanded by British law limiting Hollywood access to the domestic market.

At low-budget Twickenham Studios, with David Lean as an editor and protégé (and ingenue Ida Lupino as his biggest star), Vorhaus turned out a half-dozen B films that mixed documentary-style footage of working-class life with predictable romance.[35] When the British film industry slumped in the middle 1930s, Vorhaus returned to Hollywood and signed on to Republic, a move that he later regarded as a great mistake, fixing the rest of his career at a low level. The now-forgotten *King of the Newsboys* (1938) was nevertheless a true slum bildungsroman-drama written hurriedly by Vorhaus about an adolescent boy and girl dreaming of getting out but seeing the garbage scow on the East River as the real metaphor of their lives. He becomes the editor of a tip-sheet daily, she a gangster's moll, and they both taste bitterness before the end.

Vorhaus moved on to Bobby Breen Productions for two curious semi-adolescent dramas squeezing in social themes around the songs of the pre-pubescent sensation. The first, *Fisherman's Wharf* (1939), was a proletarian drama to the nth degree, the script rewritten and botched by the producer but still retaining some strong material. Little Bobby launches the film memorably with a chorus from Italian opera, working steadily on a ship hauling in a line, while his stepfather (played by Leo Carrillo) commands Italian-American clansmen to help bring in the catch. All goes well for this tightly knit and happy cooperative until an outsider convinces Carrillo that he should turn the co-op into a capitalistic enterprise. Normality is restored along with strained father-son relations. Some moments of the film not only are cinematically beautiful but are actually touching—all that can be demanded from a B production.

At first glance, another Bobby Breen film, *Way Down South* (1939), offered further interesting possibilities. Vorhaus persuaded producer Sol Lesser to hire famed poet Langston Hughes, assisted by African-American actor Clarence Muse, to do the script about an antebellum plantation where a boy grows warmly sympathetic toward a slave about to be sold "down the river."[36] With Lesser's own rewrite, the interracial drama disappeared into a scene or two at the beginning and end of the film, climaxing in the saving of a plantation uniquely benign to its owned humans. What remains strongest is an early dance sequence of slaves first carrying on in a historically appropriate harvest celebration and then magically moving into a jazzy modernism, in what seems a spiritual and transhistorical emancipation.

Three Faces West (1940) for Republic was Vorhaus's near miss. The first of the top-drawer antifascist Westerns, starring John Wayne, it might have projected Vorhaus and coscripter Sam Ornitz to something higher. Unfortunately, a less knowing screenwriter was put on the set for rewrites, and, according to Vorhaus, the significant elements of the plot never were integrated adequately. Even at Republic, success offered no prospect of choosing future films. Vorhaus's war success was limited to less prestigious features in the military-documentary line. He'd switched back to British-based B production companies even before his permanent exile and his disappearance from film work entirely.

Pink Kids

But Vorhaus's low-budget Bobby Breen features did point up a zone of major success for left-wing writers: family or children's films. It was never something that Hollywood radicals would have chosen, but once placed before them, it seemed (and would continue to seem for decades after the blacklist) the most natural venue for a social message. From another angle, what the horror film allowed the radical writers from the early and middle 1930s, the family film permitted from the middle 1930s onward. The box office success of *Dracula* and *Frankenstein* was met and exceeded many times by Shirley Temple and all the lesser Shirleys (like Jane Withers, teen favorite Deanna Durbin, and a host of cute child actors in such films). At or close to the bottom of the heap could be found the proletarian pugs known variously as the Dead End Kids and, later, the Bowery Boys. Left-wing writers fitted their scripts nicely into the available categories, no doubt because of their feelings for class but almost as much due to their feelings for the troubled child, the loner, or the outsider in a world dominated by less-than-friendly grown-ups.

Almost from the beginning of the thirties, these were often not merely films about children but also New Deal films, redolent with the social messages that thirties audiences understood best. Later, the neighborhood ragamuffins could become war orphans, from America to China to practically all parts of Europe. If Americans enjoyed cheering on the underdog but too often were served up little heroes with no meaningful context, left-wingers seized the opportunity to revisit tragic scenes through the eyes of society's ultimate innocent victims.[37]

The Mayor of Hell, written by Edward Chodorov, was the earliest of these New Deal dramas. But the first big-star kid's feature written from the Left was *Peck's Bad Boy* (1934), an adaptation of the extraordinarily popular nineteenth-century children's (or family) book series. Thanks to Jackie Cooper, the hottest Hollywood child actor after Shirley Temple, and to a brother-in-law high in the industry, screenwriter Marguerite Roberts got the chance for a career breakthrough en route to decades of rich and varied experiences, from *Dragon Seed* for Katharine Hepburn to *True Grit* for John Wayne. For the rare woman writer in the early years of the talkies, a kid's movie was seen by the studios as a "natural" domain, and Roberts successfully adapted the series' plot into the story of a young boy and his adoptive father divided when the father's sister moved in with her own son.[38] Francis Faragoh, Sam Ornitz, Albert Maltz, John Howard Lawson, Ian McClellan Hunter, Carl Foreman, and a variety of lesser talents would work similar avenues of children under stress, almost invariably triumphant in the end.

Hugo Butler was, however, the champion writer—within the Left crowd, at least—of the 1930s–40s kids drama. Son of old-time (and politically conservative) screenwriter Frank Butler, married to radical actress Jean Rouveral (who played children and teens, in W. C. Fields and Hopalong Cassidy films, respectively), Butler moved rather automatically into the industry, from the middle thirties onward, for the next few years, mostly in nondescript films.[39] In 1938, he earned sole script credit for both *The Adventures of Huckleberry Finn* and the first filmed version of *A Christmas*

Carol; the next year for costory for *Young Tom Edison;* and in 1943, sole screen adaptation for the perennial *Lassie Come Home.* Although he was to write naturalistic, noir, avant-garde, and assorted other curious material for directors ranging from Jean Renoir and Luis Buñuel to Robert Aldrich and Joseph Losey, the kids films remained his triumph, not only because he had the touch but because studio productions in the Golden Age gave his work the showcasing that subsequent efforts lacked.[40]

The film adaptation of Twain's classic, the nation's oft-acclaimed greatest novel (along with *Moby Dick*), was bound to be portentious. *The Adventures of Huckleberry Finn* had been made as a silent feature in 1920, and Paramount produced a version in 1931 simply titled *Huckleberry Finn,* with Jackie Coogan as Tom Sawyer, Junior Durkin as Huck, Clarence Muse as Jim, and Mitzi Green as Becky Thatcher, the sweetheart who brings Huck around to his responsibilities. MGM's successful *Adventures of Tom Sawyer* in 1938 prompted the studio to purchase the rights to *Huckleberry Finn* from Paramount to create another vehicle for that rising kid star Mickey Rooney. The writer's assignment went to Butler. The studio wanted light comedy much in the same vein as the 1931 version, and Butler provided plenty of it. But he successfully recuperated both the novel's racial melo-drama—within the limits of what was permitted at the time—and the angst of the orphan boy on the run. Unlike Lester Cole's version of *The House of the Seven Gables,* he couldn't add an outright abolitionist to slave-era Missouri, but he made slavery so cruel and wrong for its victim Jim that the film carried weight in a moment when a new wave of racist terror was sweeping through the south.

This *Huckleberry Finn* has Huck taking to the road (actually, the river) to safeguard his guardian, Widow Douglas (played by Elizabeth Risdon), from paying a ransom to his no-good "Pap." He comes across Jim (played by Rex Ingram), who has run off after learning that the widow was going to sell him in order to pay off Pap, but Jim also seeks to join his wife in a free state. This telling detail, missing from the original, negates the infan-tilization of Jim in Twain's work. The faked death of Huck, as per the novel, prompts murder charges against the absent and escaped Jim. The two escapees on their riverboat tangle up with a pair of card sharks as Twain wrote, and amidst burlesque Shakesperean performances (with Huck in drag as Juliet), Huck uncovers their plot to return Jim for the reward.

Although depicted as uneducated and highly superstitious, Ingram's

Jim was a great deal more than a typical contemporary Stepinfetchit character; he was, rather, the full-blown companion-character for Mickey Rooney's Huck. Toward the end of the film, as Jim is captured (bringing Huck to town after a snakebite) and rushed in his jail cell by a mob of lynch-hungry rednecks, Huck steers a steamboat himself, racing dangerously across the shallows toward home. Rushing in to save his friend, he guarantees the slave emancipation at the cost of promising to become an apparently good little boy and then ends the film (pipe viewed in his back pocket), slyly suggesting that he will go on being that delightful rascal, Huck. Perfect for Rooney, *The Adventures of Huckleberry Finn* also successfully pushed race-social themes to the maximum and must have played badly, indeed, in the south. If, as his widow, Jean Rouveral Butler, later recalled, young Butler regarded his skill not as "art" but as workmanlike adaptation, he had captured the art of the artisan; his politics gave his work an edginess that it would otherwise have lacked.[41]

MGM, highly pleased with Butler's work, assigned him to script *Young Tom Edison* (1939), along with Dore Schary and Bradbury Foote. A fictional teenhood for the young inventor makes Rooney a mechanical Huck with the same traits Butler had drawn upon so well. This Huck means no harm, but through his indifference to social rules and his fanatical determination to experiment, he causes the family (but especially his father, played by George Bancroft) endless grief, but finally saves the day with his budding genius.[42]

Butler had meanwhile soloed on the first sound remake of *A Christmas Carol* (1938), in many ways the best version of the century. Handled so as to make the ambivalent character Scrooge (in Jean Rouveral Butler's words) into "a lonely kid, someone who nobody ever loved," Butler managed to avoid or transmute the overfamiliarity and maudlin gush marking future remakes.[43] He transformed the Ghost of Christmas Past into a fantastic nymph of sorts, a Victorian fairy (or semierotic Tinkerbell) with powers of real wisdom as well as past and future vision. Not surprisingly, Bob Cratchit's impoverished household becomes the proletarian family circle incarnate, and the dramatic change in Scrooge raises the hope for wider human reconciliation, rather as Dickens intended, a point Americans seem destined to accept only in the Chamber of Commerce view of charity as an adjunct to sales.

Lassie Come Home (1943), the first in the film series (not to speak of the later television series, heavily populated with blacklisted writers under pseudonymous credits), would be Butler's final children's film, as such, a distinct loss to the genre. His strong supporting teenage and child characters in films like *From This Day Forward* (1946) and *The Big Night* (1951), not to mention a later award-winning semidocumentary on the world-champion Mexican Little Leaguers of 1956 (*Los Pequeños Gigantes,* aka *Little Giants*), showed he possessed the talent but had little opportunity for it within Hollywood's mainstream.

Lassie Come Home, from Butler's solo script, had it all cinematically, aided by the inspired casting of Roddy McDowall and a devastatingly charming eight-year-old Elizabeth Taylor sharing love for the doggedly English dog. The film, obviously written to inspire strong feeling in American audiences for their embattled British cousins, also played very heavily upon the class values of Lancashire. Born and educated in Canada, Butler was expressing British and Communist as well as Hollywood wartime values in bridging those class lines. Adapted from Eric Knight's popular 1940 novel of the same name, the film also played up the rapport of adult and child stars Donald Crisp and McDowall as a father-and-son team who had won millions of fans in *How Green Was My Valley.* When the collie is sold to an aristocrat by the desperate family and travels hundreds of miles (including an extended stop with an aged couple who have lost their son in the war) to return, the courage of the nation becomes the real subject. (The film was dedicated in the credits to the author, "a man of two countries," and the narration begins, "The people of Yorkshire . . ."). Throughout, working-class dignity operates at the center—along with canine lovability. It's difficult to demonstrate that an all-around better dog film has ever been made.[44]

My Friend Flicka (1943) provided Francis Faragoh his last hit and gave Roddy McDowall another niche in history as the horse-loving boy who set the pace for others in film and television (*Flicka,* like *Lassie,* made the transition; only Rin Tin Tin, the original canine star, could claim similarly lasting audience power). Adapted from novelist Mary O'Hara's work of the same name, *Flicka* saw a boy in the contemporary West thrown and potentially crippled for life by a horse that apparently refused to be conquered. Threatened with extermination (by Roddy's otherwise kindly father, played by Preston Foster), Flicka is saved with the help of friendly ranch hand (and future blacklistee) Jeff Corey, and brought around by a boy learning to overcome adversity, naturally with the help of a mother's love (supplied by Rita Johnson). Perhaps, as some critics suggest, *Flicka* previews the later Disney live films by showing what can be done, dramatically and commercially. But it would be better to say that *Flicka* along with a circle of similar films brought to the screen the strongest of children's literature and won their viewers' young hearts legitimately and with good purpose.[45]

National Velvet (1944), coadapted by comedy writer and future blacklistee Howard Dimsdale, with Helen Deutsch and Theodore Reeves, from the novel by Enid Bagnold, raised the dramatic and box office potential another notch to the best of the entire genre. Mickey Rooney and Elizabeth Taylor were seemingly into their teens by now (actually, Taylor was a precocious twelve), thus deemed capable of puppy love pointing vaguely toward something stronger. As a young English girl in a middle-class family, she wins a prize horse in a raffle, trains it for the Grand National Steeplechase, and rides it herself successfully in disguise as a boy—although she and the horse will for reasons of gender be disqualified after they win. The working-class stable boy played by Rooney has been there all along, considering himself unworthy of her.

The emotionally gripping climax so typical of left-wing writing highlights the role of future blacklistee actress Anne Revere, pointing out that a Hollywood offer (!) might indeed earn pots of money, as suggested by kindly dad Donald Crisp, but to accept it would be pure materialism for girl and (the clinching argument) extremely unhappy for horse. Values count for more, all around. Amid a raft of nominations for the movie, including an Oscar for Best Editing, Revere won for Best Supporting Actress. Rooney exited the best of his career with this role and, arguably, so did the always subsequently overacting adult Taylor, whose cleavage was subsequently the heart of her characterization. (She later remembered *Velvet* as "the most exciting film I've ever done.") The U.S. Congress accepted the film into its then-small official Library of Congress collection on the grounds that it reflected "the contemporary tastes and preferences of the American people."[46]

Dead End (1937) had earlier played a curious and inadvertent role in the emergence of adolescent melodrama, but it was Hellman's own extraordinary "bad kids" drama, *These Three* (1936), that had earlier marked out a higher standard. Taken from her Broadway drama *The Children's Hour*, the first lesbian-themed theater successfully performed at the highest dramatic levels in the country, *These Three* was diminished seriously by taming the conflict into a heterosexual one. But the dramatic center—the effects of a child's lies directed against a female teacher and supported by a wealthy grandmother who insists upon "respectability" in a woman's profession—was successfully maintained. The apparent realization of heterosexual happiness at film's end does not diminish the destruction of the educational experiment or untangle the psychological complexity of the "bad" child's behavior. If the homosexual theme hovers just beneath the surface in the emotional tension bewteen the two women friends who together create a school and find a man coming between them, so do the difficult questions Hellman raised about Hollywood's truly childish approach to family issues.[47] She was also way ahead of Hollywood in other departments.

Hollywood and Race

The Little Foxes (1941), drawn from her own Broadway hit, can be seen as the finest of Hellman's Hollywood work and in many ways her signature film. A historical epic about turn-of-the-century days in the south and a family drama about social corruption and personal disloyalty, it manages as well as any American play ever to transmit into film, thanks in no small part to the sympathetic direction of left-liberal William Wyler. No one gets to escape from the claustrophobic family, and Bette Davis, who had drawn quite close to the Popular Front projects (she starred in half a dozen future blacklisted writers' films between 1940 and 1946), provided an unforgettable performance as the schemer who needs release and has chosen betrayal as the only path open to her.[48] A close look at these films of hers shows that here, as in *They Won't Forget* and *Among the Living,* degrading racial values as the core southern experience are often implied if not stated outright. This was, it must be remembered, the era of *Gone With the Wind,* the biggest and most important Hollywood hit since that other subcategorical race film, *The Jazz Singer.* The idea that lynch mobs and postbellum madness should dominate the regional scene marked out a contrasting view, to say the least.

Scholars have by now thoroughly established what every racist and every Hollywoodite knew in 1935 or 1940: that Communists and their al-

lies took the propaganda lead and did the footwork in the antiracist impulse of New Deal political and social-cultural life. By the middle 1930s,
competing radical movements like the old Socialist Party had a major antiracist hero or two (although none in Hollywood), but the Popular Front
had the numbers and the determination to force the issue in almost every
avenue available. If they seemed less strident on issues of colonialism after
several of the colonizing nations of Europe became possible allies against
fascism, they nevertheless operated in social networks from Harlem high
society to neighborhood ethnic clubs to urge issues of race equality and
even themselves live (although as little was made of this as possible) the
then-rare interracial marriages.

Communists deeply felt and often observed, from the pages of *New
Theater* to the *Daily Worker* and the *New Masses,* that the time for a change
in films toward dignified racial characterizations was long overdue. If Rex
Ingram as Jim in *Huckleberry Finn* marked a curious early moment of hope,
Paul Robeson's disappointments in low-budget race films (*The Emperor
Jones, Song of Freedom*) and Hollywood big-budget films (*Showboat, King
Solomon's Mines*) were especially bitter. By these extremely modest standards, *In This Our Life* (1942) offered a sign of change. Adapted by Howard
Koch from Ellen Glasgow's popular novel, it had Ernest Anderson as an
earnest law school student (and son of a family maid) who is wrongly accused of driving a hit-and-run car that Bette Davis's character, a rebellious
but self-centered modern southern belle, actually drove. Though just as
selfish as her tobacco magnate uncle (who patronizes her in ways that betray the borderline incestuous desires of an old man), Davis dies in a car
crash, sparing a good black youngster and his family.

Anderson manfully bore the "good black" image that Hollywood had
sometimes (usually with left-wing screenwriters) bestowed upon African-
Americans and would continue to give to those whose possible contradictions and complexities it viewed as a bad commercial risk. To take another
example from Left lore, Dooley Wilson reprised the "good black" role sans
education as Bogart's right-hand man Sam in *Casablanca.* Whatever the obviously severe limitations, these images were nevertheless surely better
than the existing alternatives of the happy and superstitious darky, the chat-
tering maid, the comical thief, or the laughable pseudo-gentleman. Indeed,
a friendly witness or two reminded the House Committee, as a prime example of thought control, that Hollywood Party sentiment (in a later era, it

would have been called "political correctness") had wrongly made the writer feel guilty enough to refuse to write blackface minstrel comedy.[49]

Tales of Manhattan (1942), a story anthology of an overcoat passed unwittingly from protagonist to protagonist, bringing new experiences to each one, climaxed in a southern church with the coat, cash in its pockets, falling miraculously from the sky (actually, from an airplane) upon parishioners who saw the hand of "de Lawd" and devoted it to their religious institution. The presence of left-wing screenwriters brought no cheers from the Left; it seemed to patronize without uplifting. Robeson, who played the minister, expressed his particular bitterness by giving up movies altogether: It was his last Hollywood flim appearance.[50]

But the African-American story in Hollywood had only begun. The Office of War Information (OWI) signaled shortly after its 1942 formation that it had a full agenda of Hollywood priorities to build victory spirit on the home front, including the improvement of race relations. Although mostly a lip-service response to the campaign led by the NAACP's Walter White and 1940 liberal Republican presidential nominee Wendell Wilkie to improve film treatment of African-Americans, it provided encouragement for some projects, almost inevitably with Left connections.[51]

Cabin in the Sky (1943) was the first A film with an all-black cast. Directed by Vincente Minnelli, it came out of a 1940 Broadway hit written by lefty lyricist John Latouche and one of Yip Harburg's familiar collaborators, Vernon Duke. Harburg and Harold Arlen were hired by MGM to write the score for the film, and their collaboration brought the memorable "Happiness Is a Thing Called Joe." *New Masses* film critics no doubt reflected one common attitude among Harlem intellectuals: that the biblical-style themes posing a temptress (Lena Horne) against the workaday "good woman" Ethel Waters over the soul and body of an uncertain man (Eddie "Rochester" Anderson) did not escape stereotypes, essentially re-creating *The Green Pastures* atmosphere that whites liked to believe benignly about African-American life. But Horne and Waters, with Rex Ingram in the background, plus Louis Armstrong, Duke Ellington, and the phenomenal addition of the Hall Johnson Choir, made the film a commercial success and a showcase for American black talent. That was surely progress of a kind.

Stormy Weather (1943) went much further. Unlike *Cabin in the Sky* or anything else yet seen (and too infrequently seen since), *Stormy Weather*

brought into light the kinds of comedy routines—absent the sexual innu-
endos—typically seen in black honky-tonks or nightclub musicals. The
story line was thin, tracing the careers and lives of a prominent black-
entertainment couple around their music and dance routines. But Bill
("Bojangles") Robinson, himself an African-American show business legend, transcended the limitations of the part in which he meets, loses, and
finally regains his protégée, played by Lena Horne. Left-winger Hy Kraft,
a Broadway writer with a single film credit and several successful theatrical outings under his belt, filled out the story through the "book" he developed for *Stormy Weather* from an original story by Jerry Horwin and
Seymour B. Robinson.[52]

At the first moment of the film, a retired tap dancer (Robinson) is
busy teaching his routines to neighborhood children when he receives an
entertainment-world paper celebrating his accomplishments as a "magnificent contribution of the colored race." Scanning the quotations from old
friends, he reminisces about his return as a hero of the First World War, his
discovery of a new talent in Horne's character, and the deep reality of going
back to casual labor on a riverboat. Next he is a waiter in a Beale Street bar
in Memphis who shows his stuff when a successful Horne and her promoter
come by. Discovered, he determines to put on a show in Harlem but runs
out of money; by a fortunate accident, he meets his old sidekick working as
a lowly bootblack. Things work out, and eventually Cab Calloway reunites
the couple for the home life that Horne's character has postponed.
Notwithstanding the Hollywood finish, the reality of unrewarded talent
and a subproletarian life for ordinary African-Americans is never far from
the surface.

The film's most memorable features include the longest cinematic appearance of Fats Waller—singing, playing piano, and jiving—amidst a
career (and geographical) move to Hollywood that otherwise proved a total
letdown. The Katherine Dunham dance troupe, the dancing Nicholas
Brothers, Calloway, and, of course, Horne and Robinson meanwhile kick
up a storm like nothing seen previously in film. If it all sounds merely entertaining and awfully tame, consider that Twentieth Century-Fox mulled
pulling the film from distribution and that less than half of Fox's affiliated
first-run theaters even showed it. This was the moment of racist riots
against wartime black populations moving into Detroit—along with the
anti-Chicano "zoot suit" riots in Los Angeles—and the very appearance of

crowds of dynamic blacks on film obviously seemed potentially dangerous. That *Stormy Weather* still made money testified to the sensation of other kinds stirred by its performances.[53]

Hollywood left-wingers itched to go further, but with a single exception their efforts had to await the last few years of the forties as the blacklist closed in. The only African-American writer on the blacklist, Carlton Moss, failed to receive on-screen credit for his one semidocumentary feature film, *The Negro Soldier* (1944). Written for Frank Capra's "Why We Fight" documentary series for the War Department, in which none of the writers featured got credit, it has Moss himself as a Harlem minister recognizing Armed Forces personnel in the church, then narrating the story of black soldiers (starting with the present, featuring Joe Louis in training camp) across American history. If *The Negro Soldier* practically skipped over the Civil War as too divisive a subject, it firmly implanted Crispus Attucks at the Boston Massacre leading to the American Revolution, and went on to narrate a wider African-American history, including Booker T. Washington and George Washington Carver; the founding of black colleges; the role of Jesse Owens at the 1936 Olympics in Berlin; the symbolism of Joe Louis knocking out Max Schmeling; and ended in an evocation of war for the fight against global injustice. Capra himself later insisted that the idea for the film began with reports of discrimination within the Armed Forces, but it seems likely that reports of low morale among blacks prompted the War Department effort. Repeatedly delayed by concerns about the racial sensitivities of whites, with unrevised prints actually destroyed and showings banned from military facilities in the south (where a large percentage of training was held), it had a troubled history and an imperfect outcome but nevertheless remains a milestone.

Every mention that Moss made of a segregation in early scripts was cut, all depictions of black officers dropped, and any indication of African-American anger, even at the Germans, was deleted. As Moss reflected decades after he had turned to making educational films for public schools, a Hollywood still locked in the segregation era of American public life (including most L.A. facilities) was not likely to have accepted him even as a non-left-winger. Initially asked to write *Pinky* for Elia Kazan's direction, he was dropped when he refused to depict an interracial romance as an inherent "tragedy." For him, the real tragedy was the blindness of the studio system and wider America.[54]

Nor were left-wingers entirely innocent in this atmosphere. Compliant, one-dimensional maids and the occasional foot-shuffling comic darky could be found in their thirties films, if fewer than in others' films. Jerome Chodorov coscripted the high-profile Bob Hope comedy *Louisiana Purchase* (1941) with lots of gags about southern politicians (including one filibustering by reading *Gone With the Wind* in Congress—à la *Mr. Smith Goes to Washington*) but plenty of smiling darkies as well.[55] Sidney Buchman wrote and produced the enormously successful film *The Jolson Story* (1946), which garnered a half-dozen Academy Awards and nominations for the tale of the repugnant real-life figure who made his fortune mimicking black culture (in clubs and among GIs, he was better known for demeaning sexual material about women). No less than John Howard Lawson provided some script material for the sequel, *Jolson Sings Again* (1949), which was virtually as bad, even though it deleted all blackface scenes, and once more starred Larry Parks, a leading Communist official in the Screen Actors Guild. Perhaps all that can be said is that the writers rationalized such films with their political stands, and genuinely tried to do better.[56]

The success of the Hollywood struggle was, however, wholly dependent upon the New Deal and patriotic antifascism. In that sense, the Hollywood Left was also a shadow movement, trying to find its own way amidst daily union and international issues but nearly always subject to forces beyond its control. The Popular Front spirit, indeed, carried the Beverly Hills Left forward better than the Party cared to know.

Growing Up and Growing Out

The FBI never lost a keen interest in Communist behavior in Hollywood, viewed as key to the interracial labor political struggles that J. Edgar Hoover considered to be organically connected parts of one giant subversive program. Internal documents now available offer milestones in the trail that the Bureau traced, mainly through the reports of its informers (including "F-10," the Bureau's code name for Ronald Reagan), leading straight back to the last years of the Depression and the formation of a leftwing Hollywood academy.[57]

However hilariously inaccurate the FBI (and much of later personal testimony to HUAC) might be and often was in details, marking down the likes of Dore Schary, Philip Dunne, and Dudley Nichols as "PL" ("party-liners"), they grasped the larger threat of seriously written pictures. *The Grapes of Wrath, Mr. Deeds Goes to Town, Mr. Smith Goes to Washington,* and the like *were* subversive to the America as seen and protected by Hoover and his spies.

Passing their own infantile stage of blindly denouncing Hollywood, Communists advanced toward a more sophisticated perspective as the decade drew to a close. Lewis Jacobs's *The Rise of the American Film* (1939), arguably the first sustained intellectual treatment of the subject, was not much more than a survey volume. But Jacobs treated films as the potential "people's art," maturing and growing toward their responsibility to become, for the modern age, what Greek theater had once been for the dawn of western civilization.[58] The change was coincidental. Only a few years earlier, Jacobs had been among the founders of the left-wing documentary film movement.

The formation of a secret Party school for Hollywoodites in 1938 had marked a modest step, improved upon in the League of American writers school (1940–43), established under difficult political conditions but open to the public. The LAW school set the tone by drawing more would-be studio employees—and FBI agents.[59]

Hollywood left-wingers (and not only writers or directors) were fast advancing toward their own ways of thinking about films, closer to pioneering Hollywood pedagogue John Weber's recollection that "a person could be an honest, dedicated Communist only if he or she was at the time a humanist, not a cold devotee of certain notions about social revolution." Translated into film work, "Marxism was not some hardline Bolshevik dedication . . . [but] dedication to the future of humanity" in another vein, whose ore had yet to be assayed.[60]

1. It has mostly been passed over, of course; Lester Cole devotes only one sentence to it in his autobiography, purely as an example: "An escapist 'entertainment' is political to the degree that it denies the existing social realities and, as in the film, *The President's Mystery,* I sought to inject such reality when the subject called for it." Cole, *Hollywood Red: The Autobiography of Lester Cole* (Palo Alto: Ramparts Books, 1981), 159. The movie title does not appear in the index.

2. Director Karlson was an interesting figure. Of Jewish-Irish background, the son of a trouper who moved from Dublin's Abbey Players to become a star on the Yiddish stage, he started out in law and worked his way up, though never far up, into films. His credits include several pre-blacklist films written by lefties: *G.I. Honeymoon, Bowery Bombshell,* and *The Big Cat.* He was especially admired by Hollywood liberals for *Black Gold,* an interracial family drama.

3. Cole, *Hollywood Red,* 145–50.

4. Ibid., 57–69, 81–84. The British journalist was Cedric Belfrage, later a founder of the progressive weekly *National Guardian* and author of *Promised Land.*

5. Three of Cole's other films at the time deserve mention. *The Man in Blue* (1937), a heredity-versus-environment film based on a story by Kubec Glasmon, has a slum boy pull a bank job after he has been falsely accused of an earlier crime. He finds his true self in prison with the help of a self-taught convict known as The Professor. *I Stole a Million* (1939), with Cole supplying a story for Nathanael West's script, featured George Raft as the taxi driver who has been cheated by a taxi-fleet capitalist on payments he has been making to buy his own cab, and falls into becoming a career criminal. *The Jury's Secret* (1938) exposes the class truths behind respectability, when a tycoon (and claimed philanthropist) tries to prevent a town from rebuilding after a calamitous flood. This attack upon respectability was initially rebuffed by the Breen Office, and the final version retracted some of the more outrageous accusations; *American Film Institute Catalog, Feature Films, 1931–1940, A–L* (Berkeley: University of California Press, 1993), 1079–1080; *M–Z,* 1299–1300.

6. Contemporary sources suggest that a future blacklistee, perhaps Cole himself, made uncredited script contributions to *Dragonwyck,* but no hard evidence has been produced on the subject.

7. To mention only one not discussed further in this book: *Dance, Girl, Dance* (1940), scripted by Tess Slesinger and Frank Davis and directed by Dorothy Arzner, the director's next-to-last film. Regarded as Arzner's cult film, it has Maureen O'Hara as a trained ballet dancer who comes to work in a chorus, then switches over to burlesque, and finally gains her vindication in professional ballet. Her telling off the patrons of the burlesque is one of the strongest gender speeches in contemporary cinema, but by no means as unique as some scholars insist, and pale indeed compared with Susan

Hayward's speech in *I Can Get It for You Wholesale*. See Gerald Peary, *Cult Movies: The Classics, the Sleepers, the Weird and the Wonderful* (New York: Gramercy Books, 1981), 59–63.

8. Ella Winter, "Battleship Hollywood," *Black & White* I (June 1939), 7. Winter's title, a play upon *Battleship Potemkin,* shows how strong the old metaphors remained.

9. Maurice Rapf, *Back Lot: Growing Up with the Movies* (Latham, NJ: Scarecrow Press, 1999), 48–49.

10. David Bordwell and Kristin Thompson, "Technological Change and Classical Film Style," in Tino Balio, editor, *Grand Design: Hollywood as a Modern Business Enterprise, 1930–39* (Berkeley: University of California Press, 1993), 109–41.

11. See, e.g., Beverly Heisner, *Hollywood Art: Art Direction in the Days of the Great Studios* (Jefferson, NC: McFarland & Company, 169–73, 286–89. *Becky Sharp* thus gave the hardworking British film commentator Graham Greene a welcome sensation: "the forgotten film gave me even a certain hope for color." Graham Greene, *Ways of Escape* (New York: Pocket Books, 1980), 45.

12. John Bright was in a unique position to see the exploitation of the technicians as well as the writers during the early years of sound. See his comments in his interview by Patrick McGilligan, *Tender Comrades: A Backstory of the Hollywood Blacklist* (New York: St. Martin's Press, 1997), 132.

13. Bordwell and Thompson, 140.

14. See Alan Casty, *The Films of Robert Rossen* (New York: Museum of Modern Art, 1969), a pamphlet-length volume prepared for a MOMA showing of Rossen's films; and Brian Neve, *Film and Politics in America* (London: Routledge, 1992), 18–27. For a later discussion of Rossen, see Chapters 5 and 8.

15. Neve, building on the work of others, points out that the sensational studio publicity campaign tended to overwhelm the Hays Office–dictated rewrites, making any adult viewer naive, indeed, to think these high-paid "hostesses" were not prostitutes, ibid., 19.

16. On the Curtiz-Rossen collaboration, see James C. Robertson, *The Casablanca Man: The Cinema of Michael Curtiz* (London: Routledge, 1993), 56–57. Rossen also wrote the sentimental *A Child Is Born* (1940), an adaptation from the play *Life Begins,* by Mary McDougal Axelson. This cinematic melodrama concerns a father in trouble with the law, wrestling with his conscience at the time of a son's birth.

17. See the treatment of the film in the *American Film Institute Catalog of Motion Pictures Produced in the United States, Feature Films, 1941–1950, M–Z* (Berkeley: University of California Press, 1999), 2097–2098.

18. The rules of the sea, virtually unchanged since the time of the American Revolution, deprived seamen of the least democratic redress. A heartrending labor-oriented film version of *Two Years Before the Mast* (1946), from the famed novel by Richard Henry Dana, starring Alan Ladd and cowritten by Melvin Levy, was accompanied by a political publicity effort featuring the Three Stooges successfully urging the passage of the La Follette Seaman's Act.

19. Walter Bernstein interviewed by Paul Buhle, in *Tender Comrades*, 45–46.

20. Abraham Polonsky interviewed by Paul Buhle and Dave Wagner, July 1997, Beverly Hills.

21. See John Wexley interviewed by Patrick McGilligan, in *Tender Comrades*, 698–721; unfortunately, Wexley has nothing to say about the film itself. His next credit was for coscripting *The Amazing Dr. Clitterhouse* (1938), a Runyonesque tale of a professor who falls among affable thieves. It is memorable mostly for being the first credit of coscripter John Huston, who devotes less than a sentence to the film in his autobiography, *An Open Book* (New York: Ballantine, 1972), 82, and fails to credit Wexley's role. Huston nevertheless remained good friends with Wexley. In two more years, Huston was at Warners working on *High Sierra* and *The Maltese Falcon*.

22. An all-too Hollywood melodramatic adventure follows, and Cooper gets to ask rhetorically, "What's better work for an American than fighting for democracy?" But the script was far from the best thing in the film. Villain Akim Tamirof was nominated for a Best Supporting Actor Oscar (other nominations were for Best Cinematography and Best Score), and a descendant of Leo Tolstoy actually worked as a technical adviser! See *American Film Institute Catalog Feature Films, 1931–1940* (Berkeley: University of California Press, 1993), 741–42.

23. See Bernard F. Dick, *The Merchant Prince of Poverty Row: Harry Cohn of Columbia Pictures* (Lexington: University Press of Kentucky, 1993), especially Chapter 6, "CapraCohn," 89–118. The description of Columbia as a resident of Poverty Row is, however, a stretch.

24. See Joseph McBride, *Frank Capra: The Catastrophe of Success* (New York: Simon and Schuster, 1992), 412–22. One of Roosevelt's favorite politicians, Senator James F. "Jimmy" Byrnes of South Carolina, reported that he walked out of

the theater at the end of the film, concluding he'd just seen "a picture that is going to tell . . . the people that 95 out of 96 senators are corrupt . . . exactly the kind of picture that dictators of totalitarian governments would like to have their subjects believe exists in a democracy." (McBride, p. 421.) See also the excellent section on Capra in Brian Neve, *Film and Politics in America: A Social Tradition* (London: Routledge, 1992), 28–49.

25. Starring Jean Rogers, *Heaven with a Barbed Wire Fence* was also memorable for the feature film debut of Glenn Ford, one of the left-wing writers' favorite character actors of the 1940s and very early 1950s.

26 The film's protagonist is predictably saved from further self-discovery by a loyal hometown boyfriend, but the point has been made.

27. Jeanine Basinger, *A Woman's View* (Hanover: Wesleyan University Press, 1993), 488–89, 495–97.

28. Bruce Cook, *Dalton Trumbo* (New York: Scribner's Sons, 1977), 140–41.

29. Ring Lardner, Jr., interview by Ronald L. Davis, Southern Methodist University Oral History Program, January 11, 1985, 5–7. This transcript was kindly made available to us by Lardner. As he handed it over (in 1993) at his Central Park West apartment, the phone rang and he answered—it was "Kate" Hepburn checking facts for her own memoirs.

30. Ring Lardner, Jr., interview, 8–9.

31. Stewart wrote one more screenplay-adaptation for Hepburn, *Without Love* (1945), a Hepburn-Tracy matchup from another Philip Barry play, in which lonely scientist Tracy is in WWII Washington working on a secret project, and happens to move into the basement of an elegant house of blueblood Hepburn who is affianced to the snobbish Keenan Wynn. Agreeing to abandon all romantic pretensions after their respective past disappointments, they strive for an unromantic, businesslike, companionate marriage. Inevitably, after assorted complications, they also fall in love. *Without Love* was one of the biggest box office films of 1945.

32. Interesting for the day, *Beauty for the Asking* had the protagonist creating her own cosmetic empire based upon her personal invention of a superior face cream. In the process, she loses her fair-weather boyfriend to her financial patroness, eventually sees him beg for a return, and takes a favorite alternative in these kinds of films—the nice guy conveniently waiting in the wings, in this case a helpful male employee who will neither betray nor stand in the way of her worldly accomplishments.

33. In later years, Jarrico was fond of recalling his naïveté. Thanks to him for several generous interviews (by Paul Buhle) in 1991–92. A reading of *RKO Classic Screenplays: Tom, Dick and Harry* (New York: Frederick Ungar, 1968) recalls Jarrico's quick wit.

34. Paul Jarrico interviewed by Patrick McGilligan, *Tender Comrades,* 336–38.

35. Especially notable is *Cotton Queen* (1936), near-documentary in its depiction of the working class at play, if also predictable in its cross-class romantic plot. See Bernard Vorhaus interviewed by John Baxter, in *Tender Comrades,* 675–81.

36. According to American Film Institute research, Muse was hired as actor, technical adviser, and dance director for the film. The exact relation of the Hughes-Muse original and the shooting script remains unknown. See *American Film Institute Catalog: Feature Films, 1931–1940, M–Z* (Berkeley: University of California Press, 1993), 2361.

37. The proletarian or lower-middle-class family and the spunky teen also had a larger role for left-wing writers in the B districts. Edward Eliscu, more usually a lyricist, found his scripting métier with affable pre-sitcom family adventures like *Little Miss Nobody* and *Every Saturday Night* (both 1936) for Jane Withers, the Shirley Temple of Fox's B unit.

38. Roberts's coscripter on *Peck's Bad Boy* was sometime playwright, later friendly witness Bernard Schubert, who had earlier written *Don Q, Jr.* for tennis star Bill Tilden in 1927, a play dubbed by *Variety* "the lemon of the year." The same year as *Peck's Bad Boy,* John Howard Lawson made uncredited script contributions to an adaptation of Stevenson's *Treasure Island,* directed by Victor Fleming. If Cooper was not quite at his best—as some critics complained—Wallace Beery was perfectly splendid as a roguish, constantly prevaricating, potentially murderous but still somehow lovable pirate Long John Silver.

39 Jean Rouveral Butler's mother had written the play *Skidding,* upon which the Andy Hardy series was based, and she worked on contract scriptwriting through the 1920s. Jean Butler's films as actress included W. C. Fields's *It's a Gift* (1934) and Hopalong Cassidy's *Bar 20 Rides Again* (1935). Jean Rouveral Butler, interviewed by Paul Buhle and Dave Wagner, *Tender Comrades,* 155–60.

40. Renoir's film *The Southerner* (1945), for which Butler did not get credit, and *The Big Night* (for Losey, 1951) are considered in Chapter 8. He suffered from

hypertension and died of a stroke at fifty-four. *Sodom and Gomorrah* (1963) and *The Legend of Lylah Clare* (1968), coscripted by Butler in his last years, are among Aldrich's least successful films from any point of view. Hugo and Jean Butler's papers are in the American Heritage Center, the University of Wyoming, Laramie.

41. Jean Rouveral Butler interview with Paul Buhle and Dave Wagner in *Tender Comrades*, 163. It is worth adding that future blacklistee and Oscar winner Waldo Salt, Butler's close friend, also made a script contribution.

42. Spencer Tracy as *Edison, the Man* (1940), with costory by Butler (and Dore Schary), was totally predictable by contrast, and in violent contradiction with the real-life wily entrepreneur who valued his inventions less than his financial standing and spent his vital energies trying to monopolize the film industry.

43. Jean Rouveral Butler, interviewed with Paul Buhle and Dave Wagner, *Tender Comrades*, 161.

44. Butler also wrote the script for *Barnacle Bill* (1941), an often delightful family drama with a roughneck soldier (played by Wallace Beery) brought to task by would-be fiancée Marjorie Main, and his child, Virginia Weidler, whom he likes but who symbolizes the need for him to settle down and accept his family duties.

45. *The Strawberry Roan* (1948), a Gene Autry color vehicle with a script by Julian Zimet that looks a great deal like a Flicka knockoff, has a lad who is spiritually crippled grow fond of a horse that nevertheless throws and apparently cripples him physically. The wrathful ranch owner and dad orders the horse shot, but foreman Gene hides him, eventually returning to the ranch with the boy mounted and recovered. Gene doesn't even get to kiss the girl, but the roan in question has found a wild mare and sired a future heart winner. See the *Variety* review by "Whit," April 28, 1948, for special praise of the film's commercial potential.

46. Quoted in the American Film Institute Catalog, *Feature Films, 1941–1950, M–Z* (Berkeley: University of California Press, 2000), 1666–67.

47. Bernard F. Dick, *Hellman in Hollywood* (Rutherford, NJ: Fairleigh Dickinson University Press, 1982), 36–47. The film starred Miriam Hopkins and Merle Oberon, with Joel McCrea at the apex of the triangle and Bonita Granville as the bad little girl. The 1961 remake, again by William Wyler, with Shirley MacLaine and Audrey Hepburn in the key roles, is somewhat less successful

dramatically, but broke taboos on lesbianism and features an exceptionally strong performance by MacLaine as a "butch" character. Hellman had already found the Philistine side of Hollywood work in *The Dark Angel* (1935), a silly World War I British drama of blindness and stiff-upper-lip nobility.

48. Dick, *Hellman in Hollywood,* 58–71.

49. See David Lang's testimony, *Communist Activities in the Motion Picture Industry, Hearings before the Committee on Un-American Activities, House of Representatives* (Washington, D.C.: Government Printing Office, 1951), hereinafter referred to as *Motion Picture Hearings.*

50. Screenwriters included Donald Ogden Stewart, Alan Campbell, and Henry Blankfort, along with Ferenc Molnár, Samuel Hoffenstein, Ladislas Fodor, László Vadnay, László Görög, and Lamar Trotti. According to contemporary materials, Robeson described the outcome as "very offensive."

51. See Clayton R. Koppes, "Regulating the Screen: The Office of War Information and the Production Code Administration," in Thomas Schatz, *Boom and Bust: American Cinema in the 1940s* (Berkeley: University of California Press, 1997), 273.

52. Kraft's only previous film credit was for *Champagne Waltz* (1937), a literally bubbly comedy about music and love interests in Vienna and Manhattan. He was known best at the time for the theatrical hit *Cafe Crown,* set in the famed Yiddishist Lower East Side institution, the Cafe Royale, about the effort of an aging star (Morris Carnovsky) trying to persuade a prosperous figure (Sam Jaffe) to back a new production of *King Lear. Cafe Crown* marked the debut of Sam Wanamaker, and was revived in 1964 by the blacklisted Kraft, with Sam Levene, Theodore Bikel, and Alan Alda. Several other post-blacklist Kraft plays also featured Jaffe, another blacklist victim.

53. See *American Film Institute Catalog of Motion Pictures Produced in the United States, Feature Films, 1941–1950, M–Z,* 2335–36.

54. We express our gratitude to Moss (or rather, to his memory) for his granting an interview to Paul Buhle in 1992. See also *American Film Institute Catalog, Feature Films, 1941–1950, M–Z,* 1675–66.

55. Based on a musical by Irving Berlin and shot in color, *Louisiana Purchase* got Academy Award nominations for Cinematography, Art, and Art Direction.

56. See Chapter 8, on the later and better 1940s films about African-American life.

57. *FBI Papers, Reel 5, #100–15732,* 2–5.

58. Lewis Jacobs, *The Rise of the American Film* (New York: Harcourt, 1939), 538–39.

59. See Chapter 2 on the first, informal Party school of Hollywood and its two teachers, Weber and Arthur Birnkrandt.

60. John Weber interviewed by Paul Buhle in *Tender Comrades*, 688–89.

WAR ON TWO (OR THREE) FRONTS

THE MCCARTHY-ERA IMAGE OF wartime Hollywood with rampant Communist subversion—and what was almost worse, Communist respectability, personal prestige, high salaries, and influence—remains a fascinating distortion of American cultural life. The image was wildly exaggerated but not entirely false, leaving aside the issue of what exactly was being "subverted." From a cinematic view, nearly all the charges offered only a sidebar to more complex and more important developments.

If the didactic (even more, the musical) pro-Russianism of a handful of films was more than understandable in moments when the Red Army and civilians took the German punishment for the West, Hollywood conservatives and FBI agents nevertheless rightly glimpsed a certain anticapitalism—even as they refused to admit that the images corresponded with widespread popular sentiment. But making a political statement was never the key issue, especially not during wartime. Intuitively, because of the opportunity before them but also because of their complex critical and personal identification with major trends, the Hollywood left-wingers sought to extend the useful metaphors, visual as well as dialogue, and subtly transform them into something beyond the previous reach of film. And yet they were studio artists first and foremost, working within the limits of their domain.

The changing structure of the industry had already begun to give a small handful of independent producers a little-precedented freedom, even while a financial keystone of the older independent production was being lost. During the war, major and some relatively minor studios gained "essential war industry" status that gave them access to the raw film stock denied the real Poverty Row operations. The actual number of independents declined sharply from more than ninety in 1939 to fewer than twenty in 1944, losing out an overall share of production—along with foreign films, many of them blocked out for the duration of the conflict—from half to less than a fourth. Monopolism (or oligopolism) in the raw sense flourished as never before.[1]

But these stark figures were in some ways deceptive. The astronomical rise of film production to meet consumer demand during the same period of global warfare prompted the multiplication of "B" production units that in many ways replicated or improved upon the function of the vanished independents. Meanwhile, the studio system showed signs of a sort of preparatory disintegration from within. Back in the 1930s, a few determined stars and their handlers—more at the bottom of the prestige scale than at the top—had joined the shift toward independent production efforts; in the emerging monied era, far more in the upper strata made plans to do so.

Along with the new independent producer and independent-minded director came the day of the writer, albeit more subtly and indirectly. This is not to say that the producers and studios, shadowed by the bankers, lost their overarching influence on the general shape of the industry. But from the top layers to the bottom, handfuls of artists enjoyed a surprising degree of autonomy. Noir, as we shall see, notoriously owed its proliferation to small budgets and short shooting schedules made possible by technological savings. But so did the wartime films in almost every imaginable genre besides noir. The big films remained big (with some important thematic shifts), and the stock B films changed subtly in some scripts' suggestion of something more tantalizing than the same prewar genres offered.

Meanwhile, accelerating changes in technology, from improved lenses to movable dollies—some of the most important of these pioneered by intimates and staunch allies of the Left like James Wong Howe and Edgar G. Ulmer—also went a long way toward putting the successful director into the driver's seat within the prestige units of the regular studios. The vast expansion in film production wore the studio bureaucracy thin, the skyrocketing profits encouraged execs to give hands-on artists their head, and the mechanical improvements made films more appealing as well as actually cheaper in some respects to produce. Under these conditions, even the run-of-the-mill director could stretch his legs a bit. The end of the war, as expected, brought a veritable explosion of these efforts almost as real as the explosion of strikes rocking the nation during 1945–46.

According to some distaff interpretations of cinematic wartime, the late 1930s shift toward the "dialogic camera" method, in which characters gain a greater equality with one another and project multiple viewpoints for the audience to assess, came to a screeching conceptual halt with the antifascist effort. Technicians, directors, and actors therefore conveyed, in this view, a single, indisputably patriotic antifascist message. The validation of the popular disdain for the wealthy classes, the emphasis on "the people" (as in *ordinary* people) at the proper foundation of national life all diminished as Hollywood emphasized class and social unity—with the powerful now decisively revalidated. What has been called the "conversion narrative," the abandonment of oppositional values to the benefit of hierarchical institutions like the American military purportedly saving the world, spelled the end of the 1930s dream, notwithstanding moments of noir to come.[2]

This perspective contains some real insights into the ways that "Doctor New Deal," in FDR's own phrase, was abandoned for "Doctor Win the War," never to return: Military and defense mobilization became the accepted engine of economic growth, and idealistic efforts morphed from toppling the powerful into unifying the society. But in an inversion of screenwriters' own experience, this view both exaggerates the freedoms of the prewar (at the least, pre-1940) Hollywood system and drastically underestimates the empowering character of subtle and not-so-subtle shifts during wartime.

The formation of the Office of War Information in early 1942 and its Bureau of Motion Pictures (BMP)—its "reviewing unit" run by ardent New Dealer Dorothy Jones—would prove a formidable setback for Hays Office censorship. The decree that studios should ask, "Will this help win the war?" was to validate, over the next four years, scenes and emphases, from Nazi sadism to evocations of the heroic Red Army, that could not possibly have passed muster previously. Subsequent charges of left-wing influence could not have been entirely mistaken when the BMP's 1942 pamphlet *Manual for the Motion Picture Industry* read like an applied version of Vice President Henry Wallace's then ubiquitous tract, *Century of the*

Common Man. By the end of the decade, Truman's anti-Communist liberal supporters along with conservatives would declare the same Wallace an agent of Communist aims.[3]

Back in 1942, the universal acceptance of antifascist themes earlier scorned freed screenwriters and directors to attempt entertaining "message" films like *The Talk of The Town* to validate "the people" as heroes and heroines in overalls or khakis, to claim that the very point of national unity was to create a world and an America different from the one they were leaving behind—even while exercising new levels of nostalgia for homely virtues. America mobilized for social change was a New Dealish notion fiercely resisted by conservatives before the war; now it often seemed as if empowerment at the top (in new government agencies) and at the bottom (in the will of ordinary folk to exercise initiative and do more than their part) went hand in hand.

The change of mood also allowed filmmakers to risk popular depiction, in nearly unprecedented ways, of predatory merchants and grasping government officials, albeit far away in other lands or back in the old West. Wartime, really from the onset of Hitler's invasion of France, marked not the simple eclipse but the filmic coming-of-age of New Deal themes. Only in hindsight, by extracting the contradictions, did it also appear to mark their negation. From inside Hollywood, also from the large parts of liberated Europe and Asia where the previous ruling classes had been discredited, it looked like a different ending of the real-life war narrative lay ahead.

Seen in a different light, then, 1940–45 properly constitutes the climax as well as the finish of the "Classic Hollywood" bundle of conventions in place since the beginning of sound. So thoroughly did that era of unquestioned studio dominance shape world cinema and what viewers take "movies" to be that we forget the obvious: Nearly all the top studios came to power before 1945, and most of the top stars of the previous era survived afterward only by rehashing the same roles with slightly altered settings. Even the genres rapidly dimmed, with the best of screwball comedies, costume dramas, musicals, swashbucklers, and biographies already "in the can" by the time President Harry Truman had introduced the world to the fear-shadowed epoch of atomic warfare.[4]

Russophile films like *Song of Russia* and *Mission to Moscow,* Russophile moments like the landing of the American navy crew of *Action in the North Atlantic* in the Soviet port of Murmansk (where John Garfield and his buddies can simultaneously hail the Red Fleet and admire Russian women's legs), offered the evidence HUAC wanted but occupied a very small space in left-wing film work. Though this space would doubtless have been larger if studio leadership and the daunted but game censors of the Hays Office had permitted, the more manageable subjects like romance, comedy, musicals, family movies, mysteries, and above all the new-minted (or suddenly acceptable) antifascist genre happened to be where the vast majority of jobs opened. Films like *Casablanca* and *Watch on the Rhine* had direct political points to make, but from another and far less obvious standpoint so did Judy Canova vehicles, all about a less-than-gorgeous but decidedly characterful hick making her way—as warbler, male impersonator, or even inadvertent striptease artist—into the new world of Rosie the Riveter theater audiences. Likewise, *National Velvet, Lassie Come Home,* and *My Friend Flicka* might conceivably have been produced at any time. But they *were* produced when the home front badly needed boosting. New young stars like Elizabeth Taylor and Roddy McDowall emerged along with the left-wing writers who wrote their memorable parts.

To take a genre case in point: Canova's sudden rise (thanks in career terms to the erstwhile opera singer's shrewd adoption of a hillbilly persona) can be attributed not only to a booming entertainment-hungry audience but also to the dawning truth that the very success of the familiar film stereotypes had begun to invite takeoffs, an early form of camp with its own distinctive rules. Audiences laughed with her self-conscious mocking of female gentility, her sheer silliness and democratic impulses in left-written films like *Sis Hopkins* (1941), *True to the Army* (1942), or *Singin' in the Corn* (1946). In the first, Canova is tricked into singing and stripping in a burlesque theater, a scene that the Hays Office found objectionable on numerous counts, including breast exposure; in the second, she sneaks her way into an army camp and takes part in a presumably all-male musical as a multiple cross-dresser; and in the last, she presides over the return of a small Western town to the Indians from whom the land had been stolen generations previous.[5]

Horror-to-comedy offers yet better examples, as we have seen. Frankenstein, Dracula, and monsters of various types and shades associated above all with Boris Karloff and Bela Lugosi had practically exhausted classic horror within a decade. The world obviously trembled with other horrors by 1941. But more to the point, a return of the same creatures was more likely to inspire laughter than dread in the self-trained film audience, thanks in no small part to the inspiration and extremely clever scripting of several left-wingers and the huge success of one of their movies, *Hold That Ghost.* From then on, monsters and ghosts of all kinds, as well as specialized creatures like the Invisible Man, Mr. Hyde, Frankenstein, and Dracula, reappear with Abbott and Costello in tow. Whenever innocent Lou met the monsters and reality-principle Bud predictably scorned the little man's reports as fanciful, audiences erupted in a succession of released tension and downright hilarity. Meanwhile, the more inventive horror films became so vividly psychological that late-in-the-century shockers like *Pulp Fiction* had nothing on their predecessors save enhanced special effects and an absence of censorship.

Yet the real story was the war itself, the home front, and that movies-intensive zone of soldiers, sailors, and airmen training while entertaining (often, unintentionally confounding and confusing) themselves and civilians. The simple fact that thousands of films were being made for a domestic audience willing and eager to go more often—and able to afford it—rendered this celluloid outpouring improbably significant as a kind of social history of and for the masses.

The cinematic advances making possible ever greater degrees of realism were restrained until the end of the fighting mainly by the compulsion to deliver patriotic messages. Hollywood's Communists, second to none in boosting the war effort, nevertheless often seized the occasion to move ahead. Especially for the many left-wing writers and directors involved in Armed Forces and assorted government documentaries, this camera-realism was a natural impulse and the unprecedented skill-sharing experience of wartime, if destined never to be used to its full potential.

Thematic antifascist imperatives gained status and a quirky sort of leverage as studios strained to prove their sincere commitment to the war effort. Sadly, left-wing writers craved to do more plots about Partisans behind enemy lines and about Europe's (and Asia's) fascist-collaborationist businessmen than could interest audiences or persuade studio execs. But (accounting for all the vulgarities of mistranslation) dozens of the hardest-hitting political films on international issues ever seen on American screens were made at this moment. At the same time, a Hollywood that had routinely kept African-Americans in cheerfully subservient roles now began to yield to political attacks upon the domestic racism that spawned homegrown Hitlers as breakthroughs to dignity first arrived the only way they could, i.e., in splashy musicals. Even women's status rose in the same shadow, turning the weepy films of the 1930s into more characterful pieces that might conclude in the happy yielding of "I know the answer but he hasn't asked the question yet," but still showed a contrasting narrative of women's strength right up to the Hollywood ending.[6]

The servicemen's film, purportedly drawing upon training-camp shows but really reviving vaudeville traditions one last time cinematically, verged into the wartime big-budget musical. Here, the Gene Kelly–Frank Sinatra special fairly blew apart the genteel Fred Astaire predecessors of the thirties and recuperated the excitement of theater with some of the manic energy of the Marx Brothers. Meanwhile, prosperity and probably the absence of paterfamilias on the home front practically introduced the teenager as a cinematic staple. What did the bobby-soxers do when not either swooning for Frankie or nabbing the occasional Axis spy/saboteur? They mugged, sang, and danced on high school or college campuses, in malt shops or on amateur stages, eager to grow up in a different world that could be both more secure and more exciting.

Unsettling and nonaffirming was the home-front film with a more mixed message. Foreshadowing noir but less dangerous than dysfunctional, a handful of films portrayed (especially in the last years) civilians who treated the situation selfishly, couldn't handle the stress, or who needed a severe shock to come to their senses. At best, perhaps, their characters glimpsed something wrong that victory over Germans, Italians, and Japanese could not solve; hardly observed outside the noir frame, this melancholy notion would position the "problem" films ahead.

Opportunity in any case knocked and the radicals responded, sometimes with a naïveté that they would rue later on, but also with an unprecedented enthusiasm. Did they perceive that they were finishing off an old era as well as edging toward a new one? It's an important question that can best be taken up by considering first the films themselves, the screenwriters' collective efforts, and then (in the following chapter) the reshaping of film criticism.

Pacifism to Box Office Boffo

To say that the Hollywood Left greeted the U.S. declaration of war in December 1941 with a sigh of relief would be a considerable understatement. The Hitler-Stalin period, with its terrible loss of both credibility and allies, had ended as far as the veteran antifascists were concerned when the Germans invaded the Soviet Union months earlier. But their own status remained very much in doubt until America needed the Russians as allies. Meanwhile, the Red Army retreat riveted Hollywoodites at large with the fear of total German victory in Europe. Now suddenly, amidst the ongoing crisis, it was an American-Russian military alliance and the pledging of U.S. goods to Russians willing to lose millions of citizens and keep fighting that offered a way out of despair.

Shrewd political analysts, in Hollywood as well as in New York, Paris, London, and the Red zones of China, could see the scenario unfolding: Communists and their sympathizers across the globe would once again be the foremost source of antifascist energies; and the United States would simultaneously become, perforce, the all-powerful ally that antifascism had always lacked. In their own peculiar narratives, later friendly witnesses confirmed this view, fairly gushing about the patriotism or apparent patriotism of the wartime Party milieu. Meta Rosenberg (at the time married to director Irving Reis, who taught occasionally at assorted Party schools in Hollywood) later swore to HUAC investigators that she detected "no conflict in my mind in terms of attitude of the party toward the war effort and the attitudes of the Government toward the war effort."[7] Quite to the contrary, the Party out-patrioted everyone else in Hollywood, from films to sales of war bonds and, above all, in mobilizing public support for the servicemen. Richard Collins, who coscripted *Song of Russia* with Paul Jarrico, likewise told the House Committee that Party members were useful to the studios and especially helpful to fellow screenwriters "because they had a more international viewpoint [and] . . . were in a good position to help in many cases where there were [assignments] that had to do with our allies, Britain, China . . . Soviet Russia, the underground movements, and so on."[8]

So, in a real sense, the Left's Hollywood moment had come. The politically shaded films on international themes that had been impossible to make as late as 1938–39 became barely possible in 1940, and sometimes wildly popular as well as widely admired by 1941–42. Left-wingers across the country, emphatically including artists well as intellectuals, rapidly enlisted in the war effort, bringing many talented writers and directors from Broadway or radio into documentary war work around Hollywood. Suddenly, a new generation of writers and directors took shape, working between war assignments (or waiting for them), finding ways to entertain and educate in the permissive atmosphere where Communists were, for the moment, anyway, both artistic and more than symbolic political representatives of heroic Russia.

In retrospect, the pacifist mood that the Communists sought to embrace in their unpopular days, before 1936, and again briefly during the Hitler-Stalin Pact period, had scarcely offered serious possibilities for Hollywood film. Not only was the mood evanescent; Hollywood would not permit much railing against the munitions makers and militarists who were (in real life as well as left-wing fiction) the first and final beneficiaries of any war. Isolationism of the America First variety enrolled actor Robert Young and a small handful of other personalities during 1939–40, but had few if any advocates in the studios whose moguls were mostly Jewish and whose bankers planned to take large profits from prospective war orders.

Few moments of pacifistic film stand out in the 1930s after the aforementioned *All Quiet on the Western Front* and *The Man Who Reclaimed His Head.* But Waldo Salt's script for *The Shopworn Angel* (1938) has Margaret Sullavan as a glamorous singer of doubtful morals who suddenly comes to grips with the horrors of war, through losing her heart to cornball-sincere trainee Jimmy Stewart, the point hammered home with war footage and Stewart's inability at first to thrust his bayonet into the training-field dummy. The serialized juvenile-aimed *Adventures of Captain Marvel* (1940), coscripted by Sol Shor, closes with a Superman-style figure hurling the "death ray machine" into a pit, warning that no government should possess the power to destroy life with such concentrated energy. Like the fullest popular treatment of the implied pacifist theme—*They Gave Him a Gun* (1937) written by Maurice Rapf, with Spencer Tracy losing his girl to a doughboy buddy who learns to kill and makes himself into a hired killer— these antiwar moments are mostly plot afterthoughts, gestures toward the broad popular sentiment that rarely reached films.

By contrast, we have seen how Republic Westerns like *Saddle Pals*

(1938), out of the normal line of sight of studio caution against antifascist themes but firmly in the saddle of patriotism, had already broached political issues of "foreign enemies" and restricted materiels without bringing down anything like the wrath experienced by Lawson's *Blockade*. Still, *Confessions of a Nazi Spy* (1939), written by Wexley and directed by independent-minded leftish émigré Anatole Litvak, would remain the singular opening shot, with all the dangerous implications of the genre—including stock footage, in a later rerelease that Wexley despised, of the Russian invasion of Finland as a counterpart totalitarian threat to that of the Germans.[9]

The plot of *Confessions of a Nazi Spy* treated a real-life case of an innocent recruited into the German-American Bund (a fascistic organization strongest in Wisconsin and Long Island, but elsewhere no competition for native racist-fascist groups like the Silver Shirts and the Ku Klux Klan), and thence into espionage, with the assistance of the German embassy. Nevertheless, Warner Brothers received warnings from the Dies Committee against the slurring of a "friendly country"! Wexley later swore that he'd seen Dies personally exiting from Jack Warner's office, and that the executive urged him to include Communist characters along with Nazis as subversives to be curbed. Wexley refused, naturally. But opening *Confessions of a Nazi Spy* in New York with armed guards was not just a publicity stunt, even though it may also have served that purpose well. Real-life Nazi sympathizers actually burned down a theater in Milwaukee that was playing the film; this was nothing compared to Poland, where two of the film's distributors were assassinated.[10]

Despite all this, *Confessions* remains in most ways a typical Warners picture, substituting German-American Bundists for criminals, insinuating the resentments that prompted confused Americans to get mixed up in a dangerous as well as unpatriotic business, and straightening it all out with the help of savvy lawmen at the end. These particular criminals were, of course, no more lovably picaresque than the hoods in *The Public Enemy*, and had moreover no social or psychological justifications (such as poverty or oppression or bad childhoods) to do as their predecessors did. Henry O'Neill, playing a deserter from the German Army, tries to straighten himself out with homeland authorities through a spy mission, but is picked up and leads the trail to the wrongdoers. Paul Lukas, the dentist who doubles as the leader of the Bund, was carefully coached to speak and offer mannerisms closely akin to the Fuehrer himself. After some struggle, the studio allowed posters very much like those used in real life by the Bund. Adding to the drive for realism, Wexley's coscripter Milton Krims actually attended Bund meetings in disguise, and an official of the studio's story department shot interiors of pro-Bund restaurants in Manhattan's Yorkville, as well as drawing upon the "look" of Bund publications.

But the plot hinged most improbably upon Edward G. Robinson as an FBI agent. As every Hollywood radical (or liberal) knew, the FBI in real life was never as interested in the Bund as in Communism. High agency officials including Hoover himself regarded Jews as likely subversives; not all that far from Nazi ideology in another key respect, he and many of his agents considered movements for black equality a Communist-inspired effort at promoting a biologically impossible egalitarianism.[11] In the film, the pursuit of a respectable ally against fascism thrust the Bureau forward—at the very moment when the real-life FBI intensified its campaign against Communists, from the labor movement to antifascist fund-raising campaigns. Did Wexley hope to defy and thereby change reality or merely find a convenient hook upon which to hang the action? Or was the urgency of the Nazi threat so great that every other consideration had to be subordinated? In any case, hardly a charge made against "foreign subversion" in *Confessions of a Nazi Spy* would *not* be turned against Communists during the Pact and with more concentrated ferocity during the decade after the war.

Or consider *Beasts of Berlin* (1939, aka *Goose Step*), a more extreme oddity made by a small production company with exiled German actors, its distribution attempted unsuccessfully not once but three times—again in 1941 and 1943, with the title altered—in an attempt to find the elusive antifascist audience. Its plot, probably uncommercial in any case, lionized an underground anti-Nazi movement within Germany, a favorite Communist fantasy destined to be realized only at the last moments of Hitler's power, and then suppressed by the Allies themselves. The film's heavily political tone, with Communists, socialists, and Catholics sharing danger and prison camp life, found no audience resonance. Shepard Traube, a talented theatrical director with scarcely a film credit before or afterward to justify his blacklisting, had determinedly seen the doomed production through.[12]

These two films practically (and astonishingly) constituted Hollywood's net contribution to explicit antifascism before 1940. In the Senate hearings of 1941, definite precursors to the postwar Red hunt, conservatives accused Hollywood of bending public will toward prowar sentiment. But it was the fear of profit loss far more than government regulation that caused leading executives to back off after the first of the strong antifascist films. Shrinkage of studio earnings in Germany and Italy represented a major loss of markets, something they continued to avoid by generally vetoing antifascist film projects even after Hitler's invasion of Belgium and the declaration of war by Great Britain in September 1939.[13] But the sense of inevitability as well as the horror stories coming from central and eastern Europe unleashed, over the course of 1940 and the first two-thirds of 1941, a cinematic near-revolution (at least in retrospect) that understandably unnerved those who correctly feared that the shooting war for America was around the corner.

A full half of the first ten additional films described by scholars as "unequivocally anti-Nazi" came from Left-wielded pens or directors' chairs. The legion of heartrending exotics began with director Irving Pichel's *The Man I Married,* retitled from *I Married a Nazi,* starring Joan Bennett (shortly afterward linked romantically with Orson Welles's producer, the reliable progressive John Houseman), quite wonderfully showing how an ordinary American comes to consciousness, step by step, about the evil mentality and evil worse deeds of the Nazis. In the film, Bennett's German-born husband, played by Francis Lederer, insists upon returning home; as they travel, he falls for a Nazi dame, compelling Bennett to scheme an escape to America with her son. A brief highlight shows Czechs in a cattle car en route to a slave-labor camp after Lederer in a facing train coach gives his wife a mini-sermon on German "efficiency."

Escape (1940), written by Marguerite Roberts, and *Four Sons* (1940), by John Howard Lawson, described European families divided against themselves. Mervyn LeRoy directed Roberts's film, and Norma Shearer (then at the peak of her popularity) stars as a Nazi general's mistress who suddenly realizes what is happening around her and assists a young man (Robert Taylor, in the first of the "Communistic" features that the conservative actor would later regret) in getting his Jewish mother out of a concentration camp to freedom. *Four Sons,* a remake of a 1928 silent film (now anti-Nazi rather than antiwar), has a Czech family divided over the German takeover *Anschluss*. Son Don Ameche and his mother finally resolve to save Jews—and save themselves as moral beings—by resisting the supposedly friendly invaders.

Escape could be described as predictable, if only (by virtue of the near absence of such films up to 1941) in retrospect: The evil of the prospective enemies cuts right through to the bone of every bad character, and the problem is getting the others to recognize the dangers that it poses to themselves and the world at large. Yet the treatment of the themes was strong and the attack on anti-Semitism exceptionally bold for the moment. *Four Sons*, Lawson's first political film after *Blockade*, was much subtler and more challenging. The depicted appeal of German nationalism to the Sudetenland Germans—ethnically German citizens of Czechoslovakia thanks to the doubtful nationality carved out of the defunct Austro-Hungarian Empire by the Versailles Treaty—had firm roots in reality. Pro-Nazi organizations developed a genuine popular base, although Lawson is quick to place the responsibility upon the petite bourgeoisie. The shift of a potential bride from a loyal Czech to his pro-Nazi sibling symbolizes the complex set of connections on both sides; the multiple tragedies that find all the brothers dead (except the one lucky enough to be working in a Manhattan factory) offer no easy Hollywood ending. As with *Blockade*, we see instead the horror to which the world is belatedly awakening.

Back home, fictionally speaking, the future blacklistees had already begun preparing the ground for the great national unity effort ahead. Sidney Buchman's historical epic about the American Revolution, *The Howards of Virginia* (1940), starred Cary Grant as an eighteenth-century Real American Hero who would happily have stayed on the farm but instead rises to the occasion of national crisis in 1776 and becomes a political figure. Leaving aside the obvious holes in the yeoman myth (city folk launched the real American revolution, and fading rural America was still a center of isolationist sentiment during the 1910s), *The Howards of Virginia* naturally bent the facts. To make the historic case for national patriotism, Buchman had to brush aside race issues and glamorize yeoman farmer Grant's personal victory over an arrogant, downright un-American pseudo-aristocracy.[14]

The Sea Hawk (1940), written by Howard Koch and notably directed by Michael Curtiz, was the silliest but easily the most enjoyable of the costume-drama, cryptically antifascist features. Using the baldest possible historical metaphors, the threat to freedom-loving England from ominous Continental enemies was set back in the days of the Spanish Armada. Errol Flynn as the privateer persuades Queen Elizabeth of the nation's precarious situation. With his help, she fends off Quisling-like advisers who advise peace (but really are working for the Spaniards) and seek to weaken English defense forces. The Spanish Armada is strong, but the slavish Spaniards cannot overcome Free Englishmen (never mind that privateers got their crews through impressment, a life-or-death servitude) under the command of the great swashbuckler Flynn, at once courageous and amiable, his screen persona getting ready for a glorious war in the present.[15]

Things changed, although not violently, even before the bombs fell on Pearl Harbor. Antifascist projects stuck for years began to move forward, and writers floated plots that exposed this or that danger of fascism, prompting decent people to find the reasons and the courage to resist. Donald Ogden Stewart, riding high after triumphs with *Holiday* and *The Philadelphia Story,* would naturally be the first prestige writer to leap into the breach. *A Woman's Face* (1941), an MGM vehicle for Joan Crawford taken from a French play, provided the occasion.

Ostensibly, it offers a dramatic murder trial, with flashbacks, of a facially disfigured governess who has conspired against her Swedish employer (played by a distinguished exiled German actor, Albert Bassermann) but has her own tale to tell. She was sent by a lover (played ominously by another refugee, Conrad Veidt) who has coerced her into a dozen painful operations and now manipulates her into planning the murder of a child for the sake of an inheritance. At the last moment, notably after Veidt reveals that he is a Nazi sympathizer, she instead shoots the schemer and saves the boy from drowning. As in so many films of the next few years—and not so far from life in many sections of Europe—the aristocratic remnants take Hitler's part as their final revenge against democracy, and their potential salvation. Antifascists, by opposing them, essentially complete the bourgeois revolution, as European socialists had sought to do peacefully in the good old days before the first great war. That Stewart was the leading figure in a Hollywood Peace (i.e., antiwar) Mobilization at the time of the film's premiere was the fate of the moment for someone who insisted upon defending the Soviet Union at an unpopular time for American radicals.[16]

Then again, wouldn't audiences focusing on the romantic-dramatic plot likely miss a minor point of political contradiction? [17] Stewart's script for *Keeper of the Flame* (1943), which he regarded as the most radical film of his that Hollywood could accept, strove to drive it home to the heartlands—literally. Real-life aviator-hero Charles "Lindy" Lindbergh, son of a Minnesota antiwar congressman during the First World War, had himself been suspiciously eager to accept invitations and medals from the fuehrer and harshly critical of the drift toward war. In Stewart's rendering of I. A. R. Wylie's novel, the film opens with a dramatic funeral of a nationally beloved native son and with reporter Spencer Tracy on hand to get the real story. Interviewing a determinedly reclusive widow (Katharine Hepburn), he becomes more and more convinced that she knew about the washed-out bridge where his car plunged him to his death, and he finally discovers the reason. The late hero had worse than feet of clay. With the support of powerful industrialists and bankers, he was planning a Mussolini-like coup against FDR's regime, aiming to head up a "march on Washington" the following morning!

Stewart had politically erred twice over, and the Left would one day pay a price. Whatever the sins of American fascists, plotting armed coups had not apparently been among them (joining Klansmen and reactionaries of either party to take over state government was more in their line, quite successful in several states during the 1920s–30s and much later in the South). In swiping at figures like Lindbergh, Stewart actually assisted the attack upon pacifists, civil libertarians, and others who had their own legitimate reasons for resisting the way in which the nation entered the war and the ways in which it fought, including the bombing of civilian targets and the use of the atomic bomb. Moreover, the real March on Washington (MOW) had been the plan for the African-American movement led by A. Philip Randolph, successfully threatening a massive rally if Roosevelt did not concede racial discrimination in many walks of national life and begin to make amends.

That said, *Keeper of the Flame* is a brilliant and badly underrated film, not only because Tracy draws out Hepburn step by step, raising her confidence in herself rather than breaking her down, but also because the familiar idea of rich and ruthless totalitarians attains here as high a statement ever made in a major film (along with Capra's 1941 *Meet John Doe*), themes relegated to B productions within a few years. According to Stewart's account, mogul Mayer was horrified and "walked out in a fury" from the heralded New York premiere "when he discovered, apparently for the first time, what the picture was really about."[18] Obviously at the height of his powers, a little short of fifty, Stewart was all but finished as a screenwriter.

Casablanca (1942), according to some commentators of later decades, is only very remotely political, a cinematic means of affirming the necessity for American responsibility in the world only by insisting that political activity may be necessary on rare occasions and in small doses. Merely "the most popular and typical of American films," according to this reading, its meaning and its triumph subordinate everything to the love story.[19] Strangely, however, not only did principal screenwriter Howard Koch fail to see the film this way (left-wingers could always deceive themselves, no doubt), but so did contemporary critics and presumably audiences as well. Not that they missed the love story, but the overall picture seemed an inspiration "to inject a cold point of tough resistance to evil forces afoot in Europe today," as Bosley Crowther wrote in *The New York Times*.[20]

Koch himself recalled studio aspiration to "make another *Algiers*," John Howard Lawson's moneymaking 1938 adaptation of the exotic French love story of the Casbah's likeable crook (played by the dashing Charles Boyer) who finally abandons a safe haven for his route to beloved Paris but is betrayed to the local police by his spurned native ex-lover. En route to *Casablanca*, brothers Julius and Philip Epstein had written a first adaptation of an unproduced play, *Everybody Goes to Rick's*, and Koch came in for last-minute rewrites that turned out to be more than half the screenplay, specifically emphasizing the political elements. The shooting progressively caught up with the script, pressures increased exponentially, and Koch managed to bring out a suppressed or only cynically expressed idealism epitomized by Bogart's Rick: "something," as the screenwriter put it later, "worth a personal commitment and sacrifice," from both Bogart's character and Bergman's. To give up everything for love had been the way of film, and not only American film. To give up love for a different "everything," the commitment to defeat fascism and create a new world no matter the personal cost, was part of the new mood. *Casablanca* gave that impulse the shape it retained decades after the memory faded of the promise that had been lost during the war; only *Citizen Kane* stood higher in the last third of the century as the Hollywood Golden Age cult film par excellence.[21]

At any rate, the floodgates had now opened for films increasing in number and poised to capture Academy Awards as well as entertainment-hungry wartime audiences. Not all those who had suffered for their union efforts or unwillingness to be bullied by the studios found outlets; relative old-timers Bright and Ornitz, to name only two, had practically exhausted their options.

But most of the writers rising by 1940, not only the A screenwriters like Dalton Trumbo but the B screenwriters like Lester Cole, hastened to take advantage of the opportunities that had not heretofore existed. Cole called the recollective wartime chapter of his memoir "Hollywood Discovers an Ally," by which he obviously meant his left-wing milieu, and the discovery went the other way as well. The writers suddenly found the industry aching to place them in features more closely suited to their talents than anything before, and better funded and promoted than anything after. As Cole quickly grasped, studio betrayals of the screenwriters' intent—a transformation from hard-hitting scripts into suds and worse—would nevertheless remain common. Hammy and plainly unintelligent acting by politically conservative stars like Ginger Rogers and Robert Taylor also had a way of muffing the best-intended scripts.[22]

But at least sometimes the message got through and the art associated with the message worked superbly, because the writer's views *were* respected and taken seriously. Among the several hundred war-related features made during actual wartime and the following year, left-wing writers and directors contributed only several dozen; but by critical reception, box office totals, Academy Award nominations, and above all the sharpness of political themes, they were very often the outstanding films of the age.

The change meant the most both to younger writers who had little luck during the 1930s but hadn't lost heart, and to those coming late into the system from the stage or elsewhere. During the war years, a small galaxy of future left-wing directorial stars appeared for the first time in the Hollywood firmament: Edward Dmytryk, Jules Dassin, Joseph Losey, Cy Endfield, John Berry, and Adrian Scott (the last en route to becoming a producer). Albert Maltz and Dalton Trumbo became two of the best-paid writers in the business. Comedy writing partners Bobby Lees and Fred Rinaldo hit the top, and dramatic screenwriters Michael Wilson, Alvah Bessie, Carl Foreman, Ben Barzman, Marguerite Roberts, Ben Maddow, Michael Blankfort, and Isobel Lennart (the last three destined to become reluctant friendly witnesses) made real names for themselves. A host of B screenwriters, including Western writers Julian Zimet, Louise Rousseau, and Morton Grant and comedy writers Connie Lee, Karen De Wolf, Val Burton, and Howard Dimsdale, moved quickly forward, if not to notability then at least to series that sustained them for years.

These were not the films they would have chosen for themselves, of course. Marguerite Roberts's coscripting of *Honky Tonk* jump-started her series of high-budget Westerns in later decades, but the genre was by no means her career choice. The antifascist film may well have been, if not her métier, at least a better avenue for her artistic expression.[23] *Dragon Seed* (1944) marked her high point in this genre, a film anticipated in many ways by *The Good Earth* (1937). Producer Irving Thalberg's last grand gesture at "quality" film before his untimely demise and also Hollywood Red novelist-screenwriter Tess Slesinger's best credit, *The Good Earth* was cleaned up from Pearl S. Buck's rather sexier and more political hit novel of the same name. Intended to be shot in China, its shooting was badly hindered and the film itself actually censored by Jiang Jeshi's (Chiang Kai-shek's) corrupt and collapsing government. With yellow-face acting, a mixture of social catastrophe (here a famine) and Confucian dignity, love of land, and the female protagonist (played by Luise Rainer) who rises above her oppression and child-bearing to the historic occasion, it nevertheless anticipates *Dragon Seed*'s framework and characterization.[24]

But the latter film had Katharine Hepburn, and with her, a world of difference. Hepburn's boldest antifascist film is ruined for later viewers by the use of Hollywood actors (including Hepburn) in Asian makeup for the starring roles, and by the stylization of "Chinese" culture. But it remains nevertheless exceptionally strong in its own terms. Seen not altogether inaccurately at its release as a sort of sequel to *The Good Earth* (albeit without any of the same characters), it was adapted from a Buck novel, too. This is a modern women's film displaced to occupied Asia, with Hepburn the young wife insisting (to the scandal of her husband and his family) upon her right to learn to read. As father-in-law Walter Huston repeatedly pronounces platitudes ("there is a saying . . ."), she convinces husband Turhan Bey to purchase a book for her (significantly titled *All Men Are Brothers*) and learns she is pregnant only as Japanese bombs fall. After the occupation begins, the local merchant predictably becomes chief collaborator, and spies upon the resistance force that now includes the married couple. Any well-educated viewer would know what the movie does not state outright: The patriots are preparing for Mao's army to retake China from the Axis.

At the end of the film, the pair return from the mountains to encourage farmers to burn their crops, depriving the Japanese of sustenance, and Hepburn leads the rhetorical charge with a fiery appeal, leaving their new child with the now patriotically antifascist grandparents. A better future awaits the survivors. Despite the made-up slanted eyes and the hokey accents that reviewers rightly jibed, *Dragon Seed* was the seventh most popular film of the year, earning Academy Awards for supporting players and for cinematography as well as a healthy profit. Roberts's career at MGM was made. But this was the last high-budget, progressive film to be produced about China for a very long time to come.[25]

Watch on the Rhine (1943) meanwhile marked Dashiell Hammett's only vindication as screenwriter, and also partner Lillian Hellman's last artistic success until *Julia,* decades later. If there were suggestions from within the Hollywood Left circle that Hammett had actually rewritten most or all of Hellman's screenplays, *Watch on the Rhine* was certainly the best evidence of his otherwise unacknowledged contribution, adapting her timely Broadway triumph. It was also (along with the interracial drama *In This Our Life*) the best evidence that Bette Davis could deliver a credible antifascist performance by playing against type. And it all came together: not only a commercial triumph and instant critical raves, but an Oscar nomination for Best Screenplay, Paul Lukas's Oscar for Best Actor, and the industry's own *Film Daily* naming it as one of the ten best of the year.

Watch leaned heavily upon the old innocent-America-learns-the-truth ploy. A German intellectual played by Lukas arrives in the United States with his American wife (Davis) and their three kids, ostensibly to seek shelter among relatives. Her mother is hosting houseguests, including a Romanian count (played by George Couloiris) who is secretly working for the Germans, and a countess (Geraldine Fitzgerald). Already planning to deliver a major financial boost to the Underground and learning that a fellow antifascist who saved his life has been arrested by the Gestapo, Lukas prepares to leave for Germany even as the odds mount against his survival there. Cast entirely against her usual screen role, Davis bravely accepts the probable fate of her husband, and in the near future of her oldest son, who has also determined to return to Europe. The antifascists (read: Communist partisans), she explains to her fearful but well-meaning mother (played by Lucile Watson), not only care about the world but are ready to "do something" about it—obviously unlike quavering liberals. Watson's genteel (and female-dominated) Virginia home with pleasant and obviously well-treated black servants comes off badly to later generations of viewers, but must have been intended to domesticate the seemingly wild-eyed European antifascists. The film nevertheless works because of the Lukas-Davis connection as much as the surrounding plot. She's the American innocent who has figured out the truth, while he's the international adventurer, Old World intellectual, and activist combined. Together, they can convince Americans to join the great fight. (Watson, the American successfully convinced, also got an Oscar nomination.)

Hellman had risen to the occasion, as did those others who finally got the assignment to script (or direct) something like the antifascist films that they had longed to do for years. These might be as minor as *Night Plane from Chungking* (1943), strictly low-budget material coscripted by Lester Cole. An antifascist version of the wrecked plane (or ship) stories in which loyalties sort themselves out, the jungles of Asia provide the background this time, with lots of betrayals, a heroic self-sacrifice by an agent of the Free French, and an agreement by American sweethearts to meet again after the war is over. They might be major, like *A Guy Named Joe* (1943), written by Dalton Trumbo, and starring Spencer Tracy, Irene Dunne, and Van Johnson, about a dead pilot (Tracy) who comes back as a ghost to guide his replacement and even get his girl. Sentimental to the point of maudlin and beyond, shot (after several government-rejected scripts) with the active cooperation of the War Department, *A Guy Named Joe* got an Oscar nomination and was one of the ten highest grossing films of the year.[26]

Most of the wartime Left's films inevitably fell in between the little and the big, the silly and the successfully dramatic. Some of the best and politically strongest were destined never to become box office smashes because they dramatized the struggles of occupied Europe without a dashing American on the scene.[27] Two other European-based films deserve special consideration.[28] *Mademoiselle Fifi* (1944) is a gem of a historical metaphor, undoubtedly the best of the period (and one of the most mistakenly overlooked of the Left-written films). Produced by Val Lewton as a wished-for exit from horror films—he never successfully made the shift—and directed by young progressive Robert Wise, it was coscripted by Austrian refugee

Josef Mischel from several stories by Guy de Maupassant. Set at the moment of the 1870 Prussian invasion of France (i.e., just before the Paris Commune), it shows a little laundress, played brilliantly by Simone Simon, defying both invaders and bourgeois French collaborators. The coach trip by eight countrymen is a metaphor for France itself, seventy years later; the Germans commanding them find most of the passengers offended at bad manners but altogether willing to take orders.

When the honor of Simon's character is in effect demanded by the Prussian officer as the price for the trip's continuation, they insist that she give in. Ultimately, she murders him—not because he assaults her but because he has insulted France, while the wavering liberal of the crowd is restored to courage and joins what is in effect the Resistance.[29] Never romantically attached, the two resisters give each other courage for the difficult struggle ahead. Preview audiences objected most to the French obeisance, obviously wanting a happier picture of the middle classes.

The Moon Is Down (1943), adapted by Nunnally Johnson from a play based upon a most unusual Steinbeck novella and directed by Irving Pichel, might be described as a philosophical *Edge of Darkness*. Here, too, a little Norwegian town sees a Nazi occupation, this time to keep a mine operating to serve the future conquest of Britain. But instead of a single hero, the hero is the entire people, and the mayor (played with brilliant modesty by Henry Travers) merely what he and his predecessors have apparently always been, the echo of the citizens' nature as well as their wishes. These Norwegians are not the occupying type: they want only freedom, and therefore they have learned slowly what they must do to resist the German tyranny. The Germans, as the mayor patiently explains to the Nazi colonel (played by Cedric Hardwicke) after his captors place him under house arrest, have on the other hand never learned anything at all, because in war after war they seek to impose themselves upon others. After British fliers drop hundreds of single sticks of industrial-use dynamite with parachutes, and the sabotage steadily expands, the mayor and fifty other villagers are lined up for hanging. All hell breaks loose as they go to their martyrs' deaths, singing the Norwegian national anthem.

Nazi Hardwicke is no fool or martinet. He even finishes Socrates's death speech that the mayor recalls from boyhood oration. He believes in orderly occupation and he seeks to persuade his opposite number that only by working the mine and obeying assorted commands will the village be spared calamity. Thereby, Steinbeck (via screenwriter Johnson) once more entered the ranks of the most radical writers because the apparently calm and reasonable demand for "order" was the practice of every political leader during moments of crisis. Attacked by critics on these points in story and theatrical form because the Nazi figure seemed too reasonable (a great deal too much like an American law officer, perhaps), the movie flew in under the patriotic radar and was named one of the year's ten best by the National Board of Review.[30]

Reworking the Genres

Dorothy B. Jones, writing in the *Hollywood Quarterly* in 1945, properly assailed the overwhelming majority of war films (not specifying those leftward-written) for their mere manipulation of action plots to function within the now popular war themes.[31] Certainly that was the case with the discovery of spies, as in Hitchcock's *Saboteur* (1942), which lists Dorothy Parker with a screenwriting co-credit. Parker claimed later not to have any memory of what she contributed to the script, and the claim has a certain logic. Here we have another case of the false accusation: Munitions worker Robert Cummings is accused of torching the factory when actually he was handed a fire extinguisher full of gasoline by the real saboteur. The premiere was attended by eighty U.S. senators and 350 congressmen, thus guaranteeing, along with the Hitchcock imprimatur, a notable success owing precious little dramatically or politically to real contemporary issues.[32] But the old crime-and-mystery game could take interesting and unexpected turns in the hands of a dexterous writer. Universal was looking to relaunch the Sherlock Holmes character and successfully cast Basil Rathbone (with Nigel Bruce playing his assistant, Watson) as the most unforgettable of subsequent screen versions. They chose John Bright as coscripter of the first entry, and *Sherlock Holmes and the Voice of Terror* (1942) marked the transfer of the great detective from Victorian England to the present day.

Curious antifascists they are. Always the unintending comic relief, Watson is an aristocratic duffer who through no ill intent bears all the prejudices of his class. For him, the boys from the right schools are gentlemen and patriots, the lower classes made up of ruffians and potential traitors.

Holmes sees so accurately beyond the stereotypes that he can root out those racist and anti-Semitic Nazi sympathizers who, in real life, could be found easily—before the war, that is—within the House of Lords and the British Foreign Office. The film's "Voice of Terror," delivering radio warnings before bombing military and civilian targets to demoralize the English public, is a German spy who has passed himself off as an aristocrat (replacing the real one secretly murdered twenty years earlier). In the best moment of the film, Holmes enters the London slums to rally the patriotism of the petty thieves, prostitutes, and gamblers to the cause, beseeching them to search out elusive clues to the bombers' identity. The same slum proletarians save Holmes's skin later on, and as the film fades after the crime has been solved, he tells Watson that "a wind is blowing from the East" that will transform the world. His uncomprehending companion nods, and Holmes murmurs, "Good old Watson," as if he were about to say good-bye to a world that must pass.

Critic Jones understandably had her eyes on the product, not the screenwriters' intent. Had she written a few years later and focused on the writers most drawn to the left-led journal where her essay appeared, she would have discovered how the other genres offered ways forward unanticipated before wartime, both for careers being launched (or relaunched) and for "entertainment" films rarely subject to the Popular Front treatment in previous times.

The patriotic musical-comedy genre began curiously, as a declension of Hollywood's most radical musical theater. *Meet the People,* eventually made into a film in 1944, began as a project of the Hollywood Theater Alliance, in turn an outgrowth of fund-raising for the Hollywood Anti-Nazi League. Brothers Ben and Sol Barzman, inspired by Harold Rome's union-sponsored *Pins and Needles,* had a year or two earlier created a West Coast counterpart, *Labor Pains.* Its grand successor was *Meet the People.* Jay Gorney supplied the music, Edward Eliscu the lyrics, jokester Henry Myers the book, and Mortimer Offner directed. They successfully prevailed upon future friendly witness director Danny Dare to choreograph, and the "topical musical revue" took shape. "Miss Hollywood" is a sleeping beauty unaware of the world of strikes, war, and starvation until a prince sticks a pin in her and invites her to come out of her stupor to "meet the people." It was full of sharp-edged, funny numbers (like the antiracist "It's the Same Old South," which Jimmy Rushing and Count Basie later recorded) and great dance routines. So successful was the production that it stirred Hedda Hopper to raves and it moved to one of L.A.'s biggest theaters.

Then it went East and flopped, as Hollywoodites familiar with New Yorkers' prejudices against their theater had gloomily anticipated. But MGM assigned Yip Harburg (whose own satirical musical, *Hooray for What?* had been a modest Broadway success in the later 1930s) to produce a film version, with a script by his frequent collaborator Fred Saidy (and S. M. Herzig). Harburg, Harold Arlen, Burton Lane, Sammy Fain, and Gorney collaborated on new tunes, dumping most of the stronger political ones of the theatrical version, and the script became a home-front love story between a Broadway songbird played by Lucille Ball and a shipyard worker played by Dick Powell. Managing to get himself a date with the star (conveniently on hand for a war-bonds drive), he explains that he is a playwright and that his brother, a collaborating composer, is fighting in the Pacific. The two have written a workingman's musical, and Lucy manages to get it into production. But the brothers' heartfelt effort about patriotic workers making a battleship to defeat fascism is rendered into a silly Broadway costume drama. Refusing to sell out, he exercises his option to close the show before it opens. Boy and girl, who had just fallen in love, part unhappily until Ball takes a job as a welder in his Delaware shipyard and convinces the real workers to produce their own show, celebrating the shipyard's three-hundredth finished project, based on Powell's original idea. Notwithstanding some further romantic confusion, the singing and dancing proles have successfully invited the public to "meet the people."[33]

It was a big comedown from the edgy political original, whose creators felt demeaned and denied. But *Meet the People* had its earnest and happily producing workers, Spike Jones giving Hitler (as a dressed-up chimp) the Bronx cheer, and a big climax number, "It's Smart to Be People," taken from the original, which laid on the Popular Front theme about a mile thick. Once proper society had been all the thing, Ball explains lyrically, but now the day of "the people" has arrived.[34]

Low-budget home-front films combined youth and war themes in sometimes unconsciously hilarious ways. *You Can't Ration Love* (1944), co-scripted by Val Burton and directed by Lester Fuller, saw a small college adopt a student's plan to ration the available males with coupons—something that actually seems to have happened at Berkeley. Forgotten singing bobby-soxer Betty Jane Rhodes uses up her coupons quickly, then stages a show for an all-female (and obviously man-hungry) audience that practically rips the clothes off a dean in attendance!

The swing fashion, seen through the late thirties as white teenagers' entry into black music and a source of rebellious identifications (the Young Communist League put on a Socialism in Swing concert at Madison Square Garden in 1939), now became willy-nilly a potential source of unity among the nation's youth, GIs, and even the long-haired intellectual set. A squadron of B's like *Babes on Swing Street, Swing Out, Sister, Henry Aldrich Swings It,* even *Swing in the Saddle* (where ranchers help solve the manpower shortage through a sort of workforce co-op) all carried the same idea forward.

The upscale version of all this patriotic musical reverie was *Thousands Cheer* (1943), one of producer Joe Pasternak's Popular Front–leaning un-classics, scripted by Paul Jarrico and Richard Collins, with lyrics and tunes by the likes of Harold Rome, Burton Lane, Yip Harburg, Fats Waller, and Mabel Wayne. Gene Kelly is a working acrobat who has been drafted but falls in love with an operatic soprano played by Kathryn Grayson. He tries to convince her officer dad to get him out of service, and has to learn the stern lesson that, as in acrobatics, everybody must do his or her part if all are to survive. (In boot camp, we find the real louse if not villain in a rich draftee who tries to take advantage of his money and contacts.) As a morally reformed Kelly ships out, the couple make up. *Thousands Cheer* didn't have much of a plot and the music wasn't so great, either, but at the windup Grayson leads an anthem to the UN that, with its onstage Russians and red flag, was an astounding musical-moment tribute to U.S./USSR unity.[35]

Westerns now also had their moment and their most skilled left-wing screenwriter, even if he gained fame later, only by leaving the cowpokes behind. Michael Wilson, born in 1914 in McAlester, Oklahoma—at the time a Socialist Party hotbed and the town where Steinbeck's *Grapes of Wrath* begins a generation later—the son of a salesman and of the declassed daughter of a president of the Southern Baptist Convention. When the boy was nine, the family moved to a suburb of Los Angeles, and he grew up there and in the Bay Area, at first rather lonely and bookish but by his senior year in high school an all-around athlete, fraternity member, and president of the student body of Berkeley High.[36]

Close observation of the local labor movement changed Wilson, and

his first published fiction, in *Esquire,* treated the efforts of shipping companies to use students as strikebreakers. He studied for a year in Paris during
1937–38, traveling on to the Soviet Union. French films impressed him
greatly, reviving his childhood memories of adventure-filled double features. Back at Berkeley with a fellowship, he was recruited into the
Communist Party, soon to become campus organizer, teaching classes in
Marxism. He met and married Jewish architecture student Zelma Jarrico,
sister of Paul Jarrico, by this time a Communist and a screenwriter.
Wilson's arrival in Hollywood coincided with the fall of France, for Communists one of those weighty events that foreshadowed the combination of
politics and screenwriting reaching new heights during the war.

Wilson, intending to become a novelist, had never remotely contemplated film work, and jobs came hard for years. But he found himself politically comfortable within the Hollywood Left, and much appreciated. As a
former college instructor, he had pedagogical experience that was put to
work almost immediately. Friendly witness David Lang, whose credits
were almost entirely B comedy films like *People Are Funny* or *Cheezit the
Cops!,* recalled to the House Committee that he had been drawn into the
Party through a Hollywood Marxist study class with Wilson, and went on,

> At that time he was not too well known [as a screenwriter] but had
> been a functionary within the party for some time [sic]. He was quite
> a bright man. He had exceptional background in the philosophies of
> the Communist Party. They had enormous confidence in his ability to
> teach this particular subject. He was [also] quiet; he listened . . . [37]

Wilson filled in the educational gaps, from Hegel and Marx to Schopen-
hauer, in ways that made Lang both self-conscious of his ignorance and
want to acquire more culture. According to his own testimony, Lang
thereby became a better writer if (in reality) never much more than a B
script-jockey.

Wilson himself meanwhile learned the trade, working first on *The Men
in Her Life,* a Loretta Young vehicle, after fifteen (!) other writers, fever-
ishly revising the script just hours ahead of the shooting.[38] He jumped at the
chance to write three Hopalong Cassidy pictures for producer Harry Sherman at $200 per week. When his wife went to work in war plants, Wilson
joined the marines, serving in the Pacific. By the time he had returned in

1945, Hollywood was ready for him—at least for half a dozen precious years. Looking back from the end of his career, Wilson observed that the B picture work that would have seemed repellent during his first months in Hollywood had actually proved useful and, more than that, meaningful in the social themes that could be pursued even in a Hopalong Cassidy film. Although he continued to regret his inability to write the serious novels he intended (or the full political life that screenwriting made impossible), he was hooked.[39] Surrounded by a Jewish left-wing writers' milieu, he had found a spiritual home as well, until the blacklist drove him abroad.

Carl Foreman, who rose from a working-class Chicago Jewish family to attend law school and then fell back during the recession of the later 1930s into a carnival barker, bummed his way to Hollywood in 1940, and found his own way into B pictures through left-wing contacts. In *Bowery Blitzkrieg* (1941), to which Foreman contributed without credit, the boys characteristically turned away from crime after ridiculing authority in various forms. Foreman wrote a few more B's. (He gained his first credit in *Spooks Run Wild* (1941), then emerged most amazingly with a string of stunning realist films—most notably *Champion, The Men, Cyrano de Bergerac,* and *High Noon*—before the political curtain came down. He credited his skills, in later interviews, to experience at the lowest levels, learning the ropes in left-led scriptwriters' workshops.

Jules Dassin offers a director's equivalent to Wilson and Foreman. Singularly among the Hollywood Left, Dassin grew up in Harlem, in a Yiddish-speaking lower-middle-class family. As a teen he joined the ardently left-wing ARTEF (Jewish Workers' Theater), working unpaid as an actor and scene director for an artistic lifetime of a half dozen years, learning at the feet of Benno Schneider and himself directing fully for the first time in Jewish summer camps. He was, in fact, a rare American-born actor among an otherwise almost completely immigrant milieu, noted for its high-quality productions but isolated by the hostility of the Yiddish theatrical mainstream toward ARTEF.[40] It is notable that when ARTEF collapsed, in 1940, only a few of its members went west to Hollywood: Schneider (who never realized his secondary ambition as a director in English theater or films, becoming instead a mere adviser to a mogul), David Opatoshu (who played many supporting roles in radio and films, late in life scripting *Romance of a Horsethief,* the final film directed by Abraham Polonsky, in 1971), ARTEF child actor (and future progressive director) Sidney Lumet, and Dassin himself.

Thanks to ARTEF contacts, Dassin got into MGM, assigned to direct *Nazi Agent* (1942), in which Conrad Veidt played both the evil brother (the figure of the title) and the good brother, a right-thinking German immigrant who has fled Nazism and substitutes himself for his murdered brother, pretending to be an espionage agent while keeping the authorities informed about the workings of the ring. He regarded his next assignment, *Reunion in France* (1942), with Joan Crawford and John Wayne, a mere farce, because he was denied the kind of story conferences that would have lifted the film from unlikely melodrama into something better.

Dassin had, in retrospect, even less respect for the next MGM assignments leading into the postwar years.[41] But *The Affairs of Martha* (1942) was a horse of another color: a wrongly forgotten class farce, based on an original script by future blacklistee Lee Gold and future friendly witness Isobel Lennart, and with Marsha Hunt as a maid at a fancy Long Island estate. She possesses, however low her station, a mighty secret: She has married the inebriated young master of the house, although he doesn't actually remember, and has written an exposé novel that a publicist is pushing in the New York dailies, rousing terrible fear among the rich that their intimacies will be revealed. And what revelations! Not only adulterous trysts, but financial swindles, crooked war deals, and so on. As employers threaten their serving staff to compel identification of the culprit, a servants' general strike nearly emerges. Some delightfully silly performances, and class-conscious phrases uttered by Marjorie Main as cook, highlight the film. Perhaps Dassin—this time substituted at the last moment for Sylvan Simon—again felt he could not make the picture his own or he did not wish to.

Antifascist Apex

Perhaps a talent like that of Edward Dmytryk had all along been perfect for wartime exploitation. Dmytryk had never directed a quality film before wartime, and his métier consisted of programmers like *Confessions of Boston Blackie* and *Secrets of the Lone Wolf,* both released in 1941. Then came war and *Hitler's Children,* shot for a minimal budget of $200,000 in late 1942 but succeeding beyond RKO's wildest dreams, raking in $3.5 million in film rentals. What could explain it? Assorted industry commentators noted Dmytryk's cost-conscious use of footage from Hitler's Germany. But liberal screenwriter Emmett Lavery's eye for the sentimental and Dmytryk's shrewd talent for sensationalism (not excluding a certain sadism more than recurrent in his films) melodramatically adapted the timely revelation novel *Education for Death* by an American educator who had spent time in Hitler's Germany (and upon which the Disney studio had already shot a half-hour semidocumentary).

As the film opens, before the credits, we see the volume *Education for Death* literally dripping blood. The image of absolute horror is best realized not in actual book-burning, but when American-born German schoolgirl Bonita Granville is sent to a camp for unfit women to be sterilized, and there whipped on her bare back—just the kind of action strictly forbidden by an earlier Hays Office. Building up to this penultimate moment, a teacher in an American Colony School of provincial Germany of 1933 stresses critical thinking, critical even toward the New Order. As the children gather to celebrate America's Memorial Day, Nazi authorities demand custody of the school's German and Polish nationals, especially its Jews, driving home the patriotic-freedom message. At other moments, *Hitler's Children* manages to place lovers of classical music and officials of the Catholic Church against Nazism. Neither identification had much real-life accuracy. But accuracy wasn't what Dmytryk and his writers had in mind; he had carefully rallied all the forces of civilization against the emerging evil.

What gave the film its thematic fillip was the Nazi youth (played by 1930s white-hatted cowboy star Tim Holt) in love with Granville, an innocent patriot who gradually opens his eyes to the horror. Granville's honesty and perky charisma—equivalents of those qualities that made Gary Cooper so attractive to sophisticated European women in 1930s and 1940s movies—send Holt upon a heroic suicide mission. He pretends to recant, for a nationwide radio broadcast, criticisms he had made of the State; and then utters an all-out attack on Nazism, precipitating his own execution-style murder in the last moments of the film.

It was definitely not a Hollywood ending, but early 1943 was hardly a normal time. Astonishing Hollywood, *Hitler's Children* broke all records for advance-ticket sales after special preview presentations featured announcements that receipts would be delivered to the League of Nations.[42] As Dmytryk observed later, he made the film perfectly assured of Communist support and comradeship, at that curious moment a genuine plus with the studios.[43] No one was more conscious of the values of this alliance than the shrewdly self-promoting director.

Dmytryk went on to his best days with war themes, big stars, and heavy studio support: *Tender Comrade* (1943), written by Dalton Trumbo, a great romantic-sloppy favorite with the pairing of real-life reactionary Ginger Rogers and real-life progressive Robert Ryan that had women war workers plotting a cooperative lifestyle for the duration.[44] He also expertly fitted themes later identified as noir into the continuing antifascist themes, like *Cornered* (1945). One of his most timely was *Till the End of Time* (1946), about ex-soldiers' desperate effort to achieve a normal life. Even better-timed for box office effect was *Crossfire* (1947), about the wave of potentially murderous anti-Semitism and violence quotient that still persisted among veterans and warned of an American-style Hitlerism.[45]

Thanks to Left writers and progressive themes as well as his own keen eye for the exploitation flick, Dmytryk had decisively advanced his career beyond B detectives and *Captive Wild Woman* (1943, in which an ape with an implanted brain of a woman reverts to ape-type in moments of jealous rage, i.e., instinctual cross-species femininity). But to his lasting resentment, no one on the Left took him to be the auteur of significant or artistic film.[46] That honor went to several writers and directors of different kinds of films made during wartime, but especially to the one film coscripted by Bertolt Brecht and to the ongoing experiments in cinematic realism.

Hangmen Also Die! (1943), directed by Fritz Lang, with a score by Hanns Eisler, succeeded artistically if not politically in creating the collective protagonist that left-wingers had discussed for a decade. If not the proletariat, it was the citizenry of Prague united against the Nazi occupiers. It was also inspired by real-life events: the assassination by a Czech Resistance figure of a Nazi deputy protector known as the "Hangman of Europe" who was especially vicious against Jews. Brecht, under active investigation by the FBI, wrote a draft. John Wexley, assigned to work with him because of Wexley's sympathies and fluency in German, did extensive rewriting, then successfully appealed to the Screen Writers Guild arbitrators for sole screenwriting credit. ("Bert" Brecht got an adaptation credit along with Lang).

The story line probably failed to appeal to American audiences because romance played no role. Anna Lee, as the daughter of a Czech professor (Walter Brennan), accidentally encounters the former physician (played by Brian Donlevy) who has killed the Nazi, and her father feels morally compelled to invite the desperate man to spend the night in their flat as the Gestapo combs the streets. When they cannot find him, the Germans arrest four hundred Czechs, including Brennan, and announce that the prisoners will be executed unless the assassin can be found. The announcement prompts extreme guilt on Donlevy's part, overcome only when others convince him that he represents, in effect, the Czech nation. After various intrigues, the Resistance underground dupes the Germans into accepting the theory that a collaborationist beer brewer (played with special brilliance by Gene Lockhart) is the real key to the Czech operation. When the collaborator is executed (significantly, running toward a church), the Nazis close the book on the case: They have failed to break the will of the Czechs.

The cine-story also had the expressionist touch that made it, at least to some serious observers, the artistic triumph that left-wing film-watchers had long awaited. The most talented *New Masses* reviewer, Joy Davidman, argued that "Here, the mass is, correctly, the logical extension of the individual—not, romantically, the individual's antagonistic and contrasting background" as in even well-intended war films.[47] But no model had thereby been established for other war films; indeed, the commercial failure of *Hangmen Also Die!* probably pushed Hollywood in the other direction, toward assuring audiences of a romance or at least the thrill of American men in patriotic conspiracy or armed conflict.

Most of the other war films written by left-wingers fit into three or four patterns. Easily the best remembered are the international action pictures with big stars: *Action in the North Atlantic* (with Humphrey Bogart), *Destination Tokyo* (with Cary Grant), *Blood on the Sun* (with James Cagney), *Northern Pursuit* (with Errol Flynn), *Somewhere I'll Find You* (with Clark Gable and Lana Turner), *Back to Bataan* (with John Wayne), and *Mr. Winkle Goes to War* (with Edward G. Robinson). Scads of less-remembered films, from *Action in Arabia* to sentimental home-front features like *Sunday Dinner for a Soldier,* as well as the variety musicals that carried the same messages of hope, solidarity, and American self-confidence, kept audiences coming back to the pictures.

Later critics suspicious of these films' self-consciously virtuous approach to the individual within the world scale have sometimes condensed their critique into a scathing commentary on one film: *Pride of the Marines* (1945).[48] It's an intriguing point because Albert Maltz's script, written for a cast featuring John Garfield, Dane Clark, and Eleanor Parker, was indeed hailed and shown repeatedly on Guadalcanal Day by local marine veterans and boosters—until Maltz was hauled in front of HUAC.

Pride of the Marines shows Garfield, family, and fiancée talking as little as possible about the international situation until they hear of the Pearl Harbor attack on the radio, and Garfield correctly observes in a strictly nonpolitical way that he will soon be in the thick of it. Unprepared for the savagery of war, he returns from battle both blinded and bitter, symbolically emasculated and unable to return to the community. In the end, after a lengthy (and for the audience no doubt exhausting) psychological struggle led by Parker, he becomes convinced with a vengeance of the value of his sacrifice for the community. Like the blinded Cagney in *City for Conquest,* he now sees things as he has never seen them before.

But it was the strangeness of the scene on Guadalcanal, with Garfield at once astoundingly heroic and virtually psychotic, that must have struck viewers (especially veterans) as psychologically realistic in mowing down the enemy—at least as much so as the pain of the blinded soldier resisting rehabilitation. Italian-born cinematographer Sol Polito, much admired for his technical skills and a favorite of directors like Michael Curtiz, was fortuitously substituted at the last moment for a flu-ridden cameraman.[49] But Delmer Daves's direction of Maltz's script and Garfield's acting gave *Pride of the Marines* almost everything that so many other war films lacked. When Carl Foreman wrote *The Men* (1950), a remarkably realistic film about the rehabilitation of war veterans and the last such until Waldo Salt's *Coming Home,* he (and Marlon Brando) had an enormously useful example to draw upon.[50]

The documentary quality of *Objective, Burma!* (1945), coscripted by Lester Cole (on a story by Alvah Bessie, one of the rare future blacklistees who had seen previous military duty—in Spain), stood highest, for good and also curious reasons. Situated spuriously in the American paratrooper role in Burma (where the Chinese and the British Indian forces, not mainly

U.S. forces and certainly not paratroopers, fought alongside partisan Burmese guerrillas), it nevertheless featured a jungle trek with fine camera work by James Wong Howe (much of the footage actually shot in the Van Nuys Airport). Facts apart, the film also had a fairly realistic story line: A company of troops is ordered to parachute into the jungle, destroy a radar station, and march to an abandoned airstrip where they will be picked up.

They succeed in their first mission, but before they can get to the airstrip, the well-placed Japanese decimate them. Now bearing the wounded, they need to make their way through heavy jungle. Along the way, a newspaper reporter (played by William Prince) explains the historic and political significance to his younger buddies. The film was as much as banned for a time from English audiences, but received plenty of attention, including an Oscar nomination for Bessie's original story, and additional nominations for editing and music. It also included a few extraordinarily racist "Yellow Peril" phrases—added by a last-minute screenwriter—that Cole found outrageous but could not manage to get deleted and obviously did not feel strongly enough to abandon his credit over.

Action in the North Atlantic was less miraculous and more meticulous in its production, even more than in its plot. It glorified the merchant seaman and, in a memorable scene ashore in the Manhattan seamen's hall, highlighted the real-life Communist-guided National Maritime Union's self-educated rank and file who understood perfectly the political meaning of the struggle against fascism. Again, the plot ultimately hinges upon the goal that unifies the crew, this time the compelling need to deliver war goods to Murmansk, i.e., the Red Army just going on a heroic counter-offensive against the retreating Germans as the film reached theaters. Its technical adviser was one of two survivors of a U-boat attack on a merchant marine vessel.

According to one scholar's view, *Action in the North Atlantic* is virtually a remake of *Battleship Potemkin*. In cinematography, director Lloyd Bacon followed Lawson's suggestions into Soviet-style montage, with a virtual absence of mise-en-scène (it could be said that many B films achieved that goal without trying), and a narrow-focused cutting and tonal montage, light and shadow, for its effects. Bernard F. Dick insists that the film actually repeats the five-part structure of the earlier film by having the ship torpedoed (as with the opening of *Potemkin*). One wonders if anything could imitate Eisenstein's mass spectacles, but this interpretation is surely right on many small points, such as the pause in the action through a homecoming, which in *Action* counterpoises a dedicated captain (Raymond Massey) with his wife and seaman Bogey with bar singer Julie Bishop, who he resolves to marry after his life as a skirt-chaser. The return to the sea and a picturesque "gathering of the ships" follows (much as in *Potemkin*). Then comes the U-boat attack, counterpart to the massacre at the Odessa Steps that precipitated the 1905 Russian Revolution.[51]

In the more mundane narrative subtext, protean proletarians like Sam Levene (who gets the antifascist monologue), Dane Clark, Alan Hale, and others squabble, but good-naturedly learn to cooperate and risk their lives to best the enemy. Some sailors don't make it, especially because the final attack on a German sub has the Americans ramming it just as Russian planes (a sailor looks up and shouts, "They're ours!") appear. The ship limps into Murmansk, where the masses meet them as comrades (in *Potemkin,* the sailors in mutiny cry, "Brothers!" to a Czarist crew that waves back). This is surely the Communist-style happy ending. Yet the film attracted less ire than a half dozen others that spent heavier effort portraying either happy Russians or their partners, the compliantly subverted Americans. Production styles, let alone such fine points as camera angles, didn't interest investigating committees.[52]

To add to the remarkable qualities of *Action,* according to publicity Bogart had urgently sought to include a black merchant marine captain, insisting, "In the world of the theater or any other phase of American life, the color of a man's skin should have nothing to do with his rights . . . "[53] The scene, if made at all, was cut. But much remained, and gained public admiration. Not only did the writer of the original story (Guy Gilpatrick) get an Oscar nomination, but the film was adopted by the merchant marine for training sessions and considered by the critics a roaring-good adventure story perfect for pumping up the home-front audience.[54] If screenwriter Lawson did not achieve all he wanted here, in film style and public reception, he achieved all he would ever reach in Hollywood.

Many other films also sought earnestly to replicate war action. In seeking realism or publicity value for *Thirty Seconds Over Tokyo* (1944), MGM turned to one of the pilots of the famed "Doolittle Raid," the first time land-based planes had taken off from a navy ship and the first American bombing mission over the Japanese mainland. Around and after this military plot (conducted with considerable War Department assistance) in Florida and California, Dalton Trumbo scripted an amazing political-unity sentiment. Airman Van Johnson (playing commander of the ship) and his crew are sensitive enough for qualms about killing Japanese civilians (who, they insist, they do not hate) and lucky enough to crash-land just off the coast of a part of China where the Chinese Red Army, even if not described as such, evidently holds sway. There, amid recovery from injuries, they get the full picture of the true American-loving Asians (a Chinese children's choir sings "The Star-Spangled Banner," and despite obvious poverty, their hosts offer rare and precious gifts). Van Johnson loses a leg but comes home to a pregnant Phyllis Thaxter. Despite these evident crypto-Reds, the film received high praise from the National Board of Review, and *Look* called it one of the five best of the year. Premier Jiang Jeshi (Chiang Kai-shek) apparently attended the Chinese premiere of the film, although his nationalists had done precious little against the Japanese and were in the process of retreating steadily before the peasant-based Communist forces. The era of America "losing China" and likewise of John Wayne's cinematic war against the "Chicoms" was obviously still ahead.[55]

More generally, footage was simply tacked on to the narrative to increase enthusiasm and attendance. *Back to Bataan* (1945), written by Ben Barzman and Richard Landau and directed by Dmytryk, began with the prologue "This story was not invented," against a background of former Japanese prisoners of war marching—although their presence was, historically speaking, strictly an epilogue to the Filipino Resistance plot of the film. Barzman himself had suggested the docu-dramatic opening.[56]

The movie is more interesting because it foreshadows in some ways the skimpy but demonstrably radical postwar anticolonialist film genre and manages almost to make the real-life unabashed racist John Wayne a heroic supporter of the natives. Wayne plays an American army colonel assigned to organize guerrillas against the Japanese army about to invade early in the war. He finds a symbolic Resistance leader in the grandson of a famed *independista,* played by the multi-nonwhite-racial Anthony Quinn. Whether the admired grandfather resisted only the Spanish in times of yore, or continued (as did the bulk of the independence fighters) to battle the incredibly brutal and efficient American invaders during the 1897–1909 conflict remains undescribed. But Quinn's character has a bigger problem: His sweetheart works as a spokeswoman for the Japanese collab-

Dynamite (1929) starred Charles Bickford (center) as an honest coal miner drawn into a world of privilege that was about to cave in. It was written by John Howard Lawson, then a famous expressionist playwright. The upper-class swell (above) was played by Conrad Nagel; the debutante (below) by Kay Johnson.

Museum of Modern Art Film Stills Archive

The Public Enemy (1931) was the *Pulp Fiction* of its day. John Bright's screenplay enraged moralists and delighted audiences with its casual mixture of tabloid news and hard-boiled fiction. It made James Cagney a star. Edward Woods (left) played his best friend. *Museum of Modern Art Film Stills Archive*

Writers Henry Myers and Joseph L. Mankiewicz teamed up for the richly eccentric *Diplomaniacs* (1933), in which the comedy team of Robert Woolsey (left, with razor) and Bert Wheeler (right) led a peace delegation to Geneva and prevailed over arms dealers with gospel songs. The bearded prospector is Dewey Robinson. *Museum of Modern Art Film Stills Archive*

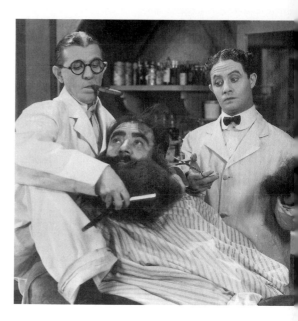

In *The Mayor of Hell* (1933), boys reorganized a repressive reformatory into a participatory democracy with the help of New Dealer James Cagney (second from left). The script was written by Edward Chodorov, who was later blacklisted. Other players included Dudley Digges as the cruel headmaster and Madge Evans as the nurse with a conscience. Frankie Darro played the "mayor" of the reformatory. *Museum of Modern Art Film Stills Archive*

The odd title of *The Man Who Reclaimed His Head* (1934), adapted by Samuel Ornitz from a French pacifist play, had less to do with the horrors of war than the price paid by intellectuals when they sell their talent to those who secretly despise them. Claude Rains played the lead. The child is Linette Verin. *Museum of Modern Art Film Stills Archive*

Theodora Goes Wild (1936) proved that Irene Dunne (left) could be funny while puncturing the pretensions of politics, class, and the sexual double standard, as writer-producer Sidney Buchman did in his screenplay. Dunne's foil was Melvyn Douglas (right). *Museum of Modern Art Film Stills Archive*

Poet and fabulist Guy Endore co-wrote the script for *The Devil-Doll* (1936) with Garrett Fort and Erich Von Stroheim. The film is about a wrongly convicted French businessman who miniaturizes victims to sneak into the home of a stock-market swindler to steal jewels. In this scene, two mad experimenters, played by Henry B. Walthall (left) and Rafaela Ottiano, shrink a servant, played by Grace Ford. *Museum of Modern Art Film Stills Archive*

Lester Cole, later one of the Hollywood Ten, wrote *The President's Mystery* (1936), which examined the life of a man who gave up his wealth to join the workers' cause. The story about a failed canning company that was converted to a producers' cooperative was about as radical as Hollywood ever got about economics, and was based on a story suggested by FDR himself. Two of the lead roles were played by Betty Furness (left) and Henry Wilcoxon. *Museum of Modern Art Film Stills Archive*

Marked Woman (1937), Robert Rossen's screenplay for Bette Davis (left), was as tough and smart as Davis herself. Scenes of solidarity among sex workers were daring in more ways than one. Humphrey Bogart played the district attorney.
Museum of Modern Art Film Stills Archive

In *Destry Rides Again* (1939), Jimmy Stewart (center) got to play the sheriff as a social philosopher from *Mittel-Europa,* abjuring sidearms in favor of parables. American leftists and German refugees lovingly mocked every Hollywood Western convention in this enduring fable. Costarring were Brian Donlevy (left) and Marlene Dietrich. *Museum of Modern Art Film Stills Archive*

Back Door to Heaven (1939) was John Bright's screenplay contribution to one of the best of the narrow stream of films with Christian Socialist themes. The child lead was played by Jimmy Lydon (center). *Museum of Modern Art Film Stills Archive*

Blues in the Night (1941), an early assertion of black–Jewish solidarity, was written by Robert Rossen with a focus on music, this time with an acknowledgment of the roots of jazz. Band members included Billy Halop (drummer), Peter Whitney (bass), Elia Kazan (clarinet), Jack Carson (trumpet), Priscilla Lane (vocalist), and Richard Whorf (guitar). *Museum of Modern Art Film Stills Archive*

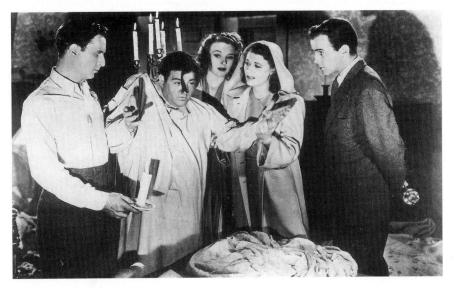

Hold That Ghost (1941) was an early hit for Bud Abbott (left, with candle) and Lou Costello (second from left), thanks to a story and script by writing partners Robert Lees and Fred Rinaldo, who were later blacklisted. Joan Davis, playing an actress who specialized in screaming for radio, is holding Costello's left hand. *Museum of Modern Art Film Stills Archive*

Honky Tonk (1941), with a screenplay by Marguerite Roberts and John Sanford, showed how a ruthless businessman (Clark Gable) acquired so much political power in a Western town that he could ask the governor to call out the National Guard to suppress his enemies in a civic reform movement. Lana Turner (left) and Claire Trevor (right) costarred. *Museum of Modern Art Film Stills Archive*

Was Katharine Hepburn's dead husband a homegrown fascist? In *Keeper of the Flame* (1942), written by Donald Ogden Stewart close to the peak of radical Hollywood's influence, Spencer Tracy helped her find out. *Museum of Modern Art Film Stills Archive*

In *Talk of the Town* (1942), a snooty law professor (Ronald Colman, right) gets an eerily prophetic lesson in the practical politics of dissent and repression from Cary Grant (left), in a script written by Sidney Buchman and Irwin Shaw. Jean Arthur (center) costarred. *Museum of Modern Art Film Stills Archive*

Hitler's Children (1942) was director Edward Dmytryk's unusual attempt at B movie–antifascism in a political-horror-exploitation film, with Tim Holt (right, a cowboy star) in the lead role. The actress is Bonita Granville.

Museum of Modern Art Film Stills Archive

Hugo Butler's unerring instinct for children's stories was evident in *Lassie Come Home* (1943). He wrote without condescending to them, as in this story that depicts the essential "democracy" in the affection between a poor boy (Roddy McDowall) and his dog, lost to a rich family. *Museum of Modern Art Film Stills Archive*

Stormy Weather (1943) was a knockout musical with Lena Horne and Bill (Bojangles) Robinson that moved black–Jewish artistic cooperation to a new level in Hollywood. Among its writers was Hy Kraft, who returned to Broadway after the blacklist. *Museum of Modern Art Film Stills Archive*

A rarity in Hollywood history was *Meet the People* (1944), a self-referential musical that asked the movie industry to produce films more engaging to working people. The four stars were (left to right) Virginia O'Brien, Bert Lahr, Lucille Ball, and Dick Powell. *Museum of Modern Art Film Stills Archive*

One of the most effective early examples of film noir was Bernard C. Schoenfeld's screenplay for *Phantom Lady* (1944), a moody mystery most often remembered today for Elisha Cook's drum solo. The lead roles were played by Ella Raines and Franchot Tone. *Museum of Modern Art Film Stills Archive*

The U.S. working class went to war and beat the fascists in *The Story of G.I. Joe* (1945). The film was both acted by Hollywood rebels (including Burgess Meredith as Ernie Pyle, second from left) and written by them as well (Leopold Atlas, Guy Endore, and Philip Stevenson). Publicity did not suffer from the fact that nine real war correspondents appeared in cameos in the film, including the unidentified three who posed with Meredith in this publicity photo. *Museum of Modern Art Film Stills Archive*

One of the most controversial creations of radical Hollywood was *Pride of the Marines* (1945), starring John Garfield and written by Albert Maltz. Although it may have been one of the strongest of the antifascist war films as a narrative, critics felt the parade-ground scene at the end prepared the way for postwar jingoism and the blacklist. *Museum of Modern Art Film Stills Archive*

According to *Our Vines Have Tender Grapes* (1945), written by Dalton Trumbo, American socialism would resemble life in a small Wisconsin town, where life's troubles would be no harsher than squabbles among children, and adults would act with patience and wisdom. The children were played by James Craig and Margaret O'Brien.

Museum of Modern Art Film Stills Archive

In *Ruthless* (1948), written by Alvah Bessie and Gordon Kahn, a pair of capitalists (Zachary Scott, left, and Sydney Greenstreet) would rather die than give up the advantage of a pair of hands around their competitor's throat.

Museum of Modern Art Film Stills Archive

The Long Night (1947) was lost until 2000, when a movie with a reputation as a plodding remake of a French classic was revealed as an important bridge between political films in prewar France and American film noir. It was written by John Wexley and starred Henry Fonda and Barbara Bel Geddes.

Museum of Modern Art Film Stills Archive

Give Us This Day (1949), one of the most powerful social dramas made in the shadow of the blacklist, was directed by Edward Dmytryk in exile in England, with Ben Barzman writing and Sam Wanamaker (left) in the lead role. It was based on the Pietro di Donato novel *Christ in Concrete* (1939). *Museum of Modern Art Film Stills Archive*

A major contribution to neorealism posing as exploitation was *Caged* (1950), a women's-prison movie starring Eleanor Powell. It was cowritten by Virginia Kellogg and Bernard C. Schoenfeld. *Museum of Modern Art Film Stills Archive*

In *The Lawless* (1950), a nearly lost B classic directed by Joseph Losey, the lawless are not the poor but are those who are indifferent to exploitation and injustice. It starred MacDonald Carey as a liberal newspaper editor and costarred Paul Rodriguez (left). The police officer in this scene was played by Ian MacDonald. *Museum of Modern Art Film Stills Archive*

The classic *High Noon* (1952), with Gary Cooper, was written in the middle of congressional hearings in Hollywood. The writer, Carl Foreman, was forced off the set before filming was finished, but not before completing a script that depicted the frozen liberalism of the moment.
Museum of Modern Art Film Stills Archive

orators. Actually, she's an Allied spy (played by Fely Franquelli, her only major film role) and she secretly lectures him on the struggle after Bataan falls to the Rising Sun. Resistance courage is further bolstered by American schoolmarm Beulah Bondi, who adds to the usual missionary-teacher operation stirring antifascist ideas and personal courage under fire.

After a heroic guerrilla (played by a short-lived Hollywood favorite Third World Kid, Ducky Louie) steers a Japanese tank over a cliff, the guerrilla struggle ensues with Quinn at the helm, cheered by the presence of American subs to fight until the bitter end. According to contemporary publicity, Wayne wanted the Filipinos to be shown freeing themselves (with Quinn a less indecisive figure) rather than relying upon American guidance, but one suspects that this bit of goodwill was also left-wing doing.

The most admired film for Left critics—putting aside the propaganda value of *Mission to Moscow*—was not nearly so realistic but nonetheless firmly bore the Russian quasi-realist stamp. *Sahara* (1943), written by John Howard Lawson drawing upon a 1937 desert-adventure Soviet film, *The Thirteen*, was a vision of internationalism with antiracism tossed in to boot. Directed by Zoltan Korda with a score by Miklos Rozsa, it premiered at an army camp on the first anniversary of the activation of the IV Armored Corps, and was dedicated to the "Armored Corps of the Army Ground Services" that had cooperated with the production.[57]

Sahara was star-spangled all the way, not only by virtue of Bogart but also J. Carrol Naish (who won an Academy Award nomination for his portrayal of an antifascist Italian), future friendly witness Lloyd Bridges, and the first African-American actor to be slated for multiple serious roles, Rex Ingram. It is set in northern Africa, as a tank commander is ordered to retreat south, through the desert, from the Nazi invasion of Libya. Aboard the injured vehicle ("Lulubelle," the only designated female in the film) and running badly short on supplies, he and his two men nevertheless pick up assorted Allied stragglers—British soldiers (including the British Sudanese, Ingram), a South African, a French soldier—and even Italian and German prisoners. All looks hopeless as news of a German battalion comes, but the men decide together on a suicide mission of delaying them until the British regroup. They also know that the tank could easily break down, or that the group could simply run out of water and die in the desert.

Intuitive sympathies prompt Naish to refuse to aid the German officer and to sacrifice himself for Bogey's crew (a reminder that Italians are *never* seen as the enemies in WWII films, and after the real-life invasion they become the main civilian landscape for European end-of-the-war dramas). The Nazi beast has already exposed his species when he sneers—as any Red-baiting Dixiecrat congressman would surely do back home—at Ingram (playing the Sudanese), the supposed racial inferior. All turns out well because the good guys deceive the Germans by promising to deliver precious water in return for their surrender. And when things look hopeless even for the victors of the standoff, the shooting just happens to open up a well: miraculous doings indeed. In the closing moments, the survivors learn that the British have held the Germans back at El Alamein. Africa can be won, and perhaps even the Africans themselves will be liberated.

Downright Russian was Lawson's last wartime film, *Counter-Attack.* Released four months before Japan's surrender and once more directed by Zoltan Korda, it was based upon a modestly successful play by two other Hollywood Reds, Janet and Philip Stevenson, in turn based upon an earlier Russian theater piece. It is a peculiar film, with master cameraman James Wong Howe mostly confined to a theatrical-style subterranean cellar where two beleaguered Russians hold an outnumbering seven Germans prisoners while they fight sleeping and anxiously await a Russian troop movement.

This is, albeit from a technical standpoint barely involving the narrative, an apotheosis of the Russian engineers, as the tribute in the film's prologue reveals. They have constructed an underwater bridge that will provide the means for a tank counterattack against the invading Germans, but they need to discover the position of the enemy reserves while keeping their own operation secret. One of the paratroopers (played by Paul Muni) and a guide (played by Marguerite Chapman) survive the collapse of a factory that the Russians have captured from the Germans. Now they remain trapped in the rubble and duel philosophically with the Germans while they uncover a Nazi officer (Harro Meller) who sneakily pretends to be an ordinary soldier. Outside, Muni's dog (a German shepherd!), clawing at the rubble, painstakingly leads rescuers to his master.

Odd bits like the phrasings of the apparent antifascist German schoolteacher (played by another future blacklistee, Ludwig Donath) must have escaped the audience's attention and that of most critics as well, who wrote off the film as a dull parlor-style drama. Certainly it would have benefited by appearing a year or two earlier, when Russian heroism held great popular admiration. But Lawson really needed big-screen action for his pictures to transcend his own basically theatrical instincts, and now, except for the exteriors of *Cry, the Beloved Country* (1951), he had run out of chances.

Of the average big-time war-drama films written from the Left, *Destination Tokyo* (1943) was more standard issue, albeit of a superior sort. Produced by Jerry Wald for Warners, and coscripted by director Delmer Daves and Albert Maltz, it was clearly a Cary Grant vehicle, with the genteel submarine captain gently running herd over his proletarians. He must command, but after he unseals the orders to conduct the near-impossible— entering Tokyo Bay within the submarine net, torpedoing ships, and somehow escaping again—he grants the crew's anxieties instead of denying them. John Garfield as the sentimental tough guy and (inevitably) ladies' man contrasts with the scared kid, the lively cook, the surgeon-on-demand (an ordinary sailor who has to make an emergency operation on a ruptured appendix), and so on across the character types. Unity is the issue from start to finish, and, as usual in these cases, class unity was pushed by Communists as a central theme, as achievable as regional unity and more achievable than racial unity, which was still as much as forbidden from the screen.

On close examinations of such films, later accusations of Hollywood's Communist subversion properly seem not only wildly disproportionate but downright ironic. The three movies most often accused of Communist propaganda—*Mission to Moscow, Song of Russia,* and *The North Star,* all of them released in 1943—hardly fill the bill.

The first, virtually assigned to Hollywood by the American ambassador to Russia, Joseph E. Davies (and reportedly assigned to him by FDR), was a talky non-drama with plenty of stock footage. Mostly, it recounted Davies and his wife's 1936–38 visits to Russia, amidst the Moscow Trials period, foreshadowing Munich, the Hitler-Stalin Pact, Hitler's conquest of France, and the Japanese attack on Pearl Harbor. Actors chosen partly for lookalike qualities with the characters they portrayed (Walter Huston as Davies, Ann Harding as his wife, Gene Lockhart as Molotov, Oscar Homolka as Litvinov, and, in a cameo, Manart Kippen as mustachioed Stalin) frequently seem strangely impassive, almost like talking scenery. The homespun Huston dominates virtually the whole picture as he gleans insights and offers his straight-from-the-shoulder response to critics of the Russians.

Never before or after did any Left-written film contain anything like this degree of outright propaganda for Russia's importance or for Russian Communism. But *Mission to Moscow*, for all its docu-drama, was also real Hollywood in its often grotesquely caricatured narrative realism. Since silent days, a similar degree of imaginative leaps had been common fare about any manner of American (and other) subjects, historical or current, not at all infrequently romanticizing human rights violations in the name of progress, notably when aimed at unruly nonwhite natives of any kind. *Gone With the Wind*, Hollywood's biggest film for a decade, would be hard to beat as historic justification of a system vastly more widespread, brutal, and lasting than Stalinism. Likewise, the usual treatments of warrior-colonizers, whether Euro-Americans in the Indian or Mexican-American Wars, the British in India, or practically anyone white in Africa, and so on, earned no censure outside the left-wing press.

And yet there were important differences. Even before Koch's narrative takes proper shape, an on-screen appearance by the real Joseph Davies prepares the audience for the seriousness of the narrative presentation ahead and the reality of Russo-American alliance to halt the greatest threat that civilization has ever seen. Then the real film begins: A fictional Davies is called in from a long-desired fishing trip by a summons from FDR, whom we hear but do not see as Davies accepts the assignment to find out the truth about the Germans and the Russians. Soon, he and his family stop by Germany and perceive in the military buildup the Nazi global aggression destined to come.

Russia marks the greatest possible contrast: He visits a steel plant, a tractor factory, a dam, a mine, and a cooperative farm; in his absence, cinema soap opera veteran Harding as Marjorie Davies chats with the wife of Premier Molotov, a Communist beauty. In this fictional Russia, pragmatism actually rules the all-important production process, and go-getters rise from lowly positions to factory managers based upon American-style hard work. Meanwhile, the beauty of the culture comes alive in the Moscow Ballet: the ballerinas' femininity providing more evidence that Russian women, even while rapidly advancing toward economic equality with their male comrades, remain feminine in the truest sense. In short,

Russia is "different" but has not seceded from human nature. In various ways played to the hilt, it embodies the ideals that productive capitalists like Davies himself, a former corporate lawyer, can readily appreciate once they cut through the cobwebs of the familiar anti-Communist propaganda.

The lowest point in the film, from any retrospective viewpoint, soon arrives when Davies returns to Moscow and observes a moment of the notorious Moscow "Frame-Up" trials. Having detected supposed signs of sabotage in his travels, he is easily convinced by confessions that Trotsky has masterminded the sabotage and intends to aid the impending fascist invasion so as to overthrow Stalin. From there on, the film veers toward Russian benevolence (medical assistance to the Chinese civilians wounded during the Japanese invasion) and Soviet preparedness for war heroism—with footage of a militarized May Day parade so lengthy and dull that audiences must have seized the moment for a bathroom visit. As he is leaving, the Germans invade Austria and he meets with Churchill, urging British support for common resistance to the Nazis. As the film rushes toward a conclusion, when British Prime Minister Chamberlain as much as encourages the Germans to dismember Czechoslovakia, Hitler gladly takes the hint and pushes his aggression into France and Russia. Touring the United States, urging the retraction of the Neutrality Acts, Davies fails to convince the American politicians of the dangers until the bombs fall in Pearl Harbor and the newfound allies are forced together. Davies has been painfully vindicated, and the Russians even more so.

The most outrageous portions, with Trotsky as a sort of Russian Benedict Arnold or Aaron Burr, constituted a fairly small segment of the film. But the documentary quality of the credulousness toward Stalin's leadership and perspicacity would become a most painful memory to Hollywood—after the Cold War opened. Jack Warner, defending the film retrospectively, insisted that it had the same purpose in production as the famed *Air Force* (1943) and *This Is the Army* (1943), adding, "if making *Mission to Moscow* in 1942 was subversive activity, then the American Liberty ships . . . were likewise engaged in subversive activity," pleading most uniquely that the film was produced "only to help a desperate war effort and not for posterity." *Variety* had at the time of the film's appearance called it "Hollywood's initial effort at a living history," and the film's technicians received an Oscar nomination for Best Art Direction. But philosopher John Dewey, the most prestigious defender of Trotsky's innocence (and himself locked for years in a destructive factional war against Communists within New York's teachers' union), accused the film, in a letter to *The New York Times,* of "totalitarian propaganda."[58] Dewey truly anticipated the Hollywood future. In hundreds of films to come, the white hats and black hats would still be distributed with vigor—and with a Manichaean quality no less than that of *Mission to Moscow* itself, if aimed at the Russians as the essence of evil.

Howard Koch, according to his memoirs, got the idea of how to write the script while reading Davies's book of the same title, as he started a cross-country train trip from Los Angeles with a new secretary (Margaret Gruen, a screenwriter of minimal credits before blacklisting), who became his second wife. Actually, the story is rather more complicated. Erskine Caldwell wrote a first draft, although how much of this script remained in the final version is unknown. Davies, whose name appears above the title in the credits, also had something rather different from the filmed version in mind, hoping to see Fredric March cast as the ambassador, and Olivia de Havilland as his wife (in real life Marjorie Post, heiress to a breakfast-cereal fortune). Warners actually spent an unprecedented half million dollars on publicity after early favorable notices, but audiences didn't warm particularly to a film without a dynamic love story or a more adventuresome hero than an ambassador. Koch himself, looking back in his memoirs, called the project "Mission Improbable," based on scanty information but fueled by a deep desire to get out of Hollywood and to contribute to the antifascist effort.[59] The talented screenwriter believed in it as much as he did in a film that he did not get to script, the biopic, magnum box office flop *Wilson* (1944), meant to apotheosize the United Nations by pointing toward the beleaguered presidential supporter of its predecessor, the League of Nations. Indeed, *Mission's* opening evoked the memory of Wilson as champion of the League. Koch remained consistent—if strangely sympathetic to political leaders who ordered rebels and mere dissenters crushed through state authority (in Stalin's case vast numbers murdered or imprisoned, in Wilson's mere tens of thousands silenced by the suppression of the radical press, sent up for long jail sentences, or deported)—but the world did not.[60]

Song of Russia, another of Joe Pasternak's Popular Front musical études, should have been memorable only for its songs by Jerome Kern and lyrics by Yip Harburg, excerpts from *Swan Lake,* the *Nutcracker Suite, The Sleeping*

Beauty, Humoresque, assorted Tchaikovsky, Rimsky-Korsakov, and so on. Its
story line was awfully thin: A New York Philharmonic Orchestra conduc-
tor (played by Robert Taylor) tours Russia in 1941 and falls for a talented
amateur pianist (played by Susan Peters) and follows her back to her village. Named after Tchaikovsky and based upon collective farms, this is obviously a worthy place because classical music lies at the center of local
culture, and because the musicians work cheerfully in the fields with the
masses. The sweethearts, now married, perform together for a national
radio broadcast, but at that very moment the Nazi invasion comes. The village lies in ruins, and they quickly pledge to help rebuild, but the two are
persuaded by appeals from Russian authorities to come to America and
spread the word.

The backstory found Jarrico and Richard Collins working from a story
by Leo Mittler, Victor Trival, and Guy Endore, with advisers (including
former Seattle Sunday school teacher and labor poet Anna Louise Strong,
since the 1920s an American living intermittently in Russia and glamorizing it for U.S. audiences) providing Russian documentary material. It was
rewritten in the last stages by Boris Ingster to tone down the pro-
Communism. Meanwhile, John Wexley was placed on the set, not really to
write but with the full-time task of reassuring conservative star Taylor
(who respected the playwright, politics aside) by making further, if strictly
minor, script changes for his character. The film duly appeared to good notices. A few years later, of course, *Song of Russia* was taken to be proof of the
Communist infiltration of Hollywood.

Of all these stories and controversies, easily the silliest concerns *The
North Star,* Goldwyn's personal entry into the Russia films, directed by
Lewis Milestone, with an original script by Lillian Hellman (and minor re-
vision by Edward Chodorov), shot by James Wong Howe, and with music
by Aaron Copland and lyrics by Ira Gershwin. It was, from its beginnings,
a troubled production. Hellman claimed that FDR had personally urged
the film project upon her and director William Wyler as a documentary on
the war in Russia. Wyler even consulted with Russian officials on production details. But Goldwyn's initial hesitancy and the prospective director's
enlistment in the army threw the project into doubt until Milestone
stepped in. Hellman was so upset that she bought back her contract from
Goldwyn, ending an eight-year engagement.

Judged outside Cold War political lines, it might have been a forgotten operetta patched into a war action film. It opened to prewar life in the village, where the happy dwellers (the screenwriters were forbidden to use the phrase "collective farm") seem rather like Munchkins after the Wicked Witch has been disposed of. At a festival they sing and dance quaintly to a Copland tune as the radio ominously announces German troop movements within Poland. Alas, a walking tour of some villagers to Kiev becomes a nightmare when German planes pound them. The village leader announces that men will head for the hills to become guerrilla fighters and those left behind will burn the village with its crops. The invading Germans act like beasts (even forcing children to give blood for transfusions to the *Wehrmacht* injured), and we see most of the inhabitants die in one terrible way or another—but the surviving guerrillas rally to blow up the gasoline stores. Reentering their village, armed only with clubs, they drive the German survivors out. They leave the smoking ruins, vowing to make this the last war for a free world.

The normally conservative *Motion Picture Herald* praised the film, and so did nearly all the early reviewers, with the noted exception of the Hearst press. If the Hearst countercampaign slowed down initial receipts, the film did well, and its documentary-drama (not to mention melodrama) style played excellently to American and British audiences. Taylor later testified against his own work, and in the wake of the 1956 Russian invasion of Hungary, Goldwyn sold an altered version to television, dropping a half hour of footage and adding a voice-over likening the Nazi invasion of Russia to the Russian invasion of Finland. It was a sad end to an odd saga all around.[61]

Looking Back and Ahead

Postwar films about the war had the possibility of presenting a less restricted tale of GIs and their work. Hollywood risked reminding audiences of a war that many obviously wanted to forget. And yet, with thousands of troubled veterans and tens of thousands more flatly disappointed in the aftermath, with some liberal-radical moods and social movements from Depression days taking new forms, the right audience existed for a cinematic breakthrough.

One of the best war films ever made, *The Story of G.I. Joe* (1945, aka

G.I. Joe), offered audiences the only slightly fictionalized story of famed war correspondent Ernie Pyle. The script by Leopold Atlas, Guy Endore, and Philip Stevenson—two future blacklistees and a friendly witness (Atlas)—adapted two of Pyle's reportage books and starred the screen progressive Burgess Meredith. (Pyle, who died in the Pacific Theater earlier in the year, never got to see the film.) Under William Wellman's direction, the cinematography, with little panning and hardly more tracking, is just a camera's-eye view (with many close-ups) of the unshaven, often terrified infantrymen of Company C marching first through North Africa and then Italy, repeatedly pounded by the Germans, sharing their feelings with the journalist while occasionally seeking and even more occasionally finding love with the locals.[62]

When journalist Pyle learns he has won a Pulitzer Prize, he has no time and less reason to celebrate as the stress, exhaustion, and deaths surround the company's leader (played by Robert Mitchum without a hint of melodrama), most un-Hollywoodishly killed at the end. Widely lauded at the time as the most realistic of the non-documentaries, *G.I. Joe* earned back its $2 million budget and won Oscar nominations for Mitchum, the screenwriters, and for Best Song, and placed on the *Times*'s ten best list. It showed that a war film might also be a peace film, with the horrors experienced by the soldiers barely offset by the prospect of victory somewhere ahead.[63]

G.I. Joe might be readily compared with a small film that suddenly got large. Famed director Fred Zinnemann always thought of his career as beginning with the retelling of events in Europe, including *The Search* (1948), coscripted by Paul Jarrico and others. The full trauma of the war (including Zinnemann's own trauma of losing most of his family in the Holocaust) was lost on many Americans, who to his eyes seemed both ignorant of and indifferent toward events not affecting them directly. On leave from MGM and deeply influenced by Italian neorealism, Zinnemann turned to the UN Children's Relief Agency and its clients, many of them youngsters separated from parents who might still be alive. Shooting in the refugee camps in Germany and among children in Switzerland, preparing Montgomery Clift and others to act among real inhabitants of the camps, he urged his writers to focus on a single story, which understandably concerned a Jew who did not "belong" to any German parent but would finally be recognized by a desperately searching mother. Clift objected bitterly to any softening of the message, threatening to quit if he were not allowed to improvise one pivotal speech telling a Czech mother that her child had died—and won his point. Notwithstanding a certain flatness of style and much amateur acting, the film movingly portrays the lost feeling of the youngest war survivors. Child actor Ivan Jandl won a special Oscar for Outstanding Juvenile Performance, and Clift along with the two credited screenwriters were nominated as well. Critics treated the film respectfully but with a certain distance: It was to be appreciated, not enjoyed.[64]

This might have been the greater moment for cinematic realism than noir. But almost before new projects could be envisioned let alone made, political censorship associated with the Cold War had begun to chill opportunities. Ring Lardner, Jr., and Albert Maltz wrote a wartime spy thriller, *Cloak and Dagger* (1946), with an added zinger. In their script, an atomic scientist, rescued from behind the lines in Italy, warns the audience at the end of the film that in the hands of anyone, atomic bombs constituted a menace to humankind. That message, as Lardner recalled, didn't make it into production. Fritz Lang, no radical but a refugee with a conscience, later told anyone who would listen that he had agreed to direct the film only *because* he had so believed in the omitted final speech, and "God help us Americans if we think we can keep the atomic power for ourselves alone."[65]

Without the political punch line, *Cloak and Dagger* receded into a stock treatment that could have been set almost anywhere, anytime: A seemingly unlikely American civilian undertakes a dangerous mission abroad and finds a gorgeous dame in the process. This American (Gary Cooper) happens to be a scientist himself, sent by the Office of Strategic Services into the arms of danger—and of a tough Resistance fighter (Lilli Palmer, in her American screen debut) who ultimately sends him home while she fights on. Real-life OSS chief "Wild Bill" Donovan, happy enough to employ talented left-wingers like Polonsky for the duration of the war, even wanted to pick the cast, beginning with his personal friend James Cagney.[66] But America's favorite gangster turned down the part. By the time *Cloak and Dagger* was released, the OSS had become the CIA, and agency holdovers had set themselves upon a totally different agenda.

Attempting to put aside the dire implications, Hollywood left-wingers looked toward the extension of the unity sentiment. Their version of peace coincided nicely with the niche-marketing that would become more and more Hollywood's future. The family film had already become a natural haven for the Communist writer who specialized in the humane, heartwarming family (or family-and-animal) saga. The brief and badly mistaken blush of postwar optimism prompted an extraordinary romanticization of homespun values, the saga of a peace-loving American people working out their problems. Heavy with the schmaltz, it was the extension of antifascism by other means.

The Romance of Rosy Ridge (1947), a domestic historical drama, articulated most literally the craving for peace and global reconciliation. Screenwriter Lester Cole (drawing upon a novel by MacKinley Kantor) considered it his favorite work, perhaps because his script suffered few changes. In the years shortly after the Civil War, the Missouri Ozarks region remains bitterly divided by sentiment and differences literally inflamed by a series of mysterious barn burnings directed at both Union and Confederate veterans' farms. An enraged Reb father played by Thomas Mitchell vows revenge just as a cheerful drifter, played by Van Johnson, makes himself a friend by working hard and playing the harmonica for all, wooing daughter Janet Leigh (in her first major film feature) along the way. Johnson's britches have faded so badly that Gray or Blue has disappeared, and only late in the day, with the daughter betrothed to the stranger, does Dad learn that Johnson fought for the Union.

A barn dance for all proposed by Johnson tests the ability of the nation to come back together. Although a riot is narrowly averted through the insistence of decent folk on civilized behavior, reconciliation will not come easily. But come it does—in small ways, at least. Admitting his veteran status, Johnson explains that the Rebel son and brother of the farmer and daughter had died in his arms, improbably urging the nominal foe to go and help the family back on its feet. Now's the time to close ranks, although the absence of minorities and race issues from this Missouri location surely makes closure less difficult.

Our Vines Have Tender Grapes (1945), written by Dalton Trumbo from a novel by George Victor Martin, was similarly said to be Trumbo's favorite film of his own work, and for much the same reason that Cole liked *The Romance of Rosy Ridge*. Here the reconciliation is achieved within the goodness of small-town life demonstrated by the willingness of its inhabitants to share and share alike in the face of crisis. In Norwegian-American Wisconsin, early in the century, modest farmer Edward G. Robinson and his wife,

Agnes Moorehead, rear their child, played by Margaret O'Brien in her best dramatic role at any age. At the opening moment of the film, O'Brien tosses a rock at a squirrel to impress her cousin and inadvertently kills the animal, touching off the kind of emotional crisis typical of childhood. Robinson, alarmed but also moved by his daughter's soft heart, gives her a new calf to raise. Various adventures ensue around the appealing tomboy, including a near-fatal accident in a makeshift rowboat during a spring flood, and, more important, a childish unwillingness to share her skates with a poor neighbor boy. Despite her father's old-fashioned wish to keep her on the farm, she struggles for education, encouraged by a sophisticated new schoolteacher from Milwaukee, played by Frances Gifford, who is in turn trying to decide whether to seek her destiny elsewhere when she finishes her doctorate in education, or allow herself to be wooed successfully by an idealistic local newspaperman. O'Brien delivers a strikingly socialistic recitation on the Nativity, and in a church meeting to raise money for a family to rebuild their destroyed barn, shames the rest of the town by donating the calf. They, too, one family after another (and Gifford as well, in choosing to stay) will offer up sacrifices for the common good. Trumbo took the title from the same biblical verse as Hellman's *Little Foxes*: "Take us the foxes, the little foxes that spoil the vines; for our vines have tender grapes." But in his moment of optimism, he reversed Hellman's meaning.

Finally, and with the highest cinematic acclaim, Tess Slesinger and Frank Davis adapted a novel by Betty Smith (whose own successes had up to now been her plays for the Federal Theater) pinpointing the loving center of society within the hard-pressed slum family. Placed back at the turn-of-the-century city, *A Tree Grows in Brooklyn* (1945) wove the tale of an impoverished but colorful family shadowed by the drunkenness of the singing waiter father, played with great sentimentalism by James Dunn, and the consequent desperation of the mother, played by Dorothy McGuire. Actress Peggy Ann Garner is the teen determined to become a writer, and it is she who notices the near-destruction of a beloved nearby tree, its apparent rebirth in the spring a symbol of hope amidst so much trouble. Elia Kazan's directorial debut (with his theatrical collaborator Nicholas Ray also debuting as dialogue director), *A Tree Grows in Brooklyn* was shown widely to U.S. troops stationed abroad. It earned an Oscar nomination for screenwriting and was one of the first films chosen for inclusion in the Library of Congress: in short, an instant classic.

These three films offered fair samples of what the postwar Left might accomplish in cinematic "Americanism," with the full backing of the studios. But the optimism that made this work notable was quickly fading, never to return.

1. Lary May, *The Big Tomorrow: Hollywood and the Politics of the American Way* (Chicago: University of Chicago Press, 2000), 146–47.
2. Ibid., 147–48.
3. Thomas Schatz, *Boom and Bust: American Cinema in the 1940s* (Berkeley: University of California Press, 1997), 269–71. See also Clayton R. Koppes and Gregory D. Black, *Hollywood Goes to War: How Politics, Profits and Propganda Shaped World War II Movies* (Berkeley: University of California Press, 1987).
4. See, e.g., Robert Ray, *A Certain Tendency of the Hollywood Cinema, 1930–1980* (Princeton: Princeton University Press, 1985), 25–26.
5. *Sis Hopkins* was coscripted by Edward Eliscu; *True to the Army* was adapted by Val Burton; and *Singin' in the Corn* was an original by Richard Weil.
6. From the last moments of *Somewhere in the Night* (1947), scripted by Howard Dimsdale and Joseph L. Mankiewicz (and adapted by Lee Strasberg), by heroine Nancy Guild to hero John Hodiak after the murder was solved.
7. *Motion Picture Hearings,* 1951, 285. Irving Reis, whose death at age forty-six in 1953 may be attributed in part to the stress of that era, had been founder and director of radio's *Columbia Workshop,* which gave Orson Welles and a number of later Hollywood radicals like Abraham Polonsky their radio backgrounds; in Hollywood, Irving Reis directed among others *Weekend for Three, Crack-Up,* and *Three Husbands,* all written by left-wingers.
8. *Motion Picture Hearings,* Richard Collins' testimony, April 12, 1951, 227.
9. Wexley went on to write the narration for Litvak's documentary *The Battle of Russia* (1943), the fourth collaboration between writer and director: *City for Conquest* and *The Amazing Dr. Clitterhouse,* like *Confessions of a Nazi Spy,* had all been Warners projects for the two.
10. John Wexley interviewed by Patrick McGilligan, *Tender Comrades* (New York: St. Martin's Press, 1997), 715; *American Film Institute Catalog, Feature Films, 1931–1940, A–L, 387.*
11 Joseph Breen ardently opposed the production of the film, advising Jack Warner to abandon the project. But admitting its basis in fact, he could not persuade the mogul. Paramount exec Luigi Luraschi, who apparently

worked closely with the Central Intelligence Agency a decade later, warned that the film was not "smart showmanship." See Koppes, "Regulating the Screen," 267.

12. Actually, he had shortly before directed *Mystery Train* for Republic, under a pseudonym. Traube's theatrical work included producing and directing all the way from the early 1930s to the early 1970s, mostly of mysteries or romantic comedies of no particular political implications; his artistic apex may have been 172 performances of Sidney Kingsley's *The Patriots* (1943), depicting Thomas Jefferson versus rival Alexander Hamilton during the 1790s—a clear reference to the present. See Edwin Bronner, *The Encyclopedia of American Theater* (New York: A. S. Barnes, 1980), 71, 90, 179, 193, 217, 315, 339, 365, 407, 474, 479, 525. The Shepard Traube oral history, 1977, Academy of Motion Pictures, Los Angeles, pointedly avoids any discussion of his involvement with the Left or his subsequent blacklisting. *Beast of Berlin* also had hero Alan Ladd, in his first major screen appearance, still in training, so to speak, for a great career in Hollywood's coming antifascist industry.

13. Bernard F. Dick, *Star Spangled Cinema: The American World War II Film* (Lexington: University of Kentucky Press, 1985), 65–67.

14. An update of this down-home-patriot theme was Howard Koch's coscript (with three other writers) for *Sergeant York* (1940), which starred Gary Cooper in an expanded version of a true story from the last war. A former boozer turned Bible fundamentalist and deeply moral pacifist-farmer who changed his mind and with his keen shooting talents became a military hero, then turned down million-dollar endorsement offers and returned to his rural home with Cooperesque (better: Jimmy Stewartesque) modesty. The overplayed hick treatment of "mountain holler" Tennessee might be too much for future generations (or any native Tennessean) to bear. Koch suggests that his script was the decisive one: Howard Koch, *As Time Goes By: Memoirs of a Writer* (New York: Harcourt, Brace, Jovanovich, 1979), 71–75.

15. See Koch, *As Time Goes By,* 42–47, for an amusing commentary on *The Sea Hawk.* As antifascist fables go, *Jennie* (1940) was potentially head and shoulders above all this disingenuousness and not surprisingly lost out in studio machinations. Twentieth Century-Fox set Maurice Rapf and Harold Buchman under B director David Burton on a project about a Pennsylvania girl who sees in her authoritarian German-American father the shadow of the Reich. During the early reels a tough, almost literally feminist yarn, *Jennie* suffered a similar fate to many other similar projects, down to television's *All*

in the Family (taken over from a British television show and adapted in part by a few quiet friends-of-the-left studio survivors): Father has to be made lovable despite everything. In this case, a softening and reconciliation on all sides bring a weakling husband into the desired career, and a baby for the protagonist finally settles the issue all around.

16. Donald Ogden Stewart, *By a Stroke of Luck: An Autobiography of Donald Ogden Stewart* (London: the Paddington Press, 1975), 256.

17. Not only audiences. Jeanine Basinger, in *A Woman's View* (Hanover: Weslyan University Press/University Press of New England, 1993), 150–51, comments at length on how the plastic surgery on her face allows Crawford to become "womanly," insisting that as a now beautiful woman she wishes to be loved rather than powerful; this interpretation neatly passes over the growing self-assertion that allows her to cast off her maidenly illusions and strike a blow against the fascists.

18. Stewart, *By a Stroke of Luck,* 262.

19. Robert Ray, *A Certain Tendency,* 89–93, 3–5.

20. Bosley Crowther, " 'Casablanca,' With Humphrey Bogart and Ingrid Bergman," *The New York Times,* November 26, 1942. Among the overabundant literature on *Casablanca,* see the reflections on the role of the director: James C. Robertson, *The Casablanca Man: The Cinema of Michael Curtiz* (London: Routledge, 1993), 76–80.

21. Howard Koch, *As Time Goes by,* 82–84. *Yank on the Burma Road* (1942), co-scripted by Hugo Butler, Gordon Kahn, and future friendly witness David Lang, offered another, Republic B version of premature antifascism, this time in a gutsy Manhattan cabbie played by Barry Nelson, who earns headlines by catching a bank robber single-handedly and then accepts a Chinese partisan offer to drive a truck through the Burma Road (i.e., to the Red Army). The film was finished in November 1941, but a narrative tacked on after Pearl Harbor reminds the film audience, "This is a story of one American who tackled Japan a little before the rest of us—what he started the Yanks will finish!" It was notable also for the use of many Asian-American actors, including Keye Luke in a supporting role.

22. Paul Jarrico interviewed by Larry Ceplair, UCLA Oral History Project, 1978.

23. *Somewhere I'll Find You* (1942) had reporter and skirt-chaser Clark Gable falling for a fellow reporter, Lana Turner, who is also his brother's girl, as war nears. Like so many other antifascist heroes of the time, Gable plays a militant lefty liberal whose porcine press boss refuses to believe the Japanese will

attack the United States—and who steals the boss's clothes in order to insert a headlined antifascist wake-up message in the tabloid! Lana, also a reporter, takes an assignment in Indochina, and the blackballed Gable follows. He finally turns her up in Vietnam, smuggling children away from the Japanese invaders. After further adventures, climaxing in her work at a repeatedly bombed field hospital, they do find each other as he dictates (for her typing—from heroine to secretary!) a story about the attack on (and U.S. forces' withdrawal from) Bataan at the hyper-didactic last moment of the film. Some Hollywood lore, true in this case, also attaches here: Gable, brokenhearted at his wife Carole Lombard's recent death in a plane crash, enlisted in the air force immediately after finishing *Somewhere I'll Find You.* He had more hits ahead (including *The Hucksters,* an advertising satire written by another left-winger), but a good case can be made that no writers suited him as well as Roberts did.

24. *The Good Earth*'s associate producer was Albert Lewin (see Chapter 8); hugely expensive to produce, it was heavily publicized, won two Oscars (including one for Rainer), and was named one of the year's ten best by the *Film Directory Year Book,* but never recovered its costs.

25. Roberts still had ahead of her, in the same genre, the stiff-upper-lip drama about wartime Britain *If Winter Comes* (1947), with Deborah Kerr, a veddy veddy English saga about love and identity in wartime Britain; and another on the same general themes set in postwar France, *Desire Me* (1947), with Greer Garson and Robert Mitchum. Marguerite Roberts and John Sanford interviewed by Tina Daniell, *Tender Comrades,* 576–79. Ironically, the melodramatic spy thriller about China and the Cultural Revolution, *The Chairman* (1969), was scripted in part by Ben Maddow, back from the blacklist after giving names privately.

26. Steven Spielberg remade the film in 1989 as *Always,* with the heroes in the present day, firefighting their way toward romantic-psychological resolutions.

27. *The Cross of Lorraine* (1943), scripted by Ring Lardner, Jr., like *Tonight We Raid Calais* (1943), by Waldo Salt, and *Paris After Dark* (1943), by Harold Buchman, saluted the courage of French civilians lighting their crops and heading into the hills to join the Resistance, and fighting it out with Nazi officers on Paris streets; precisely accurate they may not have been (and the screenwriters knew it), but such films successfully conveyed the message of hope that it had not been possible to deliver even a few years earlier. *Hotel*

Berlin (1945), a "Grand Hotel" ensemble drama by Albert Maltz, went so far as to urge the message that not all Germans were monsters. Anti-fascist resisters—here seen naturally as hidden Jews and the lower classes, inevitably including softhearted prostitutes—carried on as best they could and awaited a signal for final action.

Waldo Salt, born in Chicago and educated at a private school in British Columbia and a military academy in California, graduated from Stanford at twenty, taught a year at Menlo Junior College, and made uncredited contributions to assorted films before *The Shopworn Angel.* In addition to *Tonight We Raid Calais,* Salt cowrote *Mr. Winkle Goes to War* while serving as a civilian consultant to the Office of War Information (OWI), where he also wrote army documentaries. He had few other credits before the blacklist, of which the best known were *Rachel and the Stranger* (1948) and *The Flame and the Arrow* (1950), the latter independently produced by Burt Lancaster's partner (and future friendly witness) Harold Hecht. It was Hecht who managed to get Salt off the list, in 1962, via Hecht's production of *Taras Bulba.* In the following years until his death, Salt wrote two award-winning films, *Midnight Cowboy* (1969) and *Coming Home* (1978). He also wrote the widely praised *Serpico* (1973) and one of the most personally rewarding, his adaptation of Nathaneal West's surreal dark comedy-drama of Hollywood, *The Day of the Locust* (1975).

Léonide Moguy had not much of a career in France and none in the United States. But *Paris After Dark* allowed some of the nearest evocations of the Partisans, the Communist-linked members of the Resistance. It was also nearer the facts than strictly "Made in America" efforts. Ring Lardner, Jr., observed later that when *The Cross of Lorraine* appeared after the war in France, it understandably brought adverse reaction—the French knew the circumstances better.

28. To mention another, *In Our Time* (1944) was far from realistic, but as co-scripted (an original) by Howard Koch, directed by Group Theatre–veteran Vincent Sherman for Warners, and starring Ida Lupino and Paul Henreid, it was a major antifascist work of popular explanation. Going back to the months before the German invasion of Poland, we find an English decorator's assistant traveling through Poland searching for antiques. She meets and falls in love with an aristocrat who is determined to take over the family estate from his pro-Nazi uncle and to reorganize production, and mechanize and make it a profit-sharing (almost a cooperative) enterprise with the peasants. Then the

invaders come, and as the armed resistance melts away, they torch the farm and the family manse; one day a new and different Poland will arise. Bosley Crowther complained, "So much chin-lifting and orating have not been seen on the screen" since the early 1930s, showing the film's vice for earnestness and talkiness. "In Our Time," *The New York Times,* February 12, 1944.

29. Bernard F. Dick, *The Star-Spangled Cinema,* 150–51.

30. The Hays Office sought to suppress a scene in which a young widow (played by Doris Bowdon) invites a Nazi officer into her bedroom and stabs him to death with her scissors. Pichel himself had a supporting role as the innkeeper (his last film-acting job of importance). Future friendly witness Lee J. Cobb plays the friendly town doctor, at first ambivalent about resistance and then proudly marching to his death as sabotage erupts.

31. Dorothy B. Jones, "The Hollywood War Film," *Hollywood Quarterly* 1 (October, 1945), 1–19.

32. The same was surely true of *Mr. Lucky* (1942), cowritten by Adrian Scott, one of those lovable-gangster films but this time with a wartime twist of draft-shirker wiseguy Cary Grant falling for relief volunteer Laraine Day and becoming a patriot. It was just another Damon Runyon knockoff. Cary Grant purchased the original story himself, and Dudley Nichols wrote one of the drafts of the film.

33. Nancy Lynn Schwartz, *The Hollywood Writers' War,* 164, 166; also Edward Eliscu interview, *Tender Comrades,* 241.

34. A special nationwide broadcast from San Francisco on the founding of the UN in 1945 featured "It's Smart to Be People," and another fresh number by Harburg, "We're in the Same Boat, Brother," made famous in folk circles by a Leadbelly recording. Eliscu had meantime become involved in another and more typical home-front musical, *Something to Shout About* (1944), best remembered for introducing black nightclub singer Hazel Scott. Meanwhile, both real and fictional training-camp musicals had grown out of the mobilization of millions of young men and women. *Hey, Rookie* (1944), presented by the Yard Bird Club of Fort MacArthur and moved to the Belasco Theater in Los Angeles, morphed into a picture about a drafted musical producer who rediscovers his love for theater as romance emerges and the guys put on a show. It is arguably most notable for the film debut of leftish Manhattan nightclub comedian Jack Gilford. Henry Myers, Edward Eliscu, and Jay Gorney wrote songs, devised a thin script around the music, and served as associate producers. A handful of other pictures reproduced the scene with

comic mix-ups (conspicuously including cross-dressing) to add to the romance and songs of the base musical.

35. Kelly's only dance in *Thousands* was a memorable solo with mop-and-broom, but in *Anchors Aweigh* (1945) he tore up the stage, including an animated sequence with Jerry, of Tom and Jerry cartoons, certain to be in any future *That's Entertainment!* anthology of Hollywood (and enough for Kelly to win an Oscar nomination). On shore leave in California with fellow sailor and wolf Frank Sinatra (contrasted to the shy Kelly), the two naturally try to meet dames, run into fellow native Brooklynites, and finally manage to arrange a screen test for Kathryn Grayson. Written by Isobel Lennart, it was already a preparation for postwar musicals like *It Happened in Brooklyn* (1947, also written by Lennart), with Sinatra and Peter Lawford in a story hardly removed from the original, as GIs finding their way back into domestic life. *Knickerbocker Holiday* (1944), coscripted by future blacklistee Harold Goldman, with songs by Kurt Weill (including "September Song"), among others, was the hammy historical metaphor for the American Freedom saga, in the struggle for freedom of the press against the Dutch overlords of New Amsterdam. It was taken from a Maxwell Anderson Broadway hit of 1938.

36. Michael Wilson, "I Am the Sum of My Actions," oral history by Joel Gardner, UCLA, 1982. Tragically, Wilson was ill when the interview was conducted in 1975, and died before he could take his interlocutor beyond the years of his war service to his later, Oscar-winning career, his exile to France, and his return.

37. Like most of the new writers, Lang himself had been admittedly ill-educated, in his case an eleventh-grade drop-out, a veteran of the school of hard knocks from gas stations and tango parlors to the lower end of film cartoon work, and thence to junior writer status when the war boom hit.

38. Based on the novel *Ballerina,* by Lady Eleanor Smith, *The Men in Her Life* has artist Young choosing between men who either demand she give up her career as dancer, or share her triumph, a narrative complicated by her having a daughter whom she eventually (in the happy windup of the film) instructs in dancing. Communist Paul Trivers shared screenwriters' credits with Frederick Kohner.

39. Telephone interview with Abraham Polonsky, August 8, 1999, during which Polansky recalled Wilson's dismay; Jarrico had said on more than one occasion that Wilson might have been happier and less frustrated as a novelist, but this was not a realistic solution for a writer whose great talent evidently

lay in the screen. According to a 1971 interview, Wilson wrote scripts for Thomas Wolfe's *Look Homeward, Angel,* Lillian Hellman's *Montserrat,* Howard Fast's *April Morning,* and several originals, all unfilmed. He added, "these shelved properties represent much of my better work." "Michael Wilson," *Film Comment* 6 (Winter 1970–71), 99. Most of the unused script materials can be found in the Michael Wilson Collection, UCLA.

40. See Edna Nahshon, *Yiddish Proletarian Theatre: The Art and Politics of the ARTEF, 1925–1940* (Westport, Connecticut: Greenwood, 1998), 182, 204.

41. But in this blanket judgment he is surely mistaken. *Young Ideas* (1943), co-scripted by Ian McClellan Hunter, was indeed a bobby-soxer farce about a popular female novelist and her efforts to have romantic love, family, and artistic fulfillment all at once. *The Canterville Ghost* (1944), based on a short story by Oscar Wilde and rewritten as wartime alliance comedy, has GIs stationed in a castle where a self-frightened ghost (played by Charles Laughton to the hilt) resolves a family dilemma by encouraging his descendent into a brave act that saves the GIs from a saboteurs' bomb. Dassin only stepped into the director's chair after thirty-eight days of shooting, when Norman Z. McLeod was bounced at Laughton's insistence. Dassin could not have felt the film was his own.

42. Other Left-led films could offer some of the same sado-sexual grotesqueries (very minor, of course, compared to real life) without similarly happy box-office results. *Hitler's Madman* (1943), an independent feature cowritten by noted Yiddish playwright Peretz Hirschbein and future friendly witness Melvin Levy, saw Czech female students rounded up to be sent to the Russian Front as sex-fodder for German soldiers. The father of one of the girls (who hurls herself off a building rather than accept this fate) sets a suicide charge for the sabotage bombing. As in real life, the village of Lidice is then stripped of its population—men shot, women and children sent to concentration camps—and burned, so that the very ghosts of the dead must rise up to swear revenge through cinema. That the film opened with a poem on Lidice by Edna St. Vincent Millay, and that October 25, 1942, was named National Lidice Memorial Day, apparently did the film little good. Politics without warming heroic scenes and a convincing love story, preferably with top stars, did not sell tickets. The film was based, in part, upon an unpublished story by another future blacklistee, Bart Lytton; MGM, taking over production, insisted upon adding scenes that included starlets like Ava Gardner and scenes written by a third writer, Doris Malloy. The actual production company, An-

gelus, based upon private funds of German refugees and others, did not survive this feature.

43. "Reminiscences of Edward Dmytryk," interview by Robert and Joan Franklin, 1959, Columbia University oral history project, transcript in Columbia University Archives.

44. *Behind the Rising Sun* (1943), which purported to be the true story of an American journalist jailed by the Japanese before the war, has Tom Neal in yellowface trained in the United States as an engineer. Son of the powerful man destined to be propaganda minister, Neal looks on as war crimes are committed against Chinese civilians and remains apparently unshaken when his fiancée's sister is sold into slavery; at the end, horror stricken, he dies in a suicidal plane crash, precipitating his father's committing hari-kari. All in all, it was Dmytryk's kind of film.

45. See Chapter 7 for a further discussion of *Cornered* and Chapter 8 for *Crossfire*. Additionally, Dmytryk directed *Counter-Espionage* (1942), a British anti-Nazi spy thriller, part of the Falcon series; and *Seven Miles from Alcatraz* (1942), about lifers who nevertheless feel patriotic enough to resist the Nazis in their own way, among a half dozen other nonwar films at the time.

46. For comments on *Give Us This Day* (1949), see Chapter 8. *Mirage* (1965), the most interesting of the mainly dreadful features that Dmytryk made after his friendly testimony, offered a fascinating view of the security state. Meanwhile, his explanations for his behavior toward ex-comrades grew less credible as he successively retold the story.

47. Joy Davidman, "But the People Live," *New Masses* 47 (March 4, 1943), 28–29, an essay that began, "Once in five years, perhaps, a film appears which so perfectly realizes its subject and its medium that criticism is struck dumb," naming *The Informer* and *The Grapes of Wrath* as its proper predecessors. Davidman did not, however, so much as mention the writers' credits.

48. See Dana Polan, *Power and Paranoia: History, Narrative, and the American Cinema, 1940–1950* (New York: Columbia University Press, 1986), 86–88. But it might be said in Polan's defense that he is less concerned with *Pride's* sloughing off the unruly 1930s past than some of his readers, especially Lary May, seem to be.

49. His other film credits spanning 1914 to 1949 included *Three on a Match, I Am a Fugitive from a Chain Gang, Gold Diggers of 1933, 42nd Street, Confessions of a Nazi Spy, City for Conquest, The Sea Hawk, Sergeant York, The Sea Wolf, Rhapsody in Blue, Cloak and Dagger,* and *The Long Night.*

50. Some of the other most realistic war films, like many of the unrealistic ones, drew upon war footage. The forgotten *Three Russian Girls* (1944), adapted by Aben Kandel and future blacklistee Dan James from the Russian film *The Girl from Leningrad* (1941), drew from 50,000 feet of Russian film stock of battle scenes taped by Soviet cameramen, and some of the film's action scenes were taken directly from the Russian version. The plot of Russian nurses assisting the troops in the defense of Leningrad brings a former dancer into an unrealized romance with an American flyer from a downed plane. Amazingly enough, *Three Russian Girls* received an Academy Award nomination for its Russian-sounding score. Daniel James was later best known (or unknown) for his pseudonymous (as "Danny Santiago") writing of the celebrated Chicano (in this case, Jewish Chicano) novel *All Over Town*. He had few film credits.

51. Bernard F. Dick, *The Star-Spangled Screen: The American World War II Film* (Lexington: University Press of Kentucky, 1982), 222–24. The fact that the talented and fluid director Bacon attempted nothing like this style in his many other films (including a half dozen, notably *Marked Woman* and *Footsteps in the Dark,* written by left-wing writers) strongly suggests that Lawson's script was a sort of shadow direction, perhaps by way of the commitments and perceptions of the actors, with whom Bacon was usually in sympathetic touch.

52. Ibid., 223–24.

53. *AFI Catalog, Feature Films, 1941–1950* (Berkeley: University of California Press, 2000), 18.

54. Thus Bosley Crowther, (" 'Action in the North Atlantic,' Thrilling Film of Merchant Marine, Starring Humphrey Bogart, Opens at the Strand," *The New York Times,* May 22, 1943) has precious few criticisms and overwhelming praise.

55. Occasionally, progressive war films merely stuck together footage, adding very minimal plots. *Corregidor* (1943), coscripted by Edgar G. Ulmer, wove a thin love triangle around action in the Pacific.

56. Thanks to Norma Barzman in a July 2000, phone call for making this suggestion.

57. Among other interesting connections, *Sahara*'s associate director, Abby Berlin, took over the Blondie series in the early forties and as such worked intermittently with left-wing screenwriters Connie Lee and Karen De Wolf.

58. *AFI Catalog of Feature Films, 1941–1950, M–Z,* 1565.

59. A leader of the international tribunal that vindicated Leon Trotsky (shortly afterward assassinated by Stalin's agents), Dewey had his own good reasons to assault the film. But to call it "totalitarian" blurs both the normal distortions of Hollywood and Dewey's own hardly less extraordinary record of public misrepresentations aimed at silencing opposition to U.S. entry into the First World War. Perhaps he recognized his earlier self in Koch. *AFI Catalog of Feature Films, 1941–50, II,* 1565.

60. Howard Koch, *As Time Goes By,* 109–31.

61. See *AFI Catalog of Feature Films, 1941–1950, II,* 1720; Joseph R. Millichap, *Lewis Milestone* (Boston: Twayne, 1981), 115–18.

62. Bernard F. Dick, *The Star-Spangled Screen,* 140–41. In the film's most controversial moment, a GI's marriage with a nurse is followed by the couple seen together under a blanket, their entwined feet sticking out the back end of a truck—something previously unimaginable for the Hays Office.

63. We wish to acknowledge e-mail correspondence with Lee Atlas's daughter, Antonia Atlas Dosik, in our analysis of the film.

    Contrast *G.I. Joe*'s triumph with the kind of small film that could deliver a message if only it could find its audience at the bottom of a neighborhood double bill. Republic's *Identity Unknown* (1945), shot with the simplest possible sets and only a handful of actors, was written by Richard Weill to blend all the suffering and loss of the war into a single soldier. An amnesiac knows (or thinks he knows) only that he is the sole survivor of four GIs found after a Nazi attack on a farmhouse. Played by Richard Arlen, "Johnny March" (as in "Johnny Comes Marching Home Again") approaches each of four bereft families, hopeful of being recognized and brought back into daily life. Emotion-charged visits to widows, an orphaned son, and aging farm parents end in the revelation to an army psychiatrist that although he is none of these four (having landed by plane shortly before the attack)—actually, a college history teacher brought back to himself through the recognition of otherwise meaningless facts!—he is nevertheless connected to all of the four families for whose loved ones' principles he also fought.

64. See *AFI Catalog of Feature Films, 1941–1950, II,* 2100–01. Jarrico remarked that when queried by a Screen Writers Guild committee about his status on the film, he jokingly asked for "subtractional dialogue," i.e., his taking out weak lines. He was credited only with a script contribution, and in the Cold War atmosphere, he did not seek arbitration. The joke cost him an Oscar

conomination. Jarrico interview with Paul Buhle, Santa Monica, September 1991.

65. *AFI Catalog of Feature Films, 1941–1950, I,* 443; Ring Lardner, Jr., interviewed by Ronald L. Davis, SMU Oral History Program, January 11, 1985, 16–18.

66. Polonsky was the only Hollywoodite who directly conducted media warfare against the Germans. Sent behind German lines near Paris during the Normandy invasion, he broadcast to German soldiers and civilians, urging surrender. His OSS status was viewed by the FBI and congressional investigators, a few years later, as posing special dangers of an unspecified kind. See Paul Buhle and Dave Wagner, *A Very Dangerous Citizen: Abraham Lincoln Polonsky and the Hollywood Left* (Berkeley: University of California Press, 2001), 75–77, 145.

6

FILM COMMENTARY AND
THEORY IN MIDPASSAGE

A CULTURAL MOVEMENT'S THOUGHT has often been summed up in the contents, status, and symbolic historical role of its leading journal. The *Masses* of the Greenwich Village 1910s crowd and later the *Partisan Review* as the organ of New York intellectuals offer obvious standards. But things could never be so simple in Hollywood, where the real influence was inevitably measured in the success of the commercial product. Orson Welles's collaborator and formidable film artist John Houseman recalled the contradiction simply, in the 1979 memoir *Front and Center,* by noting that during the years 1945–50, the *Hollywood Quarterly* "created no major stir and exerted not the slightest influence on the filmmaking of its time." Even so, it was "the first serious cultural publication in which members of the motion-picture industry were collectively involved."[1] The distinguished journal was also the butt of Red-baiters seeking to ferret out Communist influences in Hollywood. The *Hollywood Quarterly (HQ),* the *only* serious effort from within American filmmaking to grasp the significance of the effort beyond box office and bottom line, could also only be the work of the Hollywood intellectuals, the Hollywood Left.

The source of the controversy around the *HQ,* as Houseman further recalled, lay precisely in the exceptionally high profile of the enterprise. Its twin sponsors, the Hollywood Writers Mobilization and UCLA, bestowed the university imprimatur upon the film talent and friendly academics. It was a marriage signified by the Advisory Board: two prominent psychologists, a historian, and the head of the University of California Press on the one side; John Howard Lawson, Dudley Nichols, Howard Koch, and John

Houseman on the other. Somewhere in the middle was Kenneth Mac-Gowan, a former producer for Eugene O'Neill, a sometime film producer, and, within a year of the *Hollywood Quarterly*'s launch, the dean of theater arts at UCLA. Lawson and Koch, despite their high degree of public prestige, were headed for the blacklist, and the best part of Nichols's remarkable career was over. After a few brilliant years, the *Hollywood Quarterly* set upon a process of disguising its origins, purged of its original editorial and advisory boards, drifting toward collapse and renamed twice before settling in as the *Film Quarterly*. Only during the later 1960s did the journal, in the hands of unaffiliated left-winger (and soon to be noted utopian novelist) Ernest Callenbach, quietly begin to reassert its then distant progressive origins as a point of pride.[2]

The belated vindication of the original *HQ* had unimpeachable logic. The American Film Institute, which would sponsor the *Film Quarterly* and publish (in cooperation with the University of California Press) the definitive scholarly guides to American cinema, could easily if somewhat indirectly be traced to the same historical sources. Where else could film scholarship originate? Initial success had cursed the *Hollywood Quarterly* by making it a most unique intellectual object of the Red Hunt, but it had also set into place a solid foundation for the most thorough cinematic scholarship in the United States and arguably anywhere outside of Paris. Apart from their films and their leading role in the early decades of the talent guilds, this was the finest and certainly the most scholarly accomplishment of the Hollywood intellectuals.[3]

"There is no recognizable aesthetic for our contemporary fiction film, the kind people are going to see nowadays," wrote director William Wyler following the grand public and critical reception of *The Best Years of Our Lives*. "The people who make pictures, and face problems, have to solve them on their own hook, without any connection or communication with other minds on the creative level."[4] Dudley Nichols, providing an overview essay for *Best Film Plays of 1943–1944*, spoke similarly from deep inside Hollywood: "One of the great lacks of the cinema so far has been its deficiency in perceptive criticism," the inability or simple lack of extra needed energy of filmmakers themselves to analyze their art, and the great difficulty of understanding it from the outside.[5] If the field was now "open for a great deal of serious work," Wyler hardly needed to add, the *HQ* was the main place to do it.[6]

The *Hollywood Quarterly*'s existence depended heavily upon the troubled politics of the Hollywood Left, a phrase that had come to mean something very different from the previous decade. In ways that confirmed anti-Communists could not comprehend and that Communist leaders often bitterly resented, the Popular Front pulled subtly away from the Party apparatus—and nowhere more so than in cultural activities. The logic of detachment had always been present in Hollywood, for the good reason (among others) that Hollywood Reds had never been and could not be integrated into the local or regional party structures, or effectively disciplined. Despite much personal misbehavior (ranging from drinking to womanizing) and privately voiced disagreements expressed on an almost daily basis, not a single expulsion was recorded. Instead, as Guy Endore recalled decades later, informal discussions after the formal branch meetings often contradicted Party decisions, much as free-spirited writers learned to ignore Party directives aimed at their own scripts.[7]

Party leaders, unable to browbeat the successful writers, generally ignored the undercurrent of political opposition, choosing simply to impose formal political positions rather than disciplining offenders. Those writers, directors, and others sufficiently distressed by political sectarianism and unwanted demands upon their time simply stopped paying dues. No one broke violently from the Party with anything like the dissenting manifestos of the 1930s *Partisan Review* circle, and in truth, the assorted personal complaints whether justified or not would likely never have come to light if not for later "friendly" testimony and subsequent, largely self-serving memoirs. The *HQ,* inevitably implicated in these complex ongoing negotiations, reflected the Party's gingerly approach to allies but also, by its very presence, declared a new position of intellectual independence in matters of film theory. It took no direct political stances, but neither did the Party seek to insert itself into the discussions of its contents. Even the nominal Advisory Board continued the pursuit of balance, with noted academics alongside longtime Communists like John Weber, himself by the late forties (after successfully founding the Screen Story Analysts Guild) an executive at the William Morris Agency.[8]

Nothing is so revealing of this complexity as the story-behind-the-story in the much-discussed Maltz Affair. With Albert Maltz at the height of his career, the *New Masses* editors responded eagerly, in the first week of February 1946, to his submission of an essay entitled "What Shall We Ask of Writers?" On behalf of the magazine board, Isidor Schneider assured Maltz that it "met with virtually unanimous approval," and looked forward to "vigorous and high level discussion." [9] He got both and then some.

In response to Maltz's insistence that "the accepted understanding of art as a weapon is not a useful guide, but a straitjacket" and that artistic freedom must include the right to admire artists who were politically suspect (or worse), the Party leaders fired back with heavy guns. The next two issues of the *New Masses* were filled with attacks on Maltz and his positions from the likes of Mike Gold, Howard Fast, old-time functionary William Z. Foster—and John Howard Lawson. Maltz, they insisted, had been taking dangerous liberties with the supremacy of political commitments over artistic tastes. A few others defended Maltz in the *New Masses,* but these voices were fairly drowned out by the accusers.

In the next few years and for decades to follow, unsympathetic accounts of the Hollywood Left, whether by friendly witnesses or Cold War ideologues—most notably Arthur Schlesinger, Jr.'s totemic *The Vital Center* (1949)—cited the semiofficial Party response to Maltz's "deviations" as proof of a totalitarian Communist effect on popular culture, the decisive refutation of any democratic claims to the contrary.[10] The heavy-handedness of the Party is indeed apparent, but what would explain the obviously crossed signals first encouraging Maltz and then mostly but not quite entirely damning the widely admired screenwriter for his pains?

For starters, Maltz may have had the right inspiration at exactly the wrong historical moment; the onslaught of the Cold War brought the downfall (almost certainly engineered from abroad) of Popular Front Party leader Earl Browder. That meant the return of hard-liners, most of all William Z. Foster, from the bureaucratic exile that they had suffered since 1935, and back into positions of power. The effect was similar to that of Jimmy Carter's liberal appointees to the National Endowment for the Humanities (among other agencies) being replaced by Reagan-era conservatives during the early 1980s. In the Communist case of the 1940s, the very V. J. Jerome who had (through John Howard Lawson) successfully killed off the promising *New Theater and Film* years earlier now evidently sought to finish off his other nemeses. But the story was also considerably larger than this Union Square bureaucratic intrigue.

Back in 1941, a very different political era, Maltz had announced that with several film and novel projects on hand and with a draft board summons sure to come, he no longer had time for Communist Party meetings. According to his own recollection, Lawson called him on the carpet before Los Angeles headquarters (a most unusual act for Hollywoodites), and he still refused. The matter had been left hanging, or perhaps implicitly resolved in Maltz's behalf, an entirely different handling than he received in 1946.[11] As the Cold War revived, and the national Party leaders made the firm decision to condemn him, the fat was in the fire. Or was it?

At a pivotal meeting in actor Morris Carnovsky's basement in 1946 (and with several prominent New York attackers actually on hand), the defense of artistic independence was vigorously supported by Abraham Polonsky, John Weber, and screenwriter Arnold Manoff against the evident prestige and weight of the Party's national leadership. Robert Rossen, along with Lawson, led the attack, which was in effect an insistence upon Party prerogatives against what amounted to the experience of a semi-autonomous Popular Front impulse and the collective screenwriters' experience that Party officials could not comprehend in the ways that they evaluated (rightly or wrongly) trade-union activity or agitation on the "Negro Question." Most curiously (within what unfriendly outsiders often called a "totalitarian" organization), the discussion was vigorous and the defeated dissenters still remained unpunished. Controversy within American Catholicism was rarely so benign—to offer a comparable case—and purges of dissenting Protestant brethren from their own denominations hardly unknown, either. Some Hollywoodites later dated to this moment the first move by local members to dump Lawson as their leader. The next logical move, a year or so later, was to discuss among themselves putting forward Polonsky as Lawson's replacement. But Polonsky was deeply involved in his filmmaking, and by that time it was too late for the collapsing movement, anyway.[12]

The Maltz controversy was, in short, best seen as a continuation of an old discussion on increasingly unfavorable ground for Party guidance, with the stakes set artificially higher than ever. But no one really wanted to call in the bet. To the disgust of Polonsky and his fellow dissidents, Maltz this time capitulated "downtown," to Los Angeles leaders, a week after the basement meeting. Shortly following the capitulation, Party leaders hurried—as only a modern papacy might, after doling out punishment—into dramatic ameliorative symbolism. In a highly publicized midtown Manhattan forum, a jam-packed audience of 5,000 cheered the victim's personal appearance and watched as the very heads of the Party declared that the discussion had strengthened both freedom of art and freedom of expression within Party ranks, with leaders and rank and file now joined more firmly in opposition to political regimentation of any sort!

Unlike the original Inquisition, or the McCarthyite inquisition soon to come, this Mother Church desperately wanted its prodigal sons to come home and not merely to repudiate their sins, let alone name other sinners.[13] The Communist Party had by 1946 become dependent upon Hollywood in ways that no other institutional inquisitor was every likely to become dependent upon its victims. To double or treble the irony, the most vehement attackers of Maltz at the historic Carnovsky basement meeting (aside from Lawson and the New Yorkers) had been the weak links in the chain, future friendly witnesses like Rossen drifting first one way and then another with their private shifts of fortune.

After all, Albert Maltz was not merely a leading screenwriter. Together with his friends, he provided many thousands of dollars for Party projects each month, not to mention the prestige garnered by his participation. By Polonsky's estimation (and his own experience in defying commands that he appear for disciplinary hearings "downtown"), Maltz certainly could have resisted successfully. In effect, Communist leaders in New York had unsuccessfully tried to turn Hollywood into a distant Party branch of Brooklyn or the Bronx, where their authority was likely to be absolute. But organizational opportunism alone could not have performed this miracle of circumlocution.

Unlike either theater or novels where left-wing writers often bore the brunt of ideological corrections, criticisms of films were usually applied to the aims of the studio capitalists. At worst, left-wing writers and directors—the Communist critics repeatedly suggested—had gone along willingly with the usual mystifications of class struggle and individual escape. The growing influence of Party members in Hollywood, from unions and publicity campaigns and the films themselves (usually seen as the least likely locus of real political impact), had also considerably softened the old Manichaeanism. Although no more power was attributed to them in the workplace (i.e., the studios), their importance in the movement nationally was widely if sometimes resentfully accepted. The wartime drive for antifascist unity had still more effect in the same direction. Amidst a formally rigid political apparatus, a theoretical or intellectual language about cinema developed in parallel with the cinematic "language" screenwriters had begun to deploy as they moved past the limits of the 1930s.

These thinkers moved ahead largely on instinct and personal experience, leavened with large doses of informal discussions and a dash of formal Marxism. Outside of the *Hollywood Quarterly* and the intellectual crowd around it, outside of the rare sympathetic review-essay about a particular film in the *Daily Worker* or the West Coast *People's Daily World,* some of the best critical left-wing writing on films came from screenwriters or former screenwriters. Predictably, some of the most hackneyed criticism was delivered as well by screenwriters who insisted upon an aesthetic of didacticism that they obviously could not effect in their own films and by those who considered their own lack of success in Hollywood as proof positive of the studio system's near-total iniquity. Critic status in the *New Masses* or *Daily Worker,* like Party status in Hollywood, compensated for life's disappointments. According to later accounts, Hollywood left-wingers doggedly read the reviews and argued about them, however much they may have disagreed with particulars and perspective.[14]

Many interesting points were in fact scored, all the way from the beginnings of Communist commentary in the early 1930s through the last-minute observations of the early 1950s. But despite many efforts, no cogent and coherent critical formulae emerged for the appropriate left-wing Hollywood film. Perhaps the Marxist critics lacked the energy, the political support, and the theoretical education. Most of them also palpably lacked the requisite inside experience. Alternatively, it was a dubious task to begin with, undertaken in future decades by academic auteur and deconstructionist critics with more formal training but too often bearing a similar degree of theoretical overkill and real-life inexperience behind the camera.

Abraham Polonsky, the most promising of the new faces in Hollywood, could say flatly that he did not insert "political" themes into film dialogue simply because his films embodied, as a whole work of art, his understanding of Marxism. Most regrettably, he arrived in Hollywood so late that only a few films with Polonsky's touch suggest the possible outcomes of that self-consciously unified conception. The best of the other left-leaning writers and directors arrived at roughly similar conclusions, usually sans Marxism. Some of the most talented of them, including Dudley Nichols, Orson Welles, and John Huston, drew deeply upon the political sentiments and the accumulated wisdom within the Popular Front milieu while holding back from formal membership or extended links with the Party as such.[15]

The field of perceptions behind Polonsky's quip never became common coin on the Left. No doubt the lack of formal dramatic training, even more the mundane quality of assignments available to most Communist writers, militated against sophisticated artistic visions. They intuitively understood the need for a humane cinema, and according to some recollections, Party discussions drove home in particular the message of anti-racism. Many of them concluded, at the simplest level, that the politically charged line of dialogue was likely to be the only possible active expression of commitment within the filmmaking process. The "insertion method" of political screenwriting, as it was known in Party circles, actually suited some of the projects assigned to them during the wartime production boom and the Russian-American alliance. Skeptics wondered if audiences noticed what amounted to throwaway lines about the Red Army, the Partisans, or the American spirit of cooperation.

The same writers, as self-educated (for the most part, ill-educated) in politics as aesthetics, were also the most likely to trust the judgment of the local Party leaders, often with the consequence of being advised to work in some more suitably "social" theme than they had intended.[16] But only a small portion of scripts written by any writer would actually be produced in any case. More to the point, studio exec conservatives and (after 1945) front-office anti-Communist liberals who sought to dictate film politics had vastly more clout and consequently more success than dogmatic Reds, at least in getting films made if not in producing hits or admired cinema. The studios, after all, still owned the means of production; in spite of any and all changes, as Dudley Nichols put it, every writer learned that the "control of production is in a mysterious place called the front office" where the "Chief Engineers of the studio-machines rack their brains to produce a standard product."[17] Independent production companies with the greatest promise of intelligent political drama flickered into and out of existence as persistent undercapitalization, distribution problems, and the incipient decline of movie attendance all reinforced the foreboding blacklist.

All these problems reflected the shadows behind the very real accomplishments of the Communists and the Popular Front. The great opportunity of Hollywood radicals, it was clear from 1936 onward, lay in successfully mobilizing everyone left of center around particular issues and the larger sense of progressive coalitions. Paradoxically, the weakest Communist Party of the Western world had in some ways the most opportunities—at least for that particular style of cultural mobilization, if not for the obviously deferred project of confronting capitalism.

The lower-middle-class cadre that filled the Party's peripheries at its late-1930s apex had already offered a demographic and "taste" prediction of its mid-1940s heights. In Greater New York, Jewish substitute schoolteachers, social workers, dentists in working-class neighborhoods, and children of the middle class who had thrown themselves body and soul into the labor movement continued (with a partial lapse of 1939–41) to pack Madison Square Garden, Irving Place, the Bronx Coliseum, and Manhattan Community Church on many evenings and weekend afternoons for concerts, rallies, and theater, not to mention openings of left-wing artists at the ACA Gallery and summer berths in several dozen resorts promising hearty meals, invigorating exercise, holiday openings, and a progressive atmosphere.[18]

Constituencies like these, less dense (and usually less Jewish) but no less real, stretched out from Boston and cultural centers of the south like Chapel Hill to Chicago, Milwaukee, the Northwest, and of course California. Aging ethnics and their children, Yankee spiritual descendants of abolitionists and women's rights activists, African-American intellectuals, and Chicano community activists felt the stirring of national promise for what future conservatives would curse as multiculturalism. Wartime respectability of the Left reinforced the basic program with a vengeance and a larger following than ever.

These were the people—Yankee or Finn, African-American or Hungarian, as well as Jewish—who could glimpse in John Garfield their own denied aspirations in Depression America and see in antifascism the hope of the world. They also found in Hollywood's New Dealish and "Win the War" pictures an identification with the mainstream that hard-bitten older Communists or the Wobblies of yore had never imagined. Apart from the 1940 election, they could likewise throw themselves directly into FDR's campaigns as an extension of their own enthusiasms and as an arm of the industrial union movement—the CIO's invention of the Political Action Committee (PAC), a form of electoral campaign organization, ironically enough, created to overcome the financial power of rich Republican contributors. The elaboration of a "progressive" culture around the New Deal, the labor movement, and the leftward edge of the Democratic Party showed vividly that there was no going back to old days of expecting more or less imminent revolution—and that the broad constituency of the Popular Front had no desire for anything like that, anyway.

Radicalism by now comprised a series of "fronts" or movements that held a common set of values but depended upon networks of well-placed contacts within assorted labor or political mainstream institutions—likewise, within media culture—to remain strong and credible. Earl Browder, Party leader since the early 1930s, when Moscow had designated his status, drew the logical conclusion only a few years before his 1945 ouster. As the Red Army fought desperately to regain ground lost to the Germans, Browder and other American Communist leaders pronounced the dissolution of the Party itself. Penning his last major opus (*The Road to Teheran*) in 1945, Browder predicted postwar amity between the United States and the Soviet Union. One is tempted to say that the leadership had already adopted the "Hollywood Model": formally dissolving the Communist Party for the Communist Political Association, an organization suitably reorganized into Democratic Party–style political clubs and intended to be open rather than cloistered. From the self-styled vanguard of the workers, the Communists had become (in their vision, at any rate) the spark plug or gingergroup of the liberal-labor alliance with as many celebrities as possible.

And it seemed, at least for a moment, to work. In the mini-world of screenwriters themselves going off to war (sometimes only a few miles away to what Hollywoodites called "Fort Roach" after the studio head who turned over the property for the duration), veteran screenwriter Hugo Butler drafted a pamphlet based on Browder's document, submitting it to the delighted response of his army base commander: here was a soldier who understood what fighting for democracy meant, and could put it across to the troops.[19] Others, from Hollywood veterans to New Yorkers en route to Hollywood careers, delivered scripts for Armed Forces documentaries with millions of overseas and home-front viewers.

The same 1944, back in Hollywood, saw the final reelection campaign of Franklin Roosevelt with left-wingers in unprecedented positions of influence, from labor mobilization to entertainment. Ironically, the radicals had poured on the steam for a ticket that now included not Henry Wallace (vice president since 1940, controversial and widely loved for his midwestern homilies and *Lost Horizon*-like Hollywoodesque mysticism) but Missouri's Harry Truman, whose combination of domestic welfare state extension, civil rights advocacy, Cold War globalism, and political repression would make him the worst of all nightmares for radicals.

The impending crisis was complicated for the Hollywood Left because the talents of outspokenly left-wing writers, directors, and a handful of actors were still highly coveted, and because Hollywood liberals accurately saw a new era of censorship ahead. As late as the spring of 1945, almost coinciding with the calamitous Conference of Studio Unions strike, progressive political gatherings could rally Walter Huston, Lena Horne, Eddie Cantor, Charles Boyer, Humphrey Bogart, Edward G. Robinson, Charles Laughton, and Robert Young, not to mention reliables like Charlie Chaplin, Bette Davis, and Katharine Hepburn. Robinson publicly urged the Left's favorite attorney, Robert W. Kenny, to challenge Earl Warren for the governorship of California, an imagined victory that would have given left-wingers unprecedented access to the halls of regional and even national power.[20]

It all melted away—or was melted away with the modern book-burning fires of the FBI, the Justice Department, the tabloid press, and the local Red Squads—so fast that Hollywoodites could hardly figure out what was going on. Their rise and fall may not have been so much exceptional as indicative of newer cultural-political trends within the Left and the wider society. If the middle class with its liberal sympathies and sometimes bohemian or sex-egalitarian impulses, its real and wished-for ties with unions, minority communities, and movements or governments abroad, constituted the new turf of the Left, Hollywoodites lived it, portrayed it fictionally, and continually helped sustain its self-conscious existence. The disasters that fell upon radicals were consequently a tragedy not only for participants and for American culture at large but for the process of radicals' self-clarification, fatally interrupted just when the new ground rules were becoming clear.

Criticism Reconsidered

Left-wing aesthetics had entered a merry chase from the desperate early 1930s through the early years of the Popular Front, as we have seen. The disappearance of *New Theater and Film* left not exactly a vacuum, but highlighted, at least in retrospect, an avoidance of the problems posed for radicals involved in either the WPA New Deal theater or in Hollywood. How much did theoretical background of a Marxist quality matter or even enter into such discussions? It's an interesting question because Communists (like socialists before them, and followers of Trotsky even more intensely or at least studiously so) considered Marxism to be a chief sign of intelligent insight into a complex society and world. But Marx and Engels had left precious few guidelines for aesthetic considerations, and some of their writings plainly contradicted Communist efforts to judge artists of any kind along political lines. Marx in particular dearly loved Shakespeare and Goethe, was a personal friend of the sentimental Heinrich Heine, and devoured (as did Engels) with relish the novels of Balzac, Dickens, Thackeray, Charlotte Brontë, and Elizabeth Gaskell. They did not disdain these novelists for making money sans guilt, and Marx pointedly admired Balzac in particular while pointing out the stupidity of his royalist politics. Like other nineteenth-century advocates of *Bildung,* they wanted art to entertain and to instruct by being true to human experience.

Marx's most intensely philosophical observations would have been inaccessible to Marxists of the day. In an unpublished manuscript preparation for writing *Das Kapital,* he proposed that "the object of art, as well as any other product, creates an artistic public, appreciative of beauty. Production produces not only the object for the subject, but also a subject for the object." [21] Any number of subsequent Marxist writers in the United States and more frequently in European circles sought to claim theoretical authority on literature and on culture more generally. An aesthetics philosopher in Moscow formulated in 1933 the notion that capitalism, as it socialized production, also moved simultaneously toward the abolition of art as such. By becoming completely realized human beings, ordinary people as well as extraordinary ones would "live" their art. [22] Even if this formulation were accurate, it provided no guidelines for art and artists under capitalism. A few scattered theoreticians of mass culture, Walter Benjamin in Germany or Mikhail Bakhtin in Russia, advanced sophisticated ideas about popular culture, but they had no contemporary impact. [23]

A glance at American Communist writings or the advertising for Party-sold booklets of the 1930s disproves any grand claims made by Party specialists to real aesthetic theorizing. The stubborn crudeness of theory purporting to explain current political lines—whether in defense of "'socialist construction" in Russia or the antifascist front against capitalism or (still worse by far) heretics and heresies—was palpable, more so with every drastic overall shift from class struggle and potential war threats to anti-interventionism to all-out war support. It should be added that in questions of culture, even their best-versed opponents on the Left were also wandering around in the dark, denouncing the Communist "artists in uniform" but scarcely able to come up with workable alternatives, especially for areas of popular culture.[24]

For many film activists of the later 1930s, the vision of producing radical documentaries continued to pose a seeming celluloid alternative to commercial films' slickness and packaging. Fictional films clearly offered less political or artistic promise, even if (as was clearly impossible) radicals could have raised the money to make the kinds of movies that Americans loved to watch.[25]

Despite the attendance of some of *New Theater and Film*'s key writers in Lee Strasberg's classes on theatrical direction, the magazine's collective eyes remained upon the documentary for one other very good reason: the extraordinary talent close at hand. Film and Photo League (FPL) members included Joris Ivens, Leo Hurwitz, Ralph Steiner, and Irving Lerner. The first two were to remain permanently alienated from Hollywood, the second two destined for unsuccessful careers in commercial film after working years further in documentaries. All were outstanding figures in the small but vital nonfiction film world, central to it in ways that very few Communists could ever be in Hollywood. Of the other FPL luminaries, only Elia Kazan and Ben Maddow, near the heart of the documentary operation, managed to make the transition to significant success—until the blacklist and belated friendly testimony temporarily wiped out Maddow and gave Kazan a different direction. But other major cultural figures, including Henri Cartier-Bresson, Willard Van Dyke, Earl Robinson, Paul Robeson, Marc Blitzstein, and Erskine Caldwell, helped shape individual FPL films, and several of them worked on Pare Lorentz's twin New Deal classics, *The Plow That Broke the Plains* (1936) and *The River* (1937).

Left-made documentaries, memorably *Heart of Spain* (1937, a major fund-raiser as well as conscience-raiser, directed by Ivens), *China Strikes Back* (1937), and *People of the Cumberland* (1938), climaxing in *Native Land* (1942), featured serious talent including Paul Strand, Maddow, Lerner, and

Hurwitz, with a bevy of public supporters including Lewis Mumford, George Seldes, Max Lerner, Archibald MacLeish, Vera Caspary, Aaron Copland, Malcolm Cowley, Waldo Frank, Lillian Hellman, Max Lerner, Lewis Milestone, Clifford Odets, Irwin Shaw, New Dealer Gardner Jackson, and poet Muriel Rukeyser. But by 1940 the peak energies had been gathered, the radical and independent "documentary era" quickly transmuted into wartime war work with Hollywood bosses, the government, and even the Armed Forces. Even the "message" of *Native Land* was transformed into a quasi-patriotic one of defending inherent "American" freedoms from the likes of antiunion employers. This would-be canonical epic itself never actually made it to major theaters; by the time it appeared, most of the FPL veterans were in Hollywood.[26]

Such documentary or semidocumentary experiments, unmarketable to commercial movie houses, had even less chance in a mass culture society than the early 1930s left-wing theater that melted into Federal Theater and the Group Theatre. One of their chief negative features (at least in retrospect) was to detract attention from subtle but important shifts in the film capital. "There are many fine, charming people in Hollywood," wrote Joris Ivens, arguably the leading documentarist, after a visit in 1937,

> At home they play with their children, read a great deal, take an interest in art. But at the office they write and produce bad films that their own children, and the rest of the world as well, will see. They distort, consciously or unconsciously, the fundamentally healthy illusions of human beings and project them on the screen as a new kind of reality. Their work constitutes a moral disarmament of the masses.[27]

Now and then, a *New Masses*—more rarely, a *Daily Worker*—remark about an individual film up to 1938 or so contradicted these generalizations. Chaplin, of course, regularly got good marks, as did *Mr. Deeds Goes to Town, Mr. Smith Goes to Washington, The Story of Louis Pasteur,* and a handful of others. But the exception mainly proved the rule, even as the reviewers dropped the old heavy-handed condemnations for light satire. As late as 1939, Lewis Jacobs's *Rise of the American Film* was greeted with the telling phrase, "Study of the American movies has matured if the medium itself has not."[28] The same *New Masses* reviewer went on to conclude, "Now is a good time to go to a meeting instead of a movie," because the movies were judged to be so bad and, obviously, the meetings so important.[29] Two small-circulation magazines personally published by screenwriter Guy Endore during the Pact Period, *The Clipper* and *Black and White*, mostly refurbished, with several important exceptions, the by now familiar mordant comments about Hollywood films. Endore's contributors, when not supplying fiction or cracking the usual jokes about the industry, obviously wanted to turn their attention to more interesting and encouraging subjects. Like the novelist of *What Makes Sammy Run?*, they dealt with daily life in Hollywood as a painful joke.[30]

But something of importance had happened, nonetheless. If by 1939 the writers' workshops run by the League of American Writers out of New York had—like their predecessors the John Reed Clubs—run their course, in Hollywood the work had just begun. The informal (and secret) classes held for film industry workers from early 1938 until the Pact had begun a preliminary discussion of film that left behind warm memories but no records. The League of American Writers' Hollywood branch, which had scarcely existed before, reconvened this activity in the fall of 1939 with a formalized "School for Writers" whose "faculty" consisted of Lawson, Lester Cole, Donald Odgen Stewart, Fred Rinaldo, Robert Lees, George Sklar, Viola Brothers Shore, Cedric Belfrage, Robert Rossen, and W. L. River, in addition to crucial non-Communist allies Irving Reis, Boris Ingster, Meyer Levin, Irwin Shaw, Dore Schary, and Sheridan Gibney.[31]

Under these curious circumstances, just as the liberal alliance with the Left faded and Hollywood Communists began to anticipate an early witch hunt, some 150 students nevertheless enrolled in a variety of classes on the novel, radio, motion picture analysis, playwriting, the short story, the history of the stage, and the history of American literature (Lawson's chosen specialty).[32] Significantly, screenwriting classes with formal lectures were soon abandoned for workshops: just what the bulk of the students really wanted. Aspiring screenwriters sought not historical background or formal aesthetics but hands-on instruction and perhaps a leg up on those who had not taken classes from such well-connected workshop leaders.

Soon, workshops tutored by Paul Jarrico and Federal Theater veteran Michael Blankfort, among others, developed script originals for submission through Hollywood agencies. "As a result," a report claimed, some students "sold stories to magazines, landed jobs in studios, sold material to radio networks and succeeded in interesting important agents . . . "[33] Future semesters promised more screenwriting classes taught by the likes of Gordon Kahn, Paul Jarrico, Richard Collins, and Gertude Purcell (the last two future friendly witnesses), with radio, journalism, and short-story classes as well, all to be taught at the school's new building in Hollywood.

According to participants, the political but also technical issues of writing were pressed home with great seriousness. For instance, what were the consequences when a writer succumbed to pressure to write shallow characters and plot? Can movies that contain only male actors really develop full characterization? Is a love relationship justifiable as the center of a story, or a mere diversion from the social side? These nonrhetorical questions came to a simple point: How could writers in a commercial industry with inescapable managerial supervision survive without cynicism and perhaps even do (at least some) memorable work? For all the continued talk about the near impossibility of achieving anything decent in film, a certain focus emerged, or at least a forum for discussion about the contrary possibility. This was an accomplishment of no small measure, especially for young would-be writers like Carl Foreman, fresh to Hollywood and broke (Dore Schary advanced him the $18 tuition).[34]

How can the apparent contradiction of simultaneous political crisis in the Left and a pedagogical boom be reconciled? The answer was well known to Hollywoodites. During the last two or three years before Pearl Harbor, hundreds of young writers decided to try their chances in film. For the most experienced of them, the blush had vanished from the rose of the stage, partly because they were older and more experienced than they had been early in the Depression and partly because the WPA Federal Theater was on the verge of abolition (and was closed, by congressional fiat, in 1939). There could be no going back to the days of agitprop now, any more than local activists could return to the now vanished movement of the unemployed. For still other young radicals, from their own perspective watching the rise of "interesting" films and noticing, in many cases, their friends and relatives making a living writing something, it was worth a try.

To take a case in point: Alfred Lewis Levitt, recently fired for union activities while working as an animation story writer for Terrytoons in New Rochelle, New York, heard that a former Jewish camp counselor of his, Michael (Mickey) Uris, had married another counselor from the same camp, film actress Dorothy Tree, and that both were working in Hollywood. It gave Levitt someone to "look up," a social introduction to match his political introduction, transferring from one Communist branch to another in 1940. Within weeks of arrival, Levitt and his wife, Helen Slote (who would soon be hired as John Garfield's personal secretary), were attending the premiere of *Confessions of a Nazi Spy,* costarring Tree. The Levitts met Donald Ogden Stewart, Ella Winter, Guy Endore, and his wife, Harriet Endore. By the summer, they went to the same stretch of beach as the Endores, director Shepard Traube, and even Groucho Marx; meanwhile, Levitt took work (no doubt through a connection) as a reader for David O. Selznick.[35] War service as a documentary cameraman on bombers delayed his entry as a full-fledged screenwriter, and then he had only a few years of credited work ahead of him before the blacklist.[36]

Registration at the LAW school had meanwhile reached three hundred or more, with its pedagogical functions now ironically playing the least visible role. The league threw itself into a flurry of political activities, from an Exiled Writers Committee (with a gala dinner and nationwide radio broadcast that included Paul Muni, future congresswoman Helen Gahagan Douglas, and screenwriters Garson Kanin, Dalton Trumbo, Earl Robinson, and Sheridan Gibney), to a 1930s-style "Living Newspaper," local radio broadcasts, rallies, and assorted campaigns for civil liberties and peace (i.e., resistance against the larger shift toward intervention and a more conservative social policy of winning the war in place of New Deal reformism). Such Party politics, going up against popular Jewish sensibilities and patriotic antifascist sentiment so successfully encouraged earlier, threatened the more practical work like screenwriting classes.

And yet, if held in the fervid atmosphere of the Pact and in New York rather than in Hollywood, the League of American Writers Congress of June 1941 for the first time foregrounded an LAW screenwriting discussion. By this time, most of the biggest names had withdrawn from the league, and the prestigious biannual LAW national conventions were a thing of the past. One of the few giants who remained was the congress's past president (and compiler of published proceedings), Donald Ogden Stewart. Other than Stewart and John Howard Lawson (intermittently stationed in New York, and by his own lights still more playwright than filmmaker), screenwriters had been almost entirely absent since the LAW's 1935 inception. Held in the literary locus classicus of Manhattan, such events (in the decades before convenient air service) offered logistical diffi-

culties for West Coasters, and the overwhelming majority of the participants shared a serious prejudice against Hollywood in any case. Now the
shoe was truly on the other foot.

Perhaps the world of Left-connected cultural luminaries had become
so much smaller that the Left screenwriters simply looked larger. Perhaps
the American love affair with Hollywood had started paying off heavily for
the Left. Or perhaps the organizers had discovered a waiting audience, even
in New York, of would-be writers along with the merely curious. Whatever the case, the Screen Writing Session was slated for the opening night
of the congress, with papers read by Michael Uris, John Bright, Charles
Page (a non-screenwriter who directed the LAW chapter in Hollywood),
and documentary filmmaker Paul Strand, with Viola Brothers Shore chair-
ing the session. As Stewart observed sharply, amid good-humored remarks
on assorted political subjects, the LAW had finally come to the point where
screenwriters themselves would be speaking about films rather than the
critics (and mostly hostile critics at that, he did not add) of earlier years.[37]
Was the Left finally coming of age in mass culture, or was it only the Hollywood Left?

Under these most peculiar circumstances, sympathetic film discussion
became almost respectable. "The films talk, why shouldn't we?" asked
Shore rhetorically (though not altogether: She had been a silent screen titlist), launching the discussion. "The films talk but what do they say? This
is what we are going to try to find out at tonight's panel." Amid the entirely predictable political resolutions of the moment ("that organization
of pressure by . . . labor organizations, churches, liberal and progressive organizations of all kinds . . . [writing] to Hollywood, to the producers, saying that when they produce pro-labor, pro-peace, pro-democratic pictures
the people will come back" to the movies[38]), a certain deepening of
thought had begun to take place.

The panel discussion did not deal wholly with film content. Uris's
presentation focused on the bread-and-butter issues: the struggle for
unionization and improvement of screenwriters' conditions in an atmosphere of staff cutbacks and vast profit-taking. The very availability of
more writers, along with a streamlining of production techniques, had led
to a writers' crisis. When "jobs are shorter, pressure greater," plenty of
writers willing to work for $50 a week, and B pictures being turned out in
as short as two weeks' time, pay scales fell sharply. Younger writers were

being inducted into a sort of factory for the working indigent, where those who built up résumés over several years now faced increased competition from low-wage workers, and the high- (or moderately-) priced writers were brought in at the end of the scripting process for a brief and not especially remunerative polish. The familiar artisanal (rather than proletarian) demand that studios designate 1 percent of production costs for writing remained far beyond realization. Still, working for such minimal gains as a two-week guarantee, now increasingly afraid of the potential repression and regimentation that war mobilization might bring (and at this moment still unable to anticipate the pleasures of uniting with the Hollywood establishment against fascism), the SWG seemed exceptionally beleaguered. But it was also placed strategically at the head of an embattled constituency.

Next, John Bright, apparently presenting a collective position of the Hollywood writers' group, delivered an updated and fairly sophisticated Marxist interpretation of the screenwriters' struggle in the changing conditions of filmmaking.[39] The hard-bitten, authentically proletarian intellectual who had never before even appeared at a literary congress (and whose name would have been unknown to readers of the left-leaning press) was suddenly at the center of the left-wing writers' attention.

Bright sought to interpret optimistically for listeners the expansion and consolidation of the industry both physically and financially, as containing further steps toward the objective socialization of labor and the promise of workers' rising consciousness of their own creative capacity. To take a leading example, sound offered "the greatest single advance toward realism the film had ever made," enhancing the dramatic potentiality of shock value but also offering the prospect of a deep personalization, the realization of social relations at the core of film:

> The emphasis must be on people, their lives, their problems, and their relationship with one another. This is no denial of "ideas" per se, because ideas, once they become concrete, become things that people "do" rather than things they "say." Ideas expressed through people, springing from their objective circumstances, are not denied. But ideas for themselves, abstract and symbolic, tend to make the pictures coming out of these vast technological processes as cold in their end result as the machines which make them possible . . .

Sound really makes this emphasis meaningful. It becomes meaningful because sound allows for real characterization, for subtle shadings and for depth of psychological study. Sound makes the conventional theories of film composition impossible—because what is said is most important.[40]

All Quiet on the Western Front (to which, we may be reminded, future Westerns' writer and blacklistee Gordon Kahn made a script contribution) had thereby brought the antiwar message home, Bright reminded his listeners, via the personalization of war, catapulting the "screech of artillery shells and of serial bombs right into the Theater." If released from its capitalist integument, the potential of this breakthrough was practically limitless. Indeed, "technological progress and political progress" could now be viewed as virtually synonymous, with *The Grapes of Wrath*'s grainy film stock and single-source lighting and *Citizen Kane*'s pan focus making "middle range" combinations of action and conversation natural, allowing for a realism and compression of meaning heretofore unimaginable.[41]

These technical observations, at a more general level, had already been valid a half dozen years earlier. But now, even if the studios continued to isolate writers from cutters and cameramen, even if producers mortally feared directorial initiatives and so on, the diffusion of knowledge and the appearance of a handful of genuinely masterful films had still shown the way forward toward a future revolutionized Hollywood.[42] This was a Hollywood that workers themselves—screenwriters being mental workers, but no less workers for that—could make real. They most of all needed a sense of themselves, of their own power and potential.

Bright might easily have added that what they did *not* need was a condescending Communist Party (for which he personally showed intermittent fondness and contempt) so much as a developed understanding of their own circumstances and prospects. The suggestion, if unstated, nevertheless clearly rankled. Lawson, rising from the floor to read his own prepared statement on the issues, either could not accept such a straightforward message or perhaps could not allow himself to be upstaged by a lesser light. Lawson insisted that since all of Hollywood's innovation could be applied to reactionary purposes (something that Bright would not have denied), political content had therefore to be placed foremost. This was an unworkable demand for Hollywood films, and Lawson knew it perfectly well. His outburst betrayed not only personal frustration with his film career but an insecurity in his theoretical grasp of the issues—and an inclination toward political dicta as a resolution. Formal discussion at the LAW reached its end point here, and so did the LAW proper. The organization never convened again.[43]

Perhaps the most important point of Hollywood discussion had already been reached in the short-lived *Clipper* by another political oddball at least as curious as Bright: British-exile novelist, newspaper "personality" interviewer, and past film publicist Cedric Belfrage. He chose *Citizen Kane* as the supreme example of what radical innovators could do in Hollywood, the proof that showed the way forward. This was a more obviously left-wing choice than critics (except perhaps those on the Right) were able to admit for decades—not only because *Kane*'s factual basis happened to be the Red-baiting William Randolph Hearst, of course, but because of Orson Welles himself.

That Welles of the Mercury Theatre days had been surrounded by future blacklisted writers like Howard Koch and that he so depended upon the Popular Front-ish John Houseman as his producer could have been no secret. The notorious 1938 "War of the Worlds" radio broadcast hoax caught savants of the Merc flat-footed: no one expected it to be taken seriously. The arrival of America's bad boy and mass-artistic genius in Hollywood has been made legend again and again. Right down to gofer William Alland, who drove Welles westward from New York and turned up as the narrator of *Citizen Kane* with back to the camera, Welles was surrounded by helpful, sometimes worshipful Communists.[44]

From Cedric Belfrage's trained eye, seeing *Citizen Kane* was "as profoundly moving an experience as only this extraordinary and hitherto unexplored media of sound-cinema can afford," the proof positive that the ensemble of brilliant mise-en-scène, dialogue, timing, camera work, and everything else artistically inherent in movies was truly possible at the heart of production for the mass audience. Clichés Hollywood-style thereby fell one after another, from plot to lighting. Some unthinking critics, observed Belfrage, were quick to insist that the great majority of Hollywood's technicians simply be replaced after such an extraordinary show of skill: A new broom would sweep everything clean. Belfrage the longtime intimate observer of the film process had the opposite conclusion: that Hollywood's unionists possessed (in some cases, created) the skills and for years had been "hoping and trying for a chance [like this] . . . but always the film salesman, speaking through the producer, has had the last word." Until *Kane,* that is. The "biggest man in Hollywood" had done it himself, recognizing diverse skills as the maestro must, pulling them all together as "great works of art in any medium have always been up to now."[45]

John Bright would shortly speak up in a narrowed circle of Communist and near-Communist intellectuals. Belfrage had the luxury of using a near personal outlet, beyond the control of Party ideologues, for his inner thoughts. Both spoke to the same idea, but Belfrage most successfully swept away the Hollywood Left's own negativism, at least in regards the unique realized oeuvre. *All Quiet on the Western Front* had a decade earlier shown the political potential of the mainstream film, but *Citizen Kane* realized the medium's potential in message and technique, implicitly lifting up the dignity and revolutionary self-consciousness of the workers in a future film industry.

The LAW as a national body disappeared overnight with the German invasion of Russia in June 1941, although the LAW school in Hollywood survived until 1943. Its lively component emerged a few weeks after Pearl Harbor as the Hollywood Writers' Clinics. The task of the clinics, it was early and wisely declared, should be not merely to produce better movies (i.e., the short-term political results), but to produce better screenwriters. Most remarkably, the clinics treated all participating writers more or less equally, hashing through scripts by some major writers like Paul Jarrico, John Bright, and John Howard Lawson, along with younger would-be screenwriters. The collective examination could be harsh. But through this venue, wide-ranging, open discussions were being held for the first time on issues of movie art and politics. It might be remembered that the Hollywood Party had begun with study groups, handing down the line on given texts to potential recruits; now the discussion could go the other way, inventing a language or text (never actually written) beyond existing Marxist or other standards.

According to the recollections of Paul Jarrico, the sharpest disagreements came down to what might be described as the division between "historians" and "humanists." The historians sought to understand the characters, who they were, and how they got that way. The humanists, on the other hand, looked to the story as story, probing less for historical motivation and more for interpersonal conflicts. These differences were fruitful, for neither position specified certain or didactic results. Indeed, writers and would-be writers asked themselves collectively whether the shallowness of the plots and characterization that some among them had written could be evidence of a lack of respect for the Hollywood film's real potential. They wanted to discuss such recurring concerns as whether heterosexual romance was an indispensable part of film (a major issue for writers beginning to make war films) or a market mechanism. They wanted, in short, to place upon their own agendas the questions of the commercial film becoming an art form as well as a way of making a living.[46]

The backward look of future friendly witnesses was more suspicious and sour but not necessarily in contradiction to the blacklistees' recollections. David Lang remembered the "top-echelon writers who were at the service of all members of the party to discuss scripts, originals, stories that were in work at the studios and to improve, from their point of view, the material and the quality of the script." The sense of collectivity and of gratitude, of "being helped by the functionaries," infused the young writers with a sense of loyalty. Prodded by obsessed anti-Communist congressmen to say whether improved scripts also meant more and better jobs, hence more influence for the Party in Hollywood generally, Lang admitted "that was part and parcel of the whole thing."[47] On the other hand, George Beck, a comedy writer encouraged by the Writers' Clinics to do serious drama, belatedly realized that he was in actuality just "like any comic wanting to play Hamlet." Under artistic-minded as much as political-minded Communist influence, he claimed, he had mistakenly sought to exceed his natural limitations.[48] Perhaps these two examples are not so different after all: Both Lang and Beck remained B writers, as did nearly all of the screenwriters who were to become friendly witnesses.

It was hardly surprising, then, that the deeper theoretical issues might be mooted in favor of practical and sometimes immediate ones facing screenwriters with plentiful assignments. Shortly after the LAW school was disbanded, in 1943, the People's Education Center was launched, a full-blown Popular Front school with some of the same teachers as the old LAW school, the same general approach to historical questions, the same mixture of uncertainty about how screenwriting fit larger theoretical understanding, and the same valuable lectures of writers and directors on how good movies were made at Writers' Clinics. But mobilization was the order of the day. Far from conflicting with Party programs, mobilization gave them new meaning and emphasis.[49]

The Writers Congress

The 1943 Hollywood Writers Mobilization congress was by its nature and timing an almost entirely different enterprise, conceived and heralded in such a manner that its intimate connection with the history of the LAW and the formal training sessions would not have been apparent at first sight and was perhaps meant to be somewhat concealed. Rather, it essentially reconstituted the Hollywood Anti-Nazi League (HANL to HWM, one might say) of progressive spectacle as politics, adding in large doses of volunteerism, from selling war bonds to gathering actors and actresses for appearances at servicemen's canteens. Convening on the day after Pearl Harbor—strongly suggesting that the formation had been planned for months—it not only rose to the occasion but operated at a frantic pace. Probably from its first moments, its organizers had intended to make the most of the respectability of the left-wing screenwriters and their connections with academic life. After months of planning and preliminaries, the full operation came together. The New York literati, their best days with the Left now over, had nothing to compare.[50]

The opening days of October saw leading Hollywood personalities like movie execs Darryl Zanuck and Dore Schary (one might say, rather than literary figures like Edmund Wilson or Archibald MacLeish of the 1930s congress salad days) at UCLA sharing the dais with the university's highest officials and an audience that included many of Hollywood's brightest.

The HWM intended above all to be practical. The urgency of the war circumstance and the eagerness to become part of a broader movement focused the 1943 convention's sessions on the strategic goals of antifascism, along with such pressing issues as the fate of the exiled writer. Aesthetics occasionally entered discussions, for instance, of how the movies would sensitively handle the all-important issue of "collective guilt," the role of ordinary Germans in fascism and war. Nor did writers wish to discuss their continuing conflicts with the studios here. In an odd way, the narrow 1941 conference *entre nous* the left-wing intellectuals had actually placed more focus on screenwriting, while the newest congress emphasized the writers' political role in Hollywood.

The meetings opened at UCLA with the most favorable endorsement imaginable. On White House stationery, the president sent "greetings . . . with a deep sense of the significance of a gathering of writers in these times." Vice President Henry Wallace and recent Republican presidential hopeful Wendell Wilkie along with Robert Sproul, president of the University of California, added their own salutations. But it was Roosevelt (or his staff in any case) whose words obviously meant the most. The official communication went on to say that the Writers Congress

> is a symbol, it seems to me, of our American faith in the Freedom of Expression—of our reliance upon the talents of our writers to present and clarify the issues of our times. Already, the men and women gathered there have rendered great service in elucidating for the nation the issues of this war and the nature of our enemies.[51]

The phrasing of such presidential sentiments no doubt closely resembled the content of similar letters sent out to the attending meetings of all kinds of patriotic organizations, especially if not only during the war. But surely, the Hollywood patriots were a bit different.

Congress Chair Marc Connelly, to whom Roosevelt addressed the communication, had already been named by FBI operatives as a probable Communist (a false charge, but one suggestive of the popular playwright's allies), and the "men and women" on hand included dozens who would be on the blacklist within a few years. John Howard Lawson and Robert Rossen were central figures throughout, painstakingly preparing the documentation of the event in a prestigious university press volume of the following year, themselves supplying the overviews and the conceptual glue that held the book together. Francis Faragoh's keynote talk became the preface, and Richard Collins along with Paul Trivers (an unsuccessful writer and a future blacklistee, rumored to be Jack Lawson's political second-in-command) among others prepared the forewords and summaries.

The Hollywood Left, as Edward Dmytryk wryly recalled decades later, was already now way out in front of anyone else with war support.[52] By the time the congress adjourned, they had almost a hammerlock on the writers' colony. As hundreds of liberal, Popular Front, and quietly Communist participants and audience came together, even some of those émigré intellectuals of the Anti-Nazi League burned by the Hitler-Stalin Pact found their way back. Thomas Mann, Lion Feuchtwanger, and a handful of prominent Latin American intellectuals eagerly took part. In the proceedings volume's inclusive phrase, "men and women of many callings who shared kinship with the craftsman of the word" had arrived at a common destiny.[53] Indeed, the congress's most noteworthy feature was undoubtedly the presence, not of writers turned uniformed servicemen or of industry executives (although both of these could be found in numbers), but of cartoonists, radio writers like scriptwriter Norman Corwin, and the future celebrity broadcaster Chet Huntley; lyricists including Hanns Eisler, Oscar Hammerstein II, and Earl Robinson; and the personal appearance of, or messages from, such seemingly unlikely and admired figures as communications scholar Paul Lazarsfeld, sociologist Robert K. Merton, and the usually cautious NAACP luminary Walter White.[54]

Unlike many a successful wartime institution, the congress also had a long-term aim. According to several speakers, a new phase of filmmaking and, more to the point here, screenwriting was on the verge of arrival. In a sermon-like exercise of faith, Robert Rossen as much as admitted that his Depression-era scripting had rather suddenly become obsolete. Having previously "never doubted that my approach to content was right," he insisted that he suddenly had difficulty writing about the "strata" that he had written about and known personally all his life. The "sullen, bewildered little man who rebelled against society" and the "girl who wants nothing in life so much as one last fling . . . and then to settle down in life with a man she doesn't love," or the "old philosophical gent who sits on park benches or tenement roofs and spends several reels talking about the futility of life" (this last one was not a notable feature of Rossen's films, at any rate)—all these characters had as good as vanished.[55]

In their place, people who knew society needed them had gone to work in war industries or gone to war willingly. Those erstwhile subproletarians and others who had "come out of the bewilderment and confusion that beset them" were now "taking an affirmative and positive point of view toward life."[56] So were capitalists, at least a few of them. Those who found dignity were willing to fight and die for it, if necessary.

Instead of exposing the social rot and the fatal blows of fate against human striving, Rossen insisted, he found the need and the purpose to write about "people who were going to win, despite any condition." The greatest problem of writers was to understand why the change had taken place, and to adapt themselves to where the ordinary American had already traveled:

> We've been so steeped in the cynicism of the last twenty years that we find it hard to think of characters such as the ones I've been talking about in any other terms but as people who must be crushed by destructive social forces. We're still thinking in terms of the last war and not in terms of this war: we're still afraid that things will go back the way they did in the last war. We are still afraid of being betrayed, and that fear goes deep. We've been sick, and this has reflected itself in everything that's been written in the last twenty years. Our stories have been stories of frustration, of defeat—our characters have always gone down to their doom . . . Well, the average man isn't afraid of being betrayed. He doesn't think it can happen any more.[57]

That average man (and presumably woman) was only waiting "for us to write him." Nothing less would do. Higher-ups were surprisingly eager to affirm this kind of sentiment. Darryl Zanuck hailed *Watch on the Rhine* ("a marvelous piece of entertainment") as just the ticket for the popular presentation of positive entertainment, the proper successor to *The Grapes of Wrath*–type Depression picture.[58] Edward Dmytryk argued somewhat immodestly that *Hitler's Children* and *Behind the Rising Sun* offered necessary insight into real-life horror, thereby connecting the moviegoer with the antifascist cinematic heroes and showing what Americans were fighting (or working) for.[59]

Discussions of documentaries even went a measurable distance to resolving the conflict between the radical documentarians and the supposed Hollywood wool-spinners. Joris Ivens, Kenneth MacGowan, James Wong Howe, and "Sergeant Ben Maddow" described the ways in which the documentary had become part of the antifascist effort and in the process established a ground for realism that filmmaking would take unto itself. It was an understandable optimism of the moment, with so many left-wing writers engaged in documentary work.[60]

A Writers' Credo adopted unanimously by the audience at the end of the conference drove home the central message. The "obligation to seek and find the truth," an obligation without limits, nevertheless found itself channeled in very particular ways: toward freedom of expression (including the need to oppose "the divisive racist doctrines that pollute the free air of America and that imprison the great creative energies of the Negro people and of other national minorities") in tune with patriotism as "a deep reality, an expression of the common man's profound and reasoned faith in our democratic way of life." [61] Democratic sentiment was here to stay—or so the participants were able to convince themselves.

Had *The New York Times* reviewer of the proceedings volume exaggerated or overdrawn the conclusion that Hollywood's writers were preparing to take over the town? Very possibly, but only because he seemed to read between the lines, or to hear the voices in the hallways that never got into the formal addresses. [62] The LAW school and the writers' workshops had been about learning to think cinematically, in radical ways; the congress had been about reorganizing an industry (actually, several industries, including radio and publishing), albeit under the banner of patriotic unity.

As if called into rethinking by these promising notes, at the opposite end of the country, intelligent and more encouraging voices of the cultural Left could also belatedly be heard. No doubt the perception of political openings in film by Pearl Harbor emboldened shifts in left-wing attitudes. But the appearance in the *New Masses* columns of Joy Davidman, the promising poet whose *Letter to a Comrade* won the Yale Series of Younger Poets Award in 1939, itself marked a significant left-wing advance.

The American-born daughter of Jewish immigrants growing up in the Bronx, Davidman reputedly broke the scale in youthful IQ testing, and read widely in childhood, but she suffered acutely from a range of health problems—from a bent spine to hyperthyroidism to the cancer that finally killed her at forty. Stephen Vincent Benét had taken a special interest in her writing, spurring her beyond poetry to a D. H. Lawrence–style novel about a free-loving woman. Spending six disappointing months at MGM in Hollywood in 1939, with most of her attention given to left-wing social affairs, she returned to New York to work on staff at the *New Masses* and to edit the League of American Writers' 1943 volume of international writers, *War Poems of the United Nations.* By the time that volume appeared, she had married a radical folksinger and borne a son, dropping her output to occasional book reviews and poems. She abandoned the Left a few years after the war.[63]

But her brief span of critical writing on films encompassed some of the most interesting in Communist (or any other Left) publications to that time. She had obviously stayed in Hollywood long enough to develop an immanent critique of filmmaking, especially film writing, in a commercial context. *The Sea Wolf* (1941), which Communist interpreters given to reductive logic might easily have been written off as exploiting the works of Jack London (immensely popular in the Soviet Union, more so than in the United States, by this time), she pronounced the "much needed proof that the film industry is not run entirely by Mongoloid idiots with adenoids." Sans cinematic innovations of the kind that made *Citizen Kane* great, *The Sea Wolf* was nevertheless "a rattling good adventure tale" and expressed the "brotherhood of man against the doctrine of the superman" and pathos without sentimentalism, played brilliantly by Edward G. Robinson, Alexander Knox, Ida Lupino, and John Garfield.

If *The Sea Wolf* had entirely lacked a political edge—in fact, it was adapted for the screen by Party member Robert Rossen—Davidman might not have been able to credit it with such accomplishment. But by this time a growing number of films (not all written by left-wingers) had attained the combination of political and artistic qualities that Marxist-minded critics could admire. The invasion of Russia by Germany shortly followed the LAW Congress in which screenwriting was on the agenda.[64]

Scarcely more imaginable for didactic theorists like V. J. Jerome or John Howard Lawson was the possibility that better movies could arrive *without* the organized political pressure of a progressive film community. The idea that liberal-leftish films by the dozens could make significant money and even a handful could win Academy Awards, that Dalton Trumbo would both join the Party and simultaneously become the highest-paid writer in Hollywood—this was far beyond the purview of the pre–Pearl Harbor understanding of Communists.

By the close of 1942, it looked as if the Left had never been marginal in Hollywood. The previous year's films, like *Among the Living, Here Comes Mr. Jordan, Honky Tonk, The Little Foxes, The Maltese Falcon,* and *Tom, Dick and Harry,* had registered their success. Buchman got an Oscar for *Mr. Jordan,* Jarrico shared a nomination for *Tom, Dick and Harry,* and *The Little Foxes* won the ringing accolades of critics. The new season brought *Casablanca, The Glass Key, In This Our Life, My Sister Eileen, The Talk of the Town, This Gun for Hire,* and *Woman of the Year,* not to mention *Saboteur,* a half dozen other antifascist features earlier postponed, and the distinctly interracial *Tales of Manhattan.* At the bottom of the barrel, military musicals, leftish Westerns, and oddball episodes of the Henry Aldrich and the Blondie series all made money and paid salaries. In the same two years, Jules Dassin, Joseph Losey, Carl Foreman, and other newcomers (some of them latecomers from theater and documentaries) also got their first regular screen credits. This moment of high industry prestige and higher expectations was perfect for the master political stroke.

In this atmosphere, serious critics like Joy Davidman could admire even those previously unadmirable escape films, "the strain-lifters, the cheerer-uppers, the movies to which soldiers on leave take their girls" and which films themselves had "suffered a sea-change since Pearl Harbor with more straining, the contemplation of sex and death shadowing through the merry-making." [65] It was something to behold.

Not that writers weren't still continually frustrated by studio realities, but even these might not be quite what they had seemed. Arnaud d'Usseau, a successful playwright and unsuccessful screenwriter whose shifting back and forth from New York sometimes found him defending arch Party aesthetic positions from a distance and then ignoring them when actually working at the studios, had correctly observed back in 1939 (perhaps about himself) that "a writer who comes to Hollywood and is soon dissatisfied only sees pictures in terms of his own craft." Their quite natural "investment as artists" made it difficult to see things any other way, even what was beneath their collective noses: that Hollywood now represented popular drama as Washington represented politics and Manhattan represented finance, and that Hollywood had discovered a new way of telling a story. [66]

But how good was the story and how much had the democratic spirit of wartime changed the Hollywood framework after all? The answers could be daunting. Davidman, the undoubted feminist (even if the word "feminism" had fallen into deepest ill repute) of the *New Masses,* complained sharply that the Hollywood version of woman's life as aspiring only to love and to have children remained, one way or another, even in gender-satirical films like *Tom, Dick and Harry,* or *Woman of the Year.* Ginger Rogers of the former movie, so affably dumb, could not possibly be Nora of *A Doll's*

House. The character played by Katharine Hepburn in *Woman of the Year* was incredibly talented, but was so incapable of handling ordinary household duties, Davidman complained, that her dependence upon gruff Spencer Tracy would become unavoidable, anyway.[67]

Charles Humboldt, soon to be key editor of the new left-literary magazine *Mainstream,* added to Davidman's commentary that a female film protagonist was invariably made to pay heavily for any successful striving. Real life offered up plenty of this punishment, but Hollywood films seemed to relish it. The alternative to punishment seemed to make her strong or able only in contrast to a ridiculous boyfriend or husband, ditzy Blondie with super-bumbling Dagwood Bumstead.

If war work and wartime popular culture offered a rare opportunity to challenge sex stereotypes, Humboldt asked, "would it not be more realistic to demand that our films show women in the middle of struggle for their freedom, than to recount a victory that has not yet been won?"[68] That kind of thought did not carry the *New Masses* readers very far, perhaps because so little of it could be found in war-production posters, contemporary radio drama, popular magazine stories, let alone Hollywood films. Neither Rosie the Riveter nor Superwoman, both of them wartime creations, had to overcome real-life problems. But like the left-wing demand for dignified African-American dramatic parts, Humboldt's challenge seemed at least to go in the right direction, toward what films might be able to do under the proper circumstance.

Nor should it be surprising that the Hollywood Writers Mobilization conference at UCLA in 1943 should have produced so little of a programmatic nature. As *The New York Times* reviewer of the proceedings volume had also pointed out, "concrete ideas upon how to use the potent media of film and radio" remained scarce.[69]

The *Hollywood Quarterly*

The appearance of the *Hollywood Quarterly* in the fall of 1945 provided a direct successor to the proceedings volume of the 1943 Hollywood Writers Mobilization in more ways than one. The publication of that volume by UCLA had already set a larger process in motion. UCLA psychology professor and key mover Franklin Fearing, who seems to have been blissfully unaware of the dangers posed to himself despite the steady drumbeat of the tabloid press in California, more than anyone made the transition from symposium to quarterly publication possible. The "Red" taint had been brushed over if not brushed away by wartime mentality—more so by the romance between UCLA academics (including a few high-ranking administrators), the most prestigious left-wing writers, and the few studio execs farsighted enough to welcome serious dialogue.

An opening "Editorial Statement" sought to verify the new journal's independent outlook. "One of the first casualties" of the war had been the Hollywood myth of films as "pure entertainment," because films (and radio) had "reflected the anxieties and hopes of the long crisis." What role would these media play in the victorious "creation of new patterns of world culture and understanding?" Modestly, the *HQ*'s editors considered themselves "not so incautious as to attempt an answer," and therefore placed the journal's task to "seek answers by presenting the record of research and exploitation" on various lines. The very lack of precedent for serious research here seemed the most daunting prospect. But a start could be made; if successfully accomplished, "the editors will feel that the *Quarterly* has justified itself indeed."[70] This tone was already a long way from the "searchlight of Marxism" so familiar to left-wing publications of almost every stripe.

HQ institutionally secured a decisive measure of freedom from Party control by virtue of its academic and formally nonpolitical status. Fearing naturally served as editor. His protégée Sylvia Jarrico, screenwriter Paul Jarrico's wife and a returning student at the university, was its managing editor.[71]

That John Howard Lawson and Howard Koch, the scriptwriter of *Mission to Moscow,* shared the editorial board of the journal with Fearing and other various respectables seems almost incredible even by the Cold War–leaning standards of 1946. Lawson's resignation the following year was regretted (he was, a journal note mentioned blandly, "compelled to resign because of pressure of literary work in addition to his writing for the screen") as if politics had been a nonissue. Non-Communist Kenneth Mac-Gowan left the board with Lawson, en route to the distinguished academic career that might otherwise have been denied him. But in replacement the board gained two novelist-screenwriter liberals, James Hilton and John Collier, along with two cerebral radicals, highly respected avant-gardist Abraham Polonsky and hardly respected B film director Irving Pichel.

These last two were among the most remarkable intellectual figures in the history of Hollywood. Most other left-wingers including some top screenwriters and directors certainly considered themselves intellectuals, but they rarely set down their thoughts about screenwriting and what might be called political aesthetics. Polonsky and Pichel wrote lucidly about cinema, even if the opportunity and incentive to put their thoughts into print had to be confined to a few years between the war and the black-list. Their essays, written mostly in terms of film particulars rather than cultural generalizations, nevertheless spanned many of the issues raised by the Hollywood Left.

Polonsky's essay on the multiple-Oscar-winning *The Best Years of Our Lives* offered a close examination of the possibilities and limits of the con-temporary Hollywood system. The film captured middle America, provid-ing the audience "a landmark in the fog of escapism, meretricious violence and the gimmick plot attitude of the usual movie." In doing so, it illumi-nated the struggle for content as the way forward in film. The postwar ad-justment of the film's three protagonists—banker, blue-collar worker, and lower-middle-class battle victim with hooks for hands—was stitched to-gether all too typically Hollywood-style, but the effort to inject realism through detail and what Polonsky called "emotional texture" had broken through stereotypes. If all Hollywood filmmaking and particularly screen-writing were, in a sense, writing under censorship, an aspiration could nev-ertheless be declared to "make imagination live."[72]

This strategy confronted censorship on different grounds from those usually applied by the Hays Office. The struggle for content demanded stark realism about postwar adjustment: seeing through the false promises of peace and prosperity for all, made in return for past sacrifices and in re-sponse to the restlessness of postwar society. While *The Best Years of Our Lives* opened up the crucial issues, it finally supplied merely personal an-swers signifying nothing very much. Life recommenced more or less con-tentedly in all quarters, with occasional twinges reminding audiences of unresolved issues somewhere below the surface. If *The Best Years* was a suc-cess, it resembled the war itself, whose victory was definitely partial. Vul-gar optimism and vulgar despair ruled together in the aftermath.[73]

Polonsky's essay on the British suspense drama *Odd Man Out* and Chaplin's *Monsieur Verdoux* asked how film art could reconstruct reality, in a world shadowed by the new threat of atomic warfare, without giving way to celluloid versions of the metaphysical consolation proposed by contemporary philosophers. *Odd Man Out,* a daring film about an Irish nationalist on the run, offered a genuine glimpse of darkness but ended in meaningless moralizing. Meanwhile, Chaplin, beginning from the wildly imaginary premise of a bigamist, adulterer, and murderer who is after all a sweet fellow, moved through a critique of bourgeois morals toward a higher realism that the stock realists themselves could not reach.[74] Anticipating future friendly witness Elia Kazan's emphasis in *Viva, Zapata!,* Polonsky skewered the lionization of the Irish rebel who was destined to remain an outcast because a ruling authority was inevitable (even needed and desired by plain folk) to keep the rebels of the world from getting out of hand. The problem of artists in a world still yearning to be free was the handiness of such a comfortable solution, about as meaningful as the intervention of a ghost or angel into some apparently insoluble dilemma, and usually no more inventive.[75]

Polonsky the noir master was especially struck about this time by the surrealist low-budget French classic, Jean Vigo's *Zero de conduite* (*Zero for Conduct,* 1933), which first reached specialized American audiences after the war and met with distinctly unfriendly reviews. The rebellion of French schoolboys against tyrannical authorities offered images themselves run riot, demonstrating (for him, at least) that film art could lift a kind of realism up to new heights. But this was not a particularly useful observation in Hollywood, or for that matter in most of the Hollywood Left (probably the writers of slapstick comedy would have appreciated it best). *Hollywood Quarterly* provided only a small opening—most readily for left-leaning animationists—for the kind of exploration that he had in mind, a beginning with no succeeding steps.[76]

Irving Pichel wrote, over a period of a few years, considerably more than Polonsky. Perhaps the older figure with a large backlog of practical experience on stage and at various levels of screen work had saved up these thoughts for the moment when they might be heard and even make a difference.[77] He was no philosopher in any case, but an earnest technician. Thinking aloud in the manner of Dudley Nichols, Pichel came squarely to issues that interested most of the industry's readers of the *HQ:* technical details and plot themes, especially in areas little discussed, such as animation, film music, or color technique. The intersection of these and more general trends with the all-pervasive business end of moviemaking constituted daily life, intangibles that the sometime actor and casting director, all-around Hollywood artist and auteur understood as well as anyone in the movie capital.

For Pichel, the very slimness of the "slim literature" on films written by those working in films, and not just in Hollywood, testified to the difficulty, as old as Greek theater of antiquity, of the artist discussing his own art form. The Greeks had left that work to the philosophers, but the artist did have something crucial to say, especially in the least-understood, most swiftly evolving modern art forms. For his part, Pichel formulated by moving cautiously from the particular to the general.[78] Thus, for instance, he approached the implications of camera movement as the growing technical capacity (and personal skill) of the cameraman to "move the spectator" so effectively that the camera imitated the function of the eye. The machine now "operates as the mind does when one reads a story, visualizing with the author's account and actions" from character to character, scene to scene. But just as important was the enhanced imaginative capacity, for the same camera "objectifies magically, as no other medium can, the wish to be able to come closer, to see more early and intimately than life or the earlier forms of theater art have allowed us."[79] And yet, for Pichel, the story nevertheless had to remain supreme, every shot dealing in one way or another with the characters' narrative development.

If the film industry's mass-production process had robbed the erstwhile theatrical director (and Pichel here clearly meant himself) of his treasured prerogatives, first of all preventing him from collaborating creatively with the screenwriter (because screenwriting and filming took place on different schedules), the possibility of unifying concept and the method was nevertheless inherent in the progress of filmmaking. Welles offered the best example on this side of the ocean, but Pichel pointed to the British example of director David Lean. *Great Expectations* (1946), a much-awarded instant classic, brought Dickens to life neither by seeking to reproduce the Victorian world nor by treating the characters psychologically in the "modern" film fashion, but by capturing the story with such concision that the "disparate arrangement of elements of consciousness and experience, are real as efforts of the artist's mind to discover meaning and design in human life.'" As in Hamlet, the protagonist "is more real as symbol and synthesis than any actual man who may have lived."[80] Lean had, in short, prepared cinema to leap forward—further than Pichel himself ever had the opportunity to go.

And the same might be said for the *Hollywood Quarterly* in its promising early days. Who else would write so knowledgeably (as well as lovingly) about screen animation as Bugs Bunny creator Chuck Jones, no left-winger but neither averse to such company; about French film as Georges Sadoul, a near-Communist and famed historian-critic; or, from the academic side, Kenneth MacGowan, who offered a pointed contrast between Disney's politics (of which he disapproved) and Disney's contributions to animation (which he praised highly)?[81]

The *HQ* writers sought to make their political points mainly through the observation of genre. Dorothy B. Jones, who would a decade later write the prestigious critique, on behalf of the Fund for the Republic, of politics in blacklisted screenwriters' work,[82] delivered an early assessment of the war film, more survey than analysis, and ending with Hollywood's considerable contribution to film's "vital role in world affairs" and Hollywood's own advance in "social awareness and in new techniques of filmmaking."[83] In Jones's view, as we have seen, the filmmakers lacked the knowledge for the most sophisticated subjects (like the United Nations) and too easily turned home-front films into spy thrillers no different from detective yarns and murder mysteries; but a minority of war action films (like *Bataan, Sahara, Action in the North Atlantic, Guadalcanal Diary,* and *Gung Ho!*) avoided the clichés of American superheroes or the kind of trivialization inevitable in pure "entertainment" genres like musicals, and vividly conveyed the real issues of the war. Regrettably, Jones's query came a year or two too early, before the best films on battle or the home front would be released.

Franklin Fearing followed up Jones's lead two years later with an assessment of film and the veterans' return. By this time, Polonsky's critique of *The Best Years of Our Lives* had already covered some of the most vexing issues of Hollywood realism's successes and failures. Fearing, the psychologist, wanted to deal specifically with the filmic response to grief. He pointed to *A Medal for Benny* and *Thirty Seconds Over Tokyo* as successfully dealing with the all-important current issue of GIs getting past their war traumas and successfully readjusting to civilian life. The earliest of the high-quality war-theme films, like *Since You Went Away,* tended to reveal either extreme nostalgia for a prewar world lost or frustration at the one gained. The chief danger, as Fearing made clear, was in films now blaming the trauma of the present upon the "weaknesses imbedded in the human psyche" that were beyond self-correction, even beyond therapy.[84] The promising alternative demanded a creative rethinking of the relationships between military and civilian life, not only for future life in the United States but across the globe. To grasp the reasons for the suffering, and the prospects of salvation for the "family of man," could turn the trauma into something like its opposite. But sadly for Fearing as well as his magazine colleagues, the world situation offered ample new reasons for fear—and no greater understanding.

No contributor to the *Hollywood Quarterly* stood higher in Hollywood estimation than screenwriter Dudley Nichols. In the last important critical essay that he would pen, Nichols described wartime filmmaking as embodying the special qualities of method and intention that might possibly remake cinema. *Counter-Attack,* John Howard Lawson's rewrite of a Russian feature, struck Nichols as admirable for its use of a highly confined set. But Nichols celebrated *G.I. Joe* as "pure film," among the purest ever made. The bedrock realism and the capture of humane emotion must have seemed to the master screenwriter and critic at the level of his own best efforts, perhaps even beyond.[85]

Only rarely—and this is altogether notable—did the *Hollywood Quarterly* fall into what might be called the special pleading of the Left so often seen in the *Daily Worker* and other Communist-linked organs over issues of political censorship or the antisocial themes multiplying in contemporary films. Lester Cole thus retold, with considerable risk to himself and no small degree of personal ax-grinding, the story of the censorship of *Blood on the Sun.* He had written a screenplay about Japan during the 1920s and the Japanese government's "Tanaka Document," a purported plan for Asian conquest that fell into the hands of the State Department. The toned-down version let American officials off the hook and even lowered the rhetoric of attack upon the Japanese, bowing (at least according to Cole) to the Hearst newspapers' call for a negotiated rather than unconditional surrender in the current conflict—a way to end the war without shattering the class systems of the capitalist world. The *Hollywood Reporter,* ever eager for a Red scandal, leaped at the opportunity to smash the new journal. Warning in a front-page editorial about Communist efforts to take over movies, the paper plunged the *HQ* into its first serious controversy.[86]

The difference between Cole's script and the finished film appeared considerably less important within a few years, when the real-life issue of Unconditional Surrender had been rendered moot by the dire implications of the A-bomb's use. Many a peace activist also wondered about the original Unconditional Surrender demand as predictive of the aggressive Cold War rollback or "total victory" syndrome. But this was not the worst result of the always-egotistic Cole overstepping political boundaries. According to later accounts, the writer's spleen turned Cagney—whose brother William had produced the film and presumably made the political decision—away from his left-wing pals and toward willingness to cooperate with their sworn enemies.[87] At any rate, Cole's essay was the *Quarterly's* lowest note, as well as the most costly.

John Houseman meanwhile pondered, in a more philosophical vein, the meaning of the abundant psychologically overwrought postwar films. As much as he enjoyed *Body and Soul* with its psychological intricacies, *Crossfire* seemed to him the most complete example, amazingly unified within its twenty-three-day shooting schedule and B budget, its narrowing of the issues to anti-Semitism, and its mise-en-scène of dark interiors and narrow streets. By contrast, Houseman savaged director Jules Dassin's *Brute Force* as "deeply . . . immoral, chiefly by reason of its complete unreality" with criminals as the victims and the ostensibly kindly warden as culpable.[88] Likewise, he found in the "tough guy" films of the postwar era an absence of the morality of their 1930s counterparts, perhaps even a widespread feeling of fear among people "turning away from the anxiety and shock of the war . . . afraid to face their personal problems and the painful situations of their national life."[89] Veteran exponent of a more hopeful drama and film, Houseman was unnerved by noir.

Ben Maddow, trying to unify the current experience with the works of Eisenstein, provided in the very first issue what might be called a sort of artistic/philosophical credo of the *Hollywood Quarterly*. Great cinematic work had been done, in Russia as elsewhere, but now it was time to move on.

Compression and selection, the great principles of filming historical drama, had never been surpassed after the Russian master's *Potemkin* and *Alexander Nevsky.* If Einsenstein himself had more recently insisted that films must look to own their traditions, Hollywood obviously needed to comprehend that tradition—but not as the later Eisenstein did himself, for the potentialities of that machine, the camera, which gives the cinema its unique breadth and freedom . . . is the supreme, the untiring eye of the camera that can grasp and hold details, that can fill even the corners of the frame with the abracadabra of reality; an overturned chair, or the texture of weathered ironwork; an indifferent dog, the opening of a door that is irrelevant, or a face, close for a moment, that is not part of the central action beyond. All such actions have been ruthlessly stripped from [Eisenstein's later, heavily nationalist film] *Ivan* [*the Great*].

Finally, it is the movie camera alone that can follow and hold—and by editing sustain, heighten and contradict into drama—all the tumult of human events, all their violent concurrence in the three-dimensional space of the screen; this freedom . . . Eisenstein has [now] put aside in order to freeze and monumentalize an era . . . Thus *Ivan* is a great film, in motive and in plan; but it is not a good one.[90]

Hostile critics of the *HQ* looked upon such phrases as typical Communist homage to the art and politics of the so-called Workers' Fatherland.[91] Maddow intended the opposite: an almost unthinkable criticism of Russia's leading mass artist and the father of revolutionary cinema that also placed the mundane and secular work of Hollywood artists in a context of their own. Maddow had thereby made a declaration similar to Maltz's, albeit without flying the colors of rebellion from familiar Party positions on art and culture. As Pichel and Polonsky had stressed, the task at hand was *not* to monumentalize through grand historical gestures and melodrama but to use the advances of screenwriting and camera work to capture society, social relations, and the contradictions and the promise of human behavior. Although the studio system and the radicals' own failures of imagination had limited that effort, the promise of something better should lie ahead.

If a crypto-Marxist critique was the *Hollywood Quarterly*'s most controversial feature, its commentary on less-considered areas by hands-on specialists may have been its most unique. Adolph Deutsch, vice president of the Screen Composers' Association (not a union, but with some of the functions of one), an important participant in the Hollywood Writers Mobilization and a more important figure in the forgotten Musicians Congress the following year, the composer for the score of *The Maltese Falcon* and *Action in the North Atlantic,* assayed his recent work on *Three Strangers.* The composer had nothing too remarkable to say about this bit of exotica (coincidentally written by John Huston and Howard Koch), which plays upon the tragic consequences of a meeting between several psychologically damaged people; but in focusing attention on the uses of sound in tandem with images and action, he pointed readers toward aspects of film barely recognizable to even most industry insiders. Like more theoretical essays on music and separate essays on stage design and color, Deutsch's contribution gave dignity to the craft of virtually anonymous (if sometimes well-paid) studio workers.[92]

Even before the *Hollywood Quarterly* ended its formal relation with all left-wingers, the journal had become more academic, less an organic extension of filmmakers' dialogue, than its founders had wanted. By Polonsky's estimation, "It wanted to be better . . . [but] never got to the heart of what films were about. It couldn't survive the attack on radicals in the university and in Hollywood."[93] This was surely too modest, because a real start had been made. Radicals wanted to keep the politics of film, in the broadest sense, as a central part of the discussion, without monopolizing or manipulating the discussion. Yielding ground, they hoped to prevent harm from falling upon the journal on their account, so that their formal withdrawal was only a final step.

The failure of the project might be seen as the reversal of the victories won and loss of the high ground taken at the 1943 Writers Congress. It is, perhaps, useless to speculate about what the *Hollywood Quarterly,* maintained at the levels reached in 1945–47, might have effected in Hollywood—almost as useless as to speculate how America (or the world) might be a different place if Henry Wallace had been retained as FDR's vice president in 1944 or if FDR had not died in office before completing his fourth term. But it is tempting to wonder about the dialogue that did not take place in California and could not take place elsewhere.

Labor Crises and Left Self-Immolation

Things had meanwhile also collapsed on Hollywood's labor front, with considerably more direct consequences for screenwriters. The resentment of the moguls toward unionism burst out first in May 1941, during an especially bitter nine-week strike at Disney. It was directed most ironically at an employer whom left-wingers quietly admired as a hands-on producer who strove for perfection rather than the mere bottom line. But "Uncle Walt," as he liked to think of himself, also brooked no compromise and flatly refused to bargain. That the strike opened during the Hitler-Stalin Pact period when the Left had lost its allies worsened the picture considerably.

But things were still far from dire. In California generally and especially in Southern California, the late arrival of wide-scale unionism created an all-out rush for members. At the studios, dissatisfaction with the International Alliance of Theatrical Stage Employees (IATSE) and hopes of wider unionization had toward the end of the 1930s prompted a few craft locals to form the rival Federated Motion Picture Crafts (FMPC), a move immediately challenged when FMPC members struck in 1937 for higher wages. For the first time in Hollywood, strikers found themselves confronting both employers and the IATSE-connected mob, whose imported goons broke picket lines with saps and brass knuckles and then moved in on the painters' hiring haul, mauling everyone on hand. The Los Angeles Central Labor Council passed a resolution labeling the Hollywood IATSE "a company union and a scab-herding agency," no overstatement of the case. The tough leader of the painters, Herb Sorrell, was also the founding figure of the Conference of Studio Unions (CSU) in 1940, bringing together the FMPC with the former "IATSE Progressives" who carried off their craft locals from the mobbed-up international.[94]

The lines were now drawn. Sorrell, who had apparently once been a Communist but regarded himself as a free agent (and was said to resent local Party leaders as much as they resented him), remained in the AFL but obviously envisioned an inclusive industrial unionism in the studios as the ultimate solution to labor conflicts. The studios not incorrectly saw the CSU as a stalking horse for this goal. For a middling entrepreneur like Disney, the threat all but demanded no-holds-barred response. Some later anti-Communist figures of note, fast-rising actor-unionist Ronald Reagan among them, were to comment that the very possibility of industrial unionism signaled subversion and potential revolution, notwithstanding the non-Communist status and leadership of so many industrial unions elsewhere (including some uncomfortably squeezed into the AFL). Perhaps that was the way they had seen things, from the Hollywood perspective of "talent guilds" and exclusionary craft unions, all the way along.[95]

IATSE, however, also entered the fray with some major handicaps.

Local leaders George Browne and Willie Bioff, tainted by investigations of the Senate's La Follette Committee into union corruption, were finally forced out of local leadership in 1941 as the evidence against them accumulated. As Gerald Horne observes, even the ritual playing of "Dixie" (a sort of race affirmation of whites-only IATSE) at the union's 1940 annual convention seemed this time to signal defensiveness or desperation rather than the old craft triumphalism.[96]

IATSE still held an ace or two. During the torrent of Red-baiting and the HUAC hearings of the Pact period, IATSE leaders melodramatically presented their union as the first line of defense against the Communist control of Hollywood. Even amidst the wartime Soviet-American alliance, the baiting continued. Not long after the imprisoned Bioff offered state's evidence in 1943, Chicago mob rival Sam Giancana hatched a neat public relations plan. IATSE's Hollywood unit suddenly boasted a new leader: Roy Brewer, with no history of mob involvement if also a strangely sparse history as a dues-paying union member of any kind.[97] Although the Los Angeles IATSE executive board remained unchanged, its longtime collaboration with the mob apparently as firmly entrenched as ever, Brewer soon claimed to have cleaned house, producing a show business union at once ferociously anti-Communist and respectable.

This cosmetic operation came just in time. Studios making money hand over fist in the new and more efficient, factory-like facilities quickly succeeded in centralizing the filmmaking process, but also brought studio workers together as never before. Under these changed conditions, unionized carpenters under CSU jurisdiction went out on strike for better pay. IATSE responded by offering to replace the strikers with its own, more compliant members. Timing was entirely against the CSU, because the picket lines went up in March 1945, and the war was to continue until August. Sworn to prevent strikes and resolve wartime labor disputes, Communists could not bring themselves to back Sorrell and the CSU in this dispute. In retrospect, the Left and the would-be industrial unionists may very well have fallen together into a carefully laid trap.

Despite proposals from the National Labor Relations Board to settle the jurisdictional dispute and the strike on amenable grounds to all, the conflict sputtered on. After the Japanese surrender, Communists belatedly threw their support behind the strikers, buoying the now-flagging effort. During the early days of October, when picketers announced a more forceful stand against strikebreakers, mobsters again made an appearance, wading into crowds with chains, rubber hoses, and blackjacks. At the front gates of Warners, local firemen and policemen knocked down CSUers with hose spray and clubs, while out-of-town Teamsters (defying a local Teamster vote in solidarity with the strike) sent buses with human and material deliveries crashing through the lines. Even Frank Sinatra, closely associated with the Left during the war years but more closely associated with the mob from his earliest days as a nightclub singer, announced his decision to cross the lines with mob help if needed. Old friends of liberalism and unionism like Judy Garland, Olivia de Havilland, the Three Stooges, and even former Party elector Lucille Ball also crossed (although Bette Davis and Edgar Bergen held fast, while Eddie "Rochester" Anderson, Roy Rogers, Dale Evans, and boxing champ Joe Louis all made appearances at a strike benefit). The strike was crushed, and the CSU suffered a body-blow.

Hollywood's labor war wasn't quite over. In July 1946, the CSU won an amazing 25 percent pay increase with a quickie strike, and a "Treaty of Beverly Hills" seemed to promise amity. Soon, the National Labor Relations Board—still bearing Roosevelt appointees—ruled that the CSU was entitled to one small further victory, the jurisdiction of set decorators who, in fact, had already voted to join it. Producers and the IATSE now reset the trap, instigating a studio lockout of CSU members and threatening to fire any IATSE members who refused to cross the picket line. The new, aggressively anti-Communist leadership of the Screen Actors Guild (especially Reagan, his close friend George Murphy, and Robert Montgomery) persuaded the membership in a succession of heated meetings to allow SAG members to cross lines without violating rules of union solidarity. Violence by mob muscle-men and police resumed against picketers (sometimes also by studio unionists against scabs), and loyal IATSE members were rewarded with a generous wage increase. Studio production schedules had suffered in the conflict, but by the end of 1946, its members facing growing legal troubles from picket-line arrests and subsequent convictions, the CSU was as good as dead.[98]

Within a year, Herb Sorrell and other die-hard CSUers had been effectively blacklisted from any studio jobs. Most members swallowed hard and rejoined the IATSE, whose leaders rapidly further pressed the advantage. With congressional hearings on tap, local IATSE leader Roy Brewer emerged as star witness, a prime exemplar of the vastly more conservative union movement that took shape nationally in the Cold War years under building-trades conservative George Meany and a merged AFL-CIO.

In all this, Hollywood Communists could hardly be blamed. Private suspicions of Sorrell's ambitions leading unionists into strategic disasters were sadly vindicated, although the combination of the studios, IATSE, the police, hired sluggers, and the commercial press would have made even modest victories unlikely in the deteriorating atmosphere. But on the political front, if FBI infiltrators within the Hollywood Communist branches had devised Party policies from 1947 onward, they could not have done any worse than the group around John Howard Lawson, or received more destructive assistance than they did from the national Party apparatus.

As the *Hollywood Quarterly* basked for a moment in the sun and then all but disappeared, *New Masses* film commentary (likewise that of the *Daily Worker*) went into a kind of reverse gear back to pre-1940-style condemnations of Hollywood. Since the movies' Left personalities were under increasingly sharp attack from leading Hollywood executives, the simple (and simplistic) reasoning went, the industry had gone (or returned) to the dogs. Or perhaps the more hard-bitten Communist film critics had merely moderated their true sentiments during wartime and now returned to a reductionist normal.[99]

If conservatives therefore complained that films had become "too serious," unlike those joyful escapist days of old, *New Masses, Daily Worker,* and *People's World* writers insisted in time-worn fashion that contemporary films were *not* serious, or, if serious, not clear-mindedly political in their efforts.[100] *Life With Father,* Donald Ogden Stewart's witty antipatriarchal screenplay, offered nothing to *New Masses* critic Joseph Foster. *The Bishop's Wife* (written by Leonardo Bercovici) was if anything worse, a recipe for escapism, and so was *The Lost Moment,* the same writer's adaptation of Henry James. (Communist critics were perfectly capable of being insulted on behalf of a highly elitist American novelist, as well as of the working class and the "Negro people.")[101] *It's a Wonderful Life* was dreadful, almost beyond words (possibly, Communist critics did not know how many Red Hollywoodites had worked on the script).[102] *Home of the Brave,* hailed as a liberal triumph in Hollywood itself, had to be scored as "progress" for having a full-blown black character, and yet its compromising solution to problems ("dangerous conceptions . . . so attractively packaged, colored with such dexterity that it is all too easy to be taken in") revealed the cold soul of Hollywood.[103] Never mind the film's left-wing writers and actors! Similar polemics against critically acclaimed left-written realist films like Carl Foreman's *Champion* simply drove home the old, old point: nothing good could be done in Hollywood.[104]

If the 1948 "Unity Awards" created the previous year by a Popular Front–laden committee of Hollywood liberals aimed at urging more films with positive social content (including African-American racial dignity) hailed *Crossfire, Gentleman's Agreement, Cass Timberlane,* and *Body and Soul,* the first two barely got a friendly nod in the Communist press. The third was treated as well-made tripe, and the last considered too sentimental for the required realism.[105] On the rare occasion when a film like *Monsieur Verdoux* appeared with unimpeachable political (as well as artistic) credentials, the main purpose of the review was to point to the exception that proved the rule and to pronounce it "miles ahead of anything else being done on the West Coast."[106]

For that matter, most discussion of Hollywood was not even about films (let alone techniques of filmmaking) anymore. For some years, from 1947 onward, issues of repression and persecution of the screenwriter Party faithful ruled film talk. Hollywood became, for just a moment, a rallying center for anti–Cold War sentiment surrounding Henry Wallace's Progressive Party presidential bid—but mainly as a celebrity cry in the growing night. Stars like Lauren Bacall, who previously had been treated with little admiration from the Communist press, suddenly gained great (but short-lived) attention, at least in their political appearances. By the time the ferociously baited Wallace campaign had practically shut down in the shadow of the coming elections, hardly anything remained but the inclination to protest and bewail a newly reactionary and perhaps always hopeless Hollywood.

Now was the moment for V. J. Jerome, last seen urging the demise of *New Theater and Film* and apparently waiting a decade for his opportunity to swoop down on the Hollywood Left's "illusions." He launched missive after missive in *New Masses's* successor, *Masses and Mainstream,* attacking a favorable *Daily People's World* review of the updated version of an earlier volume, now titled *Theory and Technique of Playwriting and Screenwriting,* by none other than Jerome's longtime political devotee John Howard Lawson.[107] Seeking to apply his theatrical understanding to the evolution of film, Lawson had mostly rehearsed Lewis Jacobs's liberal narrative history of Hollywood, *The Rise of the American Film,* adding some brief and only somewhat favorable comments on film trends during the war and on the worrisome political winds afterward. He was more interested in technical problems of structure, characterization, and sound track than in political aesthetics. For perhaps the last time, Lawson wrote mainly as an artist.[108]

But Jerome flatly declined to see Lawson's reserved optimism about American film at its best as anything but myopia bordering, in a lesser figure, on deviationism. The "fallacy in the idealization of the cinema" in Lawson's writings should now be seen for what it was, namely the pseudo-merger of mass entertainment and "people's art." If Hollywood could produce the latter, then films would be antiracist rather than racist. But "under capitalism . . . the film serves monopoly [capitalism] . . . as its most potent ideological weapon to master the minds of millions."[109] Hollywood was, as twenty years earlier, practically the Main Enemy. Jerome's *The Negro and American Films* pressed the issue over almost a hundred pages of polemics.[110] Subject closed—or at least Jerome must have thought so.

Lawson responded by flagellating himself. Four years earlier Albert Maltz had agreed to the criticism of his call for an art independent of immediate political judgments. Lawson, who may have drafted the official criticism of Maltz, more than capitulated to his own critic:

> It is symptomatic of the general level of Marxist criticism in the United States, that, aside from Jerome's comment, my work on playwriting and screenwriting has been favorably reviewed and uncritically accepted without discussion of its erroneous formulations. It is left to the author to acknowledge his shortcomings . . . [111]

Nothing from within the Communist camp in the United States would be better calculated to confirm Cold War overgeneralizations, for Lawson certainly did acknowledge his purported errors. He had, he admitted, been far too optimistic, even irresponsible, in spreading the illusions of Hollywood as a positive force in society.

In the last serialized essay making up his pamphlet *Film in the Battle of Ideas,* Lawson doggedly struggled for some slight positive message. He admitted that his formulation describing films as "one of the most essential parts of the cultural superstructure . . . utilized with special care and attention by the ruling class" might be taken as a confession of futility. But only, he insisted, by those who refused to see a struggle in culture similar to that in the factory or the courts. "Audience protest" could "force concessions in the content of the films," especially if combined with the struggle for independent production. In the meantime, the struggle for those concessions should not feed "reformist illusions" about the "celluloid poison that is dishonestly labeled entertainment."[112]

Lawson imagined an escape hatch for the handful of his remaining comrades—if film could encompass working-class, African-American, and Mexican-American life as well as that of the foreign born, begin to treat women characters with real dignity, and make room for pacifist sentiments and a counter-history to official propaganda. These remained mere noble sentiments, notwithstanding all the faulty logic that accompanied them. Lawson may even have been right to attribute the sharp decline in film attendance, accompanied by the sudden shutdowns of hundreds of theaters in the early 1950s, to something more than competition from television. Intelligent movies had indeed sharply diminished in number. But he could not foresee that the only way back up was through the system, albeit a revised system that allowed independent productions for stars and others able to make their own bank deals, with major studios continuing the films' distribution. And it would not happen in the short run.

That reality, and the hopelessness of appealing for "mass pressure" from entertainment-starved audiences who were more likely to turn on the newly acquired television set than bother with unwanted films (like the anti-Communist clunkers), made Lawson's position worse than untenable. It had returned to the old theatrical and documentary impulse to abolish Battleship Hollywood altogether, when only Hollywood itself could do that.[113]

The struggle over cinematic meaning before the collapse into political reductionism had foreshadowed the academic discussions decades ahead. In a global and transpolitical sense, film theory gained a degree of specificity only after 1945, with the beginnings of international dialogue. A sense grew, if by no means rapidly or coherently, that differences in approach might ultimately aid in the construction of a unified theory by focusing attention on a wide range of elements. Everything in the *Hollywood Quarterly* suggested that this development was natural and indeed inevitable. By the time that criticism split into theories that sought to explain cinema as an art form, and still more academic ones that sought to analyze it as a social fact of life through sociology, psychology, or other social scientific methods, the Popular Front had long passed.[114]

Amid attack and self-attack, the Hollywood Left was as good as dead by 1947. And yet, what could explain John Howard Lawson's successful script for *Cry, the Beloved Country,* shot in Africa and released just a year earlier than his pamphlet, with many remarkable scenes of suffering but unbroken humanity? Or something so obscure and silly as Laurel and Hardy's last picture, *Utopia,* written by Howard Dimsdale, about a hapless pair who inherit an island of uranium ore? Or the appearance of *Death of a Salesman, The Prowler, Captain Scarlett, Martin Luther, High Noon, The Robe,* and *Roman Holiday* (the last two not credited to the real screenwriters), most of all the Oscar-winning *A Place in the Sun,* all within the same several years?

Somehow, almost inexplicably, the work went along in the semi-autonomous world of mass entertainment until the final blows delivered by the Hollywood hearings—and even afterward. Against hardened class analysis, against constant prediction, good films continued to be made, very often by those on their way out of the Communist Party but not out of the Left.

The political atmosphere, the repression, the FBI campaigns against unions and civil rights groups, the tabloid headlines, and a crescendo of war scares all seemed to rule out any further advances in the theory or practice of American filmmaking. Through it all, the work continued where it had flourished in the first place—deep in the genres, virtually out of the sight of everyone except knowledgeable urban audiences. Many of the Left's best screenwriters did their finest work here. Nowhere had this been more true, since 1946, than in film noir, a genre that seemed to thrive on political and personal disappointment. No one would have guessed in 1938 or 1944 that the fantastic convergence of Hollywood-style realism, German aesthetics, and Freudianized Marxism would become the very emblem of the Los Angeles Popular Front.

1. John Houseman, *Front and Center* (New York: Random House, 1979), 156–57.

2. Our thanks to Ernest Callenbach for this characterization of himself, in e-mail correspondence with the authors, August 2000. See also Brian Hen-

derson, "Introduction," to Brian Henderson and Ann Martin, editors, *Film Quarterly—Forty Years, a Selection* (Berkeley: University of California Press, 1999), 1–2.

3. The AFI's later sponsorship of *American Film,* under the editorship of Peter Biskind, produced the nearest political counterpart to the *Hollywood Quarterly,* but it was more a journal of often acute political-cultural journalism, sans the often scholarly tone of the original that lay at the root of both film studies and serious film criticism.

4. William Wyler, "No Magic Wand," *The Screen Writer 2* (February 1947), 2.

5. Dudley Nichols, "Writer, Director and Film," in John Gassner and Dudley Nichols, editors, *Best Film Plays of 1943–1944* (New York: Crown Publishers, 1945), xxv.

6. Wyler, "No Magic Wand," 2.

7. "Reflections of Guy Endore," interview by Guy Rogers, UCLA Oral History Program, 1964, 143–45.

8. These conclusions are drawn from discussions with Abraham Polonsky and with John Weber, who has no memory of a practical involvement beyond lending his name to the Advisory Board. The same relative detachment would apply to *Screen Writer,* whose editorial board was also a balancing act.

9. Isidor [Schneider] to Maltz, February 6, 1946, Albert Maltz Papers, State Historical Society of Wisconsin.

10. Arthur Schlesinger, Jr., *The Vital Center: The Politics of Freedom* (Boston: Little, Brown, 1949), 123–24.

11. "The Citizen-Writer In Retrospect," Albert Maltz Oral History, UCLA, interview by Joel Rogers, 1976, 511–15.

12. The discussion about replacing Lawson was evidently informal, but recorded in FBI documents several years later by a well-placed informer. FBI Documents L.A. 200365 and 10022184 [1951]. When Lawson went to prison, Michael Wilson and Paul Jarrico effectively took over the much-reduced Communist branch, until they also left the Party.

13. Bernhard J. Stern to Albert Maltz, April 29, 1946, Maltz Papers. Stern, an editor of the journal *Science and Society,* was to lead a shift of that journal away from the Communist orbit in the early 1950s. Paraphrasing, Stern cited the speech by Party leader Foster declaring "that the movement was opposed to thesis literature. He said that he did not wish to confine the artist within the narrow limits of the concepts of the class sruggle, that the artist must have

interests as wide as the world and boundaries as full of life as humanity it-self." So the issue was only political loyalty after all.

14. This recollection from John Weber, in a letter to Paul Buhle, February 10, 2000.

15. Never in the Communist Party but closely allied with Communists in the Screen Writers Guild, Nichols signed a noninterventionist manifesto of the 1941 LAW Congress, a document considered at the time and later only likely to be signed by those closest to the Party.

16. Albert Maltz, "The Citizen-Writer," 514–15, pinpoints Endore as a partic-ular victim of Lawson's ego rather than of general Party policies in Holly-wood or elsewhere.

17. Dudley Nichols, "The Machine from the God," in John Gassner and Dudley Nichols, editors, *Best Film Plays, 1945* (New York: Crown, 1946), xxvii.

18. See Daniel Walkowitz, *Working with Class: Social Workers and the Politics of Middle Class Identity* (Chapel Hill: University of North Carolina Press, 1999), for a rich picture of the cultural lives of the lower-middle-class (and mostly Jewish) Left.

19. Jean Butler, interviewed by Paul Buhle, *Tender Comrades.*

20. Horne, *Class Struggle in Hollywood,* 112–14.

21. Karl Marx, *The Grundrisse,* edited and translated by David McLellan (New York: Harper and Row, 1971), 26.

22. Mikhail Lifshitz, *The Philosophy of Art of Karl Marx* (New York: New York Critics Group, 1938), translated by Ralph B. Winn.

    This particular document was not likely known in Hollywood, but its sentiments—straddling the "proletarian" position that the working class could create art, and the Hollywood feeling that commercial popular cul-ture was perhaps an inevitable transitional form—would have coincided roughly with the views of many writers. Thanks to John Weber for his pri-vate reflections on the primitive state of aesthetics within the Hollywood Left.

23. The only school of artists and culture critics to take up the cudgels for pop-ular culture was the surrealists, heavily influencing Benjamin but severely confined in their capacity to influence the American Left by virtue of their support of Trotsky. The situation was different in the French film industry, for complicated reasons; see Chapter 7, below.

24. As a would-be revolutionary artists' federation called for by Trotsky and sur-realist leader André Breton came to nothing, other non-Communist left-

wing cultural projects dissolved or turned rightward. The *Partisan Review,* still nominally socialist in 1940, was moving toward an avant-garde position attacking popular culture. See Paul Buhle, *Marxism in the United States* (London: Verso, 1991 edition), 159–83, 206–16; and Paul R. Gorman, *Left Intellectuals and Popular Culture in Twentieth Century America* (Chapel Hill: University of North Carolina Press, 1996), 137–56.

25. Expert commentary on Yiddish-language film in the Communist-connected *Morgn Freiheit* and the participation of radicals in the creative process of U.S.–made Yiddish features might seem to transcend these limits, but were like the films themselves an extension of Yiddish theater, again as alternative to the mainstream. J. Hoberman provides many fine examples of *Morgn Freiheit* commentary on Yiddish film in *Bridge of Light.*

26. See Russell Campbell, *Cinema Strikes Back: Radical Filmmaking in the United States, 1930–1942* (Ann Arbor: UMI Research Press, 1982), 146–48, and the last chapter, 237–73. An illuminating oral history of Leo Hurwitz with bitter comments about his difficulties in Hollywood during the war (most especially, the engagement of erstwhile comrades in moneymaking pictures) is in the Federal Theater (FT) Project archives, recently removed from George Mason University to the Library of Congress. Special thanks go to Lorraine Brown of the FT Project for making this interview available.

27. Joris Ivens, "Notes on Hollywood," in Herbert Kline, editor, *New Theater and Film, 1934–1937* (New York: Harcourt Brace, 1985), 299. Interestingly, Kline now relocated to Hollywood was by 1941 one of the instructors of the LAW school—but was unreconciled to Lawson and didn't fit into the Party picture.

28. James Dugan, "American Movies," *New Masses* 33 (December 5, 1939), 24. This was a generous remark about the critic-historian's volume. In truth, Jacobs's *Rise of the American Film: A Critical History* (New York: Teachers College Press, Columbia University, 1939) is extraordinarily bland, so apolitical (or carefully distanced from Jacobs's former Left ties) that the "educational" function of films in explaining the turn-of-the-century imperial conflicts or the First World War, and the Negrophobic politics of Griffith's *Birth of a Nation* are hardly criticized. Only a relatively small portion of the book discusses sound films, and is more of a categorization than a commentary. Despite a few highly suggestive chapters (the best of them on Chaplin), *Rise* works most adequately as a primer on technology and technique as well as film influences before 1930.

29. Dugan, "American Movies," 24.

30. Endore recalled that the two magazines had been nominally the organs of the League of American Writers Hollywood branch, but this sponsorship was purely a matter of form. His brief but valuable retrospective observations can be found in the introduction of the reprint version, *"Black and White/Clipper,"* reprinted in Joseph Conlin, editor, *The Radical Press in America, 1890–1950* (Westport: Greenwood Press), 554–61.

31. Not just prospective screenwriters took the opportunity to gain training in the workshops. Gerda Lerner, decades later one of the founders of women's history, took classes here, was encouraged to write fiction by Viola Brothers Shore, published her first story in *The Clipper,* and learned U.S. history from John Howard Lawson.

32. Gibney, coming from a genteel background (Phillips Exeter Academy and Amherst College), had won Oscars for the story and screenplay of *The Story of Louis Pasteur,* a cinematic left-wing favorite; he also wrote *I Am a Fugitive from a Chain Gang,* collaborated with Edward Chodorov on *The World Changes,* and later, with Norma Barzman on *The Locket,* shifted to television as well as the stage in the blacklist years and after. Gibney served several terms as president of the SWG. Schary, of whom we hear more in Chapters 6 and 8, began as an actor, making his debut on Broadway in John Wexley's *The Last Mile,* wrote the story for *Boys Town,* coscripted *The Raven* with Francis Faragoh, and collaborated with Hugo Butler on *Young Tom Edison* and *Edison the Man,* among his other features. Schary shifted into the executive end of the studios in the 1940s, becoming known for "message" pictures (including *The Boy with Green Hair*), until a bout of McCarthyism turned him from Left to Center.

33. "The School for Writers: an Editorial Article," *The Clipper* 1 (October 1941), 19. This commentary was presumably written by Guy Endore and elaborates in somewhat different terms the remarks made in the "Opening Remarks" at the LAW Congress earlier that year.

34. Schwartz, *The Hollywood Writers' Wars,* 164.

35. Alfred Lewis Levitt interview with Larry Ceplair, *Tender Comrades,* 446–47.

36. During the blacklist, Levitt worked odd jobs, ran his own photo studio, collaborated pseudonymously with his wife on a half dozen television sitcoms and variety shows (most notably *The Donna Reed Show* and *The Ghost and Mrs. Muir*), and penned several family films. He is best remembered in

screenwriting circles for having tutored aspiring young African-American film and television writers, and also for working within the Writers Guild to secure limited pensions for blacklistee writers from a special fund, and to recover lost credits. See Alfred Lewis Levitt, interviewed by Larry Ceplair, *Tender Comrades,* 441–69. We wish to acknowledge Levitt's eagerness to talk and his candor in an interview with Paul Buhle in 1994. See also "Interview with Alfred Lewis Levitt" and "Interview with Helen Slote Levitt," both by Larry Ceplair, UCLA, 1988.

37. "Opening Remarks: League of American Writers Congress, 1941," LAW Papers, Bancroft Library, University of California, Berkeley. Unpaged.

38. Resolution, 1941 Congress, LAW Papers.

39. Ibid.

40. "The Shadows Find a Voice," *New Masses* 37, July 22, 1941, 27.

41. John Bright, "Not Words—Machines," 1941 Congress, LAW Papers.

42. "The Shadows Find a Voice," 27–28.

43. The LAW Congress also featured a collective telegram from the Hollywood chapter and the election of a Resolutions Committee (including Marc Blitzstein, Dashiell Hammett, Viola Brothers Shore, and Lawson as chair) whose work may have effectively closed out the LAW, sine die.

44. Interview of William Alland by Paul Buhle, Los Angeles, 1992. Alland, with a slight background in theater, had attached himself to Welles of Mercury Theatre days, and in the later 1940s wrote the first radio series based upon children's psychiatric experiences. Late to arrive in films (and a cooperative witness in the last of the Hollywood hearings, in 1953), Alland produced family pictures in considerable numbers for a decade, all in the B genres and mostly in Creature Features, most notably the "3-D" *Creature from the Black Lagoon.* He insisted to his interviewer that his fantasy films had an ecologial message. By the time of the interview, several years before his death, Alland had gone through all his money and lived in a trailer park, supporting himself meagerly through phone sales of *Los Angeles Times* subscriptions.

45. Cedric Belfrage, "Orson Welles' *Citizen Kane,*" *The Clipper* I (May 1941), 12–14. Belfrage may, indeed, have deeply influenced Bright's LAW paper through discussions. The best recent reevaluation of *Citizen Kane* is Michael Denning, *The Cultural Front: The Laboring of American Culture in the Twentieth Century* (New York: Verso, 1996), 362–94.

46. See Schwartz, *The Hollywood Writers' Wars,* 192–94, for a valuable discussion of the issues and contemporary perceptions of them, drawn from Schwartz's conversations with Paul Jarrico and others.

47. "Testimony of David Lang," *Motion Picure Hearings,* Los Angeles, 1953, 347.

48. "Testimony of George Beck," *Motion Picture Hearings,* Los Angeles, 1953, 1823–24.

49. *Communism in the Motion Picture Industry, Hearings of the House Committee on Un-American Activities, 1951* (Washington: U.S. Government Printing Office, 1951), 287.

50. One of the few accounts of the congress is in Servio Giovancchini, *Hollywood Modernism, Film and Politics in the Age of the New Deal* (Philadelphia: Temple University Press, 2001), 168–71.

51. Frontispiece, *Writers Congress: The Proceedings of the Conference held in October 1943 Under the Sponsorship of the Hollywood Writers Mobilization and the University of California* (Berkeley: University of California Press, 1944).

52. "A Conversation with Edward Dmytryk," Columbia University Oral History Project, 1959, in Columbia University archives.

53. "Preface," *Writers Congress,* xi–xii.

54. Producers Darryl Zanuck, William Dozier, and Kenneth MacGowan were the biggest names. Among writers not notably on the Left, Leonard Spielgass, Emmet Lavery, Harry Kurnitz, Arch Oboler, Dudley Nichols, and James Hilton could be counted. Left-wingers of various callings giving presentations included James Wong Howe, Ben Maddow, Abe Burrows, John Hubley, Ben Barzman, Vladimir Pozner, and Dalton Trumbo.

55. Robert Rossen, "An Approach to Character, 1943," *Writers Congress,* 63.

56. Ibid., 64.

57. Ibid., 66.

58. Darryl Zanuck, "The Responsibility of the Industry," *Writers Congress,* 33.

59. Edward Dmytryk, "The Director's Point of View," *Writers Congress,* 45.

60. See Joris Ivens, "The Documentary Film and Morale," Kenneth MacGowan, "Ambassadors of Good Will," James Wong Howe, "The Documentary Film and Hollywood Techniques," and Sergeant Ben Maddow, "The Writer's Function in Documentary Film," in *Writers Congress,* 75–79, 90–103.

61. "An American Writers' Credo," *Writers Congress,* 611–12.

62. W. McNeil Lowry, "A Writers' Congress and Its Credo," *The New York Times Book Review,* September 24, 1944. Just as likely, the reviewer was close to the Hollywood Left.

63. Davidman eventually abandoned her husband as well, converted to Christianity, and after a transatlantic correspondence moved to England to marry the famed Christian mystic writer C. S. Lewis, a romance recorded properly enough in film first through a 1985 BBC documentary, and then as *Shadowlands* (1993), with Anthony Hopkins and Debra Winger. Perhaps, one might suggest, she had finally made it (posthumously) in the movies after all. These autobiographical details supplied by Alan Wald, to whom thanks are once again owed.

64. See Herbert Biberman, "Hollywood Skips the Next War," *New Masses* 36 (August 2, 1940), 7–8. The article's title was drawn from a Guy Endore pamphlet, *Let's Skip the Next War,* and Biberman was able to report several major local rallies and demonstrations. Biberman failed to report the actual disarray of the pre-1939 Hollywood Left and its cultural projects. An antiwar successor to the stage show *Meet the People,* it was so entirely unsuccessful that it finished off the Hollywood Theater Alliance created a few years earlier by Henry Myers, Henry Blankfort, and others.

65. Joy Davidman, "The Will and the Way," *New Masses* 45 (October 27, 1942), 29.

66. Arnaud d'Usseau, "A Screenwriter Speaks," *New Masses* 32 (September 12, 1939), 29–32. This piece was described as a letter to a *New Masses* editor, responding to Edmund Wilson's stuffy review of Nathaneal West's novel *The Day of the Locust* and insisting that screenwriters had deceived themselves about their profession.

67. Joy Davidman, "Women: Hollywood Version," *New Masses* 44 (July 14, 1942), 28–30.

68. Charles Humboldt, "Caricature by Hollywood," *New Masses* 51 (July 28, 1944), 29–30.

69. W. McNeil Lowry, "A Writers' Congress."

70. "Editorial Statement," *Hollywood Quarterly* 1 (October 1945), n.p.

71. Interview with Sylvia Jarrico by Paul Buhle, Pecoima, 1993.

72. Abraham Polonsky, " 'The Best Years of Our Lives': A Review," *Hollywood Quarterly* 2 (April 1947), 257–60.

73. Polonsky, "The Best Years," 260.

74. Polonsky, "Odd Man Out," 402.

75. Ibid., 406.

76. His next notable philosophical statement on film would appear not until 1961—and then in a French journal, *Presence du Cinema,* influenced by

surrealism. We produce a portion of it in *A Very Dangerous Citizen,* 196–97.

77. Not destined to be a critic, Polonsky was en route to becoming a novelist, something he probably would have pursued even if the blacklist had never occurred. Pichel, for his part, had only a few years of life ahead.

78. Irving Pichel, "Book Reviews: The Creator as Critic," *Hollywood Quarterly* 2 (October 1946), 212–13.

79. Irving Pichel, "Seeing with the Camera," *Hollywood Quarterly* 1 (January 1946), 139–40. See also Pichel, "The Creator as Critic," *Hollywood Quarterly* 2 (October 1946), especially 212–13, and Pichel, "A Long Rope," *Hollywood Quarterly* 3 (October 1946), 416–20, an important essay on Alfred Hitchcock.

80. Pichel, " 'Happy Breed' and 'Great Expectations,' " *Hollywood Quarterly* 2 (October 1946), 411.

81. At the time of the publication, Sadoul, a former surrealist, had become general secretary of the *Federation Francaise des Cine-Clubs* and one of the most influential film critics in France. Chuck Jones, working at Warner, was creating such characters as Bugs Bunny, Porky Pig, Daffy Duck, Tweetie Pie, Speedy Gonzalez, the Road Runner, and Wily E. Coyote.

82. See Dorothy B. Jones, "Communism and the Movies: A Study of Film Content," in John Cogley, editor, *Report on Blacklisting* I (Washington: the Fund for the Republic, 1956), 196–233. This is all the more poignant because the Fund for the Republic also served as a "pass through" for key CIA intellectual projects as the "Communism in American Life" series of heavily funded scholarly volumes planned by the executive board of the American Committee for Cultural Freedom (with Arthur Schlesinger, Jr., as its most influential figure). See Sigmund Diamond, *Compromised Campus: The Collaboration of the Universities with the Intelligence Community, 1945–1955* (New York: Oxford University Press, 1992), 133–34.

83. Dorothy B. Jones, "Hollywood War Film, 1942–44," *Hollywood Quarterly* 1 (October 1945), 1–2.

84. Franklin Fearing, "Warriors Return: Normal or Neurotic," *Hollywood Quarterly* 1 (October 1945), 97–109, especially 108. At a time when Marxists continued as a group to be very critical of Freud, the definitely non-Marxist (and non-Communist, albeit left-wing) Fearing reflected such sentiment in suggesting a "pessimistic and defeatist" view, n. 3, 108. See also Fearing,

"Psychology and the Film," *Hollywood Quarterly* (1946), 108–21; and the distinguished Lawrence S. Kubie, "Psychiatry and the Films," *Hollywood Quarterly* 2 (January 1947), 113–17. Fearing critiqued *The Dark Mirror,* a "doubling" film written by Vladamir Pozner, noting that here for the first time *any* film had shown the Rorschach test. Both Fearing and Kubie pointed to the need for more research into the area of psychology and films.

85. Dudley Nichols, "Men in Battle," *Hollywood Quarterly* 1 (October 1945), 34–39. Serious scholarship on Nichols is practically limited to Cheryl R. Kiley, "The Career and Films of Dudley Nichols," unpublished dissertation, St. Louis University, 1982. See Chapter 8 on his problems during the writing of *Pinky,* his last important film.

86. See Cole's self-serving account in *Hollywood Red,* 217–221, which includes a reprint of the characteristically Red-baiting *Reporter* story.

87. Lester Cole, "Unhappy Ending," *Hollywood Quarterly* 1 (October 1945), 80–83; see Robert Sklar, *City Boys* (Princeton: Princeton University Press, 1992), 158–59, on Cagney's estrangement from the Left, thanks more to a long drift from the middle 1930s than Sklar perceives (and not excluding a certain civil liberties support of Communists in 1947, hastily abandoned thereafter), but Lester Cole's rant certainly irked the liberal star.

88. John Houseman, "Violence, 1947: Three Specimens," *Hollywood Quarterly* 3 (October 1947), 63.

89. John Houseman, "Today's Hero," *Hollywood Quarterly* 2 (October 1946), 162.

90. Ben Maddow, "Eisenstein and the Historical Film," *Hollywood Quarterly* 1 (October 1945), 26–28.

91. As in the *Hollywood Quarterly* "exposé" by the *Hollywood Reporter,* reprinted in the Cole volume.

92. Adolph Deutsch, "Three Strangers," *Hollywood Quarterly* 1 (January 1946), 214–19. See also Frederick W. Sternfield, "The Strange Music of Martha Ivers," Edward Biberman, " ' . . . In Glorious Technicolor,' " and Mordecai Gorelik, "Hollywood's Art Machinery," all in *Hollywood Quarterly* 2 (October 1946), 214–23, for other examples.

93. Quoted by Nancy Lynn Schwartz, *Hollywood Writers' Wars,* 234.

94. Gerald Horne, *Class Struggle in Hollywood, 1930–1950: Moguls, Mobsters, Stars, Reds and Trade Unionists* (Austin: University of Texas Press, 2001), 52–54.

318 ★ RADICAL HOLLYWOOD

95. The bitterly anti-Communist International Ladies Garment Union, initially part of the CIO, had returned to the AFL, giving Communists and their allies less competition for leadership there. But contrary to postwar recollections of troublesome Communists, it was CIO compliance with wartime government directives that gave the organization its final membership boost upward—a fact that gave the suspicious-minded more reason to view the "Rosenfeld" administration as Communist and Jewish infiltrated, in anti-CIO propaganda usually the same thing.

96. Horne, *Class Struggle in Hollywood,* 55.

97. In Nebraska, Brewer managed to get himself elected to the presidency of the weak Nebraska Federation of Labor at age twenty-three. He served nominally as an AFL executive while spending most of his time working with the New Deal agencies to enforce industrial codes. His promotion to Hollywood leader was a surprise to IATSE members, most of whom had never heard of him, but was hardly a shock: They had never really chosen their own leaders.

98. Horne, *Class Struggle in Hollywood,* 202–17.

99. The *Daily People's World,* aiming at a broader audience than the *Daily Worker,* actually carried Hollywood cheesecake shots and other celebrity photos through the period, spicing a weekend culture section with wire-service chatter about new films. Hollywood writers thus almost never contributed to the paper that loyal Southern California rank and filers distributed free on weekends, nor did the paper seek to intervene in cinematic issues (apart from political questions). Two more ironies in a long series.

100. See, e.g., David Platt, "Hollywood Invokes the Supernatural," *Daily People's World,* January 14, 1948.

101. Joseph Foster, "Entertainment Only," *New Masses* 66 (January 13, 1948), 21.

102. Joseph Foster, "You Have Troubles?" *New Masses* 62 (January 21, 1947), 26–27. See Chapter 7.

103. Warren Miller, "Film: Home of the Brave," *Masses and Mainstream* 2 (July 1949), 81. The Party folded *Mainstream* into *New Masses* in 1948 and began a new series, with a much-condensed magazine format and the new title.

104. Warren Miller, "Trading Punches," *Masses and Mainstream* 2 (August 1949), 86–89. David Platt had a somewhat more sophisticated view of the studios'

role. "Back Where I Started: Warner Brothers Completes a Circle," *Daily People's World,* January 27, 1948, recalls that Warners had made reactionary films until the middle 1930s, switched to a progressive line for business reasons, and converted again in the face of the Cold War, by 1948 foremost in anti-Communist pictures.

105. The "Unity Awards," described as a "Poor Man's Academy Awards," were held in 1947–48 in Los Angeles hotels, and then abandoned. See *Fan: The Movie-Goers Magazine, Souvenir Edition* [1948], in the Maltz Papers. An essay in this edition featured ads for interracial entertainment in Los Angeles, and an essay urging that "the Negro problem" be solved by the making of interracial films with strong and characterful African-American characters.

106. "Monseiur Verdoux," *New Masses* 63 (April 29, 1947), 11.

107. John Howard Lawson, *Theory and Techniques of Playwriting and Screenwriting* (New York: G. P. Putnam's Sons, 1949).

108. Ibid., especially Book Two, 309–439.

109. V. J. Jerome, "The Roots of Hollywood's Racism," *Masses and Mainstream* 3 (October 1950), 48–49.

110. V. J. Jerome, *The Negro in Hollywood Films* (New York: International Publishers, 1950).

111. John Howard Lawson, "Hollywood: Illusion and Reality," *Masses and Mainstream* 5 (July 1952), 33. This essay was reprinted as a self-abnegating chapter in Lawson's *Film in the Battle of Ideas,* 15–22.

112. John Howard Lawson, "Can Anything Be Done About Hollywood?" *Masses and Mainstream* 5 (November 1952), 38–40.

113. Writing *Film: The Creative Process: The Search for an Audio-Visual Language and Structure* (New York: Hill and Wang, 1964) a decade later, Lawson had nothing new to add to this picture. American films had not been particularly interesting, except as marvelous examples of a terrible example. That apparently included his own films, none of which, with one or two exceptions, evidently gave him much satisfaction. He admired the beginnings expressed in Chaplin and Welles, and he hailed the political, cinematic, and even psychological advances of film in wartime, especially for the purposes of the documentary. A "neorealism" chapter included only Italian pictures, and the next, "The Decline of Hollywood," dissolved after *Monsieur Verdoux* into a political description of the blacklist. Nothing else of the postwar period had stuck with him, except the partial breakthroughs on race and the

democratic tradition in the two films coscripted anonymously by Nedrick Young, *The Defiant Ones* (1958) and the treatment of the Scopes "monkey trial," *Inherit the Wind* (1960).

114. Francesco Casetti, *Theories of Cinema, 1945–95,* translated by Francesca Chiostri, et al. (Austin: University of Texas Press, 1999 edition), 8–10.

Politics and Mythology of
Film Art—The Noir Era

THE SUBJECT OF FILM NOIR opens wide the Pandora's box of film's social, artistic, and political meaning. The final, concentrated phase of Hollywood film styles before McCarthyism and arguably the only fully realized American "art film" genre, noir has ironically gained its wide currency via French nomenclature. For all its familiarity and virtue as a quick key to a complex sensibility, the phrase continues to disguise more than it reveals. When its explicators summon the usual influences onstage like so many suspects in a police lineup—German expressionism, Cagney-era gangster films, tough-guy crime novels, pulp psychoanalysis, and the naturalism of the war experiences stuffed deep in the veterans' duffel—there generally seems to be confusion about the motive. What *was* the point of the protagonist's disorientation, alienation, or betrayal? The deeper political meaning often remains hermetic or distinctly secondary, especially in the auteur perspective. But in real-life Hollywood, film noir perhaps more than any other film genre expressed the artists' political worldview and the politics of contemporary film production.

Acutely described as "the unique example of a *wholly* American film style," noir did not lack international connections on that account.[1] Far from it. The new global generation of radical filmmakers emerging in the 1920s–40s shared a sensibility that can be traced, notwithstanding locally inflected traditions, from one country to another and from German expressionism to the French Popular Front to certain films of the 1940s Hollywood Left—not forgetting pre-fascist and post-fascist counterparts in Rome and Tokyo. The later American critics' adoption of noir phraseology was, then, an interesting species of self-reflection in the rearview mirror, an acceptance of categories confirmed abroad.

The global continuities are all the more remarkable given the lack of conscious coordination and virtual absence of theoretical work—a weakness, as we have seen for Hollywood, exaggerated by the constrained outlook and bureaucratic mentality of Communist cultural functionaries. Rather than organized and regularized as knowledge in the way that the *Hollywood Quarterly* might have realized in more favorable circumstances, the experience was simply shared and discussed in private by those with similar conditions (and some international contacts). A quietly converging approach, from the admiring theft of a camera angle or lighting effect to the unconscious appropriation of a mood or theme, marked the shared practice.[2]

The preliminary forms of noir appeared in early-1930s France among a group of filmmakers gathered around the cultural magazine *Commune* that included Jean Vigo, Luis Buñuel, and Man Ray. These artists shared one outstanding trait: a determination to preserve the energies and techniques of 1920s surrealism. They combined this impulse with the use of news documentary and theatrical agitprop styles, recast within popular cinema emphasizing working-class characters and locales. Critics dubbed this heightened sense of visual style and language "poetic realism."[3] Films in this mode quickly gained the loyalty of many ordinary French men and women, capturing the mood of hopelessness fast setting in with the approaching war.[4]

Given the context of interwar France and of 1940s America, film noir, a child of poetic realism, could no more escape the impact of Freudianism than of contemporary left-wing social and political life. As it was, these filmmakers and their political-intellectual circles became steadily more attracted to psychological issues, especially intrigued by what Marxist doctrine could *not* explain: why working people so often did not act in their own collective self-interest. The famed German intellectuals of the Frankfurt School, facing a more extreme form of the same dilemma, chose dialectical theory; one is tempted to say that the French filmmakers and their American counterparts, chose dialectical cinema.

Here, in any case, lies the original hidden political meaning of the term "film noir." The phrase was coined in the summer of 1939 by Georges Altman in his review of the newly released Marcel Carné film, *Le Jour se lève*, literally the dernier cri of the French artistic Left and the original version of one of Hollywood's most underappreciated noir efforts, *The Long Night* (1947). *Le Jour se lève* correctly prophesied the violence about to be inflicted—not only by the German invaders but by French collaborators as well. This foreknowledge is summed up with exquisite irony when the film's protagonist, played by Jean Gabin, the ineffable countenance of the French working class, sets his alarm clock to go off before work the next morning even though he knows full well that he will be dead when the alarm rings.

Film noir gained major currency among French intellectuals, however, only when American murder films held back from distribution in Vichy France hit the Paris screens in 1946. The combination of *The Maltese Falcon, Double Indemnity,* and *Murder, My Sweet* moved a Parisian critic to recoin the phrase; a decade later, with the accumulation of similar American films and the publication of French translations of detective stories by Hammett and Raymond Chandler, a critical volume, *Panorama du film noir américain,* nailed down the expression. American reviewers and the first generations of U.S. film scholars borrowed back the fascination and the name of the genre that was by then receding into cinematic history.[5]

Film noir, the style if not the term, came to Hollywood on the verge of the industry's grimmest phase. Eastern and central European refugees had, of course, fled fascism to escape not only censorship and unemployment but a worse fate. The approaching blacklist in Hollywood was nevertheless familiar in many ways: the third such to fall on those who abandoned Germany in 1933 and France six years later. Noir understandably became, during the Hollywood Left's reaction against the loss of patriotic hopes so real in the Good War, both an emotional outlet and practically the only remaining sphere open for dissenting political expression. The descending edge of the political sword would indeed drive many European filmmakers back to Europe after 1949, among them a large handful of Jews for whom the barely concealed anti-Semitism of the blacklisters could only have been a muted reprise of the familiar. And yet, even for these artistic travelers, the American studio experience would be decisive.

The subsequent flourishing of noir imitations and retrospectives during the last quarter of the twentieth century has encompassed everything from college courses and museum exhibits to television drama and experimental literature, supplying Hollywood's own would-be auteurs of the

1970s and later with a ready public for their products. European directors of the 1950s had long since predicted this move by styling an existential-ism of modern moral chaos within an Americanized commodity culture.[6]

Even in an earlier era, the moral victories that came cheaply to movie cops or to spotless heroes enforcing contemporary laws and norms (even liberal ones, like abhorrence of anti-Semitism) generally revealed only Hollywood's self-indulgence and exploitation of contemporary contro-versy. The deeper issues of moral erosion and individual alienation in the midst of postwar prosperity proved both far harder to express and also less bankable than the national self-congratulation of the war years. But a con-siderable section of the reduced post–World War II film audience, self-selected in its quest for serious film art, appeared ready for the maturity these themes demanded.

The FBI's 1940s movie-industry informers, knowledgeable of indus-try gossip if often obtuse to artistic fine points, had early on fretted about the political content of noir without using the term, scoring certain crime films as prejudicial toward business (or what was often the same thing, "American values"). Presumably on that basis, FBI agents selected the production of Abraham Polonsky's *Force of Evil* for the one telephone-tap transcript apparently ever made by 1940s Hollywood field agents: a con-versation between the writer-director and the novelist, Ira Wolfert, from whose work Polonsky loosely adapted the plot and characters. Perhaps it goes directly to noir values, in this case sans paranoia, to note that the two speakers referred casually to what the federal agents likely listening to their conversation might think![7]

One more irony abided. The heavy hand of censors in deep sympathy with FBI attitudes may actually be said to have contributed to the birth of noir. From the establishment of the Hays Office to the end of the studio era, they insisted upon so many omissions that a multitude of meanings had to be conveyed within ambiguous gestures. As we have seen, the treat-ment of capitalist or police-authority villains, the use of sexual imagery and sex-related speech—to say nothing of negative observations about American society and the American role in the postwar world—were al-most invariably conducted by stealth. More rigorous self-censorship of the industry was very much on the agenda as the investigating committees and scandal-mongers threw around accusations of cinematic subversion. William Wyler, director of *The Best Years of Our Lives,* notoriously insisted in 1947 that he would likely never be allowed to make such a film (itself loaded with assorted artistic compromises) in Hollywood again.[8]

Noir's challenge to censorship arguably offered a more deft political challenge than the 1930s social-film shockers like *The Grapes of Wrath* and was potentially more powerful because of its artistry. *Double Indemnity* (1944) stunned Hays Office previewers and excited Parisians a few years later not because of explicit sex or violence, but because of its amoral approach to law and order, to adulterous violations of marriage's sacred bonds, and of course to cold-blooded murder. In the midst of military conflict, Hollywood's censors frequently backed down, no doubt in part because the Office of War Information had successfully put czar Joseph Breen on the defensive. Even under these conditions, perhaps Breen would not have accepted political points scored against the American wealthy classes or for unionism. But in giving way to seemingly apolitical amorality, he established one of the precedents for the more subtle (and differently armed) cultural war against the office, waged more steadily and more effectively by the studios for commercial reasons during the decades to follow.

Interestingly, the challenge to propriety had been preceded by less-noticed fissures of censorship rules within other zones. In film's lower orders, cowboy pictures and minor costume dramas had sometimes implied rape and regularly shown unpunished violence, not to mention an aristocratic or simply upper-class immorality. Subvisible to censors' attention, which was locked on the big films, such items routinely slipped past, recuperating at least some of the pre-censorship moments of daring in the big-budget features *The Sign of the Cross, She Done Him Wrong,* or the militantly antibourgeois *Dinner at Eight* (albeit without uncovering the female flesh occasionally on display before the Code).

War films showing explicit torture (like *Hitler's Children* and *Behind the Rising Sun*) also pushed the envelope with every gesture at battlefield or behind-the-lines realism. The *Pride of the Marines* scene of an American innocent played by John Garfield heroically firing his machine gun for hours, slaughtering incoming Japs with a frenzy bordering upon homicidal mania, eluded censorship on patriotic grounds and thereby damaged the rules dictating no realistic violence. For that matter, the suggestion that powerful and beloved Americans (e.g., the Charles Lindbergh–like figure in *Keeper of the Flame*) might actually be Nazi collaborators or homegrown fascists rather than naive dupes would likely never have made the cut earlier. The powerful (and accurate) revelation expressed in a plethora of films that wealthy European conservatives were likely to view the rise of fascism as a healthy response to the threat of Communism, and that they often welcomed the invaders while profiting personally, also was clearly owed to the changed atmosphere.[9]

The end of the war brought the close of the Office of War Information and its liberal Motion Picture Board. The Hays Office officially became the Breen Office in 1945. Joseph Breen aspired to a return to the old days—but the studios naturally resisted for better reasons than the ones they might have used as debating points a few years earlier. With the end of studios' theater-chain ownership dictated by the Supreme Court in 1948 and independent productions springing up on all sides, not to mention a new generation of European imports, the familiar giants now lacked the power as much as the will to enforce the once-accepted standards. A new day was dawning, along with a new audience at the movie houses, peppered with veterans unwilling, in this way as well as many others, to go back to a cloistered past.

The permitted sadism in *The Dark Corner* (1946), *Champion* (1948), and *The Big Clock* (1948), or—to take a key starring figure in point—Robert Ryan in *Crossfire* (1947), *Caught* (1949), *Clash By Night* (1952), and *On Dangerous Ground* (1952) surely had its origin here as well. Much of the pain inflicted in film after film had a thirties quality. Better, it offered an update: The cruelty then had not only social causes but social cures; a decade later, it still had social causes, but possible cures had been practically ruled out. The unwilling boxer who becomes a brute—a part written so beautifully by Carl Foreman and played so perfectly by Kirk Douglas in *Champion*—begins throwing punches to help his crippled brother, but thanks to his rise to celebrity and wealth is soon beyond salvation himself. As the perceptive feminist critic Barbara Deming later observed, this "No Exit" conclusion to years of seemingly successful struggle or the seemingly courageous adventure becomes a general condition of a certain kind of later forties film. Whenever the protagonist tries "to escape a condition of life in which [he and the heroine] no longer believe," a "helplessness" overwhelms them.[10]

The shift from the ambience of the censored thirties is most literal, in a different sense, in *Clash By Night* (1951). Adapted from an Odets drama, its screenwriter was former Popular Front lyricist Alfred Hayes, who had

most recently worked in Rome scripting (albeit without credit) scenes of
Paisan, the neorealistic classic directed by Roberto Rossellini.[11] Set in the
considerably less romantic ruins of contemporary Monterey, California,
Clash opens realistically with a proletarian scene of boats bringing back the
catch for the fish-processing plant, then sweeps in to show a young Marilyn
Monroe, rising sleepily and unwillingly from her lonely bed at the call of
the alarm clock, then walking to the plant for her production-line job of
fish sorting. Soon enough, we learn that the catch is down, part of a larger
melancholy drift: Monterey's happiest days as a working-class town are
now well behind it, and the urgency to get out has become supreme.

Altogether, the opening is among the best depictions of work in any
Hollywood film. The camera in *Clash* then suddenly moves from the factory floor to a nearby exterior, where a lone woman, played by Barbara
Stanwyck, comes into view, evidently walking from a train or bus station
with a suitcase in hand. She enters a bar and asks for a coffee and a brandy
(she doesn't know or has perhaps only forgotten: whiskey is the substitute
for genteel strong drink in this town). She is, we will soon learn, the former
mistress of a prominent California politician now dead, and she has most
unwillingly returned to the hometown that she despises. Unlike the kindly
but simple Monroe character who soon happily marries a local, Stanwyck
doesn't belong here.

The struggle that continues is not class against class but gender
against gender, quickly following Stanwyck's acceptance of a marriage proposal from the dumb if doggedly loyal ship's captain. She hasn't the will to
quarrel with him, but she also accepts the love (or lust) of the brooding
Robert Ryan, a perpetually enraged prole who has been deserted by his
stripper ex-wife. The adultery that takes place offscreen is not even an issue
by this time. The Hollywood ending, which demands Stanwyck accept
her life because she won't desert the baby she has had with the captain, is
mere cliché, tacked on to the narrative in the pre-Code manner of bringing
the flagrantly adulterous woman back home.

Noir filmmaking at large treated the remaining censorship of sexuality in a similarly diffuse manner. As noir scholars have often pointed out
and aficionados have always known, the suggestion—or more properly, the
fetish—now rules, not realized in the outlined breast or rear so much as in
styles, especially clothing accessories. No better example may exist than
the murderous couple in *Gun Crazy,* quite apart from the omnipresence of

the phallic weapon. Peggy Cummins's sideshow outfits, tawdry in multiple ways, yield to retro Western wear as if she and John Dall had been planning cheerfully, even campily, for a final, suicidal, and thereby sexualized shoot-out. Left-wing noir writers, who generally tended away from the femme fatale, were perfectly capable of projecting a fetishized Jane Russell (torch singer in *His Kind of Woman,* 1951) or Lizabeth Scott (twisted schemer in *Too Late for Tears,* 1949) and occasionally proposed outfits for these purposes.

The politics of censorship could not of course entirely explain how the noir era and noir films managed to push issues in every sense so far and so quickly. Apart from the absence of visualized sex and gore, American films would not be so daring for decades. To some degree it was certainly the *approach* of the blacklist that paradoxically helped create some of the finest films Hollywood ever made. The dread and the accompanying abandonment of even the most determined optimism crystallized artistically the deep foreboding that often marked the Left-written films from the early horror and crime features to the later poverty-and-fatalism (even if such conditions were reversed in the last reel) films of Rossen and others. Gnawing loneliness within the supreme individualism of American life, disillusionment whenever the American Dream of material success evaporated, leaving nothing behind—these had only been held at bay. Now such sentiments and others closely related burst the integument, releasing artistic energies to their fullest.

Thanks to the public craving for films and also to the studios' reluctance to lose their writing talent, the message came across. It was a scary society, and some scarily beautiful movies could be made about it. Films had the public value that certain kinds of "alternative" popular music offered at various points from the 1960s onward, a measuring of the distance between national rhetoric and personal reality. Here, in Polonsky's words, "where the moral authority is, in the undestroyed element left in human nature," was the nub of the matter.[12]

Long before subpoenas went flying in 1947, the moviemaking machine commenced slipping into the hands of East Coast financiers who would increasingly dictate the terms of studio survival. But this insight fails to appreciate the long-standing quest of studio workers—not only writers, directors, and producers on the Left, but also stars like James Cagney and Hedy Lamarr—who wanted to shake free of studio control and to produce their own films. A crucial moment had been reached in the early postwar years and would soon pass, but before it did, an intelligent section of Hollywoodites had begun to think out loud about the possibilities of film. Noir was, more than anything else, the testing ground for possibilities.

The fact that they were usually tested under conditions of low production values is even more astounding. The notorious noir film use of single-source (or high-contrast) lighting and assorted technical devices was also a product, if never a simple consequence, of limited budgets as well as of scenes that could not easily be filmed within Code requirements. *Crossfire,* a relatively major studio film set at a half-million dollars, had most of its budget devoted to name actor salaries. Shot in the studio in under four weeks, it radiated minimalist black art, featuring the repeated use of a few symbolic props and tacky low-budget sets, registering cinematic shocks by sudden changes of lighting. Rewritten from *The Brick Foxhole,* a novel by Richard Brooks about a gay GI bashed to death, the film saw a decisive plot shift to a Jewish GI and enjoyed heavy marketing to the industry and public as a social-theme feature in which the police nail the unmistakably American bigot and killer, expertly played by Robert Ryan. Director Dmytryk bragged that it made him "Mr. RKO" until he received his subpoena.[13]

Seeking to make the most of such raffish appeal to audience tastes, Warner Brothers withdrew in 1945 from what had become the Motion Picture Association of America (MPAA), forecasting the thoroughgoing breakdown of the system during the decade to follow. Soon enough, political censorship would be tightened as other forms eased. If HUAC had been looking seriously for subversive art and subversives in art, its investigators would have been right on target, noir their prey a hundred times more than the wartime films with the notorious spectacle of smiling Russian faces.

Starting Out Noir

By one popular line of argument, the breakthrough 1941 (and third) adaptation of Hammett's *The Maltese Falcon,* directed and scripted by John Huston for Warners, provided Hollywood a set piece for noir. Bogart was made for the part, although he had shortly before been dropped from top billing because of what the studio considered too many appearances as a heavy in B films. Here he occupied almost the entire screen, on camera at virtually every moment as the betrayed private eye, a taciturn borderline-personality figure who pursues the villains (including a marvelously perverse Sydney Greenstreet). Bogey ends up discovering the center of the murderous conspiracy in Mary Astor, the very femme fatale that he longs for. Hammett had never conceived of a more brilliant device for illustrating commodity fetishism than this miniature statue, a miserable fake despite all the crimes committed to possess it. The whole misadventure confirms what could rightly be called the Noir Mood, as does the black-and-white cinematography of San Francisco with its wonderfully dark urban setting of winding streets, hills, and narrow alleys.

This Gun for Hire (1942), written by Albert Maltz and hard-boiled novelist W. R. Burnett from a gripping novel by Graham Greene (cinematically reset from the UK to Los Angeles in the process) and directed by Frank Tuttle, took the noir mood a step further, because protagonist Alan Ladd plays a criminal with serious mental problems (he confesses in a railroad car to singer Veronica Lake, whom he has kidnapped, that he is the product of childhood abuse; he may be the first outlaw who *knows,* as he stutters out, that he needs a "psy-psy-psychiatrist"). When he discovers he has been betrayed by his employer, an industrialist-traitor, he takes up a patriotic task (i.e., murder) to accomplish, but the change of political valence in no way throws off the sadness that life has handed him, or offers a means to escape fate as he passes from hired gun to the doomed agent of murderous justice.[14] If *This Gun for Hire* really launched noir, it was because audiences craved a glimpse at the deeper psychosexual reality that lay beneath the zeal of the collective war effort.[15]

Murder, My Sweet (1944), directed by Edward Dmytryk, written by progressive John Paxton, and produced by his frequent collaborator Adrian Scott, may be said to have completed the basic set of noir images, including a badly beaten detective (in an especially notable out-of-focus drug sequence), a devious upper-class lady, and a plot so tangled that not even the most determined viewer could follow along easily. Based on Raymond Chandler's 1940 novel *Farewell, My Lovely,* which earned its classic status through the film, *Murder, My Sweet* added a crucial flashback element that Scott had proposed, beginning with the detective dazed and blinded in a police interrogation, barely managing to piece together the events that swept upon him. Offering Dick Powell an utterly unfamiliar casting, with Claire Trevor in the femme fatale role and Anne Shirley as the good dame, the film ends with a pile of corpses, including those of the client and Trevor. Hardly anyone gets out alive.

During the next five years, the Left-written and Left-directed noirs would become almost as thick as blackflies in a north woods summer day, with a bite every bit as nasty. In 1946 alone, *Crack-Up* (scripted by the otherwise forgotten Ben Bengal) has an art lecturer nearly convinced that he has somehow become a murderer during "lost" memory time. *The Strange Love of Martha Ivers,* written by Robert Rossen, boasts Barbara Stanwyck as a murderous factory owner who keeps a neurotic and wimpy Kirk Douglas on a leash decades later because he saw the crime and shared in its rewards (Bosley Crowther described her as twice as bad as the murderous plotter of *Double Indemnity*). *They Won't Believe Me,* directed by Irving Pichel, features Robert Young as a man with a mistress who tries to murder his wife, fails, and is in the process of being convicted for the murder that he didn't commit when he throws himself out the window to his death.[16] *Undercurrent,* a more traditional endangered-woman film (and one of Donald Ogden Stewart's last big films) casts Katharine Hepburn against type, fearfully encountering yet another of those cinematic male characters who has come back from the war disturbed and unable to control his potentially murderous paranoia.

To say that left-wing screenwriters and directors had good reasons for their growing desperation about the politics and culture of the society (most especially the state) is obvious. That they transformed that sensibility into classic cinema is still little understood. Edgar Ulmer, working within his familiar subterranean budgets but now more often with left-wing writers, had shown in more than one way with *Detour* (1945) what could be done and how. Reputedly on a budget of under $30,000 and less than seven days' shooting time, Ulmer had projected a loner and loser (played by Tom Neal) into a road picture where loss of everything, including identity, lies unalterably ahead. Flashing back upon his journey, away from the nightclub singer back east who won't marry him because of his poverty, he hits the road and finds himself picked up by a woman while hitchhiking, then is locked with her into a blackmailing scheme and an accidental death that looks like murder. From a budgetary standpoint, all Ulmer had at hand to suggest the ambience of L.A. was a parking lot. But "parking lot Los Angeles" is, after all, the authentic look of an anonymous and unglamorous, average American tomorrow. Throughout the film, Neal moves but never advances, drawn ever closer into the grasping hand of fate. Ulmer insisted that he had invented the portable dolly for *Detour* because he had no choice: The usual technical operations were far beyond his budget.[17]

Ulmer's *Ruthless* (1948), cowritten by Gordon Kahn and Albert Maltz, politicizes the low-budget tale of a whole life gone wrong. There is nothing stylistically interesting about the film, but its script is steady, as a dead-set careerist lower-class boy played by Zachary Scott advances financially and socially through life, betraying childhood friends, businessmen, and lovers, one after another. When at the end he suddenly faces his past and drowns in a struggle with an equally venal capitalist played by Sydney Greenstreet, someone says that he was "not a man but a system," deservedly plunged into the welcoming waters of the deep.[18]

Nowhere was that man-as-system more literally realized than in *The Big Clock* (1948), with script construction and dialogue credits by future blacklistee Harold Goldman from left-wing fiction writer Kenneth Fearing's novel of the same name. The clock of the title stands at the center of the Janoth magazine empire, setting the time precisely (or in totalitarian fashion) for every clock in the giant Janoth Building, where protagonist Ray Milland is an admired editor of *Crimeways* magazine (a pulp whose scale eerily resembles Henry Luce's Time-Life empire). Played brilliantly by Charles Laughton, Janoth himself is a cross between William Randolph Hearst and Luce, who articulated the imperial vision of the "American century." Janoth is above all a megalomaniac and tyrant (not so far, actually, from the real Luce), making the film a Laughton vehicle, brilliantly captured by lighting and camera work to bring out a gross ugliness of spirit.

Quitting the magazine for working him too hard, Milland relaxes in a bar while waiting for his wife, runs into a blonde, misses his train, and squires the blonde around for the evening, not guessing that she is the great man Janoth's mistress, though he almost spots Laughton leaving her apartment. Later and unbeknownst to Milland's character, Laughton returns, quarrels violently with her, kills her, and adroitly plans to implicate his editor as the murderer. Janoth thus pleads with his star editor to return from vacation to help the magazine locate the real killer; as Milland uncovers clue after carefully planted clue, they lead ever more obviously to himself.

This plot device, executed with great smoothness, is exceded only by another. On the run from Laughton and the cops, Milland hides inside the clock, thus symbolically entering the arena of supreme (mechanical) control and, albeit inadvertently, stopping the Machine. The fact that our protagonist is hardly to blame for his dilemma and that the film can arrive at a traditional happy ending takes some of the edge off the noir—but not too much, for the Janoths still control the nation and indeed the planet. Their dreams of total control are mad, but they have the power to pursue the plan to the apocalyptic end.

Another noir of the same kind, *Caught* (1949) was so literal a depiction of the Big Man that industrialist-turned-mogul Howard Hughes immediately recognized his own image in the unsold script and reputedly insisted upon Robert Ryan as the only actor capable of portraying him! Screenwriter Arthur Laurents, never quite blacklisted but as much as driven out of Hollywood for his political connections and his homosexuality, provided the adaptation from Libbie Block's novel *Wild Calendar*. John Berry directed until he was replaced with the more prestigious Max Ophuls.

Caught is mainly a women's film, with Barbara Bel Geddes as a working-class girl and department-store model convinced that marrying rich is the only way to get out from under.[19] She attends stenographic school and gets hired by millionaire Smith Ohlrig (Ryan)—sounds a bit like "oil rig," the newest class of southwestern barons—an industrialist who hardly has time for women but perversely proposes to her after his psychoanalyst warns him against marrying for the wrong reasons. The tabloids hail their union as a Cinderella wedding, a match made in the heaven-bound fantasies of its female readers; but Ohlrig can never escape his own neuroses, including a bout of psychosomatic illness, his need to bully, and his obsessions with making money and controlling people for purposes that even he cannot grasp.

Bel Geddes's leaving him and his Long Island estate for an apartment on the Lower East Side is a window of escape from this life. If her earlier craving for upward mobility sets her up for noir consequences, the prospect of a useful life of social services lifts the film's mood. Meeting a dedicated pediatrician (James Mason in his American film debut), she begins a new life. Then, after a temporary reconciliation with Ohlrig, she realizes that she is pregnant, and that he is so determined to get her back or to seize the child that he will make her life a misery. (He succeeds in one key way: She loses the child in a miscarriage.) She gets away this time, and in a partial return to noir he is the one now caught, trapped within his circle of flunkies and yes-men—a strangely passive moral for a left-wing film, but perhaps the only one possible in a high-quality drama, short of killing him off artificially.[20] Most unfortunately, the film's complicated plot didn't inspire audiences, and its failure finished off Enterprise Studios, which had for a few years the largest percentage of left-wingers working at every level of production and the largest degree of creative control for filmmakers like Robert Rossen and Abraham Polonsky.

At the other thematic end from the manipulative capitalist were society's scum, prison inmates, and those apparently headed in the same direction or to an early grave. *Caged* (1950), regarded as the best women's prison film ever made (a genre given over almost exclusively to exploitation sub-features) and scripted by future friendly witness Bernard Schoenfeld in collaboration with Virginia Kellogg, revived an old Warners-style social drama of a victim (Eleanor Parker as a young woman caught up in a small-time robbery with her boyfriend, who died in the stickup) becoming further victimized through the brutality and crookedness of the prison setup. Here again, as in the prison films of the Depression years, the top authorities become the real criminals, and the inmates are finally saved from brutalization by the action of prison reformers. The claustrophobia of the prison, the sadism of the matrons (with more than a hint of brute lesbianism), the helplessness that turns the presumably rehabilitated protagonist back to prostitution—all serve to underscore the true noir feel.

In a similar vein, *Brute Force* (1947), Jules Dassin's first serious dramatic film (Bosley Crowther called his direction "steel-springed"[21]), was scripted by Richard Brooks, a friend of the Left. Working from an unpublished story, Brooks shows the sadism behind prison walls and makes a case for the moral innocence of a circle of cellmates led by the morally tortured Burt Lancaster as a con with a dying wife.[22] His opposite number is the prison's head screw, played brilliantly by Hume Cronyn, a lackey who enjoys doing the dirty work for a warden, and carefully explains the logic of the necessary viciousness.

Around Lancaster ranges a cell full of hard-luck guys whose fantasies and dreams, mostly involving a past life with a beloved woman, briefly make them more human than the authorities, but whose hopes are quashed by the alternating submissiveness and bestiality of the cons around them. In order to make a successful escape, Lancaster has to arrange the murder of an informer—in a unique camera moment of a laundry press coming down to crush the informer, seen from the victim's perspective—and his project is thereby tainted. During the moment of the break, the violence nevertheless expresses a Fanonesque poetics of liberation, all the more because the effort is doomed, a "revolutionary suicide" uprising of inmates. The metaphor for the prison-house vision of the postwar world is also inescapable, even if Dassin himself understandably complained a half-century later that Lancaster's cellmates were obviously too good-heartedly innocent to be in jail.[23] Producer Mark Hellinger helped Dassin escape a B-film contract at MGM and named him director for the semi-noir police drama *The Naked City* (1948), Dassin's biggest Hollywood triumph (if by no means his most important work before his exile).

But perhaps the most striking element of *Brute Force*—absent from *Naked City,* but increasingly apparent in other left-wing noirs—was the figure cut by Roman Bohnen, the warden who relies upon others to do his dirty work while retaining his almost saintly image of the prison reformer. Bohnen also bore a remarkable resemblance to FDR in his imperial vision of a superstate that would be unthinkable for Communists in their usual effort to valorize the dead president against brusque Harry Truman, his all-too-live successor. For many future historians, Roosevelt had ceased to be a reformer after 1939. His drastically revised policies of mobilization for war rather than domestic reform (with much radical involvement) encompassed the fearful nationalism mirrored in the screenwriters' own demonization of foreign "agents" in *Confession of a Nazi Spy* and other films, which legitimized the repressive actions of the state and may even have helped make Truman's moves possible.

This dread insight into liberal betrayal, as aesthetic as political and perhaps intuited rather than reasoned out, came across writers unpredictably, as much so as the job offerings that made the noir genre possible. More than a few of the earlier noirs, produced as the war ended or shortly after, still bore the print of antifascism, but now figured it very differently. *Cornered* (1945) was written by John Paxton, based upon an unpublished story by John Wexley, and produced by Adrian Scott.[24] A follow-up to *Murder, My Sweet* with Dick Powell again in the starring role, this international adventure brought a GI just released from a POW camp to Argentina, bent on avenging the murder of his French war bride. Here (as in real-life Buenos Aires), the smell of Vichy France was thick, and high Nazi officials found sanction in return for generous bribes to government officials. Traumatized by his wartime treatment, Powell suffers from repeated blackouts (an echo of the detective's drugging in *Murder, My Sweet*) and hardly realizes that he has beaten to death the object of his search, a former Vichy official who is busy defending the network of hidden Nazis.

The mysterious young woman with whom Powell's character falls in love is none other than the wife of the Nazi villain, although when pressed she makes a strong case that she had been forced into the marriage during wartime. He also discovers a secret group sworn to bring ex-Nazis to justice. But no matter what he does to assist them, the postwar world remains in darkness—and not only because he has lost his true love. The expressionistic devices that made *Murder, My Sweet* an innovative film recur here, with almost compulsive repetition but still used quite effectively.

More noirs or semi-noirs, however, used the war itself to explain the psychological disturbance that military victory could not cure.[25] *Act of Violence* (1949), the very best of the veteran-as-noir-protagonist mini-genre and one of the several early films that showed director Fred Zinnemann's promise, had Van Heflin as an ex-sergeant who had saved himself by betraying to the Nazis the breakout plan of his troops from the POW camp where they were interned. He has apparently escaped his secret sin entirely, because we see him as the proud architect of a suburban development outside Los Angeles, accepting an award from the mayor under flags practically proclaiming the success of American consumerism as the true victory won in the war.

But Heflin has a nemesis whom we see at the opening moment of the film: a maddened (what else?) ex-GI, Robert Ryan, limping from a Manhattan street, up a flight of stairs with his gun and a plane ticket for L.A. (obviously airports lacked security in those days). Ryan is the only survivor of the attempted escape, and by the time he tracks down his former commander, Van Heflin is at an L.A. salesman's convention where silly men wear party hats and stagger around drunk, chasing dames—America's furiously growing greed sector. We already know that the sergeant's credulous wife has no knowledge of her husband's dark secret, and we soon learn that he knows his own rationalizations (that the plan was doomed to fail, and he could minimize the losses of life) were empty.

Heflin flees from Ryan down the empty nighttime streets of a remarkably working-class, noir Los Angeles, where an aging hooker (Mary Astor in her last good role, proclaiming, "I couldn't *live* without kicks!" A drug reference?) takes the ex-sergeant in tow, finds him a hit man, and sets up the final confrontation between the two psychologically damaged veterans, as the wife and the madman Ryan's girlfriend (played by Janet Leigh, suddenly arrived from New York) try desperately to pull them back from a mutual disaster. This extraordinary film has somehow escaped serious notice outside Zinnemann scholarship, due likely to its near-miss of big stars, originally announced as Gregory Peck and Humphrey Bogart. Still, as Zinnemann scholar Wheeler Winston Dixon points out, *Act of Violence* was a "dress rehearsal" for the most famous part of the director's career (with such later films as *From Here to Eternity, The Nun's Story, A Hatful of Rain,* and *The Sundowners*—the last two written respectively by a credited blacklistee, Carl Foreman, and a regretful friendly witness, Isobel Lennart).[26] For the first time (and unlike the small-scale production of *The Search*), the promising director was in full technical command of his material. Stripping away unnecessary dialogue for "the look" that made his films so impressive, Zinnemann lay bare the hidden costs of the boom mentality. When the boosterish Heflin confesses bitterly to his wife, "I was an informer!" he also casts considerable light on contemporary Hollywood.[27]

Lives of Crime

The further American society advanced from the antifascist optimism of the war years, the more drastic the situation of the writers and the clearer that left-wing writers and directors were about to make their final stand. The real dimension of noir was, of course, not so much deranged GIs or inmates abused in prison facilities but crime and the criminal running rampant: a working metaphor of society's inner logic.

The new artistic wave that had begun to crest through independent production companies most ironically ran into the obstacle of court decisions ending the compulsory "block booking" of theater chains by studios and freeing movie-house owners to pick and choose their own selections. The antitrust move, more than a decade in the making, slowed down during the war, and acquired a favorable preliminary judgment (against a particular movie chain for practicing restraint of trade) in a 1944 Supreme Court decision considered crucial to further successful litigation. A further series of lower-court decisions encouraged non-chain theaters to sue, and here the death of Franklin Roosevelt became decisive. The Truman presidency had no grand vision of corporate reform, but did harbor deep suspicions of Hollywood. Attorney General Tom Clark, who would compile the punitive "Attorney General's List" aimed at purportedly subversive organizations (many of them mere cultural organizations with left-wing ties, others defunct antifascist entities), forged ahead. In early 1948, the Supreme Court ruled against eight studios and two theater circuits, compelling divestiture. After brief resistance, a badly sagging Hollywood hierarchy consented. Less power for the studios by this time meant *more* power for the bankers. This was a crucial fact not only for the Hollywoodites who were busily setting up political defense committees and attempting a publicity barrage to stave off the worst prospects of the Red Scare, but also for anyone who looked to independent productions for real freedom.[28]

Hollywood's establishment, confused and divided, sought out a variety of remedies. As a group, the moguls were quite willing to throw a handful of left-wing screenwriters to the lions in order to satisfy the political emperors in Washington. Some studios meanwhile took up schemes like the rerelease of old favorites, presumably a surefire method to returning the family audiences that were beginning to disappear into television-viewing. But others responded to the deteriorating conditions by encouraging the desires of stars and directors to set themselves up independently, in production companies loosely tied to studios via distribution schemes. This project inspired wider visions of an American cinema artistically untrammeled, successfully reaching a self-selected audience sophisticated enough to appreciate the accomplishment.

Only with this encouragement could Joseph Losey have directed *M* (1951), an intentionally close-to-the-original remake of the Fritz Lang 1931 classic reset for Los Angeles in the present. It was enormously ambitious for Superior Films (owned by a father-and-son team, Seymour and Harold Nebenzal, the former actually the producer of the original), with a writing staff that included Waldo Salt. Superior did not long outlast the effort. The film was doubtless hard for U.S. audiences to watch, because the set pieces of Weimar cinema, especially the crucial communitarian solidarity of the demimonde, seemed out of kilter with American crime's anarchic individualism, but also because the psycho-erotic sadism of a child murderer, played to the hilt by David Wayne, was decades ahead of the contemporary Hollywood mind-set.

Wayne has already murdered four children when the film opens, and he lures his next victim, a little girl, by buying her a balloon from a blind vendor—further cinematic insignias that belong more to the world of *La Strada* than they do to American murder dramas. It is the balloon vendor who identifies him by sound, and marks the killer for a kangaroo court conducted by the underworld "community" to remove the pressure (or perhaps it is the stain: They are only criminals, not monsters) that his actions have placed upon them. By contrast, the police, led by Howard da Silva, have scarcely a clue, and barely manage to halt a lynching after Wayne is movingly defended by a Sidney Carton–like ex-attorney, personally broken and barred from official duties. The defendant speaks of his madness on his own behalf. Not even the original (with Peter Lorre in the starring role) had so strong an emotional undertone as this murderer, who obviously suffers from Oedipal conflicts while slathering over a child's shoelaces.

M's reputation suffered first of all from its being a remake of a classic and, in the long run, even more from the pathos that lay (according to Losey himself) in the repressed homosexuality and unresolved mother complex of the killer. It succeeded artistically to the degree that it did thanks to Lang's earlier work, the production staff (including Robert Aldrich as assistant editor), and a distinguished cast that included future blacklistees Luther Adler and Karen Morley along with da Silva. Losey never regarded it as adequate to its intent.[29]

The most avant-garde of Reds, Losey made two more films before his exit from United States. *The Prowler* (1951) was shot for Sam Spiegel and Horizon Pictures with two alternative titles, *The Cost of Loving* and *The Cost of Living,* its screenplay credited to Hugo Butler but actually scripted by Dalton Trumbo, by this time very much a name on the hot sheet. A political shocker (if visually unexperimental), it has Van Heflin once again as a seeming straight arrow who hides his psychopathic character. This time he's a cop who checks out a report of a prowler at the home of a radio disc jockey (John Maxwell) and his wife (played by Evelyn Keyes). He later returns to seduce the woman and quickly makes plans to murder the husband, getting her and the insurance policy as part of a larger scheme to set himself up as a respectable motel proprietor in Nevada. Keyes remains unaware that Heflin is the murderer and, after he proposes to her, fails to grasp the reasons for his panic when she announces that she is pregnant. Heflin knows what she doesn't: that her first husband was sterile. Like the Heflin character of the tortured veteran of *Act of Violence,* the cop is a public success (albeit more modestly, a milk-drinking former high school sports hero who constantly mulls his prospects for his big chance) and a private horror. Eventually, he will be stopped, in one of those desert scenes that highlight desolation and failed escape.

Losey, according to his biographer, had devised *The Prowler* upon many viewings of Billy Wilder's *Double Indemnity,* the images of California sun-based bourgeois splendor tempting adultery and murder. But it was a more political version, inevitably, and also a cheaper one, and was shot in nineteen days. Losey relied so heavily upon interiors that he became known, for a moment, as a sort of American von Stroheim. Not surprisingly, it was the one film that he showed around in Britain to get exile work, eventually leading to such memorable features as *Accident, The Go-Between,* and *Galileo.*

Losey's last film before exile, *The Big Night* (for yet another fly-by-night company, Philip A. Waxman Productions), offers as its highlight a phantasmagoria of night very much like *Act of Violence,* but through the eyes of a naive adolescent. Losey collaborated on the screenplay, but the main work was done by an uncredited Hugo Butler, now also on the run, adapting a novel by coscripter Stanley Ellin. Critics pilloried the film when they bothered to notice it at all, and with production costs at $300,000, *The Big Night* was probably predestined for failure (distributor United Artists lost heavily on its investment). But it has extraordinary moments. John Barrymore, Jr., plays a teenager who is teased by peers, in an early scene, as too shy for girls (perhaps a "sissy") and then, on his birthday, watches with horror in his father's tavern as the beloved parent is beaten and humiliated for failing to fight back.

Grabbing his father's gun, he goes out to take revenge and thereby enters a demimonde world of fight fans, hoods, and an older woman, played by Joan Lorring, who seems uncertain about whether she should assume the role of mother or lover. After a chase punctuated by observing a frenzy of orchestrated violence in the boxing ring, he shoots the newspaperman who set up the beating. There, in a dark apartment, his intended victim tells the boy about the suicide of a woman after an affair with the boy's father, whose Catholicism forbade him from divorcing his abandoning wife. The newspaperman, brother to the suicide, is no more guilty or innocent than anyone else. Barrymore ultimately returns home, accepting arrest after waving around the gun and obviously ruminating suicide and learning that the wounded man has not died. Few critics bothered even to analyze the film, but later scholars have saluted the allegorical horror-ridden journey of maturation-by-fire.[30]

The Big Night was a remarkable effort, considering the pressure on all parties, but also a small-scale film that surely attempted too much narrative and made too many demands upon its young star. Dorothy Comingore, one of the supporting actresses, was about to be placed on the blacklist, declared an unfit mother for legal purposes by her screenwriter-husband, friendly witness Richard Collins, and figuratively driven from pillar to post until her death by alcoholism a decade later.

A few years earlier, Clifford Odets had tried something similar. Already deeply discouraged by his Hollywood experiences but still game, he hooked up with his admired friend, theatrical maven Harold Clurman, writing from a Cornell Woolrich novel and for Clurman's direction *Deadline at Dawn* (1946). Perhaps not for decades would so much concentrated artistic promise as Odets and Clurman disappoint, despite some remarkable and rarely appreciated moments. This time the innocent is a young sailor played by fresh-faced Bill Williams, on leave in Manhattan. A conniving, blackmailing woman has been murdered, and because he had gone to see her, Williams is the logical suspect. Luckily for him (if most improbably to the critical viewer) he has hooked up with an embittered taxi dancer, played by Susan Hayward, and a philosophical cabdriver played by that seasoned antifascist favorite, Paul Lukas. Into the night they go, looking for clues as the morning closes in and the sailor is due back to his ship.

George Lipsitz has observed that Odets captured the thinking of the working-class neighborhood at a time of tumultuous change—when street-corner philosophers had a great deal to say about antifascism, city general strikes, and the uncertainty and restlessness that seemed to seize a population coming out of depression and war.[31] If some critics complained that Odets was patronizing his proletarians, stylizing their dialogue, delivering a pseudo-poetry that confused more than illuminated, more sympathetic ones observed that like playwright Philip Barry (but at the other end of the social spectrum), Odets created a verbal world of his own, with inverted word order, lilts, and nuances that captured a sincere "authenticity" for the worlds that the neighborhood characters inhabited.[32] Before the GI Bill, cerebral-minded workers, autodidacts, and often enough left-wingers remained proletarians, more by chance than by choice. The war and the emergence of a Popular Front further detached them from the old premises of Marxism, and from the rigors of the Communist Party proper. "The horror and terror you feel is from being alive," says Lukas supportively to Hayward, a phrase that would pass for nihilism except that Lukas emphasizes the living as the lesson itself.

The cabbie, a crypto-Marxist who is fond of justifying his statements by prefacing them with "Statistics show . . . ," has had a tragic life since his wife deserted him and their small daughter. Like so many real-life 1946 Marxists, he wanted and expected modest upward mobility for himself, beyond casual labor and into a useful profession. It turns out that he committed the crime—as he confesses when all other possibilities have been exhausted for helping the sailor—in order to spare his daughter the blackmail planned by the woman that he murdered.

Only one film bore Odets's full creative stamp as writer and director: *None But the Lonely Heart* (1944), the best blue-collar use and in one or two ways the best (as well as most humane) dramatic work that Cary Grant ever did. Odets's themes work better in London than in New York, perhaps because the stylization seems more suited to a fixed-class structure, perhaps because Grant is perfect as the Cockney drifter, as is Ethel Barrymore (who won an Academy Award for the part) as his mother, the hard-pressed shopkeeper. Vagabond lover, get-rich-quick schemer, trapped by class and by the sense of impending disaster between the wars, Grant abandons the fellow ghetto dweller who loves him (Jane Wyatt) for a played-out gangster's moll (June Duprez) who tells him she only has a few good kisses left in her.[33]

Dying of cancer and eager to assist her son, Barrymore accepts stolen goods and is sent to prison—the last crushing blow to his dream of freedom. He wants a different world, not just a change of luck, but as his mum says, it won't happen in *this* world. As in so many films of this kind, an old

Jew (in this case a seemingly unlikely pawnbroker) offers the socialistic, ethical alternative, impractical and abstract but humane: "Everything with a kiss." Tragically, there was no alternative for the nearly played-out Odets, either. When the House Committee called him up to testify, he had no fight left in him, his own opinion of himself driven so low by Hollywood that giving names was only one more self-abasement.[34]

A half dozen years later it would be entirely too late for political themes. But so long as a bottom-budget *Superman and the Mole Men* (1951) could depict an all-too-typically American, redneck crowd ready to lynch hapless little creatures (the Man of Steel tells them they are acting "like Nazi storm troopers" and takes their guns away), a civil-liberties argument could still be made for dissent and for "different" people.[35] Cyril Endfield, the veteran B director who would go on to become a noted director in British exile (*Zulu* and *Sands of the Kalahari* are his best), guided the extraordinary *Try and Get Me!* (aka *The Sound of Fury*, 1951), scripted by the progressive Jo Pagano from his own novel about a real-life 1930s San Jose, California, lynching of two convicted murderers, and produced by a one-shot operation, Robert Stillman Productions.

It's another sunny California story of heartbreak and murder with the era's purported optimism sadly belied. Frank Lovejoy stars as a hard-luck veteran who moves to the West Coast with a sickly wife and a cheery child, confident of the prosperity promised to all hardworking whites. No such luck. As he broods on his personal failure and as his relationship with his wife appears in danger of collapse, he agrees reluctantly to set out with a small-time hood (played brilliantly by Lloyd Bridges) in a string of neighborhood grocery- and liquor-store robberies. The paucity of the take propels them, led and goaded by Bridges, to kidnap the son of a rich local merchant. Lovejoy doesn't realize that Bridges has no intention of letting the victim live. In the lag time between the murder and the arrests, Lovejoy meets and begins to launch into a near romance with a simple, lonely woman (Katherine Locke).

Then comes the moment of reckoning, making all these developments a prologue, in a sense, to the cinematic message. Rising local newspaperman Richard Carlson has been looking for a big story, and this is it. Dramatizing the kidnap-murder to the hilt, he practically evokes a lynch-mob atmosphere that leads a crowd to break into the jail and beat the killers to death. If the frustration registered in the noir mood establishes a basis for American brutality, nowhere is the disappointment or disillusionment with the American Dream so clearly linked to the sign of the vigilante.

The Underworld Story (1950), likewise directed by Enfield and scripted by Henry Blankfort, does *Try and Get Me* one better in its portrayal of journalistic corruption and legalized lynching.[36] Reporter Dan Duryea is a seedy big-city journalist who specializes in shaking down businessmen; he loses his job and borrows heavily from a mob boss in order to buy a half-interest in a suburban weekly. Unwittingly, he walks into a big story when the daughter-in-law of the state's newspaper magnate is found murdered in the family mansion. He cashes in ruthlessly by selling it to competing news services and attempting to collect a $25,000 reward when a suspect, the dead woman's black maid, walks into the office seeking help from an old friend, none other than the former editor, played by Gale Storm in the usually bubbly comedienne's best screen dramatics. When the dead woman's family organizes a vast publicity drive to railroad the maid, Duryea actually follows the story, and experiences a change of heart (along with romantic prospects for Storm); he also finds himself haunted by the mob, personified by his creditor, played by Howard da Silva. The liberals who lead the defense campaign look a lot like the real-life Civil Rights Congress—as many in the noir audience would have recognized—at that moment frantically pursued by the FBI, baited by the Committee, and finally destroyed after several dramatic campaigns for southern African-American defendants.

Compared to that series of complications, a distinctly crisp noir like *The Asphalt Jungle* (1950), the last of John Huston's crime pictures (and his only collaboration with Ben Maddow, both working from a W. R. Burnett novel), had to make up in taut script and empathetic characters what it lacked as social drama. In this case, the talent (actors Sterling Hayden, Louis Calhern, Jean Hagen, James Whitmore, and Sam Jaffe, with a cameo for young Marilyn Monroe) and the backing (by MGM) made the results look almost easy. A criminal genius and a corrupt lawyer plot a grand jewel heist, but personal problems and a falling-out among thieves foreshadow doom. As the cops close in, double crosses and a suicide leave Hayden alone and wounded, on the run, heading for a horse farm reminiscent of his vanished childhood, but he dies in a field en route. Crooked cops and an atmosphere of social decay render the criminals, if by no means heroic, then no worse than others around them. Hayden, who in real life would soon become a self-hating friendly witness destined to drown in a swimming pool after years of alcoholism, is more than perfect. Like Lovejoy in *Try and Get Me,* he shows himself to be a plain Joe burdened with an inescapable fate.

Decades after the blacklist, as campus and film festival devotees relished and recuperated old noirs from obscurity, the avant-garde *Gun Crazy* (1950) would gain acclaim far beyond its makers' expectations or even, according to later reports, their conscious intentions. Artistry apart, there was a contemporary reason for this film's spectacular return: It had set the plot and characterization, with a certain crude stylization that became vastly more appealing in time, for that cinematic explosion of 1967, *Bonnie and Clyde.*

Critics at first despised *Bonnie and Clyde* for its violence and apparent nihilism; after the box office figures revealed a generational mega-trend, they changed their minds (or their tastes). *Gun Crazy* never possessed the elements necessary for a big hit, and its gestures became laughable to some audiences by the 1980s, but Dalton Trumbo (fronted by MacKinley Kantor and friend-of-the-left Millard Kaufman, from a Kantor short story) rendered the sexually frustrated gun hobbyist John Dall and the sideshow fancy shooter Peggy Cummins as the perfectly perverse pair. He can only "shoot" with bullets; she craves the money that crime can bring and she tempts him with sex (or threatens to leave him behind, sexless) while expressing her own erotic connections with guns and brutality. As critics have observed, other couples-on-the-run (until Bonnie and Clyde, of course) tend to repress their sexuality and play up an innocent domesticity.

The power of *Gun Crazy* to burst past conventional sentimentalism (expressed best, perhaps, in *They Live By Night,* directed by Nicholas Ray) has also been attributed to Joseph Lewis's direction. Within the sharp budgetary limits of a King Brothers independent production and his own "B" experiences, Lewis manages to play up all the kinky angles. Later director Martin Scorsese and screenwriter Jay Cocks elevated Lewis into the pantheon of auteurs, and Lewis's *New York Times* obituary claimed *Gun Crazy* perfectly captured a postwar mood and cinematic style. As Lewis himself said: "There's no more audience. There are only accomplices." [37]

Actually, noir as art usually works best with the fatalism of good but confused people who become trapped, drawn steadily into a life of degradation until they become lost. *Quicksand* (1950), with Irving Pichel directing the first good dramatic lead in Mickey Rooney's adult career, is a small gem. Rooney, the common prole, is a garage mechanic who urgently wants to impress a girl above his real prospects. He borrows $5 out of the till, fully expecting to be able to replace it before his boss's return the following Monday morning. When he can't and the small-minded manager threatens him with jail, he naively buys an expensive watch on credit and pawns it— not realizing there's a law criminalizing just such a maneuver. Now all he can do is something far out of his league, like a robbery. Meanwhile, we learn that his would-be squeeze (played by Jeanne Cagney) is the former girlfriend of amusement-gallery manager and evident weirdo, Peter Lorre.

Here the noir is laid on thick: Within the dark and cluttered arcade, the automaton-like machines programmed for skill and luck seem to reflect proprietor Peter Lorre's creepy character. Like the fun-house mirrors all around, they distort everything, reminding Rooney that his life is out of control. Here, too, escape cannot be found, but the film requires no fireworks or multiple murders, just small-time tragedy for small-time people.[38]

Similarly small films have become inescapable favorites of many viewers, the noir cinefiles whose number and global dispersion have only expanded in subsequent decades. But the famous films remain the standards of the genre for all the obvious reasons. That naturalist classic, *An American Tragedy,* by Theodore Dreiser, had become Hollywood tragedy when successive efforts to make a film version of the novel came to nothing. *A Place in the Sun* (1951), the adaptation written by Michael Wilson and directed by George Stevens, won a handful of Oscars and a Golden Globe Award for Best Film-Drama. Forty-six years later, the American Film Institute named it one of the best one hundred U.S. films. By that time, Wilson was dead, and two other Oscar-winners, *The Bridge on the River Kwai* and *Lawrence of Arabia,* were belatedly credited to him.

The casting of *A Place in the Sun* was spectacular: Montgomery Clift as the earnest working-class lad with an embarrassingly lower-class mother (Anne Revere), on the rise and wooing the capitalist's daughter (Elizabeth Taylor). Then his old girlfriend, played by a chubby and brilliantly proletarian Shelley Winters, turns up pregnant. Without altogether consciously intending to do so, dragged down by his own unconscious desires for American-style success, he arranges for her drowning. Only on one point, albeit a crucial one, did the movie fail, and for that Wilson paid what he rightly considered a terrible artistic price: the tragedy, exposure in a publicity-ridden trial, and Clift's character's self-realization of the darkness within himself became a Hollywood-style apotheosis of the change-of-heart, an uplifting ending that the audience could enjoy and approve. Without it (and the award-winning black-and-white cinematography), sad to say, the film might have failed commercially. But no other writer could have come closer to the real message.

Working on a slim budget without the prospect of the renown that *A Place in the Sun* could attract, writer-director Abraham Polonsky nevertheless managed to make the crime film that he wanted, with an unforgettable Manhattan set. *Force of Evil,* with a crooked Wall Street lawyer played by John Garfield posed against the "honest" brother (Thomas Gomez) who put him through law school and now runs a small numbers operation, neatly brought together themes of corporations as a higher form of enterprise. Garfield, fronting for a new syndicate, aims to put the little crooks out of business and offers to let his brother in—for a stiff cut of the profits. Gomez refuses, and will die before Garfield can redeem himself. Behind the evident costs of postwar materialism, the seduced include Gomez's secretary, played by Beatrice Pearson, whom Polonsky shows to be secretly (perhaps unconsciously) eager for her corruption at the hands of Garfield. That corruption, a lack of innocence on all levels, is seen to collapse into itself as our protagonists are destroyed along with any potentiality of love or redemption. Unlike the films of Robert Rossen, with whom Polonsky had worked a year earlier on *Body and Soul,* no hope could be found here: It was a noir world indeed.

Sexual Politics and High-Art Anxiety

The elaborate angst of Montgomery Clift in *A Place in the Sun,* like the perpetually self-tortured persona of Burt Lancaster in a half dozen left-written noir films, raises the uncomfortable issue of what one critic has aptly called the "masochistic aesthetic."[39] Female masochism was a well-worn Hollywood cliché, of course, so it is not really the presence of masochism that is at issue, but *male* masochism. An emotion seen sporadically in leading cinema, such masochism remains so frightening that, until the appearance of noir, it takes place mostly within the interstices of the plot, via side glances at failure at breadwinning or implicitly homosexual "sissy" characteristics. Since reviewers of, say, Cagney's mom-loving murderer in *The Public Enemy* (or nearly any other of his crime films, down to *White Heat*) declined to describe his behavior as masochistic, perhaps the audiences did not, at least consciously, see it that way, either. Filmgoers had matured or perhaps sharpened their tastes.

Phantom Lady (1944), adapted by Bernard Schoenfeld from the 1942 novel of the same title by William Irish (aka Cornell Woolrich), was directed by Robert Siodmak for Universal. On the surface, the film seems straightforward. The protagonist, played by Alan Curtis, has been having trouble at work as an architect and at home with his wife. He meets a mystery lady in a bar and takes her to a show, moving toward a romantic interlude, but breaks it off when she announces her intention to go home. Returning to his apartment, he finds his wife strangled with one of his neckties. He now desperately needs to contact the woman for an alibi but can remember only her outsized hat, as the police draw him deeper and deeper into a web of details further incriminating him. His loyal secretary (played by Ella Raines) meanwhile sets herself on finding the woman and finally does.

Behind these fairly standard plot features, Curtis's disorientation and the displacement of his "male" role to Raines highlight the troubling noir context. Ridiculed by his wife from beyond the grave as he relives her laughing at him, he has every reason to kill her—as the police inspector played by noir favorite Thomas Gomez concludes immediately. Unlike the childish Bill Williams of *Deadline at Dawn,* Curtis has a distinguished career, but that accomplishment proves no psychic protection. Raines, nicknamed "Kansas," sports a masculine suit and hairstyle, puffs on cigarettes with all the authority of Lauren Bacall, and marches through the film undemurely taking charge.

Ultimately, she will find the mystery woman (a psychotic whose life has been shattered by another man), meeting other characteristically weak males along the way. A spaced-out hipster musician played by another favorite noir "type," Elisha Cook, Jr., helps lead her to the real killer, a self-described Nietzschean (but subliminally feminine) architect in the same firm, played by Franchot Tone. The heterosexual ending with Raines happily prepared to continue as a secretary and simultaneously go out to dinner with her boss/husband "every night" is as irrelevant as an old popular joke's punch line. Raines is clearly in charge; emotional weakling Curtis is in for a surprise if he imagines that he can ever dominate her.[40]

But what Left reading can we give to the dyad of male weakness and female strength? There's no doubt that the postwar period saw a rise of male uncertainty, accompanied by some of the most strident and unabashed misogyny ever seen in twentieth-century America. The high rejection rate of U.S. soldiers for psychological reasons that were often reduced to "insufficient manliness" (rather than, say, a mundane reluctance to be killed) prompted psychologists to warn against the phenomenon soon known in the parents' magazines as "momism." Sometime screenwriter Philip Wylie delivered the crowning polemic in 1942, A *Generation of Vipers*. For what seemed like the nth time (but not nearly so often as in decades to come), the nation and indeed the world was said to depend upon American men's revitalization. An educated society listened as it rarely did to a screenwriter's prosaic advice: the wildly polemical screed attacking Mom for all modern ills was selected by the American Library Association as one of the all-important nonfiction works of the century, sold in the hundreds of thousands, and remained on college English course syllabi through the early 1960s.[41]

This was Freudianism's (or pseudo-Freudianism's) most unattractive possible femme fatale: the homely, bonbon-eating middle-age monster who enslaved father and son and administered at least symbolic castration on a daily basis. If Freud found women's love narcissistic, he regarded that narcissism as a mostly charming quality necessary for the continued procreation of the race. Mom, by contrast, denied real maleness and thereby prompted the psychic explosions that result in war and worse.

Homosexuality itself deserves a side glance here. The Hays Office certainly did not want to permit any depiction of homosexuals, not even those who would be punished for their sins. But films that dealt with psychological issues, especially those of a violent demimonde, repeatedly raised the issue; noir put it in a nearly plain if by no means sympathetic light. One would be hard-pressed to find more than a handful of pre-1950 films with lesbian themes—leaving aside the "man haters" who have chosen life on their own—most of those being women's prison dramas.[42] Gay men were fair game, however.

A handful of "prissy" or just plain fat men gained dramatic stature for their hinted homosexuality, usually tied with scheming and/or sadism of some kind: Clifton Webb (in *Laura*); Sydney Greenstreet (repeatedly, but most especially in *The Maltese Falcon*); William Conrad (*Body and Soul*); Raymond Burr (*Raw Deal*); William Bendix (*The Dark Corner*); and perhaps even the psychopathic Richard Widmark characters. Was it better to have implicitly gay men absent or nefarious?

In a world where, according to Momist theories, Hitler, the Japanese, and the Russians (as Communists, that is) all apparently suffered from mother domination, the American dilemma could hardly be surprising. *Modern Woman: The Lost Sex,* a 1947 scholarly best-seller by psychologist Marnya Farnham and former muckraking anticapitalist writer Ferdinand Lundberg, capped off the popular response and that of many experts from therapist to psychological theorist. Feminism was a "psychic disorder," luring women away from their homes into improper and socially destructive roles; nothing less than comprehensive psychotherapy of American females, one by one, could return matters to a proper gender balance.[43] The severely repressed fifties lay just ahead.

Although the musical *Lady in the Dark* (1944) probably best matches the gender ascription of this formula, with a psychoanalyst literally prescribing the abandonment of the protagonist's career so that she can enjoy a "normal" female life, the more conservative noirs offered plenty of examples as well: *Detour, Double Indemnity, Scarlet Street, Gilda,* not to mention *I Was a Communist for the FBI* (with the seductive Party member/dangerous public schoolteacher who pretends to commit the worse sins in the true pursuit of patriotism). From the Left end, no careful observer doubts that the female lead of Hammett's *Maltese Falcon* holds the whip and will use it, or underestimates the assorted scheming females of *The Strange Love of Martha Ivers, Farewell, My Lovely, Too Late for Tears,* and of course *Gun Crazy.* If anything positive can be said for these almost feline schemers, it must be that, like Satan in Milton's *Paradise Lost,* they somehow get all the best lines—and even more, the best poses. The forgotten actress Jean Gillie, in the equally forgotten *Decoy* (1946), written by Ned Young from an unpublished story by future friendly witness Stanley Rubin, begins with her character dying on the couch, unabashedly recalling her sinful life and, at the film's end, laughing at the cop who listens sympathetically. Any woman who would run over a confederate (and would-be lover) repeatedly in her car and derive pleasure from it must be at least as bad as the rebelliously feminine neonoir film ladies of the 1980s–90s. Something of the same might possibly be said for the gay characters of forties films: No longer completely in the closet, they gained permission to be bad.

But it would be far easier to make the case for the victimized female in films written or directed by left-wingers, and more important to make the case for strong women like the one Ella Raines plays in *Phantom Lady,* virtually compelled to wear the pants for the duration of the drama or simply inclined to a more equitable balance than society offers. Seen at her best, she is no delicate wallflower but a tough girl with realism and courage, like Lucille Ball in *Dark Corner* (another helpful secretary, as scripted by Schoenfeld), or Ida Lupino as a charismatic singer-pianist who has the guts to gun down sadistic tavern-owner Richard Widmark in *Road House,* a critically praised film written and produced by Edward Chodorov.[44]

To be sure, Left noir's women could have been more consistently forceful on their own behalf. Too often, like Joan Crawford in *Possessed,* a nurse desperately in love with a man she cannot have, they are just mentally unbalanced, overstressed from conditions beyond their control.[45] Or they are out of the picture's center, holding the hand of the apparently doomed hero, his captive Shelley Winters as she hopelessly tries to maintain a relationship with her lover John Garfield, the man holding a gun to her family in *He Ran All the Way.*

A good argument might be made for arrested development of female noir character. Given a few more years and more freedom of action, more working-class women (also more women of color) like the dark-skinned immigrant Italian that Valentina Cortesa plays in *Thieves' Highway* (1949) would surely have blossomed. Protagonist Richard Conte, returning home to a troubled blue-collar California after the war, finally accepts her love, although she appears to have traded her body for food and the chance to escape postwar Europe. *Body and Soul*'s Lilli Palmer—a sculptor and an individual in her own right—bonds with the boxer's mother, Anne Revere, against the corrupted son and husband. *They* hold the community values intact, whatever he may do; and his victory is to return to them. Such things didn't happen often, despite the continuing slippage of the Breen Office's influence during and after the war. Femme fatale actresses could complain (and later did) that with the eclipse of the genre there was nowhere to go in Hollywood; their commercial subjectivity had been used up.

In June 1950, Bosley Crowther used his considerable influence to complain that two of the most important films later identified as *noir,* John Huston's *The Asphalt Jungle* and Jules Dassin's *Night and the City,* had actually treated criminals more sympathetically than the police, and had manipulated audiences through "shadiness and shock" to do so. This made Crowther particularly anxious, because MGM had previewed *The Asphalt Jungle* to "a number of literary lights" and secured their praise of the film to use in advertising it. None of the testimonials seemed to show cognizance of the film's disturbing elements, all the more because the performances were, Crowther observed, "simply superb in their disclosure of straight personality," the absence of disturbance usually revealing the Hollywood version of the criminal mind. Even W. R. Burnett, the author of the book upon which the screenwriter based the film, declared it the best adaptation of his work—in Crowther's view having "evidently forgotten" *Little Caesar,* which properly depicted the lawless as "obscene and grossly inhuman." The *New York Times*'s copyeditors or perhaps Crowther himself subtitled the *Night and the City* section of the piece "Same Thing." For even if "Mr. Dassin has a fine old time shooting his scenes from grotesque angles and generally working for a dark, malevolent mood," it was just "a lot of amoral maundering in London's supposed lower depths."[46]

Crowther was no doubt influenced by the descending Cold War mood at a moment when some of his distinguished colleagues at the *Times* (notably the obituaries editor, Alden Whitman) went onto the blacklist. But something else must have bothered the critic who had always kept his eye out for the well-turned left-wing film. The old war movies like *Action in the North Atlantic* that had stirred him were not only part of a now-distant era but had also carried the optimistic side of patriotic idealism to new heights. Noir painted an ugly and disturbing picture of humanity and especially of American society. Like the treatment of corrupt journalists in *The Underworld Story,* it was all too much to take.

If there were something to Crowther's charges—and left-wing noir was vastly more artistic, less garish, and less exploitative than the politically conservative imitations that routinely highlighted sadism and half-exposed breasts—it came back to the problem of an absent heroism and lay firmly in the difficulty of settling upon a comprehensive, alternative aesthetic. Discussing *Force of Evil* a decade or so later with a critic, Polonsky described the possibilities of creative control as "an experiment in which each of my resources was freed of the dominance of the other two"—image, actor, and word became equals. By thus varying the "speed, intensity, congruence and conflict for design emotion and goal," emancipation of language from the "burden of literary psychology and the role of crutch to the visual image," he had come up with a method that he "would have tried again and again" until the remaining problems were solved.[47] But time ran out.

That observation could stand for the best left-wing work at large. Huston, whose *Treasure of the Sierra Madre* had made such an impact upon audiences and critics and who would go on undeterred after *The Asphalt Jungle* (although personally saddened by the blacklist, as well as artistically deprived of the collaboration by some of his closest friends, like actor Sam Jaffe), was free to continue the experimentation that began with his screenwriting career under John Wexley's guiding hand on *The Amazing Doctor Clitterhouse*.[48] The luckiest of the blacklistees were working again within a decade, but as writers under pseudonyms and with vastly less creative influence, or as directors with considerably lessened production facilities. The great experiment, along with the era that made it possible, was over.

It is tempting to evaluate the artistic impact of noir on the Left and the Left on noir along a rather different trajectory as well. Of all the influences on the Hollywood radical film, the least understood continues to be 1930s France. Popular Front idol Jean Renoir is the key figure here. He had become a political-artistic refugee in Hollywood by 1941, adding his prestige as one of the world's most respected directors to American film at just the moment when native talent was asserting its artistic authority. Renoir's work also conspicuously connected Europe's cinematic radicals with non-Party Hollywood progressives Dudley Nichols and Burgess Meredith (recently memorable for his participation in *The Story of G.I. Joe* and his special interest in French cinema).

Here we see the impact of surrealism again, for French artists never forgot the silent film lesson that movies entered and explored dreams. At the highest level of film art (but not one often approached by the surrealists themselves), storytelling could evoke the dreamlike state artistically without abandoning the narrative that made the movies dear to ordinary viewers. Among major French filmmakers, Renoir had most successfully captured this dreamlike quality and applied it to the larger narrative.

The famed French director made *Swamp Water* (1941) shortly after settling in Hollywood. Adapted from a novel by Dudley Nichols and produced by Irving Pichel, it treats a literal border situation, lost trappers on the outskirts of Georgia's Okefenokee Swamp. The protagonist, played by Walter Brennan, is hit on the head and awakens to discover that he is being held captive by a prison escapee (played by Walter Huston) who convinces Brennan of his innocence, precipitating a life together through various picaresque, rural (white) southern adventures. The project ran into trouble almost immediately. Zanuck threatened to fire the director because his painstaking attention to detail slowed down the shooting; with no love lost, Renoir announced he was breaking his contract with Twentieth Century-Fox upon the film's completion. Pichel, eager to make *Swamp Water* work, took over the second unit himself, and served as the film's dialogue director. It was no use. It was not a success, regarded at the time as muddy as its subject, a mere regional adventure tale weakened by ineffective dialogue and poor casting. *This Land Is Mine* (1943), coproduced by Renoir and Dudley Nichols, although far from the best of the antifascist dramas about the heroic French Resistance, was heavily promoted and broke industry records for gross receipts on opening day. But it made no claims whatsoever to ambience, replicating the usual Hollywood techniques.[49] Mere success left the émigré director hungering for real artistic triumph.

Renoir's most artistic and least Hollywoodish American film was his follow-up, *The Southerner* (1945), scripted mainly by an uncredited Hugo Butler, and in smaller part by William Faulkner—the novelist's only notable screenplay contribution.[50] Perhaps the successful version of *Swamp Water* in terms of ambience, it seemed to American audiences excruciatingly slow and documentary-like, the tale of a poor white family and their struggle to maintain dignity and a sense of community amidst exceptionally hard times.

The director's next entry, *Diary of a Chambermaid* (1946), a thirties-style, heavily theatrical film and certainly Renoir's most antibourgeois American effort, was set in 1880s France, where a maid played by Paulette Goddard plots to become rich but ends by giving away a booty of silver to a rural village for its annual celebrations. *Diary* was evidently intended to reveal the fascist mentality of the maid's employers, but lost its political punch in the United States.[51] *The Woman on the Beach* (1947), Renoir's last U.S. film, was barely above average noir, with borderline psychotic veteran Robert Ryan falling for the wife of a blind painter and barely pulling himself back from disaster. Coscripted by Renoir and Frank Davis, it had at best some compelling moments in Ryan's battle-fatigue nightmares. Disappointment with the film and its reception turned Renoir back to France, where he later made a practice of denying his past associations with the Hollywood Left.[52]

Hollywood adaptations of leftish French films were blunted by a lack of resources and the inevitable mismatch of French and American creative ambience. Yet here and there a singular success left its stylistic stamp upon American and European filmmakers. Fritz Lang's *Scarlet Street* (1945), remade from Renoir's *La Chienne* (1931), is the undoubted classic. Lang turned to Dudley Nichols for the screenplay of *Scarlet Street*. With Nichols's script and the original Renoir film before him, Lang incorporated the German gestures from his earliest years (the rain-slicked streets reflecting the light of lampposts that could have been shot in Berlin), the French commitment to exploring the lives of urban workers and criminal types, and the physiognomy of American deviancy in the figures of Edward G. Robinson and Dan Duryea as the professor corrupted by a showgirl and the criminal mind spinning the deeper plot. *Scarlet Street* also foregrounded the latest technical advances in camera dollies, film stock, lenses, and lighting, their improvements collectively expanding the visual vocabulary of noir dramatically. Director Lang thereby completed an aesthetic-political trajectory, a real-life noir-ridden journey from Paris to Berlin-in-exile in Hollywood.

Anatole Litvak renewed his collaboration with John Wexley for the foremost transcontinental artistic achievement: *The Long Night*. Its original, *Le Jour se lève* (1937), which so perfectly predicted both Vichy France and noir Hollywood, had been the genius collaboration of director Marcel Carné and screenwriter (also noted poet) Jacques Prévert. The sexual politics of the story seem simple at first glance. There is François (Jean Gabin), the working stiff who can't get ahead and has no wish to do so until he meets Françoise (Jacqueline Laurent). Like him, she is an orphan, cast into the workforce with no particular ambition except to daydream about travel. In her loneliness, she has met and been seduced by a much older man, the preposterous petit bourgeois Valentin (Jules Berry), owner of a traveling nightclub dog act. Valentin's assistant, Clara (played by the celebrated actress-representative of the Parisian working class, Arletty), has worked with Valentin for three years, but now, jealous of Françoise and fed up with Valentin's cruelty to his dogs, she wants out. Meanwhile, François wants Françoise to marry him, but she cannot give up her infatuation with the older man, who both tantalizes and disgusts her, so François bides his time in the company of the older and wiser Clara. But because Françoise will not give up her attachment to either man, there comes a conflict that can have only a deadly resolution.

Stripped of its contemporary details, it is a classic theatrical formula that can be played either for laughter or for tears: A young couple's love is blocked by the unjust interference of an older man and is not resolved until the third act, either in a wedding or a funeral. But the contemporary details, the specific historical content, transform the bones of comedy or tragedy into social allegory. The orphans François and Françoise are the dispossessed workers of the interwar era who were born into the country that shares their name but which has abandoned them. Valentin, the vicious old man who trains dogs for tricks by secretly torturing them and likes to treat young women in the same way, is clearly the delusional faction of the French bourgeoisie that has turned its back on the victims of society and is all too eager to welcome the fascists into France.

This is where allegory finds its political footing. If there was a theme common to all the films of the French Popular Front, it was, as historian Marc Bloch wrote in 1940, "that striving of the masses to make a juster world [with a] touching eagerness and sincerity that ought not to have been without effect on any man animated by ordinary human feelings."[53] That is, the loss of the most elementary sense of kindness and solidarity created the conditions for the nation's collapse. It was modern Europe's tragedy that if, psychologically speaking, the working class could not summon the power to act on its own behalf, the bourgeoisie could act in no other way. (As Valentin says at one point, "Should I be blamed for being more imaginative?")

No doubt there is so much allegorical weight in the narrative that its realism is compromised from time to time. In the opening scenes, François shoots Valentin, who spins out of the top-floor room down a flight of stairs with a bullet in his groin and expires on the landing. The rest of the story is told in flashbacks as François, with the cops outside, tries to figure out how he has gotten himself into this fix and why he does not care much whether he lives or dies. Throughout the film, the familiar cinematic question remains of how a young man filled with such "eagerness and sincerity" could be willing to bait a veritable firing squad over something as slight as disappointment in love.

Eventually, the viewer comes to understand that François the orphan has been dispossessed not only of his past but also of his future. Helping him and the audience think it through are the traffic-jamming throngs in the streets. As the police set up their command post, deploy their troops in crowd control, and position snipers, the milling onlookers become an increasingly restless, jeering crowd yelling their support for François.

In the American version, the perfectly cast Henry Fonda plays Joe, the American vet whose experience of the Depression and the Second World War have obviously left him an orphan of another kind.[54] The narrator of the opening scene situates the tale in the square of a small Ohio town and describes the statue of a Civil War soldier in a Union uniform as honoring "the GIs of 1865." The stone figure presides over the rest of the film as a kind of guardian spirit that actually increases in stature (from lower camera angles) as the cops close their cordon. The whole crowd here seems to be made up of vets and their families, enraged at their own social dispossession following so much personal sacrifice. Fonda, doubly serving Hollywood's need for a happy ending and the Left's determined pursuit of African-American dignity, asks a black vet for a light after he gives himself up and descends toward the police car. To the vet's insistent "You gonna make it, Joe?" comes Fonda's answer, "Yeah, I think we're just about gonna make it."

Artful film it was, predicting what Hollywood might have done without the blacklist. But Wexley and Litvak knew just what they were attempting politically. Produced only a year or two after the high point of industry-wide strikes to maintain wartime living standards, this working class learns that it will have to stand together or return to the miserable conditions prevailing before the war. When the cops try to shoot the lock off the door of his room, Joe pushes a large chest of drawers against the door. As in the original, when the bullets slice through the back of the chest and throw open its unlocked front, a strip of cheap photos of JoAnn (i.e., Françoise) unexpectedly flaps into view, taped to the back of the door. But in the U.S. version, a last bullet also rips through the army blouse of Joe's corporal's uniform; prominent on the left shoulder is a patch of the 7th Armored Division, which would have been recognizable to most of the audience of 1947 as representing combatants in one of the bloodiest scenes of the European theater, the Battle of the Bulge. When the cops use a machine gun to blow out the windows and lights, the point is once again made that the armed State loyally served in battle only a few years before will not be an ally in the struggles ahead.

It is too early to say whether the newly rediscovered and restored (as of 2000) *Long Night* will survive scrutiny as a permanent part of the essential line of film noirs. As it stands, *The Long Night* is a substantial artistic and political effort that suffers in part from the effort of transplanting from a culture so distant in the habits of daily life; but because it captures so well a precise moment in the postwar hopes and fears of a civilization, film noir would be badly reduced without it.

In his autobiography, Carné concluded his discussion of *Le Jour se lève* with "small regret" that in some details, social allegory might have been too heavy to carry the simplest demands of realism.[55] It was a reasonable worry, present in the making of many of noir's most splendid adventures. American filmmakers, for their part, were required to sink the social allegory so deep into the story line to avoid political censorship that, in many cases, it would be years before critics and film historians would find the submerged meanings and bring them finally into the light. "I hated him," Barbara Bel Geddes says of the Valentin character in the remake, "for knowing I wanted to be kissed, that I never really was—hated him for all that he guessed about me. Yet in a way I was glad."

It is the same dark dimension that Abraham Polonsky reached in *Force of Evil* when he has shyster lawyer John Garfield tell Beatrice Pearson, "You're wicked. Really wicked . . . 'Cause you're squirming for me to do something wicked, make a pass at you, bowl you over, sweep you up, take the childishness out of you, to give you money and make you sin. That's real wickedness." Ostentatious innocence, in other words, is in reality an invitation to corruption. No better statement could be made about a postwar American society emerging as the behemoth of the planet, flattening the opposition of the weak everywhere, using up the natural resources and the hopes of would-be imitators while insisting all along upon its own lack of resemblance to earlier, now-fallen empires.

·   ·   ·

A braham Polonsky once said sagely of his fellow *noiristes,* "If they're reflecting this general sense of jeopardy of life, which is what exists in all film noir, then it's a correct representation of the anxiety caused by the system."[56] He had unerringly identified the heart of the global continuity that joined Frenchmen René Clair, Jean Renoir, Max Ophuls, Julien Duvivier—refugees at the beginning of the war—with Fritz Lang, Robert Siodmak, William Dieterle, Billy Wilder, and Otto Preminger, among others sympathetic to the Left, who had started their careers in 1920s Germany before expatriation. If ever there was an opening to the influence of French and German filmmaking on Hollywood popular genres, of a synthesis of realism (in its various expressions), naturalism, and social fantasy (with its elements of surrealism), this would be it.

Americans who had just begun to reflect more formally on their experience in making serious film art, prompted by the Depression and World War II as much as their own cinematic aspirations, were by the onset of the Cold War richly prepared for the influence. Before Hollywood could be reduced to a kind of empty stage set with the loss of so much of its finest talent, the Hollywood Left, including its European allies, reacted to the loss of patriotic hopes that had been so real shortly before by creating a vital new style. They created it not only for the deep aesthetic satisfaction it provided, but as the only opening that remained for expression of political dissent. It would be—along with the Ashcan School of the 1910s and the black-and-white folk music and folk-rock cycles of the 1930s–50s and 1960s–90s—the most single important mass-artistic achievement borne of the American Left in the twentieth century, both a response to artistic possibility and an alternative to the retreat into the accommodationist political aesthetic ("artistic free enterprise," in Henry Luce's cogent phrase) of the New York intellectuals' high modernism.

Frank Capra's *It's a Wonderful Life* (1946), with script sections drafted by Albert Maltz and Dalton Trumbo, the entirety polished by Michael Wilson, may be said to have foretold the end.[57] A perennial television favorite notable for its upbeat moral, *Wonderful Life* could hardly be less buoyant before the Hollywood ending, or more underappreciated as a demi-noir. James Stewart is scarcely less empathetic than in *Mr. Smith Goes to Washington,* still a small-town innocent but now a small-town savings and loan officer who ponders whether his existence has counted for anything.

The saga of the town falling into the clutches of an evil capitalist, of the unlucky banker's son, doomed never to escape insular Bedford Falls, his disgrace, near-suicide, and redemption, thanks to a guardian angel, is all engrained in American viewers' memories. Made by an independent production company (Liberty Films) that went bankrupt five years later, considered by its director a commercial disappointment despite winning several Oscar nominations (including one for Capra himself), and gaining cult status only in the 1970s, *It's a Wonderful Life* came close to fulfilling its own darkest suggestions. Generation after generation of die-hard fans predictably await the film's few cheery moments and its sudden reversal of mood, doubtless weighing (and personalizing) the sources of their own anxieties and hopes for release, and have testified to its life-giving powers.

But perhaps this is the wrong testimony. Back in 1945, it boded ill that only divine intervention could salvage a realistically desperate situation of fading older America, and reminded even the God-fearing that a guardian angel might *not* be coming to save them. James Stewart, cast before the war as the pious and often perky American facing the real enemies of democracy but also registering occasional moments of self-doubt, now began a morose series of film roles as the confused American, sometimes pleasantly so (*Harvey*), more often the victim (*Vertigo*). Hollywood, itself up against incipient decline, had captured this most representative figure perfectly.[58]

The noir sensibility, not merely an affirmation of popular culture but the incarnation of its critical power, was so successful that it would be imitated and reimitated through subsequent decades of the next half century, including a proliferation of retrospectives in college courses, museum exhibits, and documentaries. That even film noir would prove unable to resist such commodification would be no surprise, but the impact of the original accomplishment was far from over in an increasingly noir world.

1. "Introduction," to Alain Silver and Elizabeth Ward, editors, *Film Noir: An Encyclopedic Reference to the American Style* (Woodstock, NY: The Overlook Press, 1992 edition), 1. Our emphasis. This indispensable volume, through

its careful if by no means exhaustive cataloging of films and its spare introduction, remains the best source on noir and one not likely to be displaced.

2. Jean Vigo actually issued such an aesthetic manifesto of film in the middle
1930s, doubtless inspiring Abraham Polonsky to issue a similar commentary
(with apparently just as little effect), as we have seen, in a French magazine in
1961. See Paul Buhle and Dave Wagner, *A Very Dangerous Citizen: Abraham
Lincoln Polonsky and the Hollywood Left* (Berkeley: University of California
Press, 2001), 196–97, for the bulk of Polonsky's manifesto, published in *Presence du Cinema*.

3. "Poetic realism," a term originally designated for literature, was applied first
in relation to Pierre Chenal's film *La Rue Sans Nom* (1933); Chenal, a French
Communist, later directed the first version of *Native Son* (1950), starring the
novel's author, Richard Wright. Poetic realism usually designated dark urban
dramas, set within the Parisian working class, foregrounding doomed romantic narratives connected with criminality. See Ginette Vincendeau, "Poetic
Realism," in *Companion to French Cinema* (London: British Film Institute,
1996), 115–16. During the 1930s, the phrase resonated with contrasts to
contemporary Hollywood films.

4. The structure of the French film industry also played an important role: By
contrast with Hollywood, French screenwriters and directors continued
working in a sort of artisan mode of production of less specialization of tasks
and slower work, anachronistic in some respects but artistically freer, especially for the fluid relations to burgeoning film journalism. See Richard Abel,
editor, "Culture and Politics: The Popular Front Era," in *French Film Theory
and Criticism: A Historic Anthology, II,* 152 (Princeton: Princeton University
Press, 1988), and Jonathan Buchsbaum, *Cinema Engagé: Film in the Popular
Front* (Urbana: University of Illinois Press, 1988), 12.

5. Nino Frank, "A New Kind of Police Drama: the Criminal Adventure," trans-
lated and reprinted in Alain Silver and James Ursini, editors, *Film Noir
Reader 2* (New York: Limelight Editions, 1999), 15–19; see also Jean-Pierre
Chartier, "Americans Also Make Noir Films," published in 1946 and
reprinted in the same volume, 21–23. The first coining of the term "film
noir," "Le Jour se lève: une oeuvre noire et pure," had appeared in *La Lumiere,*
June 16, 1939, but mentioned no American film except *I Am a Fugitive from a
Chain Gang,* and spoke to the point more generally, of a "violence which is excruciatingly gloomy, but perfectly pure" expressing the essence of the best
cinema.

6. James Naremore, *More Than Night: Film Noir in Its Contexts* (Berkeley: University of California Press, 1998), 38; and see Steve Neale, *Genre and Hollywood* (London and New York: Routledge, 2000), the very cogent Chapter 4, 151–177, that summarizes decades of research on noir.

7. See the appendix to *A Very Dangerous Citizen,* 235–38, for the text of the phone tap, mainly notable because the participants evidently knew that the conversation was being overheard.

8. William Wyler, statement in "Hollywood Strikes Back," radio broadcast transcript, undated [aired October 1947]. In Albert Maltz Papers, State Historical Society of Wisconsin.

9. Among the many films in this category: *Hangmen Also Die!, Mademoiselle Fifi,* and *Four Brothers.*

10. Barbara Deming, *Running Away from Myself: A Dream Portrait of America Drawn from the Films of the Forties* (New York: Grossman, 1969), 108.

11. Hayes is an especially fascinating case. In the late 1930s he had written the lyrics for "The Ballad of Joe Hill" ("I dreamed I saw Joe Hill last night . . ."), soon to be one of Paul Robeson's biggest performance numbers, in a Jewish summer camp of the late 1930s. Stationed in Rome with the army during wartime, he began work with Italian filmmakers, although his exact screenwriting contribution to *Paisan* remains unknown. He almost certainly contributed one of the film's six episodes, likely the one about a black GI who encounters a scarred and impoverished city. A young Federico Fellini and the director Rossellini got the screenwriting credits (including a nomination for Best Screenplay). Hayes had a few mediocre screen credits after *Clash By Night,* but mainly returned to writing novels. He had never really been part of the Hollywood scene, out of the Party (if he ever joined) before his sojourn there, and probably for those reasons managed to escape the blacklist.

12. Quoted by Ian Hamilton, *Writers in Hollywood, 1915–1951* (New York: Carroll and Graf, 1991), 299.

13. Edward Dmytryk, *A Hell of a Life But Not a Bad Living* (New York: Times Books, 1978), 88–89.

14. This film not only made Ladd's career as noir hero (although normally, if barely, on the other side of the law), but also brought back from obscurity longtime Party member and once-prominent silent film director Frank Tuttle, by this time near the end of a career spent mostly working in the B's.

15. Maltz recalls working out of Tuttle's house during his first job in Holly-wood, a mansion complete with a swimming pool and gym, when "I had come to Los Angeles with one suit only." "Albert Maltz: Citizen Writer," interviewed by Joel Rogers, UCLA Oral History Project, 1975–76, 494–95, 509–10.

16. Based on a James M. Cain story, *They Won't Believe Me* costars Barbara Stanwyck, as the mistress, and Rita Johnson (especially notable as the miserable wife).

17. George Lipsitz, *Time Passages: Collective Memory and American Popular Culture* (Minneapolis: University of Minnesota Press, 1990), 194–207.

18. Not that critics much noticed the film's merits. "Plodding and deadening" was *The New York Times*'s phrase for the one-sided condemnation of the rich. "TMP," "Films," *The New York Times,* September 4, 1948.

19. *Variety* called it an "out and out soap opera on film," potentially appealing "to a certain age group among the femmes," given sufficient exploitation of the Cinderella theme. "Caught," *Variety,* February 23, 1949.

20. See the very different analysis of *Caught* in Mary Ann Doane, *The Desire to Desire: The Woman's Film in the 1940s* (Bloomington: University of Indiana Press, 1987), 155–75. Doane has absented the screenwriter and director, removed capitalist Ohlrig from the picture, along with James Mason, and focused upon the female self-image or "gaze" of Barbara Bel Geddes as demonstrating the "impossibility of female spectatorship." (175). To us, this argument is analytically untenable.

21. Bosley Crowther, "Brute Force," *The New York Times,* July 17, 1949. Crowther wittily concluded, "The moral is: don't go to prison; you meet such vile authorities there."

22. Screenwriter Brooks would also pen the scripts for *Key Largo, The Blackboard Jungle, Cat on a Hot Tin Roof, Elmer Gantry, In Cold Blood,* and *Looking for Mr. Goodbar.*

23. Jules Dassin interviewed by Patrick McGilligan in *Tender Comrades,* 207.

24. See Dmytryk, *It's a Hell of a Life But Not a Bad Living,* 68–72, for the director's claims that the script had to be toned down because of Wexley's propagandistic speeches and because a Party committee headed by Lawson insisted on reshooting scenes in the script that he had eliminated. Most improbably, Dmytryk insists that this incident caused him to leave the Party and prompted Albert Maltz to write his manifesto for freedom of expression in

the *New Masses*. Dmytryk had better reasons to leave; and Maltz, as we have seen, had other, larger, and better reasons to demand artistic freedom. Wexley himself explained the conflict over *Cornered* as coming from Dmytryk's unsuccessful effort to depoliticize the film. See Wexley interview with Patrick McGilligan and Ken Mate, *Tender Comrades*, 716.

25. Among the other films of mentally wounded GIs, the best-named of all was surely *Kiss the Blood Off My Hands* (1948), a title first considered too shocking by a weakened Breen Office but was later accepted. The film project began with former documentarian Ben Maddow and erstwhile *New Yorker* writer Walter Bernstein adapting the novel of the same name by Gerald Butler. When Bernstein returned to New York and a distinguished career in early television drama, the final (but thoroughgoing) rewrite went to Leonardo Bercovici. The story of *Kiss* wasn't much: A distraught GI kills a man in a London pub and takes refuge in the room of a shy nurse, played by Joan Fontaine. Burt Lancaster as the GI offers up another version of the emotionally masochistic character that he played with more effect and complexity in half a dozen other films, and yet as the victim of war he remains compelling.

Likewise, *The High Wall* (1947), adapted from a novel and play by Sidney Boehm and Lester Cole, stands out as one of the early appeals for recognition of post-traumatic stress disorder. A top-grade production by Left ally Robert Lord for MGM made a fine sympathetic-patient drama in which a wartime brain injury has caused the incarceration of an ex-pilot (played by Robert Taylor) found next to his murdered wife's body. A kindly female doctor (played by Audrey Totter) draws him through nightmares and seizures of anxiety to the answer and his vindication. Almost better than all this is the villain played by Herbert Marshall, a religious-book publishing executive. See Lester Cole's passing comments on *High Wall* in *Hollywood Red* (Palo Alto: Ramparts Books, 1970), 256.

26. Wheeler Winston Dixon, "Early Films of Fred Zinnemann," in Arthur Noletti, Jr., editor, *The Films of Fred Zinnemann: Critical Perspectives* (Albany: SUNY Press, 1999), 42–52. Dixon points out that the forced ending, a sort of psychological reconciliation, was almost certainly the product of Breen Office pressure.

27. *Act of Violence* was written by the future blacklistee Robert Richards, who cheerfully told HUAC questioners that he devoted his final pre-blacklist years to writing screenplays about stool pigeons. Named and abandoned by

his wife, Sylvia Richards, according to old friends he made a miserable living by brewing moonshine whiskey, but drank much of it himself.

28. Gordon Kindem, "SAG, HUAC and Postwar Hollywood," in Thomas Schatz, et al., *Boom and Bust: American Cinema in the 1940s* (Berkeley: University of California Press, 1999), 323–28.

29. David Caute, *Joseph Losey: A Revenge on Life* (New York: Oxford University Press, 1994), 91–94.

30. Ibid., 95–96.

31. George Lipsitz, *"A Rainbow at Midnight": Labor and Culture in Cold War America* (Urbana: University of Illinois Press, 1994), 283.

32. Keenly observed by Bernard F. Dick, *Radical Innocence: A Critical Study of the Hollywood Ten* (Lexington: University of Kentucky Press, 1989), 129.

33. Dassin would soon direct a pathetic but unlovable version of the same haphazardly calculating character with Richard Widmark, in his earliest exile film, *Night and the City.*

34. It was also notable that *None But the Lonely Heart* had Mordecai Gorelik as production designer. A veteran avant-gardist and ardent follower of Brecht, Gorelik had served as stage technician for productions at New York's Provincetown Playhouse and worked often in the Yiddish Art Theater (as well as designing sets for Lawson's *Processional* and *The Loud Speaker*). He worked intermittently in films, including also *Give Us This Day* and *A Hatful of Rain.*

35. The first of the Superman films and parent to the 1950s television series, *Superman and the Mole Men* had no specific left-wing connections except its supporting actor Jeff Corey; its screenwriter (and director of the first *Superman* television series), Lee Sholem, had been a frequent collaborator with Harold Buchman, leading one to wonder whether he may even have fronted for his old collaborator. The film ends with Lois Lane's speech for coexistence (apropos the Molemen: they have their world, we have ours). With its comic strip background of young socialists and a future revival among a circle of noted film progressives, including Christopher Reeves, Margot Kidder, Jackie Cooper, Richard Pryor, and gray-listed exile Sam Wanamaker, Superman had been and remained a natural for the crypto-left treatment.

36. *The Underworld Story* was Henry Blankfort's only artistic credit. A successful small businessman before he came to Hollywood, he devoted his best energies in the 1940s to theatrical projects while writing several Joe Palooka films.

After being named by his more famous cousin, screenwriter Michael Blankfort, he returned to business. Our thanks go to Jeff Blankfort, Henry Blankfort's son, for much information. *The Underworld Story* was bombed by the critics, perhaps because it expressed such burning criticism of newspapermen: See Bosley Crowther, "The Screen," *The New York Times,* July 27, 1950.

37. Lawrence Van Gelder, "Joseph H. Lewis, 93, Director Who Turned B-Movies Into Art," *The New York Times,* September 13, 2000. Lewis's two strangest and arguably best films, *Gun Crazy* and *Terror in a Texas Town* (1958), both owed their scripts to blacklisted left-wingers. A true cult film, *Gun Crazy* went in and out of fashion with subsequent genre audiences, but Lewis himself proudly appeared at a screening at UCLA only weeks before his death.

38. *Quicksand,* despite its general cinematic flatness, has a succession of recurring, obsessive images, giving the film a near-surrealist character.

39. Tony Williams, "Phantom Lady, Cornell Woolrich and the Masochistic Aesthetic," reprinted from *Cine/Action!* (Summer 1988) in Alain Silver and James Ursini, editors, *The Film Noir Reader* (New York: Limelight Editions, 1996), 129–30.

40. Tony Williams, "Phantom Lady," 129–43. Siodmak's hit psychological dramas for Universal (especially *The Killers,* 1946) cast a Germanic tone in his American work. The more prominent brother of screenwriter Curt Siodmak, he had collaborated with young Edgar Ulmer, Billy Wilder, and Fred Zinnemann on *Menschen am Sonntag* (1929) before leaving Germany, hitting his peak in the postwar period before abandoning blacklist Hollywood for France in 1953. Other features of his that incorporated left-wing writers include *The Dark Mirror* (1946), *The Crimson Pirate* (1952), and the anti-Stalinist adventure *Escape from East Berlin* (1962), coscripted by blacklistee Millard Lampell.

41. See Mari Jo Buhle, *Feminism and Its Discontents: A Century of Struggle with Psychoanalysis* (Cambridge: Harvard University Press, 1998), 125–30.

42. The female crime-ring boss who puts herself above and beyond the reach of any man was a popular subtheme since the days of nineteenth-century pulp novels and their pirate captain ladies. Nearly a century later, they offered a more suitable subject for Bob Hope or Abbott and Costello comedies. But *Lady Scarface* (1941), coscripted by future friendly witness Richard Collins, offers an exceptional Mildred Coles as a leader who explains her choice clearly when she refuses the potential love interest played by Dennis O'Keefe.

43. Mari Jo Buhle, *Feminism and Its Discontents,* 134–39.

44. Interestingly, *Road House* was adapted from an unpublished story by Margaret Gruen (whose career was abbreviated by marriage to Howard Koch) and Oscar Saul, a former Federal Theater dramatist and close friend of the Left. *Road House* was directed by Jean Negulesco.

45. *Possessed* (1947), coscripted by future friendly witness Sylvia Richards, gained Crawford an Academy Award nomination for her portrayal of the distraught figure who wanders the streets at the beginning of the film, is brought into a mental hospital, and is guided by a kindly psychologist to recall her disappointment in love.

46. "Sensationalism," *The New York Times,* June 18, 1950.

47. William Pechter, "Abraham Polonsky and *Force of Evil,*" in *Film Quarterly* 15 (spring 1962), 50.

48. Huston devoted a chapter of his autobiography to recalling his struggle against the blacklist, as a member of the Committee for the First Amendment and a member of the Screen Directors Guild. He devoted only a few paragraphs to *The Asphalt Jungle.* See John Huston, *An Open Book* (New York: Ballantine, 1980), 94–95, 145–55.

49. *This Land Is Mine* stars Charles Laughton as a shy (and eventually martyred) schoolteacher who becomes a voice for liberty. Completing the international ensemble, it had production designer Eugene Lourie brought from Paris for sets, and a former key member of the Moscow Art Theater, Leo Bulgakov, as dialogue director. Nichols's artistic intentions are expressed in his writing in the *Hollywood Quarterly* (see Chapter 6) and also in "Writer, Editor and Film," in John Gassner and Dudley Nichols, *Best Film Plays of 1943–1944* (New York: Crown Publishers, 1944), xxi–xxx.

50. It may be remembered that *Intruder in the Dust* was adapted by Ben Maddow from a Faulkner novel. Butler's own script version of *The Southerner* is preserved in the Hugo and Jean Butler Collection, American Heritage Center, Laramie, Wyoming.

51. Funded largely by producer Benedict Borgeaus, *Diary* was supposed to have been made by RKO with Burgess Meredith, with Renoir and Goddard as coproducers, but disagreements forced Renoir into a more insular operation. It was rewritten by Meredith himself (his only screenwriting credit), following a draft by Dudley Nichols. The National Board of Review named it one of the ten best films of the year, and it earned a small profit, but it marked the end of Nichols's collaboration with Renoir. A rather more successful version of *Diary* was directed in 1964 by Luis Buñuel.

52. Credits vary in some accounts, including a coscript for Dudley Nichols (who actually withdrew from the project), but the American Film Institute Catalog listing should be considered definitive: *American Film Institute Catalog of Motion Pictures Produced in the United States, Feature Films, 1941–1959, M–Z* (Berkeley: University of California Press, 2001), 2818.

53. Marc Bloch, *Strange Defeat,* translated by Gerard Hopkins (New York: Octagon Books, 1968 edition), 166–67.

54. It was produced by the Hakim brothers and Litvak himself, with Barbara Bel Geddes as the object of yearning, Ann Dvorak as the experienced Other Woman who comforts Fonda (and apparently sleeps with him, in part of the slippage of postwar censorship), and a delightfully hammy Vincent Price as the dog-act master who only apparently (in a concession to the Breen Office) has seduced Bel Geddes. The film lost a cool million dollars at the box office before being promptly forgotten. It may be remembered that Litvak had earlier directed *Confessions of a Nazi Spy.* His largest hits were just ahead: *Sorry, Wrong Number* (1948), *The Snake Pit* (1948), and *Decision Before Dawn* (1951); not blacklisted but under political suspicion, he worked mostly in Europe during the 1950s and finally abandoned the United States for Paris in 1961.

55. Carné, *Ma vie a belle dents* (Paris: L'Editions Archipel, 1996), 127.

56. Interview with Abraham Polonsky, in *Film Noir,* video documentary, coproduction of the New York Center for Visual History, KCET/Los Angeles and the BBC.

57. Credited screenwriters are listed as Frances Goodrich, Albert Hackett, and Capra himself. Wilson actually received credit for a script contribution, while Maltz had to satisfy himself with a glowing letter from a film executive (in the Maltz Papers) and Trumbo with a mere paycheck. Jeanine Basinger's *The It's a Wonderful Life Book* (New York: Knopf, 1986) makes no mention of Wilson, effectively wiping him from the record. The evidence of his work is clearly displayed in the Michael Wilson Papers, UCLA.

58. Ignorant of Wilson's role, Danny Peary nevertheless captured the pathos of the film in *Cult Movies: The Classics, the Sleepers, the Weird and the Wonderful* (New York: Gramercy Books, 1981), 165–66, paralleling Stewart's psychological state to that achieved in Anthony Mann's tortured Westerns and Hitchcock's *Vertigo*—in short, the fullest range of emotion that Jimmy Stewart or perhaps Frank Capra ever offered, but absolutely a continuity with their other work.

8

To the Bitter End

N 1949, MERE DAYS BEFORE Darryl Zanuck came to Jules Dassin's tenement to warn the talented young director to clear out fast, handing him the script for *Night and the City,* to be made in England, Zanuck had Dassin and a skeleton crew plan to work secretly outside San Francisco on an adaptation of an Albert Maltz novel. With the film made and Walter Huston in the starring role, the plan went, it would be too late to halt production; through Maltz, the blacklist would be broken. According to Dassin's version, Maltz blew the chance when he answered a *Hollywood Reporter*'s query instead of begging off.[1]

It seems unlikely that such a project, even if successfully produced, would have changed the outcome of events. But the perception that the blacklisting *could* be halted—or else strictly limited to the Hollywood Ten—was as real as the scheming by Zanuck, producer Jerry Wald, and a few other exceptionally powerful figures determined not to lose their best writers and their prospects for "important" films. In real-life Hollywood, left-wing writers beyond the Ten saw the offers dry up week after week and month by month, until they got subpoenas to appear before investigating committees. Then the studios and agents stopped making excuses.

At the same time, the presence of Jewish names throughout filmmaking, the prominence of Jews in patriotic antifascist movements, and the near-total Jewish reluctance to break an ancient commandment against informing continued to weigh heavily on the minds of the ascending Right. A 1949 report to the FBI on "the background of the racial question" by a Hollywood "member of the Jewish race" warned in the stiffest terms:

Cutting across the present situation in the Hollywood studios is the Jewish Question, aided by the propaganda of the Communist Party. In fact more and more behind the scenes of the House Committee and all of the agencies of government or state investigating Communism in the United States are being charged with attacks on the Jews; that underlying this whole matter of anti-communism is anti-Semitism. This charge is being made by Communists and thousands of Jews who are not Communists.

A careful check of Jewish publications, such as the B'nai B'rith Messenger, a weekly, Jewish Voice, New Frontiers, etc., shows the Jews themselves raising this issue. And so far not one Jewish organization has upheld any investigation of Communism or opposed the Communists openly. On the contrary, the tone of these publications are [sic] favorable to Communists, especially in the present situation in Hollywood.[2]

Of course, Jews had the best of reasons to resist anti-Communists.

By 1947, the Jew-baiting by HUAC's congressional delegation, marked by frequent reading-into-the-record of unfriendly witnesses' "real" (i.e., birth) names, was an old story. Mississippi congressman John Rankin, not HUAC chair but its true voice and conscience, was an unabashed Negrophobe and not much better about Jews. Answering an audience of critics with the declaration, "I never saw such a wilderness of noses in my life," segregationist Rankin attacked his Hollywood critics for "the communism of Leon Trotsky that is based upon hatred for Christianity . . . [that] hounded and persecuted the savior." Worse than poisoning adults, Hollywood Reds were putting "loathsome, lying, immoral, anti-Christian filth" in front of innocent American children.[3]

Making famed anti-Semites like Gerald L. K. Smith respectable by giving them a sympathetic spotlight at the hearings (Rankin defensively told objecting reporters that Smith needed to be heard because "Russian Jews control too much of Hollywood propaganda"), HUAC stiffened the backbones of Hollywood's liberal conscience, which had abandoned the Communist Party or had never joined, though they had participated in assorted antifascist fronts, and now viewed the interrogation as another chapter in the Jewish history of heroic resistance and treacherous collaborators.[4]

The Hollywood blacklist therefore was an affront as well as a huge embarrassment to Jewish popular opinion and would remain so even when many American institutional and intellectual leaders praised the FBI and approved the purgative purposes of McCarthyism (if not Joe McCarthy, the repugnant personality). Editors of those publications that did not cave in early on obviously believed that the blacklist both could be defeated and had to be defeated for the sake of Jewish liberalism and Jewish participation in American culture.[5]

The FBI informer who warned against Jewish resistance to the blacklist had, however, clearly missed a countertendency. *Commentary* magazine (the official publication of the ostensibly liberal American Jewish Committee, based in New York) and the more conservative sections of the B'nai B'rith's Anti-Defamation League, especially the Los Angeles office, eagerly jumped into the Red-hunting business with florid praise for the FBI, despite the well-known anti-Semitism in the Bureau—all in the name of higher Jewish interests. But the overwhelming majority of Jewish supporters of the blacklistees and of civil libertarian opponents of the blacklist never became supporters of the blacklist, but were merely frightened into silence.

The staggered dates of the two HUAC hearings, 1947 and 1951, must also be kept clearly in mind. Conservatives and Cold War liberals, not to mention the FBI and the attorney general's office, were hard at work consolidating their victories pursuing and demonizing influential individuals and the ordinary rank and file of all who resisted them. But director John Berry, in the midst of guiding John Garfield's final screen appearance before the star's second, fatal heart attack, nevertheless recalled a moment in early 1951 when "we were combative. We had a feeling we would come off. We knew things were dangerous and all that, but so what? This was before the hysteria went wild."[6] That is to say, just before the fate of the Ten spelled doom to everyone save those who chose to betray friends and erstwhile comrades.

Amazingly enough, the creative development of more critical and realistic films continued right to the wire and even a bit beyond. *A Place in the Sun* came out in 1951 only weeks before Michael Wilson fell under the blacklist.[7] It was almost an old story by that time, although individual hopes to escape its worst effects had lasted until the artist personally fell victim. No blacklistee, as far as is known, resentfully looked forward to another colleague taking the fall.

A Place in the Sun and the final noted work of the soon-to-be black-listees, *High Noon,* alone would merit serious attention. Situating these two films amidst lesser efforts gives us a clearer picture of the possibilities that managed to survive for a time.

The 1947–48 season saw also more than modest successes with left-connected major star features such as *Gentleman's Agreement, Another Part of the Forest, Forever Amber, It Happened in Brooklyn, Boomerang, My Favorite Brunette, The Wistful Widow of Wagon Gap, Life With Father, Cass Timberlane, The Hucksters, Portrait of Jennie, Laura, Pinky,* and *Possessed,* not to mention ecstatic reviews and the occasional Oscar for smaller, more intensely moral films like *The Search.* Three years later, in 1950, as Hollywood's iron curtain prepared to fall hard, the noir and melodramatic classics *The Asphalt Jungle, Broken Arrow, Caged, Harriet Craig, The Men, Give Us This Day, Quicksand, Try and Get Me, Night and the City, The Underworld Story, All the King's Men,* and *Young Man with a Horn* all appeared. Even in the several years after 1950, credits still could be seen on such serious films as *Death of a Salesman, The Lusty Men, The Prowler, Saturday's Hero, I Can Get It for You Wholesale, He Ran All the Way, Cyrano de Bergerac,* and *Cry, the Beloved Country,* and as unserious as Burt Lancaster's *The Crimson Pirate,* Martin and Lewis's *Jumping Jacks,* and *Abbott and Costello Meet the Invisible Man.* But it was very nearly over, even for younger screenwriters, like Bernard Gordon, who hadn't yet been identified in FBI reports and managed to script a film or two under their own names before falling victim.[8] After 1952 (and a bit later, in many cases), numerous films written by talented hands—*The Robe, The Brave One, Roman Holiday,* and *The Defiant Ones* among the famous, but many more from *Friendly Persuasion* to *A Hatful of Rain* with a lower profile—could be credited to other writers. An era had truly come to its crashing conclusion.[9]

It was an especially stark turnaround for some of the rising artists. Thus, for example, the year of the first postwar hearings, 1947, saw a giant hit in a future Christmas-season television perennial, *The Bishop's Wife* (remade in 1996 as *The Preacher's Wife*). Screenwriter Leonardo Bercovici was a relative newcomer to films. After a highly successful career as a radio writer and producer, and a few years as a wartime documentary filmmaker (as well as impresario for Charlie Chaplin's famed Carnegie Hall event—which was formally an appeal for a Second Front, but was in effect a tribute to the Red Army), he stepped into a major Hollywood career. After *The Bishop's Wife,* this newly high-prestige figure was offered a long-term writer-producer-director's contract with Hal Wallis for a guaranteed $2 million per year. Unfortunately for Bercovici, success came too late. A subpoena finished off his Hollywood career. Following his wife's suicide at the height of the 1951 hearings, Bercovici spent nearly all the rest of his productive years in Italy, intimate with that nation's film giants but working mostly as a script doctor.[10]

Hollywood left-wingers would doubtless have experienced difficulty in a time of steep Hollywood decline even without the blacklist. The once-continuous succession of big hits slowed suddenly after 1946 and virtually stopped by 1949. American theatrical rentals of biggies topping $3 million fell from forty-three films to nineteen in those years; those making more than $4 million dropped from eighteen to five. Studio and exhibitor profits sank by a staggering two-thirds in that brief period.[11]

More stunning and arguably different in meaning from the straightforward decline of industry profits was the unprecedented public disinterest in new American films. Reissues, along with foreign-made films, became big business for the first time. To what extent can this drop-off be attributed to the disappearance of the gripping wartime films and immediate postwar noir, absences that made the "art" crowd now more likely to discover Italian, British, and French cinema? It's an interesting question, not likely to be answered definitively. But the rise of the university cinematheque crowd after 1950—some of the longest-lived college-based film societies dated to 1948 or 1949—surely owed much to a *different way of seeing films.* Like the "art house" crowd in large cities (and, for that matter, albeit in a very different sense, the emerging drive-in movie fans), the college crowd was by its nature a niche audience. That was the sort of niche that the top-drawer blacklistees-to-be had in mind, dictating the form of their never-to-be-made pictures.

The near-collapse of the studio system, Hollywood's Cold War–style search for the "ultimate weapon" in the blockbuster, and the multiple effects of television upon the industry all leave huge margins of error for any attempt at counter-history. But one can certainly see what the future blacklistees (and a handful of future friendly witnesses) wanted. If the antifascist and war patriotism films and their rediscovery of a democratic America were succeeded by noir, there were still deeper impulses apparent since the exposure of the American success story in the mob films of the early 1930s and reinforced in the last years before the blacklist. These impulses opened up the nation's self-created mythos. Noir, women's films, family films, slapstick comedy, and musicals all with left-wing slants would surely have continued in any case. But the search for a new, more complex understanding of national identity was key to content.[12]

Many reasons far from Hollywood can be found for this trend. The war and its aftermath had, for instance, badly shaken the "progressive" view of history that had held dominance among advanced professionals and popularists since the 1920s. That view, with its roots in the old ideas of the yeoman farmer as the soul of democracy, a perspective that interpreted large-scale capitalism (or at least monopolism) as the reinvasion of European ("foreign") systems of privilege, had been iconoclastic and even radical in its day. Charles Beard (along with his wife and collaborator, Mary Beard), the most widely read American historian of that or any other era, had rebuked the champions of the First World War, urged the history of women, and at first resisted the state-oriented economy of the New Deal in favor of decentralized democracy.

During the 1930s, the Beards yielded increasingly to the popularity of Franklin Roosevelt and the larger impulse (very much shared by the Popular Front) to grant greater legitimacy to the American saga as the evolution of the world's bastion of freedom. Certain underlying weaknesses in the Beards' view, especially an inability to see race at the center of the picture, cast increasing doubt upon their totemic texts. But Charles Beard's remaining suspicions of Roosevelt and dread of the likely permanent militarization of American life offered critics the opening that they had been seeking to overturn the Progressive mind-set entirely.[13]

Cold War liberals (and not only historians), many of them shifting away from their youthful left-wing leanings, savaged Charles Beard from two directions simultaneously. The first view took the stage immediately. Now, more than ever, a strong state was needed to combat Communism, and American idealism demanded a global crusade for free society, naturally including free markets. Harry Truman, despite many liberals' initial reservations about him, proved the man of the hour to root out subversives (including all those insufficiently critical of Communists) at home and unite Americans for global stewardship. The Beardian view, which resisted centralization of power as erosion of democracy, was not only out of tune but by now very nearly subversive itself.

From a different psychological angle but one suited for a similar political outlook increasingly salient by the early 1950s, American society was seen as fiercely if for the most part benevolently individualistic, its "genius" realized in a collective unwillingness to accept the ideological platitudes, Left or Right, that had proved so destructive elsewhere in the world. Richard Hofstadter, a former Communist who rose to the pinnacle of scholarly and popular-intellectual renown with this upside-down Marxist view, thus lucidly explicated what would become known as "consensus" history. Along with a host of roughly like-minded younger Jewish intellectuals (including Daniel Bell, David Riesman, and S. M. Lipset), most of them ex-socialists, Hofstadter ruled out the class struggle as historically outdated, pronounced race conflicts resolvable with patient efforts, and fretted about the apparent boredom and restlessness in a society whose major problems had already been solved.[14]

A generation older than these intellectuals, noir filmmakers (also mostly Jewish) might have happily granted individualism as the core of American experience. But they saw little benevolence in its manifestations, and deeply mistrusted the newer liberal impulse to fit the history of American race relations into a past misfortune (now, according to the liberals, being swiftly overcome) along with the very existence of class tensions. For these Hollywoodites, continuing racism at home looked a great deal like colonialism and, indeed, like neocolonialism—a category that the new liberals firmly refused to accept in any form. The next round of radical scholarship, emerging in a decade or so, would vindicate in scholarly terms the view that the Left noir filmmakers held: All American history had been contest and conquest, most often of nonwhite peoples. Intellectually, left-wing filmmakers were already there—with a serious narrative problem.

The problem might be characterized as a paucity of accepted heroic archetypes and splendid national victories, the social equivalents (in Hollywood terms, the thrilling background) to romance. Popular Front themes, especially during the war, had given the Left a major stake in the national myths, while offering the means to alter them subtly. Noir, by contrast, found the socially misunderstood hero or nonhero at the end of the film go down in a hail of gunfire or disappear down a dark alley. In time, other kinds of heroes could be found, like the public defender (subject of *The Defenders,* a 1960s dramatic television series written in part by blacklistees under pseudonyms and starring outstanding liberals), woman's rights crusader, black or Chicano activist, even union organizer.[15] None would entirely suit the noir mood. The more complex and difficult task was to identify social problems within the lives of troubled subjects, so as to investigate the subtler effects of capitalism's continuing stresses, to globalize the story where possible, and to explore alternatives lost, forgotten, or simply never tried.

It goes almost without saying that filmmakers under the gun were scarcely able to work out common strategies. But a revised radical sense of history, free of many Popular Front illusions, pushed them suddenly forward, as they saw time running out. Had they been given just a few more years, they would for instance certainly have seized upon the "youth rebellion" theme—Hugo Butler and Carl Foreman had actually taken options on the story-basis of "The Wild One," and Clifford Odets spiritually advised Nicholas Ray on the set of *Rebel Without a Cause*—and presumably have taken it further and differently from its sensationalizing Hollywood uses in the next few years. Many of them wanted badly to treat the threat of nuclear war and the first hints of irreversible environmental damage. Likewise, they urgently wanted to work with racial themes, and some of them showed a sharpening interest in gender themes restyled for women's striving for careers.[16] And so on.

The keenest now seemed to grasp intellectually or artistically that what they had always meant to do was make the big statement about American life. They wanted to claim their own status as American artists and to offer their maturing view of how the crisis about them might be met.

Political Disaster in the Making

The background to the last phase of pre-blacklist activity can only be characterized as defeat after defeat, from politics to civil liberties. The crushing of the 1946 studio strike might be taken as the death knell of the Hollywood Left, but it was not perceived as such, any more than Churchill's "Iron Curtain" speech of the previous year, warning that an aggressive Communism now threatened civilization, seemed to demonstrate an irreversible Cold War. All that might be reversed with changing political-labor moods. But the administering of the loyalty oath, Truman's Executive Order 9835 in March 1947, mandating compulsory declarations of loyalty—in practice, oaths disavowing either left-wing connections or homosexuality—by all federal employees, sent the chill up the spine of everyone who remained (or had ever been) on the Left.

That same month, a subcommittee opened hearings in Los Angeles to "investigate" the defeated strike, whose legal procedures dragged on even as the IATSE locals mopped up the remains of the Conference of Studio Unions (CSU). Tomorrow's big-fish right-wingers now showed their hands: Richard Nixon, a freshman congressman who made his name here, and Ronald Reagan, a secret FBI collaborator who was rapidly emerging as the spokesman for the conservatives in the Screen Actors Guild (and Hollywood at large).[17] In May, HUAC received a special appropriation of $75,000 for its investigations, and in June, Attorney General Tom Clark announced that he had uncovered a Communist plot to take over the labor movement through fomenting strikes and creating legal barriers against the power of lawful authorities to keep order. (This was an amazing revelation, since AFL locals rather than Left-led unions had led the bulk of the dramatic citywide general strikes of the postwar years, and surviving Communist union leaders, by now, mostly directed a tactical retreat.) California legislative leader Jack Tenney, not to be outdone, had his own agents infiltrate various Hollywood organizations and political meetings, and used blunderbuss attacks upon the *Hollywood Quarterly* as opening shots in his own carefully crafted war.

Worse was to come shortly. HUAC commenced its Hollywood hearings in May, under Chairman J. Parnell Thomas (a southern congressman destined for prison on corruption charges, but not soon enough). The Motion Picture Alliance for the Preservation of American Ideals greeted its coming. Indeed, an alliance executive director threw another bucket of blood in the lion's cage by warning that many current pictures contained "sizeable doses of communist propaganda." Which ones? *The Best Years of Our Lives, The Strange Love of Martha Ivers, Margie, A Medal for Benny, The Searching Wind, Watch on the Rhine, The North Star, Mission to Moscow,* and *Pride of the Marines.* Not all were current; in fact, some went back to 1942. But all of them had left-wing screenwriters, except *Margie* (based on short stories by former *New Masses* columnist Ruth McKenney, author of *My Sister Eileen*) and *A Medal for Benny* (directed by Irving Pichel).[18] J. Edgar Hoover himself testified to the Committee, giving it his blessings; he was immediately followed by Jack Tenney, who provided nearly four hundred pages of dubious evidence about the Red infiltration of Hollywood. The assorted friendly witnesses included Jack Warner, Robert Taylor, Roy Brewer, and Ginger Rogers's mother, Lela, protecting the apparently naive star—the same year Ginger asked Abraham Polonsky to write a script for her—from Red manipulation.[19]

If a vastly stronger Hollywood Left had inadvertently opened itself to attack with the success of the 1943 Hollywood Writers Mobilization Congress, a weakened Left walked squarely into disaster with the runup to the Wallace campaign of 1948. The Hollywood Independent Citizens Committee of the Arts, Sciences and the Professions (HICCASP) had been launched in 1945, with many of the key people in the Hollywood Democratic Party's recent heroic reelection effort for FDR. It seemed well positioned to defend the legacy of the New Deal against an unpopular, evidently rightward-moving president. James Roosevelt, the FDR scion who was widely believed to be his father's political heir to a White House future, came out to California in early 1946 to become HICCASP president. On its board stood Hollywood royalty in vice presidents Olivia de Havilland, Lena Horne, Linus Pauling, Dore Schary, and Frank Sinatra, with E. Y. Harburg as secretary.

But with the fall elections looming and the Republicans looking stronger by the moment, a centrist Democrat (ironically another famous son, Will Rogers, Jr.) far less inclined to defend the Hollywood Left against persecution was chosen for senatorial nomination over the HICCASP choice of Roosevelt, who defected to Rogers, Jr.—an act that retrospectively seemed to some like the real beginning of the end. If the Democratic liberals were moving against the Left, what hope remained?

The dip centerward had no good effect for the Democrats, in any case. Wavering in their commitments to expand New Deal programs, fraught with the kinds of scandals that would fill newspaper pages during Truman's second administration, Democrats were routed by Republicans in the fall elections, in California as well as elsewhere. The GOP now stood in command of Congress for the first time since 1932, and the "Red" issue offered an inviting opportunity to go after the administration, notwithstanding Truman's staunch anti-Communist credentials. Hollywood hearts grew faint; HICCASP's membership so drastically narrowed that it increasingly lacked the necessary charisma to keep the worsening attacks at bay.

Jack Tenney sent out subpoenas to some of HICCASP's most prominent figures only a few weeks before the 1946 election, including former Screen Writers Guild president Emmett Lavery (a progressive and very non-Communist Catholic), who found himself defending the movies in ways that subtly revealed the changing state of affairs. Did "Marxist" ideas find their way into films? To that charge, now heard more and more widely, Lavery had the answer: The studio executives, "the Skourases, the Schencks, and Mr. Zanuck . . . are as alert as this committee to not allow Marxist doctrines in pictures." [20]

It was an adept response, and may even have reflected the Communists' own disappointments in being blocked from creating "message" pictures. But to make this the defensive basis of the argument (and to make it against all Marxist-appearing ideas and not just Communists' ideas) was tantamount to abandoning in advance the idea that film workers of any political leaning had the perfect right to create—whether write, direct, or produce—films outside the dictates of studio taste. It also as much as warned against independent productions for their possible lack of internal censorship. This line of reasoning already pointed to the weakness of the First Amendment defense of Communists, former Communists, and just plain libertarians facing the blacklist. Rather than insisting that they had as legitimate a right as radicals (no less than conservatives or liberals had the right) to make films reflecting their political perspective, they took the position that no one had a right to ask them about their affiliations and outlook. Given the circumstances, this line of defense was understandable. No alternative would likely have worked, anyway. But as Irving Pichel observed, they had all but conceded the game in advance. [21]

The Left's biggest public event to date mirrored the defensive approach, while trying hard to put things in the best celebrity light. In May 1947, Hollywood Fights Back played to a packed crowd at Gilmore Stadium (the management of the Hollywood Bowl had turned the event's organizers down flat). Chief headliner Katharine Hepburn praised Roosevelt's third-term vice president, Henry Wallace, and cursed the climate of attack. "Silence the artist," she said, "and you silence the most articulate voice the people have. Destroy culture and you destroy one of the strongest sources of inspiration from which a people can draw strength to fight for a better life." Immediately after her peroration, Wallace himself reiterated her attack on the Red-hunting Right. If anyone knew that Hepburn was speaking lines written for her by Dalton Trumbo, no one revealed it.[22] But nothing could stop the downhill rush.

The internal disputes of the SAG and SWG in these years had the same now-familiar ring. Communists and their allies had influenced the writers far more than the actors over the years, by virtue of their role as founders of the SWG and because the memory of the conservative Screen Playwrights as company unionists still rankled. But in both talent guilds, issues that had sometimes figured as anti-Communists versus Communists, which just as often divided members over practical matters that could cut across such boundaries, now flared up into straight-out political wars. As the Cold War moved ahead, the middle bloc that had shifted from side to side, including some close personal friends of the Left back in the 1930s, now moved solidly in the direction of the Right. Frequently, these defectors convinced themselves that they were protecting Hollywood as well as their own careers: They could simply take the political issues off the table, or balance a somewhat liberal agenda (such as fair hiring practices for minorities in a few regions of studio work) with flat-out anti-Communism.

In the SAG, which never had many radicals but did occasionally elect some of the Left's hardest workers to its own high offices, the issue was the continued toleration of Communists who were also good, solid unionists, widely recognized either as heroic pioneers or those still willing to take the time for details and endless negotiations that other members would rather ignore. By the summer of 1947, the Taft-Hartley Act had taken effect, stipulating that all union officers had to sign anti-Communist affidavits in order for their union to remain certified as a legitimate bargaining body. The SAG contract continued until 1949, and the Left could hope that the act might be overturned in the Supreme Court by then. But the Right seized the moment, electing a slate with no Communist members and no Left supporters.

The SWG battle was more protracted and in that sense nastier, not only due to history but because left-wingers ran the house organ, the *Screen Writer,* and because Left writers were still some of the biggest names as well as the most respected artists in the business. Oddly enough, the worst split took place over an American Authors Authority (AAA) plan proposed by James M. Cain (otherwise no radical) and supported by Emmett Lavery to compel studios to share film profits with the screenwriters. Turning writers into lesees could have made them something akin to the credited "Creative

Producers" of today. It would certainly have been a step upward, however improbable. When studio execs denounced the AAA plan as "communistic," left-wingers threw their remaining energies into supporting their remaining liberal allies, especially Cain and Lavery. The AAA plan nevertheless died a painful death.

The Taft-Hartley Act marked the Left screenwriters' final undoing, although SWG liberals like Phil Dunne—having opposed the Communists outright on other matters—eloquently opposed the act's interference in the free election of union officials. It was all to no avail. As with the SAG, the SWG's removal of left-wing officers was a decisive step toward the official action toward both guilds blacklisting their own members a few years later by demanding a loyalty oath signature as condition of membership. No one without a card worked in films, at least not over the table, and in the case of the actors—with precious few exceptions—not at all. Thus, many of the earliest and most hardworking figures of the organizations that established the status of screen actors and writers were ungratefully heaved out into the darkness. Others, non-Communists like actress Jane Wyatt who simply refused to testify against her colleagues on ethical grounds, found work only in television.

The prospect of television, of the 1948 Supreme Court decision to break up movie theater chains, and most important of unemployment might have been enough to impel most of the SWG members to try to get rid of the problem by getting rid of Communists as elected representatives. After the 1947 guild election swept assorted Communists from office (defeated secretary Stanley Rubin and defeated treasurer Leo Townsend both became friendly witnesses), only the mopping up remained.

J. Parnell Thomas had foreshadowed and helped arrange the worst of this by building upon his initial foray into the film world and avowing, in the late spring and summer of 1947, to root out all Hollywood Communists. Thomas was, in this respect at least, as good as his word. In September, subpoenas went flying out to forty-five men and women, conservatives as well as radicals, but including nineteen men (no women) already marked by investigators to become the true targets.

The nineteen already offered an interesting cross section of the potential victims that the committee savants had in mind: producer-director Adrian Scott; directors Herbert Biberman, Edward Dmytryk, Lewis Milestone, Robert Rossen, and Irving Pichel; actor Larry Parks; and writers

Alvah Bessie, Bertolt Brecht, Lester Cole, Richard Collins, Gordon Kahn, Howard Koch, Ring Lardner, Jr., John Howard Lawson, Albert Maltz, Samuel Ornitz, Waldo Salt, and Dalton Trumbo.

The FBI had long since identified all (accurately, with the exception of Milestone and the possible exception of Brecht) as Hollywood Communists. But it had passed over many others as well, from the most famous of Red writers, Donald Ogden Stewart, to the party's informal social chairman, Robert Lees. Also absent were its most cerebral figures apart from Lawson, Abraham Polonsky and Michael Wilson; several of the most talented writers of family films (including Francis Faragoh and Hugo Butler); its most famous lyricist, E. Y. Harburg; and its notorious two-fisted bohemian, John Bright. Why not them?

Chance may have played a role in it—Dmytryk and Scott were considered on the block for having made the hated *Crossfire,* Koch and Milestone for *Mission to Moscow*—but the fact that thirteen out of the nineteen were Jews and that none had served in war combat was inescapable.[23] Vets and heroes like Dashiell Hammett might have embarrassed the Committee deeply; Polonsky or Harburg might have found a witty way to ridicule them instead of responding with the outraged morality and countercharges that witnesses like Lawson offered before the camera. (Lardner, Jr., was to provide the brightest moment of the dark days by suggesting that he could answer the question of his affiliation "but I would hate myself in the morning.")[24] In any case, Hollywood conservatives Ayn Rand, Louis B. Mayer, and Adolph Menjou—who specialized in collecting evidence, in this case an old pamphlet of the Hollywood Writers Mobilization, with the names of the Reds identified by philosopher and Red-hunter Sidney Hook—had preceded the unfriendlies, establishing the Left's collective guilt.[25]

The planeload of prospective unfriendly witnesses nonetheless left Hollywood for Washington cheerfully determined. Howard Hughes even offered to charter a second plane of supporters. They came back wilted by the overwhelming power of the Committee and of the vitriolic tabloid press.

Actually, only eleven of the nineteen prospective unfriendlies had testified before the Committee adjourned, satisfied with its political spectacle. Brecht immediately afterward fled the country. That left ten: the Hollywood Ten. Why not Kahn, Parks, Salt, Collins, or three of the five directors, Milestone, Rossen, or Pichel? No doubt it was partly because the others had sufficiently exposed themselves to attack by announcing their refusal to testify. More probably, the FBI had narrowed the list to current Party members for investigatory purposes, and had good reason to suspect a softness in Rossen (who had quit the Party), Pichel (according to FBI informants, terrified), and Collins (who some have suspected, in hindsight, of *being* one of the informants, although neither his previous work nor his testimony gives us any solid reason for thinking so). Whatever the pattern of accidents and conspiracies, the die had been cast.[26]

Roland Kibbee, a screenwriter of B musicals and a future friendly witness, probably responded best to the situation with firm irony. Penning a straight-faced satire of Red-baiting in the *Screen Writer,* he recalled recently returning from San Francisco (in an ironical aside about the much-attacked longshore union leader, "a city which I am told is controlled by Harry Bridges") to Los Angeles, where he determined to write "not the usual hogwash about mad writers, illiterate producers and wild parties" but a stark revelation of "the first soviet community within the continental limits of the United States."[27]

Entering a zone of snarling proletarians, passing by drive-ins where a "Stalinburger" was the *faire du jour,* he was guided around by "Comrade X" and then trailed by Secret Police ("their thin disguise of lavender blouses, rouged cheeks and peroxided hair did not fool me for a moment"). Visiting Ciro's (full of starlets "all of whom are members of the Young Communist League . . . [who] lure unsuspecting writers . . . under the influence of orange juice . . . into the ranks of the Party") and going on to the RKO Collective, he watched awed as Comrade X flashed his Screen Writers Guild card and police guarding the studios "withdrew instantly, bowing, scraping and stammering apologies." The SWG, known only by its dreaded initials, actually controlled Hollywood. Entering the ultra-lavish guild headquarters under a portrait of Ring Lardner, Jr. (known as "Ring," in this comic construction, because he had to be telephoned to approve of all light entertainment pictures), he interviewed a studio mogul who proudly wore the "coveted Order of John Howard Lawson" medal but who nonetheless cowered before writers' commands. They, too, had limits on their power, however: *Important* scripts had to be approved in Moscow.[28]

Earlier that year, Irving Pichel—who offered humor only through his often puckish characters—had a deeper observation. Censorship was nothing new. Since the earliest Greek theater, drama arose under the fiat of religious teachings. Inasmuch as the dramatists shared with official and unofficial moralists the desire to instruct, the real nub of the problem lay in the "distinction between the story as truth and as homily." The sophisticated dramatist, curious as to *why* homilies fail to persuade people to act properly, always takes up the issue of human misbehavior—something at the root of every comedy or tragedy. Drama thus probes for the reasons that Eve took the apple and so many subsequent Adams and Eves have continued to do so; it seeks to "explain the difference between fantasy and reality."[29]

Hollywoodites, then, should declare "clearly the function we ask the screen and screen entertainment to fulfill . . . We do not know whether we intend to view life as it is or as it ought to be," in other words, the real America or idealized America.[30] These were wise words, even a wise course of action in another age. But now it was too late for such wisdom to do much good.

Late Flashes

And yet brilliant and interesting films, some of them written by left-wingers before and some after the warning signals, continued to be made and to attract audiences. From talented obscurities and future foreign talents to Oscar winners, the Hollywood Reds went out with a flash.

A small handful of the most brilliant films, including not only *The Long Night* but also notably *Give Us This Day* (1949), were simply buried.[31] *Give Us This Day* was made under the most inauspicious circumstances. Ben Barzman, who had an acclaimed hit in *Back to Bataan,* had finished scripting (with Al Levitt) *The Boy with Green Hair* and was beginning a new Dore Schary vehicle for Lana Turner. He got a pleading message from Dmytryk, already blacklisted and desperately trying to make a new film. If an admired feature could be made by one of the Hollywood Ten working under his own name, the blacklist might be broken. The estimable Sam Wanamaker, by this time refused stage work in New York, would star. The production company would be British; plans to shoot on Manhattan's Lower East Side (originating with a certain sense of poetic justice) had to be abandoned.[32]

Give Us This Day was based on Pietro di Donato's vividly impressionistic 1939 novel, *Christ in Concrete*. Widely considered the finest and most poetic depiction of the Italian-American working class, the novel moved impressionistically through a common bricklayer's tragedy. Barzman and Dmytryk followed the lines of the novel pretty carefully, aware perhaps without knowing it that their achievement was likely to be an unrequited love of cinematic art, realized within the simplest of sets. Shifting in and out of the heavily Italian dialect that fills the novel, *Give Us This Day* opens with the bricklayer's wife (played by Italian actress Lea Padovani) slamming the door on her unfaithful husband, who returns to his American mistress, played by Kathleen Ryan. Cut off from his children and keenly aware of his wrongdoing, he looks back on the past decade as one of disappointment and ruin.

Back at the dawn of the 1920s, as a second-generation American (but also deeply Italian) craftsman, he nearly loses his life while working on a future skyscraper. Realizing that a single man's death meant leaving nothing behind he is obsessively drawn to a photo that his best friend shows him of a girlfriend and her family back in Abruzzi. In the face of the girlfriend's sister, he sees the woman that he dreams of marrying and sends back word to Abruzzi for her hand. But her family insists that he be a man of means, a homeowner. The marriage pact and her immigration assured, he plays a trick by borrowing for a few days' honeymoon the Brooklyn house that he hopes to own when he is actually able to put down $750. The nuptials have scarcely begun when the real owner appears and reveals the truth. The couple move to a Manhattan tenement, and there the hope and common tragedy of working-class life unfolds.

Wanamaker and Padovani act their domestic roles with dignity and (especially for her) a large degree of Catholic fatalism as they welcome the arrival of babies and mark on a kitchen wall the cash they save toward the house that remains unsold. The stock-market crash intensifies the desperation for personal success, as jobs grow scarce and their savings dwindle perilously. The old friend becomes a foreman and sets up a competition for the workman who can lay the most bricks. Wanamaker wins the $100 prize, which Padovani turns over to the impatient owner of their would-be dream house. Now Wanamaker himself becomes foreman and drives his fellows hard, ignoring well-placed fears of a dangerous demolition project because of their faith in him. Tragedy strikes when a wall caves in upon a worker. Wanamaker's friends break with him and, emotionally disoriented, he turns toward the Other Woman. By this time the story has caught up to the film's opening scene, and only more tragedy can follow. A wall collapses on him as well, and he falls into a hole. As he is being buried alive by liquid cement, he dies pleading with his absent wife for forgiveness. Insisting to authorities that no one can place a dollar amount on love or dreams, she is awarded $1,000 by a compensation committee. Her late husband has bought the family a house after all.

The sharply etched film was applauded in New York and in Europe, where it was given a special award by Italian motion picture critics. But American Legionnaires picketed showings, and a hasty change of title (to *Salt for the Wise*) fooled no one.[33] In short, the film was effectively suppressed and lost, not even emerging in the wave of campus and art theater rediscoveries a quarter century later. This was a tragedy several times over. Dmytryk never before or after made a real art film. More important, until the brilliant performance of Padovani, the Left had almost never successfully taken Catholic faith at its face value, choosing instead to place the usually conservative religion within the parentheses of antifascist patriotism or community egalitarianism. Without condescending or caricaturing, the makers of *Give Us This Day* had captured the Mariolatry of "woman's religion" so central to Italian Catholicism.

All the King's Men (1949) offers a counterpoint in several important ways to this lost blue-collar film. The most highly awarded movie by a prospective blacklistee, *King's Men* was Robert Rossen's triumph and very likely his corruption. Succeeding brilliantly on his own terms as writer-director, Rossen delivered the artistic self-congratulations of the parliamentary democratic system that rightward-drifting American liberals longed to hear by this time. Faithfully adapted from Robert Penn Warren's novel, it raked over the memory of the late Louisiana governor Huey Long, considered by Franklin Roosevelt the "most dangerous man in the country" until Long's assassination, occurring in time to remove him from the 1936 election. Contrary to the film, what made Long so dangerous was not his demagoguery or manipulation of state government (the last more closely resembled the ordinary Chicago politics of mixed crime and corruption than it did the crypto-fascist treatment given in the film), but that the son of a prominent Louisiana socialist had built his machine on a multiracial basis, preached antibusiness populism (however little he practiced it), and threatened to break the two-party stranglehold on American politics.

Rossen brilliantly restaged history as a social psychodrama. John Ireland is the newspaperman who buys into the lore of the boss played by Broderick Crawford only to expose him in the end. Mercedes McCambridge, as the alter ego and probable lover of "the Kingfish," is overwhelmed by his power and therefore sacrifices her life to him, though knowing better. Crawford's ability to speak for the masses readily becomes a power smothering all decency and wounding everyone who loves him.

The reception of the film must have been almost everything that Rossen had dreamed of: Oscar nominations for Best Picture and Best Screenplay, awards for Best Actor (Crawford) and Best Supporting Actress (McCambridge). It was also the last film that Rossen made before he was compelled to testify twice—the first time unfriendly; then, following several apparent heart attacks in Mexico, compliant. The resuscitation of his Hollywood career followed.[34]

Close behind *All the King's Men* in critical prestige and public reception (as well as unfavorable FBI reports) were the famed "conscience" films, an obvious source of what the Bureau called "Communistic or anti-American propaganda." Agent R. B. Hood, stationed in Los Angeles, issued a memo to Bureau Chief Hoover in 1948 warning against *So Well Remembered* (1948), *Crossfire* (1947), *Gentleman's Agreement* (1948), *Monsieur Verdoux* (1947), *Body and Soul* (1948), and *The Best Years of Our Lives* (1946), with the particulars of Communist-sympathetic producers, directors, actors, and, in one case, score-composer carefully noted.[35]

It certainly was a good if by no means comprehensive list of roughly current films that later Hollywoodites would consider both high art and public service, even if Howard Koch did not write *Gentleman's Agreement* as Agent Hood insisted. The Bureau, like the House Committee, had always considered attacks upon anti-Semitism as particularly suspicious (even as Jewish friendly witnesses insisted that Russian anti-Semitism had driven them into patriotic American causes). Hoover and his associates had likewise nurtured a grudge against Charlie Chaplin since the 1920s, although the high-living Chaplin's actual left-wing activities extended no further than financial contributions, picnics on the grounds outside his mansion, and an occasional appearance at a wartime pro-Russian rally.

Did the Bureau consider *Till the End of Time,* a sort of bargain-basement *Best Years of Our Lives* with a fist-swinging attack on anti-Semitism, to be safe, or Hellman's propagandistic *The Searching Wind* beneath notice, or assorted noir, anti-prison, and other antiauthority films not worthy of consideration? If so, their ignorance did not last long, as the Bureau continued to prepare documentation of Hollywood political activities for exposure and potential blacklisting. Generally, outside the work of major figures, they were interested in personalities and politics rather than in film per se.

Gentleman's Agreement was for several reasons a prize subject for investigators. The screen adaptation by Moss Hart of Laura Z. Hobson's best-selling novel, produced by Darryl Zanuck for Twentieth Century-Fox and featuring some of the best talents in the business, bowled over the critics.[36] Here, Hollywood had truly succeeded, doing well by doing good. From the FBI standpoint, supporting actors John Garfield, Anne Revere, and Sam Jaffe were all proven cases of Red taint; Gregory Peck (thanks mostly to his wife), Albert Dekker, and Jane Wyatt all went on the suspect list.[37]

But far worse was the plot. At the suggestion of his boss, magazine writer Peck goes underground—without changing appearance, language, or any other characteristic, he announces his identity as a Jew—and then suffers many of the slights and insults to himself and his family that were altogether normal for the contemporary Jewish middle classes. Cynics, some of them on the Left, sharply observed that the film actually warned Americans never to discriminate, at least not against Jews, for fear the target might turn out to be a Gentile! Producer Zanuck, explaining his passion for the film, unintentionally went his critics one better, explaining that he had once spent hours at a hotel desk before he could prove that he wasn't Jewish. Perhaps not so ironically, Zanuck had turned down an earlier, somewhat similar script by Ring Lardner, Jr., as "too Jewish." The Connecticut WASPs of *Gentleman's Agreement* offer easy targets, but Peck's screen wife, Dorothy McGuire, provides some of the most painful scenes as she gamely goes along until in her frustration admits that she's *glad* to be non-Jewish in the same way that she's glad she's not poor, and insists that she shouldn't be made to feel ashamed of her good fortune. Their son, played by Dean Stockwell, adds to the sentimental side by becoming the innocent mocked by schoolmates for no reason other than his presumed ethnicity.

But it is Garfield, as the returning Jewish soldier tired of hearing liberal talk about the "poor little Jews," who hits the hardest, virtually demanding social change; and Anne Revere, the protagonist's mother, who vows to live on to see a better world. Coming at the film's climax, her speech constitutes the classic Popular Front declaration of faith in American democracy. By the time the film appeared, the witch-hunt had begun, and not only within the film community. Nevertheless, whatever ill effects Kazan's subsequent moral compromises were to have upon left-wingers, cinematic free speech, and dissenting social causes generally, he had *Gentleman's Agreement* (and one more genuine conscience film to come, *Pinky*) to his lasting credit.

Crossfire, typical of Dmytryk's films, was indeed a virtual B version of *Gentleman's Agreement,* with action scenes and sadism prominent. As critics have often noted, what began as a Richard Brooks novel treating various veterans' frustrations including homophobia became a project about the suddenly salable issue of anti-Semitism. Adrian Scott had optioned the novel, and John Paxton (neither of them Jewish, either) worked on a treatment, by which time Dore Schary became the head of RKO. The casting of Robert Ryan as the anti-Semite was the genius stroke. The film featured a simple *policier* plot of detective Robert Young tracking down the anti-Semitic killer, war veteran Ryan, and convincing GI Robert Mitchum to help turn in his fellow veteran. Single-source lighting made the best use of a short shooting schedule and a relatively modest budget of a half-million dollars.

So Well Remembered, the least-remembered of these FBI-identified conscience classics, was the more radical by far. RKO had chosen Irving Reis to direct the joint venture with the British J. Arthur Rank Studios about life in Depression England, but Reis chose not to go abroad, and producer Adrian Scott persuaded Edward Dmytryk to take the helm. Paul Jarrico joined John Paxton on the script about the hardworking newspaperman— played ably by John Mills—in a dark industrial town of the 1920s who crusades against the cruelty and stupidity of the upper classes but finds himself mainly fighting his in-laws as he marries up into the literal bosom of privilege. One could say (and the *New Masses* did say) that the social criticism melted into the romantic dilemmas, and that the complaints about British stodginess were appeals for no more than American New Deal–style measures (especially since "socialism," often exhorted if unpracticed by the postwar Labour government, was never mentioned in the film). The indictment of "privilege" was nevertheless evidently enough for the FBI, and perhaps (along with the romance) a real factor in the modest success of the film.

Agent Hood might well have argued (although he didn't) that *Monsieur Verdoux, Cyrano de Bergerac, Death of a Salesman,* and *Body and Soul* were the tainted features of the highbrow set—not because they contained any red-hot propaganda or outright criticisms of capitalism but because they captured artistic possibilities of film, and especially the possibilities of film as seen through the talents of Chaplin, Robert Rossen, Abraham Polonsky, John Garfield, Anne Revere, Lilli Palmer, and Canada Lee. *Death of a Salesman* might easily be described as decades ahead of its time in an avowed critique of American psychology; *Body and Soul* belonged to the spirit of the disappearing thirties when it was made, and could have been made again only by stripping out the implicit proletarian Jewishness essential to the mise-en-scène.

Monsieur Verdoux shocked Hollywood censors. But because nothing in the film could reasonably be described as lewd, Chaplin successfully confronted Joseph Breen himself in what the film master called a "Shavian dialogue" during which the moralist objected most ardently to the satire of Catholic values.[38] But Breen had the last laugh. The Catholic Legion of Decency picketed the film across the country, while the right-wing tabloids took the opportunity the accelerating Cold War provided to accuse Chaplin of being a "fellow traveler." His once-fabulous financial success, gradually wearing thin, ended here.[39] Chaplin's name had enough magic to prevent outright disappearance à la *Give Us This Day,* but not to make his film a success.

Cyrano de Bergerac, likewise, should have had everything going for it, including Stanley Kramer's production, Michael Gordon's direction, Carl Foreman's script, and José Ferrer (then close to the Left, later a friendly witness) as its star. It was a serious art effort, albeit laid upon a turn-of-the-century French theatrical hit about the long-nosed poet and soldier who cannot connect romantically but finds his nobility in death. An earlier-intended Orson Welles version, never made, would probably have suffered the same fate of well-intentioned artiness, but with greater dignity and better prospects for later revival.

Death of a Salesman (1951), scripted by Stanley Roberts, was another story. Arthur Miller, author of the fabled stage hit, had by this time been dragged through the yellow press as a potentially dangerous anti-anti-Communist and unpatriotic ingrate (since he *was* successful) to boot. Paramount initially intended to run a trailer with the film praising real-life American salesmen, to salve the sting of the message, but apparently abandoned the idea, and the film, leaving it to disappear quietly.

Body and Soul captured much of what was familiar in the work of the Hollywood Left and distilled it in romantic, even sentimental ways that Polonsky's artistically purer *Force of Evil* could not possibly permit. The "fable of the streets" picked up the lower-class boxer where *Golden Boy* left off. Only this time, he was no fiddler and no Cagneyesque puncher with a brother yearning to become a composer. No, John Garfield's character was only the son of a Lower East Side candy-store owner who happened to be gunned down accidentally in mob crossfire. Facing together with his mother (once more the role brilliantly played by Anne Revere) the shame of welfare and the psychological impossibility of his situation, he turns into something that she says she would rather see him dead than become: a fighter, but not "for something," as she pleads, just for money. Polonsky, writing for director Rossen, created a wonderful romance-and-sex counterpart in the artist played by Lilli Palmer, whom he woos, wins, and discards on his way up to the top.

By a notable contrast to *Monsieur Verdoux*'s old-fashioned look, Polonsky utilized the latest cinematic innovations, inventing some of his own along the way and often contesting director Rossen's control. Unlike both the charmingly Chaplinesque dialogue and the Warners standard, Polonsky injected a sharpness in the inherent sentimentality of the ghetto boy turning away from his mother's values only to return to them later. (Thanks to his suggestions, cameramen trained in the war scooted around on roller skates, shooting from moving angles never seen before in Hollywood features.) The dialectical break from community, the subsequent angst, and the return to a (somehow transformed and uplifted) common cause etched lasting images and made the picture a hit.

But there was another, more structural reason for the beauty and depth of *Body and Soul*. It was produced by the fledgling Enterprise Studios, launched two years earlier as one of the early group of "independents" with enough backing to hire stars and bring forth quality films. Himself on loan from Paramount, Polonsky joined with Rossen in creating Enterprise's first real hit. The company was felled by the decline of movie revenues and by the blacklist taking away its best talent, but Polonsky's brief success had, among other small accomplishments, made the artist's own creative control of *Force of Evil* possible.

In the dawning era of sympathetic pictures about racism involving (for the first time) African-Americans in other than cheerfully subservient roles, Canada Lee's portrayal of Garfield's sparring partner captured keen attention. Lee, punch-drunk from treatment by his former mob bosses (who have become Garfield's bosses), lashes out at their arrogance and abuse. And then he dies, leaving Garfield to chew over their command that he throw the championship match and win big for himself: He has already bet his life savings on his opponent.

Garfield's victory over his worst impulses and his victory over his more literal opponent are philosophically guaranteed as he comes to understand that he has betrayed his black sparring partner. In cinematic history, the two endings of the film—Garfield killed by the mob, or triumphant over them ("Whaddaya gonna do, kill me? Everybody dies!")—represented the contrary spirits of Rossen and Polonsky. In a sense, Rossen was truer to noir, and Polonsky to the Warners tradition that almost always had to have a happy ending. But Polonsky had something else in mind: a knockout blow for the working class's enemies, with Garfield the proletariat's symbolic representative, during the last moment when sweeping labor victory over postwar capitalism could be still imagined.

African-Americans were then engaged in real-life working-class struggles as they had never been previously—at a turning point akin to Reconstruction. Black workers had won their place in industry and the bottom levels of unions during the wartime labor shortage. Subsequent walkouts, including wildcat strikes against the bureaucratic encrustation of the unions, frequently found them foremost, a fact of particular poignancy to labor education veteran Polonsky, whose United Auto Workers faction had put black workers' advancement squarely upon the agenda.

Body and Soul was certainly not the first left-wing film that placed African-Americans in roles of greater dignity. As we have seen, *The Adventures of Huckleberry Finn* drove home an antilynching message, *Sahara* offered a perfect setting for a progressive antiracist statement, and all-black casts of *Cabin in the Sky* and (especially) *Stormy Weather* offered virtually nonstop entertainment. *New Orleans* (1947), coscripted and produced in part by

Herbert Biberman for the independent Majestic Productions (and distributed by United Artists), featured fabulous takes of Meade Lux Lewis, Zutty Singleton, Woody Herman, Louis Armstrong, and Billie Holiday (her only film appearance), shot partly on location in New Orleans.

Most remarkably, Armstrong was on camera as an actor, a bandleader whose girlfriend (played by Holiday) introduces a visiting classically trained singer (Dorothy Patrick) to the blues. The owner of the bar where the great trumpeter performs is also Patrick's potential beau, who tries to spare her the disgrace of association with disreputable music and himself. After various complications (including a panic in the city about white debutantes coming unchaperoned to hear jazz, and the consequent threat from a local grand jury to have the navy close New Orleans's Storyville), jazz triumphs in Manhattan—albeit with Woody Herman in the spotlight. Almost hidden in the film is Dutch émigré composer and actor Richard Hageman as the kindly Germanic composer who comes to see the necessity of dialogue between the classics and jazz and helps diva Patrick see it, too.[40] *New Orleans* escaped right-wing picketing, perhaps thanks to the obscurity of its connections, but despite bravura notices in *Variety,* it lacked the backing and big (white) stars to do much business.

Left-wing cinematic drama about African-American life meanwhile took several more, however ambiguous, steps upward with a trio of serious films near the end of the 1940s. *Home of the Brave* (1949), written by Carl Foreman and produced by Stanley Kramer, was destined to remain on the cutting edge for decades. *Intruder in the Dust* (1949) was a Faulkner tale scripted by documentary veteran Ben Maddow. *Pinky* (1949) could be accurately described as the last film of Elia Kazan's that failed to celebrate the superior qualities of American life.

Home of the Brave, an independent production, began as an Arthur Laurents play about a Jewish soldier persecuted by fellow GIs. That a victimized Jew could become black as easily as a victimized gay soldier could become Jewish in *Crossfire* was unsurprising in Hollywood, where it was just part of the transfer of victimhood.[41] But in this case the shift foreshadowed the weaknesses as well as the strengths of a movie. The plan for a small group of volunteers to be sent on a reconnaissance mission on a Pacific island almost collapses before beginning, because of the racism of one of the soldiers, played brilliantly by Frank Lovejoy, toward its black member, played by Hollywood unknown James Edwards. After a series of quarrels with Edwards, Lovejoy happens to be killed by the Japanese, dying in the black soldier's arms. On the survivors' return to safety, Edwards suffers a hysterical paralysis. An army psychologist (played by Jeff Corey) gets to the heart of the problem in relieving Edwards of his guilt, permitting him to feel "like any other soldier," not white or black but just a soldier.

From a doctrinaire Communist perspective—especially as the romance of American-Soviet unity during the Good War faded—the film seemed a sellout. But from the Hollywood Left's view it was a measured triumph. Associate producer Robert Stillman assured the artistic integrity of the production by putting up the money (most of it his father's) himself. Most important, Edwards had no resemblance to a character out of minstrelsy; the actor achieved dignity on his own terms.[42]

Intruder in the Dust, produced and directed by Clarence Brown, could rightly be called the first truly good film adaptation of a William Faulkner novel, and the model for many a future southern race-issue film and television show (most prominently, *To Kill a Mockingbird* and television's *I'll Fly Away*). The nephew of a prominent local lawyer encounters an especially stubborn, elderly black man (played by Juano Hernandez, an overnight Hollywood favorite for black male roles after his film debut here), who at first is disliked by the boy, then gains respect from him when Hernandez rescues him from an icy river. Hernandez's character, then arrested on trumped-up charges, is the truly powerless one, and David Brian plays the uncle/lawyer who defends him. The one-on-one quality of the film somewhat separates the theme from any critique of a system of racism, but in the finale an incipient redneck uprising is quelled by the good white people of the town (notably led by Elizabeth Patterson as an ultra-dignified, elderly southern lady), reinstating some kind of decency against racist disorder. Bosley Crowther praised the film to the skies, calling it "probably this year's pre-eminent picture and one of the great cinema dramas of our times."[43] Ralph Ellison famously dubbed it the only black-connected film that could be seen without a black audience to correct mistaken white impressions.[44] *Intruder* did not receive a single Oscar nomination, however; Hollywood liberalism was still way behind the keenest critics.

Pinky had the biggest backing and the best chance for box office gold.

Zanuck's baby (for which he picked two frequent liberal allies of the Screen Writers Guild's Left, first hiring and then firing Dudley Nichols, finishing up with Philip Dunne) and Kazan's stepchild, it was intended to raise many issues of interracial love without resolving them. Adapted from a novel by Cid Ricketts Sumner, *Pinky* offered the definitely contemporary story of a light-skinned young lady (Jeanne Crain) returning to the south from a northern nursing education. We learn in a flashback that her fiancé (who does not at first suspect her racial identity, but then insists that it makes "no difference') sees her return as a mere interlude before a "normal" life elsewhere, an idea that she shares. But she finds her aged mother, predictably if also well played by Ethel Waters, is impoverished and ill in her tiny ghetto shack.

Pinky vows to stay only long enough to see her mother through to the end, and in the process she is vividly reminded of the insults, dangers (like threatened sexual assault), and all-around humiliation that southern blacks face on a daily basis. Filling in for her mother's servant job with an aged heiress (Ethel Barrymore) at a "big house," she inherits the mansion from another of the screen's Good Southern Ladies. She renounces her chance for personal happiness via escape from blackness (and the south), instead determined to establish a clinic and nursery school, with the help of a kindly local doctor, to service the African-American community.

Some liberal reviewers glimpsed, amidst flattering comments, an implied paternalism (right at "the picture's core," Crowther complained).[45] The first writer called into the studio to be hired for the prospective script happened to be Carlton Moss, a rare African-American behind the camera and very likely the only black Communist in Hollywood.[46] Moss had a stronger and more searing view of *Pinky*. The romantic problem of the film as explained to him by Kazan and Zanuck was to show *why* a relationship between a white man and a woman of color would be bound for tragedy. To Moss, this was a completely unacceptable premise. Pointedly illegal under the miscegenation laws in California and the entire south, interracial liaisons flourished in practice, by the later 1940s, as never before. The film's logic, as Moss observed after leaving the project, actually carried race relations backward by denying the possibilities already lived by millions of determined Americans.[47] Dudley Nichols, according to his biographer, struggled to work within the limiting premise to keep the racial dimension sharp-edged, so that the film would not fall back into a mere love story with a "social service" conclusion. Zanuck and perhaps Kazan as well had never seriously considered anything else.[48]

In truth, it was easier to write sympathetic films about Chicanos or Indians. No doubt the distancing regionalism and local color lent a comfort that African-American themes could not so easily allow contemporary movie audiences. Then again, censorship remained a real force: The Breen Office was quicker to note possible affronts to the southern (meaning, of course, white southern) film audience than to any other object of potential racial controversy. At any rate, coming years after *Robin Hood of El Dorado* (about Joaquín Murieta), and several half-serious treatments of Zapata and the Mexican Revolution (none by left-wingers) during the 1930s, the satirical *A Medal for Benny,* released back in 1944 and directed by Irving Pichel, signaled a new era in treating racism against Chicanos.[49] Taken from a short story by John Steinbeck, this home-front feature captures the hypocrisy of an ag-biz township in rural California where Mexicans do the hard labor and chamber of commerce types recognize their presence as little as possible. The town fathers find themselves embarrassed almost beyond endurance when it turns out that a dead Chicano lad was a major war hero in the Pacific and will be remembered by a grand military ceremony on his home grounds. Screenwriter Frank Butler, by wartime a great enthusiast of the Russians, almost certainly had an assist from his son, Communist screenwriter Hugo Butler. But the best of the film is a Twainesque commentary on businessmen unable to squeeze modern California into their preset images. Strictly minor drama-and-comedy fare, *A Medal for Benny* got nominations for three Academy Awards.[50]

By 1950, Joseph Losey could direct *The Lawless,* a film as starkly naturalistic as any Chicano-themed film made in Hollywood could be for decades into the future. Like so many other daring films, it was a B-level independent, this time by the "Dollar Bills," William Pine and William Thomas, of Pine-Thomas Productions, hitherto known for low-budget, near-exploitation features.[51] Reflecting the climate of postwar racial conflict, it was filmed on location in California, in Grass Valley and Marysville, and was shot in just over twenty days, with Anglo townspeople happily throwing rocks and overturning cars, as directed. *The Lawless* suffered from the producers' cost-cutting interference as well as from the personal intervention of Breen, who complained that the depicted "willingness" of whites to persecute Chicanos and the successful manipulations of the sensation-mongering press together constituted "a very great disservice to this country of ours, and to its institutions and its ideals." [52] The film's key themes and some of its vivid footage nevertheless survived.

As *The Lawless* opens, two Chicano fruit pickers decline to work overtime on a Saturday, and as a supervisor taunts them, an embittered ex-GI (played by Maurice Jara) turns to fight but is held back by his pal (played by Lalo Rios, a "discovery" of Losey's from the Chicano theater circuit). They drive off in Jara's jalopy but run a stop sign and hit a car driven by two Anglos their own age. Racist phrases lead to fisticuffs. Soon we see the parallel worlds of teenagers, the Chicano shack versus the American middle-class lifestyle; the dichotomy is echoed in the town's two newspapers, the Spanish-language weekly and the Anglo daily. A social-minded Chicana works at the former, and a new owner is publishing the latter. Inevitably, a romantic tension brings the full social circumstances to light. Over the course of the film, actress Gail Russell (her face evidently darkened for the part) will convince MacDonald Carey to become a crusading liberal journalist, despite his reluctance to entertain controversy of any kind.

A nearly hidden historical reference gives us a strong political clue that the audience probably missed. Carey was a noted antifascist (i.e., Popular Front) journalist, while Russell was an educated youngster with a liberal father who, years back, subscribed to certain publications in which the writer's work appeared. Carey has been defeated somewhere along the line—we don't have to ask where or how—so badly that he only wants to live a small-town life. She calls him back to the colors on the postwar issue most important to the American Left: the struggle against racism.

A brawl erupts at a dance in the run-down Chicano neighborhood, an event that the area tabloid melodramatically reports on its front page as "Fruit Tramps Riot." Rios flees the dance after inadvertently slugging a cop who grabbed for him and sets out on a series of misadventures, including multiple car theft, a terrible beating at the hand of a vicious cop (derided by other police for his crude behavior), and finally an incident in a barn with a teenage farm girl who accidentally hits her head and tells police that she has been assaulted. Now all hell breaks loose in redneck land as Carey finds the boy and, after final equivocation, prints the truth. The crowd wants blood, but eventually settles for tearing apart his newspaper office, beating Rios and Russell. Sickened by the whole thing, Carey decides to leave town. But after Rios tells him that in his eyes he looks like the Chicano sibling who died in the Battle of Normandy(!), he determines to stay, with his new sweetheart, and publish a liberal weekly. Almost all was foretold in the didactic introductory message across the screen as the film opened: "This is the story of a town and some of its people, who, in the grip of blind anger forget their American heritage of tolerance and decency, and become the lawless."

The film premiered in San Antonio and received warm press reviews. But Paramount boss Y. Frank Freeman swiftly pulled it from distribution. *The Lawless* got still better notices in the UK (where it appeared as *The Dividing Line*), accurately forecasting Losey's future career there. Looking back from 1957—when he had still not made his best-remembered features—he called it the "closest to the kind of film I'd have chosen to make," chosen, that is, if Hollywood had remained his artistic home.[53]

Suspiciously controversial when close to home, Mexicans, like Cubans, could be pleasantly picturesque at a distance, as illustrated best by *Fiesta* (1947), an Esther Williams musical coscripted by Lester Cole and described in *Variety* as a "Technicolor trailer for Mexican-American good will." Ordinarily, as in the Lees-Rinaldo script for the comedy *Holiday in Havana* (1949), a cheerful solution to any dilemma was eventually reached because a returning native, home from a U.S. education, could romance pale-skinned Latin Americans without raising any racial hackles. Action plots of bullfighting or conga drum contests, spirited women (in *Fiesta,* one actually fights the bulls for her musical-minded brother, putting off her wedding day; in *Holiday in Havana,* another asserts her right to become a Cuban carnival singer) just barely keep the story lines going outside of the songs and dancing.

But as prospective blacklistees looked south for their own relocation, the treatment of Mexican culture managed a bit more realism. *The Brave Bulls* (1951), scripted as John Bright's own farewell to Hollywood, was a semidocumentary pro-bullfighting picture directed by Rossen with Mel Ferrer in the starring role and Anthony Quinn, in one of the films where he Third Worldishly played his own real-life Mexican-American identity. *The Brave Bulls* was, at the very least, a dignified production, and it got respectable notices.[54]

Despite the best intentions of the Reds and their allies, Hollywood hadn't come very far with nonwhite leads up to 1950. But the liberal themes of race were to become swiftly more important in the near future. While American diplomats struggled to maintain the sympathy of leaders and critics within the "underdeveloped" world of nonwhites—many still fighting against the vestiges of colonialism—Hollywood sought to identify the brave, self-directed, but ultimately patriotic African-American. In Sidney Poitier (considerably more militant than the parts provided for him) they found their perfect protagonist. At the same time, they needed to balance an increasingly tempered racial paternalism and even egalitarianism with the need for social controls over restless natives, whether in Africa, the Pacific, the Caribbean, or Harlem.[55]

The woman's film had a richer and more complex history, as we have seen. The bored housewife in search of romance, the career woman wanting love, and even the temptress were rarely depicted with the one-dimensionality of the masochistic sacrificer for husband and children, a cinematic fact that often made the morally doubtful roles more interesting—except perhaps when the morally pure woman challenged male public prerogatives. Wartime conditions (even *She's a Soldier Too* was a trick title; lead Beulah Bondi was only a cabdriver) with women working and teen girls showing early signs of generational restlessness should have offered more dimensions, but home-front films were normally escapist in the true sense of musical entertainments with thin plots.[56]

To this generalization, *Tender Comrade,* as we have seen, offered a remarkable if limited exception. In the film's best scene—save for the factory collective of Riveter Rosies deciding to live together and share their worldly goods—Ginger Rogers struggles to explain to an uncomprehending Robert Ryan that women want something beyond a husband, home, and children. One of Trumbo's best pieces of writing, directed none too expertly by Dmytryk (in one of his first A films), it survives the schlock of the film's remainder, the news of Ryan's battlefield death and the consolation for Rogers of a baby to love and to teach the lessons of sacrifice for democracy.

The angst of the postwar era not only brought a conservative and psychoanalytic onslaught against women's advance from the home, but simultaneously placed the "woman question" (in familiar Left parlance) higher on the left-wing agenda. Los Angeles boasted a powerfully Hollywood-connected Congress of American Women (CAW) branch, led from the rank and file by a young Gerda Lerner. Part of the Women's International Democratic Federation (WIDF), an alliance of some 80 million affiliated women in over forty countries, with prominent women anthropologists, African-American writers, and aged suffrage veterans of note along with actresses, the Congress might easily have become an important political body, with Hollywood as a focal point of publicity. Instead, it was destroyed by Cold War pressures.[57] *New Masses* and other organs meanwhile regularly complained about the inadequacy of gender filmic treatments, seeking a positive and straightforward message that was only possible after the women's liberation movement had made waves through the media. Hollywood's radicals working against the formulae managed some powerful if contradictory message films.

A few of the best known could be characterized as stories about the power of women to act as wickedly as men. This strategy had been pioneered by noir and the crime film, but fresh efforts located the female figure in more historical terms, drawing on popular current novels or older materials. *Forever Amber* (1947), coscripted by Ring Lardner, Jr., and Philip Dunne from a Kathleen Winsor novel, presented Linda Darnell as a lowborn wench not quite as amoral and ruthless as Becky Sharp, but with the same personal strategy. Betrothed to a farmer in the age of Cromwell, she is romantically drawn to a soldier-turned-privateer. Scheming for her own rise, she is sent to prison, breaks out to join a gang, marries an elderly lord, acquires assorted lovers, including a king, but ends up with only the consolation of sending her son off to sea with her first amour, his father. Lardner later said the film was interesting part of the way through but too often gutted of meaning by Breen and Dunne (assigned to clean up the script of any and all questionable areas). Still, despite the censorship and some less-than-convincing scenes by Darnell, the character had the life of a modern woman, unconquered by the odds.[58]

Another Part of the Forest (1948), prequel to *The Little Foxes* and, like it, a treatment of the meanness that racist and exploitative southern life forces upon its (white) inhabitants and above all its women, had also proven itself on Broadway. It was shot for Universal-International back-to-back with another film bearing strong left-wing connections, *An Act of Murder* (1948), and even shared some of the cast. The latter featured a plea for the understanding of euthanasia, and sympathetic hints to the earlier "radical" career of a lawyer gone sour, played by Fredric March. Michael Gordon, one of the final blacklistees to turn friendly witness, directed the two films almost simultaneously. *An Act of Murder* was coscripted by WPA Federal Theater veteran Michael Blankfort; *Another Part of the Forest* found its screenwriter in Vladimir Pozner, a Russian émigré who later returned to Europe, and was disfigured in Paris by a right-wing terrorist's bomb.[59]

It could be rightly argued that these films and multiple others at the B level never really abandoned the basic masochism of the woman's film, especially when sex reared its tempting head.[60] But a few of the more remarkable films had women proudly challenging the accepted limits of their social status. *The Girl in White* (1952), an overly earnest drama written by Philip Stevenson and directed by John Sturges, recounted the real-life saga of Emily Dunning, the first woman to work as a doctor in a Manhattan public hospital. June Allyson was predictable in this turn-of-the-century melodrama, yet the telling was emphatic: It was made at a moment when real American women were rushing into the lowest levels of white-collar jobs, becoming nurses and secretaries instead of doctors. As unlikely a professional woman as Lana Turner revealed determination in *A Life of Her Own* (1950), albeit as a model, in a feature written by Isobel Lennart and directed by George Cukor.[61] Too many, like *The Lady Takes a Sailor* (1949), showed women strong in the first reel, then undergoing assorted comic trials and finally accepting their status as happy brides and prospective mothers. Still, here and there a real gem emerged.

Life With Father (1947), a modest triumph for Donald Ogden Stewart, was an especially keen adaptation of a hit Broadway play based upon a *New Yorker* series of remembrances about upper-crust family life in the gaslight era. Businessman Clarence Day (played by William Powell, in what he later declared to be his best film role) played Father, who firmly believes that he is in charge (and is allowed, in formal terms, to continue believing it) but who yields in every case to the prerogatives of wife and sons. Irene Dunne, as benignly conspiring Mother, is really in charge as the boys head into adolesence and maturity.[62]

Stewart had a more subversive gender effort just ahead, the last film (as he recalled) that he would be allowed to make in Hollywood. Assigned one of Sinclair Lewis's lesser works, *Cass Timberlane,* and finding it hopelessly dull as film material, he transformed it from a personal melodrama between a middle-aged respectable judge in a small commercial town and his young wife into a class-society drama between the town's respectables and the others. Between social evenings with Chaplin, Hepburn, Bertolt

Brecht, and others, Stewart turned out a combination genre script at once highlighting country club snootiness, marital restlessness (even adultery), and the inevitable Hollywood windup. Lana Turner was scarcely adequate for her part, but it was her best opportunity since *They Won't Forget* to be something more than a desired sexual partner.[63]

For better and mostly for worse, other important left-wing films about women fell into the familiar victim category, if now improved by clearer social contextualization. The first film made about (and on the set of) Las Vegas, *The Lady Gambles,* written by Roy Huggins, a future friendly witness of later *77 Sunset Strip, The Fugitive,* and *The Rockford Files* fame, found an emotionally troubled Susan Hayward unable to resist the lure of the game. Better yet, *Smash-up* (1947), an alcoholism script by John Howard Lawson, from an original story by Dorothy Parker (who ought to have known the subject well) and Frank Cavett, and produced by Walter Wanger. It was a well-rehearsed female version of *The Long Weekend,* with Hayward as a singer who drops her own career to marry a rising crooner and have a baby. Soon lonely and bored, she loses herself in alcoholism. Her self-hatred, jealousy, and plainly alcoholic behavior are obvious, even if the conclusion (she rushes into her home, set on fire by one of her cigarette butts, rescues her baby, and instantly reforms) pushed melodrama to the extreme. Still, Hayward got an Oscar nomination. *Smash-up,* like other films with desperate women realistically portrayed, had real trouble getting past Breen, but survived with some effect.

The least remembered films were often more lively ones—films like *Calamity Jane and Sam Bass* (1949), where women took on tomboy or mannish roles; or films where they acted and sang over the top, like Maureen O'Hara as a thoroughly improbable, British-raised Bedouin princess and nationalist-revolutionary singer-leader in the exceptionally silly but delightful *Bagdad* (1949), based on a story by Tamara Hovey.[64] Or again, they could be small-scale experiments in uncomfortable themes, like *Not Wanted* (1948), about illegitimate birth and an impoverished immigrant mother, actually written by Paul Jarrico and coproduced by Ida Lupino in her first, exceedingly low-budget outing. Such daring starts were practically abandoned in the Hollywood era ahead, when busty Jane Russell, a grown Elizabeth Taylor, and Doris Day played strictly for laughs or overwrought melodrama, and talented actresses usually found more serious parts in television drama.

I Can Get It for You Wholesale (1951), written by Abraham Polonsky and directed by Michael Gordon, was in any case the premier achievement of the contemporary woman's film. Based upon a nearly anti-Semitic novel that the screenwriter basically discarded, it explored the life of a hardworking female executive in the ferociously competitive garment district. Susan Hayward is the businesswoman who confronts Dan Dailey, her would-be fiancé but also her best salesman, with her determination not to be subjected to the double standard in business or sex, and Sam Jaffe plays her cryptically socialistic elder employee who lays out the humane principles that are more important than commercial success. The ending had to be softened for the sake of Hollywood romance. But the rest of the film was unstinting in showing what the next generations of women would need to know about their emotional as well as their legal rights, the stresses of playing in the big time where men's rules yield unwillingly, if at all.[65]

One could ask also if subsequent writers would make such good use of the male protagonists who lean toward the temptation of less-than-solidly married women, like Robert Mitchum in *Rachel and the Stranger* (1948) or *The Lusty Men* (1952). Perfect as the semi-repentant loner destined to remain on the outside, Mitchum outlived his era without ever outliving his role.[66]

In the best passages of his ham-fisted *Film in the Battle of Ideas,* John Howard Lawson assessed the roles offered to women as either the criminal, femme fatale or both; the man-hater who must be made to learn better; or the primitive child, a male's dream of submission. None of these roles offered female actors the scope of their own subjectivity, and even those that revealed a capacity for choice in love finally ended in the voluntary acceptance of submission as the price of fulfillment.[67]

Social Fantasia

The second half of the 1940s, as widely noted, saw a veritable explosion of supernatural themes, from cloying angels to helpful ghosts, scoring some of the decade's biggest hits. Communist film critics, especially as the era closed, bitterly and perhaps understandably concluded that the old bogey "escapism," due for a vivid revival, was Hollywood's reactionary answer to the grim political situation of the emerging Cold War. But as with the upsweep of supernatural themes following the Civil War, whose massive casualties prompted supernatural best-sellers and buoyed a spiritualist movement briefly threatening to become a major religious denomination, the 1940s response to mass death had an authentic mass appeal. Like the distinctly socialist wings of spiritualism in generations past, the radical pursuers of fantasy usually had something different to offer from the standard Judeo-Christian reaffirmation of the social order.

Here Comes Mr. Jordan (1941) was upbeat, an ingeniously comic ghost-story successor to the Topper literary and cinematic escapades. It was also a multiple Academy Award winner (Best Original Story and Screenplay, plus nominations for Best Picture, Best Actor, and Best Supporting Actor) for coscripter Sidney Buchman and others. A boxer and amateur flier accidentally snuffed out ahead of his time inherits the body of a millionaire playboy and parries with a conflicted angel (Edward Everett Horton). The complications, romantic and otherwise, delighted audiences so much that left-wing writers working on wartime and postwar themes might well have continued along these fundamentally cheerful supernatural lines. Aside from certain Abbott and Costello features, they didn't.

Happy Land (1943), produced by Kenneth MacGowan and directed by Irving Pichel for Fox, was a home-front set piece. An Iowa community is hit by the news that one of their boys, the son of a beloved pharmacist, played by Don Ameche, has been killed in action. An embittered Ameche declares that his would-be heir, unmarried and childless, has died for nothing. Then the spirit of Gramp (Harry Carey) intervenes to lead Ameche down the long memory road from his own hero's return in 1919, through courtship, marriage, and child rearing. Meanwhile, Ameche "adopts" a war buddy saved by his son's life-saving last act, and reconciles himself to the loss. The themes of memory, and whether a life was wasted or well spent, were wartime favorites but also typical of Pichel and, in his hands, plainly weird.

As the glare of the Hollywood 19 (the unfriendly witnesses of 1947) publicity intensified upon him, Pichel directed one of the strangest of the many strange postwar films. *The Miracle of the Bells* (1947), scripted by Ben Hecht, turned the novel by Russell Janey upside down (prompting some amusement and irritation among contemporary reviewers) to create the epic of a Pennsylvania coal patch whose impoverished and suffering inhabitants have produced a symbolic redeemer in a would-be screen actress (played by Alida Valli) determined to play Joan of Arc on camera.[68] The story begins after her death, i.e., her sacrifice for them. Press agent Fred MacMurray, the narrator of the film, recalls how he fell in love with her as he encouraged the former burlesque dancer to take over the Joan part when the assigned star takes a powder. Valli, unbeknownst to him, is actually dying of the endemic miner's disease, lung failure, but necessarily lasts just long enough to finish the picture, which the producer (an exceptionally sly Lee J. Cobb) then decides to shelve as a certain loser. MacMurray tours her home district to execute a publicity stunt of having churches ring their bells for her memory, and his plan gets across when the little church manned by a people's priest (Frank Sinatra) has its angelic pillars actually turn toward her body during the funeral service.

The scientific explanation of mineshaft rumblings underground is at once rationally and spiritually convincing, the ghosts of a vanished proletariat claiming their own. As worshippers fill the streets in her memory and the building of a new hospital specializing in lung research is announced, the release of the Joan of Arc film becomes inevitable, uniting working-class strivings, religious sentiment, and Hollywood production. Unfortunately, the real movie, a multimillion-dollar production by Jesse L. Lasky Feature Play Company, was a bomb. The setting if not the theme was altogether too thirties, and not even an a cappella performance by then teen heartthrob Sinatra brought out the crowds.

Again, if not for Pichel's predilections for this kind of theme, *The Miracle of the Bells* could be written off as a mere failed commercial experiment. But even when turning out pure entertainment, the director clearly had something else on his mind. Thus, *Mr. Peabody and the Mermaid* (1948) took fantasy in a new direction with Nunnally Johnson's adaptation of a novel drawn teasingly between eros and nostalgia. Far away on a Caribbean island, a duffer at the cusp of middle age, at fifty (William Powell, in what he described as his all-time favorite role), innocently adopts a beautiful if nonspeaking mermaid who adores him and even agrees for his sake to wear a bathing suit! His wife is understandably discomfited, but back at home he consults a kindly psychologist who explains carefully that middle-aged men (and women, too) have *precisely* these kinds of fantastic visions. The standard critics were mildly amused; the *New Masses* sniped at the film as yet one more product of Hollywood escapism. But what kind of escapism did Pichel have in mind when his next picture, *The Great Rupert* (1950), featured a trained squirrel that "discovers" hoarded money and awards it to a needy vaudevillian played by Jimmy Durante?[69] Perhaps it was only studio work, the best that the journeyman director could get by this time. But perhaps not. In one of his last published essays, Pichel suggested that the true "function of dramatic fiction" must be to "present the conflict between human desires and the curbs to their fulfillment," exploring experimentation on behalf of desire. He complained against the failure of all screen commentators (and he obviously meant left-wingers as well as others) who had not "declared clearly the function we ask of the screen and screen entertainment to fulfill," suggesting

> We totter along a wavering line between objective realism and sententious maxim . . . We do not know whether we wish to show the world the America we live in or the America we dream about. We do not know whether our business is with wish-fulfillment or wish-denial. We do not know whether we are purveying escape from life into dreams or escape from limited lives into the expansion of life through vicarious experience.[70]

Pichel had worked steadily since early sound films in a world where the only corporate purpose was moneymaking. But it was still possible, in the later 1940s, to imagine something different, to explore coherent alternatives beyond anything that the Left had so far articulated. He thus urged a "new Aristotle"—obviously a collective Aristotle this time—to meet the pressure for censorship with positive and constructive visions, for only then might the confusion between the story's function as truth-telling and didacticism be resolved, combining realism with an artistic inventiveness surpassing realism without abandoning it.[71]

It was too late for this to happen in a more than personal way. But Pichel turned his studied, final attention to spiritual themes. *Day of Triumph* (1953) returned to biblical times to draw out the quixotic struggle of the Zodakite sect, those early Christians who tried to turn the religious moment into a communitarian revolution and were crushed, their very memory suppressed by the Church. *Martin Luther* (1953), Pichel's last major film—sponsored by the Lutheran church and distributed largely in religious circles—recast the great rebel as society's conscience against the

Inquisition-like (or HUAC-like) trial by papal agents. It quietly put aside Luther's real-life firm attachment to the wealthy classes and his urgings for them to suppress the restless and communitarian-minded masses as ruthlessly as necessary. In that sense, *Martin Luther* was a final artistic compromise in a life of careful compromises but also strange directorial efforts, many of them as out of place in Hollywood as Edgar Ulmer's independent cheapies. But it was also a monument to Pichel's highly personal cinematic vision.

Leonardo Bercovici had something distinctly different in mind, less spiritual, more psychoanalytic. Bercovici later admitted having introduced into the original story of *The Bishop's Wife* (1947) a seemingly risky, quasi-romantic attraction between Loretta Young as the woman of the title and angel Cary Grant, who has come down to enliven the efforts of her pious but soul-weary husband to build a new church. An angel with erotic leanings? In fact, as later feminists enjoyed pointing out, Grant is everything that an earthly female could want, a witty companion eager to toss a football to sonny or talk seriously with a daughter, while David Niven as the bishop must slowly learn to humanize himself outside his clerical routine.[72] It was one of the biggest money-winners of the year.

Bercovici's next important project, *Portrait of Jennie* (for which he received an "adaptation" credit that he considered entirely inadequate), is suffused with a fantastic nostalgia. This time, Manhattan portrait painter Joseph Cotten is on the verge of suicide when he's pulled back by a strange girl dressed in the apparel of earlier generations. That she is innocently childlike, though a child who apparently grows up by years every few times he sees her in Central Park, marks her as an appealingly vulnerable apparition. But apparition she is, more so in the green tinting of the last reel and the Technicolor of the final scene when she has to die. One can easily imagine that, like Mr. Peabody's mermaid, she is never more than the artist's fantasy of the unrealizable, a crutch against the fearful emptiness that is the real spirit of the postwar age.[73]

Ex-Marxist Albert Lewin, formerly Irving Thalberg's personal assistant and then writer-director of six of his own films, carried these themes further with explicit references to surrealism. The supernatural *The Picture of Dorian Gray* (1945), the Catholic Legion of Decency–condemned *The Private Affairs of Bel Ami* (1947), and, above all, *Pandora and the Flying*

Dutchman (1951) create universes more out of control than Marxists had allowed themselves, since at least the abandonment of the horror field proper way back in the 1930s.[74] *Pandora,* with James Mason as the ship's captain condemned to wander through eternity until he finds a woman willing to die for him, moves through two hours of absolute strangeness to a forceful rejection of apparent reality for some inner meaning connected simultaneously with eros and doom. Intimately close to Hollywood's Marxists, yet unwilling or unable to be part of their struggle or to make his way independently as an avant-gardist, Lewin rose and fell with their era—like so many others more successful but fatally bound to the film styles that the Depression, the war, and the Left had done so much to create.

Family Films

It should not be surprising that children's epics and films about children offered a first glimpse of the problems at hand or that left-wing writers should be so good at them. The delicate humanism required for noncondescending treatments of children's pleasures and thoughts had never been far from circus-style slapstick comedy, the depiction of misunderstood creatures (semihuman monsters, potential pets, or free-spirited beasts of the field), and the proud accomplishments of the heroic child.

Our Vines Have Tender Grapes (1945) offered, as we have seen in Chapter 5, a wider vision, a whole American world in miniature, captured in small-town turn-of-the-century Wisconsin. Here, individual striving versus community sentiment could be measured. But Walt Disney's *So Dear to My Heart* (1949), set in Indiana during a similar era, might do nearly as well. The semi-animated musical whose memorable rendition of "Lavender Blue" (the Dilly Dilly song) by then Popular Front folksinger Burl Ives was perhaps its emotional high point, touching sentimental chords in all but the crustiest viewers.[75]

Despite his conservatism and paternalism, despite his proud membership in the Motion Picture Alliance for the Protection of American Ideals, and even despite his eventual role in the blacklisting, Walt Disney could relish making a film like this. Left-wing veterans of Disney Studios have often looked back sentimentally upon their days with the larger-than-life innovator who was surely a megalomaniac but shared none of the cynicism of his fellow moguls.[76] More than a few Communists saw in him, despite his formal politics and resistance to unionism, the implied promise of a different kind of cinema, though it proved a promise unfulfilled.

Maurice Rapf had tried harder to capture bits of the national epoch in a catastrophic (from his standpoint) production of Disney's *Song of the South* (1946). The screenwriter later recalled how even the best intentions could go badly awry. "Uncle Walt" had personally pleaded with him to work on *Song,* promising to make a unique, semi-animated, antiracist film about black southerners and white southerners if only Rapf would provide a preliminary script: "You're against Uncle Tomism and you're a radical. That's exactly the kind of point of view I want brought to this film."[77]

Rapf worked faithfully from the premise that the "Uncle Remus" stories of the antebellum south about a wily rabbit outwitting more powerful animals were, in fact, part of the "Papa Legba" African diaspora folklore hinting at slave resistance. The results might just have been, with a little effort and luck, a stunning and subtly political film of enduring value. Perhaps responding to the growing climate of conservatism—or perhaps merely carrying through on a deceitful intention—Disney double-crossed Rapf, giving the white folks a mansion and turning Uncle Remus into a kindly savant for white kids who reveled in the innocent joys of happy-go-lucky black culture. Still, brilliant animation as well as a deep love for the characters marked the film. As one of the credited screenwriters, Rapf sympathized with picket lines organized by the NAACP and left-wingers around theaters showing the film, providing still one more embittering experience for the rightward-moving Disney.[78] More than a half century later, aficionados could get their hands on *Song of the South* only by ordering a videodisc from Japan; the Walt Disney Company remained too embarrassed to reissue it, after a mercifully brief revival during the 1960s.[79]

Outside the noirs, the overtly (and perhaps overly) political climax of 1940s Left film was another family movie. *The Boy with Green Hair* (1948), directed by Joseph Losey in his biggest-budget outing to date, was produced by Adrian Scott and scripted by Ben Barzman and Alfred Lewis Levitt: a powerful team whose members would never be reassembled. The most forceful antiwar film made at the historic moment when "peace" was defined as a Communist cry to disarm a threatened America, it very nearly didn't get made at all. Dore Schary, still close to the Left, had encouraged Scott, but in midproduction Howard Hughes took over RKO. Hughes determined to reverse its message into a Cold War warning of "preparedness" for the next global conflict. Before production finished, Scott was thrown off the set. But happily, new producer Stephen Ames quietly saw the film through, convincing Hughes along the way that the film had been altered even though nothing essential had been changed.

Not treated too kindly even by sympathetic critics, the film telegraphed its punches in triplicate from the first moments onward. The device of a boy (the inevitable war orphan, this time played ably by Dean Stockwell) who gains insight into distrust and other worldly maladies when his hair suddenly turns green was clearly fantasy. And yet at moments, the film has great power. Stockwell's guardian, kindly old Pat O'Brien—in real life a political conservative, but one serious about drama, especially Irish drama—at once sees that he must assist the boy in standing up against authority figures who treat him as a freak who might prove dangerous in a world where control is all-important.

Little Stockwell meanwhile stumbles across grown-ups talking casually about the inevitability of another world war (although no probable enemy is named) and the necessity for more and more weapons. In a dreamlike sequence, he comes upon child refugee survivors of the last war who appeal to him to spread the message that peace is still possible. This all might fall flat if the magnetism between O'Brien and Stockwell were not so convincing; instead, it succeeds as a fractured but viable message. As screenwriter Levitt recalled, what suffered in the attempts to placate or lull Hughes was "not the content but the aesthetics," leaving the picture considerably uneven.[80]

Another failed effort suggests that the Left had only begun to tinker with form. Talented comic screenwriter Henry Myers, in his final film effort, joined with lyricist-writer Edward Eliscu and several animation veterans from Disney picket lines to create an *Alice in Wonderland* "puppettoon" with then-famed puppeteer Lou Bunin. The film was doomed despite the eagerness of the postwar, leftish French government to assist shooting in Paris, for the simple reason that Disney suddenly restarted his own apparently abandoned or hopelessly delayed version of *Alice,* putting the two features head-to-head in release. The left-wing version's Manhattan premiere in 1951 came but two days before the much ballyhooed Disney version, its animation technically perfect and featuring voices like Ed Wynn's and Jerry Collonna's for flair—an unmercifully one-sided competition.

The previous Hollywood *Alice in Wonderland* dated to 1933 and offered a sort of Hollywood who's who in various cameo voice roles, from Gary Cooper to W. C. Fields. The Bunin version was saddled with a live-action Alice, who was, at nineteen, too pubescent by far for the part, thanks to legal complications of bringing a younger British girl to Paris. Furthermore, the film's semi-animated cutouts of various creatures, its motley color, and too many cheery (or cheesy) tunes were at best inconsistent in both technique and characterization.

And yet, unlike the Disney version that turned the carefully structured Lewis Carroll fantasy into a series of silly encounters with a tagged-on moral of good behavior, the Bunin version with its abundant faults stands as the most serious filmic effort to remain loyal to the intent of the fantasy writer's masterwork. The various characters don't look especially good, but they radiate a splendid Victorian craziness and a sometimes deft political edge—when not interrupted by one of Alice's songs. A monarchical tyrant, the Red Queen, in the absurdity of her power, really does want to cut off heads. Her minions, so like the Hollywood yes-men, would happily cut off Alice's to preserve their own standing. Compared with that, Disney's *Alice* was (as Eliscu put it with deadly accuracy) "like a picture about childhood with Shirley Temple."[81]

A spate of other family pictures included at least a few nuggets, most innovatively within sports features, a category admirably suited to the entertainment-crazed postwar years. John Bright penned *The Kid from Cleveland* (1949), which was produced and directed by Herbert Kline, the former editor of *New Theater and Film*.[82] The kid in question, played by Russ Tamblyn, is the orphaned son of a navy dad killed in the Pacific, headed for juvenile delinquency when a kindly sportscaster (played by George Brent) arranges for him to become the assistant batboy of one of the first racially integrated teams in baseball. In this rather murky and at times psychoanalytic tale, no opportunity is missed to put across the multicultural message: The immortal Satchel Paige and outfielder Larry Doby personally coach the boy, while the Native America pitcher Early Wynn has a walk-on. Hank Greenberg, for a decade the most famous Jewish baseball player, and Bill Veeck, the first important Jewish team owner, also figure prominently. The team even becomes his collective godfather until the complications get sorted out. On the ball field, through example of cooperation and mutual respect (not to mention stock footage from the 1949 World Series, one of the rare happy moments of the heavily working-class and ethnic, declining industrial city of Cleveland), the lad learns self-confidence. Lynn Bari as his mother finds solace, and reconciles herself to a replacement husband, the boy's stepfather.[83] This is a follow-up war story, in other words, with some of the familiar elements now strung out into children's themes.

Go, Man, Go! (aka *The Harlem Globetrotters,* 1951), written by one-shot left-wing screenwriter Al Palca and produced by Sidney Buchman, ventured into "race pride" territory for the story of a medical-student-turned-athlete and the famous black touring basketball team. Thomas Gomez as real-life coach Abe Saperstein watches over the players in a fatherly but highly respectful fashion, while the individualistic Bill Walker learns the need for teamwork the hard way, with help from wife Dorothy Dandridge. The plot was thin, the footage of famed Globetrotter court antics even more than the hard-driving ball play the real attraction of the picture, some of it too much in the minstrelsy-clown tradition for later tastes. But the best of these films, *Saturday's Hero* (1951), written by former Almanacs folksinger Millard Lampell, with cocredit to producer Sidney Buchman, offered a powerful critique of the corrupt system by which muscled boys are given scholarships, excused from classes, hailed as gridiron heroes—and see everything taken away when they become injured and useless for alumni purposes. Rather like other sports features, *Saturday's Hero* was just the sort of movie that a parent could take a child to, and be surprised by the truly educational message about sports as the mirror of American society. To shift the metaphor: As usual, left-wing ideas were coming in under the radar.[84]

Only a certain type of aficionado and hardly a cineaste would seek to recuperate *Bedtime for Bonzo* (1952), Val Burton's last screenplay (with collaborator Lou Breslow) before the blacklist struck him down. It was not so much the Disneyesque plot (actually foreshadowing two Disney films pseudonymously written by Al and Helen Levitt about a professor with a chimpanzee) with a prof trying to raise a chimp as human and meanwhile court a girl, which is memorable, but rather *Bonzo*'s star: Ronald Reagan.[85]

The Western Revisited

It's most ironic that the socially critical Western would occupy both the topmost and the bottom drawer of the left-wing film. Cowboy screenwriter Julian Zimet, admitting that the narrative framework of Westerns left little room for realism and narrowed film's social meaning to the salvational powers of the lone cowboy, nevertheless pointed out to fellow screenwriters that this genre (at the time including slightly over 50 percent of all films produced) also showed that "right is more frequently on the side of the poor than on the rich," and that "the history of our country has been largely a struggle by little people for their rights against great interests."[86] Screenwriter Louise Rousseau, perhaps the only open lesbian screenwriter at work in Hollywood, testified to the Committee that the Westerns offered a rare opportunity to present historically accurate bits of American history—an opportunity that, she noted bitterly, was about to be taken away from her.[87]

The rightward shift of John Ford from *The Grapes of Wrath* and *The Informer* to *Fort Apache* might well be taken as the dominant note of the day. Marguerite Roberts, assigned to script *Ambush* for militantly right-wing director Sam Wood, recalled the impossibility of altering its anti-Indian orientation. *Last Outpost* (1951), scripted by a near-future friendly witness David Lang, even featured Confederate and Union Army brothers, divided by the war, reunited in fighting the common enemy: the Red Man's threat to white civilization. (It was also Ronald Reagan's first Western starring role, as one of the reconciled brothers.)

But the "conscience Western" also already had a certain aura, and not apparently for liberal audiences only. Until the ax fell and even afterward, a subordinate trend could be detected in the search for the "good" Indian and in the critique of corruption, cruelty, and even (as time went on) ecological degradation that accompanied Western development. The anti-Western lay in the future, with an abundance of socially critical films—a handful by former blacklistees or the occasional erstwhile friendly witness—suggesting what presumably might have been done earlier sans the blacklist.

Of the many smaller but artistically successful Westerns written on the Left, *Roughshod* (1949) displayed its progressive wares with suitable modesty. Coscripter Hugo Butler, working from a story by Peter Viertel and under the directorship of progressive Mark Robson, helped fashion a gendered drama of "bad" women who prove themselves "good" enough for the hardiest of men.[88] Four saloon girls (i.e., borderline prostitutes) driven from town by bluenose "reformers" gain assistance from a handsome would-be rancher (Robert Sterling) en route to his own spread, and his preadolescent brother (Claude Jarman, Jr.). Favorite noir femme fatale Gloria Grahame plays the liveliest of the dames, and as one after another of them takes the hand of a cowboy (or returns home to aggrieved parents), she leans toward Sterling, though he cannot yet accept her past. Eventually, through her heroism, she shows Sterling that her past should not be held against her. If this were a mark for recovered purity through abnegation and tearful pleas for forgiveness, the moral of the story would not be even mildly radical, but Grahame's character neither wants nor begs for this kind of vindication. He will take her not at all, or on her terms—and he does. Perhaps anticipating saloon-keeper Kitty (the coming era's Western queen, Amanda Blake) in television's *Gunsmoke,* such full-bloodedness leaves the idealized women of the Breen Office far behind.

Broken Arrow (1950) and *Devil's Doorway* (1949) unmistakably trace the sources of American madness back to the imperial conquest of Indian territory. Of the two, *Broken Arrow* is the better known, not only for its success at the box office, since Jeff Chandler's Oscar for Best Supporting Actor and the film's Golden Globe Award for "Best Film Promoting International Understanding"[!] have made it a minor classic. It was, indeed, among the first films written partly under the blacklist. Michael Blankfort, later a friendly witness, lent his name for Albert Maltz's script, with Delmar Daves directing. Guy Trosper—named by FBI sources as a "CPL" (Communist Party Liner) and possible earlier Party member and who was, at the least, intimately close to a host of Hollywood left-wingers—scripted *Devil's Doorway* with the vastly better director Anthony Mann.

Mann created the more memorable images and more lasting authority even with the burden of the stolid Robert Taylor playing the lead, as an unidentified Indian who returns home after fighting for the Union in the Civil War and receiving a Congressional Medal of Honor for bravery in action. Unlike other Native Americans in the area, Taylor's family has almost completely assimilated. They have cut their hair short, raise cattle, and in every other noticeable way assert their identities as citizens of the republic rather than of the reservation system. Taylor even falls for a white woman, although the relationship ends. But in matters large and small, from being denied a drink in a saloon to fighting a swindler to retain ownership of ancestral lands, Taylor learns that he still has no civil rights, and like Jesse James of repeated Left treatment, he must go into open rebellion— without sympathetic white settlers or a narrative of heroic outlawry. His is, rather, the doomed rebellion of the excluded.

Specifically, *Devil's Doorway* insists that no opportunity for equality exists for Indians or anyone else in a society dominated by the representatives of Eastern corporations, Eastern law, and Eastern finance. When Taylor has been robbed of all choices except to fight back against the government he served, he takes up arms against his old comrades in the cavalry, using tactics he learned in the Civil War, wearing his battlefield uniform and even the Congressional Medal of Honor. At the end of the battle, he rides slowly toward the camera and is asked where the rest of the warriors are. "We are gone," he says, his lips already cold with death. He then pitches forward off his horse, out of camera range. It is such a stunning moment of American cinema, a *J'Accuse* of such power, that the Fox management remained understandably uncertain about releasing it, until *Broken Arrow* had proved a hit.

Devil's Doorway nevertheless remains a New Deal Western politically for the simple reason that it asks for Indians to be allowed into the system. *Broken Arrow* shifts the logic of the Western by insisting that not only should Indian culture be recognized as worth saving, but Indian sovereignty be established and respected. Here the excluded, with an admittedly large degree of sentimental bathos, are not trying to get in but are trying just as hopelessly to get *out*.

Jimmy Stewart plays a former cavalry scout in an Arizona frontier town of the 1870s seeking to open lines of communication with Cochise (Jeff Chandler, with Jay Silverheels, the future Tonto of television and a prominent Indian culture activist of note, as the young Geronimo), hidden away in the Chiricahua Mountains. Taking his life into his hands, Stewart enters Cochise's land as the lone white diplomat for peace, arguing that the chief should show his willingness to deal with whites by saving the United States mail from attack. In the meantime, Stewart wins the confidence of other Apaches in Cochise's band by saving the life of an Indian boy and by learning the language and customs of the tribe, then risks it all by wooing the shy maiden played by Debra Paget in redface. He also seeks to calm white townsfolk, led by an enraged Will Geer (who was almost immediately blacklisted after this role) and others seeking to string him up. Later, the rednecks break the peace by attacking Stewart and the Apache in a streambed.

Broken Arrow has come under attack in recent years for historical inaccuracy, along with a failure to use Indian actors (Paget was more convincing, a few years later, as Queen of the Nile—although perhaps not to Egyptian moviegoers). But it remains a strong and at times moving narrative.[89] Indeed, *Broken Arrow* can be compared only with *Dances with Wolves* in its effect upon viewing audiences; whatever its limits, it remains the only screen representation of the massacre of eighteen Arizona Apache men, women, and children at Aravaipa Creek in 1871 by whites from Tucson who wanted to keep the war going, in part because of the loss of federal subsidies following an earlier negotiated truce.

Dramatically and cinematically, the left-wing Western reached its apex in *High Noon,* screenwriter Carl Foreman's final contribution before departure from the United States and from screenwriting as a profession.[90] It stands in the foreground not merely of blacklist films but of the Western as a genre and American movies as a whole, one of the very few blacklist movies that has been studied carefully from many different ideological positions and one of the relative few from the Left that early generations of post-blacklist filmmakers borrowed from without embarrassment. There was little to add to the debate, however, particularly insofar as the dissident Western had been established as a critique of empire. On the other hand, the real critical content of *High Noon* has rarely been set down with any clarity.

The original of the aging sheriff torn " 'twixt love and dooty," as Tex Ritter helpfully explains in the film's title song, can be found in a *Collier's* short story.[91] The story's focus is not the existential quality of the stand that he takes, alone facing the return of criminals on the twelve o'clock train that he captured years earlier, but the final gunfight scene in which he triumphs against all the odds. When Foreman undertook to rewrite this simple story for the formidable team of producer Stanley Kramer and director Fred Zinnemann, the writer was at the peak of a career gained the hard way. After two Dead End Kids/Bowery Boys films and a stint in the U.S. Army

Signal Corps, Foreman wrote a comedy, *So This Is New York* (1947), produced by Stanley Kramer and based on a quality property: Ring Lardner, Sr.'s story "The Big Town," about a South Bend family that vacations in New York and becomes starstruck with Broadway and the racetrack.[92] The film went nowhere. But Kramer was the writer's meal ticket. Their association lasted through four of the more critically successful films of the postwar era—*Home of the Brave, Champion, The Men,* and *High Noon*—which were part of the wave of films enriching the content of American cinema, both as art and as mass communication, well beyond the ability for the old studios to control it. Indeed, three of these remain among the most influential films ever made in Hollywood.

Champion (1949) appeared at a key moment in the boxing genre, by now made familiar by *Golden Boy* and *Body and Soul:* Can a working-class lad succeed in the ring and still have the strength to resist the twin temptations of hubris and gang-style corruption? The problem was audience overfamiliarity and the consequent need for some new approach. Foreman formulated his response, according to film colony lore, in a most remarkable way. He insisted that, with the sympathetic encouragement of director Mark Robson and of Oscar-winning film editor Harry Gerstad, he had created the jumpcut, shunning the usual fades for a sudden advancement of the story. Had it been done in American films before? Perhaps, but not often or effectively. More important than precedent was the artistic premise that the American film audience was sophisticated enough to go with the innovation. In other words, the all-crucial mass filmgoer was coming of age, prepared for whatever the writer, director, actors, and technicians could dish out.[93]

The Kirk Douglas character of *Champion* boxed his way out of economic desperation, but in becoming a champ, turned cruel. Dumping his kindly wife for a chippy, he makes his crippled brother into a spokesman and apologist for his increasingly appalling behavior. Even in death he seems to command the loyalty of silence. Foreman was closing a door, one might say, on a time and opportunity that no longer existed, with the shocking naturalism of the shadows and canyons in the boxer's increasingly depraved face reflecting everyone's despair.

In *The Men* (1950), a story of war-maimed GIs fighting despair (again directed by Robson), Foreman took up the question: When is it worth even trying to go home? What is most striking about this film from the vantage point of fifty years later, apart from the acting of a young Marlon Brando in the part that made his career, is the extraordinary sense of detail. The uncontrollable shaking of the paralyzed Brando's leg on his wedding night and the look on the face of his bride (Teresa Wright) when she realizes what she has given up are, taken by themselves, well worth the price of admission.

Beyond the texture of *The Men,* the *fact* of the film counts more than anything. Many films had been made in their vein after the First World War, though none done with such frankness, and only *Coming Home* (1978, written by Waldo Salt, back from the blacklist and relying upon vets' own testimony), after Vietnam, imparted more medical information about the sexual implications of impaired spinal cords. Despite the plea for tolerance that is their public face, these films are covertly coded messages to the veterans themselves: Don't put up with everything they ask of you, and don't believe everything they tell you. If he had done nothing else but *The Men,* Foreman would be remembered among war veterans for all time; perhaps it was this realization that led him in exile years to put much of his remaining cinematic energy into inflated war epics. But his real triumph was, as of 1950, still to come.

When evicted from the set of *High Noon* (1952) by the producer's fear of HUAC, Foreman left behind a work claimed as the favorite movie of two presidents (Eisenhower and Clinton) and innumerable fans who regard it—with the possible exception of *Casablanca*—as the best American movie ever made. It is easy enough to guess why American presidents like the film so much. The man with the nuclear gun who thinks to himself that he often must do the hard thing, the unpopular thing, would also like to think of himself as spiritually resembling Gary Cooper. But the political story cuts a good deal deeper, and while Foreman developed some of the themes in other films before his masterpiece, in *High Noon* he made a decisive intervention into the evolving national narrative called the Western: his own critique of capitalist society.

Naturally, his technique combined indirection and disguise. Given the times, with coworkers and friends being hauled up in front of committees and thrown out of the artistic enterprise they had come to master just a few years earlier, it would have been a greater surprise if his technique had been more overt. But to measure just what kind of detail Foreman wove into his narrative to reveal its larger pattern, consider a passage that, while cut from the script, was hinted at clearly enough as a critique of the small-minded townsfolk: "For behold, the day comes, burning like an oven, when all the arrogant and evildoers will be stubble; the day that comes shall burn them up, says the lord of hosts, so that it will leave them neither root nor branch."

The audience is directed to the passage when the parson asks the church congregation to turn their Bibles to the last book of the Old Testament: Malachi IV, 1. This is the scene of the movie in which everyone's motives are revealed. The pastor issues the call to text at a crucial moment, when the figure of the sheriff looms in the doorway, a man turned down by everyone else in town and reduced to going to his biggest critics, the pinch-nosed minister who is still upset that Cooper married his new Quaker bride in a civil ceremony and a congregation that never much approved of him in the first place. No doubt, in a town this size, they know of his bohemian mentality and his earlier intimate relations with an unflinching Chicana businesswoman.

While the excised quote from Malachi is interesting, it merely buttresses the surviving piece of dialogue that comes next and is the evidence of Foreman's indirect accusation that the townspeople themselves are the true evildoers. The pastor's narrow nostrils flare at the sight of Cooper, and the mayor (Thomas Mitchell) comes to the pulpit to quiet things down. He thanks the sheriff for long years of service to the town. But that was then and this is now, Mitchell makes plain. The best thing for everyone would be for the sheriff simply to leave because—the mayor gathers himself up to explain—"People up North are looking hard at the town," an aria that would be sung by the baritone at the end of the second act if *High Noon* were reimagined as an opera. As an example of the standard American political speech conflating the interests of finance capital with the public interest, the mayor's speech indeed approaches the quality of verse, with delicate internal echoes and long and short rhythms that alternate from one line to the next.

People up North are thinking about this town,
Thinking mighty hard,
Thinking about sending down money,
Money to put up stores and to build factories.
That would mean a lot to this town, an awful lot.
But if they're going to be reading about shooting and killing in the streets—

What are they going to think, then?
I'll tell you.
They're going to think this is just another town.
And everything we worked for will be wiped out in one day,
Everything we worked for in five years will be wiped out.

It comes down to the same thing Cooper has heard all morning: Get lost before the bad guys return. Issues of revenge and/or justice are no longer on the table, simply because Cooper and his style of heroics have lost their cost-effectiveness.

For this reason, and not merely the reluctance (or cowardice) of ordinary citizens to join an impending gunfight, Cooper throws his star into the dirt of Main Street at the end of the film. He and his wife, a pacifist who stopped to take up the weapon she hated in order to save her husband's life, actually saved a town that not only didn't deserve to be saved but didn't *want* to be saved. The judge, first to saddle up when he learned that the man in the black hat was coming back, turned out to be right after all: Hadleyville was only "a dirty little town in the middle of nowhere." For the sheriff, of course, that would be beside the point: Most of America and nearly all the touted heartland is "nowhere." Such an unbending character, like Foreman himself, had to either shift with the changing tide or get out of town—their role was finished.

Cold War liberal writer Robert Warshow, a shrewd critic who may be said to have understood the film the way that a cop in a cruiser understands a minority neighborhood, insisted that the sheriff's noble gesture made the film a "social drama of a very low order . . . altogether unconvincing and displaying a vulgar anti-populism."[94] With *The Men*, Foreman had shortly before been one of the screenwriters who successfully challenged postwar American cities, particularly small towns, for their ungrateful response to the maimed veterans and black soldiers returning home. From the promise of the immediate postwar years, the historical situation had changed decisively. American villagers had grown glum and suspicious. In Foreman's version of Hadleyville, one can therefore search in vain for happy faces of the saloons or listen for the laughter and joyous gunfire of hardworking cowboys of *Destry Rides Again*—in short, the optimism of the Popular Front years. One finds instead sneers and tight lips, squinty eyes, and the vast silence of the plains.

The change from Bottleneck of *Destry* to Hadleyville of *High Noon* is reminiscent of the changes in the real town of Silver City, New Mexico, from the time blacklisted filmmakers arrived in 1951 (when they were welcomed with fiestas and good food and feelings) to scout locations and enlist the help of townspeople in the making of *Salt of the Earth*—to the moment they left in 1954 with the film negative in the can but chased by vigilantes and assorted armed thugs who had been inflamed by the network of professional anti-Communists in the news media.[95] So it was that Sheriff Cooper and his Quaker wife had become the infamous "elitists." Warshow and lesser critics could indeed identify the American people with Hadleyville, a town that pinned its hopes for the future not on social justice but on outside investment. And these same critics were in some metaphoric sense now properly inhabitants of the town themselves, perhaps gathering in a room over the saloon to discuss their contributions to a local newspaper eager to make Hadleyville (with the quiet financial assistance of railroad executives) attractive to compliant intellectuals as well as to outside investors.

In his last interviews Foreman left little doubt that he intended all along for Hadleyville to represent the people and events of Hollywood in that period. He called the film "a parable about Hollywood and McCarthyism." As he was writing it, he recalled, he watched

> a community beginning to crumble around the edges as these high powered politicians came in . . . putting this community through an inquisition that was getting more and more painful for a lot of people, and people were falling to the wayside one way or another. They were either capitulating to these gangsters—political gangsters from out of town—or they were being executed by them here. And I could see that my time was coming sooner or later—it was just being delayed by a couple of years or so—and I wanted to write about that. I wanted to write about the death of Hollywood. So all that shaped the writing of *High Noon*. That was very conscious, see.[96]

It would be hard to see Western myths, essential American myths of justice and conquest, first merged, then torn apart more successfully. The thematic reversals foreshadowed what a *New York Times* critic would call "Mock Twain": *Cat Ballou* (produced in 1965 by reluctant friendly witness and longtime Kirk Douglas collaborator, Harold Hecht), featuring the drunken and foolish badman Lee Marvin, succeeded by the militant Indian Western *Tell Them Willie Boy Is Here* (written and directed by Abraham Polonsky), the rotten antihero Western *Hud* (directed by fellow blacklistee Martin Ritt), and the lampooned-hero Western *True Grit,* written by Marguerite Roberts and starring, in his only Oscar winner, John Wayne as a thoroughly ludicrous version of himself.

If one wanted a few more examples (from a score of possibilities) of the kinds of films the victims of the blacklist would surely have made, no single genre comes to mind. Going all the way back to 1944–46, Odets's beautifully stylized *None But the Lonely Heart* about British working-class (and demimonde) life could be placed along the unstylized proletarian soaper, *From This Day Forward.* Jack Barry's first directorial outing is no work of genius, but the film moves honestly and directly from a GI's search for a job to factory work that doesn't last, through ups and (mostly) downs, hoping to live a different and less limiting kind of life without losing the closeness of the past.

It was a hopeless dream, given the state of America, and the wistful couple at the end of the picture looking out with determination over a Bronx footbridge might more realistically have seen, through the mist, new thoroughfares ripping apart the neighborhoods, the drugs and hopelessness that descended upon them, and the escape, for the fortunate, into a bland, homogenized, deeply white-bread suburbia. Notwithstanding its sentimentalism, *From This Day Forward* recounted the events and psychology better than the vastly celebrated, schematizing *Marty* a decade later.

The late left-wing art film *Cyrano de Bergerac* or *Death of a Salesman,* not to mention Losey's *M,* all quested after something more serious than *this* Hollywood was ever likely to offer. Notwithstanding *A Streetcar Named Desire, On the Waterfront,* or *Come Back, Little Sheba,* notwithstanding the plaudits laid before cinematic artists (the ones not working underground, of course) after the pervasiveness of television had lifted up movies as art form, the American art movie was a flop. Perhaps this failure was predestined, but the worthwhile productions were so few and so scattered that Hollywood talent never really had a chance to hold on to the audience that was rapidly drifting away from films.

Naturally, younger and older audiences on campuses and in cinema clubs and big cities flocked increasingly to see European and Japanese films once the Cold War had eased and American society seemed less terrified of anything different. Late 1950s and early 1960s showings of assorted Ingmar Bergman classics, of *Jules and Jim, The Seven Samurai,* and so on, might have reminded the most perspicacious in the audience that film-makers around the world had drunk deeply from the vintage of the older Hollywood film. Most of us (and this includes the two authors), only beginning to watch the classics on late-night television, felt wonder-struck that movies could ignore the virginal games of Doris Day, the regressive physical humor of Jerry Lewis, or the cowboys-and-Indians violence that still served as main neighborhood fare, and reach for something entirely different.

The failure of the 1960s American art film imitations can be viewed as a self-inflicted national insult, another example of the newly rich dragging home foreign trinkets without grasping their meanings in an older culture.[97] We had no way of knowing that even if everything were suddenly possible, as the emerging counterculture proclaimed, the older and firmer bases for resistance—the working-class autodidacts, the collective experience of antifascism, the popular resentment against a system that failed human needs—had been swept away. The organic basis for the screenwriter's (and director's, and actor's, and cinematographer's, and so on) best radical work no longer existed, and the community of critical filmmakers, once scattered, could not be reconstituted.

On the other hand, if Hollywood never did make radical dreams come true, it never totally disappointed, either. *The Defiant Ones* or *The Brave One, Odds Against Tomorrow,* little films like *No Down Payment* and big films like *Fail-Safe* heralded a return of at least selective richness from the doldrums of blacklist days. Hollywood's large social and artistic rebellions, when they came again over a bad war and endless racial divides, injustice, and the assorted dreadful effects of an imperial world order, made for many further fine pictures, in a trajectory that is still far from finished. But despite raging successes in the rebellion market, despite a virtual abandonment of censorship (on the Golden Rule: Those who have the gold make the rules, even among the avant-gardists), the collective spirit or purpose remained simply absent. Many young filmmakers, and many audiences around the world, continued to gaze at the stunning films of the Hollywood past and to wonder how they had disappeared—and why.

By the next turn of the century, a distempered and badly aging literary critic, Norman Podhoretz, complained of Philip Roth's *I Married a Communist* that even a distinguished novelist who had contempt for Stalinism and evidently shared both the hawkish-Israeli and acquisitive-American values of the new-new rich of Podhoretz's crowd nevertheless looked back upon the past Jewish-heavy radical movements as containing the most *memorable* events and personalities of a lifetime.[98] That was the key, as well, to *The Way We Were* as an amazingly enduring icon, not just the love story but the protagonist Katie (realized perfectly in Barbra Streisand), rebelling in the forms that her era offered, trying to give America a gift that it didn't want, not Russian-style Communism at all, but gay Jewish screenwriter Arthur Laurent's version of a different Jewish, American, and global future from 1945 onward.

"Print the legend," Frank Capra was reputed to have quipped, a way of substituting convenient images for life, naturally including his own work. For us, now so removed by decades from Hollywood's Golden Age and by death from its survivors, the images captured on celluloid really do capture truths if the often shadowy story behind the story can only be illuminated. The chief point of *Radical Hollywood* is to get readers to watch and watch again dozens or, even better, hundreds of these films—not just those before the blacklist, but those by familiar hands in the era to follow—and come to their own conclusions.

1. Jules Dassin interviewed by Patrick McGilligan, in Patrick McGilligan and Paul Buhle, editors, *Tender Comrades: A Backstory of the Hollywood Blacklist* (New York: St. Martin's Press, 1997), 207–08. The novel was *The Journey of Simon McKeever,* an ostensibly nonpolitical story of a man with severe arthritis who hitchhikes from San Francisco to Los Angeles.

2. FBI Document LA 100–15732, n.d. [1949], "Communist Activity in the Entertainment Industry: FBI Surveillance Files on Hollywood, 1942–1958" (Brandeis University). [No italics in the original.]

3. Quoted in Neal Gabler, *An Empire of Their Own: How the Jews Invented Hollywood* (New York: Doubleday, 1988), 356.

4. Ibid., 356–60.

5. Ibid., 375–76, 378–80. The head of the Hollywood branch of the American Jewish Committee Against Communism, the most extreme wing of the Jewish anti-Communist tendency, was conservative screenwriter Morrie Ryskind.

6. "John Berry," interviewed by Patrick McGilligan, *Tender Comrades*, 74.

7. *5 Fingers* (1952), a distinctly lesser film also written by Wilson—he got no credit—is nevertheless a stunning piece of work as well, with James Mason as a lowly valet to haughty wartime British diplomats, successfully betraying them and escaping with a bundle, but offering the Germans vital information that they do not use.

8. Gordon tells his story in *Hollywood Exile, or How I Learned to Love the Blacklist* (Austin: University of Texas Press, 1999). Of his films written under several names, *Flesh and Fury* (1952) is closest to the familiar empathetic proletarian themes, with Tony Curtis starring as a deaf boxer who finally must confront his own conscience.

9. Among the undisclosed 1950s credits later restored, along with Albert Maltz's scripting *The Robe*, were Dalton Trumbo, for the Oscar-winning *The Brave One* as well as for *Roman Holiday* (using as a front Ian McClellan Hunter, who had not yet been blacklisted); Foreman, for *A Hatful of Rain;* Michael Wilson, for *Friendly Persuasion;* and Abraham Polonsky, for *Odds Against Tomorrow.* Major script-doctoring credits, in some cases wholesale rewrites, are almost certainly destined never to be revealed; the most inventive of rewriters, Abraham Polonsky, refused to name them even to his biographers, on a point of honor to those "fronts" whose names he utilized.

10. "Leonardo Bercovici," interviewed by Paul Buhle, *Tender Comrades*, 40–41.

11. Thomas Schatz, "The Postwar Motion Picture Industry," in Schatz, editor, *Boom and Bust: American Cinema in the 1940s* (Berkeley: University of California Press, 1997), 291–93.

12. Some of the best efforts at recasting national history never reached production; Adrian Scott left a handful of would-be historical epics behind, and these can be viewed in the Adrian and Joan Scott Papers, American Heritage Center, Laramie, Wyoming.

13. A recent observation on Beard's misdirection offers helpful details: J. Samuel Walker, "The Not-So-Strange Career of Charles Beard," *Diplomatic History* 25 (Spring 2001), 251–74.

14. See Paul Buhle, "How Sweet It Wasn't: Scholars and the CIA," in John McMillian and Paul Buhle, editors, *A Movement to Change America: The New Left Re-Examined* (Philadelphia: Temple University Press, forthcoming), an essay on this trend within American intellectual life.

15. *The Defenders* (1961–65) had, however, less pseudonymous left-wing work than the almost exclusively blacklistee operation produced in the UK, *The*

Adventures of Robin Hood (1955–58), whose writers included Ring Lardner, Jr., Ian McClellan Hunter, Robert Lees, and Adrian Scott; or the first series of *You Are There* (1953–55), entirely written by blacklistees Abraham Polonsky, Walter Bernstein, and Arnold Manoff.

16. And some of them managed to treat these themes, others perhaps quietly assisting unblacklisted progressives in similar work. Bernard Gordon wrote *Earth vs. the Flying Saucers* (1956), about an outer space threat that brought the United States together with the Soviet Union, a few years after Abraham Polonsky's close friend Robert Wise was making *The Day the Earth Stood Still* (1951), the most progressive of the space-invader films. The Adrian and Joan Scott Papers include, along with unproduced film scripts of the 1950s, television scripts for shows made and never made, many of them heavily laden with minority characters, slum teenagers, good-hearted physicians, or social workers and the like.

17. On Reagan's Hollywood informing, see Anthony Summers, *Official and Confidential: The Secret Life of J. Edgar Hoover* (New York: Putnam, 1993), 162. As described here, the future president's brother Neil had already been spying on Hollywood meetings for the Bureau, and warned his sibling to resign from the Hollywood Independent Citizens Committee for the Arts, Sciences and the Professions (HICCASP), the liberal-left group in which he had been very prominent. Instead, the future president chose to remain—and become "Confidential Informant F-10," calling the Bureau from home, after dark, to report on SAG meetings and then making a secret appearance before HUAC.

18. *Margie,* with no other suspicious connections, was a light comedy set in the 1920s, about a spunky Indiana teenager who learns that her grandmother chained herself to a Washington monument during the suffragist parades of the 1910s, and still has the chains to prove it! Even better, she has an indulgent if nominally conservative daddy who loyally (to her, that is) opposes the contemporary American invasion of Nicaragua as imperialist and un-American.

19. Schwartz, *The Hollywood Writers' Wars,* 254.

20. Quoted in ibid., 243.

21. Irving Pichel "On Freedom of the Screen," *Screen Writer* 3 (November 1947), 1–4.

22. Schwartz, *The Hollywood Writers' Wars,* 255–56.

23. Dmytryk and Scott had of course collaborated on *Crossfire*, thus may be said to have joined themselves vicariously to Jewishness; Pichel, Collins, Koch, and Lardner, Jr., were apparently "innocent" in that sense, although all had been in their political practice also militant opponents of anti-Semitism. It's also interesting that unlike later hearings that confined themselves to either friendly witnesses or known (by the FBI, that is) Party members, the first list included Koch, Milestone, and others who had never been in the Party, either a deliberate blurring of lines or a consequence of flawed intelligence.

24. For a recent reminiscence, see Ring Lardner, Jr., *I'd Hate Myself in the Morning: A Memoir* (New York: Nation Books/Thunder's Mouth Press, 2000), 9.

25. Schwartz, *The Hollywood Writers' Wars*, 267–68.

26. Of the others, only director Milestone, never a Communist and, in any case, at the end of his career, formally escaped the blacklist without self-abnegating testimony.

27. Roland Kibbee, "Reddened Any Good Pictures Lately?" *Screen Writer* 3 (December 1947), 16.

28. Ibid., 17–20.

29. Pichel, "On the Freedom of the Screen," 3.

30. Ibid., 4.

31. See Chapter 7 on *The Long Night*.

32. See Norman Barzman interview with Larry Ceplair, *Tender Comrades*, 10–12, for further production details.

33. Tullio Kezich, "The Venice Film Festival—1950," *Hollywood Quarterly* 5 (January 1951), 373. *Give Us This Day* was finally produced by Plantagenet Films and distributed by the B-level British Eagle-Lion. Bosley Crowther complained of a certain formality or stiffness in direction, especially for Wanamaker, yet he appreciated the effort. "Films," *The New York Times*, December 21, 1949, especially praising the "quality of spirituality in Miss Padovani's performance." Thanks to Norma Barzman for making a rare print of the film—with subtitles in Danish!—available to us.

34. Rossen made several unsuccessful films hitching avant-garde themes to blue-collar backgrounds—the best of them was *Mambo* (1954)—then succeeded grandly in *The Hustler* (1961), not long before his fatal heart attack.

35. "United States Department of Justice, Los Angeles, California, February 21, 1948," by R. B. Hood. On an unintentionally comic note, Agent Hood complained that "qualified agents" were unable to take notes quickly and accu-

rately enough by viewing the films at local theaters, and needed special private showings to "more fully comply with the Bureau instructures [sic]." The studio insider (with name blacked out) would, it was hoped, both offer the private viewings and dig out the scripts.

36. Laura Z. (for Zametkin) Hobson herself was the daughter of one of the founders of the daily socialist *Jewish Daily Forward,* Michael Zametkin, and his wife, Adella.

37. As Wyatt later observed, her adamant refusal to denounce Communists within SAG caused her to lose all jobs in Hollywood, without actually being blacklisted; as a consequence she moved to television, where she costarred in *Father Knows Best* and other series. Her series costar, Robert Young, had been a noted opponent of U.S. intervention and a supporter of free speech during the 1940s.

38. Charles Chaplin, *My Autobiography* (New York: Pocket Books, 1964), 473–86.

39. Ibid., 487–92.

40. *New Orleans* might well be contrasted to the Gershwin biopic *Rhapsody in Blue* (1945), coscripted by Howard Koch. Even at that late date, Al Jolson playing himself heroically assists the young lyricist by singing "Sewanee" in blackface, and Paul Whiteman gives him the ultimate dignity by making jazz into "a lady" in Carnegie Hall (there were no black performers). *Rhapsody* had big stars, including Morris Carnovsky as "Papa" Gershwin. Like the Chopin counterpart, *A Song to Remember* (1945), written by Sidney Buchman, *Rhapsody* made European music the dignified standard to which jazz must rise. Neither film produced a sound track worth recording separately—unlike *New Orleans,* whose sound track reappeared in 1983, recuperating some of the songs cut from the original.

41. Another small irony: The working title of *Home of the Brave* was *High Noon!*

42. Warren Miller, "Home of the Brave," *Masses and Mainstream* 2 (July 1949), 79–81, grudgingly admits that *"for the first time in a Hollywood film* a Negro is the major point of interest, of audience concern; and . . . the characterization is one that, on the surface, is not offensive [italics in original]." And yet Miller goes on to argue that the moral has been trivialized into a personal issue, making the basic similarity of the human condition its only meaningful message.

43. Bosley Crowther, " 'Intruder in the Dust': MGM's Drama of Lynching in the South, at the Mayfair," *The New York Times,* November 23, 1949.

44. Quoted by Mel Watkins, *On the Real Side: Laughing, Lying, and Signifying—the Underground Tradition of African-American Humor That Transformed American Culture, from Slavery to Richard Pryor* (New York: Simon & Schuster, 1995), 165.

45. Bosley Crowther, "Films," *The New York Times,* September 30, 1949.

46. As noted above, Moss wrote (and starred in) *The Negro Soldier,* for the "Why We Fight" documentary series, but had no other opportunities for Hollywood screenwriting. Although named in the blacklist, he had a distinguished career writing and directing films on black themes for public schools, mentoring young black filmmakers, and serving as a critic of Hollywood's meager racial progress. Long before, Stanley Kramer had named the black protagonist of *Home of the Brave* "Mossy," in a bow to his friend. Robert McG. Thomas, Jr., "Carlton Moss, 88, Who Filmed the Black Experience, Dies," *The New York Times,* August 15, 1997.

47. Interview of Carlton Moss by Paul Buhle, September 1992, Hollywood.

48. Cheryl R. Kelley, "The Career and Films of Dudley Nichols," unpublished dissertation, St. Louis University, 1982, 94–103. The near-future of black-white relations in the liberal film had been cast more accurately by *Young Man with a Horn* (1950), a Kirk Douglas melodrama coscripted by Foreman, where a black trumpeter (played by Hernandez) is a plot mechanism for the protagonist.

49. We leave aside here the legendary "Robin Hood of the Pecos," the Cisco Kid, played for laughs by the quietly gay Cesar Romero but seriously by several other actors (occasionally scripted by left-wing writers, notably Louise Rousseau) in a forgotten B 1940s movie series, up to the present still unavailable.

50. At this writing, *A Medal for Benny* has not been rereleased and was viewed at the Library of Congress.

51. Liberal screenwriter Daniel Mainwaring chose a pseudonym, Geoffrey Homes, for his credit. The set design was by the credited John Hubley, fired from Disney for union activities some years earlier. Interesting light is cast upon the role of Hubley, a future independent animation creator of note, by his widow, also an animator: Faith Hubley interviewed by Patrick McGilligan, in *Tender Comrades,* 281–304.

52. See the distinctly liberal newspaper coverage: Thomas F. Brady, "Hollywood Agenda," *The New York Times,* January 29, 1950; Bosley Crowther, "The Screen in Review," *The New York Times,* June 23, 1950; and in a unique, blacklist-era case of a pseudonymous screenwriter covering the making of his

own film, Geoffrey Holmes [i.e., Daniel Mainwaring], "New Study of Migratory Workers in California," *The New York Times,* March 5, 1950. For further production details, see *American Film Institute Catalog, Feature Films, 1941–50,* 1353–54. This film has very recently come back into circulation for the first time.

53. See David Caute, *Joseph Losey: A Revenge on Life* (New York: Oxford University Press, 1994), 90. Paramount executive Luigi Luraschi, reportedly by this time in close contact with the Central Intelligence Agency, may very well have authorized the withdrawal of the film.

54. See Bosley Crowther, "Pictorial Power," *The New York Times,* April 22, 1951. But even here the censor still made the rules. American audiences, who happily sat through hundreds of war films, were considered too weak-stomached for its gory man-versus-bull killing scenes, and some minutes were lopped off to protect their delicate sensibilities.

55. In a 1996 interview with Paul Buhle, African-American actor William Marshall described himself as being "graylisted," politically suspect without being named, but nevertheless used occasionally in 1950s films when they needed an "angry African" out of control. Marshall lost patience with Hollywood, spent decades abroad in Shakespearean productions, and returned to star in the "blaxploitation" films *Blacula* and *Scream, Blacula, Scream!* A new era had begun in Marshall's absence with Martin Ritt's *Edge of the City* (1957), originally a television broadcast, with Poitier as a righteously angry longshoreman (if not quite the lead protagonist), and even more with *Odds Against Tomorrow* (1959). *Odds* star Harry Belafonte produced the film and intended a series of racial shockers—but failed to gain needed backing.

56. Actually, *She's a Soldier Too* (1944), written by Melvin Levy and starring the durable Bondi, was about women defense workers living in the mansion of a heiress—a pretty unlikely cabdriver! Women did better abroad, but here, too, mostly as nurses and teachers rather than WACs or WAVEs.

57. Gerda Lerner, wife of film editor (and later blacklistee) Carl Lerner, would become one of the founding figures of women's history. She coscripted, with him, *Black Like Me* (1964), a commercially unsuccessful antiracist film. Thanks to Gerda Lerner for an advance look at her memoirs. The CAW, still little studied, is described briefly in Amy Swerdlow, "Congress of American Women," *Encyclopedia of the American Left* (New York: Oxford University Press, 2nd Edition), edited by Mari Jo Buhle, Paul Buhle, and Dan Georgakas, 159.

58. Indeed, the Breen Office regarded censorship as having failed in the case of *Forever Amber. Temptation* (1946), directed by Pichel and adapted from the turn-of-the-century novel and play, has a British archaeologist's wife in Cairo falling for a native playboy and poisoning her hubby. Edgar Ulmer's *The Strange Woman* (1946) found Hedy Lamarr as the seductive daughter of the town drunk in mid-nineteenth-century Maine, dallying with the son of her lumber capitalist husband. Lamarr herself coproduced this film—for the first and last time, in her case—obviously eager for the strong woman role that Hollywood hadn't given her. But it was all to no avail when critics panned the film and audiences avoided it.

59. See the excellent commentary on *Another Part of the Forest* in Bernard F. Dick, *Hellman in Hollywood* (Rutherford, NJ: Farleigh Dickinson Press, 1982), 72–79.

60. We considered *Possessed,* the Joan Crawford vehicle, in Chapter 7. The remake of *Craig's Wife* (its 1936 version produced by Edward Chodorov for Dorothy Arzner's direction) as *Harriet Craig* in 1950 and coscripted by a future black-listee offered an all-time case of masochism, but not without interesting psychological angles. See Anne Froelick, interview by Paul Buhle, in *Tender Comrades,* 257.

61. The Breen Office repeatedly interfered with the production of this film, finally demanding and receiving a decisive change of ending (Turner decides not to leap to her death). Donald Ogden Stewart contributed to the script, his final script contribution before leaving for the UK.

62. See Stewart, *By a Stroke of Luck: An Autobiography* (London: Paddington Press, 1975), 279. The film was directed by Michael Curtiz, one of his last big hits, and won Oscar nominations for Best Actor (Powell), Score, and Cinematography. See James C. Robertson, *The Casablanca Man: The Cinema of Michael Curtiz* (London: Routledge, 1993), 96–97.

63. Stewart's last credit during the era was for the British-made (but U.S.-released) *Edward, My Son* (1949), based on a Robert Morley–Noel Langley play, tracing the guilt of a Canadian manufacturer and his wife as they realize that their bad example has driven their beloved son Edward to suicide (masked as an RAF death in action). Definitively downbeat without being noir, and linked to the blacklisted screenwriter, it never had a chance. Under a pseudonym, he adapted a pacifist theatrical drama into the British film *Escapade* (1955), about the idealism of youth.

64. *Calamity Jane and Sam Bass,* coscripted by Melvin Levy, starring Yvonne De Carlo as the dark, impassioned, hard-riding, and fast-shooting bandit queen, Howard Duff as the man she craves, and Dorothy Hart as the Goody Two-shoes lady *he* loves, has real-life Old West outlaws Calamity Jane and Sam all but forced into bandithood, and him uttering his love for Hart as he dies in Calamity's arms. *Bagdad,* with its highly coordinated "native" dances, codirected by the only blacklisted choreographer, Bella Lewitzky, features a delightfully hammy Vincent Price as the Machiavellian Pasha whose Turkish rule over the Arabs is undone by O'Hara's courage and royal air.

65. See the extensive treatment of this film, released only weeks before Polonsky was called before HUAC, in Buhle and Wagner, *A Very Dangerous Citizen: Abraham Lincoln Polonsky and the Hollywood Left* (Berkeley: University of California Press, 2001), 146–55.

66. *Rachel and the Stranger* placed Mitchum as drifter opposite Loretta Young, in a frontier Western written by Waldo Salt (who also wrote the lyrics of several songs in the film), from a short story by Howard Fast about the "young nation" of America growing up. *The Lusty Men* had Mitchum as a retired bronco rider tutoring an airhead played by Arthur Kennedy and falling in love with his protégé's wife, played by Susan Hayward. It was directed by Nicholas Ray—just before Ray's big hit in *Rebel Without a Cause*—and written by Carl Foreman.

67. John Howard Lawson, *Film in the Battle of Ideas* (New York: Masses & Mainstream, 1953), 50–61. Even here, the distraught Lawson overdoes his analysis, or perhaps forgives the similar treatment of gender themes by Hollywood comrades and even himself while zeroing in on Kazan and other enemies.

68. Bosley Crowther noted that in the novel (humorous and picaresque rather than somber, like the film), an atheistic local union leader was brought to see the light of day by the miraculous developments. "Miracle of the Bells," *The New York Times,* March 17, 1948.

69. Produced by Eagle-Lion Features and animationist George Pal, *The Great Rupert* was a low-cost, sentimental production not treated well by critics. See the anonymous *New York Times* review: "Films," April 14, 1950.

70. Pichel, "On the Freedom of the Screen," 3.

71. Ibid., 4.

72. "After that," said Bercovici, "everybody in town wanted my scripts. Everybody." Leonardo Bercovici interview with Paul Buhle in *Tender Comrades,* 39.

73. More interested than any of his colleagues (with the possible exception of Abraham Polonsky) in the meeting points of psychoanalysis and Marxism,

Bercovici also set out to do a Henry James adaptation different from all others. One of producer Walter Wanger's last pictures before shifting abroad and fleeing left-wing connections, *The Lost Moment* (1947) was taken from *The Aspern Papers,* for whose film rights Wanger paid a reported $200,000. It was a bad investment and an extremely odd film, but it struck a chord with the connections between memory and guilt.

74. *The Private Affairs of Bel Ami* (1947), a black-and-white film about a particularly reckless lover in nineteenth-century France, featured a canvas of ex-surrealist painter Max Ernst's "Temptation of St. Anthony" in color. Lewin sponsored a contemporary art show (banned in Boston) of various works on the theme, including paintings by surrealists Leonora Carrington and Laura Tanning. The film's assistant director was Robert Aldrich. *The Picture of Dorian Gray,* taken from an Oscar Wilde novel, again used color selectively, for dramatic effect, and won an Academy Award for Best Black-and-White Cinematography, with several additional nominations. It was the only financially successful effort of writer-director Lewin.

75. In *So Dear to My Heart,* an Indiana orphan farm boy played by Billy Driscoll finds the warmth otherwise lacking in his life in the (literal) black sheep—a born troublemaker who sees in Driscoll a human soul mate—as well as in his grandmother, played by Beulah Bondi. Ives, a neighbor wooing Bondi, sings, strums, and offers cracker-barrel philosophy for Driscoll's edification, while animated sequences express childish fantasies and expectations. The boy's disgrace at the sheep's misdeeds prepares the town to see its own shortcomings, and prepares the boy's emotional leap necessary for a satisfying conclusion. Burl Ives, so prominent in the Left during these years, turned friendly witness and successfully became a homespun national icon of sorts on television and in children's records. See Bosley Crowther, "Films," *The New York Times,* January 31, 1949.

76. Maurice Rapf, *Back Lot: Growing Up in the Movies* (Lanham: Scarecrow Press, 1999), 134–35.

77. See Maurice Rapf interview by Patrick McGilligan, *Tender Comrades,* 520–26.

78. Maurice Rapf interview, 522, though he told the story somewhat differently in Rapf, *Back Lot,* 130.

79. Ironically, Rapf was bounced from *Song of the South* to *Cinderella.* There, he insists, he succeeded in making the protagonist a "rebel," and indeed she is—supported emotionally by those mice, fellow downtrodden members of the household, and resisting the social climbing as well as the pure

meanness of her stepmother and stepsisters. Maurice Rapf interview, 522.

80. Alfred Lewis Levitt interviewed by Larry Ceplair, in *Tender Comrades,* 455.

81. "Edward Eliscu," interviewed by Patrick McGilligan and David Eliscu, *Tender Comrades,* 245. See also *The New York Times*'s coverage of the controversy about the two Alices: Bosley Crowther, "A Muchness of Alices," July 29, 1951; and Bosley Crowther, "The Screen in Review," July 30, 1951.

82. Kline had few other credits, and is remembered privately for an understandable bitterness at the Party's cultural apparatus.

83. The prologue of the film ran, "This is the story of a city, a kid and a baseball team."

84. *Saturday's Hero* marked a practical end to Lampell's film career. His Emmy-winning teleplay, *Eagle in a Cage* (1965), about Napoleon's exile, became a theatrical film but failed to restore his career. See the interview of Lampell by Paul Buhle in *Tender Comrades,* 391–403. *Go, Man, Go!* has received a new life through cable television, thanks to its athletes of color; *Saturday's Hero* has so far not been rereleased and was viewed at the Library of Congress.

85. See the illuminating treatment of *Bedtime for Bonzo* in Danny Peary, *Cult Movies: The Classics, the Sleepers, the Weird and the Wonderful* (New York: Gramercy Books, 1981), 230–32. Supporters of California governor Pat Brown showed the film at fund-raisers in 1966 as the incumbent sought to defend himself from real-life airhead, Republican candidate and GE corporate spokesman Reagan. These showings turned out badly because the actor comes across as lovable, though the best action (if not the best lines) surely belongs to the chimp. The Levitts together, under the pseudonyms of Tom and Helen August, wrote along similar lines, for Disney, *The Misadventures of Merlin Jones* (1964) and *The Monkey's Uncle* (1965).

86. Julian Zimet, "Regarding the Horse Opera," *The Screen Writer* 2 (November 1946), 18.

87. Rousseau, a collateral (indirect) descendant of Jean Jacques Rousseau and a prolific writer of Republic Westerns in the forties, set up a job-shop printing operation in Hollywood after being blacklisted; she never worked in films again. Thanks to Robert Lees in a May 1998, interview, Los Angeles, for this personal information.

88. Viertel's best screen credit was for coscripting *Saboteur,* with Dorothy Parker. Robson, who had worked uncredited with Robert Wise editing *Citizen Kane,* directed several horror films in the 1940s, including *Isle of the Dead,* but also

directed *Champion* and *Home of the Brave.* The defeat of the Left arguably cost Robson his edge. *Peyton Place* was his biggest hit. He had a fatal heart attack while shooting the action film *Avalanche Express* (1982, with a script by his longtime friend Abraham Polonsky), sparing himself the completion of the most embarrassing film that either director and writer had ever worked on.

89. The television drama version, in 1956, placed Latina Rita Mareno in the Indian princess role; a television series, 1956–58 (with reruns continuing until 1960) starred the Jewish Michael Ansara in the Jimmy Stewart role. Back from the blacklist, the same Albert Maltz would write *Two Mules for Sister Sara* (1970), which gave progressive actress Shirley MacLaine a politically strong costarring role, and also inspired a television series.

90. Foreman actually testified in a HUAC Executive Session, in 1956, albeit apparently without naming names, and his blacklisting was informal, but his Hollywood days were over. His major subsequent film work was mainly administrative, as governor of the British Film Institute and producer of World War II action and semi-comedy films (he also wrote several of them), as though other themes had lost interest for him. His success as executive producer of *Born Free* (1966) marked a high point in newly emerging political themes.

91. Published as "The Tin Star," *Collier's,* December 6, 1947.

92. He also wrote *The Clay Pigeon* (1949), a dark tale about informing and betrayal.

93. Interview of Jean Butler with Paul Buhle and Dave Wagner, *Tender Comrades,* 166; see also Lauren Rabinowitz, "Experimental and Avant-Garde Cinema in the 1940s," in Thomas Schatz, *Boom and Bust: American Cinema in the 1940s, History of the American Cinema, Vol. 6* (Berkeley: University of California Press, 1997), 445–60.

94. Essay reprinted in Robert Warshow, *The Immediate Experience: Movies, Comics, Theatre & Other Aspects of Popular Culture* (New York: Atheneum, 1972 edition), 149.

95. A recent, prize-winning treatment of the entire episode is by James J. Lorence, *The Suppression of Salt of the Earth: How Hollywood, Big Labor and Politicians Blacklisted a Movie in Cold War America* (Albuquerque: University of New Mexico Press, 1999).

96. Foreman interviewed in the 1981 American Film Foundation documentary, *Carl Foreman, Words Into Image: Portraits of American Screenwriters.* Transcript, 1–2. That the influence of *High Noon* continues is demonstrated amply by the

film's impression upon the German director Wolfgang Petersen (whose own films include *The Perfect Storm, Air Force One, Outbreak,* and *Das Boot*): Rick Lyman, "A Boy Shaped by 'High Noon," *The New York Times,* March 30, 2001.

97. A splendidly terrible example was cowritten and produced by Ben Maddow, a late and reluctant friendly witness: an adaptation of Jean Genet's *The Balcony* (1963), starring the suspiciously left-leaning cast of Shelley Winters, Peter Falk, Ruby Dee, and blacklist-returnees Lee Grant and Jeff Corey, along with young avant-gardist Leonard Nimoy. Winters plays a madam who presides over a house of ill repute during a revolutionary uprising; Falk is the crazy general-patron, and Grant a lesbian confidante of Winters. Americans had obviously seen nothing like this from the home market, and clearly did not know how to react; neither did distributors.

98. Norman Podhoretz, "Bellow at 85, Roth at 67," *Commentary* 110 (July–August, 2000), 39.

EPILOGUE

"THIS IS GENE KELLY," the transcript for the "Hollywood Fights Back" national radio broadcast of November 26, 1947, begins,

The House Un-American [Activities] Committee has called on the carpet some of the people who have been making your favorite movies. Did you happen to see THE BEST YEARS OF OUR LIVES, the picture that won seven Academy Awards? Did You enjoy it? Well, the producer of that film, Samuel Goldwyn, has been subpoenaed. I understand supporters of the Un-American Committee didn't like it. Did you like it? Were you subverted by it? Did it make you Un-American? Did you come out of the movie with the desire to overthrow the government? [1]

Kelly was immediately followed by Lauren Bacall ("This is Bacall. Have you seen CROSSFIRE yet? Good picture? . . . The American *people* have awarded it four stars, but the Un-American *Committee* gave the men who made it three subpoenas." Joseph ("Joe") Cotten, Peter Lorre, Danny Kaye, Richard Conte, Burt Lancaster, Robert Ryan (speaking against "the testimony of crackpots and subversives accepted and given out to the press as if it were gospel truth"), Robert Young, Van Heflin, Humphrey Bogart, Edward G. Robinson, Lucille Ball, William Wyler ("I wouldn't be allowed to make THE BEST YEARS OF OUR LIVES in Hollywood today"), Fredric March, John Garfield, Frank Sinatra, Judy Garland, and last but hardly least Vincent Price. The future favorite horror star announced the names of others who joined the Committee for the First Amendment but couldn't be fitted into a half-hour broadcast. These included Ava Gardner, Geraldine Brooks, Henry Fonda, Norwin [Norman] Corwin, Eddie Cantor, Katharine Hepburn, Cornel Wilde, Keenan Wynn, Benny Goodman, Rita Hayworth, Canada Lee, Margo and Gregory Peck.

This was an exceedingly modest list of Hollywood progressives. It contained no writers and only one director—other sympathizers obviously lacking star power—and not all of the left-leaning or civil libertarian actors by a long shot, doubtless because some less secure in their status must have declined the potentially unfavorable exposure.[2]

It appears from internal evidence that the radio speeches had been scripted by Albert Maltz, a detail that might be contrasted with Dalton Trumbo ghostwriting a major address for the UN meetings in San Francisco two years earlier: first time anticipating triumph (the speech was not used, as it turned out); second time pure defensiveness. Frank Sinatra, who would seem to have broken with the Popular Front during the jurisdictional warfare of 1946, nevertheless ended the radio show by asking, "If this [HUAC] committee gets the green light from the American people now, will it be possible to make a broadcast like this a year from today?" It clearly wasn't, and would not be again until the day that the HUAC closed shop in 1973, after more than two decades of legal challenges.

Still, for our purposes, Gene Kelly had put some of the right questions up front. Did American audiences intend to see the people who had worked on "their favorite movies" taken out of the scene? In the spring of 1947, before the attorney general's list of supposedly subversive political, cultural, and fraternal associations had been spelled out by the government and accepted by a mostly eager-to-dramatize press, public opinion was badly divided. By Christmas, only the courts could save the Hollywood Left—an awfully weak reed with Harry Truman now making the high judicial appointments.

The vexing question that remained for decades, beyond the usual civil liberties issues raised by the fact of the blacklist, was whether the blacklistees' removal made any real difference. Had Hollywood been changed by the Red Scare, and, if so, how?

Beyond claims to First Amendment rights, the "materialist" liberal position rested upon the familiar assumptions (whether Marxist, liberal, or conservative) about the control of the means of production. If the studios controlled content, then how could Communists (or anyone else) have possibly delivered messages unwanted by the executives to the public? This old chestnut has recently gained new meaning with the revelation that, quite apart from FBI operations, the Central Intelligence Agency planted its own representatives in the studios, engaging in a consultation process acknowledged in the private correspondence of executives at Paramount and MGM.[3]

CIA intervention, in contrast to the long-term activity of FBI operatives and the Red-baiting of the gossip columnists and the Hearst press going back to the 1930s, was apparently late in the process and unlikely to transform the sagging industry. Still, Communists were not wrong to think that the clampdown was an operation guided from the upper levels of the security-state apparatus. Repression Hollywood-style did not constitute anything like an American fascism, as many on the Left (and others outside their ranks, especially refugees from European fascism) feared during the late 1940s and early 1950s; but it was at once blatant, subtle, and pervasive, far more culturally directed than the dreaded Red Scare of 1919–21, and considerably more sustained.

What the new Hollywood powers-that-be could not do was bring in the customers. The accelerating decline in attendance began in 1948, years before even the most centralized and urban 20 percent of the population owned television sets. Attendance continued to decline for the decade often described as the worst in American film history, and by the time it recovered ground, television had become pervasive.

Historian Lary May suggests that from the late 1940s onward practically "all the amusements that had their roots in the thirties began a sharp decline," a process marked by suburbanization, ethnic assimilation to a common "white" identity, privatized family consumerism, and an abiding quest for security.[4] What recuperated the crowds for films a decade or more later is more difficult to discern, but May is surely correct to say that new stars' special attraction for a younger audience very often signaled an aesthetic of rebellion. It all began as the old system fell apart. Marlon Brando (who made his screen starring debut in *The Men*), James Dean (guided through *Rebel Without a Cause* by director Nicholas Ray, with Clifford Odets on the set as Ray's savant), Montgomery Clift (whose proudest moment had been the lead in *A Place in the Sun*), and others would be followed by the rebellious icons of Warren Beatty, Dustin Hoffman, Jane Fonda, and so on. Not that Doris Day, Fabian, or the endless succession of pretty faces and bodies played a lesser role in star charisma, but the return of the cutting edge put Hollywood back on the entertainment map.[5]

The successors to the blacklisted writers—by the 1960s and 1970s, also a large handful of returnees, including a handful of prominent actors—found their niche in the ever-newer personae and circumstances of the Outsider. They also fulfilled those personae (outright feminists, rounded-character African-Americans and other racial minorities, gays and lesbians) whose potentially pivotal roles had been ruled improper in previous generations.

By the later 1950s (and much more in the next ten years), *The New York Times* reviewers began to redeem the talented and successful blacklist-breakers, one by one, in the search for the "socially relevant" films that critics could admire. The *Times* sometimes led but mostly followed the Motion Picture Academy, whose members seemed eager to make a statement of sorts without renewing past political controversies. Sometimes chunks of missing history reappeared in an acceptance speech or in newspaper coverage of an award event, with the almost offhand remark that so-and-so had "not been working," or working only abroad, for a dozen years or more.[6] Rarely did anything like the larger story emerge. Perhaps would-be ex-blacklistees and somewhat chastened Cold Warriors shared a near-conspiracy of silence.

And so time passed, with most of the careers and many of the lives of the unfortunates on hold or simply destroyed, their legacy a mystery. One might conclude that the jury is still out on the impact of the Left in Hollywood before the blacklist, except that the jury has continued all these decades later to be all but nonexistent. At most, the story of the films has been recuperated one artist at a time; at worst, not even that, as hundreds of the films in question continue to garner large audiences on television and their most useful reviews in the clipped commentaries of newspaper "TV Week" or paperback reference guide synopses.

For that reason, early judgments have seemed until very recent years to stand still in time. Eager to deploy Billy Wilder's quip about the Hollywood Ten ("Only one of them had talent. The rest were just unfriendly."), vindictive anti-Communists sought from the early days on to dispose of the whole messy issue by dismissing the left-wing screenwriters as purveyors of bad taste.

Arthur Schlesinger, Jr.'s *The Vital Center* (1949), a totemic document of liberal zeal for the Cold War, devoted little space but great animus to the Hollywood Left. In a chapter about the "Communist challenge to America," the author sought to demonstrate the totalitarian character of the Party's cultural outreach by identifying long-gone thirties trends and institutions like "proletarian literature" and the American Writers Congress, then turned abruptly to the Maltz controversy.[7] He concluded with a sweeping generalization about the Left in Hollywood and the suggestion that in the process of corrupting the artist, Communism compelled him (or her) to voice only official opinions: "So direct political control either throttles the serious artist or makes him slick and false." Albert Maltz, John Howard Lawson, Alvah Bessie, Dalton Trumbo, and the other "fellow-traveling, ex-proletarian writers go to Hollywood and become film hacks," making Hollywood "a particularly favorable climate for the spread of Communism."[8]

The screenwriter, Schlesinger warned, was so driven by the guilt of making good money that "he believes that he can buy indulgences by participating in the Communist movement," resulting in a "double corruption . . . a corrupt criticism and a corrupt art," no mere creation of mediocre films but "a dangerous inroad upon the moral fabric of American culture" by extending Communist influence "toward lowering and softening artistic standards in a pseudo-democratic direction."[9]

Of course, Schlesinger had stacked the deck from the first mention of actual screenwriters. Few of them had ever been the pre–Popular Front "proletarian" novelists of yore, although many of them had unquestionably been, personally, both proletarians and fiction writers. Schlesinger obviously hadn't chosen tainted Oscar winners and other renowned talents like Donald Ogden Stewart, Sidney Buchman, Abraham Polonsky, Robert Rossen, or Ring Lardner, Jr., as cases at hand. Perhaps like so many other literary or politically minded American intellectuals, he didn't actually know much about writing in Hollywood, but was simply determined to make a political point.[10] A half century later, in a meditative autobiography, he recalled by name many of the beloved movies of his younger days without flagging those written by the politically repugnant, future victims of the blacklist.[11] Perhaps he had changed his mind; more likely, he had simply failed to notice the screenwriters' credits until the Cold War prompted his attention, and then he lapsed again in later decades.

Back in 1949, Schlesinger put the true killing phrase into a footnote. He would not "Wish to imply approval of the question asked by the Un-American Activities Committee," but as he urged elsewhere in the volume readers' cooperation with the FBI, he described with gleeful irony the response of the film industry, that, "rearing itself in an unwonted spasm of moral nobility, turned [the Communist screenwriters] out into the storm."[12] He had found a way to point a finger of disdain simultaneously at Hollywood commercialism and at the Hollywood Left, clinching the argument. If the studio system was as corrupt as so many believed, then it followed that Communists within it were doubly corrupt by virtue of their support for Russia and were owed no sympathy. They had brought the blacklist upon themselves.[13] As an executive of Schlesinger's brainchild American Committee for Cultural Freedom pronounced a few years later, no violation of "cultural freedom" at all had taken place in Hollywood: The "American people" had simply chosen to disgorge the supporters of their enemies.[14]

Murray Kempton's *Part of Our Time* (1955) capped this high-profile school of ostensibly liberal thought by insisting that the writers were all-around mediocrities whose hack screenwriting efforts "had not so much violated their essence as found their proper level."[15] Such a sweeping judgment, which extended from the least accomplished to Academy Award winners and those whose work had been lauded as artistically brilliant, suggested an interesting test case. Lawson, who was working steadily and with apparently rising prestige until the HUAC hearings began and continued intermittently thereafter, could count the extraordinary *Cry, the Beloved Country* (1951), not to mention more recent under-the-table work. He nevertheless came off most remarkably, in Kempton's perspective, as someone who had "long ceased to interest anyone except grave robbers and the House Committee on UnAmerican Activities."[16] How long was long? How often did a novelist (or a journalist like Kempton) need to deliver a critically acclaimed best-seller, the equivalent to a screenwriter's achievement, in order to be more than past-dated?

To be fair, by the late 1960s, Kempton basically repudiated the particular morals charge of hypocrisy that he had made against the Hollywood Ten for refusing to confess their political status. Admitting that if the blacklistees' rhetoric had been "inferior to their cause," still "they did what they could with the remaining resources of language and dignity, and . . .

they did better than we." [17] Better, that is, than those who stayed safely on the sidelines with the winners, hurling imprecations, whether political, aesthetic, or otherwise.

And still Kempton had not touched bottom. The damage was long done when the columnist, no doubt shadowed by liberal anti-Communists' tardiness in opposing the Vietnam War (also leading liberals' involvement in its crucial early phases of escalation, and the conversion of some of the most prominent to hawkish conservatism in the process), made this admission. But the cloud of the blacklistees' purported aesthetic unworthiness that hung over critical discussion of Hollywood actually thickened in the era to follow.

The courtship of academics and the film industry, symbolized early on in the *Hollywood Quarterly,* ended in something like an extended trial separation if not a divorce. Those who had written seriously about film (unless they had crucial connections, like Dwight Macdonald writing in the pages of *Esquire*), especially film insiders, had no incentive and, if they were left-wing, simply no opportunity to continue the discussion. Relations reached an all-time low in the later 1950s, by which time the organized "militant highbrows" (to borrow a phrase from Schlesinger) of the Cold War cerebral camp began to experience their own breakup. [18] With the Reds as a Hollywood milieu safely gone, the Soviet Union discredited in Hungary, and détente around the corner, there was considerably less to argue about on this score, anyway. First Couple John and Jacqueline Kennedy, flouting the threats of an American Legion boycott, attended the Washington premiere of *Spartacus* that brought Dalton Trumbo (if few of his erstwhile comrades) out of the blacklist.

For corporate Hollywood and its political friends, by the 1960s the burning issue had become the accelerated export of American products. The defense against charges of subversion had lost its relevance, and not only because the blacklistees had all but disappeared. Grizzled liberal Cold Warriors, if not the most hard-bitten conservatives, once again urged the separation of Hollywood's art or culture from political censorship. But the cultural rebellion had only begun.

In the rapidly expanding fields of higher education that drew their strength most directly from tax dollars, academic film studies meanwhile commenced on a serious scale. The new scholars, with the rarest exceptions, stayed away from the work of the blacklistees or treated the Hollywood Left, if at all, as the severely confined list of the Hollywood Ten. Serious work along these lines was still decades ahead.

The Left's tangled road back is a subject best suited to another volume. Ring Lardner, Jr.'s mid-1970s conclusions are nevertheless precise and probably universal. The blacklist, he wrote, had "wiped out scores of careers and a few lives, but there were enough of us who survived it to create a whole new subversive threat to the content of American movies." That erosion, "so far is invisible to the naked eye, which is the way we prefer it." [19] That returnees would seek *not* to be recognized as part of a milieu but only as individual writers (or directors, actors, or film editors, among other technicians) is indubitably wedded to the necessity of camouflage, even a quarter-century after the onset of the blacklist. But perhaps it is suggestive of some larger meaning as well.

The postwar repression and the collapse of the Popular Front rendered the future blacklistees, in Walter Bernstein's humorous phrase, into "disorganized Marxists" with no institutional home but a continued warm feeling in their hearts for most of the causes they had supported all their adult lives.[20] If they lost their illusions about the Soviet Union, they happily embraced other obvious issues from antiracism, labor revival, and women's liberation to antiwar and ecological sentiments. The keenest among them recognized that if the old visions of the "struggle for content" remained relevant, new strategies also had to be adopted to expand the potential of screen art. Television, at least until the 1960s, was more often than film their chief (usually if not always pseudonymous) outlet.[21]

Perhaps the humanism of Martin Ritt's films spoke most literally for cinematic politics of silenced others and for the straightforward aesthetics that they would also likely have employed. Blacklisted as an actor but successfully returning as a director in the later 1950s, he guided socially minded comedies, films of hard-pressed but ardent women (*Nuts*), working people aroused (*Norma Rae*), films upholding black pride and blasting racism in society (*Sounder, The Great White Hope*), films about kids and animals (*Casey's Shadow*), and inevitably films against the blacklist itself (*The Front*). Reduced to a microcosm, this was the further evolution of what the larger group had always had in mind.

The higher art of Joseph Losey and Jules Dassin, including efforts to recuperate theatrical traditions from Greek drama to opera to versions of the most serious contemporary drama, suggested a dimension scarcely imagined in 1940 (just barely imagined by 1950, with the poetic realism of *Give Us This Day* and the American *M*), and unlikely ever to be realized in Hollywood, if anywhere. In between leftish pop and high art, the exemplary work of screenwriter Waldo Salt's post-blacklist treasures *Midnight Cowboy* and *The Day of the Locust,* along with Ring Lardner, Jr.'s coscripted *M*A*S*H,* might safely be said to stand for others. The survivors wanted to make art and make a difference; given the heavy odds against them, not only past politics but advancing age, they did well.

Abraham Polonsky, former college lecturer on literary modernism and practically the only one among the filmmakers who managed to get his formal aesthetic views into the printed word, claimed that he sought at once to attain realism—then break its spell over cinematic art. Perhaps such a lofty goal could only have been achieved in the decade after World War II, before most of the radical filmmakers' contact with the Jewish working class of their youth disappeared. Perhaps its promise is just now being realized in films like *The Majestic* (2001), whose blacklisted protagonist played by Jim Carrey wins the heart of Lawson (!), a little California town, with his courage to stand up to the Committee. In any case, to continue the longstanding disregard for the work of the Hollywood Left would confirm an indifference toward the inner history of many of the medium's most creative spirits, and seriously damage the prospects for a different cinema today and tomorrow.

1. Marked "1:30 to 2:00 pm EST, Copy for Artie Shaw," Albert Maltz Papers, State Historical Society of Wisconsin.

2. Notably excluding the two dozen Communists or former Communists as Anne Revere, Howard da Silva, Will Geer, or Larry Parks still acting in current films, although as mostly supporting players they may have been simply less famous than the ones heard or named on the broadcast. It's also interesting that some non-Communists who were placed on the blacklist strictly for their civil libertarian views—which is to say, an unwillingness to testify against friends and former colleagues—included Marsha Hunt and Jane Wyatt. Lauren Bacall, counting on audience familiarity, didn't use her first name here.

3. Lary May, *The Big Tomorrow: Hollywood and the Politics of the American Way* (Chicago: University of Chicago Press, 2000), 203. May cites material in the

files of C. D. Jackson, unearthed through Freedom of Information Act inquiries. Frances Stonor Saunders found more. Her revelatory volume, *The Cultural Cold War: The CIA and the World of Arts and Letters* (New York: The New Press, 2000), 288–97, points to extensive CIA efforts in Hollywood, and the funding of *Animal Farm,* in two quite differently tailored versions—one for British and one for American audiences.

4. May, *The Big Tomorrow,* 224.

5. Meanwhile, television largely recuperated the themes and treatment of women's films of the 1930s. Blacklistees were generally barred from the medium, at least under their own names. Nevertheless, a dozen or so blacklistees wrote prolifically for television, and their disguised (and sometimes undisguised) credits included *Danger, You Are There, The Danny Thomas Show, The Naked City, The Adventures of Robin Hood, 77 Sunset Strip, Have Gun Will Travel, East-Side/West-Side, The Ghost and Mrs. Muir, The Donna Reed Show, The Dick Van Dyke Show,* and a handful of standard family features, including *Lassie, Flipper,* and *Daktari,* in addition to many dramatic anthology programs of the 1950s and some made-for-TV films of the 1970s.

6. Millard Lampell, "I Think I Ought to Mention That I Was Blacklisted," *The New York Times,* August 3, 1966, excerpts from an Emmy speech that he made for the *Hallmark Hall of Fame* show, *Eagle in a Cage* (later reshot for theater audiences). This was the most dramatic open break from the blacklist since Trumbo's scripting of *Spartacus,* and the most important for the lesser-known writers, who had far more difficulty making their way back under their own names.

7. Arthur Schlesinger, Jr., *The Vital Center* (Boston: Little, Brown, 1949), 122–123.

8. Ibid., 125.

9. Ibid., 125–26.

10. Would he have known of Hollywood Reds not identified among the Hollywood Ten? Leaving aside possible assistance from the FBI, whose investigatory powers he praised widely at the time, Schlesinger was known as *Life* magazine's expert on American Communism. He presumably had access to information on those writers who participated in Popular Front events and, if he wished, considerably more intimate knowledge.

11. These included *She Done Him Wrong, The Thin Man* (based upon the hated Hammett's story), *Alice Adams, They Won't Forget, Racket Busters, Mayor of*

Hell, and, most especially, *Casablanca,* his very special favorite. See Arthur
Schlesinger, Jr., *A Life in the Twentieth Century: Innocent Beginnings, 1917–
1950* (Boston: Houghton Mifflin, 2000), 141, 148, 285.

12. Schlesinger, *The Vital Center,* 125ff.

13. A half century later, enraged at the controversy around the prospective Academy Lifetime Achievement Award to be given to Elia Kazan, Schlesinger repeated his position: The blacklistees, guilty of Communism, hadn't a moral
leg to stand on, nor had American cinema suffered for their absence. Arthur
Schlesinger, Jr., "Hollywood Hypocrisy," *The New York Times,* February 28,
1999.

14. Sol Stein, Draft Statement, 1955 [no month or day noted], in American
Committee for Cultural Freedom Papers, Tamiment Library, New York University. This draft statement was prepared in support of the upcoming investigations of AFTRA, the actors' union. Protesting assorted measures of
cultural suppression in the East Bloc (and occasionally elsewhere, although
very rarely in countries allied with the United States), CCF and ACCF issued
no complaint against HUAC investigations and subsequent blacklisting in
the U.S. entertainment industry; on the contrary, their leaders urged further
vigilance. Arthur Schlesinger, Jr. and several others, reversing their previous
direction, opted out of the new campaign. Papers consulted with the permission of Daniel Bell.

15. Murray Kempton, *Part of Our Time: Some Ruins and Monuments of the Thirties*
(New York, Simon & Schuster, 1955), 184.

16. Ibid., 184.

17. Murray Kempton, "The Limits of Irony," *The New Republic,* April 15, 1968,
34.

18. See Arthur Schlesinger, Jr., "The Highbrow in American Politics," *Partisan
Review* 19 (March–April, 1953), 157–65; and in the same issue a former
Trotskyist intellectual-going-mainstream, Harvey Swados, "Popular Taste
and 'The Caine Mutiny,' " 248–56. Again, irony: Swados was attacking a film
directed by friendly witness Dmytryk, whose apostasy from the Left (and
loyalty to purported American values) the *Partisan Review* had shortly before applauded vigorously. Novelist Swados would be best known for his
portrayal of working-class life, while the screenwriters who came closest
to portraying working-class life in film were wiped out, apparently to his
satisfaction.

19. Ring Lardner, Jr., *The Lardners: My Family Remembered* (New York: Harper-Colophon, 1976), 354.

20. Thanks to Walter Bernstein for an interview with Paul Buhle in New York, in 1995, bearing these insights and others.

21. The best description of the world of the Left writer's 1950s–60s participation in dramatic television is in Walter Bernstein, *Inside Out: A Memoir of the Blacklist* (New York: Knopf, 1996), 207–79. Thanks also to successful television writers Al Ruben, Eddie Adler, and Al Brenner, none of them named in the blacklist, for interviews with Paul Buhle and Dave Wagner in New York and Hollywood, 1995–1998, on their work in various dramatic shows. These included *Have Gun Will Travel, The Defenders, The Nurses,* and *East Side/West Side.* A future volume will treat this work, and similar television writing by Adrian and Joan Scott, Abraham Polonsky, Walter Bernstein, Robert Lees, Frank Tarloff, Ring Lardner, Jr., and others, at length.

INDEX

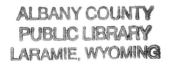